Parallel Processing for Scientific Computing

SOFTWARE • ENVIRONMENTS • TOOLS

The SIAM series on Software, Environments, and Tools focuses on the practical implementation of computational methods and the high performance aspects of scientific computation by emphasizing in-demand software, computing environments, and tools for computing. Software technology development issues such as current status, applications and algorithms, mathematical software, software tools, languages and compilers, computing environments, and visualization are presented.

Editor-in-Chief
Jack J. Dongarra
University of Tennessee and Oak Ridge National Laboratory

Editorial Board

James W. Demmel, University of California, Berkeley
Dennis Gannon, Indiana University
Eric Grosse, AT&T Bell Laboratories
Ken Kennedy, Rice University
Jorge J. Moré, Argonne National Laboratory

Software, Environments, and Tools

Michael A. Heroux, Padma Raghavan, and Horst D. Simon, editors, *Parallel Processing for Scientific Computing*

Gérard Meurant, *The Lanczos and Conjugate Gradient Algorithms: From Theory to Finite Precision Computations*

Bo Einarsson, editor, *Accuracy and Reliability in Scientific Computing*

Michael W. Berry and Murray Browne, *Understanding Search Engines: Mathematical Modeling and Text Retrieval, Second Edition*

Craig C. Douglas, Gundolf Haase, and Ulrich Langer, *A Tutorial on Elliptic PDE Solvers and Their Parallelization*

Louis Komzsik, *The Lanczos Method: Evolution and Application*

Bard Ermentrout, *Simulating, Analyzing, and Animating Dynamical Systems: A Guide to XPPAUT for Researchers and Students*

V. A. Barker, L. S. Blackford, J. Dongarra, J. Du Croz, S. Hammarling, M. Marinova, J. Waśniewski, and P. Yalamov, *LAPACK95 Users' Guide*

Stefan Goedecker and Adolfy Hoisie, *Performance Optimization of Numerically Intensive Codes*

Zhaojun Bai, James Demmel, Jack Dongarra, Axel Ruhe, and Henk van der Vorst, *Templates for the Solution of Algebraic Eigenvalue Problems: A Practical Guide*

Lloyd N. Trefethen, *Spectral Methods in MATLAB*

E. Anderson, Z. Bai, C. Bischof, S. Blackford, J. Demmel, J. Dongarra, J. Du Croz, A. Greenbaum, S. Hammarling, A. McKenney, and D. Sorensen, *LAPACK Users' Guide, Third Edition*

Michael W. Berry and Murray Browne, *Understanding Search Engines: Mathematical Modeling and Text Retrieval*

Jack J. Dongarra, Iain S. Duff, Danny C. Sorensen, and Henk A. van der Vorst, *Numerical Linear Algebra for High-Performance Computers*

R. B. Lehoucq, D. C. Sorensen, and C. Yang, *ARPACK Users' Guide: Solution of Large-Scale Eigenvalue Problems with Implicitly Restarted Arnoldi Methods*

Randolph E. Bank, *PLTMG: A Software Package for Solving Elliptic Partial Differential Equations, Users' Guide 8.0*

L. S. Blackford, J. Choi, A. Cleary, E. D'Azevedo, J. Demmel, I. Dhillon, J. Dongarra, S. Hammarling, G. Henry, A. Petitet, K. Stanley, D. Walker, and R. C. Whaley, *ScaLAPACK Users' Guide*

Greg Astfalk, editor, *Applications on Advanced Architecture Computers*

Françoise Chaitin-Chatelin and Valérie Frayssé, *Lectures on Finite Precision Computations*

Roger W. Hockney, *The Science of Computer Benchmarking*

Richard Barrett, Michael Berry, Tony F. Chan, James Demmel, June Donato, Jack Dongarra, Victor Eijkhout, Roldan Pozo, Charles Romine, and Henk van der Vorst, *Templates for the Solution of Linear Systems: Building Blocks for Iterative Methods*

E. Anderson, Z. Bai, C. Bischof, J. Demmel, J. Dongarra, J. Du Croz, A. Greenbaum, S. Hammarling, A. McKenney, S. Ostrouchov, and D. Sorensen, *LAPACK Users' Guide, Second Edition*

Jack J. Dongarra, Iain S. Duff, Danny C. Sorensen, and Henk van der Vorst, *Solving Linear Systems on Vector and Shared Memory Computers*

J. J. Dongarra, J. R. Bunch, C. B. Moler, and G. W. Stewart, *Linpack Users' Guide*

Parallel Processing for Scientific Computing

Edited by

Michael A. Heroux
Sandia National Laboratories
Albuquerque, New Mexico

Padma Raghavan
Pennsylvania State University
University Park, Pennsylvania

Horst D. Simon
Lawrence Berkeley National Laboratory
Berkeley, California

Society for Industrial and Applied Mathematics
Philadelphia

Copyright © 2006 by the Society for Industrial and Applied Mathematics.

10 9 8 7 6 5 4 3 2 1

All rights reserved. Printed in the United States of America. No part of this book may be reproduced, stored, or transmitted in any manner without the written permission of the publisher. For information, write to the Society for Industrial and Applied Mathematics, 3600 University City Science Center, Philadelphia, PA 19104-2688.

Trademarked names may be used in this book without the inclusion of a trademark symbol. These names are used in an editorial context only; no infringement of trademark is intended.

BlueGene/L was designed by IBM Research for the Department of Energy/NNSA's Advanced Simulation and Computing Program.

Linux is a registered trademark of Linus Torvalds.

MATLAB is a registered trademark of The MathWorks, Inc. For MATLAB product information, please contact The MathWorks, Inc., 3 Apple Hill Drive, Natick, MA 01760-2098 USA, 508-647-7000, Fax: 508-647-7101, info@mathworks.com, www.mathworks.com

POWER3 and POWER4 are trademarks of IBM Corporation.

X1E is a trademark of Cray, Inc.

Figure 8.2 is reprinted from *Advances in Engineering Software,* 29, W. J. Barry, M. T. Jones, and P. E. Plassmann, "Parallel adaptive mesh refinement techniques," 217–229, 1998, with permission from Elsevier.

Figure 8.4 is reprinted from A. Wissink et al., "Enhancing Scalability of Parallel Structured AMR Calculations." *17th ACM Int'l. Conf. on Supercomputing (ICS'03),* pp. 336–347. © 2003 ACM, Inc. Reprinted by permission.

Figure 8.6 is reprinted from "Mesh generation," M. W. Bern and P. E. Plassmann, in *Handbook of Computational Geometry,* J. Sack and J. Urrutia, eds., 291–332, 2000, with permission from Elsevier.

Figure 17.1 is reprinted from G. Lancia et al., "101 optimal PDB structure alignments: A branch-and-cut algorithm for the maximum contact map overlap problem." *Proceedings of 5th Int'l. Conference on Computational Biology (RECOMB'01),* pp. 193–202. © 2001 ACM, Inc. Reprinted by permission.

Library of Congress Cataloging-in-Publication Data

Parallel processing for scientific computing / edited by Michael A. Heroux, Padma
   Raghavan, Horst D. Simon.
      p. cm. — (Software, environments, tools)
   Includes bibliographical references and index.
   ISBN-13: 978-0-898716-19-1 (pbk.)
   ISBN-10: 0-89871-619-5 (pbk.)
   1. Parallel processing (Electronic computers) I. Heroux, Michael A. II. Raghavan,
Padma. III. Simon, Horst D.

QA76.58.P37645 2006
004'.35—dc22

                                                     2006045099

Royalties from the sale of this book are placed in a fund to help students attend SIAM meetings and other SIAM-related activities. This fund is administered by SIAM, and qualified individuals are encouraged to write directly to SIAM for guidelines.

 is a registered trademark.

List of Contributors

Volkan Akçelik
Ultrascale Simulation Laboratory
Department of Civil and
 Environmental Engineering
Carnegie Mellon University
Pittsburgh, PA 15213 USA
volkan@cs.cmu.edu

George Almasi
IBM Thomas J. Watson Research
 Center
Yorktown Heights, NY 10598 USA
gheorghe@us.ibm.com

Srinivas Aluru
Department of Electrical and
 Computer Engineering
Iowa State University
Ames, IA 50011 USA
aluru@iastate.edu

Nancy Amato
Parasol Laboratory
Department of Computer Science
Texas A&M University
College Station, TX 77843 USA
amato@cs.tamu.edu

Charles Archer
IBM Systems and Technology
 Group
Rochester, MN 55901 USA
archerc@us.ibm.com

Rob Armstrong
Sandia National Laboratories
Livermore, CA 94551 USA
rob@sandia.gov

Leonardo Bachega
LARC–University of Sao Paulo
Sao Paulo, Brazil
bachega@larc.usp.br

Scott B. Baden
CSE Department
University of California San Diego
La Jolla, CA 92093 USA
baden@cs.ucsd.edu

David A. Bader
College of Computing
Center for the Study of Systems
 Biology
Center for Experimental Research
 in Computer Systems
Georgia Institute of Technology
Atlanta, GA 30332 USA
bader@cc.gatech.edu

David Bailey
Computational Research Division
Lawrence Berkeley National
 Laboratory
Berkeley, CA 94720 USA
DHBailey@lbl.gov

Suchindra Bhandarkar
Computer Science
University of Georgia
Athens, GA 30602 USA
suchi@cs.uga.edu

Gyan Bhanot
IBM Thomas J. Watson Research
 Center
Yorktown Heights, NY 10598 USA
gyan@us.ibm.com

George Biros
Department of Mechanical
 Engineering and Applied
 Mechanics and Department
 of Computer and Information
 Science
University of Pennsylvania
Philadelphia, PA 19104 USA
biros@seas.upenn.edu

Rupak Biswas
NASA Advanced Supercomputing
 (NAS) Division
NASA Ames Research Center
Moffett Field, CA 94035 USA
rupak.biswas@nasa.gov

Erik G. Boman
Department of Discrete Algorithms
 and Mathematics
Sandia National Laboratories
Albuquerque, NM 87185 USA
egboman@sandia.gov

Randall Bramley
Computer Science
Indiana University
Bloomington, IN 47405 USA
bramley@cs.indiana.edu

Sharon Brunett
Center for Advanced Computing
 Research
California Institute of Technology
Pasadena, CA 91125 USA
sharon@cacr.caltech.edu

Bor Chan
Lawrence Livermore National
 Laboratory
Livermore, CA 94550 USA
chan1@llnl.gov

Sid Chatterjee
IBM Thomas J. Watson Research Center
Yorktown Heights, NY 10598 USA
sc@us.ibm.com

Edmond Chow
D. E. Shaw & Co.
120 W. 45th St.
New York, NY 10036 USA
etchow@gmail.com

Giri Chukkapalli
San Diego Supercomputer Center
La Jolla, CA 92093 USA
giri@sdsc.edu

Alessandro Curioni
IBM Zurich Research Laboratory
CH-8803 Ruschlikon
Switzerland
cur@zurich.ibm.com

Bruce Curtis
Lawrence Livermore National Laboratory
Livermore, CA 94550 USA
curtisb@llnl.gov

Kostadin Damevski
Scientific Computing and Imaging Institute
The University of Utah
Salt Lake City, UT 84112 USA
damevski@cs.utah.edu

Travis Desell
Department of Computer Science
Rensselaer Polytechnic Institute
Troy, NY 12180 USA
deselt@cs.rpi.edu

Karen D. Devine
Department of Discrete Algorithms and Mathematics
Sandia National Laboratories
Albuquerque, NM 87185 USA
kddevin@sandia.gov

Lori Diachin
Center for Applied Scientific Computing
Lawrence Livermore National Laboratory
P.O. Box 808, L-561
Livermore, CA 94551 USA
diachin2@llnl.gov

Jack Dongarra
Computer Science Department
University of Tennessee
Knoxville, TN 37996
dongarra@cs.utk.edu

Jonathan Eckstein
RUTCOR, Room 155
640 Bartholomew Road
Busch Campus
Rutgers University
Piscataway, NJ 08854 USA
jeckstei@rutcor.rutgers.edu

Victor Eijkhout
Computer Science Department
University of Tennessee
Knoxville, TN 37996 USA
eijkhout@cs.utk.edu

Kaoutar El Maghraoui
Department of Computer Science
Rensselaer Polytechnic Institute
Troy, NY 12180 USA
elmagk@cs.rpi.edu

Jamal Faik
Department of Computer Science
Rensselaer Polytechnic Institute
Troy, NY 12180 USA
faikj@cs.rpi.edu

Robert D. Falgout
Center for Computational Sciences and Engineering
Lawrence Livermore National Laboratory
Livermore, CA 94551 USA
rfalgout@llnl.gov

Joseph E. Flaherty
Department of Computer Science
Rensselaer Polytechnic Institute
Troy, NY 12180 USA
flaherje@cs.rpi.edu

Ian Foster
Mathematics and Computer Science Division
Argonne National Laboratory
9700 South Cass Avenue
Building 221
Argonne, IL 60439 USA
foster@mcs.anl.gov

Alan Gara
IBM Thomas J. Watson Research Center
Yorktown Heights, NY 10598 USA
alangara@us.ibm.com

Luis G. Gervasio
Department of Computer Science
Rensselaer Polytechnic Institute
Troy, NY 12180 USA
gerval@cs.rpi.edu

Omar Ghattas
Departments of Geological Sciences, Mechanical Engineering, Computer Sciences, and Biomedical Engineering
Institute for Computational Engineering and Sciences
and Institute for Geophysics
University of Texas at Austin
Austin, TX 78712 USA
omar@ices.texas.edu

Judit Gimenez
European Center for Parallelism of Barcelona
Technical University of Catalonia
08034 Barcelona Spain
judit@cepba.upc.es

William D. Gropp
Argonne National Laboratory
Argonne, IL 60439 USA
gropp@mcs.anl.gov

John Gunnels
IBM Thomas J. Watson Research Center
Yorktown Heights, NY 10598 USA
gunnels@us.ibm.com

Manish Gupta
IBM Thomas J. Watson Research Center
Yorktown Heights, NY 10598 USA
mgupta@us.ibm.com

Robert Harkness
San Diego Supercomputer Center
La Jolla, CA 92093 USA
harkness@sdsc.edu

List of Contributors

William Hart
Sandia National Laboratories
Mail Stop 1110
P.O. Box 5800
Albuquerque, NM 87185-1110
USA
wehart@sandia.gov

Michael T. Heath
Computation Science and
  Engineering Department
University of Illinois
Urbana, IL 61801 USA
heath@uiuc.edu

Bruce Hendrickson
Department of Discrete Algorithms
  and Mathematics
Sandia National Laboratories
Albuquerque, NM 87185 USA
and Department of Computer
Science
University of New Mexico
Albuquerque, NM 87131 USA
bah@sandia.gov

Amy Henning
IBM Thomas J. Watson Research
  Center
Yorktown Heights, NY 10598 USA
amhennin@us.ibm.com

Michael A. Heroux
Sandia National Laboratories
Albuquerque, NM 87185 USA
maheroux@sandia.gov

Judith Hill
Optimization & Uncertainty
  Estimation Department
Sandia National Laboratories
Albuquerque, NM 87185 USA
jhill@sandia.gov

Richard Hornung
Center for Applied Scientific
  Computing
Lawrence Livermore National
  Laboratory
P.O. Box 808, L-561
Livermore, CA 94551 USA
hornung1@llnl.gov

Patricia D. Hough
Computational Sciences and
  Mathematics Research
  Department
Sandia National Laboratories
Livermore, CA 94551 USA
pdhough@sandia.gov

Victoria E. Howle
Computational Sciences and
  Mathematics Research
  Department
Sandia National Laboratories
Livermore, CA 94551 USA
VEHOWLE@sandia.gov

Jonathan J. Hu
Sandia National Laboratories
Livermore, CA 94551 USA
jhu@sandia.gov

Xiangmin Jiao
Computational Science and
  Engineering
University of Illinois
Urbana, IL 61801 USA
jiao@uiuc.edu

Chris R. Johnson
Scientific Computing and Imaging
  Institute
The University of Utah
Salt Lake City, UT 84112 USA
crj@cs.utah.edu

Laxmikant Kale
Department of Computer Science
University of Illinois Urbana-
  Champaign
Urbana, IL 61801 USA
kale@uiuc.edu

Nicholas Karonis
Department of Computer Science
Northern Illinois University
DeKalb, IL 60115 USA
karonis@niu.edu

George Karypis
Department of Computer Science
  and Engineering
Minneapolis, MN 55455 USA
karypis@cs.umn.edu

David Keyes
Department of Applied Physics and
  Applied Mathematics
Columbia University
New York, NY USA
kd2112@columbia.edu

Jesús Labarta
CEPBA-UPC
Jordi Girona 1-2, Modulo D-6
08034 Barcelona
Spain
jesus@cepba.upc.edu

Sébastien Lacour
IRISA/INRIA
Rennes, France
Sebastien.Lacour@irisa.fr

Julien Langou
Department of Computer Science
University of Tennessee
Knoxville, TN 37996 USA
langou@cs.utk.edu

Andrew Lumsdaine
Computer Science
Indiana University
Bloomington, IN 47405 USA
lums@indiana.edu

Dan C. Marinescu
School of Computer Science
University of Central Florida
Orlando, FL 32816 USA
dcm@cs.ucf.edu

Lois McInnes
Argonne National Laboratory
Argonne, IL 60439 USA
mcinnes@mcs.anl.gov

Jose E. Moreira
IBM Thomas J. Watson Research
  Center
Yorktown Heights, NY 10598 USA
jmoreira@us.ibm.com

Esmond G. Ng
Lawrence Berkeley National
  Laboratory
Berkeley, CA 94720 USA
egng@lbl.gov

List of Contributors

Leonid Oliker
Lawrence Berkeley National Laboratory
Berkeley, CA 94720 USA
loliker@lbl.gov

Manish Parashar
The Applied Software Systems Laboratory
Department of Electrical and Computer Engineering
Rutgers, The State University of New Jersey
Piscataway, NJ 08855 USA
parashar@caip.rutgers.edu

Steven G. Parker
Scientific Computing and Imaging Institute
The University of Utah
Salt Lake City, UT 84112 USA
sparker@cs.utah.edu

Wayne Pfeiffer
San Diego Supercomputer Center
La Jolla, CA 92093 USA
pfeiffer@sdsc.edu

Cynthia A. Phillips
Sandia National Laboratories
Albuquerque, NM 87185 USA
caphill@sandia.gov

Ali Pınar
High Performance Computing Research Department
Lawrence Berkeley National Laboratory
Berkeley, CA 94720 USA
apinar@lbl.gov

Paul Plassmann
Electrical and Computer Engineering
302 Whittemore (0111)
Virginia Tech
Blacksburg, VA 24061 USA
plassmann@vt.edu

Padma Raghavan
Computer Science and Engineering
The Pennsylvania State University
University Park, PA 16802 USA
raghavan@cse.psu.edu

James Sexton
IBM Thomas J. Watson Research Center
Yorktown Heights, NY 10598 USA
sextonjc@us.ibm.com

Horst D. Simon
Lawrence Berkeley National Laboratory
Berkeley, CA 94720 USA
hdsimon@lbl.gov

Allan Snavely
CSE
University of California, San Diego
La Jolla, CA 92093 USA
allans@sdsc.edu

Matt Sottile
Los Alamos National Laboratory
Los Alamos, NM 87545 USA
sottile@lanl.gov

Rick Stevens
Mathematics and Computer Science Division
Argonne National Laboratory
9700 South Cass Avenue
Building 221
Argonne, IL 60439 USA
stevens@mcs.anl.gov

Valerie E. Taylor
Department of Computer Science
Texas A&M University
College Station, TX 77842 USA
taylor@cs.tamu.edu

James D. Teresco
Department of Computer Science
Williams College
Williamstown, MA 01267 USA
terescoj@cs.williams.edu

Raymond S. Tuminaro
Computation, Computers and Mathematics Center
Sandia National Laboratories
Livermore, CA 94551 USA
tuminaro@ca.sandia.gov

Bart van Bloemen Waanders
Optimization and Uncertainty Estimation Department
Sandia National Laboratories
Albuquerque, NM 87185 USA
bartv@cs.sandia.gov

Rob Van der Wijngaart
Computer Sciences Corporation
NASA Ames Research Center
Moffett Field, CA 94035 USA
wijngaar@nas.nasa.gov

Carlos A. Varela
Department of Computer Science
Renssalaer Polytechnic Institute
Troy, NY 12180 USA
cvarela@cs.rpi.edu

Bob Walkup
IBM Thomas J. Watson Research Center
Yorktown Heights, NY 10598 USA
walkup@us.ibm.com

Andy Wissink
NASA Ames Research Center
MS 215-1
Moffett Field, CA 94035 USA
awissink@mail.arc.nasa.gov

Xingfu Wu
Department of Computer Science
Texas A&M University
College Station, TX 77843 USA
wuxf@cs.tamu.edu

Ulrike Meier Yang
Center for Applied Scientific Computing
Lawrence Livermore National Laboratory
Livermore, CA 94551 USA
yang11@llnl.gov

Keming Zhang
Scientific Computing & Imaging Institute
The University of Utah
Salt Lake City, UT 84112 USA
kzhang@cs.utah.edu

Contents

List of Figures		xv
List of Tables		xxi
Preface		xxiii

1 Frontiers of Scientific Computing: An Overview — 1
Michael A. Heroux, Padma Raghavan, and Horst D. Simon
    1.1 Performance modeling, analysis, and optimization 2
    1.2 Parallel algorithms and enabling technologies 2
    1.3 Tools and frameworks for parallel applications 3
    1.4 Applications of parallel computing 4
    1.5 Conclusions and future directions 5
    Bibliography 5

I Performance Modeling, Analysis, and Optimization — 7

2 Performance Analysis: From Art to Science — 9
Jesús Labarta and Judit Gimenez
    2.1 Performance analysis tools 11
    2.2 Paraver 13
    2.3 Analysis methodology 18
    2.4 Scalability 23
    2.5 Models: Reference of what to expect 29
    2.6 Conclusions 30
    Acknowledgments 30
    Bibliography 31

3 Approaches to Architecture-Aware Parallel Scientific Computation — 33
James D. Teresco, Joseph E. Flaherty, Scott B. Baden, Jamal Faik,
Sébastien Lacour, Manish Parashar, Valerie E. Taylor, and Carlos A. Varela
    3.1 Prophesy: A performance analysis and modeling system for parallel
         and distributed applications 35
         Valerie E. Taylor, with Xingfu Wu and Rick Stevens

	3.2	Canonical variant programming and computation and communication scheduling 38

Scott B. Baden

3.3   A multilevel topology-aware approach to implementing MPI collective operations for computational grids 40

Sébastien Lacour, with Nicholas Karonis and Ian Foster

3.4   Dynamic load balancing for heterogeneous environments 42

Jamal Faik, James D. Teresco, and Joseph E. Flaherty, with Luis G. Gervasio

3.5   Hierarchical partitioning and dynamic load balancing 44

James D. Teresco

3.6   Autonomic management of parallel adaptive applications 46

Manish Parashar

3.7   Worldwide computing: Programming models and middleware 49

Carlos A. Varela, with Travis Desell and Kaoutar El Maghraoui

Acknowledgments 50

Bibliography 51

4   Achieving High Performance on the BlueGene/L Supercomputer   59

George Almasi, Gyan Bhanot, Sid Chatterjee, Alan Gara, John Gunnels, Manish Gupta, Amy Henning, Jose E. Moreira et al.

4.1   BG/L architectural features 60

4.2   Methods for obtaining high performance 61

4.3   Performance measurements 63

4.4   Conclusions 73

Bibliography 74

5   Performance Evaluation and Modeling of Ultra-Scale Systems   77

Leonid Oliker, Rupak Biswas, Rob Van der Wijngaart, David Bailey, and Allan Snavely

5.1   Modern high-performance ultra-scale systems 77

5.2   Architecture evaluation using full applications 80

5.3   Algorithmic and architectural benchmarks 86

5.4   Performance modeling 90

5.5   Summary 93

Acknowledgments 93

Bibliography 93

II   Parallel Algorithms and Enabling Technologies   97

6   Partitioning and Load Balancing for Emerging Parallel Applications and Architectures   99

Karen D. Devine, Erik G. Boman, and George Karypis

6.1   Traditional approaches 100

6.2   Beyond traditional applications 101

6.3   Beyond traditional approaches 108

	6.4	Beyond traditional models 112
	6.5	Beyond traditional architectures 115
	6.6	Conclusion 117
	Bibliography 118

7 Combinatorial Parallel and Scientific Computing   127
Ali Pınar and Bruce Hendrickson
- 7.1 Sparse matrix computations 127
- 7.2 Utilizing computational infrastructure 130
- 7.3 Parallelizing irregular computations 132
- 7.4 Computational biology 134
- 7.5 Information analysis 135
- 7.6 Solving combinatorial problems 136
- 7.7 Conclusions 139
- Acknowledgments 139
- Bibliography 139

8 Parallel Adaptive Mesh Refinement   143
Lori Freitag Diachin, Richard Hornung, Paul Plassmann, and Andy Wissink
- 8.1 SAMR 145
- 8.2 UAMR 149
- 8.3 A comparison of SAMR and UAMR 152
- 8.4 Recent advances and future research directions 153
- 8.5 Conclusions 156
- Acknowledgments 156
- Bibliography 157

9 Parallel Sparse Solvers, Preconditioners, and Their Applications   163
Esmond G. Ng
- 9.1 Sparse direct methods 163
- 9.2 Iterative methods and preconditioning techniques 167
- 9.3 Hybrids of direct and iterative techniques 169
- 9.4 Expert approaches to solving sparse linear systems 171
- 9.5 Applications 172
- Acknowledgments 173
- Bibliography 173

10 A Survey of Parallelization Techniques for Multigrid Solvers   179
Edmond Chow, Robert D. Falgout, Jonathan J. Hu, Raymond S. Tuminaro, and Ulrike Meier Yang
- 10.1 Sources of parallelism 179
- 10.2 Parallel computation issues 184
- 10.3 Concluding remarks 194
- Acknowledgments 195
- Bibliography 195

11 Fault Tolerance in Large-Scale Scientific Computing — 203
Patricia D. Hough and Victoria E. Howle
- 11.1 Fault tolerance in algorithms and applications 204
- 11.2 Fault tolerance in MPI 210
- 11.3 Conclusions 216
- Acknowledgments 216
- Bibliography 216

III Tools and Frameworks for Parallel Applications — 221

12 Parallel Tools and Environments: A Survey — 223
William D. Gropp and Andrew Lumsdaine
- 12.1 Software and tools for building and running clusters 224
- 12.2 Tools for computational science 228
- 12.3 Conclusion 231
- Bibliography 232

13 Parallel Linear Algebra Software — 233
Victor Eijkhout, Julien Langou, and Jack Dongarra
- 13.1 Dense linear algebra software 234
- 13.2 Sparse linear algebra software 238
- 13.3 Support libraries 242
- 13.4 Freely available software for linear algebra on the Internet 242
- Reading List 246
- Bibliography 246

14 High-Performance Component Software Systems — 249
Randall Bramley, Rob Armstrong, Lois McInnes, and Matt Sottile
- 14.1 Current scientific component systems 250
- 14.2 Mathematical challenges 254
- 14.3 Conclusion 264
- Acknowledgments 265
- Bibliography 265

15 Integrating Component-Based Scientific Computing Software — 271
Steven G. Parker, Keming Zhang, Kostadin Damevski, and Chris R. Johnson
- 15.1 SCIRun and BioPSE 272
- 15.2 Components for scientific computing 276
- 15.3 Metacomponent model 278
- 15.4 Distributed computing 280
- 15.5 Parallel components 282
- 15.6 Conclusions and future work 285
- Acknowledgments 286
- Bibliography 286

IV Applications of Parallel Computing — 289

16 Parallel Algorithms for PDE-Constrained Optimization — 291
Volkan Akçelik, George Biros, Omar Ghattas, Judith Hill, David Keyes, and Bart van Bloemen Waanders
- 16.1 Algorithms 295
- 16.2 Numerical examples 302
- 16.3 Conclusions 314
- Acknowledgments 316
- Bibliography 316

17 Massively Parallel Mixed-Integer Programming: Algorithms and Applications — 323
Cynthia A. Phillips, Jonathan Eckstein, and William Hart
- 17.1 Basic branch and bound for MIP 325
- 17.2 Applications 326
- 17.3 A scalable parallel MIP solver 332
- Bibliography 337

18 Parallel Methods and Software for Multicomponent Simulations — 341
Michael T. Heath and Xiangmin Jiao
- 18.1 System overview 342
- 18.2 Integration framework and middleware services ... 345
- 18.3 Parallel computational methods 347
- 18.4 Results of coupled simulations 351
- 18.5 Conclusion 353
- Acknowledgments 354
- Bibliography 354

19 Parallel Computational Biology — 357
Srinivas Aluru, Nancy Amato, David A. Bader, Suchindra Bhandarkar, Laxmikant Kale, and Dan C. Marinescu
- 19.1 Assembling the maize genome 357
- 19.2 An information theoretic approach to genome reconstruction ... 361
- 19.3 High-performance computing for reconstructing evolutionary trees .. 363
- 19.4 Scaling classical molecular dynamics to thousands of processors ... 365
- 19.5 Cluster and grid computing for 3D structure determination of viruses with unknown symmetry at high resolution 368
- 19.6 Using motion planning to study protein folding 371
- Bibliography 373

20 Opportunities and Challenges for Parallel Computing in Science and Engineering — 379
Michael A. Heroux, Padma Raghavan, and Horst D. Simon
- 20.1 Parallel computer systems 379
- 20.2 Robust and scalable algorithms 383

20.3	Application development and integration	385
20.4	Large-scale modeling and simulation	387
20.5	Concluding remarks	388
Acknowledgments		388
Bibliography		388

Index   **391**

List of Figures

2.1	Performance tools approaches.	12
2.2	The CEPBA-tools environment.	14
2.3	2D analysis.	16
2.4	Load balancing at different scales.	21
2.5	Communication bandwidth.	23
2.6	Parallelism profile of a 128-processor run.	27
2.7	Drill scalability.	28
3.1	Prophesy framework.	36
3.2	Broadcast using a binomial tree: processes are numbered from 0 (root) through 9; communication steps are circled.	41
3.3	Topology-unaware broadcast using a binomial tree: three intercluster messages (bold arrows) and six intracluster messages.	41
3.4	Topology-aware broadcast: only one intercluster message (bold arrow).	41
3.5	Tree constructed by DRUM to represent a heterogeneous network.	43
3.6	Ideal and achieved (using DRUM) relative changes in execution times compared to homogeneous partitioning for an adaptive calculation using PHAML on different processor combinations.	44
3.7	Hierarchical balancing algorithm selection for two four-way SMP nodes connected by a network.	45
3.8	Conceptual overview of GridARM.	47
3.9	A modular middleware architecture as a research testbed for scalable high-performance decentralized distributed computations.	50
4.1	Performance of daxpy on a BG/L node is shown as a function of vector length. L1 and L3 cache edges are apparent. For data in the L1 cache (lengths < 2,000), the performance doubles by turning on SIMD instructions (440d) and doubles again when using both processors on the node.	64
4.2	The performance speed-up using virtual node mode is shown for the class C NAS parallel benchmarks. The speed-up is defined as the ratio of Mops per node in virtual node mode to Mops per node using coprocessor mode.	65

4.3	Linpack performance in BG/L is shown as a function of the number of compute nodes. Performance is indicated as a fraction of the theoretical peak. Results for three different strategies are included: using a single processor on each node, offloading computation to the coprocessor with the model, and using virtual node mode to run with two tasks per node.	66
4.4	Performance of LINPACK on large-scale BG/L systems.	66
4.5	Comparison of the default mapping and optimized mapping for NAS BT on up to 1,024 processors in virtual node mode. Mapping provides a significant performance boost at large task counts.	67
4.6	The computational performance for sPPM is shown for systems including IBM p655 at 1.7 GHz (top curve) and BG/L at 700 MHz using virtual node mode (middle curve) or coprocessor mode with a single computational task per node (lower curve). The x-axis indicates the number of BG/L nodes or the number of p655 processors.	68
4.7	Weak scaling results for UMT2K on BG/L and an IBM p655 cluster. The x-axis indicates the number of BG/L nodes or the number of p655 processors, and the y-axis indicates overall performance relative to 32 nodes of BG/L in coprocessor mode.	70
4.8	Results for CPMD with 138,000 atoms on BG/L.	71
6.1	Cutting planes (left) and associated cut tree (right) for geometric recursive bisection. Dots are objects to be balanced; cuts are shown with dark lines and tree nodes.	101
6.2	SFC partitioning (left) and box assignment search procedure (right). Objects (dots) are ordered along the SFC (dotted line). Partitions are indicated by shading. The box for box assignment intersects partitions 0 and 2.	102
6.3	Use of multiconstraint graph partitioning for contact problems: (a) the 45 contact points are divided into three partitions; (b) the subdomains are represented geometrically as sets of axis-aligned rectangles; and (c) a decision tree describing the geometric representation is used for contact search.	104
6.4	Comparing the nonzero structure of matrices from (a) a hexahedral finite element simulation, (b) a circuit simulation, (c) a density functional theory simulation, and (d) linear programming shows differences in structure between traditional and emerging applications.	107
6.5	Example of communication metrics in the graph (left) and hypergraph (right) models. Edges are shown with ellipses; the partition boundary is the dashed line.	108
6.6	Row (left) and column (right) distribution of a sparse matrix for multiplication $u = Av$. There are only two processors, indicated by dark and light shading, and communication between them is shown with arrows. In this example, the communication volume is three words in both cases. (Adapted from [9, Ch. 4].)	109
6.7	Irregular matrix distribution with two processors. Communication between the two processors (shaded dark and light) is indicated with arrows.	110

List of Figures

7.1 Permuting large entries to the diagonal. Dark edges in the graph correspond to edges in the matching in the bipartite graph of the matrix on the left. The matrix on the right is the permuted matrix with respected to the matching where columns are reordered as mate of the first row, mate of the second row, etc. 129

7.2 Directed graph for the sweep operation. 134

7.3 Branch-and-bound algorithm. 137

7.4 Cutting planes close the gap between IP (Integer Program) and LP feasible regions. 138

8.1 Examples of AMR using structured and unstructured grids. The left figure shows fine detail in an impulsively sheared contact surface computed using patch-based structured AMR [3]. The right figure shows the accurate suface and volume representation of the fuselage and engine cowl of an RAH-66 Comanche helicopter with an unstructured AMR grid [37]. . 144

8.2 On the left is a comparison of maximum element error as a function of the number of grid vertices in an unstructured, tetrahedral mesh calculation [8]. The AMR computation requires significantly fewer points to achieve a desired accuracy. On the right is an image of the two-dimensional version of this problem showing refinement around the transition region and areas of high elastic stress. 145

8.3 An outline of a parallel adaptive solution method for PDEs. 145

8.4 Scaling properties of a three-level scaled SAMR simulation of a moving advecting sinusoidal front [68]. Remeshing occurs every two timesteps. Although the problem scales reasonably, adaptive gridding costs are clearly less scalable than numerical operations. Work to improve scaling of adaptive gridding operations is ongoing. 148

8.5 The bisection algorithm. 150

8.6 The process of the bisection algorithm is shown from left to right. In the initial mesh the shaded elements are refined; subsequently the shaded elements are refined because they are nonconforming [14]. 150

8.7 Examples of new AMR applications. The left image shows a continuum-atomistic hybrid coupling using AMR [65]. The right image shows an embedded boundary SAMR mesh around buildings in Manhattan used for flows in urban environments [41]. 154

10.1 Full domain partitioning example. 183

13.1 2D block-cyclic distribution of a matrix of order n with parameters (nprows= $n/8$,npcols= $n/8$,bs_i= 2,bs_j= 3). On the left, the original data layout, the matrix is partitioned with blocks of size $n/8$; on the right, the data is mapped on a 2×3 processor grid. 236

14.1 Ccaffeine's graphical builder: the components' uses ports appear on their right, while provides ports appear on their left. 252

14.2	Different codes in fusion energy and potential couplings among categories. (Courtesy of Stephen Jardin, Princeton Plasma Physics Laboratory.)	256
14.3	The synchronization problem in PRMI.	259
14.4	Comparison of two component architectures with a single builder that works interchangeably via model-specific glue code.	263
15.1	The SCIRun PSE, illustrating a 3D finite element simulation of an implantable cardiac defibrillator.	272
15.2	BioPSE neural source localization network. The optimal dipole source is recovered using a multistart optimization algorithm.	273
15.3	Visualization of the iterative source localization. The voltages of the true solution (disks) and the computed solution (spheres) are qualitatively compared at the electrode positions as the optimization (shown as arrows) converges on a neural source location. The solution misfit can be qualitatively interpreted by pseudocolored voltages at each electrode.	274
15.4	BioPSE dataflow interface to a forward bioelectric field application. The underlying dataflow network implements the application with modular interconnected components called modules. Data are passed between the modules as input and output parameters to the algorithms. While this is a useful interface for prototyping, it can be nonintuitive for end users; it is confusing to have a separate user interface window to control the settings for each module. Moreover, the entries in the user interface windows fail to provide semantic context for their settings. For example, the text-entry field on the SampleField user interface that is labeled "Maximum number of samples" is controlling the number of electric field streamlines that are produced for the visualization.	275
15.5	The BioFEM custom interface. Although the application is the functionality equivalent to the data flow version shown in Figure 15.4, this PowerApp version provides an easier-to-use custom interface. Everything is contained within a single window. The user is lead through the steps of loading and visualizing the data with the tabs on the right; generic control settings have been replaced with contextually appropriate labels, and application-specific tooltips (not shown) appear when the user places the cursor over any user interface element.	276
15.6	The BioTensor PowerApp. Just as with BioFEM, we have wrapped up a complicated data flow network into a custom application. In the left panel, the user is guided through the stages of loading the data, coregistering MRI diffusion weighted images, and constructing diffusion tensors. On the right panel, the user has controls for setting the visualization options. In the rendering window in the middle, the user can render and interact with the dataset.	277
15.7	Components of different models cooperate in SCIRun2.	279
15.8	A more intricate example of how components of different models cooperate in SCIRun2. The application and components shown are from a realistic (albeit incomplete) scenario.	281

15.9	MxN method invocation, with the caller on the left and the callee on the right. In the left scenario, the number of callers is fewer than the number of callees, so some callers make multiple method calls. In the right, the number of callees is fewer, so some callees send multiple return values.	283
15.10	Components of different models cooperate in SCIRun2.	285
16.1	Reconstruction of hemipelvic bony geometry via solution of an inverse wave propagation problem using a parallel multiscale reduced (Gauss) Newton conjugate gradient optimization algorithm with TV regularization.	304
16.2	An optimal boundary control problem to minimize the rate of energy dissipation (equivalent here to the drag) by applying suction or injection of a fluid on the downstream portion of a cylinder at Re = 40. The left image depicts an uncontrolled flow; the right image depicts the optimally controlled flow. Injecting fluid entirely eliminates recirculation and secondary flows in the wake of the cylinder, thus minimizing dissipation. The optimization problem has over 600,000 states and nearly 9,000 controls and was solved in 4.1 hours on 256 processors of a Cray T3E at PSC.	309
16.3	Solution of a airborne contaminant inverse problem in the Greater Los Angeles Basin with onshore winds; Peclet number = 10. The target initial concentration is shown at left and reconstructed initial condition on the right. The measurements for the inverse problem were synthesized by solving the convection-diffusion equation using the target initial condition and recording measurements on a $21 \times 21 \times 21$ uniform array of sensors. The mesh has 917,301 grid points; the problem has the same number of initial condition unknowns and 74 million total space-time unknowns. Inversion takes 2.5 hours on 64 AlphaServer processors at PSC. CG iterations are terminated when the norm of the residual of the reduced space equations is reduced by five orders of magnitude.	313
17.1	Example contact map alignment with isomorphic subgraphs with seven nodes and five edges corresponding to an alignment of seven amino acid residues with five shared contacts (bold edges) [27].	332
18.1	Overview of Rocstar software components.	342
18.2	AMPI minimizes idle times (gaps in plots) by overlapping communication with computation on different virtual procs. Courtesy of Charm group.	344
18.3	Windows and panes.	346
18.4	Abstraction of data input.	346
18.5	Scalability of data transfer on Linux cluster.	348
18.6	Speed-ups of mesh optimization and surface propagation.	349
18.7	Example of remeshing and data transfer for deformed star grain.	350
18.8	Initial burn of star slice exhibits rapid expansion at slots and contraction at fins. Images correspond to 0%, 6%, and 12% burns, respectively.	351
18.9	Titan IV propellant deformation after 1 second.	352

18.10	RSRM propellant temperature at 175 ms.	352
18.11	Hardware counters for Rocfrac obtained by Rocprof.	352
18.12	Absolute performance of Rocstar on Linux and Mac.	353
18.13	Scalability with Rocflo and Rocsolid on IBM SP.	353
18.14	Scalability with Rocflu and Rocfrac on Linux cluster.	353
19.1	Parallel clustering framework.	360
19.2	Speed-up on PSC LeMieux.	367
19.3	(a) 3D reconstruction of Sindbis at 10 Å resolution. (b) The speed-up of one 3D reconstruction algorithm for several virus structures.	369

List of Tables

4.1 The performance for CPMD using a 216-atom SiC supercell is listed for IBM p690 (Power4 1.3 GHz, Colony switch) and BG/L (700 MHz) systems. The performance metric is the elapsed time per time step in the simulation. Values marked n.a. were not available. 71

4.2 Performance of Enzo for 256**3 unigrid on BG/L and IBM p655 (1.5GHz Power4, Federation switch) relative to 32 BG/L nodes in coprocessor mode. 72

8.1 A comparison of SAMR and UAMR methods. 152

13.1 Support routines for numerical linear algebra. 243
13.2 Available.software.for.dense matrix. 243
13.3 Sparse direct solvers. 244
13.4 Sparse eigenvalue solvers. 244
13.5 Sparse iterative solvers. 245

16.1 Fixed-size scalability on a Cray T3E-900 for a 262,144–grid point problem corresponding to a two-layered medium. 306

16.2 Algorithmic scaling by LRQN, RNCG, and PRNCG methods as a function of material model resolution. For LRQN, the number of iterations is reported, and for both LRQN solver and preconditioner, 200 L-BFGS vectors are stored. For RNCG and PRNCG, the total number of CG iterations is reported, along with the number of Newton iterations in parentheses. On all material grids up to 65^3, the forward and adjoint wave propagation problems are posed on 65^3 grid $\times$ 400 time steps, and inversion is done on 64 PSC AlphaServer processors; for the 129^3 material grid, the wave equations are on 129^3 grids $\times$ 800 time steps, on 256 processors. In all cases, work per iteration reported is dominated by a reduced gradient (LRQN) or reduced-gradient-like (RNCG, PRNCG) calculation, so the reported iterations can be compared across the different methods. Convergence criterion is 10^{-5} relative norm of the reduced gradient. * indicates lack of convergence; † indicates number of iterations extrapolated from converging value after 6 hours of runtime. 307

16.3	Algorithmic scalability for Navier–Stokes optimal flow control problem on 64 and 128 processors of a Cray T3E for a doubling (roughly) of problem size.	310
16.4	Fixed size scalability of unpreconditioned and multigrid preconditioned inversion. Here the problem size is $257 \times 257 \times 257 \times 257$ for all cases. We use a three-level version of the multigrid preconditioner. The variables are distributed across the processors in space, whereas they are stored sequentially in time (as in a multicomponent PDE). Here *hours* is the wall-clock time, and η is the parallel efficiency inferred from the runtime. The unpreconditioned code scales extremely well since there is little overhead associated with its single-grid simulations. The multigrid preconditioner also scales reasonably well, but its performance deteriorates since the problem granularity at the coarser levels is significantly reduced. Nevertheless, wall-clock time is significantly reduced over the unpreconditioned case.	313
16.5	Isogranular scalability of unpreconditioned and multigrid preconditioned inversion. The spatial problem size per processor is fixed (stride of 8). Ideal speed-up should result in doubling of wall-clock time. The multigrid preconditioner scales very well due to improving algorithmic efficiency (decreasing CG iterations) with increasing problem size. Unpreconditioned CG is not able to solve the largest problem in reasonable time.	314
19.1	Assembly statistics and runtime on a 64-processor Pentium III 1.26 GZH Myrinet Cluster.	360
19.2	The increase of the amount of data and the corresponding increase in memory requirements for very-high-resolution reconstruction of the reo virus with a diameter of about 850 Å.	369
19.3	The time for different steps of the orientation refinement for reo virus using 4,422 views with 511×511 pixels/view. DFT size is $512 \times 512 \times 512$. Refinement steps of $1°$, $0.1°$, and $0.01°$. The refinement time increases three to five times when the refinement step size decreases from $0.1°$ to $0.01°$ because of a larger number of operations and also due to the memory access time to much larger data structures. The orientation refinement time is the dominant component of the total execution time, hundreds of minutes, as compared with the computation of the 3D DFT, the reading time, and the DFT analysis, which take a few hundred seconds.	370
19.4	A comparison of protein folding models.	371

Preface

Scientific computing has often been called the third approach to scientific discovery, emerging as a peer to experimentation and theory. Historically, the synergy between theory and experimentation has been well understood. Experiments give insight into possible theories, theories inspire experiments, experiments reinforce or invalidate theories, and so on. As scientific computing (also known as or strongly related to computational science and engineering; computer modeling and simulation; or technical computing) has evolved to increasingly produce computational results that meet or exceed the quality of theoretical and experimental results, it has become an indispensable third approach.

The synergy of theory, experimentation, and computation is very rich. Scientific computing requires theoretical models and often needs input data from experiments. In turn, scientists hoping to gain insight into a problem of interest have yet another basic tool set with which to advance ideas and produce results. That scientific computing is recognized as important is evidenced by the large research investment in this area. As one example, we point to the Scientific Discovery through Advanced Computing Program (SciDAC) sponsored by the U.S. Department of Energy. Although the Internet and related computing technologies have enabled tremendous growth in business and consumer computing, computing and science have been intimately connected from the very beginning of computers, and scientific computing has an insatiable demand for high-performance calculations. Although science is not the dominant force it once was in the computing field, it remains a critical area of computing for strategic purposes, and increasingly scientific computing is essential to technology innovation and development.

Parallel processing has been an enabling technology for scientific computing for more than 20 years. Initial estimates of the cost and length of time it would take to make parallel processing broadly available were admittedly optimistic. The impact of parallel processing on scientific computing varies greatly across disciplines, but we can strongly argue that it plays a vital role in most problem domains and has become essential in many.

This volume is suitable as a reference on the state of the art in scientific computing for researchers, professionals, and application developers. It is also suitable as an overview and introduction, especially for graduate and senior-level undergraduate students who are interested in computational modeling and simulation and related computer science and applied mathematics aspects. This volume reflects the themes, problems, and advances presented at the Eleventh SIAM Conference on Parallel Processing for Scientific Computing held in San Francisco in 2004. This series of SIAM conferences is a venue for mathematicians, computer scientists, and computational scientists to focus on the core enabling technologies that make parallel processing effective for scientific problems. Going back nearly 20 years, this conference series is unique in how it complements other conferences on algorithms or applications, sponsored by SIAM and other organizations. Most of the chapters in this book are authored by participants of this conference, and each chapter provides an expository treatment of a particular topic, including recent results and extensive references to related work. Although progress is made each year in advancing the state of parallel processing, the demands of our target problems require ever more capabilities. This is illustrated by the titles we chose for the four parts of this book, which could well have described the categories of interest back at the beginning of the parallel processing conference series. Our hope is that the reader will not only look at the specifics of our current capabilities but also perceive these perennial issues. By doing so, the reader will gain knowledge that has lasting value.

Michael A. Heroux
Padma Raghavan
Horst D. Simon

Chapter 1
Frontiers of Scientific Computing: An Overview

Michael A. Heroux, Padma Raghavan, and Horst D. Simon

Scientific computing is a broad discipline focused on using computers as tools for scientific discovery. This book describes the present state and future directions of scientific computing over the next 19 chapters, organized into four main parts. The first part concerns performance modeling, analysis, and optimization. The second focuses on parallel algorithms and software for an array of problems that are common to many modeling and simulation applications. The third part emphasizes tools and environments that can ease and enhance the process of application development. The fourth provides a sampling of applications that require parallel computing for scaling to solve large and realistic models that can advance science and engineering. The final chapter of this volume discusses some current and upcoming challenges and opportunities in parallel scientific computing.

In this chapter, we provide an overview of this edited volume on scientific computing, which in broad terms concerns algorithms, their tuned software implementations on advanced computing systems, and their use and evaluation in modeling and simulation applications. Some distinguishing elements of scientific computing are a focus on high performance, an emphasis on scalable parallel algorithms, the development of advanced software tools and environments, and applications to computational modeling and simulation in diverse disciplines. These aspects are covered in the four main parts of the volume (Chapters 2–19). The final chapter, Chapter 20, contains a brief discussion of new and emerging trends and challenges in scientific computing.

The remainder of this chapter provides a brief overview of the contents of the book. We discuss each of the four main parts and the chapters within these parts in the order in which they occur.

1.1 Performance modeling, analysis, and optimization

The first part of this volume focuses on one of the most prominent themes in scientific computing, namely, that of achieving high performance. This emphasis on high performance arises primarily from the need for scientists and engineers to solve realistic models of ever-increasing size at the limits of available computing resources. In this context, optimizations for higher performance often can make the difference between solving and not solving a specific problem. To enable such performance optimizations, it is critical to have tools and instruments with which to identify and measure the sources of inefficiency across all levels, from the processor architecture and system software to the algorithm and its implementation. This topic is discussed in Chapter 2 with a focus on the challenges in developing such performance analysis tools and the issues that are relevant to improving current practices.

Chapter 3 discusses how parallel multiprocessors and distributed hierarchical and heterogeneous systems further complicate the process of achieving acceptably high levels of performance. It is emphasized that parallel scientific computation must necessarily take into account architectural characteristics for performance optimizations. In addition, there is a sampling of architecture-aware optimizations which can be applied across levels, from compilers that can reorder loops to high-level algorithms that are tuned to achieve a favorable trade-off between computation and communication costs. Chapter 4 provides an overview of the BlueGene/L, which is currently the fastest supercomputer in existence, with sustained execution rates of more than 280 teraops/sec for dense matrix computations [2]. This chapter focuses on the design of the BlueGene/L processor architecture, interconnection network, and the tuning of applications and benchmarks to achieve a large fraction of the peak execution rates while scaling to tens of thousands of processors.

Chapter 5, the fourth and final chapter in this part, concerns the growing gap between sustained and peak performance for realistic scientific applications on conventional supercomputers. The authors discuss the need for high-fidelity performance modeling to understand and predict the interactions among hardware, software, and the characteristics of a diverse set of scientific applications.

1.2 Parallel algorithms and enabling technologies

The second part of this volume focuses on parallel algorithms for core problems in scientific computing, such as partitioning, load balancing, adaptive meshing, sparse linear system solution, and fault tolerance. Taken together, these techniques are critical for the scaling of a variety of scientific applications to large numbers of processors while maintaining acceptable levels of performance.

The scalability goal in scientific computing is typically that of maintaining efficiency while increasing problem size and the number of processors. This is achieved by developing algorithms that limit the overheads of parallelization, such as communication costs. If T_1 and T_P are, respectively, the observed serial and parallel execution times using P processors, the efficiency is $E = \frac{T_1}{PT_P}$. Now the total overhead $T_O = PT_P - T_1$, and thus $E = \frac{T_1}{T_1+T_O}$. Typically, for problem size N, $T_1 = f(N)$, where f is a function representing computational costs, while T_O depends both on N and P, i.e., of the form $g(N, P)$. Now $E = \frac{1}{1+g(N,P)/f(N)}$ can be maintained at a fixed acceptable level by choosing appropriate values of N for a corresponding value of P. Scientific computing algorithms are typically designed to ensure such *weak scaling*, thus allowing larger problems to be solved on larger numbers of processors in constant time.

Scientific computing has traditionally focused primarily on numeric algorithms for functions and models whose variables such as time, temperature, and velocity are continuous. However, with the development of new computational models and the need for their parallelization there has been a growth of combinatorial schemes for discrete problems, such as partitioning and integer programming. Chapter 6 provides an overview of partitioning and load-balancing schemes, which are critical for the effective scalable parallelization of most scientific applications. It includes traditional approaches such as weighted graph partitioning for computations on discretized representation of spatial domains. Additionally, models of partitioning and load balancing using multiple objectives and resource constraints, and emerging applications such as nanotechnology, clustering, and circuit simulation, are also considered. Chapter 7 provides a survey of combinatorial algorithms in scientific computing, such as those for ordering sparse matrices in a direct solver and decompositions with colorings. The authors also consider the parallelization of irregular computations such as radiation transport on unstructured grids and multipole calculations in molecular dynamics.

Many complex simulations of time-dependent partial differential equations using finite-difference, finite-element, or finite-volume methods require parallel algorithms for mesh refinement and linear system solution. Chapter 8 concerns parallel algorithms for adaptive mesh refinement (AMR) suitable for simulations with dynamic, localized features. The authors provide a survey of parallel AMR algorithms and their relative strengths and weaknesses with an emphasis on block structured and unstructured schemes. Chapters 9 and 10 concern parallel algorithms for sparse linear system solution, often the computationally intensive part of modeling applications using implicit or semi-implicit formulations. Chapter 9 provides an overview of parallel sparse solvers based on direct and iterative methods and their hybrids and preconditioning techniques for accelerating convergence. Chapter 10 concerns the parallelization of multigrid solvers, including all aspects such as coarse grid parallelism and the parallelization of the coarsening and smoothing steps.

As parallel systems and applications scale up in size, they become prone to regular failures due to the large number of components and their complex structure. Additionally, many applications will execute for several days and weeks on such high-end systems, thus increasing the probabilities of system component failures. Although fault tolerance has traditionally been an active area of research in computer science, most scientific computing applications focus on improving performance with little or no regard for fault tolerance and recovery. Chapter 11 surveys the state of the art in fault-tolerant scientific computing, including recent advances in algorithms, applications, and message-passing systems.

1.3 Tools and frameworks for parallel applications

As algorithms and parallelization methods evolve and mature, they are often packaged into tools and environments for providing specific functionality to application developers with ease of access and use. The third part of this volume comprises four chapters covering a variety of topics related to tools for improving the productivity of application developers while enabling high performance, reusability, portability, and interoperability.

Chapter 12 provides a survey of parallel tools for scientific computing, including tools for creating and developing parallel programs, libraries for managing parallelism and applying parallel numerical algorithms, and complete environments and systems for modeling and simulation. Chapter 13 focuses on parallel linear algebra software for linear system solution and eigenvalue computations. The authors discuss principal differences between dense and sparse systems and provide an overview of libraries and toolkits for dense and sparse matrix computations and load balancing. This chapter emphasizes the software aspects, and it is related to preceding chapters on the algorithmic features of such linear algebra problems.

Chapters 14 and 15 consider the development of software *components* and their role in developing large-scale scientific applications. Frequently used functions are formed into a software component with an implementation transparent to the users or other components while meeting strict interface specifications. An application developer can create new software by connecting together a group of components, thus building an application out of interchangeable pieces of software with well-defined interfaces. In scientific computing, components hide much of complexity of data structures and indexing in parallel codes with message passing. The challenges in developing scientific components without sacrificing high performance are discussed in Chapter 14 with particular emphasis on the problem of data transfers between components. Chapter 14 discusses some recent successes achieved through component technology with some observations on the limitations to interoperability in current component models and some proposals for improved abstractions for future systems.

1.4 Applications of parallel computing

The fourth part of this volume considers new and emerging computational models, simulations, and associated methodologies.

Chapters 16 and 17 consider optimization of nonlinear and linear functions with constraints. Chapter 16 considers optimization problems such as inverse acoustic wave propagation or initial condition inversion of contaminant transport. Such inverse problems are often governed by partial differential equations (PDEs), much as their simulation counterparts. However, the inverse problems seek to determine some *decision data*, such as initial or boundary conditions or source functions, unlike simulations which use such decision data to compute *state data*, such as velocity, temperature, and stress field. The authors introduce computational schemes for such PDE-based optimization and discuss their parallelization. Chapter 17 considers mixed-integer programming for the optimization of a linear function subject to linear and integrality constraints. Such optimization is used in applications like network interdiction to damage the ability of a network to transport material from a source to a destination, or to model contamination in fluid transport networks. The authors discuss the design of algorithms for such applications to effectively scale to thousands of processors to solve very large problems at regional or national scales.

Chapter 18 concerns methodology and software for designing multicomponent, multiphysics simulations for engineering. In particular, the authors focus on a system for the detailed simulation of solid rocket motors involving fluid dynamics, solid mechanics, and combustion, as well as multiple levels and types of interactions. They discuss their approach to overcome such challenges as efficiently transferring data between components, managing changing problem geometry, and maintaining mesh quality.

The fourth and final chapter in this part, Chapter 19 concerns computational biology applications which can benefit from effective parallelization. The underlying problems often involve optimization and massive data sets. The authors provide a survey of recent results for problems spanning genomics, phylogenetics, and protein structural biology, such as protein folding and reconstruction of evolutionary histories.

1.5 Conclusions and future directions

Chapter 20 concludes this volume with a discussion of opportunities and challenges facing scientific computing in the near future. These concern design and development issues for scaling and sustained performance, including processor and network design; languages and parallel programming models; power-aware high performance computing; and robust algorithms, software, and tools for high productivity application development and integration.

Bibliography

[1] SIAM, *The SIAM Conference on Parallel Processing for Scientific Computing*, 2004. http://www.siam.org/meetings/pp04.

[2] UNIVERSITY OF MANNHEIM, UNIVERSITY OF TENNESSEE, AND NERSC/LBNL, *Top500 Supercomputer Sites*, 2005. http://top500.org/.

[3] U.S. DEPARTMENT OF ENERGY, *Scientific Discovery Through Advanced Computing*, 2006. http://www.scidac.org/.

Part I

Performance Modeling, Analysis, and Optimization

Chapter 2
Performance Analysis: From Art to Science

Jesús Labarta and Judit Gimenez

Proper identification of the causes of inefficiency in parallel programs and quantification of their importance are the basic steps to optimizing the performance of an application. Performance analysis is often an art, where the skill and intuition of the analyst play a very relevant role and which requires a good understanding of how all the levels of a system (from processor architecture to algorithm) behave and interact. Proper analysis also requires measurement instruments capable of capturing the information to validate or reject the hypotheses made during the analysis cycle. The difficulty and global nature of the problem itself and the limitations of the instruments contribute to the view of performance analysis as an art. Improving the power of our instruments is a necessary step to letting analyses proceed based on measurements rather than on feelings.

This chapter discusses some of the issues that are relevant to improving current practice in this field. Many of these issues have to do with the actual power of the analysis tools (flexibility to compute and display performance indices, precision, scalability, instrumentation overhead, methodology), although other aspects, e.g., cultural, economical, are also of key importance.

The chapter looks at these issues from the perspective of a specific performance analysis environment around the Paraver visualization tool, extracting from the experience in its development and use some general observations applicable to many other approaches.

Parallel architectures and programming promise increasingly powerful computing capabilities delivered to users, enabling them to target larger and more complex problems. Unfortunately, the expected linear increase in performance with the number of processors very often is not achieved. Immediately the question arises of why it happens or how to really meet expectations. In other situations, the user may be sufficiently happy with the achieved performance without realizing that the potential of the machine and her or his algorithm may be higher than actually delivered.

Analysis of the performance of a parallel computer today is too much an art, where the experience, intuition, and sensibility of the analyst play a very important role in the way a problem is faced and the final diagnosis about how it should be solved. Engineers or scientists, designers of the systems, application developers, and users would benefit from a more formalized analysis theory and methodology that would let a broader mass of analysts to rapidly arrive at useful recommendations. We consider that three major issues will determine such evolution from art to science. The first two have a technical component and have to do with improvements in the capabilities of measurement and modeling. The third, which we could term as cultural or socioeconomic aspects, has to do with the attitude with which we face the performance analysis problem. This chapter discusses some of the issues of measurement capabilities and makes a brief incursion into the modeling aspects. The socioeconomic aspects are extremely important, with many technical implications, and will be mentioned throughout the chapter as the opportunity arises.

In a world of specialists, the first difficulty in performance analysis activities arises from the global nature of the problem. Properly understanding qualitatively and quantitatively the detailed behavior of a program and system is a difficult task. The performance of a parallel computer is the result of the convolution of many design factors at different levels of the system structure stack. The algorithm, programming model, run time, operating system, parallel architecture, and processor architecture play important roles in the resulting performance. The intricate and highly nonlinear interactions between factors within and between levels makes the analysis job a difficult one, especially in getting the details right. The performance analyst must perform a search for causes and effects in a fuzzy and ill-defined space with moving targets. In this type of situation, personal sensibility has always played an important role. Different persons faced with the same problem will most probably proceed in different directions. In this environment, it is common for a person to focus her or his interest on a subset of the above-mentioned levels, in some cases disregarding the potential impact of others or alternatively arguing that phenomena at those levels are the cause of the observed inefficiencies. It is not only end users who may lack knowledge or interest in all levels of the system structure. Engineers providing or developing one of the levels may also be too focused on their own components and thus less knowledgeable of others. Even within the analysts community, there is an important trend in rapidly pointing to the "usual suspects," like cache misses, false sharing, or communication overhead, without precise and quantified knowledge of the detailed cause in a specific situation. This attitude may result in esoteric or mysterious explanations—as also arose in other fields before they became what we today consider sciences.

To overcome such difficulties, a performance analyst should be a generalist, with a good global view of the different levels of the system architecture, capable of communicating with users as well as application or system developers. Being open minded as to where the problem could be, patient to explore a broad range of hypotheses, and scientific as to quantitatively double-check the hypotheses are qualities that the performance analyst should exercise.

The objective of performance analysis is to understand the behavior of the whole system, from architecture to application. Identifying the causes of performance losses is the first step to optimizing a design. Often, once the cause is identified, solutions can rapidly be put in place to overcome the problem. Even if the problem cannot be immediately fixed, the ability to estimate the cost of implementing a solution is extremely useful in making the appropriate planning decisions. Getting a proper estimate of the performance improvement that such a solution will provide is the other major need for planning future steps in program development. Both types of information require detailed measurement and analysis capabilities.

The ability to perform precise and accurate measurements is a key element needed to differentiate an art from a science. Instruments and measurement techniques have played an enabling role in the progress of all areas of science and technology. For very small to very large scales, humans have developed instruments to whose capability of observation have been linked many advances in science. Lack of measurement instruments is one of the difficulties that young sciences are faced with. Computer science in general and parallel programming in particular should be seen in this way.

The most widely used instruments in the performance analysis field probably are timers and print statements. Based on very coarse grain measurements like total elapsed time or total instructions and cache misses, we tend to speculate on the microscopic behaviors that result in such observed measurements. Inferring the time-varying behavior of a complex nonlinear system from a number that aggregates its actual behavior over a long period is, at the very least, risky. The approach may work properly when analyzing microbenchmarks designed to measure a specific component of the system stack. Designers make big efforts to perform these measurements under a controlled environment, trying to keep all factors stable. Unfortunately, such measurements cannot perform a full coverage of all the possible control flow paths and environment conditions that a large application will experience. A real application will have to be run in a less-controlled environment and will probably have different phases or time-varying behavior. We need mechanisms able to perform fine-grain measurements in real operation environments under realistic conditions. Tools should provide mechanisms for extracting from the raw data thus obtained the maximum information possible and should be able to associate different aspects of the observed behavior with different factors and to minimize the unexplained components.

The main idea in this chapter is that powerful tools supporting detailed quantitative analysis of system behavior are required to boost the scientific-engineering dimension that performance analysis deserves. The development of performance models is the second pillar of the performance analysis science. Based on our experience in the development and use of Paraver, we discuss issues that we consider of great importance in the direction of providing measurement instruments capable of supporting the performance analyst job. The ideas are nevertheless general and apply to a broad range of performance measurement instruments.

The structure of the chapter is as follows. In section 2.1 we briefly present the conceptual framework for performance analysis tools. Section 2.2 describes Paraver, the visualization tool developed at Centro Europeo de Paralelismo de Barcelona (CEPBA) that we will be using as the basis for the considerations in the following sections. In section 2.3 we comment on methodology issues and the required analysis power support. Section 2.4 addresses the issue of scalability, and in section 2.5 we comment on the interaction of performance analysis tools and models. Section 2.6 concludes this chapter.

2.1 Performance analysis tools

To understand the behavior of a system it is necessary to capture, during the program run, the events from which the performance indices will be derived. Performance analysis tools need mechanisms to inject probes into a system in order to capture such events. These probes typically will be segments of code capable of registering the event and possibly the summarized information that may be available through an acquisition mechanism implemented at a lower level. This is the case of hardware counters [9], for example, where hardware probes inserted into the architecture accumulate occurrences of specific events in registers that can be consulted by higher-level probes.

We can think of the captured events as points in a three-dimensional (3D) space, as shown in Figure 2.1. The temporal dimension states when an event happens, while the spatial dimension corresponds to the process (or processor) where it happens. Different types of events may be captured in a given run, and this is what we associate with the third dimension. Two basic approaches can be used in the acquisition process to determine the time when events are captured. In instrumentation mode, every event relevant to the targeted performance analysis is captured. It is then the occurrence of every event that determines its time coordinate in our 3D space. In sampling mode, an external mechanism determines when performance data are collected and thus the temporal coordinate of the event. In this situation, only a subset of the relevant events is actually captured. Both in instrumentation and sampling modes, summarized information provided by lower-level instrumentation mechanisms may also be added as an attribute to the events.

The captured data must be transformed in performance indices and presented to the analyst. This can be in the form of summarized profiles in which the time and space dimensions have been collapsed. Such summarization can take place during the run itself or offline. Online summarization results in the need to emit less information to a storing device, while emitting all the captured data to a tracefile does not lose information in the summarization process. Trace-based approaches also enable detailed offline analyses. Typical profilers follow the online summarization approach. Other tools [1] actually obtain

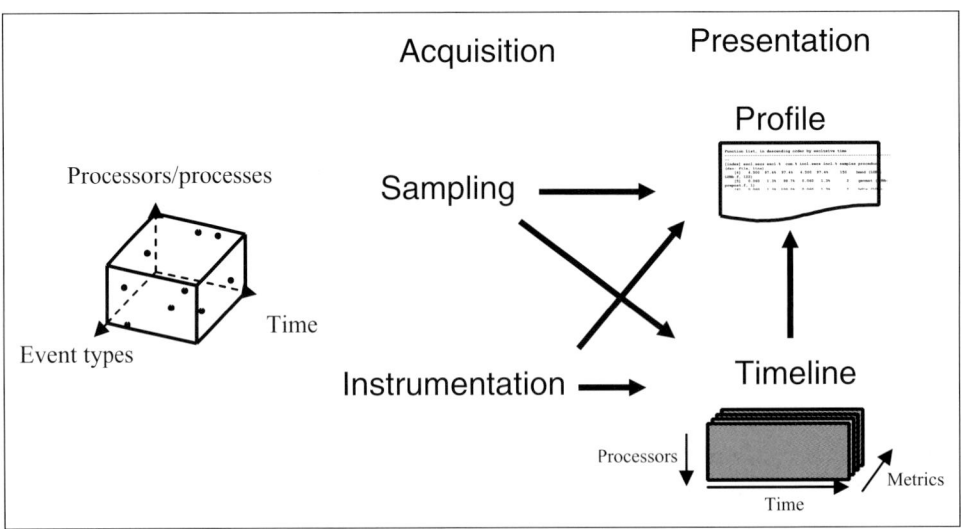

Figure 2.1. *Performance tools approaches.*

a trace so that elaborated statistics can be computed offline before the presentation process. The presentation can be in pure textual form or through a graphical user interface (GUI) (i.e., Xprofiler [7], CUBE [8]), offering the user a clearer perception of magnitudes and letting the user navigate the set of precomputed statistics.

Timelines [10, 11, 12] are an alternative representation wherein both spatial and temporal distribution of events and metrics are presented to the analyst. This approach is based on the idea that being able to observe the time distribution of events and their correlation is key to understanding the detailed behavior of a parallel program. The interaction between qualitative visual inspections and precise statistics computed on demand for selected regions of the space-time domain opens the door to deep insight into system behavior.

Other presentation forms, in the line of classical data visualization in the engineering or biology fields, would perform a spatial display of a given performance index for each process. The actual 3D structure on which to superimpose the selected index can match the parallel computer architecture or the partitioned problem domain. The first approach may help us understand performance issues related to network topology, for example, while the second may explain the relationship between computational load and the decomposition structure.

We would like to stress in this section one point that we consider of vital relevance if performance analysis is to become a scientific discipline to support program developers and users. The consideration is an economical one. We strongly believe that performance analysis is extremely expensive if an analyst cannot face an application on which she or he has no previous knowledge and then come back with sensible observations and recommendations in a short period. Minimizing the time to assess an application performance is an important requirement for the analysis tools and methodologies. In particular, requiring the analyst to enter into details of the source code in the initial phases of a study is not an ideal situation. Spending, in some cases, several months in analysis before being able to make sensible comments or suggestions to a program developer on how her or his application behaves is a tremendous economic load that can be justified only in very special environments. To be a popular discipline capable of helping all classes of users, performance analysis has to be applicable and to deliver results in very short times. It is true that deep analysis may then require a look at the source code, but in a focused way, as indicated by the initial analyses. These considerations do have some technical implications, of which we would like to stress two: the need for dynamic instrumentation and the need to automatically capture the structure of an application. We will comment more on this in section 2.3.1.

2.2 Paraver

The CEPBA-tools environment (see Figure 2.2) is organized around Paraver, a display tool conceived as a general browser of the raw performance data stored in a tracefile. The design philosophy of Paraver is to avoid semantics in the tool itself so that it could actually browse any type of data represented as a sequence of time stamped events (i.e., stock exchange time series or manufacturing plant schedules).

The environment includes several tracing packages for different parallel programming models (MPI, OpenMP, mixed, MLP) and platforms as well as other types of activities, such as OS kernel scheduling (AIXtrace, SCPU, LTT) and nonnumeric applications (JIS, WebSphere). All of these share with Paraver a fairly neutral trace format with three major

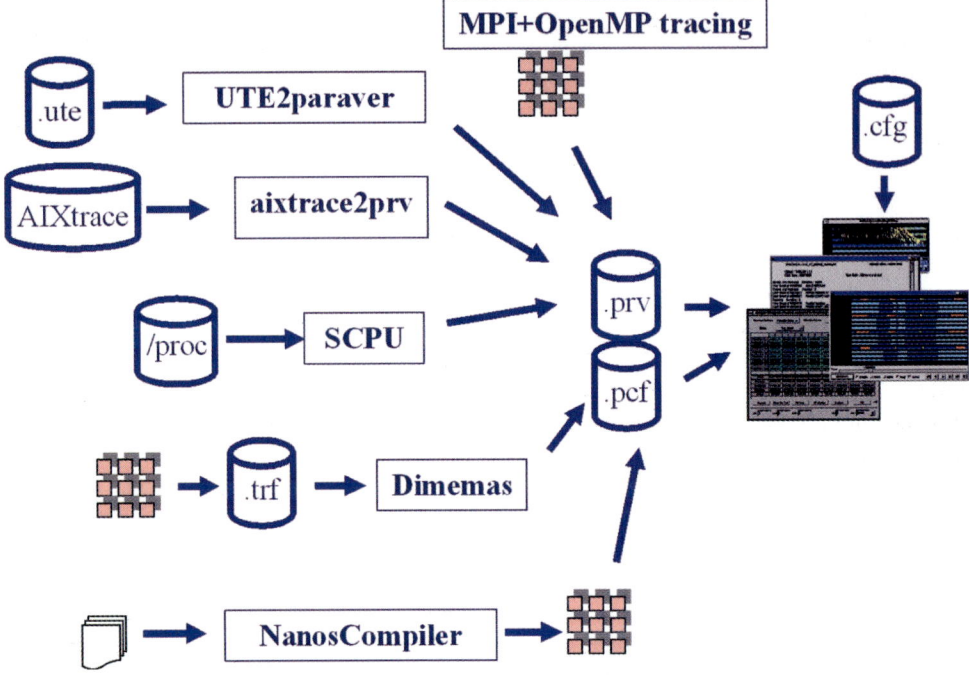

Figure 2.2. *The CEPBA-tools environment.*

types of records: state and event records that describe local activity within one thread, and communication records that represent the interaction between pairs of threads. The first such record type encodes in an integer the state a thread is in between two timestamps. The encoding of such a state is totally up to the tracing tool, but typical choices are to represent states such as running, waiting, or fork-joining overhead. Event records represent a punctual event in the program execution and thus contain a single timestamp field. Two additional integers are available to encode the desired information. Normally, a tracing tool will reserve the first integer to encode the *type* of event (i.e., function call, cache miss counter, iteration) and the second integer to represent the specific *value* associated with that event (i.e., function identifier, actual cache count, iteration number). Communication records include the identification of the source and sink threads, the tag and size of the message, and timestamps of the start and end of the communication. Additionally, the record includes two timestamps where the tracing package can indicate when the message actually left the sending processor and arrived at the target processor, if such information is available (i.e., in traces generated by Dimemas [13] or if the internals of the message passage interface (MPI) implementation are also traced [14]).

2.2.1 Timelines and performance indices

Paraver provides a flexible mechanism with which to transform the record data into functions of time that can then be represented as timelines. Paraver as such has no knowledge of what a function or cache miss is. Nevertheless an analyst knowing how the tracing package encodes the events can specify through a GUI how to generate a given performance index. The performance indices computed in this way are piecewise constant functions of time. Let t_i be the ith instant of change of the function and S_i be the value taken at that time; then the function of time ("semantic value") is

$$S(t) = S_i, t \in [t_i, t_{i+1}).$$

The typical colorful timeline displays of other tools can in this case be obtained by translating values to colors, either through a table or by a gradient encoding mechanism. Putting the emphasis on functions of time offers a conceptual framework where a large range of mathematical formulations can be applied to achieve a tremendous analysis power and a precise specification of the actual metric reported. Furthermore, as the analyst can specify how to generate the semantic value through a GUI, the color representation mechanism can now be applied not only to predefined views but to any performance metric that may arise as the analysis progresses.

Let us describe some example of how $S(t)$ can be defined. Assume that we focus on events of a given type (i.e., entry-exit user functions, cache misses) and let t_i be the instant of the ith such event and v_i its associated value.

We can define $S_i = v_i$. This will generate a function of time whose value during an interval between two events is the value associated with the event at the beginning of the interval. Such a mechanism is typically used with event types that encode the entry-exit of routines (user functions, MPI calls) to generate functions of time that take as their value the identifier of the routine during its whole duration. This mechanism is also useful when events with the value of a given variable are emitted to the trace when it changes. The essence in all these cases is that the information of the new value that will hold for the following interval is known to the tracing tool at the beginning of the interval. Other alternatives are to select as $S_i = v_{i+1}$. In this case, the value during a given interval is determined by the event at the end and matches those situations where the tracing tool is able to obtain only the information relative to an interval when it finalizes. This is the case with hardware counters, for example, but could also be the case with return values for a routine. The choice of $S_i = v_{i+1}/(t_{i+1} - t_i)$ can be used to build a function of time that reports for each interval between two samples of a hardware count the rate of its corresponding performance metric (i.e., MIPS, Mflops, cycles/us). Other choices are to report the duration of the intervals ($S_i = t_{i+1} - t_i$) or are related to communication records ($S_i = \sum \text{Bytesarriving}[t_i, t_{i+1}]$) that can be used to derive relevant metrics for message passing programs.

Two major mechanisms with which to generate new performance indices are to apply composition of functions ($S'(t) = f \circ S(t)$) and to derive new metrics combining other metrics ($S(t) = S_1(t) <op> S_2(t)$). In the first case, besides arithmetic operations (add, mod), other useful nonlinear compositions can zero out of a function of time whose value is not within a desired range or generate binary functions if a given condition (i.e., value within a given range) is satisfied or not. Deriving functions of time by pointwise combination of other views through arithmetic operations is a powerful mechanism for obtaining new metrics (i.e., miss ratios, instructions per cycle or ratio of loads per store) and also for focusing a metric on only the regions of interest. Multiplying an Mflops window by a window equal to one inside a given user function and zero outside has two major uses: first, it eliminates from a graphical representation information that may divert the analyst's perception and lets the analyst concentrate on the region of interest; and second, it is an enabler of further detailed quantitative statistic such as histograms or correlations for just the specified function.

2.2.2 Statistics

Putting the emphasis on functions of time also offers a wide range of possibilities in terms of computing statistics. All the quantitative analysis in Paraver is supported by a two-dimensional (2D) analysis module (Figure 2.3) that computes a table with one entry per process or processor and a set of columns corresponding to the different values taken by a view that we call *control window*. For each entry in the table, Paraver computes a statistic on a view that we call *data window*. The control window determines the regions of time to which metrics are computed and decides to which column the actual accumulation goes, while the statistic selector and data window determine the actual value to be accumulated.

Let $cw(t)$, $dw(t)$ be, respectively, the control window and the data window functions of time as generated by the semantic module and CW_i, DW_i be the values taken by such functions of time at their ith instant of change. Let t_start and t_end represent the limits of the analyzed time interval and i_start, i_end be the first and last instant of change within that interval. Let $cw\_range = [cw\_lower, cw\_upper]$ be the range of values of the control window that accumulate to a given column. We define the discriminator functions

$$\delta_{cw\_range}(t) = ((cw\_lower \leq cw(t) \leq cw\_upper)?1:0),$$

$$\Delta_{cw\_range}(i) = ((cw\_lower \leq DW_i \leq cw\_upper)?1:0)$$

that return one if the semantic value is within the selected range and zero otherwise. Example statistics that can be computed for one cell in the table are

$$\text{Time} = \int_{t\_start}^{t\_end} \delta_{cw\_range}(t)dt,$$

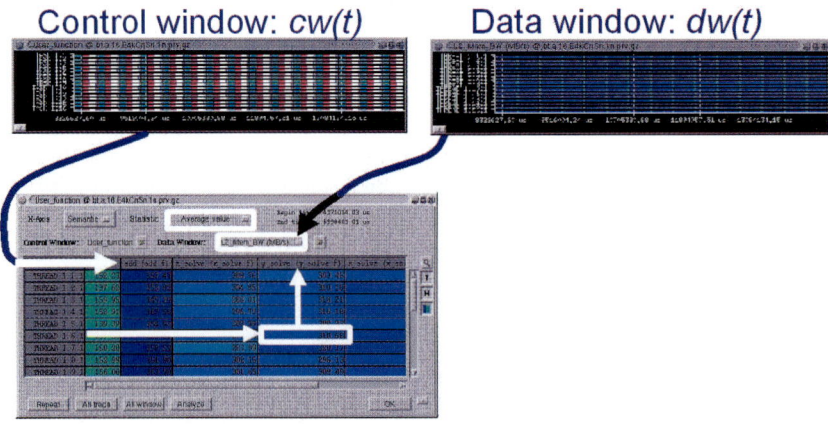

Figure 2.3. *2D analysis.*

$$\text{Average} = \frac{\int_{t\_start}^{t\_end} dw(t)\delta_{cw\_range}(t)dt}{\int_{t\_start}^{t\_end} \delta_{cw\_range}(t)dt},$$

$$\text{Integral} = \int_{t\_start}^{t\_end} dw(t)\delta_{cw\_range}(t)dt,$$

$$\text{NumBursts} = \sum_{i\_start}^{i\_end} \Delta_{cw\_range(i)},$$

$$\text{AveragePerBurst} = \frac{\sum_{i\_start}^{i\_end} \text{DW}_i * \Delta_{cw\_range(i)}}{\sum_{i\_start}^{i\_end} \Delta_{cw\_range(i)}},$$

$$\text{SumBursts} = \sum_{i\_start}^{i\_end} \text{DW}_i * \Delta_{cw\_range(i)}.$$

If the control window values are the identifiers of the function being executed along time, then there will be one column per function. The Time statistic will compute for each routine the total time it executed (a typical profile), while the NumBursts statistic would count the number of times the control flow enters the routine. If a view displaying Mflops was selected as the data window, the Average statistic would report for each routine its average Mflop ratio. SumBursts, if the selected data view represents instructions, would return the total number of instructions within the routine, something that could also be computed with the Integral statistic applied to a data window representing MIPS.

If the control window represents a continuous valued function (i.e., instructions, function duration) and the NumBursts statistic is used to count the number of occurrences, then the table will represent a histogram. If, for example, we use as the control window one that is zero when outside a given user function and the number of instructions when inside, then the NumBursts statistic would compute the histogram of the number of instructions executed within the routine. Such a histogram for all threads in a run is a precise description of the computational load balance for that function. Changing the statistic to Average and the data window to, for example, cache misses would report the correlation between the two metrics. Each entry in the table would indicate the average number of cache misses incurred as a function of the number of instructions.

The mechanism is extremely flexible, as any view can be when used as a control window as well as a data window and a rich set of statistics is provided. Which is the most appropriate statistic for a given analysis? The choice depends on the metric and even the analyst's perception or interest. Consider, for example, Average and AveragePerBurst, both of which report an aggregated statistic ultimately summarizing the sequence of values DW_i. Their values may nevertheless differ significantly as one of them takes into account the duration of the intervals, while the other just takes into account the series of values. If the DW_i represent, for example, the number of instructions within a given user function, AveragePerBurst should be used as an estimate of the expected number of instructions for an invocation of the routine. The Average statistic would weight more invocations taking more time due to worse locality behavior and would be the appropriate statistic to estimate the average MIPS.

2.2.3 Configuration files

A problem of the extremely flexible mechanisms with which to define views and statistics in Paraver is that the responsibility is moved to the user of the tool, who must concentrate knowledge of the information in the trace, how it has been encoded, and how relevant metrics can be extracted from it. Specifying how to generate a view through the GUI may also be cumbersome. To circumvent these problems, Paraver includes a mechanism by which it is possible to save into a file the information on how to build a view or statistic. In this way, an expert can hand to novice users a structured set of configuration files that would specialize the power of the tool to just the set of analyses that the expert considers relevant. We could argue that multiple performance analysis tools targeted to different uses can thus be developed by using Paraver as the core analysis engine but without needing to modify its internal implementation.

2.3 Analysis methodology

Ideally, a performance analyst equipped with a powerful instrument and facing the analysis of an application should also have a methodology stating a set of measurements to perform and how to proceed through the structured sequence, depending on the results obtained. Defining such a structured set of measurements is probably difficult, especially if we aim for a general methodology.

After the initial traversals of such a tree, the analyst will soon enter an iterative phase where she or he will generate hypotheses on the causes of the observed performance based on the observed metrics and her or his knowledge of the system or application. At this point, it is important for the tool to have the maximum flexibility and analysis power to squeeze the huge amount of information that the trace has captured.

In the following subsections we describe some issues about which we think current practice in performance analysis is not as mature as in other scientific areas.

2.3.1 Quality and structure of the data to be analyzed

The first issue faced when analyzing a trace is a general question about what the structure of the code is, how representative is the section of the program run captured, or how perturbed are the data as compared to a noninstrumented run. This initial contact with the object under observation is an important step that often does not receive the attention it deserves. Experimental scientists from archeology, medicine, engineering, or data mining devote significant time to properly preprocessing and preparing the raw data for the ulterior analysis. In performance analysis there is a certain trend in which the global data reported, is located at by, for example, a profiler, and either believed blindly or discarded it completely.

An important phase of the initial analysis should be to check whether the trace shows certain types of perturbations. A typical question is whether some processor has been preempted. This question can easily be answered on traces that contain information on the cycles hardware counter. A view computing $S_i = v_{i+1}/(t_{i+1} - t_i)$ should return a value equal to the clock frequency of the processor. A ratio less than the clock frequency has to be interpreted, assuming virtualized counters, as the process having executed for less than the total elapsed time. A typical cause may be preemptions by other processes or voluntary process yields by the run time.

Instrumentation overhead is an important concern for many users of performance analysis tools. Analysts need to be reassured that the instrumentation did not disturb the real execution of a program and will typically throw away a trace if they suspect that there has been some perturbation of the run. We strongly believe that by doing so we are often disregarding a huge amount of information that can throw light on our understanding of the behavior of a system. The probe effect is unavoidable and should always be taken into account by the analyst, verifying its potential impact on each measurement. This is naturally accepted and handled in many disciplines of science and engineering but for some reason seems to be a taboo for parallel program performance analysis. One can even think of sciences like archeology and geology, where they are happy to study a bone or stone that has suffered the effects of thousands of years or centuries of wear and still they are able to infer how such primitive civilization or epoch was. Maybe we should also learn to build plausible theories on the behavior of a system not only from its direct observation, but also from the correlation of the huge amount of different indications that even the most distorted traces have.

In this context, a view computing the distance between events in the trace can be useful to identify regions of the run with significant instrumentation overhead. If we know the amount of overhead that a probe introduces, we can clear out the intervals when the distance is larger than, say, 10 times such duration, and thus we will see only the regions of the trace where the instrumentation overhead is in the order of 10% or less of the execution. This is typically not uniformly distributed across the trace. Even if we identify some regions of a trace as potentially very perturbed, other regions may still have relevant and reliable information.

Even on very perturbed traces it is possible to obtain useful information. As an example let us discuss the case of some systems in which the implementation of the interfaces to read the hardware counters information requires a system call, which often has to acquire a lock to access some of the kernel thread data structures. If a fine-grain OpenMP application is instrumented, its elapsed execution time may be increased by even an order of magnitude with respect to the noninstrumented run, and its load balance distribution will be totally altered. Even so, if the hardware counters measure activity in user mode, the information obtained will allow the analyst to derive extremely precise histograms of the distribution of instructions per chunk. Techniques to somehow assign confidence levels to the data reported and determine the quality of the information obtained from it will be relevant not only in trace-driven approaches but also on all other performance tools.

Finding out the structure of the application is another relevant issue. Analysts often face applications for which they do not know (and may not even understand) either the actual computation being performed or the programming methodologies and practices of the developer (Single Program Multiple Data (SPMD), parallel loops, user-level synchronization, recursion, communication patterns, time-varying behavior, etc.). In this situation, determining the structure of the application is a first step to then focus on the relevant section of the program run.

In the case in which the actual code developer is performing the analysis and has obtained the trace himself, a lot of such knowledge is probably available. Even so, it is a good practice to not rely blindly on what we think is the structure and behavior of the application. It is important to verify that the trace essentially matches our preconceived structure. We have all experienced the situation in which errors in a makefile or submission script induce us to misinterpretate of the achieved performances.

If the analyst has no clue about what the program structure is, finding out is often one of the difficult and tricky parts. A first approach to get such structural information is to use a call graph profile. Once some initial trace is obtained, one typically wants to identify iterations in it, but the pattern may be complicated by different levels of iteration (time steps, different physics and domains, iterative solution methods, etc.) and other factors such as time varying behavior, problem size dependent behavior, or programming practices of the code developer.

Structural information can be useful to limit the size of the trace by just capturing a small but sufficient number of iterations. Another important use of such information is to avoid tracing a very heterogeneous mixture of granularities. Ideally, a trace should have a relatively uniform distribution of the events along time representing computations of a certain granularity level and capturing those events that may be relevant for the parallel aspects of the program behavior. If routine A computes a simple basic function (just some computation, no communications, no parallelism, no synchronization) and is called many times within a loop in routine B, instrumenting routine B will actually capture sufficiently aggregate information about routine A to identify whether there is some potential inefficiency in it. If so, an instrumented run focusing on routine A can be made to further investigate its behavior.

2.3.2 Metrics: Are simple concepts simple?

The first step to determine whether a given behavior is reasonable is to construct an appropriate performance index, metric, or property describing that behavior in a precise and quantifiable way. Our first observation in this line is that it is often not easy to specify such a metric. Very frequently, it is easy to give a qualitative description of a given behavior, but difficulties arise when trying to formalize it. Let us look at two simple cases: load balance and bandwidth.

2.3.3 Load balance

Informally speaking, a parallel computation is said to be well balanced if all processors perform the same amount of computation. If the load is imbalanced, some processors will sit idle while waiting for others, thus resulting in inefficient utilization of the resources available. Although we do talk a lot about load (im)balance, we seldom use a quantitative metric to describe it.

A first issue that needs clarification is whether we are referring to load imbalance in terms of amount of computation (useful algorithmic instructions, excluding synchronization and parallelization overheads) or in terms of time. Although both magnitudes are correlated, there are situations where a perfectly load-balanced computation leads to relatively load-imbalanced execution times. This typically happens if there is contention between the threads for some resource and the allocation algorithm is not fair. Examples of such situations are locks for mutual exclusion or contention in the access to shared data. In the latter case, processors closer to the memory module in which the data resides may be favored;

something similar may happen in the former case if no explicit effort is made to use a fair lock implementation. This observation raises the recommendation to try to quantify load balance of different magnitudes (i.e., time, instructions, cache misses) as a good approach to identifying some problems.

After choosing the magnitude, we need a mechanism to report a single number measuring the load imbalance. Different alternatives arise, although there is no general standard. One alternative is to compute the difference between the largest and smallest observed values of the selected magnitude across processors and report their difference, possibly normalized to one of them or the average. The problem is that all the processors are involved in the real system behavior, while the above index takes into account only two of them. An approach taking all of them into account would be to compute the coefficient of variation across processors. Another approach would be to report the parallelization efficiency due to the imbalance that can be computed as

$$\eta = \frac{\sum \text{Magnitude}_i}{P * \max(\text{Magnitude}_i)}.$$

Furthermore, such metrics are typically performed on the globally accumulated magnitude for the whole run. Since load balance is a property of each individual parallel region, there is a risk of underestimating it if one just looks at the global run.

Let us discuss, based on Figure 2.4, some of the issues that a detailed load-balance computation arises. The top-level display shows four iterations of the ammp SPEC OMP2001 benchmark run on 16 processors. The different colors represent the execution of different parallel loops, with light blue indicating when a processor is busy waiting outside a parallel region. The pink loop dominates the execution time. We can see that three or four threads in this loop tend to take more time than the others. If we were to compute the load balance based on the total time spent by each thread inside the pink routine for the whole program, we would find out that the application is fairly well balanced, with all the threads executing

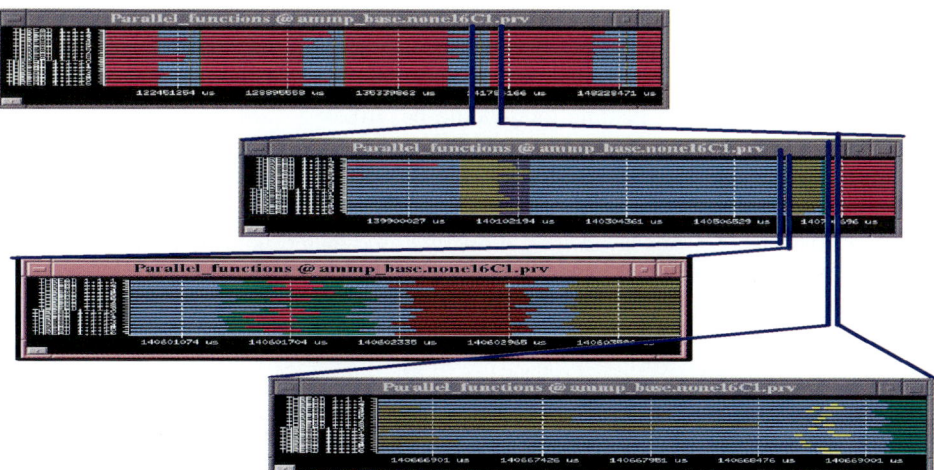

Figure 2.4. *Load balancing at different scales.*

about the same time within such parallel code. Graphically we can identify that the local load balance problem within the individual instance of the loop migrates between threads, resulting in a globally balanced execution. What would be a metric that quantitatively characterizes the load balance of the program? For loop-based OpenMP programs, we can compute for each thread and parallel routine the average fraction of time the thread is active while there is at least one active thread in that parallel region. If this statistic results in a value close to 1 for all threads, this means that all threads have been working at the same time, and this we can identify as a good load balance. If the value is close to 1 for some threads but far from 1 for others, we can infer that there has been a static load imbalance that followed a similar pattern at every invocation of the parallel region. If the value is similar for all threads but significantly different from 1, we can infer that the application had a migrating load imbalance, where all invocations of the parallel region have actual load imbalance, but it migrates between threads at different invocations.

The above example is an OpenMP one, based on parallel loops. Many situations can be found in which use of the above mechanism to estimate load balance is not appropriate. For example, in SPMD programs we may find significant skews between the invocations to a given routine by different threads. This is the case in many MPI programs but also in OpenMP programs that follow the SPMD structure. Even within the above OpenMP application (Figure 2.4), if we zoom into the two views at the bottom we can see that there will be difficulties. In these cases, the granularity of the parallel region becomes so small that skews appear in the moment each thread starts executing its part of the work. In this case the described metric will report values of less that 1 even if all threads executed exactly for the same time, but it will start skewed because of the run-time mechanism to distribute work. Furthermore, as in the case of the yellow stripes in the bottom view, the granularity may be so fine that some threads may get two chunks of work while others get none, just as a result of the contention on locks. At this granularity level it may be the case that no thread is inside the parallel work while not all of it has been performed. Classifying this behavior as load imbalance probably does not reflecting the real problem.

In summary, current practice tends to be a bit loose in the characterization of some properties of a parallel program. It is probably not realistic to think that a single metric can be computed that fits all needs and is applicable to any parallel program. In particular, it may also be difficult to display in a single metric the impact of different effects (i.e., load balance and fork-join overhead). A flexible tool should nevertheless support the computation of many such indices as appropriate for a specific situation. Blindly applying a mechanism to compute in general any property of a parallel program is risky unless we also validate that the hypotheses made about how the statistic is computed are correct. If a tool tries to report the existence or nonexistence of a property based on a rigid mechanism to compute an index that attempts to reflect such property, it should be used carefully.

2.3.4 Bandwidth

Bandwidth and latency are two words that appear pretty early in any conversation on performance. They are easily charged with responsibility for poor performances in message passing programs, yet one still seldom sees in performance tools the ability to report the bandwidth perceived by one communication or summarized for the whole application.

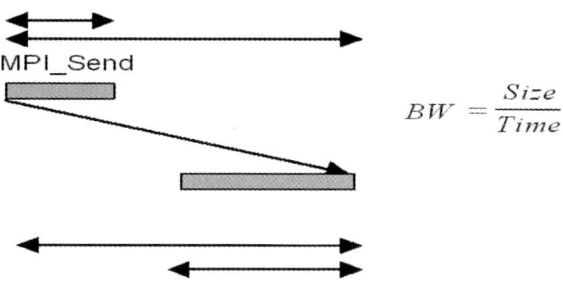

Figure 2.5. *Communication bandwidth.*

Bandwidth being a ratio between bytes and time, there is still an issue in clearly identifying what time is used as a denominator. If we take a look at the typical pattern of a message communication in Figure 2.5, the size of the message is easily identified, but one can use three possible times: the time of the MPI_send call, that of the MPI_Recv call, or the transfer time from start of send to end of receive (without going into detail about when the actual transmission is taking place). Furthermore, if we are interested in timelines reporting the evolution of such a metric, we need to project the value to the sender or receiver side and combine it with the values of other communications that may be taking place concurrently. Thus we can derive different views. An MPIcallCost view computed as

$$\text{MPIcallCost} = \frac{\text{BytesSentOrReceived}}{\text{DurationOfCall}}$$

is an indicator of how efficient the call was in handling the amount of data assigned to it. Huge values are possible, for example, in isend calls. Low values of this performance index for a given call are probably not desirable and may indicate receive calls where the sender arrives very late. A low value may nevertheless also derive from issues in the internal implementation of the MPI calls. In many platforms, it is possible to see isends for which the ratio between size and duration is small because the MPI implementation detects that the receiver is ready and performs the data transfer from within the isend call. Other implementations never perform the data transfer within the isend, and this call always returns immediately.

A receive_bandwidth view projects to the receiver timeline the transfer bandwidth (from start of send until end of receive/wait) of all incoming messages and indicates the effective bandwidth that would have been sufficient for the network and MPI layer to support in order to result in the observed communications duration. Similarly, a send_bandwidth view projects to the sender timeline the transfer bandwidth of all outgoing messages. Comparing the reported values by these views to those nominally supported by the system is a useful study that in many cases explains the low transfer bandwidth for individual communications.

2.4 Scalability

In the current environment where parallel computers up to several thousands or tens of thousands of processors are becoming available, the question naturally arises as to how applicable performance analysis tools are in such systems and what analysis techniques are appropriate for such systems.

This question has long been around. The Paradyn project [2] was motivated by this concern. This project opened the direction of dynamic instrumentation and iterative automatic search during the program run. Other current efforts follow the direction of producing online summarized information by the probes [15] and later performing statistical analyses on the results of several runs [16]. In general there is a perception that trace-based approaches face an enormous problem when scaling up to a large number of processors. Our position is that even for large numbers of processors, trace-based approaches can still be applied, offering the advantages of supporting a detailed analysis and flexible search capabilities. Certainly, blind tracing of a large system is unmanageable. The direction has to be one of intelligent selection of the traced information.

When discussing scalability of a trace-based visualization tool, two directions have to be considered: acquisition (tracing) and presentation (display/analysis).

2.4.1 Scalability of instrumentation

The acquisition problem has to do with the huge amount of information that a system can generate. This can cause problems in the process of collecting and merging the data into a single tracefile as well as in its later storage and processing by the visualizer. A frequent approach [17] is to hierarchically structure the data after partitioning in segments of reasonable size. Although this may allow a tool to display a summarized view or proceed directly to a specific segment, relying solely on the data structuring aspect of the problem just delays it.

We believe that the actual amount of information in a trace is not proportional to the amount of data. Mechanisms should be used in the tracing tools to obtain the minimal amount of data that captures the required type of information. The issue is more one of introducing intelligence in the process than what we would consider the brute force of enlarging its raw-data-handling capability. In some of the approaches we will now discuss, such intelligence will actually be the responsibility of the analyst, while in others the intelligence to automatically perform the appropriate selection can be integrated in an external driver tool or injected into the tracing tool itself. It is our belief that even if the automatic capability is highly desirable, providing the mechanisms such that the tracing tool can be directed as to what, how, and when to instrument is more important.

A common approach to reduce the amount of data captured is to use calls to stop and restart the tracing. By turning on the tracing process only for a short period we can obtain data that contain sufficient information to understand the behavior of the system. This approach will be useful in many iterative applications where the behavior is stationary along time. Tracing a few iterations will in general produce sufficient information to understand the behavior of the programs. If the user is aware that the behavior is slowly time varying, it is possible to trace several iterations at every sufficiently large interval. A similar idea can be applied to the spatial dimension if we are aware that the behavior is similar across processors. In this case it is possible to instrument a given range of processors and the interactions not only between themselves but also with others. This mechanism can significantly reduce the total amount of trace records while still recording all the detail for the selected processes. Such a mechanism has been implemented in our tracing package OMPItrace [18].

The above on-off mechanism can be controlled by explicit calls in the user code and also by arguments to the tracing package. The actual instrumentation is in any case controlled by the user or analyst. The possible interface to such a controlled instrumentation run would indicate, for example, to start instrumenting at the fifth entry to routine A and stop when exiting routine B for the 10th time.

Yet another mechanism for scaling down the size of traces is what we call software counters. This approach is also implemented in OMPItrace for some types of events. The idea is that the instrumentation probes perform some online accumulation but still emit periodically to the trace events with the summarized information. Examples of currently implemented software counters are the number of invocations of each MPI call or the total amount of bytes sent or received. A similar scheme is used for MPI calls like MPI_probe even when not using the software counters for actual data transfer or blocking calls. Fully tracing these calls would result in a lot of data and very little information, as they are often invoked in busy wait loops. In our approach, the first such call that finds no incoming message emits an event of value 0. Successive calls do not emit any record until a ready incoming message is detected. At this point, an event of value equal to the number of MPI_probes in between is emitted. From these events the analyst can extract sufficient information so as to understand the behavior of the application.

The software counters approach can drastically reduce the amount of traced information while still capturing the time-dependent aspects of system behavior. An additional advantage is its flexibility as to how to define the information emitted into the trace. We envisage a huge potential impact of the mechanism on many methodological aspects of the performance analysis process, but the actual relevance will be assessed as more experience on its use is gained.

The next step in scalability of instrumentation is to automatically detect the structure of the application and apply the above-described on-off ideas without user intervention. In [3] we presented an approach based on the detection of the repetitive pattern of the sequence of parallel functions executed by an application to turn off the generation of trace after a few iterations of an automatically detected repetitive pattern. The important thing is that the tracing mechanism is not suspended, and if the system detects a change in the structure of the application, it can still emit to the trace file the captured information. This type of semantically compressed trace can drastically reduce the size of the trace without user intervention.

These mechanisms with which to automatically detect the structure of an application should also be of interest to profilers or tools that report only summarized metrics. The idea is that properly identifying the region to analyze can result in better analyses than a blind analysis of the whole run. Analyzing a whole run may result in aggregated statistics masking slowly time-varying patterns, while blindly acquiring data during short periods without correlation with the program structure may result in incorrect statistics in the presence of rapidly varying patterns.

Manually modifying a source code to insert probes is an expensive process and assumes certain knowledge of the application to determine where to inject the timers or event calls. Even if performed by the actual developer of the code, this requires time to write and maintain. The fact that the resulting code has statements not related to its functionality is an indication that there is something at best not ideal.

Not requiring any modification of the source code is one of the strong points in profile tools based on sampling. In these tools, the control flow to the probes is fired by external events, not directly correlated to the program control flow. For instrumentation-based tools, it is necessary to precisely specify the point in the program control flow at which the probe has to be inserted. Compilation environments [19] to automatically instrument applications are an alternative when source code is available. Binary rewriting tools [24, 26] are also a possibility and have been used mostly in computer architecture studies. For performance analysis purposes they are somewhat cumbersome to use, requiring the bookkeeping of different binaries instead of directly operating on the production one. Dynamic instrumentation mechanisms [4, 5, 6, 25] are probably the most convenient alternative.

Irrespective of the mechanism used, a performance analyst should be able to specify to the tracing tool the points where she or he would like the probes to be injected as well as the type of information to capture. An abstract, high-level specification mechanism should be provided to the user to sensibly drive the tracing tool with minimal effort. Typically the user should indicate only things like trace MPI calls, use the software counter mechanism, trace this set of user functions, or use this set of hardware counters.

2.4.2 Scalability of visualization

The physical structure of a display device does pose a limit on the number of different object for which a given performance index can be displayed in a timeline. Even if we rely on color to represent magnitude and thereby reduce the required space to a minimum, index resolution cannot go below 1 pixel. A typical display cannot certainly display timelines for the range of system sizes we are considering.

The question is whether this is a real issue. What if we were able to use a display with 64,000 pixels? We would easily agree that the limit would not be the display device itself, but rather the ability of a human to properly process and classify all such information. In front of such a rich view, our visual system and mind would perform a fairly rough spatial integration and would get only a summarized perception of the program behavior. Faced with the fact that such integration will take place, the display tool now has an additional degree of freedom in performing the summarization or selection in ways that may actually increase the semantic information that is transferred to the analyst.

A first such approach is to present the information grouped by some relevant concept rather than individually for each thread. Two possible structures of integration can actually compute useful information: along the process model dimension and along the resource dimension. In the first case, it is possible to display a timeline for a single process rather than for each of its constituent threads. The function of time to display for each process can be computed by the pointwise aggregation of the functions of time of its constituent threads. It is possible, for example, to add individual functions stating whether a thread is doing useful work to report the instantaneous parallelism profile (Figure 2.6) or to add all the individual MFLOP rates to report the per-process rate. A similar mechanism adding the values of all the threads running in a node can generate a display in which a single line is presented for a node that may have several processors.

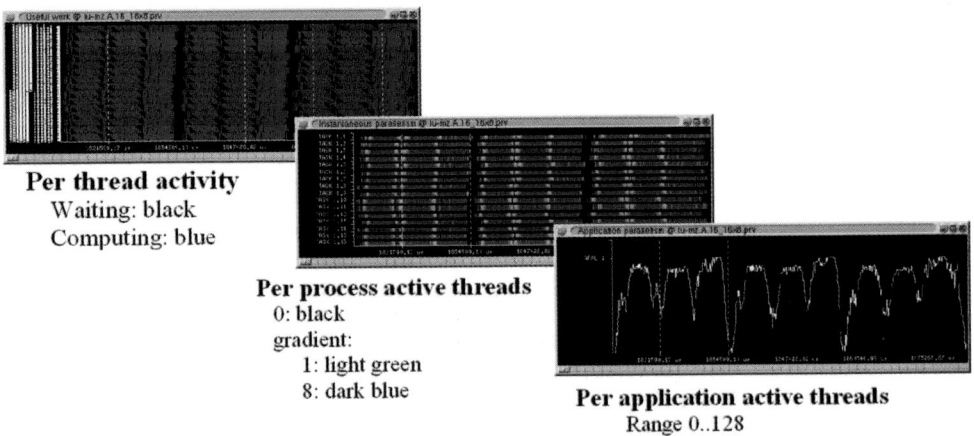

Figure 2.6. *Parallelism profile of a* 128-*processor run.*

This means of integration has the important benefit that it is not merely a representation issue but is a formal aggregation, to which all the statistical analysis capabilities described in section 2.2.2 can be applied. Precise numerical profiles can thus be obtained with specific semantics.

Let us come back for a moment to the integration process that takes place in the representation phase. We should stress the fact that even if only one of several objects (threads, processes, or nodes) is represented, such a display may often convey relevant information. The human eye has great correlation capabilities and can often identify a lot of relevant structures in sampled displays. What a tool needs to provide are mechanisms to let the analyst identify and then focus on the regions of interest.

The summarization in the display process affects not only the spatial dimension (processes) but also the temporal dimension. If the semantic value of several processes maps to the same pixel, a choice has to be made as to which value to represent. An alternative would be to select one of the possible threads, for example, randomly, the one with smallest thread identifier, etc. Another alternative would be to combine the different values by displaying an average or the maximum of all the values that map to the pixel. This mode is very useful for identifying very sparse events of extremely fine granularity but also very relevant for the analysis. Assume, for example, that our analysis module reports that a given function of an average duration of 5 microseconds is called five times by each thread in a period of 20 seconds but that it is necessary to find those invocations to deeply zoom into and study what happens around them. It is easy to build a semantic function that is one inside the function and zero outside. Like finding needles in haystacks, the chances of identifying these invocations are pretty low unless a nonlinear mechanism highlights (even if just as a single pixel) the desired regions. Paraver supports two basic modes, one selecting the maximum value and one selecting the last value that maps to each pixel. They are independently selectable for the spatial and temporal dimensions of the display.

Scroll bars are a basic mechanism used by many tools to enlarge the physical space mapped into the display. We nevertheless believe that drill-down zoom with the ability

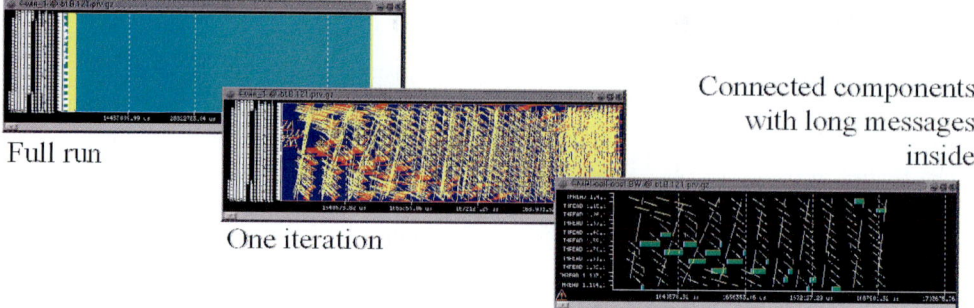

Figure 2.7. *Drill scalability.*

to undo and redo is preferable. Tools should actually go one step further in this ability to focus on a subset of the objects not necessarily contiguous in their numbering. Ideally, the selection of which objects to focus on should be based on some quantifiable statistic or property of the objects. As of today Paraver can do this based on a 2D statistic. It is possible to automatically select for display those threads with a given range of values of a computed statistic. In this way, the full power of the statistics module can be used to directly point to the relevant subset of what otherwise is an overwhelming amount of data in the trace.

Figure 2.7 exemplifies the type of capabilities we consider should form part of a properly scalable tool. The view at the top represents the whole run of a program (NAS BT class B on 121 processors). Only the initial part of the run has been traced (yellow part), while no record has been emitted since then until the end of the run (green part) because of its repetitive pattern. A zoom on the initial part is shown in the view in the middle. The view at the bottom represents a subset of the threads (4, 15, 26, 37, 48, 59, 70, 81, 92, 103, 114) involved in a connected components communication pattern. This view was obtained by manually selecting the threads involved in the communication after a slow process of just displaying messages arriving to one process, then those arriving to the senders, and so on. An automatic selection would save a significant amount of time in the process of identifying the relevant processes. The metric displayed in the bottom view is the MPIcallCost measured in MB/s. The low value represented by the light green stripes in the figure shows that some of the MPI calls in this circular communication exchange have not performed very well. The pattern rotates along the logical ring of processes. Different views like MPI calls, user functions, and duration of computation burst can be focused to display just the selected subset of processes and time interval. By analyzing them it was possible to identify that the poor performance of those MPI calls was actually due to a load-imbalance problem, curiously in a routine executed long before the invocation of the poorly performing MPI call.

This is a good example of what scalability is from our point of view. In a space of events that is certainly huge, scalability has to do with the ability to cover the huge dynamic range in terms of time, space, and size of the information that the analyst may wish to focus on.

2.5 Models: Reference of what to expect

A frequent question when analyzing a program is whether the observed performance is a reasonable one and why. This should be answered on the basis of performance models. Models are a key component of the analysis methodology in any science. They describe the relationship between the observable magnitudes, capture our understanding of the system behavior, and enable reasoning on how it should evolve. Models allow scientists to develop hypotheses for not-yet-observed behaviors that should then be validated by measurements. Observations provide new data that should be continuously contrasted with models, resulting in an assessment of the understanding of the system behavior or identifying the need to refine the model.

Although performance models are the topic of other chapters in this book and elsewhere [20, 21], we raise a couple of issues we think are relevant in this context. The first issue relates to the analysis power of the tool and the necessity to stress the importance of being able to perform precise measurements and check them against models. Very often we just look at global metrics such as elapsed time without measuring the achieved Mflops or Instructions per clock (IPC) rates, miss ratios, or communication bandwidth. The first methodological step should be to compare those measured magnitudes to either nominal values reported by the manufacturer or to previous experience, normally in the form of measured micro benchmark performance. These reference values are simple models of the system, and even if there are frequently poor approximations or unachievable upper bounds, a broad check should be performed of how far from them a given run is.

The requirement is thus for the analysis power of the tool to be able to report such measurements. By going a bit further, the tool should ease the job of the analyst in verifying the relationship between observed magnitudes and checking that they follow some simple models of program performance. As an example, an instrumented run can report hardware counts of total cycles, instructions, and level 1 and level 2 cache misses. By using the semantic module of Paraver we can build timeline views such as

$$\text{IPC\_pred} = \frac{\text{Instr}}{\text{Instr} * \text{IdealIPC} + L1\text{misses} * L1\cos t + L2\text{misses} * L2\cos t}$$

as a predictor of what the IPC should be for each section of the code based on the measured counts and values for IdealIPC, L1cost, and L2cost that could be derived from the manufacturer documentation as a first approximation. Other views computing the actually observed IPC value can be obtained by just dividing instructions and cycles. The comparison between model and observation supported by the tool offers a huge set of alternatives to the analyst. We can identify sections of the code where the match between the model and the observation is not good, leading to the identification of other factors (i.e., Translation Look-aside Buffer (TLB) misses) that have a strong impact in such sections. As another example, we can from the above expression derive a timeline for the L2cost assuming the observed IPC instead of the IPC_pred. In [22] we showed how such a view immediately pointed to memory mapping problems in a CC-NUMA machine that resulted in the cost of an L2 miss being very different for different sets of processors. Further opportunities appear by performing automated fits of the parameters. In [23] we presented Paramedir, a nongraphical version of Paraver. Paramedir can load the same Paraver traces and statistics configuration files, storing the computed results in a text file, and thus can be used for the evaluation of the cost function within an optimization code.

The second issue we would like to stress is the importance of the interoperability of tools that measure and model different parts of a computer hierarchy. Modeling tools are generally appreciated today as stand-alone prediction tools rather than as support tools for an analysis environment. Very frequently, the interest is on the tool reporting an aggregate predicted performance number, rather than the detailed internal behavior of a section of code that should then be analyzed with another tool.

One of the components of the CEPBA-tools environment is Dimemas [13], a simulator modeling the communication subsystem for message passing programs. In stand-alone mode, Dimemas can be used to estimate the performance of a hypothetical machine under construction and estimate the expected performance impact of an improvement in bandwidth, startup overhead, network connectivity, or processor performance. Nevertheless, Dimemas is integrated with Paraver and both can generate input traces for the other. By iterating between the use of Paraver and Dimemas, an analyst can greatly increase her or his understanding of the behavior of an application. Before drawing a conclusion from the measurements with Paraver, it is possible to check whether such measurements match the model or how sensitive they are to variations in certain parameters of the architecture. By being able to visualize detailed timelines, it is possible to perceive how the architecture and application characteristics interact. As a result, the integrated environment is far more powerful than just a measurement or modeling tool alone.

2.6 Conclusions

In this chapter we discussed some of the issues that we think will play a relevant role in improving today's performance analysis practices. As a first point we tried to stress the importance of extending the analysis power of our measuring instrument. Some of the capabilities these tools must support include (i) performance evaluation on production and large-scale systems, (ii) extraction of precise measurements, even from perturbed experiments, and (iii) the ability to define and quantify specific metrics as needed.

As a second point we emphasized the importance of cultural and economical aspects that often determine the attitude of users and analysts toward the performance analysis process and may impose strong limitations on what is actually achievable with our current instruments.

Models are the third component required to formalize our understanding of parallel computer performance. It is the tight interaction between models and measurement capabilities that will boost the performance analysis field into a scientific discipline, where methodology and formalism will play a role at least as important as the sensibility of the analyst.

Acknowledgments

The presentation has been based on our experience in the development of the CEPBA-tools environment and especially around Paraver and the MPI/OpenMP tracing packages.

This work is supported by the Ministry of Science and Technology of Spain (Contract TIN2004-07739-C02-01), the European Union (HPC-Europa project Contract RII3-CT-2003-506079), and the Barcelona Supercomputing Center.

Bibliography

[1] B. MOHR AND F. WOLF, *KOJAK—A tool set for automatic performance analysis of parallel programs*. Lecture Notes in Computer Science 2790, 2003, pp. 1301–1304.

[2] B. P. MILLER, M. CALLAGHAN, J. CARGILLE, J. K. HOLLINGSWORTH, R. IRVIN, K. KARAVANIC, K. KUNCHITHAPADAM, AND T. NEWHALL, *The paradyn parallel performance measurement tool*, IEEE Computer, vol. 28, no. 11, Nov. 1995, pp. 37–46.

[3] F. FREITAG, J. CAUBET, AND J. LABARTA, *On the scalability of tracing mechanisms*, Euro-Par, Paderborn, Aug. 2002, pp. 97–104.

[4] J. K. HOLLINGSWORTH, B. P. MILLER, AND J. CARGILLE, *Dynamic program instrumentation for scalable performance tools*, Scalable High Performance Computing Conference Proceedings, Knoxville, TN, May 1994.

[5] L. DEROSE, T. HOOVER, AND J. K. HOLLINGSWORTH, *The dynamic probe class library—An infrastructure for developing instrumentation for performance tools*, Int'l. Parallel and Distributed Processing Symposium, San Francisco, CA, April 2001.

[6] Dyninst. http://www.dyninst.org/.

[7] Xprofiler. http://inetsd01.bolder.ibm.com/pseries/en_Us/aixbman/prftools/xprofiler.htm.

[8] F. SONG AND F. WOLF, *CUBE User Manual*. ICL Technical Report ICL-UT-04-01. Feb. 2, 2004. http://icl.cs.utk.edu/projectfiles/kojak/software/cube/cube.pdf.

[9] PAPI. http://icl.cs.utk.edu/papi/.

[10] Paraver. http://www.cepba.upc.edu/paraver.

[11] *VAMPIR User's Guide*. Pallas GmbH. http://www.pallas.de.

[12] O. ZAKI, E. LUSK, W. GROPP, AND D. SWIDER, *Toward scalable performance visualization with jumpshot*, High-Performance Computing Applications, 13 (1999), pp. 277–288.

[13] Dimemas. http://www.cepba.upc.edu/dimemas/.

[14] R. DIMITROV, A. SKJELLUM, T. JONES, B. DE SUPINSKI, R. BRIGHTWELL, C. JANSSEN, AND M. NOCHUMSON, *PERUSE: An MPI Performance Revealing Extensions Interface*, Technical abstract UCRL-JC-149392. Lawrence Livermore National Laboratory, Aug. 2002.

[15] mpiP. http://www.llnl.gov/CASC/mpip/.

[16] J. S. VETTER AND M. O. MCCRACKEN, *Statistical scalability analysis of communication operations in distributed applications*, in Proc. ACM SIGPLAN Symposium on Principles and Practice of Parallel Programming (PPOPP), Snowbird, UT, USA, 2001.

[17] A. CHAN, W. GROPP, AND E. LUSK, *Scalable Log Files for Parallel Program Trace Data—Draft*, Argonne National Laboratory, Argonne, IL, 2000.

[18] OMPItrace. http://www.cepba.upc.es.paraver.

[19] TAU: Tuning and Analysis Utilities. http://www.cs.uoregon.edu/research/paracomp/tau.

[20] A. SNAVELY, N. WOLTER, AND L. CARRINGTON, *Modelling Application Performance by Convolving Machine Signatures with Application Profiles*, Fourth Annual IEEE Workshop on Workload Characterization, Austin, Dec. 2, 2001.

[21] D. J. KERBYSON, H. J. ALME, A. HOISIE, F. PETRINI, H. J. WASSERMAN, AND M. GITTINGS, *Predictive performance and scalability modeling of a large-scale application*, in Proc. ACM/IEEE High Performance Networking and Computing Conference SC2001, Denver, Nov. 2001.

[22] G. JOSTQ, J. LABARTA, AND J. GIMENEZ, *What multilevel parallel programs do when you are not watching: A performance analysis case study comparing MPI/OpenMP, MLP, and nested OpenMP*, Conference WOMPAT 2004, Houston, May 2004.

[23] G. JOST, J. LABARTA, AND J. GIMENEZ, *Paramedir: A tool for programable performance analysis*, International Conference on Computational Science 2004, Krakov, June 2004.

[24] A. SRIVASTAVA AND A. EUSTACE, *ATOM: A system for buiding customized porgram analysis tools*, Proc. SIGPLAN '94 Conference on Programming Language Design and Implementation, Orlando, FL, June 1994, pp. 196–205.

[25] A. SERRA, N. NAVARRO, AND T. CORTES, *DITools: Application-level support for dynamic extension and flexible composition*, in Proc. USENIX Annual Technical Conference, June 2000.

[26] M. MOUDGILL, J-D. WELLMAN, AND J. MORENO, *Environment for PowerPC microarchitecture exploration*, IEEE MICRO, May–June (1999), pp. 15–25.

Chapter 3
Approaches to Architecture-Aware Parallel Scientific Computation

James D. Teresco, Joseph E. Flaherty, Scott B. Baden, Jamal Faik, Sébastien Lacour, Manish Parashar, Valerie E. Taylor, and Carlos A. Varela

Modern parallel scientific computation is being performed in a wide variety of computational environments that include clusters, large-scale supercomputers, grid environments, and metacomputing environments. This presents challenges for application and library developers, who must develop architecture-aware software if they wish to utilize several computing platforms efficiently.

Architecture-aware computation can be beneficial in single-processor environments. It takes the form of something as common as an optimizing compiler, which will optimize software for a target computer. Application and library developers may adjust data structures or memory management techniques to improve cache utilization on a particular system [21].

Parallel computation introduces more variety and, with that, more need and opportunity for architecture-specific optimizations. Heterogeneous processor speeds at first seem easy to account for by simply giving a larger portion of the work to faster processors, but assumptions of homogeneous processor speeds may be well hidden. If all processor speeds are the same, differences between uniprocessor nodes and symmetric multiprocessing (SMP) nodes may be important. Computational and communication resources may not be dedicated to one job, and the external loads on the system may be highly dynamic and transient. Interconnection networks may be hierarchical, leading to nonuniform communication costs. Even if targeting only homogeneous systems, the relative speeds of processors, memory, and networks may affect performance. Heterogeneous processor architectures (e.g., Sparc, x86) present challenges for portable software development and data format conversions. Some operating systems may provide support for different programming paradigms (e.g., message passing, multithreading, priority thread scheduling, or distributed shared memory). Resources may also be transient or unreliable, breaking some common assumptions in, e.g., applications that use the MPI standard [37]. Finally, scalability is a concern, in that what works well for a cluster with dozens of processors will not necessarily work well for a supercomputer with thousands of processors, or in a grid environment [34] with extreme network hierarchies.

Many decisions that software developers can make may be affected by their target architectures. The choices can be algorithmic, such as when choosing a solution method that lends itself better to shared memory/multithreading or to distributed memory/message passing, as appropriate. The choice of parallelization paradigm affects portability and efficiency. The SPMD with message passing approach is often used because MPI is widely available and highly portable. However, this portability may come at the expense of efficiency. Other options include shared memory/multithreading [16, 55], a hybrid of SPMD with multithreading [8], the actor/theater model [4], and the bulk synchronous parallel (BSP) [63] model. Parallelization can be achieved by a "bag-of-tasks" master/worker paradigm, domain decomposition, or pipelining. Computation and/or communication can be overlapped or reordered for efficiency in some circumstances. A programmer may choose to replicate data and/or computation to eliminate the need for some communication. Small messages can be concatenated and large messages can be split to achieve an optimal message size, given the buffer sizes and other characteristics of a particular interconnect [58]. Communication patterns can be adjusted. The computation can be made to use an optimal number of processors, processes, or threads, given the characteristics of the application and of the computing environment [20]. Partitioning and dynamic load balancing procedures can make trade-offs for imbalance versus communication minimization, or can adjust optimal partition sizes, and can partition to avoid communication across the slowest interfaces [29, 84].

Any architecture-aware computation must have knowledge of the computing environment, knowledge of software performance characteristics, and tools to make use of this knowledge. The computing environment may come from a manual specification or may be discovered automatically at run time. Computing environment performance characteristics can be discovered through a priori benchmarking or by dynamic monitoring. Software performance characteristics can be based on performance models or on studies that compare performance.

Software can use such knowledge of the computing environment at any of a number of the common levels of abstraction. Compiler developers and low-level tool developers (e.g., MPI implementers) can make architecture-aware optimizations that are applicable to a wide range of applications. Other tool developers, such as those designing and implementing partitioners and dynamic load balancers or numerical libraries, can make their software architecture aware and benefit all users of the libraries. Middleware systems can make architecture-aware adjustments to computations that use them. Application programmers can make high-level decisions in an architecture-aware manner, e.g., through their choice of programming languages and parallel programming paradigm, by adjusting memory management techniques, or by adjusting the parameters and frequency of dynamic load balancing.

This chapter describes several efforts that were presented at a minisymposium on architecture-aware parallel computing at the Eleventh SIAM Conference on Parallel Processing for Scientific Computing (San Francisco, 2004). The first approach, the Prophesy framework by Taylor et al., analyzes the performance of applications running in parallel and distributed environments (section 3.1). Section 3.2 describes Baden's work on canonical variant programming and on computation and communication scheduling. Next, the work of Lacour et al., on topology-aware collective communication in the grid-enabled MPI implementation, MPICH-G2, is described (section 3.3). Dynamic load balancing for heterogeneous and hierarchical systems is described next, including work by Faik et al. (section 3.4), Teresco et al. (section 3.5), and Parashar et al. (section 3.6). Finally, Varela's approach to "worldwide computing" shows how a middleware layer can help manage a computation in a widely distributed and highly dynamic and transient computing environment (section 3.7).

3.1 Prophesy: A performance analysis and modeling system for parallel and distributed applications

Valerie E. Taylor, with Xingfu Wu and Rick Stevens

Today's complex parallel and distributed systems require tools to gain insight into the performance of applications executed on such environments. This section presents the web-based Prophesy system[1] [95, 96], a performance analysis and modeling infrastructure that helps to provide this needed insight. Prophesy automatically instruments application software, records performance data, system features, and application details in a performance database and provides automated modeling techniques to facilitate the analysis process. Prophesy can be used to develop models based upon significant data, identify the most efficient implementation of a given function based upon the given system configuration, explore the various trends implicated by the significant data, and predict software performance on a different system.

Prophesy consists of three major components: data collection, data analysis, and central databases (Figure 3.1). The data collection component focuses on the automated instrumentation and application code analysis at the granularity levels of basic blocks, procedures, and functions. Execution of the instrumented code gathers a significant amount of performance information for automated inclusion in the performance database. Manual entry of performance data is also supported. Performance data can then be used to gain insight into the performance relationship among the application, hardware, and system software.

An application goes through three stages to generate an analytical performance model: (1) instrumentation of the application, (2) performance data collection, and (3) model development using optimization techniques. These models, when combined with data from the system database, can be used by the prediction engine to predict the performance in a different computing environment. The Prophesy infrastructure is designed to explore the plausibility and credibility of various techniques in performance evaluation (e.g., scalability, efficiency, speedup, performance coupling between application kernels) and to allow users

---

[1] http://prophesy.cs.tamu.edu

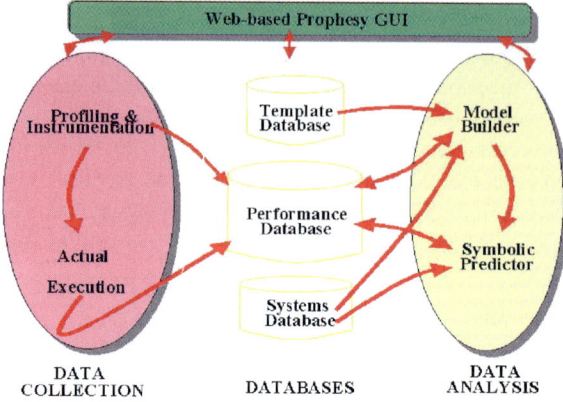

Figure 3.1. *Prophesy framework.*

to use various metrics collectively to bring performance analysis environments to the most advanced level.

The Prophesy database must accommodate queries that lead to the development of performance models, allow for prediction of performance on other systems, and allow for one to obtain insight into methods to improve the performance of the application on a given distributed system. Hence, the database must facilitate the following query types:

- Identify the best implementation of a given function for a given system configuration (identified by the run-time system, operating system, processor organization, etc.). This can be implemented by querying the database for comparison of performance data on different systems.

- Use the raw performance data to generate analytical (nonlinear or linear) models of a given function or application; the analytical model can be used to extrapolate the performance under different system scenarios and to assist programmers in optimizing the strategy or algorithms in their programs.

- Use the performance data to analyze application-system trends, such as scalability, speedup, I/O (input/output) requirements, and communication requirements. This can be implemented by querying the database to calculate the corresponding formula.

- Use the performance data to analyze user-specific metrics such as coupling between functions.

The Prophesy database has a hierarchical organization, consistent with the hierarchical structure of applications. The entities in the database are organized into four areas:

- *Application information.* This includes entities that give the application name, version number, a short description, owner information and password. Data are placed into these entities when a new application is being developed.

- *Executable information.* This includes all the entities related to generating an executable of an application. These include details about compilers, libraries, and the control flow and are given for modules and functions. Data are placed into these entities when a new executable is generated.

- *Run information.* This includes all the entities related to running an executable. These are primarily details about the program inputs and the computing environments used. Data are placed into these entities for each run of a given executable.

- *Performance statistics information.* This includes all the entities related to the raw performance data collected during execution. Performance statistics are collected for different granularities (e.g., application, function, basic unit, and data structure performance).

The Prophesy automated model builder automatically generates performance models to aid in performance analysis and evaluation of a given application or execution environment. Prophesy supports two well-established modeling techniques, curve fitting and parameterization, plus a composition method developed by the Prophesy research group [80, 81]. Curve fitting uses optimization techniques to develop a model. The model builder uses a least-squares fit on the empirical data in the Prophesy database specified by the user to generate the model. The models it generates are generally a function of some input parameters of the application and the number of parameters. The system performance terms are clustered together with the coefficients determined by the curve fitting; such parameters are not exposed to the user. The advantage of this method is that only the empirical data are needed to generate the models; no manual analysis is required. The parameterization method combines manual analysis of the code with system performance measurements. The manual analysis requires hand counting of the number of different operations in kernels or functions that are generally 100 lines of code or fewer. The manual analysis is used to produce an analytical equation with terms that represent the application and the execution environment, allowing users to explore different application and execution environment scenarios with parameterized models. The manual analysis step is the only drawback, but this step is done only once per kernel. The composition modeling technique attempts to represent the performance of an application in terms of its component kernels or functions. These kernel performance models are combined to develop the full application performance models. It is extremely useful to understand the relationships between the different functions that compose the application, determining how one kernel affects another (i.e., whether it is a constructive or a destructive relationship). Further, this information should be able to be encapsulated into a coefficient that can be used in a performance model of the application. In [80], the advantages of using the coupling values to estimate performance are demonstrated using the NAS parallel benchmarks [10]. For block tridiagonal (BT) dataset A, the four-kernel predictor had an average relative error of 0.79%, while merely summing the times of the individual kernels results in an average relative error of 21.80%.

Prophesy includes automatic instrumentation of applications, a database to hold performance and context information, and an automated model builder for developing performance models, allowing users to gain needed insight into application performance based upon their experience as well as that of others. Current research is focused on extending the tool to different application communities.

3.2 Canonical variant programming and computation and communication scheduling

Scott B. Baden

Application performance is sensitive to technological change, and an important factor is that the cost of moving data is increasing relative to that of performing computation. This effect is known as the "memory wall." A general approach for desensitizing performance to such change remains elusive. The result can be a proliferation of program variants, each tuned to a different platform and to configuration-dependent parameters. These variants are difficult to implement because of an expansion of detail encountered when converting a terse mathematical problem description into highly tuned application software.

Ideally, there would exist a *canonical program variant*, from which all *concrete* program variants unfold automatically, altering their behavior according to technological factors affecting performance. There has been some progress in realizing the notion of canonical program variants through self-tuning software. Self-tuning software has proved highly successful in managing memory hierarchy locality and includes packages such as ATLAS [93], PhiPac [12], and FFTW [35]. The general approach is to generate a search space of program variants and to solve an optimization problem over the search space. The crucial problem is how to optimize the search space. Architecture-cognizant divide and conquer algorithms [36] explored the notion of separators for pruning search trees; these enable different levels of the memory hierarchy to be optimized separately. A related approach is to customize the source code using semantic level optimizations, including telescoping languages [51], Broadway [38], and ROSE [70]. Lastly, DESOBLAS takes a different approach: it performs delayed evaluation using task graphs [56].

Another manifestation of the memory wall is the increased cost of interprocessor communication in scalable systems. Reformulating an algorithm to tolerate latency is a difficult problem because of the need to employ elaborate data decompositions and to solve a scheduling problem. Because an overlapped algorithm requires that communication and computation be treated as simultaneous activities, communication must be handled asynchronously [7, 9, 31, 76]. The resultant split-phase algorithms are ad hoc and prone to error [8], even for the experienced programmer, and require considerable knowledge about the application. The resultant difficulties have led to alternative actor-based models of execution including the Mobile Object Layer [23], Adaptive MPI [40], and Charm++ [45]. These models support shared objects with asynchronous remote method invocation. Data motion is implicit in method invocation. Other relevant work includes DMCS [22], which supports single-sided communication and active messages, and SMARTS, which uses affinity to enhance memory locality by scheduling related tasks back to back [87].

A new project called Tarragon has been started at University of California at San Diego. Tarragon supports a non-bulk-synchronous actor model of execution and is intended to simplify communication-tolerant implementations. As with the other actor-based models, Tarragon employs data-driven execution semantics [43], e.g., coarse grain dataflow [6], to manage communication overlap under the control of a scheduler. The data-driven model is attractive because it does not require the programmer to hardwire scheduling decisions into application code to manage communication overlap. As with traditional data flow [5, 25, 44] parallelism arises among tasks which are independent. Interdependent tasks are enabled according to the flow of data among them. A scheduler—rather than the application—determines an appropriate way to order computations.

A Tarragon task graph is interpreted as a logical grouping of an iteration space, along with a partial ordering of that grouping. The tasks are not objects as in Charm++ or Mobile Object Layer but an abstract description of computation to be carried out. This abstraction enables Tarragon to realize pipelining optimizations across time-stepped simulations and to capture elaborate computational structures such as time-stepped adaptive mesh hierarchies and distinguishes it from other actor-based models. Tarragon also differs in another fundamental way. Whereas the other models support shared objects with asynchronous remote method invocation, Tarragon does not support shared objects, and methods may be invoked only locally. Data motion is explicit, reflecting the Tarragon philosophy of exposing such expensive operations to the programmer.

Tarragon supports the notion of *parameterized scheduling*, which has the property that the scheduler can read attributes decorating the task graph. These attributes come in the form of *performance meta-data*, a concept which has been explored jointly with Kelly and others in the context of cross-component optimization [50]. Performance meta-data may represent a variety of quantities, e.g., affinity, priority, or other metrics. The programmer is free to interpret the meaning of meta-data, while the scheduler examines their relative magnitudes to make decisions. Parameterized scheduling differs from application-level scheduling because application-dependent behavior can be expressed via meta-data alone, i.e., without having to change the scheduler. The flexibility offered by parameterized scheduling significantly enhances the capability to explore alternative scheduling policies and metrics.

As with Charm++ and other efforts [82], Tarragon virtualizes computations. That is, the workload is split such that each processor obtains many pieces of work. Early results with a three-dimensional elliptic solver using red-black relaxation have been positive, with only modest overheads observed for virtualization factors of up to nearly an order of magnitude [72]. Virtualization enhances the ability to overlap communication via pipelining.

Tarragon is currently under development and is being applied to a variety of applications. We are also investigating compiler support for Tarragon using the ROSE [70] compiler framework developed by Quinlan. ROSE is a tool for building source-to-source translators realizing semantic-level optimizations of C++ class libraries and can extract semantic information from libraries such as Tarragon. The resultant software will in effect be a domain-specific language.

3.3 A multilevel topology-aware approach to implementing MPI collective operations for computational grids

Sébastien Lacour, with Nicholas Karonis and Ian Foster

Computational grids have a potential to yield a huge computational power. Their utilization has been made a reality by grid access middleware like the Globus Toolkit,[2] so more and more computational grids are deployed, as exemplified by such projects as NASA IPG, European DataGrid, and NSF TeraGrid.[3] In a typical grid, several sites are interconnected over a wide-area network (WAN). Within each site, a number of computers are connected over a local-area network (LAN). Some of those computers may be gathered in clusters equipped with a very-high-performance network like Myrinet. Thus, computational grids raise many issues, like *heterogeneity* in terms of computing resources and network links. As a grid is made of geographically distributed resources, possibly spread across continents, grid *networks* are inherently *multilayered*, showing large network performance gaps (bandwidth, latency) between every communication network level.

In this context, some MPI applications need to achieve high performance. To reach that goal, an efficient MPI implementation must take into account the multilayered nature of the grid network. This is particularly true for the implementation of MPI collective operations like `MPI_Bcast`. Those functions involve several processes running on a number of computers interconnected over various networks with different performance characteristics.

Topology-*unaware* implementations of broadcast often make the simplifying assumption that the communication times between all process pairs are equal. Under this assumption, the broadcast operation is often implemented using a *binomial tree*. In the example of Figure 3.2, the broadcast operation from process 0 to processes 1–9 is completed in only four steps. This implementation is efficient in terms of performance and load balancing as long as it is used within a *homogeneous* network with uniform performance.

If the 10 processes are split into two clusters (processes 0 through 4 on one cluster and processes 5 through 9 on another), then a topology-unaware implementation of broadcast incurs three intercluster messages over a lower performance network (Figure 3.3). Existing two-level topology-aware approaches [41, 52] cluster computers into groups. In Figure 3.4, the root of the broadcast first sends the message to process 5 in the remote cluster, then processes 0 and 5 broadcast the message within their respective clusters using a binomial-tree algorithm. This solution performs all intercluster messaging first while also minimizing intercluster messaging.

A computational grid like the one described above typically involves multiple sites and may also include multiple clusters at a single site. The NSF TeraGrid, for example, has a 32-bit cluster and a 64-bit cluster, both located at Argonne National Laboratory. Such grids induce three or more network levels (i.e., wide-area, local area, and intracluster) with different network characteristics at each level. In these grids, if the processes are grouped by clusters, the two-level topology-aware approach will not minimize the number

---

[2]http://www.globus.org
[3]http://www.teragrid.org/

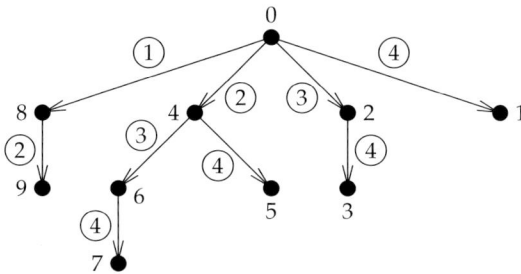

Figure 3.2. *Broadcast using a binomial tree: processes are numbered from 0 (root) through 9; communication steps are circled.*

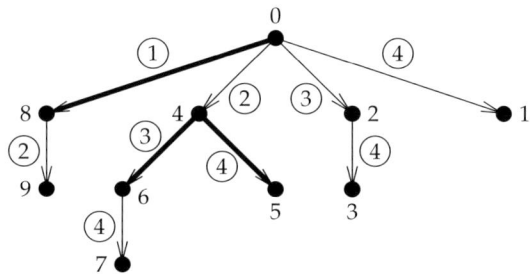

Figure 3.3. *Topology-unaware broadcast using a binomial tree: three intercluster messages (bold arrows) and six intracluster messages.*

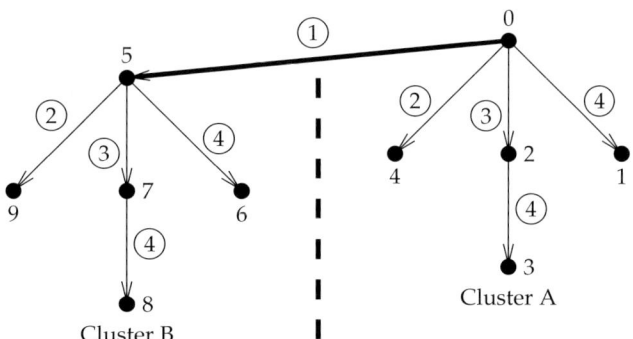

Figure 3.4. *Topology-aware broadcast: only one intercluster message (bold arrow).*

of intersite messages. If, on the other hand, the processes are instead grouped by sites, the two-level approach will not minimize the number of intercluster messages within each site. A multilevel strategy is needed, grouping the processes first by sites and then by clusters in which both intersite and intercluster messages are minimized.

Early performance evaluations [47] of the multilevel approach have shown significant performance gains for the broadcast operation. Encouraged by those results, 11 of the 14 collective operations of the MPI-1 standard have been implemented in a multilevel topology-aware manner in MPICH-G2[4] [46].

3.4 Dynamic load balancing for heterogeneous environments

Jamal Faik, James D. Teresco, and Joseph E. Flaherty, with Luis G. Gervasio

An attractive feature of clusters is their ability to expand their computational power incrementally by incorporating additional nodes. This expansion often results in heterogeneous environments, as the newly added nodes and interconnects often have superior capabilities. This section focuses on the dynamic resource utilization model (DRUM)[5] [29], which is a software library that provides support for scientific computation in heterogeneous environments. The current focus is on providing information to enable resource-aware partitioning and dynamic load-balancing procedures in a manner that incurs minimal effort to set up, requires very few changes to applications or to dynamic load balancing procedures, and adjusts dynamically to changing loads while introducing only small overheads.

A number of recent papers have addressed these and similar issues. Minyard and Kallinderis [60] monitored process "wait times" to assign element weights that are used in octree partitioning. Walshaw and Cross [91] coupled a multilevel graph algorithm with a model of a heterogeneous communication network to minimize a communication cost function. Sinha and Parashar [75] use the Network Weather Service (NWS) [94] to gather information about the state and capabilities of available resources; they compute the load capacity of each node as a weighted sum of processing, memory, and communications capabilities.

DRUM incorporates aggregated information about the capabilities of the network and computing resources composing an execution environment. DRUM can be viewed as an abstract object that encapsulates the details of the execution environment and provides a facility for dynamic, modular, and minimally intrusive monitoring of the execution environment.

DRUM addresses hierarchical clusters (e.g., clusters of clusters, or clusters of multiprocessors) by capturing the underlying interconnection network topology (Figure 3.5). The tree structure of DRUM leads naturally to a topology-driven, yet transparent, execution of hierarchical partitioning (section 3.5). The root of the tree represents the total execution environment. The children of the root node are high-level divisions of different networks connected to form the total execution environment. Subenvironments are recursively divided, according to the network hierarchy, with the tree leaves being individual single-processor (SP) nodes or symmetric multiprocessor nodes. *Computation nodes* at the leaves of the tree have data representing their relative computing and communication power. *Network nodes*, representing routers or switches, have an aggregate power calculated as a

---
[4]http://www3.niu.edu/mpi
[5]http://www.cs.williams.edu/drum

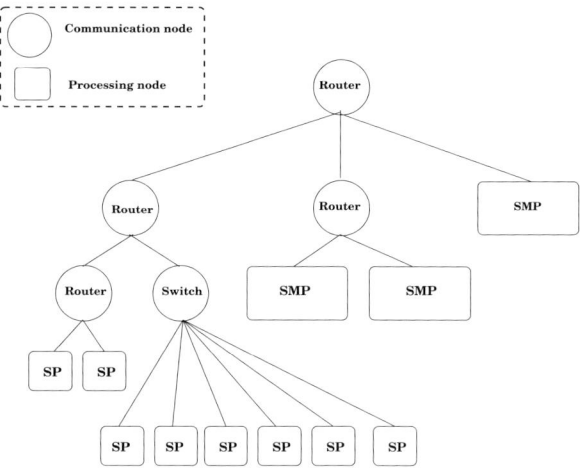

Figure 3.5. *Tree constructed by DRUM to represent a heterogeneous network.*

function of the powers of their children and the network characteristics. The model of the execution environment is created upon initialization based on an XML file that contains a list of nodes and their capabilities and a description of their interconnection topology. The XML file can be generated with the aid of a graphical configuration tool or may be specified manually.

Computational, memory, and communication resource capabilities are assessed initially using benchmarks, which are run a priori either manually or using the graphical configuration tool. Capabilities may be updated dynamically by *agents*: threads that run concurrently with the application to monitor each node's communication traffic, processing load, and memory usage. Network monitoring agents use the net-snmp library[6] or kernel statistics to collect network traffic information at each node. An experimental version that interfaces with NWS has also been developed. Processor and memory utilization are obtained using kernel statistics. The statistics are combined with the static benchmark data to obtain a dynamic evaluation of the powers of the nodes in the model.

DRUM distills the information in the model to a single quantity called the power for each node, which indicates the portion of the total load that should be assigned to that node. For load-balancing purposes, a node's power is interpreted as the percentage of overall load it should be assigned based on its capabilities. The power is computed as a weighted sum of processing and communication power, each of which are computed based on static benchmark and dynamic monitoring information.

DRUM has been used in conjunction with the Zoltan parallel data services toolkit [28, 27], which provides dynamic load balancing and related capabilities to a wide range of dynamic, unstructured, and/or adaptive applications, to demonstrate resource-aware partitioning and dynamic load balancing for a heterogeneous cluster. Given power values

---

[6]http://www.net-snmp.org

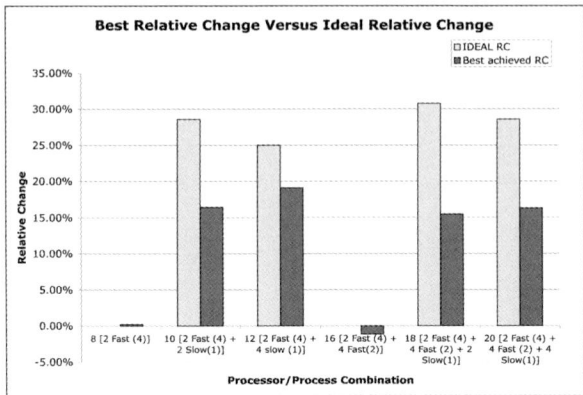

Figure 3.6. *Ideal and achieved (using DRUM) relative changes in execution times compared to homogeneous partitioning for an adaptive calculation using PHAML on different processor combinations.*

for each node, any partitioning procedure capable of producing variable-sized partitions, including all Zoltan procedures, may be used to achieve an appropriate decomposition. Thus, any applications using a load-balancing procedure capable of producing nonuniform partitions can take advantage of DRUM with little modification. Applications that already use Zoltan can make use of DRUM simply by setting a Zoltan parameter, with no further changes needed.

We conducted an experimental study in which we used DRUM to guide resource-aware load balancing in the adaptive solution of a Laplace equation on the unit square, using Mitchell's parallel hierarchical adaptive multilevel software (PHAML) [62]. Runs were performed on different combinations of processors of a heterogeneous cluster. Figure 3.6 shows the relative change in execution time obtained when DRUM is used for different weights of the communication power. The ideal relative change is a theoretical value that would be obtained if partition sizes perfectly match node processing capabilities and no interprocess communication takes place during the execution. The complete DRUM experimental study can be found in [29].

3.5 Hierarchical partitioning and dynamic load balancing

James D. Teresco

An effective partitioning or dynamic load-balancing procedure maximizes efficiency by minimizing processor idle time and interprocessor communication. While some applications can use a static partitioning throughout a computation, others, such as adaptive finite element methods, have dynamic workloads that necessitate dynamic load balancing during the computation. Partitioning and dynamic load balancing can be performed using recursive

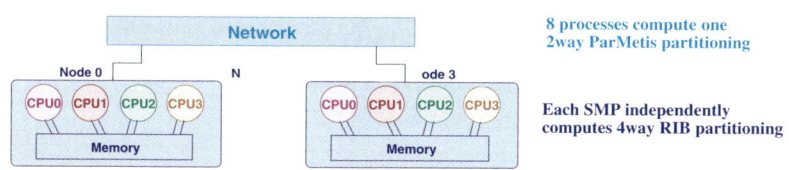

Figure 3.7. *Hierarchical balancing algorithm selection for two four-way SMP nodes connected by a network.*

bisection methods [11, 74, 79], space-filling curve (SFC) partitioning [15, 33, 61, 64, 66, 67, 68, 92], and graph partitioning (including spectral [69, 74], multilevel [14, 39, 48, 90], and diffusive [24, 42, 54] methods). Each algorithm has characteristics and requirements that make it appropriate for certain applications; see [13, 85] for examples and [83] for an overview of available methods.

Modern clusters, supercomputers, and grid environments often include hierarchical interconnection networks. For hierarchical and heterogeneous systems, different choices of partitioning and dynamic load-balancing procedures may be appropriate in different parts of the parallel environment. There are trade-offs in execution time and partition quality (e.g., amount of communication needed, interprocess connectivity, strictness of load balance) [85] and some may be more important than others in some circumstances. For example, consider a cluster of SMP nodes connected by Ethernet. A more costly graph partitioning can be done to partition among the nodes, to minimize communication across the slow network interface, possibly at the expense of some computational imbalance. Then, a fast geometric algorithm can be used to partition to a strict balance, independently, within each node. This is illustrated in Figure 3.7. Such hierarchical partitionings of a 1,103,018-element mesh used in a simulation of blood flow in a human aorta are presented in [59].

Hierarchical partitioning and dynamic load balancing has been implemented in the Zoltan parallel data services toolkit [28, 27]. (Open-source software is available at www.cs.sandia.gov/Zoltan.) Using Zoltan, application developers can switch partitioners simply by changing a run-time parameter, facilitating comparisons of the partitioners' effects on the applications. Zoltan's hierarchical balancing implementation allows different procedures to be used in different parts of the computing environment [84]. The implementation utilizes a lightweight intermediate hierarchical balancing structure (IHBS) and a set of callback functions that permit an automated and efficient hierarchical balancing which can use any of the procedures available within Zoltan (including recursive bisection methods, SFC methods, and graph partitioners) without modification and in any combination. Hierachical balancing is invoked by an application the same way as other Zoltan procedures. Since Zoltan is data-structure neutral, it operates on generic "objects" and interfaces with applications through callback functions. A hierarchical balancing step begins by building an IHBS, which is an augmented version of the graph structure that Zoltan builds to make use of the ParMetis [49] and Jostle [90] libraries, using the application callbacks. The hierarchical balancing procedure then provides its own callback functions to allow existing Zoltan procedures to be used to query and update the IHBS at each level of a hierarchical balancing. After all levels of the hierarchical balancing have been completed, Zoltan's usual migration arrays are constructed and returned to the application. Thus, only lightweight objects are migrated internally between levels, not the (larger and more costly) application data. Zoltan's hierarchical balancing can be used directly by an application or be guided by the tree representation of the computational environment created and maintained by DRUM (section 3.4).

Preliminary results applying hierarchical balancing to a parallel, adaptive simulation are promising [84]. A comparison of running times for a perforated shock tube simulation [32] on a cluster of SMPs shows that while ParMetis multilevel graph partitioning alone often achieves the fastest computation times, there is some benefit to using hierarchical load balancing where ParMetis is used for internode partitioning and where inertial recursive bisection is used within each node. Hierarchical balancing shows the most benefit in cases where ParMetis introduces a larger imbalance to reduce communication.

Studies are underway that utilize hierarchical balancing on larger clusters, on other architectures, and with a wider variety of applications. Hierarchical balancing may be most beneficial when the extreme hierarchies found in grid environments are considered.

3.6 Autonomic management of parallel adaptive applications

Manish Parashar

Parallel structured adaptive mesh refinement (SAMR) [65, 66] techniques yield advantageous ratios for cost/accuracy compared to methods based on static uniform approximations and offer the potential for accurate solutions of realistic models of complex physical phenomena. However, the inherent space-time heterogeneity and dynamism of SAMR applications coupled with a similarly heterogeneous and dynamic execution environment (such as the computational grid) present significant challenges in application composition, runtime management, optimization, and adaptation. These challenges have led researchers to consider alternate self-managing *autonomic* solutions, which are based on strategies used by biological systems to address similar challenges.

GridARM [17] (Figure 3.8) is an autonomic runtime management framework that monitors application behaviors and system architecture and runtime state and provides adaptation strategies to optimize the performance of SAMR applications. The framework has three components: (i) services for monitoring resource architecture and application dynamics and characterizing their current state, capabilities, and requirements; (ii) a deduction engine and objective function that define the appropriate optimization strategy based on runtime state and policies; and (iii) an autonomic runtime manager that is responsible for hierarchically partitioning, scheduling, and mapping application working sets onto virtual resources and tuning applications within the grid environment.

The monitoring/characterization component of the GridARM framework consists of embedded application-level and system-level sensors/actuators. Application sensors monitor the structure and state of the SAMR grid hierarchy and the nature of its refined regions. The current application state is characterized in terms of application-level metrics such as computation/communication requirements, storage requirements, activity dynamics, and

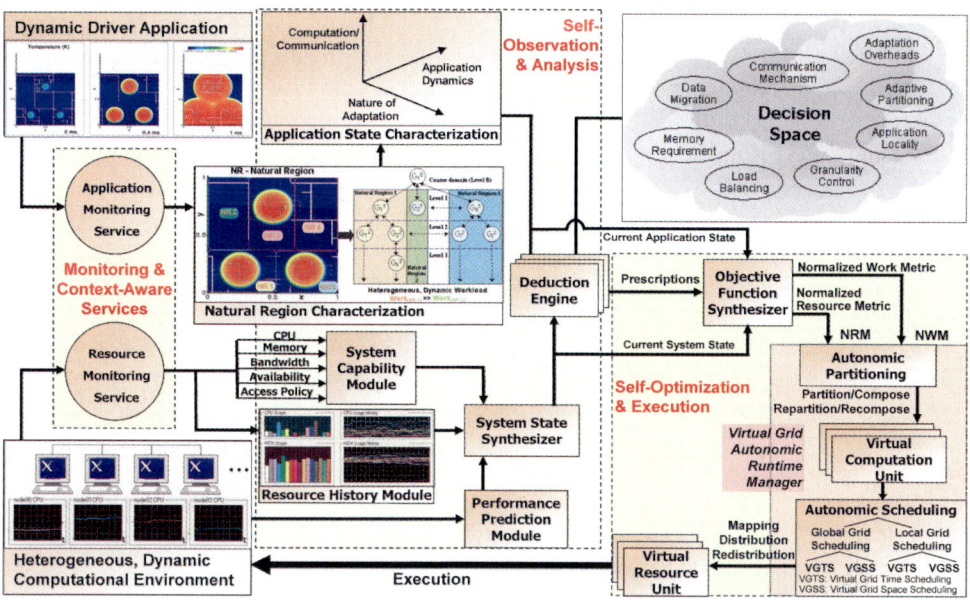

Figure 3.8. *Conceptual overview of GridARM.*

the nature of adaptations [77]. Similarly, system sensors build on existing grid services such as the NWS and sense the current state of underlying computational resources in terms of CPU, memory, bandwidth, availability, and access capabilities. These values are fed into the system state synthesizer along with system history information and predicted performance estimates (obtained using predictive performance functions) to determine the overall system runtime state.

The current application and system state along with the overall decision space are provided as inputs to the GridARM deduction engine and are used to define the autonomic runtime objective function. The decision space comprises adaptation policies, rules, and constraints defined in terms of application metrics and enables autonomic configuration, adaptation, and optimization. Application metrics include application locality, communication mechanism, data migration, load balancing, memory requirements, adaptive partitioning, adaptation overheads, and granularity control. Based on current runtime state and policies within the decision space, the deduction engine formulates prescriptions for algorithms, configurations, and parameters that are used to define the SAMR objective function.

The prescriptions provided by the deduction engine along with the objective function yield two metrics, normalized work metric (NWM) and normalized resource metric (NRM), which characterize the current application state and current system state, respectively, and are the inputs to the autonomic runtime manager (ARM). Using these inputs, the ARM defines a hierarchical distribution mechanism, configures and deploys appropriate partitioners at each level of the hierarchy, and maps the application domain onto virtual computational units (VCUs). A VCU is the basic application work unit and may consist of computation patches on a single refinement level of the SAMR grid hierarchy or composite patches that span multiple refinement levels. VCUs are dynamically defined at runtime to match the natural regions (i.e., regions with relatively uniform structure and requirements) in the application, which significantly reduces coupling and synchronization costs.

Subsequent to partitioning, spatiotemporal scheduling operations are performed across and within virtual resource units (VRUs) using global-grid scheduling (GGS) and local-grid scheduling (LGS), respectively. During GGS, VCUs are hierarchically assigned to sets of VRUs, whereas LGS is used to schedule one or more VCUs within a single VRU. A VRU may be an individual resource (computer, storage, instrument, etc.) or a collection (cluster, supercomputer, etc.) of physical grid resources. A VRU is characterized by its computational, memory, and communication capacities and by its availability and access policy. Finally, VRUs are dynamically mapped onto physical system resources at runtime and the SAMR application is tuned for execution within the dynamic grid environment.

Note that the work associated with a VCU depends on the state of the computation, the configuration of the components (algorithms, parameters), and the current ARM objectives (optimize performance, minimize resource requirements, etc.). Similarly, the capability of a VRU depends on its current state as well as the ARM objectives (minimizing communication overheads implies that a VRU with high bandwidth and low latency has higher capability). The normalized metric NWM and NRM are used to characterize VRUs and VCUs based on current ARM objectives.

The core components of GridARM have been prototyped and the adaptation schemes within GridARM have been evaluated in the context of real applications, such as the 3D Richtmyer–Meshkov instability solver (RM3D) encountered in compressible fluid dynamics. Application-aware partitioning [18] uses the current runtime state to characterize the SAMR application in terms of its computation/communication requirements, its dynamics, and the nature of adaptations. This adaptive strategy selects and configures the appropriate partitioner that matches current application requirements, thus improving overall execution time by 5% to 30% as compared to nonadaptive partitioning schemes. Adaptive hierarchical partitioning [57] dynamically creates a group topology based on SAMR natural regions and helps to reduce the application synchronization costs, resulting in improved communication time by up to 70% as compared to nonhierarchical schemes. Reactive system sensitive partitioning [75] uses system architecture and current state to select and configure distribution strategies and parameters at runtime based on the relative capacities of each node. This system-sensitive approach improves overall execution time by 10% to 40%.

Proactive runtime partitioning [97] strategies are based on performance prediction functions and estimate the expected application performance based on current loads, available memory, current latencies, and available communication bandwidth. This approach helps to determine when the costs of dynamic load redistribution exceed the costs of repartitioning and data movement and can result in a 25% improvement in the application recompose time. Architecture-sensitive communication mechanisms [73] select appropriate messaging schemes for MPI nonblocking communication optimization suited for the underlying hardware architecture and help to reduce the application communication time by up to 50%. Workload-sensitive load-balancing strategy [19] uses bin packing–based partitioning to distribute the SAMR workload among available processors while satisfying application constraints such as minimum patch size and aspect ratio. This approach reduces the application load imbalance between 2% and 15% as compared to default schemes that employ greedy algorithms. Overall, the GridARM framework has been shown to significantly improve the performance of SAMR applications [17].

3.7 Worldwide computing: Programming models and middleware

Carlos A. Varela, with Travis Desell and Kaoutar El Maghraoui

The Internet is constantly growing as a ubiquitous platform for high-performance distributed computing. This section describes a new software framework for distributed computing over large-scale dynamic and heterogeneous systems. This framework wraps data and computation into *autonomous actors*, self-organizing computing entities, which freely roam over the network to find their optimal target execution environment.

The actor model of concurrent computation represents a programming paradigm enforcing distributed memory and asynchronous communication [4]. Each actor has a unique name, which can be used as a reference by other actors. Actors process information only in reaction to messages. While processing a message, an actor can carry out any of three basic operations: alter its encapsulated state, create new actors, or send messages to peer actors. Actors are therefore inherently independent, concurrent, and autonomous, which enables efficiency in parallel execution [53] and facilitates mobility [2]. The actor model and languages provide a very useful framework for understanding and developing open distributed systems. For example, among other applications, actor systems have been used for enterprise integration [86], real-time programming [71], fault tolerance [1], and distributed artificial intelligence [30].

The presented worldwide computing framework[7] consists of an actor-oriented programming language (SALSA) [88], a distributed runtime environment (WWC) [89], and a middleware infrastructure for autonomous reconfiguration and load balancing (IOS) [26] (see Figure 3.9). SALSA provides high-level constructs for coordinating concurrent computations, which get compiled into primitive actor operations, thereby raising the level of abstraction for programmers while enabling middleware optimizations without requiring the development of application-specific checkpointing, migration, or load-balancing behavior.

Load balancing is completely transparent to application programmers. The IOS middleware triggers actor migration based on profiling application behavior and network resources in a decentralized manner. To balance computational load, three variations of random work stealing have been implemented: load-sensitive (LS), actor topology-sensitive (ATS), and network topology-sensitive (NTS) random stealing. LS and ATS were evaluated with several actor interconnection topologies in a local area network. While LS performed worse than static round-robin (RR) actor placement, ATS outperformed both LS and RR in the sparse connectivity and hypercube connectivity tests, by a full order of magnitude [26]. We are currently evaluating NTS in diverse heterogeneous grid environments.

---

[7] http://www.cs.rpi.edu/wwc/

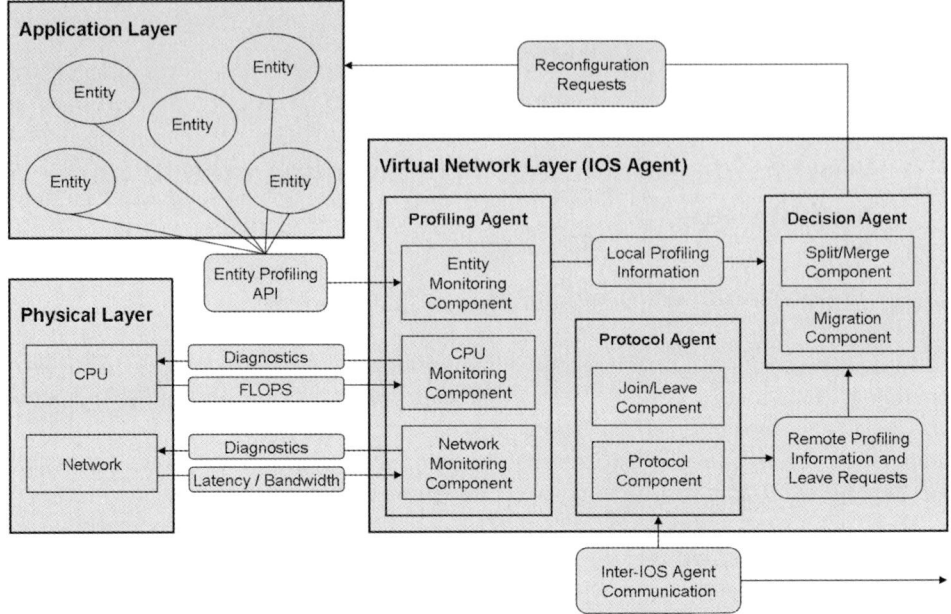

Figure 3.9. *A modular middleware architecture as a research testbed for scalable high-performance decentralized distributed computations.*

The IOS software infrastructure naturally allows for the dynamic addition and removal of nodes from the computation, while continuously balancing the load given the changing resources. The ability to adapt applications to a dynamic network is critical upon node and network failures, common in Internet computing environments. This adaptability is also critical in shared environments with unpredictable variations in resource usage, e.g., by applications running concurrently on a grid.

Our current research focuses on resource management models and their middleware implementations for nonfunctional distributed systems behavior. Examples include data and process replication for fault tolerance, and split and merge behavior to dynamically optimize the granularity of computation and migration. We are particularly interested in the interaction of high-level programming abstractions and middleware optimizations [59]. While application-level load balancing may in general afford better performance, the simplicity of the autonomous actor programming model and the availability of computing power in large-scale dynamic networks may ultimately make optimization in middleware more beneficial for scientific computing [3, 78].

Acknowledgments

J. Teresco, J. Flaherty, and J. Faik were supported by Contract 15162 with Sandia National Laboratories, a multiprogram laboratory operated by Sandia Corporation, a Lockheed Martin Company, for the United States Department of Energy (DoE) under Contract

DE-AC04-94AL85000. S. Baden was supported by the Institute for Scientific Computing Research (DoE) and National Science Foundation (NSF) Contract ACI-0326013. V. Taylor was supported in part by NSF NGS grant EIA-9974960, a grant from NASA Ames, and two NSF ITR grants—GriPhyN and Building Human Capital. Parashar's work presented in this chapter was supported in part by NSF grants ACI 9984357 (CAREERS), EIA 0103674 (NGS), EIA-0120934 (ITR), ANI-0335244 (NRT), and CNS-0305495 (NGS) and by DoE ASCI/ASAP grants PC295251 and 82-1052856. C. Varela's work was supported by a Rensselaer Seed Funding grant, two NSF grants, CISE MRI, CISE-RR, and two IBM Shared University Research grants.

Bibliography

[1] G. AGHA, S. FRØLUND, R. PANWAR, AND D. STURMAN, *A linguistic framework for dynamic composition of dependability protocols*, in Dependable Computing for Critical Applications III, International Federation of Information Processing Societies, Elsevier Science Publisher, New York, 1993, pp. 345–363.

[2] G. AGHA, N. JAMALI, AND C. VARELA, *Agent naming and coordination: Actor based models and infrastructures*, in Coordination of Internet Agents, A. Ominici, F. Zambonelli, M. Klusch, and R. Tolksdorf, eds., Springer-Verlag, New York, 2001, pp. 225–248.

[3] G. AGHA AND C. VARELA, *Worldwide computing middleware*, in Practical Handbook on Internet Computing, M. Singh, ed., CRC Press, Boca Raton, FL, 2004.

[4] G. AGHA, *Actors: A Model of Concurrent Computation in Distributed Systems*, MIT Press, Cambridge, MA, 1986.

[5] ARVIND AND R. S. NIKHIL, *Executing a program on the MIT tagged-token dataflow architecture*, IEEE Transactions on Computers, 39 (1990), pp. 300–318.

[6] R. G. BABB, II, *Parallel processing with large-grain data flow technique*, Computer, 17 (1984), pp. 55–61.

[7] S. B. BADEN AND S. J. FINK, *Communication overlap in multi-tier parallel algorithms*, in Proc. Supercomputing '98, Orlando, FL, Nov. 1998.

[8] S. B. BADEN AND S. J. FINK, *A programming methodology for dual-tier multicomputers*, IEEE Transactions on Software Engineering, 26 (2000), pp. 212–216.

[9] S. B. BADEN AND D. SHALIT, *Performance tradeoffs in multi-tier formulation of a finite difference method*, in Proc. 2001 International Conference on Computational Science, San Francisco, 2001.

[10] D. BAILEY, T. HARRIS, W. SAPHIR, R. VAN DER WIJNGAART, A. WOO, AND M. YARROW, *The NAS Parallel Benchmarks* 2.0, Tech. Report NAS-95-020, NASA Ames Research Center, Moffett Field, CA, 1995.

[11] M. J. BERGER AND S. H. BOKHARI, *A partitioning strategy for nonuniform problems on multiprocessors*, IEEE Transactions on Computers, 36 (1987), pp. 570–580.

[12] J. BILMES, K. ASANOVIC, C.-W. CHIN, AND J. DEMMEL, *Optimizing matrix multiply using PHiPAC: A portable, high-performance, ANSI C coding methodology*, in International Conference on Supercomputing, 1997, pp. 340–347.

[13] E. BOMAN, K. DEVINE, R. HEAPHY, B. HENDRICKSON, M. HEROUX, AND R. PREIS, *LDRD Report: Parallel Repartitioning for Optimal Solver Performance*, Tech. Report SAND2004–0365, Sandia National Laboratories, Albuquerque, NM, Feb. 2004.

[14] T. BUI AND C. JONES, *A heuristic for reducing fill-in in sparse matrix factorization*, in Proc. 6th SIAM Conference on Parallel Processing for Scientific Computing, SIAM, Philadelphia, 1993, pp. 445–452.

[15] P. M. CAMPBELL, K. D. DEVINE, J. E. FLAHERTY, L. G. GERVASIO, AND J. D. TERESCO, *Dynamic Octree Load Balancing Using Space-Filling Curves*, Tech. Report CS-03-01, Department of Computer Science, Williams College, Williamstown, MA, 2003.

[16] R. CHANDRA, R. MENON, L. DAGUM, D. KOH, D. MAYDAN, AND J. MCDONALD, *Parallel Programming in OpenMP*, Morgan-Kaufmann, San Francisco, CA, 2000.

[17] S. CHANDRA, M. PARASHAR, AND S. HARIRI, *GridARM: An autonomic runtime management framework for SAMR applications in Grid environments*, in Proc. Autonomic Applications Workshop, 10th International Conference on High Performance Computing (HiPC 2003), Hyderabad, 2003, Elite Publishing, pp. 286–295.

[18] S. CHANDRA AND M. PARASHAR, *ARMaDA: An adaptive application-sensitive partitioning framework for SAMR applications*, in Proc. 14th IASTED International Conference on Parallel and Distributed Computing and Systems (PDCS 2002), Cambridge, 2002, ACTA Press, pp. 446–451.

[19] S. CHANDRA AND M. PARASHAR, *Enabling scalable parallel implementations of structured adaptive mesh refinement applications*, submitted, Journal of Supercomputing, 2004.

[20] J. CHEN AND V. E. TAYLOR, *Mesh partitioning for distributed systems: Exploring optimal number of partitions with local and remote communication*, in Proc. 9th SIAM Conference on Parallel Processing for Scientific Computation, San Antonio, TX, 1999, CD-ROM.

[21] T. M. CHILIMBI, M. D. HILL, AND J. R. LARUS, *Cache-conscious structure layout*, in Proc. ACM SIGPLAN '99 Conference on Prog. Lang. Design and Implementaion, May 1999.

[22] N. CHRISOCHOIDES, K. BARKER, J. DOBBELAERE, D. NAVE, AND K. PINGALI, *Data movement and control substrate for parallel adaptive applications*, Concurrency and Computation: Practice and Experience, (2002), pp. 77–101.

[23] N. CHRISOCHOIDES, K. BARKER, D. NAVE, AND C. HAWBLITZEL, *Mobile Object Layer: A runtime substrate for parallel adaptive and irregular computations*, Advances in Engineering Software, 31 (2000), pp. 621–637.

[24] G. CYBENKO, *Dynamic load balancing for distributed memory multiprocessors*, Journal of Parallel and Distributed Computing, 7 (1989), pp. 279–301.

[25] J. DENNIS, *Data flow supercomputers*, IEEE Computer, 13 (1980), pp. 48–56.

[26] T. DESELL, K. E. MAGHRAOUI, AND C. VARELA, *Load balancing of autonomous actors over dynamic networks*, in Proc. Hawaii International Conference on System Sciences, 2004. HICSS-37 Software Technology Track, To appear.

[27] K. D. DEVINE, B. A. HENDRICKSON, E. BOMAN, M. ST. JOHN, AND C. VAUGHAN, *Zoltan: A Dynamic Load Balancing Library for Parallel Applications; User's Guide*. Tech. Report SAND99-1377. Sandia National Laboratories, Albuquerque, NM, 1999.

[28] K. DEVINE, E. BOMAN, R. HEAPHY, B. HENDRICKSON, AND C. VAUGHAN, *Zoltan data management services for parallel dynamic applications*, Computing in Science and Engineering, 4 (2002), pp. 90–97.

[29] J. FAIK, L. G. GERVASIO, J. E. FLAHERTY, J. CHANG, J. D. TERESCO, E. G. BOMAN, AND K. D. DEVINE, *A model for resource-aware load balancing on heterogeneous clusters*. Tech. Report CS-04-03, Department of Computer Science, Williams College, Williamstown, MA, 2004.

[30] J. FERBER AND J. BRIOT, *Design of a concurrent language for distributed artificial intelligence*, in Proc. International Conference on Fifth Generation Computer Systems, vol. 2, Institute for New Generation Computer Technology, 1988, pp. 755–762.

[31] S. J. FINK, *Hierarchical Programming for Block-Structured Scientific Calculations*. Ph.D. thesis. Department of Computer Science and Engineering, University of California, San Diego, 1998.

[32] J. E. FLAHERTY, R. M. LOY, M. S. SHEPHARD, M. L. SIMONE, B. K. SZYMANSKI, J. D. TERESCO, AND L. H. ZIANTZ, *Distributed octree data structures and local refinement method for the parallel solution of three-dimensional conservation laws*, in Grid Generation and Adaptive Algorithms, M. Bern, J. Flaherty, and M. Luskin, eds., IMA Volumes in Mathematics and its Applications vol. 113, Institute for Mathematics and its Applications, Springer, pp. 113–134.

[33] J. E. FLAHERTY, R. M. LOY, M. S. SHEPHARD, B. K. SZYMANSKI, J. D. TERESCO, AND L. H. ZIANTZ, *Adaptive local refinement with octree load-balancing for the parallel solution of three-dimensional conservation laws*, Journal of Parallel and Distributed Computing, 47 (1997), pp. 139–152.

[34] I. FOSTER AND C. KESSELMAN, *The Grid: Blueprint for a New Computing Infrastructure*, Morgan-Kaufman, 1999.

[35] M. FRIGO AND S. G. JOHNSON, *FFTW: An adaptive software architecture for the FFT*, in Proc. IEEE International Conference on Acoustics, Speech, and Signal Processing, vol. 3, Seattle, WA, May 1998, pp. 1381–1384.

[36] K. S. GATLIN AND L. CARTER, *Architecture-cognizant divide and conquer algorithms*, in Proc. Supercomputing '99, Nov. 1999.

[37] W. GROPP, E. LUSK, AND A. SKJELLUM, *Using MPI*, MIT Press, Cambridge, MA, 1994.

[38] S. Z. GUYER AND C. LIN, *An annotation languge for optimizing software libraries*, ACM SIGPLAN Notices, 35 (2000), pp. 39–52.

[39] B. HENDRICKSON AND R. LELAND, *A multilevel algorithm for partitioning graphs*, in Proceedings of the IEEE/ACM Conference on Supercomputing, 1995, p. 28.

[40] C. HUANG, O. LAWLOR, AND L. KALE, *Adaptive MPI*, in Proc. 16th International Workshop on Languages and Compilers for Parallel Computing (LCPC 03), College Station, TX, Oct. 2–4, 2003.

[41] P. HUSBANDS AND J. C. HOE, *MPI-StarT: Delivering network performance to numerical applications*, in Proc. IEEE/ACM Supercomputing Conference (SC98), Orlando, FL, Nov. 1998, p. 17.

[42] Y. F. HU AND R. J. BLAKE, *An Optimal Dynamic Load Balancing Algorithm*, Preprint DL-P-95-011, Daresbury Laboratory, Warrington, UK, 1995.

[43] R. JAGANNATHAN, *Coarse-grain dataflow programming of conventional parallel computers*, in Advanced Topics in Dataflow Computing and Multithreading, L. Bic, J.-L. Gaudiot, and G. Gao, eds., IEEE Computer Society Press, Piscataway, NJ, 1995, pp. 113–129.

[44] J. R. GURD, C. C. KIRKHAM, AND I. WATSON, *The Manchester prototype dataflow computer*, Communications of the ACM, 28 (1985), pp. 34–52.

[45] L. V. KALÉ, *The virtualization model of parallel programming: Runtime optimizations and the state of art*, in LACSI 2002, Albuquerque, Oct. 2002.

[46] N. T. KARONIS, B. TOONEN, AND I. FOSTER, *MPICH-G2: A grid-enabled implementation of the Message Passing Interface*, Journal of Parallel and Distributed Computing, 63 (2003), pp. 551–563.

[47] N. KARONIS, B. DE SUPINSKI, I. FOSTER, W. GROPP, E. LUSK, AND J. BRESNAHAN, *Exploiting hierarchy in parallel computer networks to optimize collective operation performance*, in Proc. 14th International Parallel and Distributed Processing Symposium (IPDPS '00), Cancun, 2000, pp. 377–384.

[48] G. KARYPIS AND V. KUMAR, *A fast and high quality multilevel scheme for partitioning irregular graphs*, SIAM Journal of Scientific Computing, 20 (1999), pp. 359–392.

[49] ——, *Parallel multilevel k-way partitioning scheme for irregular graphs*, SIAM Review, 41 (1999), pp. 278–300.

[50] P. KELLY, O. BECKMANN, A. FIELD, AND S. BADEN, *Themis: Component dependence metadata in adaptive parallel applications*, Parallel Processing Letters, 11 (2001), pp. 455–470.

[51] K. KENNEDY, *Telescoping languages: A compiler strategy for implementation of high-level domain-specific programming systems*, in Proc. 14th International Parallel and Distributed Processing Symposium, Cancun, 2000, pp. 297–306.

[52] T. KIELMANN, R. F. H. HOFMAN, H. E. BAL, A. PLAAT, AND R. BHOEDJANG, *MagPIe: MPI's collective communication operations for clustered wide area systems*, in Proc. 1999 ACM SIGPLAN Symposium on Principles and Practice of Parallel Programming (PPOPP'99), Atlanta, GA, May 1999, pp. 131–140.

[53] W. Y. KIM AND G. AGHA, *Efficient support of location transparency in concurrent object-oriented programming languages*, in Proceedings of the IEEE/ACM Conference on Supercomputing, 1995, p. 39.

[54] E. LEISS AND H. REDDY, *Distributed load balancing: Design and performance analysis*, W. M. Kuck Research Computation Laboratory, 5 (1989), pp. 205–270.

[55] B. LEWIS AND D. J. BERG, *Multithreaded Programming with pthreads*, Sun Microsystems Press, Santa Clara, CA, 1997.

[56] P. LINIKER, O. BECKMANN, AND P. KELLY, *Delayed evaluation self-optimising software components as a programming model*, in Proc. Euro-Par 2002, Parallel Processing, 8th International Euro-Par Conference, B. Monien and R. Feldmann, eds., Lecture Notes in Computer Science 2400, Paderborn, Aug. 2002, pp. 666–674.

[57] X. LI AND M. PARASHAR, *Dynamic load partitioning strategies for managing data of space and time heterogeneity in parallel SAMR applications*, in Proc. 9th International Euro-Par Conference (Euro-Par 2003), H. Kosch, L. Boszormenyi, and H. Hellwagner, eds., Lecture Notes in Computer Science 2790, Klangenfurt, 2003, Springer-Verlag, Berlin, pp. 181–188.

[58] R. M. LOY, *AUTOPACK version* 1.2. Technical Memorandum ANL/MCS-TM-241. Mathemetics and Computer Science Division, Argonne National Laboratory, Argonne, IL, 2000.

[59] K. E. MAGHRAOUI, J. E. FLAHERTY, B. K. SZYMANSKI, J. D. TERESCO, AND C. VARELA, *Adaptive computation over dynamic and heterogeneous networks*, in Proc. Fifth International Conference on Parallel Processing and Applied Mathematics (PPAM 2003), Czestochowa, R. Wyrzykowski, J. Dongarra, M. Paprzycki, and J. Wasniewski, eds., Lecture Notes in Computer Science 3019, Springer Verlag, New York, 2004, pp. 1083–1090.

[60] T. MINYARD AND Y. KALLINDERIS, *Parallel load balancing for dynamic execution environments*, Computer Methods in Applied Mechanics and Engineering, 189 (2000), pp. 1295–1309.

[61] W. F. MITCHELL, *Refinement tree based partitioning for adaptive grids*, in Proc. Seventh SIAM Conference on Parallel Processing for Scientific Computing, SIAM, Philadelphia, 1995, pp. 587–592.

[62] ———, *The design of a parallel adaptive multi-level code in Fortran 90*, in Proc. 2002 International Conference on Computational Science, Amsterdam, Netherlands, 2002.

[63] M. NIBHANAPUDI AND B. K. SZYMANSKI, *High Performance Cluster Computing*, Architectures and Systems, vol. I, Prentice-Hall, New York, 1999, pp. 702–721.

[64] J. T. ODEN, A. PATRA, AND Y. FENG, *Domain decomposition for adaptive hp finite element methods*, in Proc. Seventh International Conference on Domain Decomposition Methods, State College, PA, Oct. 1993.

[65] M. PARASHAR AND J. C. BROWNE, *Distributed dynamic data-structures for parallel adaptive mesh-refinement*, in Proc. IEEE International Conference for High Performance Computing, New Delhi, India, 1995, pp. 22–27.

[66] M. PARASHAR AND J. C. BROWNE, *On partitioning dynamic adaptive grid hierarchies*, in Proc. 29th Annual Hawaii International Conference on System Sciences, vol. 1, Hawaii, Jan. 1996, pp. 604–613.

[67] A. PATRA AND J. T. ODEN, *Problem decomposition for adaptive hp finite element methods*, Computing Systems in Engineering, 6 (1995), pp. 97–109.

[68] J. R. PILKINGTON AND S. B. BADEN, *Dynamic partitioning of non-uniform structured workloads with spacefilling curves*, IEEE Transactions on Parallel and Distributed Systems, 7 (1996), pp. 288–300.

[69] A. POTHEN, H. D. SIMON, AND K.-P. LIOU, *Partitioning sparse matrices with eigenvectors of graphs*, SIAM Journal on Matrix Analysis and Applications, 11 (1990), pp. 430–452.

[70] D. QUINLAN, B. MILLER, B. PHILIP, AND M. SCHORDAN, *A C++ infrastructure for automatic introduction and translation of OpenMP directives*, in Proc. 16th International Parallel and Distributed Processing Symposium, Fort Lauderdale, FL, April 2002, pp. 105–114.

[71] S. REN, G. A. AGHA, AND M. SAITO, *A modular approach for programming distributed real-time systems*, Journal of Parallel and Distributed Computing, 36 (1996), pp. 4–12.

[72] F. D. SACERDOTI, *A Cache-Friendly Liquid Load Balancer*, Master Thesis, University of California, San Diego, 2002.

[73] T. SAIF AND M. PARASHAR, *Understanding the behavior and performance of non-blocking communications in MPI*, in Proc. 9th International Euro-Par, Pisa, Lecture Notes in Computer Science, Volume 3149, Springer-Verlag, New York, 2004.

[74] H. D. SIMON, *Partitioning of unstructured problems for parallel processing*, Computing Systems in Engineering, 2 (1991), pp. 135–148.

[75] S. SINHA AND M. PARASHAR, *Adaptive system partitioning of AMR applications on heterogeneous clusters*, Cluster Computing, 5 (2002), pp. 343–352.

[76] A. SOHN AND R. BISWAS, *Communication studies of DMP and SMP machines*, Tech. Report NAS-97-004, NASA AMES, Moffett Field, CA, 1997.

[77] J. STEENSLAND, S. CHANDRA, AND M. PARASHAR, *An application-centric characterization of domain-based SFC partitioners for parallel SAMR*, IEEE Transactions on Parallel and Distributive Systems, 13 (2002), pp. 1275–1289.

[78] B. SZYMANSKI, C. VARELA, J. CUMMINGS, AND J. NAPOLITANO, *Dynamically reconfigurable scientific computing on large-scale heterogeneous grids*, in Proc. Fifth International Conference on Parallel Processing and Applied Mathematics (PPAM'2003), Czestochowa, Poland, Lecture Notes in Computer Science 3019, Sept. 2003.

[79] V. E. TAYLOR AND B. NOUR-OMID, *A study of the factorization fill-in for a parallel implementation of the finite element method*, International Journal for Numerical Methods in Engineering, 37 (1994), pp. 3809–3823.

[80] V. TAYLOR, X. WU, J. GEISLER, AND R. STEVENS, *Using kernel couplings to predict parallel application performance*, in Proc. 11th IEEE International Symposium on High-Performance Distributed Computing (HPDC 2002), Edinburgh, 2002.

[81] V. TAYLOR, X. WU, X. LI, J. GEISLER, Z. LAN, M. HERELD, I. R. JUDSON, AND R. STEVENS, *Prophesy: Automating the modeling process*, in Third Annual International Workshop on Active Middleware Services, San Francisco, 2001.

[82] J. D. TERESCO, M. W. BEALL, J. E. FLAHERTY, AND M. S. SHEPHARD, *A hierarchical partition model for adaptive finite element computation*, Computer Methods in Applied Mechanics and Engineering, 184 (2000), pp. 269–285.

[83] J. D. TERESCO, K. D. DEVINE, AND J. E. FLAHERTY, *Partitioning and Dynamic Load Balancing for the Numerical Solution of Partial Differential Equations*. Tech. Report CS-04-11. Department of Computer Science, Williams College, Williamstown, MA, 2005.

[84] J. D. TERESCO, J. FAIK, AND J. E. FLAHERTY, *Hierarchical Partitioning and Dynamic Load Balancing for Scientific Computation*. Tech. Report CS-04-04. Department of Computer Science, Williams College, Williamstown, MA, 2004. Lecture Notes in Computer Science (LNCS), Volume 3732, (2006), pp. 911–920.

[85] J. D. TERESCO AND L. P. UNGAR, *A Comparison of Zoltan Dynamic Load Balancers for Adaptive Computation*. Tech. Report CS-03-02. Department of Computer Science, Williams College, Williamstown, MA, 2003.

[86] C. TOMLINSON, P. CANNATA, G. MEREDITH, AND D. WOELK, *The extensible services switch in Carnot*, IEEE Parallel and Distributed Technology, 1 (1993), pp. 16–20.

[87] S. VAJRACHARYA, S. KARMESIN, P. BECKMAN, J. CROTINGER, A. MALONY, S. SHENDE, R. OLDEHOEFT, AND S. SMITH, *SMARTS: Exploiting temporal locality and parallelism through vertical execution*, in International Conference on Supercomputing, Rhodes, Greece, 1999.

[88] C. VARELA AND G. AGHA, *Programming dynamically reconfigurable systems with SALSA*, in Proc. OOPSLA 2001, Tampa Bay, 2001.

[89] C. VARELA, *Worldwide Computing with Universal Actors: Linguistic Abstractions for Naming, Migration, and Coordination*. Ph.D. thesis. University of Illinois, Champaign, 2001.

[90] C. WALSHAW AND M. CROSS, *Parallel optimisation algorithms for multilevel mesh partitioning*, Parallel Computing, 26 (2000), pp. 1635–1660.

[91] ———, *Multilevel Mesh Partitioning for Heterogeneous Communication Networks*, Future Generation Computer Systems, 17 (2001), pp. 601–623.

[92] M. S. WARREN AND J. K. SALMON, *A parallel hashed oct-tree n-body algorithm*, in Proc. Supercomputing '93, IEEE Computer Society, Piscataway, NJ, 1993, pp. 12–21.

[93] R. C. WHALEY AND J. J. DONGARRA, *Automatically tuned linear algebra software*, in Conf. High Performance Networking and Computing, Proc. 1998 ACM/IEEE conference on Supercomputing, Orlando, FL, Nov. 1998, pp. 1–27.

[94] R. WOLSKI, N. T. SPRING, AND J. HAYES, *The Network Weather Service: A distributed resource performance forecasting service for metacomputing*, Future Generation Computer Systems, 15 (1999), pp. 757–768.

[95] X. WU, V. TAYLOR, J. GEISLER, Z. LAN, R. STEVENS, M. HERELD, AND I. JUDSON, *Design and development of Prophesy Performance Database for distributed scientific applications*, in Proc. 10th SIAM Conference on Parallel Processing, SIAM, Philadelphia, 2001, CD-ROM.

[96] X. WU, V. TAYLOR, AND R. STEVENS, *Design and implementation of Prophesy Performance Database for distributed scientific applications*, in Proc. 13th IASTED Parallel and Distributed Computing and Systems Conference, Anaheim, CA, 2001.

[97] Y. ZHANG, S. CHANDRA, S. HARIRI, AND M. PARASHAR, *Autonomic proactive runtime partitioning strategies for SAMR applications*, in Proc. NSF Next Generation Systems Program Workshop, IEEE/ACM 18th International Parallel and Distributed Processing Symposium, Santa Fe, NM, 2004.

Chapter 4
Achieving High Performance on the BlueGene/L Supercomputer

George Almasi, Gyan Bhanot, Sid Chatterjee, Alan Gara, John Gunnels, Manish Gupta, Amy Henning, Jose E. Moreira, James Sexton, Bob Walkup, Alessandro Curioni, Charles Archer, Leonardo Bachega, Bor Chan, Bruce Curtis, Sharon Brunett, Giri Chukkapalli, Robert Harkness, and Wayne Pfeiffer

The BlueGene/L (BG/L) supercomputer is designed to deliver new levels of application performance by providing a combination of good single-node computational performance and high scalability. To achieve good single-node performance, the BG/L design includes a special dual floating-point unit on each processor and the ability to use two processors per node. BG/L also includes both a torus and a tree network to achieve high scalability. We demonstrate how benchmarks and applications can take advantage of these architectural features to get the most out of BG/L.

Achieving high sustained application performance has been one of the chief goals of the BG/L project [1]. The BG/L system was designed to provide a very high density of compute nodes with a modest power requirement, using a low-frequency embedded system-on-a-chip technology. The BG/L compute node is targeted to operate at 700 MHz. To obtain good performance at this relatively low frequency, each node needs to process multiple instructions per clock cycle. This can be achieved through two main strategies. First, one can make use of both processors in each BG/L node. Second, each processor has a dual floating-point unit with fused multiply-add instructions, which can perform four operations per cycle using special SIMD-like instructions. We investigate two strategies for leveraging the two processors in each node: coprocessor mode and virtual node mode. We compare the relative merits of these strategies and show that they both achieve significant gains over single processor mode.

BG/L has multiple networks, including a three-dimensional torus for point-to-point communication, and a tree for certain collective operations. For communication on the torus, the best performance will be obtained when there is good locality so that the average number of hops on the torus is small. We examine the communication properties of benchmarks and applications, and we show that in some cases very good locality can be obtained by carefully mapping MPI tasks onto the torus.

4.1 BG/L architectural features

This section reviews some architectural features of BG/L that have a significant impact on performance and that are relevant to this study. A more detailed description of the architecture is available elsewhere [1]. The design of BG/L emphasizes both single-node computational performance and scalability. For single-node performance, we focus on the dual floating-point unit and on using both processors on each node.

4.1.1 Processor characteristics and memory hierarchy

Each BG/L node has two 32-bit embedded PowerPC (PPC) 440 processors. The PPC 440 processor is a low-power superscalar processor with 32 KB each of L1 data and instruction caches. The data cache is 64-way set associative with 32 byte lines and a round-robin replacement policy for cache lines within each set. The BG/L nodes support prefetching in hardware, based on detection of sequential data access. The prefetch buffer for each processor holds 64 L1 cache lines (16 128-byte L2/L3 cache lines) and is referred to as the L2 cache. Each chip also has a 4 MB L3 cache built from embedded DRAM, and an integrated DDR memory controller. A single BG/L node supports 512 MB memory, with an option to use higher-capacity memory chips.

The PPC 440 design does not support hardware cache coherence at the L1 level. However, there are instructions to invalidate a cache line or flush the cache, which can be used to support cache coherence in software. The memory system beyond the L1 caches supports sequential consistency with respect to the memory system and the hardware locks with the exception of a fast shared SRAM accessible opnly from system space.

4.1.2 Double floating-point unit

BG/L employs a SIMD-like extension of the PPC floating-point unit, which we refer to as the double floating-point unit (DFPU). The DFPU essentially adds a secondary FPU to the primary FPU as a duplicate copy with its own register file. The second FPU is not an independent unit: it is normally used with a comprehensive set of special parallel instructions. This instruction set includes parallel add, multiply, fused multiply-add, and additional operations to support complex arithmetic. All the SIMD instructions operate on double-precision floating-point data. There are also SIMD instructions that provide reciprocal estimates and reciprocal square root estimates. These form the basis for very efficient methods to evaluate arrays of reciprocals, square roots, or reciprocal square roots.

In addition, the instruction set provides for standard single floating-point usage of the second FPU through extensions.

The special instruction set includes quad-word loads, which bring two consecutive double words (i.e., 16 bytes) from memory into a register pair in the primary and secondary floating-point units. Similarly there are quad-word store operations. The processor local bus (PLB) supports independent read and write 128-bit data transfers, matching the requirements for efficient quad-word loads and stores.

4.1.3 Torus interconnect

BG/L has a three-dimensional torus network as the primary interconnect among compute nodes. The torus circuitry, including FIFOs for incoming and outgoing packets, routing, and arbitration logic, is integrated within the compute node. Each node has six nearest-neighbor connections. The raw hardware bandwidth for each torus link is 2 bits/cycle (175 MB/s at 700 MHz) in each direction. The torus network provides both adaptive and deterministic minimal path routing in a deadlock-free manner. Each message is broken up into one or more packets, with a maximum packet size of 256 bytes, for transmission. The hardware supports variable packet sizes in the range of 32B to 256B in 32B increments.

4.2 Methods for obtaining high performance

Taking advantage of BG/L's special hardware features is important for achieving good performance on BG/L. We first describe how to exploit the double FPU for good uniprocessor performance. We then describe two different techniques for using both processors in each node: coprocessor mode and virtual node mode. We note that both approaches were used successfully on the ASCI Red machine [2]. Finally, we describe how to map applications more effectively onto the three-dimensional torus topology.

4.2.1 Using the DFPU

The IBM XL family of compilers for FORTRAN, C, and C++ share a common backend, TOBEY, which has been enhanced to support code generation for the DFPU core. TOBEY uses extensions to Larsen and Amarasinghe's superword level parallelism (SLP) algorithm [3] to generate parallel operations for the DFPU. In particular, TOBEY can recognize idioms related to basic complex arithmetic floating point computations and can exploit the SIMD-like extensions to efficiently implement those computations. The effectiveness of automatic code generation by the compiler is influenced by several factors. The compiler needs to identify independent floating-point operations using consecutive data on 16-byte boundaries in order to generate SIMD instructions. The issues are different for Fortran and C. For Fortran, the main issue is data alignment. Alignment assertions are required for cases where alignment is not known at compile time. For C and C++ there can also be pointer aliasing issues. If there is a possible load/store conflict, the compiler cannot safely issue a load for two consecutive data items. In such cases it is necessary to guarantee that pointers are disjoint in memory using #pragma disjoint or #pragma independent. Alignment assertions are provided for FORTRAN: call alignx(16, array_reference), and

C/C++: `__alignx(16, pointer)`. In applications with statically allocated global data, the alignment and aliasing issues are known at compile time, and the compiler can generate SIMD code without additional pragmas or alignment assertions. We are in the process of extending the compiler so that it can generate SIMD instructions by applying transformations like loop versioning, which use runtime checks for data alignment [4].

One can also specify SIMD instructions by using intrinsic, or built-in, functions. The compiler recognizes and replaces each such function with the corresponding DFPU instruction. For example, the intrinsic function for the parallel fused multiply-add operation is `__fpmadd()`. With intrinsic functions, one can control the generation of DFPU instructions without resorting to assembler programming.

4.2.2 Using the coprocessor for computation

By default, the coprocessor is used only to perform communication services. However, the compute node kernel supports a `co_start()` function to dispatch computation to the second processor and a `co_join()` function to allow the main thread of execution on the first processor to wait for completion of that computation. This mode of using the coprocessor can be referred to as coprocessor computation offload mode. Since the hardware does not provide cache coherence at the L1 level, the programmer needs to ensure cache coherence with software. The compute node kernel supports a number of calls to help manage cache coherence. The calls include operations to store, invalidate, or invalidate-and-store all cache lines within a specified address range, and a routine that can evict the entire contents of the L1 data cache. Further details are described elsewhere [5]. There is significant overhead associated with using the coprocessor to offload computation. It takes approximately 4,200 processor cycles to flush the entire L1 data cache; hence this method should be used only for time-consuming code blocks. Also, the code section should be without excessive memory bandwidth requirements and free of internode communication.

Ensuring cache coherence in software is a complex and error-prone task, so we expect computation off-load mode to be used mainly by expert library developers. We have used this method in Linpack and for certain routines in a subset of engineering and scientific subroutine library (ESSL) and math acceleration subsystem vector (MASSV) developed for BG/L.

4.2.3 Virtual node mode

Virtual node mode provides an easier way to harness the power of the second processor. Virtual node mode splits the available resources in the compute node, assigning half the memory to each processor and running two separate MPI tasks on each node. The two tasks share access to L3 and memory, and they share the use of the network. Communication between tasks in the same node happens through a special region of noncached shared memory. The main disadvantage of virtual node mode is that the available memory for each MPI task is reduced by a factor of 2, and the same processor handling the computation must now also handle network tasks, such as emptying and filling network FIFOs.

4.2.4 Mapping MPI tasks onto the torus network

BG/L's main network for point-to-point communication is a three-dimensional torus. Effective communication bandwidth is reduced and the latency is increased as the number of hops on the torus increases due to the sharing of the links with cut-through traffic, and so the objective is to shorten the distance each message has to travel. For a relatively small BG/L partition, such as an $8 \times 8 \times 8$ torus with 512 nodes, locality should not be a critical factor because even for a random task placement, the average number of hops in each dimension is $L/4 = 2$. The issue of task placement on the torus becomes more important for much larger torus dimensions.

Many MPI applications have regular communication patterns, and in those cases one can map MPI tasks to torus coordinates to optimize communication performance. This mapping can be done from within or from outside the application. Within the application code, task layout can be optimized by creating a new communicator and renumbering the tasks or by using MPI Cartesian topologies. This is done in the Linpack code presented in section 4.3.1 below. The implementation of MPI on BG/L allows the user to specify a mapping file, which explicitly lists the torus coordinates for each MPI task. This provides complete control of task placement from outside the application.

4.3 Performance measurements

In this section we present performance measurements for benchmarks and applications. Some performance measurements were obtained with a 512-node BG/L prototype, running at a reduced frequency of 500 MHz, while other measurements were made on a 512-node system with second-generation chips running at 700 MHz. In our experiments, we explore mathematical kernels, benchmarks including Linpack and the NAS parallel benchmarks, and several parallel applications.

4.3.1 Mathematical kernels and benchmarks

Daxpy is a level-1 BLAS routine that updates one array using values from a second array: $y(i) = a * x(i) + y(i), i = 1, \ldots, n$. Similar array update operations appear in many applications, and the daxpy kernel provides a good test of the memory subsystem. There are two loads and one store for each fused multiply-add instruction, so daxpy is load/store bound. By making repeated calls to daxpy in a loop, one can map out the performance characteristics for data in different levels of the memory hierarchy. There are a total of six load/store operations for each pair of array updates, using four floating-point operations. Without special SIMD instructions, the theoretical limit would be four flops in six cycles for data in the L1 cache. With the quad-word load and store operations, this limit becomes four flops in three cycles. Since there are two processors on each chip with private L1 data caches, the limit is eight flops in three cycles using both processors. The measured performance for daxpy is shown in Figure 4.1. When one processor is used without SIMD instructions, the observed rate peaks at about 0.5 flops/cycle, using a simple loop and compiler-generated code. This is 75% of the limit of 2/3 flops/cycle. By turning on the `-qarch=440d`

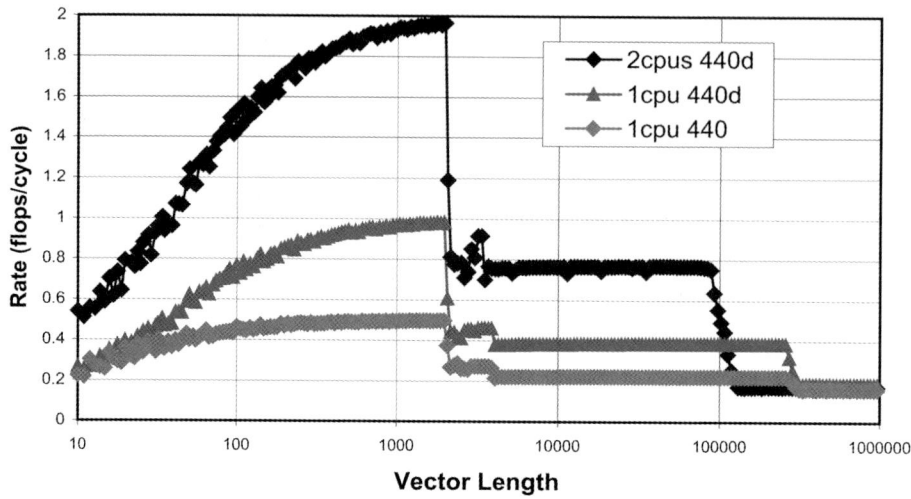

Figure 4.1. *Performance of daxpy on a BG/L node is shown as a function of vector length. L1 and L3 cache edges are apparent. For data in the L1 cache (lengths < 2,000), the performance doubles by turning on SIMD instructions (440d) and doubles again when using both processors on the node.*

compiler option to generate SIMD instructions, the flop rate approximately doubles for data in the L1 cache: for a single processor with SIMD instructions, the measured rate is about 1.0 flops/cycle for array sizes that just fit in L1. Figure 4.1 also shows the combined floating-point rate for the node, using both processors in virtual node mode. The rate doubles again for data in the L1 cache. For large array dimensions, contention for L3 and memory is apparent.

We have examined the effectiveness of virtual node mode by analyzing the performance of the NAS parallel benchmarks [6] on a 32-node BG/L system. Figure 4.2 shows the performance speed-up of the NAS parallel benchmarks (class C) resulting from virtual node mode. The BT and SP benchmarks require a perfect square for the number of MPI tasks, so those benchmarks used 25 nodes in coprocessor mode and 32 nodes (64 MPI tasks) in virtual node mode.

For every NAS benchmark, execution in virtual node mode leads to a significant performance improvement. The speed-ups vary from a factor of 2 for EP to a factor of 1.26 for IS. There are several reasons why the speed-up is typically less than a factor of 2. First, there is a loss in parallel efficiency for each benchmark (except EP) as we increase the number of tasks. Second, there is sharing of physical resources between tasks when we execute two tasks in a compute node. Those resources include the L3 cache, main memory, and interconnection networks. There are also changes in the basic computation rate due to a reduction in the problem size per task as the task count increases. (The NAS benchmarks solve a fixed total problem size.)

The other approach for utilizing both processors in a compute node is to offload some computation to the coprocessor using the `co_start()`/`co_join()` method. As previously described, this requires careful coordination between the processors, since cache

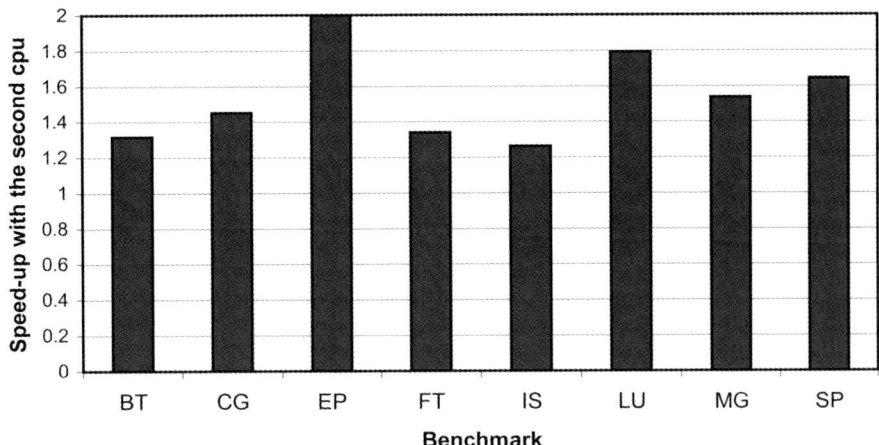

Figure 4.2. *The performance speed-up using virtual node mode is shown for the class C NAS parallel benchmarks. The speed-up is defined as the ratio of Mops per node in virtual node mode to Mops per node using coprocessor mode.*

coherence has to be managed entirely in software. Use of the second processor with `co_start()`/`co_join()` requires more programming effort than virtual node mode, but it can have performance advantages for several reasons. First, one does not need to increase the number of tasks in a parallel job, thus avoiding a loss of parallel efficiency. Second, each task has full access to all the resources of a compute node. This increases the available memory per task, for example.

We compare both approaches to utilizing the two processors in a node with the Linpack benchmark [7]. Figure 4.3 shows the performance of Linpack as a function of the number of nodes when running in three different modes: default (single processor), virtual node, and computation offload to the coprocessor with `co_start()`/`co_join()`. Performance is shown as percentage of peak for each machine size, and the results are for weak scaling (constant work per task). We change the problem size with the number of nodes to keep memory utilization in each node close to 70%.

Using a single processor on each node immediately limits the maximum possible performance to 50% of peak. In this mode we consistently achieve 80% of the maximum possible performance, which corresponds to 40% of the peak performance for the node. In virtual node mode and computation offload mode both processors in each node are busy with computations. Both approaches display essentially equivalent performance when running on a single node, achieving 74% of peak. As we increase the machine size, the benefits of computation offload mode start to show up. At the machine size of 512 nodes, computation offload mode achieves 70% of peak, while virtual node mode achieves 65% of peak.

We used the computation offload mode for subsequent Linpack runs as the BG/L system was scaled to 16,384 nodes. These results are shown in Figure 4.4. The BG/L system was ranked number 1 on the November 2004 TOP500® list with a sustained performance of 70.72 Teraflop/s on Linpack.

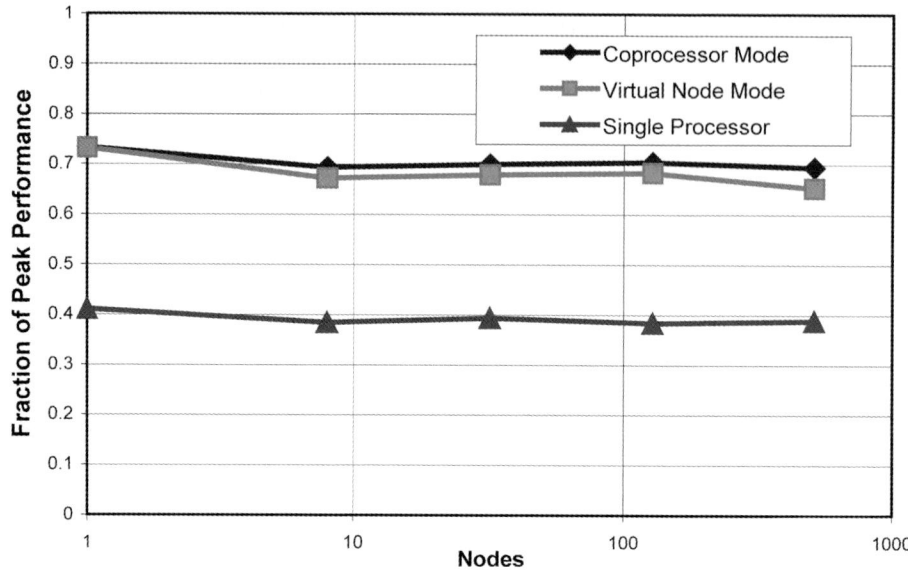

Figure 4.3. *Linpack performance in BG/L is shown as a function of the number of compute nodes. Performance is indicated as a fraction of the theoretical peak. Results for three different strategies are included: using a single processor on each node, offloading computation to the coprocessor with the model, and using virtual node mode to run with two tasks per node.*

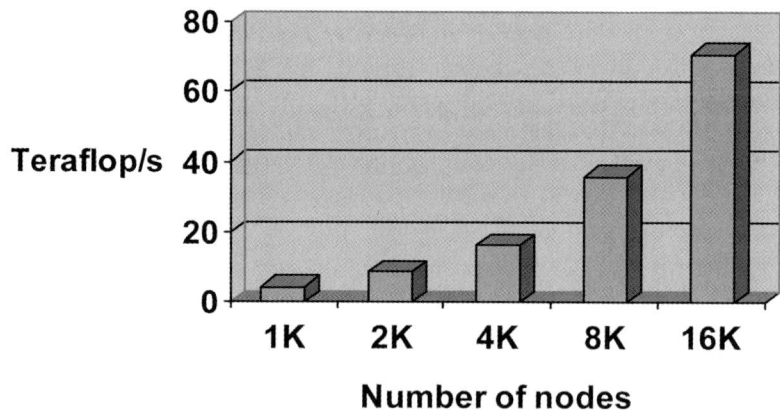

Figure 4.4. *Performance of LINPACK on large-scale BG/L systems.*

The NAS parallel benchmarks provide some interesting test cases to study the effects of task placement on the torus network. The NAS BT (block tridiagonal) benchmark solves Navier–Stokes equations in three dimensions using an alternate-direction implicit finite-difference method. The parallelization strategy distributes blocks to a two-dimensional square process mesh, and the communication pattern is primarily point-to-point commu-

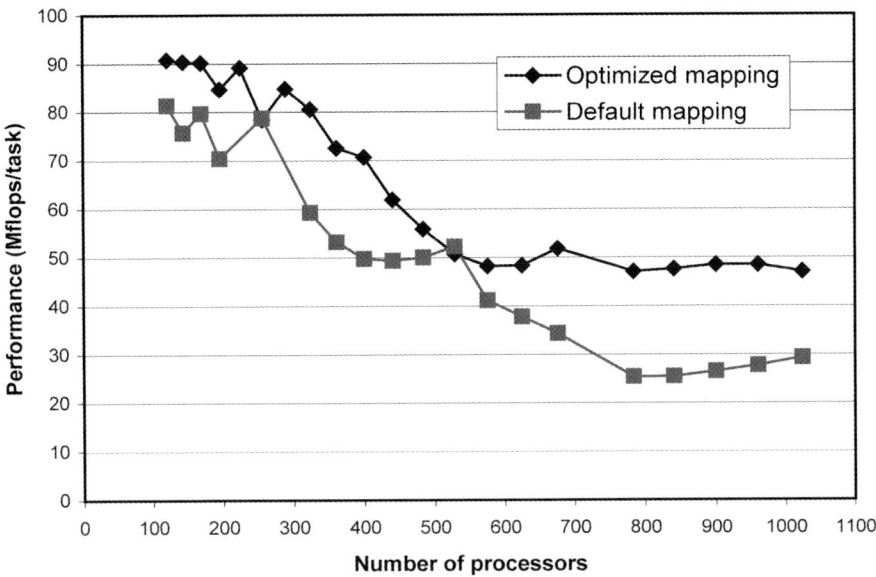

Figure 4.5. *Comparison of the default mapping and optimized mapping for NAS BT on up to 1,024 processors in virtual node mode. Mapping provides a significant performance boost at large task counts.*

nication between neighbors on the process mesh. On BG/L this two-dimensional process mesh is mapped to the three-dimensional mesh of compute nodes. The default mapping is to lay out MPI tasks in xyz order. Alternatively one can use a mapping file to explicitly specify the torus coordinates for each MPI task. The optimized mapping lays out contiguous 8×8 XY planes in such a manner that most of the edges of the planes are physically connected with a single link. As Figure 4.5 shows, optimized mapping has a significant effect on overall performance because of the better physical adjacency of communicating nodes.

4.3.2 Applications

We have examined the performance of a number of parallel applications on BG/L. In this section we describe the applications and provide performance comparisons with other parallel platforms when possible.

sPPM

The first example is sPPM, which solves a gas dynamics problem on a 3D rectangular grid using a simplified piecewise parabolic method. There is a standard version of sPPM which is an ASCI purple benchmark [8], and there is an optimized version of sPPM, which has been significantly rewritten and tuned for IBM Power3/Power4 systems. In the measurements reported here, we use the optimized version of sPPM. The optimized version makes extensive use of routines to evaluate arrays of reciprocals and square roots. On IBM pSeries systems,

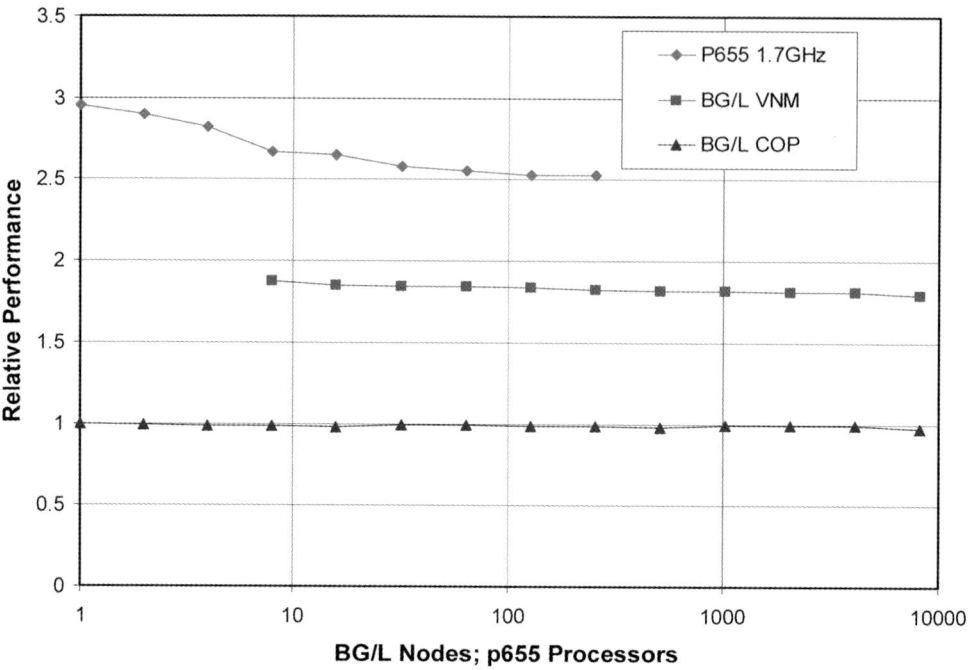

Figure 4.6. *The computational performance for sPPM is shown for systems including IBM p655 at 1.7 GHz (top curve) and BG/L at 700 MHz using virtual node mode (middle curve) or coprocessor mode with a single computational task per node (lower curve). The x-axis indicates the number of BG/L nodes or the number of p655 processors.*

these routines are supplied in the vector MASS library [9]. On BG/L, we make use of special SIMD instructions to obtain very efficient versions of these routines that exploit the DFPU. The sPPM benchmark is set up for weak scaling studies (constant work per task). The communication pattern is mainly boundary exchange with nearest neighbors for all six faces of the local rectangular domain. This problem maps perfectly onto the BG/L hardware, because each node has six neighbors in the 3D torus network.

The sPPM benchmark is highly scalable because there are extensive computations within each local domain, with a relatively small volume of boundary data for nearest-neighbor communication. The performance is compute-bound for problems that use a significant fraction of the memory available on each node. The measured performance for sPPM is shown in Figure 4.6, using a $128 \times 128 \times 128$ local domain and double-precision variables (this requires about 150 MB of memory). The performance is expressed in terms of grid points processed per second per time-step per cpu, or per node for BG/L in virtual node mode. For virtual node mode, we use a local domain that is a factor of 2 smaller in one dimension and contains twice as many tasks, thus solving the same problem on a per-node basis.

The scaling curves are relatively flat, indicating very good scalability, as expected for this application. The interconnect fabric for the IBM p655 system was the Federation switch, with two links per eight-processor node. The p655 system has a good set of hardware counters that provide insight into the computational requirements of sPPM. About 99% of the loads hit in the 32 KB L1 data cache on Power4, and the instruction mix is dominated by floating-point operations. This application makes very good use of the L1 data cache and has a small communication requirement. Less than 2% of the elapsed time is spent in communication routines. As a result, virtual node mode is very effective for sPPM on BG/L. We measure speed-ups of 1.7 to 1.8 depending on the number of nodes. The DFPU on BG/L contributes about a 30% boost to the computational performance through the use of special routines to evaluate arrays of reciprocals and square roots. In other computationally intensive regions of the code, automatic generation of SIMD instructions by the compiler has to date been inhibited by alignment issues or array access patterns. On BG/L, the measured scaling curves remain basically flat up to the largest machine that we have tested so far: 8,192 nodes using 16,384 processors in virtual node mode. On this system the sustained application performance was approximately 8.3 TFlops for sPPM, which corresponds to about 18% of the theoretical peak of 45.9 TFlops (700MHz * 4 ops/cycle * 16,384 processors).

UMT2K

UMT2K is an ASCI purple benchmark, which solves a photon transport problem on an unstructured mesh [8]. This application is written in Fortran 90 using MPI and optionally OpenMP. We use an MPI-only implementation, because there is no support for OpenMP on BG/L. The unstructured mesh is statically partitioned using the Metis library [10]. In practice there can be a significant spread in the amount of computational work per task, and this load imbalance affects the scalability of the application. By using profiling tools on IBM p-series systems, we found that the elapsed time for UMT2K was dominated by a single computational routine, snswp3d. The main performance issue in this routine is a sequence of dependent division operations. By splitting loops into independent vectorizable units, the IBM XL compiler was able to generate efficient DFPU code for reciprocals, resulting in 40% to 50% overall performance boost from the DFPU for this application.

The performance of UMT2K is shown in Figure 4.7 for BG/L and an IBM p655 cluster (1.7GHz Power4 processors, Federation switch).

The UMT2K test case shown in Figure 4.7 was modified from the RFP2 benchmark problem, following the benchmark instructions to keep the amount of work per task approximately constant. UMT2K uses an unstructured mesh, which is partitioned using the Metis library [10]. Currently, this partitioning method limits the scalability of UMT2K because it uses a table dimensioned by the number of partitions squared. This table grows too large to fit on a BG/L node when the number of partitions exceeds about 4,000. This limitation can probably be overcome by using a parallel implementation of Metis. Our measurements show that virtual node mode provides a good performance boost, but the efficiency decreases for large process counts. It should be possible to optimize the mapping of MPI tasks to improve locality for point-to-point communication. Work is in progress to provide this capability.

Car–Parrinello molecular dynamics

The Car–Parrinello molecular dynamics code (CPMD) originated in IBM's Zurich research laboratory in the early 1990s [11]. It is an implementation of density functional theory

70   Chapter 4. Achieving High Performance on the BlueGene/L Supercomputer

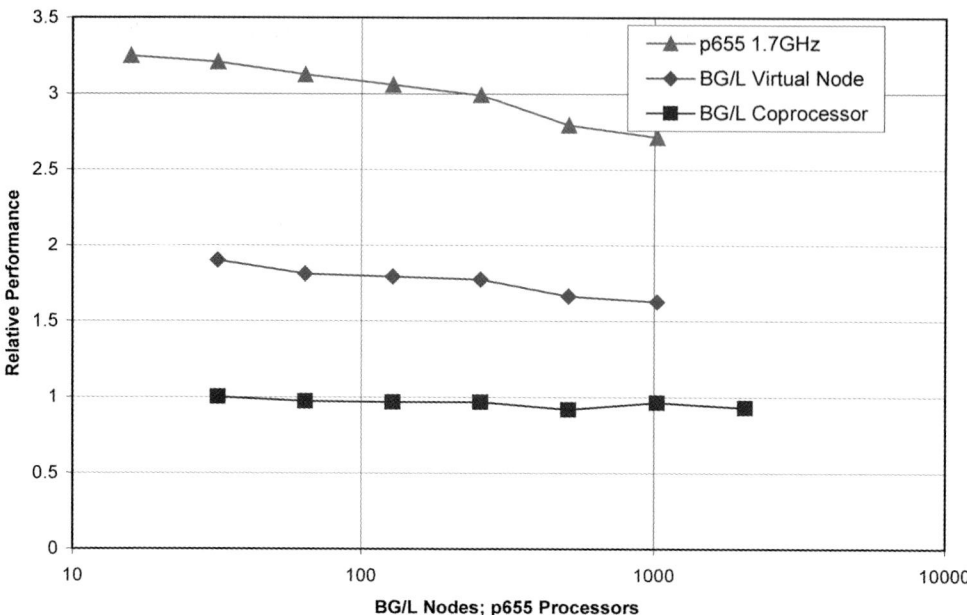

Figure 4.7. *Weak scaling results for UMT2K on BG/L and an IBM p655 cluster. The x-axis indicates the number of BG/L nodes or the number of p655 processors, and the y-axis indicates overall performance relative to 32 nodes of BG/L in coprocessor mode.*

using plane waves and pseudopotentials and is particularly designed for ab-initio molecular dynamics. The CPMD code is widely used for research in computational chemistry, materials science, and biology. It has been licensed to several thousand research groups in more than 50 countries. The application is mainly written in Fortran, parallelized for distributed-memory with MPI, with an option to add an additional level of parallelism using OpenMP for multiprocessor nodes. CPMD makes extensive use of three-dimensional FFTs, which require efficient all-to-all communication. The single-processor performance of CPMD was optimized using SIMD-enabled routines for the most common calls, such as DGEMM, DCOPY, AZZERO, and FFT. In addition, the scalability was improved using a taskgroup implementation of the FFT with a special mapping to the BG/L torus.

A test case was prepared using a silicon-carbide supercell with 216 atoms (a system that could also run on a simple workstation). The scaling behavior for this problem was studied on BG/L and on IBM Power4 p690 systems (logical partitions with eight processors at 1.3 GHz and dual-plane Colony switch). The elapsed times per time-step in the simulation are listed in Table 4.1.

This example is sensitive to latency in the communication subsystem. Small messages become important because the message size for all-to-all communication is proportional to one over the square of the number of MPI tasks. BG/L outperforms the p690 system when there are more than 32 MPI tasks, because BG/L is more efficient for small messages. The value reported for the p690 system at 1,024 processors is the best-case performance number, using 128 MPI tasks and eight OpenMP threads per task to minimize the cost of all-to-all

Table 4.1. *The performance for CPMD using a 216-atom SiC supercell is listed for IBM p690 (Power4 1.3 GHz, Colony switch) and BG/L (700 MHz) systems. The performance metric is the elapsed time per time step in the simulation. Values marked n.a. were not available.*

BG/L Nodes p690 Cpus	p690 sec/step	BG/L sec/step Coprocessor	BG/L sec/step Virtual node mode
8	40.2	58.4	29.2
16	21.1	28.7	14.8
32	11.5	14.5	8.4
64	n.a.	8.2	4.6
128	n.a.	4.0	2.7
256	n.a.	2.4	1.5
512	n.a.	1.4	n.a.
1024	3.8	n.a.	n.a.

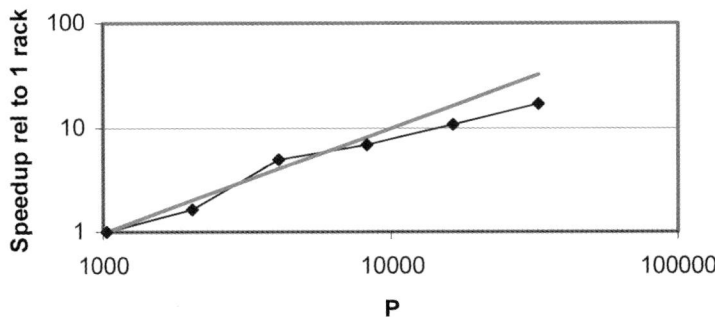

Figure 4.8. *Results for CPMD with 138,000 atoms on BG/L.*

communication. Both low latency in the MPI layer and a total lack of system demons contribute to very good scalability on BG/L. The results also show that virtual node mode provides a good performance boost, up to the largest task counts tested (512 MPI tasks). Finally, a run was done, using the new classical molecular dynamics driver for modified Tersoff potentials (developed for QM/MM calculations), with 138K atoms on up to 32K processors using virtual node mode. We can simulate 5 nanoseconds per hour on the 32K processors system. The results are shown in Figure 4.8.

Enzo

Enzo is a large-scale multiphysics code for astrophysical simulation. Its primary application is modeling cosmological processes, with particular emphasis on large-scale structure formation where self-gravity is the dominant force. Enzo combines hydrodynamics for baryonic matter (which is treated as a real gas) and particle tracking for dark matter (which is treated as collisionless particles). The global gravitational field is due to the real gas and the dark matter particles. Enzo can operate in full AMR mode or in a nonadaptive unigrid mode. Numerical methods [12] include the piecewise parabolic method (PPM) or Zeus hydrodynamics solvers (using multigrid), Fourier transforms for the global gravity solution, and various Newton iteration schemes for the real-gas effects (ionization, heating and cooling, etc.).

Enzo consists of about 35,000 lines of Fortran 90 and 65,000 lines of C++. The C++ code is primarily for managing the AMR grids and I/O. Most of the computation is performed in Fortran. The problem is parallelized by domain decomposition into rectangular subgrids, including the top/root grid (which is the only level in a non-AMR run). Message passing is done with MPI, and I/O makes use of the HDF5 data format. Enzo runs on many currently available high-end computers and is a major consumer of compute cycles at the San Diego Supercomputer Center, where it runs primarily on DataStar, a cluster of IBM Power4 processors with a peak speed of over 10 TFlops.

The main challenge in porting Enzo to BG/L was to build the HDF5 I/O library, which required extra care due to the cross-compiling environment. The version of HDF5 that was built supported serial I/O and 32-bit file offsets. These limitations can be addressed by future improvements in BG/L system software. The initial build of Enzo had very poor performance on BG/L. The problem was identified using MPI profiling tools that are available on BG/L. The performance issue was related to the way that nonblocking communication routines are completed. Enzo used a method based on occasional calls to MPI_Test. This had been observed to perform poorly on other systems that use MPICH. It was found that one could ensure progress in the MPI layer by adding a call to MPI_Barrier. On BG/L, this was absolutely essential to obtain scalable parallel performance, and it provided a performance improvement on some other systems as well. After getting Enzo up and running on BG/L hardware, experiments were done to explore ways of increasing performance. A 30% performance improvement from the DFPU was obtained by adding calls to optimized routines for vectors of reciprocals and square roots. Virtual node mode was also found to be very effective for cases that could fit in the available memory (256 MB).

The relative performance of Enzo for a test case using a 256**3 unigrid is shown in Table 4.2 for 32 and 64 nodes of BG/L and the corresponding numbers of IBM p655 processors (1.5GHz Power4, Federation switch).

This test case was computation bound at the task counts that were used in the table. In coprocessor mode, one BG/L processor (700 MHz) provided about 30% of the performance of one p655 processor (1.5 GHz). This is similar to what we have observed with other applications. Virtual node mode gave a significant speed-up by a factor of 1.73 on 32 BG/L nodes.

Scaling studies for Enzo were attempted on both systems. It was found that for a fixed problem size, scalability of Enzo is limited by bookkeeping work (integer-intensive operations) in one routine, which increases rapidly as the number of MPI tasks increases.

Table 4.2. *Performance of Enzo for 256**3 unigrid on BG/L and IBM p655 (1.5GHz Power4, Federation switch) relative to 32 BG/L nodes in coprocessor mode.*

BG/L nodes or p655 processors	Relative speed of BG/L in coprocessor mode	Relative speed of BG/L in virtual node mode	Relative speed of p655 1.5 GHz
32	1.00	1.73	3.16
64	1.83	2.85	6.27

This limits strong scaling on any system. Weak scaling studies were also attempted using a larger grid (512**3). On BG/L, this failed because the input files were larger than 2 GBytes, and the available runtime did not fully support large files. This experience makes it clear that large file support and more robust I/O throughput are needed for wider success of BG/L.

4.3.3 Polycrystal

The polycrystal application simulates grain interactions in polycrystals, including the accurate resolution of inhomogeneous anisotropic elastic and plastic fields at grain boundaries, and multiscale mechanisms of grain boundary sliding. The overall approach is to exploit the power of massively parallel computing—such as offered by BG/L and DOE ASCI platforms—to explicitly account for microstructural effects on material behavior. The computational approach is based on a Lagrangian large-deformation finite element formulation. Multiscale, atomistically informed crystal plasticity models and equations of state computed from ab-initio quantum mechanical calculations are combined with a shock-capturing method to analyze the response of tantalum under extreme loading conditions. The considerable computing effort is distributed among processors via a parallel implementation based on mesh partitioning and message passing. Each mesh partition represents a grain with a different orientation and is assigned to a different processor.

Porting polycrystal to BG/L was challenging. The build environment for polycrystal requires Python and has a complex set of environment variables and configuration files, with built-in assumptions about support for shared libraries. It was necessary to change the build process to make use of static libraries only, and it was also necessary to skip certain utilities that are normally built with polycrystal (such as mpi-python).

Polycrystal has the requirement that a global grid must fit within the memory of each MPI process. For interestingly large problems, this requires several hundred MB of memory, which is more than the available memory in virtual node mode. As a consequence, it was necessary to use coprocessor mode on BG/L. The computational work in polycrystal does not benefit from library calls to routines that are optimized for the DFPU, and the compiler was not effective at generating DFPU code due to unknown alignment of the key data structures. The overall result was that polycrystal could use just one FPU on one of the two processors in each BG/L node. Polycrystal was observed to scale moderately well. Using a fixed problem size, the performance improved by a factor of approximately 30, going from 16 to 1,024 processors. Measurements with hardware counters, combined with MPI instrumentation, showed that the scalability was limited by considerations of load balance, not message-passing or network performance. The performance of polycrystal on BG/L (700 MHz) was measured to be a factor of 4 to 5 slower per processor compared to an IBM p655 cluster (1.7 GHz Power4, Federation interconnect). The experience with polycrystal makes it clear that available memory is a major constraint and that there are important applications that will not be able to make use of virtual node mode.

4.4 Conclusions

In this chapter we have described various techniques for achieving high performance on the BlueGene/L supercomputer.

The use of optimized math libraries and the availability of double floating-point optimizations in the XL compiler suite make it possible for applications to benefit from the DFPU in each processor. The chapter shows large gains on BLAS level 1 operations resulting from the effective use of the DFPU. Our experience to date has been that optimized math libraries often provide the most effective way to use the DFPU. Success with automatic DFPU code generation by the compiler in complex applications has been limited.

The computational power of the second processor can be harnessed using coprocessor computation off-load and virtual node modes. The results shown in the chapter demonstrate close to doubling of the performance achieved by the Linpack benchmark, by deploying either computation off-load or virtual node mode. For benchmarks and applications in which computation off-load mode is not a viable option, such as the NAS parallel benchmarks, virtual node mode shows substantial gains. It often achieves speed-ups between 40% to 80%.

As the torus dimension increases, locality will be an important factor for communication performance. By judiciously mapping MPI tasks to locations in the physical network, we can achieve substantial performance improvements.

This chapter provides insight into some of the techniques we have found useful, but this is only at the beginning. As the size of the machine available to us increases, we will be concentrating on techniques to scale existing applications to tens of thousands of MPI tasks in the very near future. There are also efforts underway toward automating some of the performance-enhancing techniques, allowing for faster and more efficient application porting.

Bibliography

[1] N. R. ADIGA ET AL., *An overview of the BlueGene/L supercomputer*, in SC2002—High Performance Networking and Computing, Baltimore, MD, Nov. 2002. http://www.supercomput.org/sc2002/paperpdfs/pap.pap207.pdf.

[2] ASCI Red Homepage. http://www.sandia.gov/ASCI/Red/.

[3] S. LARSEN AND S. AMARASINGHE, *Exploiting superword level parallelism with multimedia instruction sets*, in Proc. SIGPLAN 2004 Conference on Programming Language Design and Implementation, June 2000, pp. 145–156.

[4] A. EICHENBERGER, P. WU, AND K. O'BRIEN, *Vectorization for short SIMD architectures with alignment constraints*, in Proc. SIGPLAN 2004 Conference on Programming Language Design and Implementation, Washington, DC, June 2004.

[5] G. ALMASI, L. BACHEGA, S. CHATTERJEE, D. LIEBER, X. MARTORELL, AND J. E. MOREIRA, *Enabling dual-core mode in BlueGene/L: Challenges and solutions*, in Proc. 15th Symposium on Computer Architecture and High Performance Computing, Sao Paulo, Brazil, Nov. 2003.

[6] *NAS Parallel Benchmarks*. http://www.nas.nasa.gov/Software/NPB.

[7] *The Linpack Benchmark.* http://www.netlib.org/benchmark/top500/lists/linpack.html.

[8] *ASCI Purple Benchmark Page.* http://www.llnl.gov/asci/purple/benchmarks/limited/code\underline{}list.html.

[9] *IBM Mathematical Acceleration Subsystem.* http://techsupport.services.ibm.com/server/mass.

[10] Metis home page. http://glaros.dtc.umn.edu/gkhome/views/metis.

[11] CPMD home page. http://www.cpmd.org.

[12] Enzo home page, http://cosmos.ucsd.edu/enzo.

Chapter 5

Performance Evaluation and Modeling of Ultra-Scale Systems

Leonid Oliker, Rupak Biswas, Rob Van der Wijngaart, David Bailey, and Allan Snavely

The growing gap between sustained and peak performance for full-scale complex scientific applications on conventional supercomputers is a major concern in high-performance computing (HPC). The problem is expected to be exacerbated by the end of this decade, as mission-critical applications will have computational requirements that are at least two orders of magnitude larger than current levels. To continuously increase raw computational power and at the same time substantially reap its benefits, major strides are necessary in hardware architecture, software infrastructure, and application development. The first step toward this goal is the accurate assessment of existing and emerging HPC systems across a comprehensive set of scientific algorithms. In addition, high-fidelity performance modeling is required to understand and predict the complex interactions among hardware, software, and applications and thereby influence future design trade-offs. This survey chapter discusses recent performance evaluations of state-of-the-art ultra-scale systems for a diverse set of scientific applications, including scalable compact synthetic benchmarks and architectural probes. In addition, performance models and program characterizations from key scientific areas are described.

5.1 Modern high-performance ultra-scale systems

We begin by briefly describing the salient features of the leading HPC parallel architectures that are examined in this chapter.

5.1.1 Seaborg (Power3)

The Power3 was first introduced in 1998 as part of IBM's RS/6000 series. Each 375 MHz processor contains two FPUs that can issue a multiply-add (MADD) per cycle for a peak performance of 1.5 Gflop/s. The Power3 has a pipeline of only three cycles, thus using the registers more efficiently and diminishing the penalty for mispredicted branches. The out-of-order architecture uses prefetching to reduce pipeline stalls due to cache misses. The CPU has a 32 KB instruction cache, a 128 KB 128-way set associative L1 data cache, and an 8 MB four-way set associative L2 cache with its own private bus. Each SMP node consists of 16 processors connected to main memory via a crossbar. Multinode configurations are networked via the colony switch using an omega-type topology. The Power3 experiments reported here were conducted on Seaborg, the 380-node IBM p-series system running AIX 5.1 and operated by the Lawrence Berkeley National Laboratory. Additional Power3 experiments were performed on Blue Horizon, a 144-node system located at the San Diego Supercomputer Center.

5.1.2 Cheetah (Power4)

The p-series 690 Power4 is the latest commercially available generation of IBM's RS/6000 series. Each 32-way SMP consists of 16 Power4 chips (organized as 4 Multi-Chip Modules (MCMs)), where a chip contains two 1.3 GHz processor cores. Each core has two FPUs capable of a fused MADD per cycle, for a peak performance of 5.2 Gflop/s. The superscalar out-of-order architecture can exploit instruction level parallelism through its eight execution units; however, a relatively long pipeline (six cycles) is necessitated by the high-frequency design. Each processor contains its own private L1 cache (64 KB instruction and 32 KB data) with prefetch hardware; however, both cores share a 1.5 MB unified L2 cache. The L3 is designed as a stand-alone 32 MB cache, or to be combined with other L3s on the same MCM to create a larger 128 MB interleaved cache. The Power4 experiments were performed on Cheetah, the 27-node IBM p-series 690 system running AIX 5.1 and operated by the Oak Ridge National Laboratory (ORNL). The system employs the Federation (HPS) interconnect, with two adaptors per node.

5.1.3 Ram (Itanium2)

The SGI Altix is designed as a cache-coherent, shared-memory multiprocessor system. The computational building block consists of four Intel Itanium2 processors, local memory, and a two-controller ASIC called the SHUB. The 64-bit architecture operates at 1.5 GHz and is capable of issuing two MADDs per cycle for a peak performance of 6.0 Gflop/s. The memory hierarchy consists of 128 FP registers and three on-chip data caches (32 KB L1, 256 KB L2, and 6 MB L3). The Itanium2 cannot store FP data in L1, making register loads and spills a potential source of bottlenecks; however, the relatively large register set helps mitigate this issue. The superscalar processor performs a combination of in-order and out-of-order instruction execution referred to as explicitly parallel instruction computing (EPIC). The Altix platform uses the NUMAlink3 interconnect, a high-performance custom network in a fat-tree topology that enables the bisection bandwidth to scale linearly with the number of processors. It implements a cache-coherent, nonuniform memory access (NUMA) protocol directly in hardware. A load/store cache miss causes the data to be communicated via the SHUB at a cache-line granularity and automatically replicated in the local cache. Additionally, one-sided programming languages can be efficiently implemented by leveraging the NUMA layer. The Altix experiments reported here were performed on Ram, the 256-processor system at ORNL, running 64-bit Linux version 2.4.21 and operating as a single system image. The next-generation Altix 3700 is the building block of the Columbia system, currently the world's fourth most powerful supercomputer [43], located at the NASA Ames Research Center.

5.1.4 Earth Simulator (SX-6+)

The vector processor of the Japanese Earth Simulator (JES) uses a dramatically different architectural approach than conventional cache-based systems. Vectorization exploits regularities in the computational structure of scientific applications to expedite uniform operations on independent datasets. The 500 MHz JES processor (an enhanced version of the NEC SX-6) contains an eight-way replicated vector pipe capable of issuing a MADD each cycle, for a peak performance of 8.0 Gflop/s. The processors contain 72 vector registers, each holding 256 64-bit words. For nonvectorizable instructions, the JES has a 500 MHz scalar processor with a 64 KB instruction cache, a 64 KB data cache, and 128 general-purpose registers. The four-way superscalar unit has a peak of 1.0 Gflop/s (an eighth of the vector performance) and supports branch prediction, data prefetching, and out-of-order execution.

Like traditional vector architectures, the JES vector unit is cacheless; memory latencies are masked by overlapping pipelined vector operations with memory fetches. The main memory chip uses a specially developed high-speed DRAM called FPLRAM (full pipelined RAM) operating at 24 ns bank cycle time. Each SMP contains eight processors that share the node's memory. JES is one of the world's most powerful supercomputers [43] and consists of 640 SMP nodes connected through a custom single-stage crossbar. This high-bandwidth interconnect topology provides impressive communication characteristics, as all nodes are a single hop from one another. The 5,120-processor JES runs Super-UX, a 64-bit Unix operating system based on System V-R3 with BSD4.2 communication features. As remote JES access is not available, the reported experiments were performed during the authors' visit to the Earth Simulator Center in Yokohama, Japan, in December 2003.

5.1.5 Phoenix (X1)

The Cray X1 combines traditional vector strengths with the generality and scalability features of modern superscalar cache-based parallel systems. The computational core, called the single-streaming processor (SSP), contains two 32-stage vector pipes running at 800 MHz. Each SSP contains 32 vector registers holding 64 double-precision words and operates at 3.2 Gflop/s peak for 64-bit data. The SSP also contains a two-way out-of-order superscalar processor running at 400 MHz with two 16 KB instruction and data caches. Like the SX-6, the scalar unit operates at 1/8th the vector performance, making a high vector operation ratio critical for effectively utilizing the underlying hardware.

The multistreaming processor (MSP) combines four SSPs into one logical computational unit. The four SSPs share a two-way set associative 2 MB data Ecache, a unique feature that allows extremely high bandwidth (25 to 51 GB/s) for computations with temporal data locality. MSP parallelism is achieved by distributing loop iterations across each of the four SSPs. An X1 node consists of four MSPs sharing a flat memory, and large system configurations are networked through a modified two-dimensional (2D) torus interconnect. The torus topology allows scalability to large processor counts with relatively few links compared with fat-tree or crossbar interconnects; however, this topological configuration suffers from limited bisection bandwidth. The X1 has hardware-supported globally addressable memory which allows for efficient implementations of one-sided communication libraries (SHMEM, MPI-2) and implicit parallel programming languages (UPC, CAF). All reported X1 results were obtained on Phoenix, the 256-MSP system running UNICOS/mp 2.4 and operated by ORNL.

5.2 Architecture evaluation using full applications

This section presents synopses of six full-scale scientific applications that have been recently used in evaluating these ultra-scale HPC systems.

5.2.1 Materials science

PARATEC (Parallel total energy code [35]) is a materials science code that performs ab-initio quantum-mechanical total energy calculations using pseudopotentials and a plane wave basis set. Forces can be easily calculated and used to relax the atoms into their equilibrium positions. PARATEC uses an all-band conjugate gradient (CG) approach to solve the Kohn–Sham equations of density functional theory (DFT) and obtain the ground-state electron wavefunctions. DFT is the most commonly used technique in materials science to calculate the structural and electronic properties of materials, with a quantum mechanical treatment of the electrons. Codes based on DFT are widely used to study various material properties for nanostructures, complex surfaces, and doped semiconductors and are one of the largest consumers of supercomputing cycles.

In solving the Kohn–Sham equations using a plane wave basis, part of the calculation is carried out in real space and the remainder in Fourier space using specialized parallel three-dimensional (3D) FFTs to transform the wavefunctions. The code spends most of its time in vendor-supplied BLAS3 (∼30%) and one-dimensional (1D) FFTs (∼30%) on which the 3D FFTs libraries are built. Because these routines allow high cache reuse and efficient vector utilization, PARATEC generally obtains a high percentage of peak performance across a spectrum of computing platforms. The code exploits fine-grained parallelism by dividing the plane wave (Fourier) components for each electron among the different processors [15]. PARATEC is written in F90 and MPI and is designed primarily for massively parallel computing platforms, but it can also run on serial machines. The main limitation to scaling PARATEC to large processor counts is the distributed grid transformation during the parallel 3D FFTs that requires global interprocessor communication when mapping the electron wavefunctions from Fourier space (where it is represented by a sphere) to a 3D grid in real space. Thus, architectures with a poor balance between their bisection bandwidth and computational rate will suffer performance degradation at higher concurrencies due to global communication requirements.

Experimental data were gathered for a 432 Silicon-atom bulk system and a standard LDA run of PARATEC with a 25 Ry cutoff using norm-conserving pseudopotentials [31, 32]. Results showed that PARATEC achieves impressive performance on the JES, sustaining 4.7 Gflop/s per processor (58% of peak) on 128 processors. This compares with per-processor performance of 0.7 Gflop/s (49%), 1.5 Gflop/s (29%), 3.2 Gflop/s (54%), and 1.9 Gflop/s (15%) on Seaborg, Cheetah, Ram, and Phoenix, respectively. (Ram results are for 64 processors.) The JES outperformed all other platforms primarily due to a superior architectural balance of bisection bandwidth relative to computation rate—a critical component for achieving high scalability during the global grid transformation of the wavefunctions.

5.2.2 Astrophysics

One of the most challenging problems in astrophysics is the numerical solution of Einstein's equations following from the theory of general relativity (GR): a set of coupled nonlinear hyperbolic and elliptic equations containing thousands of terms when fully expanded. The Cactus Computational ToolKit [1, 7] is designed to evolve these equations stably in three dimensions on supercomputers to simulate astrophysical phenomena with high gravitational fluxes, such as the collision of two black holes and the gravitational waves radiating from that event. While Cactus is a modular framework supporting a wide variety of multiphysics applications [14], our study focused exclusively on the GR solver, which implements the ADM-BSSN method [1] for stable evolutions of black holes.

The Cactus GR components solve Einstein's equations as an initial value problem that evolves PDEs on a regular grid using finite differences. The core of the GR solver uses the ADM formalism, which decomposes the solution into 3D spatial hypersurfaces that represent different slices of space along the time dimension. In this representation, the equations are written as 4 constraint equations and 12 evolution equations. Additional stability is provided by the BSSN modifications to the standard ADM method [1]. The evolution equations can be solved using a number of different numerical approaches, including staggered leapfrog, McCormack, Lax–Wendroff, and iterative Crank–Nicholson schemes. A *lapse* function describes the time slicing between hypersurfaces for each step in the evolution, while a *shift* vector is used to move the coordinate system at each step to avoid being drawn into a singularity. The four constraint equations are used to select different lapse functions and the related shift vectors.

For parallel computation, the global 3D grid is block domain decomposed so that each processor has its own section. The standard MPI driver for Cactus solves the PDEs on a local region and then updates the values at the ghost zones by exchanging data on the faces of its topological neighbors. On superscalar systems, the computations are blocked to improve cache locality. Blocking is accomplished through the use of temporary *slice buffers*, which improve cache reuse while modestly increasing the computational overhead. These blocking optimizations were disabled on vector architectures since they reduced the vector length and inhibited performance.

The production version of the Cactus ADM-BSSN application was run using a grid of size $250\times64\times64$ [32]. The problem was scaled with the number of processors to keep the computational load uniform. Cactus problems are typically scaled in this manner because their science requires the highest possible resolutions. Results showed that the JES reached an impressive 2.7 Tflop/s (34% of peak) for the largest problem size using 1,024 processors.

This represents the highest per-processor performance (by far) achieved by the production version of Cactus ADM-BSSN on any system to date. Comparing results at 64 processors, Seaborg and Ram are 33x and 6.4x slower, achieving only 6% and 7% of peak, respectively. The relatively low scalar performance on the microprocessor-based systems is partially due to register spilling, which is caused by the large number of variables in the main loop of the BSSN calculation. Phoenix is about 3.8 times slower than the JES, sustaining 0.7 Gflop/s per processor (6% of peak). The architectural imbalance between vector and scalar performance was particularly acute on the X1, which suffered a much greater impact from unvectorized code in Cactus than the JES.

5.2.3 Cosmology

The Microwave Anisotropy Dataset Computational Analysis Package (MADCAP) [5] implements the current optimal general algorithm for extracting the most useful cosmological information from total-power observations of the cosmic microwave background (CMB). The CMB is a snapshot of the universe when it first became electrically neutral some 400,000 years after the Big Bang. The tiny anisotropies in the temperature and polarization of the CMB radiation are sensitive probes of early universe cosmology, and measuring their detailed statistical properties has been a high priority in the field for more than 30 years. MADCAP was designed to calculate the maximum likelihood two-point angular correlation function (or power spectrum) of the CMB given a noisy, pixelized sky map and its associated pixel-pixel noise correlation matrix.

MADCAP recasts the extraction of a CMB power spectrum from a sky map into a problem in dense linear algebra and exploits the ScaLAPACK library for its efficient parallel solution. Operations include explicit matrix inversion as well as matrix-vector and matrix-matrix multiplication. Since most of the MADCAP routines utilize ScaLAPACK, code migration is relatively simple. Performance for both scalar and vector systems depends heavily on an efficient implementation of the vendor-supplied linear algebra libraries. However, explicit vectorization was required for the hand-coded calculation of the value of Legendre polynomials (up to some preset degree) for the angular separation between all pixel pairs.

To maximize its ability to handle large datasets, MADCAP generally works with many more matrices than can fit in main memory. The out-of-core disk-based storage for the other matrices in the calculation is the only practical choice, but it comes at the cost of heavy I/O. All matrices are block-cyclic distributed across the processors; when a matrix is stored to disk due to memory limitations, MADCAP generates one file per processor over which the matrix is distributed. This results in matrix I/O operations that are independent; however, the simultaneity of multiprocessor disk accesses can create contention within the I/O infrastructure, thus degrading overall performance.

Experimental data reported here were collected by MAXIMA (millimeter anisotropy experiment imaging array) [19], a balloon-borne millimeter-wave telescope designed to measure the angular power spectrum of fluctuations in the CMB over a wide range of angular scales. Simulation results using 64 processors on a dataset of 14,996 pixels and 1,200 multipoles showed that Phoenix achieved the best runtime at 2.0 Gflop/s per processor—1.1x, 2.8x, and 4.4x faster than the JES, Cheetah, and Seaborg [8, 31]. However, Seaborg sustained the highest percentage of peak (36%), followed by the JES (23%), Phoenix (16%), and Cheetah (15%). Note that all evaluated architectural platforms sustained a relatively low fraction of peak, considering MADCAP's extensive use of computationally intensive dense linear algebra functions. In-depth analysis using a lightweight version of MADCAP highlights the complex interplay between the architectural paradigms, interconnect technology, and vendor-supplied numerical libraries, while isolating I/O filesystems as the key bottleneck across all platforms [4].

5.2.4 Fluid dynamics

In the area of computational fluid dynamics (CFD), we selected the NASA Navier–Stokes production application called OVERFLOW-D [45]. The code uses the overset grid methodology to perform high-fidelity viscous simulations around realistic aerospace configurations. It is popular within the aerodynamics community due to its ability to handle complex designs with multiple geometric components. OVERFLOW-D, an extension of OVERFLOW [6], is explicitly designed to simplify the modeling of problems when components are in relative motion. The main computational logic at the top level of the sequential code consists of a time-loop and a nested grid-loop. Within the grid-loop, solutions to the flow equations are obtained on the individual grids with imposed boundary conditions. Overlapping boundary points or intergrid data are updated from the previous time step using a Chimera interpolation procedure. Upon completion of the grid-loop, the solution is automatically advanced to the next time-step by the time-loop. The code uses finite differences in space, with a variety of implicit/explicit time-stepping.

The MPI version of OVERFLOW-D (in F90) takes advantage of the overset grid system, which offers a natural coarse-grain parallelism. A grouping algorithm clusters individual grids into sets, each of which is then assigned to an MPI process. The grid-loop in the parallel implementation is subdivided into two procedures: a group-loop over sets and a grid-loop over the grids within each set. Since each MPI process is assigned to only one set, the group-loop is executed in parallel, with each set performing its own sequential grid-loop. The intergrid boundary updates within each set are performed as in the serial case. Interset boundary exchanges are achieved via MPI asynchronous communication calls. The same basic program structure is used on all target architectures except for a few minor changes in some subroutines to meet specific compiler requirements. Details about performance enhancement strategies for OVERFLOW-D can be found in [10].

Our experiments involve a simulation of vortex dynamics in the complex wake flow region around hovering rotors. The grid system consisted of 41 blocks and almost 8 million grid points [31, 33]. Results on an SX-6 platform (but not the JES) easily outperformed the superscalar machines as well as Phoenix; in fact, the runtime for eight SX-6 processors was less than 60% of the 32-processor Cheetah runtime. However, due to small vector lengths and limited vector operation ratio, the code achieved only about 1.1 Gflop/s per processor on the SX-6. Nevertheless, the SX-6 consistently achieved a high percentage of peak (14%), followed by Seaborg (8%) and Cheetah (7%), while Phoenix showed the lowest sustained performance (3.5%). Scalability on Seaborg exceeded all others, with computational efficiency decreasing for a larger number of MPI tasks primarily due to load imbalance. A hybrid MPI+OpenMP implementation [9] showed similar performance as a pure MPI approach on all systems except for Seaborg, where the multilevel results were significantly better. Note that adding more OpenMP threads beyond an optimal number, depending on the number of MPI processes, does not improve performance. The primary advantage of the hybrid paradigm for overset grid problems is that it extends their applicability to large SMP clusters. A detailed performance characterization of the Columbia supercluster using OVERFLOW-D and other NASA applications is reported in [3].

5.2.5 Magnetic fusion

The gyrokinetic toroidal code (GTC) is a 3D particle-in-cell (PIC) application developed at the Princeton Plasma Physics Laboratory to study turbulent transport in magnetic confinement fusion [23, 24]. Turbulence is believed to be the main mechanism by which energy and particles are transported away from the hot plasma core in fusion experiments with magnetic toroidal devices. GTC solves the nonlinear gyrophase-averaged Vlasov–Poisson equations [22] for a system of charged particles in a self-consistent, self-generated electrostatic field. The geometry is that of a torus with an externally imposed equilibrium magnetic field, characteristic of toroidal fusion devices. By using the PIC method, the nonlinear PDE describing the motion of the particles in the system becomes a simple set of ordinary differential equations (ODEs) that can be easily solved in the Lagrangian coordinates. The self-consistent electrostatic field driving this motion could conceptually be calculated directly from the distance between each pair of particles using an $O(N^2)$ calculation, but the PIC approach reduces it to $O(N)$ by using a grid where each particle deposits its charge to a limited number of neighboring points according to its range of influence. The electrostatic potential is then solved everywhere on the grid using the Poisson equation, and forces are gathered back to each particle. The most computationally intensive parts of GTC are the charge deposition and gather-push steps that involve large loops over the particles, which can reach several million per domain partition.

Although the PIC approach drastically reduces the computational requirements, the grid-based charge deposition phase is a source of performance degradation for both superscalar and vector architectures. Randomly localized particles deposit their charge on the grid, thereby causing poor cache reuse on superscalar machines. The effect of this deposition step is more pronounced on vector systems since two or more particles may contribute to the charge at the same grid point, creating a potential memory-dependency conflict. Several methods have been developed to address this issue. GTC uses the work-vector algorithm [29], where a temporary copy of the grid array is given an extra dimension corresponding to the vector length. Each vector operation acts on a given data set in the register, then writes to a different memory address, avoiding memory dependencies entirely. After the main loop, the results accumulated in the work-vector array are gathered to the final grid array. The only drawback is the increased memory footprint, which can be two to eight times higher than the nonvectorized code version.

Experiments were performed using a high-resolution domain of 100 particles per cell (2 million grid points, 200 million particles), allowing for significant improvements in the overall statistics of the simulation [32, 33]. The JES achieved 1.6 Gflop/s per processor or 20% of peak on 64 processors—the highest GTC performance on any tested architecture. Phoenix showed similar performance in absolute terms (1.4 Gflop/s per processor) but a lower fraction of peak at only 11%. Comparing performance with the superscalar architectures, JES is about 12x, 5.4x, and 5x faster than Seaborg (9% of peak), Cheetah (5%), and Ram (5%), respectively. The vector systems therefore have the potential for significantly higher resolution calculations that would otherwise be prohibitively expensive in terms of time to solution on conventional microprocessors.

5.2.6 Geophysics

The goal of the GeoFEM framework [16] is to model and simulate solid Earth phenomena, such as the long-term prediction of the plate near the Japanese islands and core-mantle dynamics over the entire globe. GeoFEM is being specifically developed to achieve high performance on the JES. The finite element method (FEM) used here is an approximation based on contiguous interactions, which can be reduced to solving large systems of linear equations defined over the unstructured meshes that model the underlying physical objects. Since direct methods are generally disadvantageous for solving these types of systems due to the large volume of computation involved, an iterative method such as CG is employed to address the overall degrees of freedom (DOF). To obtain a stable solution using this numerical approach requires intelligent domain partitioning as well as preconditioning for the iterative solver. The localized ILU(0) used in GeoFEM is a pseudopreconditioner, requiring only local operations within each given domain partition, thus making it well suited for parallel systems since no interprocessor communication is required.

To achieve both high parallel efficiency and vector performance for the GeoFEM iterative solvers, an intelligent reordering scheme must be utilized to mitigate the irregular nature of the underlying unstructured mesh. A reverse Cuthill–Mckee (RCM) ordering is utilized to improve data locality and reduce global communication. RCM is a level set reordering method used to reduce the profile of the underlying matrix, which improves the convergence of the ILU preconditioner but may result in a load-imbalanced computation. To create a more balanced workload, the cyclic multicolor (CM) technique, used to graph color adjacent nodes, is then combined with RCM to both balance the workload and provide fast convergence for the Krylov iterative solvers. For complicated geometries, traditional multicoloring is usually used instead of CM-RCM [27].

However, the well-known compressed row storage (CRS) representation of the underlying matrix results in short vector lengths, thus inhibiting vector performance. To address this deficiency, the descending-order jagged diagonal storage (DJDS) scheme is used to permute the matrix rows so that reasonably long innermost loop lengths are achieved. To effectively balance the computation load of each processor within an SMP using this approach, the DJDS array is reordered again in a cyclic fashion (PDJDS). On superscalar systems, the parallel descending-order compressed row storage (PDCRS) ordering is used. This approach is almost identical to PDJDS except that the matrices are stored in CRS format after reordering the rows by decreasing numbers of nonzeros. This strategy results in shorter vector lengths and is generally better suited for commodity superscalar systems with limited memory bandwidth designs.

Extensive experiments were conducted for a three-dimensional linear elastic problem with more than 2.2×10^9 DOF and solved by a 3×3 block incomplete Cholesky (IC) preconditioned CG with additive Schwarz domain decomposition [28]. Results showed that the PDJDS/CM-RCM reordering achieved 2.7 GFlop/s per processor (33.7% of peak) on the JES using 1,408 processors, while only 0.5% of peak was attained using the naive CRS approach without reordering. On Seaborg, PDCRS/CM-RCM ordering attained the highest performance; however, results were significantly poorer than those of the JES: only 0.11 GFlop/s per processor (7.2% of peak) were sustained on 1,024 processors.

5.3 Algorithmic and architectural benchmarks

The purpose of any HPC system is to run full-scale applications, and performance on such applications is the final arbiter of the utility of the system. However, the complexity of using scientific applications to identify the causes of performance bottlenecks on modern architectures has raised the importance of developing better benchmarking methods to improve program characterization and performance prediction while identifying which hardware and application features work well or poorly together. In this section, we describe both algorithmic and architectural benchmarks that strive to satisfy these objectives.

5.3.1 Scalable compact application benchmarks

Scalable compact application (SCA) benchmarks are derivatives that capture major characteristics of the full applications but avoid many of their idiosyncrasies by leaving out unnecessary details. They work with synthetic datasets that can be generated with prescribed statistical properties, so that the application signature does not change qualitatively with problem size. Moreover, any fixed-size application will ultimately lose its value as systems become more powerful. Input data for SCA benchmarks can be generated on the fly and do not have to be maintained and distributed. Considering the capability of current and future HPC systems, and taking into account that useful applications typically consume (and produce) data commensurate with the amount of computation that they do, being able to generate synthetic data greatly saves on the volume that has to be maintained, stored, and distributed. Effective SCAs have a built-in verification test that has been validated on multiple machines and configurations, so that the user knows instantly whether a run was successful. They are portable and designed to be built and run easily on any modern platform with standard tools (e.g., MPI or OpenMP), which reduces the cost and effort on the part of vendors to produce performance numbers. SCAs also represent a single path through an application, eliminating any special-purpose code not executed. This makes them easier to understand and characterize, unlike full applications, whose performance signature often depends vitally on input parameters, rendering their actual name almost meaningless when interpreting measurement results. Finally, SCAs are nonproprietary and open source, so that thorough analysis by research groups can be conducted. This makes them valuable for users outside the organization that provided the initial full-scale application from which the SCA was derived.

Microbenchmarks are codes whose performance is dominated by a single architectural feature, such as network bandwidth, memory latency, I/O speed, and clock rate. They are very useful to determine a principal machine characteristic, but application performance is typically influenced by multiple nonlinearly interacting factors, making it difficult to distinguish between the different effects. For example, it is not useful to transfer data at a high rate if the data do not embody the requested information, which takes computational effort to generate or acquire. SCAs typically feature just a few performance influence factors, making them more realistic than microbenchmarks but much easier to implement and analyze than full-fledged applications.

NAS parallel benchmarks

The NAS parallel benchmarks (NPB) [2, 30] were designed to provide a level playing field for HPC machines of various architectural specifications. This is reflected in the fact that they were first released as paper-and-pencil specifications. As standards for programming parallel computers matured, portable source code implementations were provided, first using MPI and later in Java, OpenMP, and HPF. The NPB application benchmarks lower-upper (LU) symmetric Gauss–Seidel, scalar pentadiagonal (SP), and block tridiagonal (BT), and to some extent FFT and multigrid, are SCAs that have been used extensively by vendors, compiler writers, procurement teams, and tool developers. They were especially useful at a time when unrealistic claims were being made about the computational power of emerging parallel computers and new microprocessor designs with ever-increasing clock speeds.

As parallel computing entered the mainstream, and more legacy applications were converted to run on parallel machines, new performance bottlenecks showed up that were not properly tested by the NPB. Most important, the NPB did not test the I/O subsystem, the effects of irregular and continually changing memory accesses, and the capability to solve hierarchical problems with multiple levels of exploitable parallelism. Recent additions to the NPB have addressed all these issues and also have led to larger problem classes that keep track of the growing memory size and computing power of high-end machines.

Parallel high-performance I/O is now being tested by a variation of BT, which, like SP and LU, generates a time-dependent series of solutions to a CFD problem. Real applications usually checkpoint the solution every few time-steps to recover from possible system errors or to save data for offline visualization; thus, BT was modified to write its solution to files at relatively high frequency. The reference implementation provided by NASA ARC uses either native Fortran I/O, or parallel I/O based on MPI, to write the highly fragmented data from multiple processors to the single checkpoint file.

A completely new benchmark, called unstructured adaptive (UA) mesh refinement [12], was developed to measure the effects of temporally and spatially irregular memory accesses. This code solves a stylized convective-diffusive heat transfer problem with a heat source whose location changes in time. The original NPB SCAs feature simple memory access patterns using small, fixed numbers of strides. In contrast, UA uses an unstructured Cartesian mesh whose topology changes periodically to track the moving source, inserting and removing refined mesh cells where needed, and therefore causing irregular and unpredictable memory access patterns. It utilizes a nonconforming spectral FEM of moderately high order (five), resulting in a large volume of computational work per element relative to the amount of data shared between elements. Consequently, an efficient parallel implementation of UA requires good balancing of the computational load but does not depend too heavily on the minimization of interprocessor communication. Contrasting results in the performance of OpenMP versions of MG and UA, the first featuring a small number of fixed—mostly unit—memory access strides and the latter exhibiting many irregularly strided accesses, show that UA experiences significantly larger increases in parallel efficiency as the number of threads grows [13].

The NPB multizone (NPB-MZ) version [44] was created to represent overset grid applications (e.g., OVERFLOW) with multilevel parallelism. It consists of three families of problems, each corresponding to one of the original NPB problems LU, SP, and BT. NPB-MZ solves an SCA on a collection of loosely coupled discretization meshes, called zones. The zones are arranged as a 2D, partially overlapping, tiling of 3D space. The solution within each zone is updated separately from all the others, thus offering easily exploited coarse-grain parallelism. However, at the end of each time step, neighboring zones exchange boundary values in the overlap regions. Fine-grain parallelism can be exploited at the loop nest level within individual zones.

The three MZ families are distinguished primarily by the way they tile space. LU-MZ uses a 4×4 grid of equal-size zones for all problem sizes, thus limiting the amount of coarse-grain parallelism to 16. SP-MZ also use a two-dimensional grid of equal-size zones, but the number of zones increases with problem size, thus providing increasing amounts of coarse-grain parallelism. BT-MZ has the same number and layout of zones as SP-MZ, but they differ in size, with a fixed ratio of largest over smallest zone size of 20 (for all problem sizes). Coarse-level parallelism is now not so easily exploited while simultaneously balancing the load. Current parallel implementations of NPB-MZ use OpenMP for fine-grain parallelism and message passing (MPI or MLP [42]) for the coarse grain [21]. Experiments on an IBM Power3, SGI Origin 3800, and HP/Compaq SC45 show that the best performance on a fixed number of processors for NPB-MZ is always obtained by minimizing the number of threads per process. That is, if the load can be balanced with a single thread per process, it invariably yields the best performance. For SP-MZ this is usually not a problem but is not always feasible for BT-MZ (with the same number of zones), due to the disparity in the sizes of the zones. A three-level hybrid implementation of NPB-MZ is currently being developed and will be tested on the Columbia system at NASA ARC to characterize and understand OVERFLOW performance on such platforms.

5.3.2 Architectural probes

Synthetic benchmarks like the NPB [2, 30] and those of the Standard Performance Evaluation Corporation (SPEC) [39] emphasize the proper representation of real applications but are usually too large to run on simulated architectures and too complex to identify specific architectural bottlenecks. At the other extreme, microbenchmarks such as Stream [25], Livermore loops [26], Hint [18], and Linpack [11] are easy to optimize but measure the performance of only a specific architectural feature. They present a narrow view of a broad, multidimensional parameter space of machine characteristics.

We therefore differentiate an architectural probe from a microbenchmark on the basis that the latter typically returns a single-valued result to rank processor performance consecutively—a few reference points in a multidimensional space. A probe, by contrast, is used to explore a continuous, multidimensional parameter space. The probe's parameterization enables the researcher to uncover peaks and valleys in a continuum of performance characteristics and explore the ambiguities of computer architectural comparisons that cannot be captured by a single-valued ranking.

Sqmat

Sqmat [17] is an architectural probe that complements the capabilities of traditional kernel benchmarks as tools that enhance the understanding of performance behavior of scientific codes. It maintains the simplicity of a microbenchmark while offering four distinct parameters with which to capture different types of application workloads: working-set size, computational intensity, indirection, and irregularity.

The Sqmat algorithm squares a set of matrices a given number of times. First, the values of one matrix are loaded from memory into registers; if the matrix size exceeds the register capacity, register spilling will occur—thus controlling the working set size. Accessing the matrices from memory can be done either directly or indirectly. In the direct case, matrices are stored contiguously in memory using row-major ordering. For the indirect case, a parameter controls the degree of irregularity: a fixed number of entries are stored contiguously, followed by a jump to a random position in memory. This parameter therefore captures both indirection and the degree of data access irregularity. Finally, each matrix is squared a certain number of times, thereby controlling the computational intensity—the ratio between memory transfers and arithmetic operations.

A number of important analyses can be conducted by varying these simple parameters. For example, a component of the architectural balance can be examined by measuring how much computation is required to hide the highest degree of irregularity (accessing each matrix entry at a random position) such that the achieved performance is only 50% lower than unit-stride data accesses. Results on the Itanium2 and Power4 microprocessors reveal significantly different architectural designs. The Itanium2 can hide the irregularity with a computational intensity of 9.3, showing that it is somewhat tolerant of random accesses. The Power4, however, requires a computational intensity of 74.7 for the same experiments, demonstrating that it is poorly suited for sparse matrix computations. These types of analyses help isolate architecture performance bottlenecks, helping both applications programmers and system designers.

Apex-MAP

The application performance characterization project (Apex) [40] is another effort to develop tunable synthetic benchmarks. The preliminary focus of this effort is to define performance characterizations of application data access patterns and to create a corresponding memory access probe benchmark, called Apex-MAP. Apex-MAP differs from Sqmat in that its execution profile can be tuned by a set of parameters to match the signature of a chosen scientific application, allowing it to be used as a proxy for the performance behavior of the underlying codes.

Apex-MAP assumes that the data access pattern for most codes can be described as several concurrent streams of addresses, which in turn can be characterized by a single set of performance parameters, including regularity, dataset size, spatial locality, and temporal locality. Regularity refers to the data access patterns, where the two extreme cases are random and strided accesses. The dataset size is the total volume of memory accessed, an increasingly important factor as the complexity of memory hierarchies continues to grow in modern system architectures. The spatial locality parameter controls the number of contiguous memory locations accessed in succession. Finally, temporal locality refers to the average reuse of data items and is defined independently of hardware concepts such as cache size through the use of a cumulative temporal distribution function.

Preliminary testing examined the validity and accuracy of the Apex-MAP approach on leading microarchitectures, including the Power3, Power4, and X1, using five scientific kernels (radix sorting, FFT, matrix multiplication, n-body simulation, and conjugate gradient). Results showed that application performance can be captured to within 25% across the suite of codes for a variety of memory sizes, using a few simple parameters with up to two simulated memory streams. This work has recently been extended to include interprocessor communication to capture the behavior of parallel systems [41].

5.4 Performance modeling

The goal of performance modeling is to gain understanding of a computer system's performance on various applications, by means of measurement and analysis, and then to encapsulate these characteristics in a compact formula. The resulting model can be used to obtain better insight into the performance phenomena involved and to project performance to other system-application combinations. This section focuses on the modeling of large-scale scientific computations within the Performance Evaluation Research Center (PERC) [36], a research collaboration funded through the U.S. DoE Scientific Discovery through Advanced Computation (SciDAC) program [37]. A number of important performance modeling activities are also being conducted by other groups, particularly the efforts at Los Alamos National Laboratory [20].

Performance models can be used to improve architecture design, inform procurement activities, and guide application tuning. Unfortunately, the process of producing performance models has historically been rather expensive, requiring large amounts of computer time and highly expert human effort. This has severely limited the number of HPC applications that can be modeled and studied. It has been observed that due to the difficulty of developing performance models for new applications as well as the increasing complexity of new systems, our supercomputers have become better at predicting and explaining natural phenomena (such as weather) than at predicting and explaining the performance of themselves.

5.4.1 Applications of performance modeling

The most common application of a performance model is to enable a scientist to estimate the runtime of a job when the input sets or architectural parameters are varied. Additionally, one can estimate the largest system size that can be used to run a given problem before the parallel efficiency drops to unacceptable levels. Performance models are also employed by computer vendors in the design of future systems. Typically, engineers construct a performance model for one or two key applications and then compare future technology options based on the computed projections. Once better performance modeling techniques are developed, it may be possible to target many more applications and technology options in the design process. As an example of such what-if investigations, application parameters can be used to predict how performance rates would change with a larger or more highly associative cache. In a similar way, the performance impact of various network designs can also be explored.

System and application tuning can greatly benefit from the use of performance models. For example, if a memory model is combined with application parameters, one can predict how cache hit rates would change if a different cache-blocking factor were used in the application. Once the optimal cache blocking has been identified, the code can be permanently modified. Simple performance models can even be directly incorporated into an application code, permitting on-the-fly selection of different program options. Finally, the simplification of system procurement procedures may be the most compelling application of performance modeling. Once a reasonably easy-to-use performance modeling facility is available, it may be possible to greatly reduce, if not eliminate, the benchmark tests that are specified in a procurement, replacing them with a measurement of certain performance model parameters for the target systems and applications. These parameters can then be used by the computer center staff to project performance rates for numerous system options, thus saving considerable resources during the system acquisition process.

5.4.2 PERC methodology

The PERC framework [36] is based upon *application signatures*, *machine profiles*, and *convolutions*. An application signature is a detailed but compact representation of the fundamental operations performed by an application, independent of the target system. A machine profile is a representation of the capability of a system to carry out fundamental operations, independent of the particular application. A convolution is a means to rapidly combine application signatures with machine profiles to predict performance. Overall, the PERC methodology consists of (i) accurately summarizing the requirements of applications (in ways that are not too expensive in terms of time and space requirements); (ii) automatically obtaining the application signature; (iii) generalizing the signatures to represent how the application would stress arbitrary (including future) machines; and (iv) extrapolating the signatures to larger problem sizes than what can be actually run at present.

PERC has developed a general approach to analyzing applications to obtain their signature, which has resulted in considerable space reduction and a measure of machine independence. First, a given application is statically analyzed and then instrumented and traced on an existing set of architectural platforms. Next, the operations performed by the application are summarized on the fly during execution. These operations are then indexed to the source code structures that generated them. Finally, a merge is performed on the summaries of each machine [38]. From these data, one can obtain information on memory access patterns (viz., the stride and range of memory accesses generated by individual memory operations) and communications patterns (viz., size and type of communication performed).

The second component of this performance modeling approach is to represent the resource capabilities of current and proposed machines, with emphasis on memory and communications capabilities, in an application-independent form suitable for parameterized modeling. In particular, machine profiles are gathered, which are high-level representations of the rates at which a system can carry out basic operations such as memory loads and stores and message passing. This includes the capabilities of memory units at each level of the memory hierarchy and the ability of machines to overlap memory accesses with other kinds of operations (e.g., floating-point or communication). The machine profiles are then extended to account for reduction in capability due to sharing (e.g., to express how much the memory subsystem's or communication fabric's capability is diminished by sharing these with competing processors). Finally, the behavior of a larger system can be extrapolated from validated machine profiles of similar but smaller platforms.

To enable time tractable statistical simulation, the PERC framework utilizes the convolution method, allowing quick mappings of application signatures to machine profiles. This approach closely approximates cycle-accurate predictions in a much shorter time frame by accounting for fewer details. The convolution allows relatively rapid development of performance models (full application models currently take one or two months) and results in performance predictions which can be quickly evaluated once the models are constructed (few minutes per prediction).

5.4.3 Performance sensitivity studies

Reporting the accuracy of performance models in terms of model-predicted time versus observed time is mostly just a validation step for obtaining confidence in the model. A more interesting and useful exercise is to explain and quantify performance differences while allowing architectural parameter studies. Given a model that can predict application performance based on properties of the code and machine, precise modeling experiments can be performed. For example, an in-depth study was performed [38] using the parallel ocean program (POP) [34], a well-known climate application, on the Blue Horizon system. POP has been ported to a wide variety of computers for eddy-resolving simulations of the world's oceans and for climate simulations as the ocean component of coupled climate models.

First, the effect of reducing the bandwidth from 350 MB/s to 269 MB/s was examined (equivalent to switching the network from Colony to a single rail of a Quadrics switch) but resulted in no observable performance difference. The next experiment reduced the latency from 20 ms (Colony) to 5 ms (Quadrics) and demonstrated a performance improvement of 1.3x—evidence that the barotropic calculations in POP (for the tested problem size) are latency sensitive. Finally, the system was modeled using the default Colony switch, but with an improved processor design based on the Alpha ES45 (1 GHz versus 375 MHz) and a more powerful memory subsystem capable of loading stride-1 data from L2 cache at twice the rate of the Power3. Results showed a performance improvement of 1.4x, due mainly to the faster memory subsystem. The principal observation from the above exercise is that the PERC model can quantify the performance impact of each machine hardware component. Similar experiments were conducted for varying sizes of POP problems, with results showing that POP simulations at larger processor counts become more network latency sensitive while remaining mostly bandwidth insensitive.

These types of experiments demonstrate that performance models enable what-if analyses of the implications of improving the target machine in various dimensions. Such studies are obviously useful to system designers, helping them optimize system architectures for the highest sustained performance on a target set of applications. These methods are also potentially useful in helping computing centers select the best system in an acquisition. Additionally, this approach can be used by application scientists to improve the performance of their codes by better understanding which tuning measures yield the most improvement in sustained performance.

With further improvements in this methodology, we can envision a future in which these techniques are embedded in application codes, or even in systems software, thus enabling self-tuning applications for user codes. For example, we can conceive of an application that performs the first of many iterations using numerous cache-blocking parameters, a separate combination on each processor, and then uses a simple performance model to select the most favorable value. This combination would then be used for all remaining iterations, thus enabling automatic and portable system optimization.

5.5 Summary

To substantially increase the raw computational power of ultrascale HPC systems and then reap its benefits, significant progress is necessary in hardware architecture, software infrastructure, and application development. This chapter provided a broad performance assessment of leading HPC systems using a diverse set of scientific applications, including scalable compact synthetic benchmarks and architectural probes. Performance models and program characterizations of large-scale scientific computations were also discussed.

Acknowledgments

The authors sincerely thank their collaborators Julian Borrill, Andrew Canning, Johnathan Carter, M. Jahed Djomehri, Stephane Ethier, John Shalf, and David Skinner for their many contributions to the work presented here. They also gratefully acknowledge Kengo Nakajima for reviewing the material on geophysics. L. Oliker and D. Bailey are supported by OASCR in the U.S. DoE Office of Science under Contract DE-AC03-76SF00098.

Bibliography

[1] M. ALCUBIERRE, G. ALLEN, B. BRUEGMANN, E. SEIDEL, AND W.-M. SUEN, *Towards an understanding of the stability properties of the $3+1$ evolution equations in general relativity*, Physics Review D, 62 (2000), p. 124011.

[2] D. BAILEY ET AL., *The NAS Parallel Benchmarks*. Tech. Report RNR-94-007. NASA Ames Research Center, Moffett Field, CA, 1994. http://www.nas.nasa.gov/resources/software/npb.html.

[3] R. BISWAS, M. DJOMEHRI, R. HOOD, H. JIN, C. KIRIS, AND S. SAINI, *An application-based performance characterization of the Columbia supercluster*, in Proc. Supercomputing '05, IEEE, Los Alamitos, CA, 2005, p. 26.

[4] J. BORRILL, J. CARTER, L. OLIKER, D. SKINNER, AND R. BISWAS, *Integrated performance monitoring of a cosmology application on leading HEC platforms*, in Proc. 34th International Conference on Parallel Processing, Oslo, Norway, June 2005, pp. 119–128.

[5] J. BORRILL, *MADCAP: The microwave anisotropy dataset computational analysis package*, in Proc. 5th European SGI/Cray MPP Workshop, Bologna, Italy, Sept. 1999.

[6] P. BUNING, D. JESPERSEN, T. PULLIAM, W. CHAN, J. SLOTNICK, S. KRIST, AND K. RENZE, *OVERFLOW User's Manual Version 1.8g*. Tech. Report. NASA Langley Research Center, Hampton, VA, 1999.

[7] *Cactus Code Server.* http://www.cactuscode.org.

[8] J. CARTER, J. BORRILL, AND L. OLIKER, *Performance characteristics of a cosmology package on leading HPC architectures*, in Proc. 11th International Conference on High Performance Computing, Bangalore, India, Dec. 2004.

[9] M. DJOMEHRI AND R. BISWAS, *Performance analysis of a hybrid overset multi-block application on multiple architectures*, in Proc. 10th International Conference on High Performance Computing, Hyderabad, India, Dec. 2003, pp. 383–392.

[10] ———, *Performance enhancement strategies for multi-block overset grid CFD applications*, Parallel Computing, 29 (2003), pp. 1791–1810.

[11] J. DONGARRA, *Performance of various computers using standard linear equations software*. Tech. Report CS-89-85. University of Tennessee, Knoxville, 1989.

[12] H. FENG, R. V. DER WIJNGAART, R. BISWAS, AND C. MAVRIPLIS, *Unstructured Adaptive (UA) NAS Parallel Benchmark, Version 1.0*, Tech. Report NAS-04-006. NASA Ames Research Center, Moffett Field, CA, 2004.

[13] H. FENG, R. V. DER WIJNGAART, AND R. BISWAS, *Unstructured adaptive meshes: Bad for your memory?*, Applied Numerical Mathematics, 52 (2005), pp. 153–173.

[14] J. FONT, M. MILLER, W.-M. SUEN, AND M. TOBIAS, *Three dimensional numerical general relativistic hydrodynamics: Formulations, methods, and code tests*, Physics Review D, 61 (2000), p. 044011.

[15] G. GALLI AND A. PASQUARELLO, *First-principles molecular dynamics*, in Computer Simulation in Chemical Physics, Kluwer, Dordrecht, the Netherlands, 1993, pp. 261–313.

[16] *GeoFEM Project.* http://geofem.tokyo.rist.or.jp.

[17] G. GRIEM, L. OLIKER, J. SHALF, AND K. YELICK, *Identifying performance bottlenecks on modern microarchitectures using an adaptable probe*, in Proc. 3rd International Workshop on Performance Modeling, Evaluation, and Optimization of Parallel and Distributed Systems, Santa Fe, NM, April 2004.

[18] J. GUSTAFSON AND Q. SNELL, *HINT: A new way to measure computer performance*, in Proc. 28th Hawaii International Conference on System Sciences, Wailela, HI, Jan. 1995, pp. 392–401.

[19] S. HANANY ET AL., *MAXIMA-1: A measurement of the Cosmic Microwave Background anisotropy on angular scales of $10'$–$5°$*, The Astrophysical Journal Letters, 545 (2000), pp. L5–L10. http://cdsaas.u-strasbg.fr:2001/ApJ/journal/issues/ApJL/v545n1/005389/005389.web.pdf.

[20] A. HOISIE, O. LUBECK, AND H. WASSERMAN, *Performance and scalability analysis of teraflop-scale parallel architectures using multidimensional wavefront applications*, International Journal of High Performance Computing Applications, 14 (2000), pp. 330–346.

[21] H. JIN AND R. V. DER WIJNGAART, *Performance characteristics of the multi-zone NAS Parallel Benchmarks*, in Proc. 18th International Parallel and Distributed Processing Symposium, Santa Fe, NM, April 2004.

[22] W. LEE, *Gyrokinetic particle simulation model*, Journal of Computational Physics, 72 (1987), pp. 243–269.

[23] Z. LIN, S. ETHIER, T. HAHM, AND W. TANG, *Size scaling of turbulent transport in magnetically confined plasmas*, Physics Review Letters, 88 (2002), p. 195004.

[24] Z. LIN, T. HAHM, W. LEE, W. TANG, AND R. WHITE, *Turbulent transport reduction by zonal flows: Massively parallel simulations*, Science, 281 (1998), pp. 1835–1837.

[25] J. MCCALPIN, *Memory bandwidth and machine balance in high performance computers*, IEEE TCCA Newsletter, December 1995. http://tab.computer.org/tcca/NEWS/DEC95/DEC95.htm.

[26] F. MCMAHON, *The Livermore Fortran Kernels test of the numerical performance range*, in Performance Evaluation of Supercomputers, J. Martin, ed., North-Holland, Amsterdam, 1988, pp. 143–186.

[27] K. NAKAJIMA, *Parallel iterative solvers of GeoFEM with selective blocking preconditioning for nonlinear contact problems on the Earth Simulator*, in Proc. Supercomputing '03, IEEE, Los Alamitos, CA, 2003, p. 13.

[28] ———, *Three-level hybrid vs. flat MPI on the Earth Simulator: Parallel iterative solvers for finite-element method*, in Proc. 6th IMACS International Symposium on Iterative Methods in Scientific Computing, Denver, CO, March 2003.

[29] A. NISHIGUCHI, S. ORII, AND T. YABE, *Vector calculation of particle code*, Journal of Computational Physics, 61 (1985), pp. 519–522.

[30] *NAS Parallel Benchmarks.* http://www.nas.nasa.gov/Resources/Software/npb.html.

[31] L. OLIKER, R. BISWAS, J. BORRILL, A. CANNING, J. CARTER, M. DJOMEHRI, H. SHAN, AND D. SKINNER, *A performance evaluation of the Cray X1 for scientific applications*, in Proc. 6th International Meeting on High Performance Computing for Computational Science, Valencia, Spain, June 2004, pp. 51–65.

[32] L. OLIKER, A. CANNING, J. CARTER, J. SHALF, AND S. ETHIER, *Scientific computations on modern parallel vector systems*, in Proc. Supercomputing '04, IEEE, Los Alamitos, CA, 2004, p. 10.

[33] L. OLIKER, A. CANNING, J. CARTER, J. SHALF, D. SKINNER, S. ETHIER, R. BISWAS, M. DJOMEHRI, AND R. V. DER WIJNGAART, *Performance evaluation of the SX-6 vector architecture for scientific computations*, Concurrency and Computation: Practice and Experience, 17 (2005), pp. 69–93.

[34] *The Parallel Ocean Program.* http://climate.lanl.gov/Models/POP.

[35] *PARAllel Total Energy Code.* http://www.nersc.gov/projects/paratec.

[36] *The Performance Evaluation Research Center.* http://perc.nersc.gov.

[37] *Scientific Discovery through Advanced Computing.* http://www.science.doe.gov/scidac.

[38] A. SNAVELY, X. GAO, C. LEE, N. WOLTER, J. LABARTA, J. GIMENEZ, AND P. JONES, *Performance modeling of HPC applications*, in Proc. Parallel Computing Conference, Dresden, Germany, Sept. 2003.

[39] *Standard Performance Evaluation Corporation.* http://www.spec.org.

[40] E. STROHMAIER AND H. SHAN, *Architecture independent performance characterization and benchmarking for scientific applications*, in Proc. International Symposium on Modeling, Analysis, and Simulation of Computer and Telecommunication Systems, Volendam, Netherlands, Oct. 2004.

[41] ———, *Apex-MAP: A global data access benchmark to analyze HPC systems and parallel programming paradigms*, in Proc. Supercomputing '05, IEEE, Los Almitos, CA, 2005, p. 49.

[42] J. TAFT, *Achieving 60 GFLOP/s on the production CFD code OVERFLOW-MLP*, Parallel Computing, 27 (2001), pp. 521–536.

[43] *Top500 Supercomputer Sites.* http://www.top500.org.

[44] R. VAN DER WIJNGAART AND H. JIN, *NAS Parallel Benchmarks, Multi-Zone Versions.* Tech. Report NAS-03-010. NASA Ames Research Center, Moffett Field, CA, 2003.

[45] A. WISSINK AND R. MEAKIN, *Computational fluid dynamics with adaptive overset grids on parallel and distributed computer platforms*, in Proc. International Conference on Parallel and Distributed Processing Techniques and Applications, Las Vegas, NV, July 1998, pp. 1628–1634.

Part II

Parallel Algorithms and Enabling Technologies

Chapter 6

Partitioning and Load Balancing for Emerging Parallel Applications and Architectures

Karen D. Devine, Erik G. Boman, and George Karypis

An important component of parallel scientific computing is partitioning—the assignment of work to processors. This assignment occurs at the start of a computation (static partitioning). Often, reassignment also is done during a computation (dynamic partitioning) to redistribute work as the computation changes. The goal of partitioning is to assign work to processors in a way that minimizes total solution time. In general, this goal is pursued by equally distributing work to processors (i.e., load balancing) while attempting to minimize interprocessor communication within the simulation. While distinctions can be made between partitioning and load balancing, in this chapter, we use the terms interchangeably.

A wealth of partitioning research exists for mesh-based PDE solvers (e.g., finite volume and FEMs) and their sparse linear solvers. Here, graph-based partitioners have become the tools of choice, due to their excellent results for these applications, and also due to the availability of graph-partitioning software [42, 51, 53, 75, 82, 102]. Conceptually simpler geometric methods have proved to be highly effective for particle simulations while providing reasonably good decompositions for mesh-based solvers. Software toolkits containing several different algorithms enable developers to easily compare methods to determine their effectiveness in applications [25, 27, 60]. Prior efforts have focused primarily on partitioning for homogeneous computing systems, where computing power and communication costs are roughly uniform.

Wider acceptance of parallel computing has lead to an explosion of new parallel applications. Electronic circuit simulations, linear programming, materials modeling, crash simulations, and data mining are all adopting parallel computing to solve larger problems in less time. Also, the parallel architectures they use have evolved far from uniform arrays of multiprocessors. While homogeneous, dedicated parallel computers can offer the highest performance, their cost often is prohibitive. Instead, parallel computing is done on everything from networks of workstations to clusters of shared-memory processors to grid computers. These new applications and architectures have reached the limit of standard partitioners' effectiveness; they are driving development of new algorithms and software for partitioning.

This chapter surveys current research in partitioning and dynamic load balancing, with special emphasis on work presented at the 2004 SIAM Conference on Parallel Processing for Scientific Computing. "Traditional" load-balancing methods are summarized in section 6.1. In section 6.2, we describe several nontraditional applications along with effective partitioning strategies for them. Some nontraditional approaches to load balancing are described in section 6.3. In section 6.4, we describe partitioning goals that reach beyond typical load-balancing objectives. And in section 6.5, we address load-balancing issues for nontraditional architectures.

6.1 Traditional approaches

The partitioning strategy that is perhaps most familiar to application developers is graph partitioning. In graph partitioning, an application's work is represented by a graph $G(V, E)$. The set of vertices V consists of objects (e.g., elements, nodes) to be assigned to processors. The set of edges E describes relationships between vertices in V; an edge e_{ij} exists in E if vertices i and j share information that would have to be communicated if i and j were assigned to different processors. Both vertices and edges may have weights reflecting their computational and communication cost, respectively. The goal, then, is to partition vertices so that each processor has roughly equal total vertex weight while minimizing the total weight of edges cut by subdomain boundaries. (Several alternatives to the edge-cut metric, e.g., reducing the number of boundary vertices, have been proposed [44, 41].)

Many graph-partitioning algorithms have been developed. Recursive spectral bisection [81, 91] splits vertices into groups based on eigenvectors of the Laplacian matrix associated with the graph. While effective, this strategy is slow due to the eigenvector computation. As an alternative, multilevel graph partitioners [13, 43, 53] reduce the graph to smaller, representative graphs that can be partitioned easily; the partitions are then projected to the original graph, with local refinements (usually based on the Kernighan–Lin method [56]) reducing imbalance and cut-edge weight at each level. Multilevel methods form the core of serial [42, 53, 75, 82, 102] and parallel [51, 102] graph-partitioning libraries. Diffusive graph partitioners [22, 46, 58, 105] operate more locally than multilevel graph partitioners. Diffusive partitioners transfer work from heavily loaded processors to their more lightly loaded neighbors; neighbors are defined either by the network in the parallel computer or by a processor graph induced by the application's data dependencies. Diffusive methods are faster than multilevel methods but can require several iterations to achieve global balance. Diffusive partitioners are also more incremental than other graph partitioners; that is, small changes in processor work loads result in only small changes in the decomposition. This incrementality is important in dynamic load balancing, where the cost to move data to a new decomposition must be kept low. Graph partitioners allowing multiple weights per vertex (i.e., multiconstraint or multiphase partitioning) [52, 87, 100] or edge (i.e., multiobjective partitioning) [85] have been applied to a variety of multiphase simulations.

Geometric partitioning methods can be effective alternatives to graph partitioners. Using only objects' weights and physical coordinates, they assign equal object weights to processors while grouping physically close objects within subdomains. While they tend to

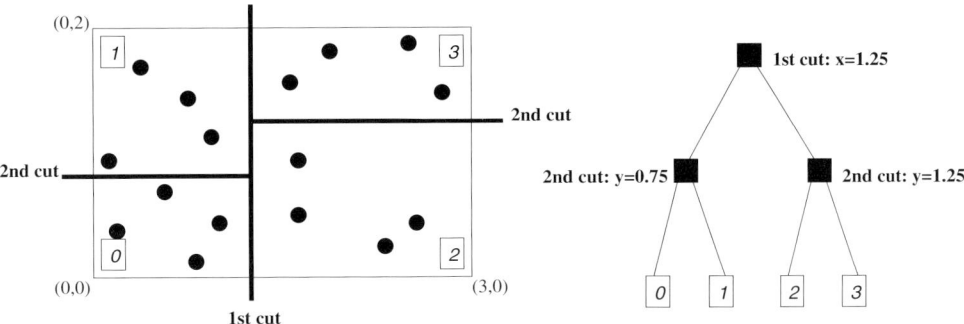

Figure 6.1. *Cutting planes (left) and associated cut tree (right) for geometric recursive bisection. Dots are objects to be balanced; cuts are shown with dark lines and tree nodes.*

produce partitions with higher communication costs than graph partitioning, they run faster and, in most cases, are implicitly incremental. Moreover, applications that lack natural graph connectivity (e.g., particle methods) can easily use geometric partitioners.

Geometric recursive bisection uses a cutting plane to divide geometric space into two sets with equal object weights (Figure 6.1). The resulting subdomains are divided recursively in the same manner, until the number of subdomains equals the number of desired partitions. (This algorithm is easily extended from powers of two to arbitrary numbers of partitions.) Variants of geometric recursive bisection differ primarily in their choice of cutting plane. Recursive coordinate bisection (RCB) [6] chooses planes orthogonal to coordinate axes. Recursive inertial bisection (RIB) [91, 94] uses planes orthogonal to long directions in the geometry; these long directions are the principal axes of inertia. (Note that RIB is not incremental.) Unbalanced recursive bisection (URB) [48] generates subdomains with lower aspect ratio (and, by implication, lower communication costs) by dividing the geometry in half and then assigning a number of processors to each half that is proportional to the work in that half.

Another geometric method, SFC partitioning, uses SFCs to map objects from their position in three-dimensional space to a linear ordering. Objects are assigned a key (typically an integer or a real number) representing the point on an SFC that is closest to the object. Sorting the keys creates the linear ordering of the objects. This linear ordering is then cut into equally weighted pieces to be assigned to partitions (Figure 6.2). SFC partitioners can be implemented in a number of ways. Different curves (e.g., Hilbert, Morton) may be used. The sorting step can be replaced with binning strategies [24]. An explicit octree representation of the SFC can be built [35, 63]. Topological connectivity can be used instead of coordinates to generate the SFC [65, 66]. In each approach, however, the speed of the algorithm and quality of the resulting decomposition is comparable to RCB.

6.2 Beyond traditional applications

Traditional partitioners have been applied with great success to a variety of applications. Multilevel graph partitioning is highly effective for finite element and finite volume methods

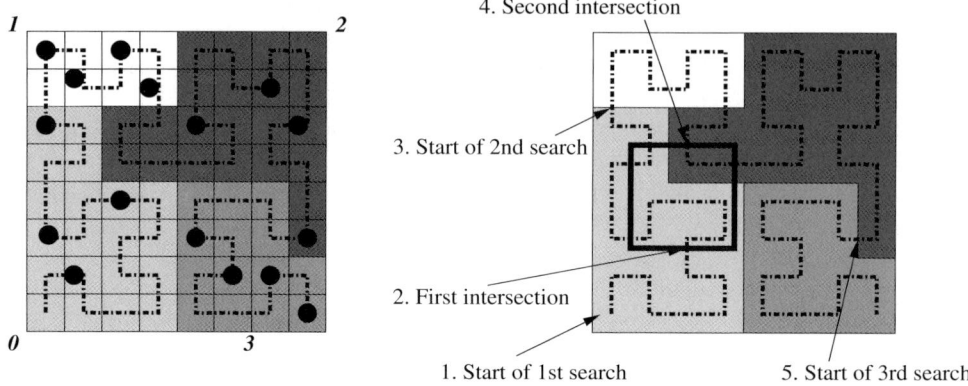

Figure 6.2. *SFC partitioning (left) and box assignment search procedure (right). Objects (dots) are ordered along the SFC (dotted line). Partitions are indicated by shading. The box for box assignment intersects partitions 0 and 2.*

(where mesh nodes or cells are divided among processors). Diffusive graph partitioners and incremental geometric methods are widely used in dynamic computations such as adaptive finite element methods [6, 26, 32, 74, 84]. The physical locality of objects provided by geometric partitioners has been exploited in particle methods [80, 104].

Some new parallel applications can use enhancements of traditional partitioners with success. Contact detection for crash and impact simulations can use geometric and/or graph-based partitioners, as long as additional functionality for finding overlaps of the geometry with given regions of space is supported. Data-mining applications often use graph partitioners to identify clusters within datasets; the partitioners' objective functions are modified to obtain nontrivial clusters.

Other applications, however, require new partitioning models. These applications are characterized by higher data connectivity and less homogeneity and symmetry. For example, circuit and density functional theory simulations can have much less data locality than finite element methods. Graph-based models do not sufficiently represent the data relationships in these applications.

In this section, we describe some emerging parallel applications and appropriate partitioning solutions for them. We present techniques used for partitioning contact detection simulations. We survey application of graph-based partitioners to clustering algorithms for data mining, and we discuss hypergraph partitioning, an effective alternative to graph partitioning for less-structured applications.

6.2.1 Partitioning for parallel contact/impact computations

A large class of scientific simulations, especially those performed in the context of computational structural mechanics, involve meshes that come in contact with each other. Examples are simulations of vehicle crashes, deformations, and projectile-target penetration. In these simulations, each iteration consists of two phases. During the first phase, traditional finite difference/element/volume methods compute forces on elements throughout the problem domain. In the second phase, a search determines which surface elements have come in contact with or penetrated other elements; the positions of the affected elements are corrected, elements are deformed, and the simulation progresses to the next iteration.

The actual contact detection is usually performed in two steps. The first step, *global search*, identifies pairs of surface elements that are close enough potentially to be in contact with each other. In the second step, *local search*, the exact locations of the contacts (if any) between these candidate surfaces are computed.

In global search, surface elements are usually represented by bounding boxes; two surface elements intersect only if their bounding boxes intersect. In parallel global search, surface elements first must be sent to processors owning elements with which they have potential interactions. Thus, computing the set of processors whose subdomains intersect a bounding box (sometimes called box assignment) is a key operation in parallel contact detection.

Plimpton et al. developed a parallel contact detection algorithm that uses different decompositions for the computation of element forces (phase one) and the contact search (phase two) [80]. For phase one, they apply a traditional multilevel graph partitioner to all elements of the mesh. RCB is used in phase two to evenly distribute only the surface elements. Between phases, data is mapped between the two decompositions, requiring communication; however, using two decompositions ensures that the overall computation is balanced and each phase is as efficient as possible. Because RCB uses geometric coordinates, potentially intersecting surfaces are likely to be assigned to the same processor, reducing communication during global search. Moreover, the box-assignment operation is very fast and efficient. The RCB decomposition is described fully by the tree of cutting planes used for partitioning (Figure 6.1). The planes are stored on each processor, and the tree of cuts is traversed to determine intersections of the bounding boxes with the processor subdomains.

The use of a geometric method for the surface-element decomposition has been extended to SFC partitioners, due in part to their slightly faster decomposition times. Like RCB, SFC decompositions can be completely described by the cuts used to partition the linear ordering of objects. Box assignment for SFC decompositions, however, is more difficult than for RCB, since SFC partitions are not regular rectangular regions. To overcome this difficulty, Heaphy and others [24, 40] developed an algorithm based on techniques for database query [57, 67]. A search routine finds each point along the SFC at which the SFC enters the bounding box (Figure 6.2); binary searches through the cuts map each entry point to the processor owning the portion of the SFC containing the point.

Multiconstraint partitioning can be used in contact detection. Each element is assigned two weights—one for force calculations (phase one) and one for contact computations (phase two). A single decomposition that balances both weights is computed. This approach balances computation in both phases while eliminating the communication between phases that is needed in the two-decomposition approach. However, solving the multiconstraint problem introduces new challenges.

Multiconstraint or multiphase graph partitioners [52, 100] can be applied naturally to obtain a single decomposition that is balanced for both the force and the contact phase. These partitioners attempt to minimize interprocessor communication costs subject to the constraint that each component of the load is balanced. Difficulty arises, however, in the

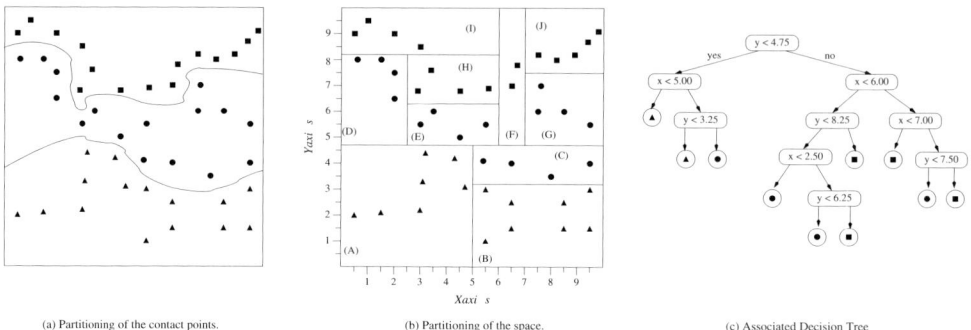

(a) Partitioning of the contact points. (b) Partitioning of the space. (c) Associated Decision Tree

Figure 6.3. *Use of multiconstraint graph partitioning for contact problems:* (a) *the 45 contact points are divided into three partitions;* (b) *the subdomains are represented geometrically as sets of axis-aligned rectangles; and* (c) *a decision tree describing the geometric representation is used for contact search.*

box assignment operation, as the subdomains generated by graph partitioners do not have geometric regularity that can be exploited. One could represent processor subdomains by bounding boxes and compute intersections of the surface-element bounding box with the processor bounding boxes. However, because the processor bounding boxes are likely to overlap, many false positives can be generated by box assignment; that is, a particular surface element is said to intersect with a processor, although none of the processor's locally stored elements identify it as a candidate for local search. To address this problem, Karypis [54] constructs a detailed geometric map of the volume covered by elements assigned to each subdomain (Figure 6.3). He also modifies the multiconstraint graph decomposition so that each subdomain can be described by a small number of disjoint axis-aligned boxes; this improved geometric description reduces the number of false positives. The boxes are assembled into a binary tree describing the entire geometry. Box assignment is then done by traversing the tree, as in RCB; however, the depth of the tree can be much greater than RCB's tree.

Boman and others proposed a multicriteria geometric partitioning method that may be used for contact problems [11, 24]. Like the multiconstraint graph partitioners, this method computes one decomposition that is balanced for multiple phases. Their algorithm, however, uses RCB, allowing box assignment to be done easily by traversing the tree of cuts (Figure 6.1). Instead of solving a multiconstraint problem, they solve a multiobjective problem: find as good a balance as possible for all loads. While good multicriteria RCB decompositions do not always exist, heuristics are used to generate reasonable decompositions for many problems. In particular, they pursue the simpler objective

$$\min_s \max \left(g \left(\sum_{i \leq s} a_i \right), g \left(\sum_{i > s} a_i \right) \right),$$

where a_i is the weight vector for object i and g is a monotonically nondecreasing function in each component of the input vector, typically $g(x) = \sum_j x_j^p$ with $p = 1$ or $p = 2$, or $g(x) = \|x\|$ for some norm. This objective function is unimodal with respect to s; that is, starting with $s = 1$ and increasing s, the objective decreases, until at some point the objective starts increasing. That point defines the optimal bisection value s, and it can be computed efficiently.

6.2.2 Clustering in data mining

Advances in information technology have greatly increased the amount of data generated, collected, and stored in various disciplines. The need to effectively and efficiently analyze these data repositories to transform raw data into information and, ultimately, knowledge motivated the rapid development of data mining. Data mining combines data analysis techniques from a wide spectrum of disciplines. Among the most extensively used data mining techniques is *clustering*, which tries to organize a large collection of data points into a relatively small number of meaningful, coherent groups. Clustering has been studied extensively; two recent surveys [39, 47] offer comprehensive summaries of different applications and algorithms.

One class of clustering algorithms is directly related to graph partitioning; these algorithms model datasets with graphs and discover clusters by identifying well-connected subgraphs. Two major categories of graph models exist: *similarity-based* models [31] and *object-attribute-based* models [29, 109]. In a similarity-based graph, vertices represent data objects, and edges connect objects that are similar to each other. Edge weights are proportional to the amount of similarity between objects. Variations of this model include reducing the density of the graph by focusing on only a small number of nearest neighbors of each vertex and using hypergraphs to allow setwise similarity as opposed to pairwise similarity. Object-attribute models represent how objects are related to the overall set of attributes. Relationships between objects and attributes are modeled by a bipartite graph $G(V_o, V_a, E)$, where V_o is the set of vertices representing objects, V_a is the set of vertices representing attributes, and E is the set of edges connecting objects in V_o with their attributes in V_a. This model is applicable when the number of attributes is very large but each object has only a small subset of them.

Graph-based clustering approaches can be classified into two categories: *direct* and *partitioning-based*. Direct approaches identify well-connected subgraphs by looking for connected components within the graph. Different definitions of the properties of connected components can be used. Some of the most widely used methods seek connected components that correspond to cliques and employ either exact or heuristic clique partitioning algorithms [28, 103]. However, this clique-based formulation is overly restrictive and cannot find large clusters in sparse graph models. For this reason, much research has focused on finding components that contain vertices connected by multiple intracluster disjoint paths [5, 36, 38, 62, 88, 89, 93, 98, 108]. A drawback of these approaches is that they are computationally expensive and, as such, can be applied only to relatively small datasets.

Partitioning-based clustering methods use min-cut graph-partitioning algorithms to decompose the graphs into well-connected components [30, 55, 109]. By minimizing the total weight of graph edges cut by partition boundaries, they minimize the similarity between clusters and, thus, tend to maximize the intracluster similarity. Using spectral and multilevel graph partitioners, high-quality decompositions can be computed reasonably quickly, allowing these methods to scale to very large datasets. However, the traditional min-cut formulation can admit trivial solutions in which some (if not most) of the partitions contain a very small number of vertices. For this reason, most of the recent research has focused on extending the min-cut objective function so that it accounts for the size of the resulting partitions and, thus, produces solutions that are better balanced. Examples of effective objective functions are ratio cut (which scales the weight of cut edges by the number of vertices in each partition) [37], normalized cut (which scales the weight of cut edges by the number of edges in each partition) [90], and min-max cut (which scales the weight of cut edges by the weight of uncut edges in each partition) [30].

6.2.3 Partitioning for circuits, nanotechnology, linear programming, and more

While graph partitioners have served well in mesh-based PDE simulations, new simulation areas such as electrical systems, computational biology, linear programming, and nanotechnology show their limitations. Critical differences between these areas and mesh-based PDE simulations include high connectivity, heterogeneity in topology, and matrices that are structurally nonsymmetric or rectangular. A comparison of a finite element matrix with matrices from circuit and DFT simulations is shown in Figure 6.4; circuit and DFT matrices are more dense and less structured than finite element matrices. The structure of linear programming matrices differs even more; indeed, these matrices are usually not square. To achieve good load balance and low communication in such applications, accurate models of work and dependency and communication are crucial.

Graph models are often considered the most effective models for mesh-based PDE simulations. However, the edge-cut metric they use only approximates communication volume. For example, in Figure 6.5 (left), a grid is divided into two partitions (separated by a dashed line). Grid point A has four edges associated with it; each edge (drawn as an ellipse) connects A with a neighboring grid point. Two edges are cut by the partition boundary; however, the actual communication volume associated with sending A to the neighboring processor is only one grid point. Nonetheless, countless examples demonstrate graph partitioning's success in mesh-based PDE applications where this approximation is often good enough.

Another limitation of the graph model is the type of systems it can represent [44]. Because edges in the graph model are nondirectional, they imply symmetry in all relationships, making them appropriate only for problems represented by square, structurally symmetric matrices. Structurally nonsymmetric systems A must be represented by a symmetrized model, typically $A + A^T$ or $A^T A$, adding new edges to the graph and further skewing the communication metric. While a directed graph model could be adopted, it would not improve the accuracy of the communication metric.

Likewise, graph models cannot represent rectangular matrices, such as those arising in linear programming. Hendrickson and Kolda [41] proposed using bipartite graphs. For an $m \times n$ matrix A, vertices r_i, $i = 1, \ldots, m$, represent rows, and vertices c_j, $j = 1, \ldots, n$, represent columns. Edges e_{ij} connecting r_i and c_j exist for nonzero matrix entries a_{ij}. But as in other graph models, the number of cut edges only approximates communication volume.

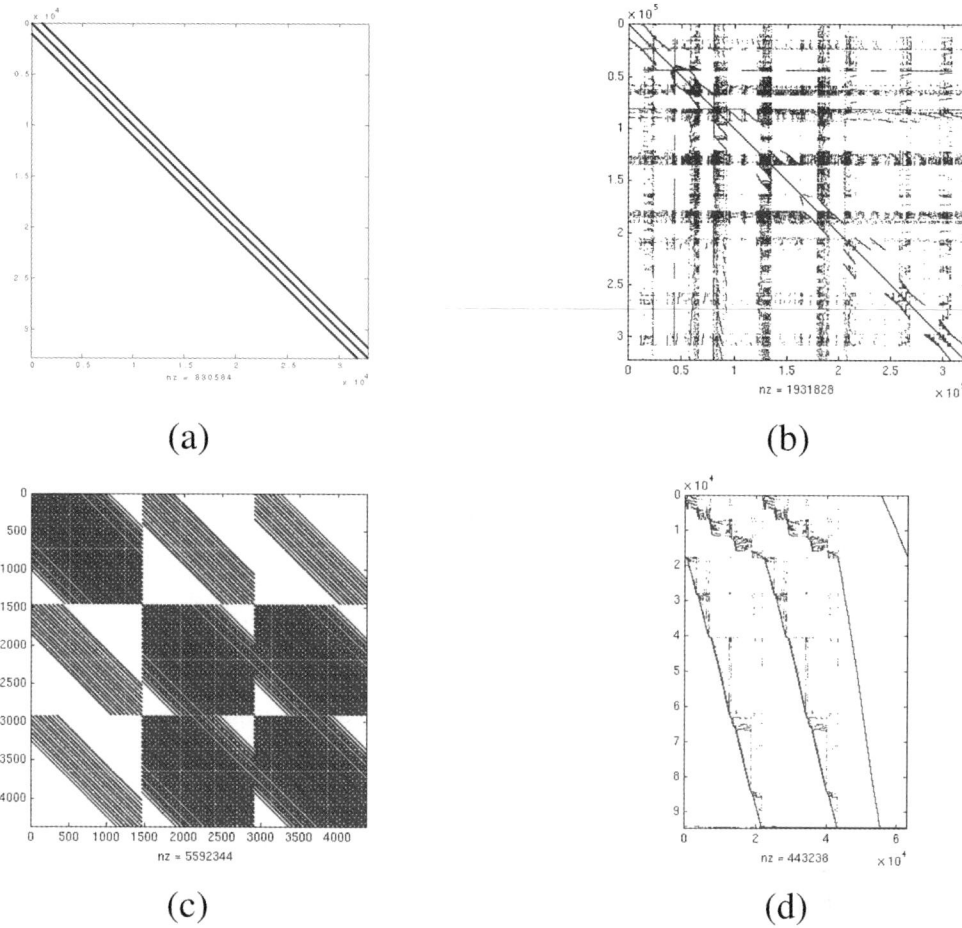

Figure 6.4. *Comparing the nonzero structure of matrices from* (a) *a hexahedral finite element simulation,* (b) *a circuit simulation,* (c) *a density functional theory simulation, and* (d) *linear programming shows differences in structure between traditional and emerging applications.*

Hypergraph models address many of the drawbacks of graph models. As in graph models, hypergraph vertices represent the work of a simulation. However, hypergraph edges (hyperedges) are sets of two *or more* related vertices. A hyperedge can thus represent dependencies between any set of vertices. The number of hyperedge cuts accurately represents communication volume [19, 17]. In the example in Figure 6.5 (right), a single hyperedge (drawn as a circle) including vertex A and its neighbors is associated with A; this single cut hyperedge accurately reflects the communication volume associated with A.

Hypergraphs also serve as useful models for sparse matrix computations, as they accurately represent nonsymmetric and rectangular matrices. For example, the columns of a rectangular matrix could be represented by the vertices of a hypergraph. Each matrix

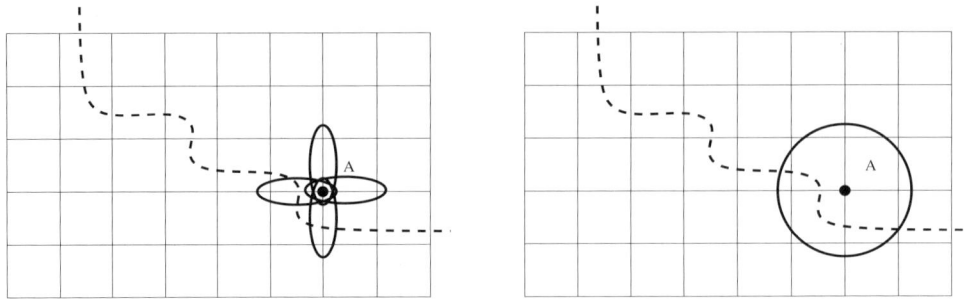

Figure 6.5. *Example of communication metrics in the graph (left) and hypergraph (right) models. Edges are shown with ellipses; the partition boundary is the dashed line.*

row would be represented by a hyperedge connecting all vertices (columns) with nonzero entries in that row. A hypergraph partitioner, then, would assign columns to processors while attempting to minimize communication along rows. Alternatively, one could let vertices represent rows, and edges represent columns, to obtain a row partitioning.

Optimal hypergraph partitioning, like graph partitioning, is NP-hard, but good heuristic algorithms have been developed. The dominant algorithms are extensions of the multilevel algorithms for graph partitioning. Hypergraph partitioning's effectiveness has been demonstrated in many areas, including VLSI layout [15], sparse matrix decompositions [17, 99], and database storage and data mining [21, 73]. Several (serial) hypergraph partitioners are available (e.g., hMETIS [50], PaToH [17, 16], MLPart [14], Mondriaan [99]), and two parallel hypergraph partitioners for large-scale problems are under development: Parkway [97], which targets information retrieval and Markov models, and Zoltan-PHG [23], part of the Zoltan [12] toolkit for parallel load balancing and data management in scientific computing.

6.3 Beyond traditional approaches

While much partitioning research has focused on the needs of new applications, older, important applications have not been forgotten. Sparse matrix-vector multiplication, for example, is a key component of countless numerical algorithms; improvements in partitioning strategies for this operation can greatly affect scientific computing. Similarly, because of the broad use of graph partitioners, algorithms that compute better graph decompositions can influence a range of applications. In this section, we discuss a few new approaches to these traditional problems.

6.3.1 Partitioning for sparse matrix-vector multiplication

A common kernel in many numerical algorithms is multiplication of a sparse matrix by a vector. For example, this operation is the most computationally expensive part of iterative methods for linear systems and eigensystems. More generally, many data dependencies in

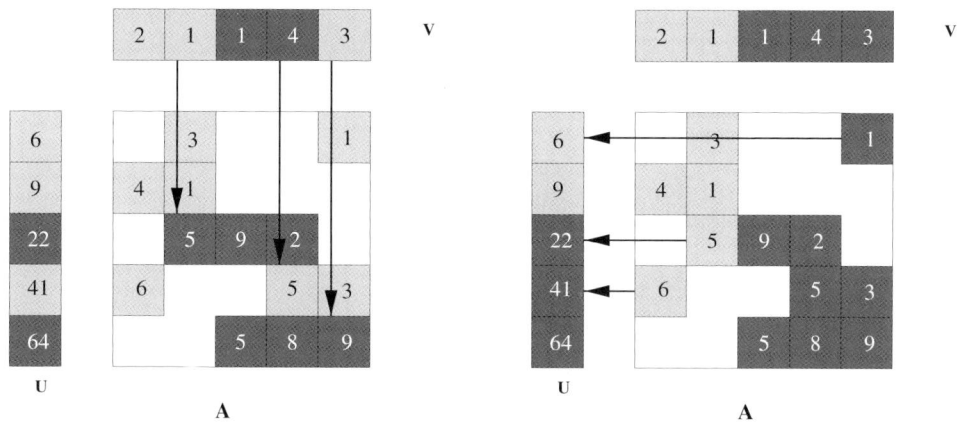

Figure 6.6. *Row (left) and column (right) distribution of a sparse matrix for multiplication $u = Av$. There are only two processors, indicated by dark and light shading, and communication between them is shown with arrows. In this example, the communication volume is three words in both cases. (Adapted from [9, Ch. 4].)*

scientific computation can be modeled as hypergraphs, which again can be represented as (usually sparse) matrices (see section 6.2.3). The question is how to distribute the nonzero matrix entries (and the vector elements) in a way that minimizes communication cost while maintaining load balance. The sparse case is much more complicated than the dense case and is a rich source of combinatorial problems. This problem has been studied in detail in [16, 17] and in [9, Ch. 4].

The standard algorithm for computing $u = Av$ on a parallel computer has four steps. First, we communicate entries of v to processors that need them. Second, we compute local contributions of the type $\sum_j a_{ij} v_j$ for certain i, j and store them in u. Third, we communicate entries of u. Fourth, we add up partial sums in u.

The simplest matrix distribution is a one-dimensional (1D) decomposition of either matrix rows or columns. The communication needed for matrix-vector multiplication with 1D distributions is demonstrated in Figure 6.6. Çatalyürek and Aykanat [16, 17] realized that this problem can be modeled as a hypergraph partitioning problem, where, for a row distribution, matrix rows correspond to vertices and matrix columns correspond to hyperedges, and vice versa for a column distribution. The communication volume is then exactly proportional to the number of cut hyperedges in the bisection case; if there are more than two partitions, the number of partitions covering each hyperedge has to be taken into account. The 1D hypergraph model reduced communication volume by 30% to 40% on average versus the graph model for a set of sparse matrices [16, 17].

2D data distributions (i.e., block distributions) are often better than 1D distributions. Most 2D distributions used are Cartesian, that is, the matrix is partitioned along both rows and columns in a grid-like fashion and each processor is assigned the nonzeros within a rectangular block. The Cartesian 2D distribution is inflexible, and good load balance is often difficult to achieve, so variations like *jagged* or *semigeneral block* partitioning have

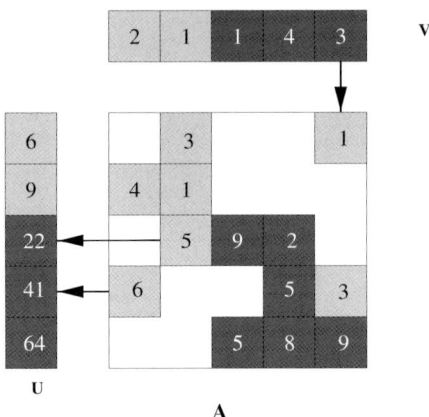

Figure 6.7. *Irregular matrix distribution with two processors. Communication between the two processors (shaded dark and light) is indicated with arrows.*

been proposed [61, 76, 83]. These schemes first partition a matrix into p_1 strips in one direction and then partition each strip independently in the orthogonal direction into p_2 domains, where $p_1 \times p_2$ is the total number of desired partitions. Vastenhow and Bisseling recently suggested a non-Cartesian distribution called Mondriaan [99]. The method is based on recursive bisection of the matrix into rectangular blocks, but permutations are allowed and the cut directions may vary. Each bisection step is solved using hypergraph partitioning. Mondriaan distributions often have significantly lower communication costs than 1D or 2D Cartesian distributions [99].

In the most general distribution, each nonzero (i, j) is assigned to a processor with no constraints on the shape or connectivity of a partition. (See Figure 6.7 for an example.) Çatalyürek [19] and Çatalyürek and Aykanat [18] showed that computing such general (or fine-grain) distributions with low communication cost can also be modeled as a hypergraph partitioning problem, but using a different (larger) hypergraph. In their fine-grain model, each nonzero entry corresponds to a vertex and each row or column corresponds to a hyperedge. This model accurately reflects communication volume. Empirical results indicate that partitioning based on the fine-grain model has communication volume that is lower than 2D Cartesian distributions [18]. The disadvantage of using such complex data distributions is that the application needs to support arbitrary distributions, which is typically not the case.

After a good distribution of the sparse matrix A has been found, vectors u and v still must be distributed. In the square case, it is often convenient to use the same distribution, but it is not necessary. In the rectangular case, the vector distributions will obviously differ. Bisseling and Meesen [9, 10] studied this *vector partitioning* problem and suggested that the objective for this phase should be to balance the communication between processors. Note that a good matrix (hypergraph) partitioning already ensures that the total communication volume is small. For computing $u = Av$, no extra communication is incurred as long as v_j is assigned to a processor that also owns an entry in column j of A and u_i is assigned to a processor that contains a nonzero in row i. There are many such assignments; for example, in Figure 6.7, u_3, u_4, and v_5 can all be assigned to either processor. The vector partitions resulting from different choices for these particular vector entries are all equally good when measured by total communication volume. One therefore has the flexibility (see also section 6.4.2 on flexibly assignable work) to choose a vector partitioning that minimizes a secondary objective, such as the largest number of send and receive operations on any processor. (Similar objectives are used in some parallel cost models, such as the BSP model [9].) Bisseling and Meesen [9, 10] proposed a fast heuristic for this problem, a greedy algorithm based on local bounds for the maximum communication for each processor. It is optimal in the special case in which each matrix column is shared among at most two processors. Their approach does not attempt to load balance the entries in u and v between processors because doing so is not important for matrix-vector multiplication.

6.3.2 Semidefinite programming for graph partitioning

Although multilevel algorithms have proved quite efficient for graph partitioning, there is ongoing research into algorithms that may give higher quality solutions (but may also take more computing time). One such algorithm uses semidefinite programming (SDP).

The graph partitioning problem can be cast as an integer programming problem. Consider the bisection problem, where the vertices of a graph $G = (V, E)$ are partitioned into two approximately equal sets P_0 and P_1. Let $x \in \{-1, 1\}^n$ be an assignment vector such that $x_i = -1$ if vertex $v_i \in P_0$ and $x_i = 1$ if $v_i \in P_1$. It is easy to see that the number of edges crossing from P_0 to P_1 is

$$\frac{1}{4} \sum_{(i,j) \in E, i<j} (x_i - x_j)^2 = \frac{1}{4} x^T L x, \tag{6.1}$$

where L is the Laplacian matrix of the graph G. Minimizing (6.1) while maintaining load balance is an NP-hard problem. By allowing x to be a vector of any real numbers, the following relaxation can be solved efficiently:

$$\min_x \frac{1}{4} x^T L x \tag{6.2}$$

$$\text{subject to } x^T x = n, \tag{6.3}$$

$$x^T e = 0. \tag{6.4}$$

The solution to (6.2) is the eigenvector of L with the second-smallest eigenvalue of L. (The smallest eigenvalue of L is zero with the eigenvector e.) The *spectral* partitioning algorithm computes the second eigenvector of L and uses a simple rounding scheme to obtain a partitioning from x [81].

In the last decade, much work has been done on SDP to approximate NP-hard combinatorial problems. SDP can be viewed as a generalization of linear programming, where the unknown variable is a symmetric semidefinite matrix. SDP can be solved in polynomial time, but current algorithms require $\Theta(n^3)$ computations per major iteration and $\Theta(n^2)$ memory and thus are quite expensive. One SDP relaxation of the graph partitioning problem is

$$\min_X \frac{1}{4} L \bullet X \tag{6.5}$$

$$\text{subject to } \operatorname{diag}(X) = e, \tag{6.6}$$

$$X \bullet (ee^T) = 0, \tag{6.7}$$

$$X \succeq 0 \quad (X \text{ is semidefinite}), \tag{6.8}$$

where X is a matrix and $\bullet$ denotes the elementwise matrix inner product. The matrix X can be considered a generalization of the vector x in (6.2); each node in the graph is assigned a vector instead of a real number. We remark that the SDP (6.5) becomes equivalent to the spectral problem (6.2) if we impose the additional constraint that $\operatorname{rank}(X) = 1$; then $X = xx^T$ for x in (6.2). A decomposition is derived from the matrix X. Since the SDP is a tighter approximation to the discrete problem, SDP solutions should produce higher-quality partitions than the spectral algorithm. (Although the continuous SDP solution X will produce a good objective value, the discrete partitioning induced by X does not necessarily have a small cut size due to the rounding step, but randomized techniques can be employed.) The SDP method for graph partitioning has been studied, e.g., in [49, 106]. Oliveira, Stewart, and Toma [71] showed that a generalization of graph partitioning, where the vertices have preference values for belonging to a certain partition, can also be modeled as an SDP. Since algorithms and software for solving SDP are quite slow, faster approximate solvers are needed. A promising approach is subspace iteration, in which X is restricted to lower-dimensional subspaces. Subspace algorithms for SDP are analogous to Lanczos–Arnoldi or Davidson-type algorithms for eigenvalue problems. Recent work [71, 72, 70] indicates that such algorithms for SDP graph partitioning are much faster than full SDP solvers and are competitive with spectral partitioning.

6.4 Beyond traditional models

While the traditional partitioning model (balancing workloads while minimizing interprocessor communication) often minimizes an application's total runtime, there are applications for which different models or goals are more important. In applications in which the total amount of work in a computation depends on the decomposition, traditional partitioning strategies are insufficient, as they partition with respect to a fixed amount of work; these scenarios, are called complex objectives. Another load-balancing issue, recently described by Pınar and Hendrickson [78], is "flexibly assignable" work; in some cases, even after the data have been distributed, there is some flexibility to assign work among processors. For some applications, the cost to move data from an old decomposition to a new one is so high that incorporating migration cost into a dynamic load-balancing strategy yields great benefit. These alternative models and goals for partitioning are described below.

6.4.1 Complex objectives

Traditional models assume that the total work (for a processor) is a linear sum of workloads associated with each task assigned to a processor. Therefore, each task is typically assigned a scalar number (weight) that describes the work (time) associated with that task. In the multiconstraint case, each task may have multiple weights associated with it.

However, there are applications in which the total work is *not* a linear sum of the weights associated with the unit tasks. A good example is sparse matrix factorization (LU or Cholesky). Assuming each task is a nonzero in the matrix A, we can balance the number of nonzeros in A between processors. Unfortunately, during LU factorization, each processor gets a different amount of *fill* in its submatrix. The fill depends on the structure of the sparse matrix and is hard to estimate in advance. Usually, there is no simple relation between the fill in L and U and the number of nonzeros in A.

Pınar and Hendrickson [77] treated such cases as *complex* objectives and used an iterative strategy for load balancing. They started with a simple linear model and balanced with respect to these weights using a traditional partitioner. After the first distribution, they evaluated (or estimated) the true complex objective and iterated using an incremental load-balancing algorithm like diffusion; the balance with respect to the complex objective improves in each iteration.

Many other applications can have complex objectives. For example, each processor may perform an iterative method in which the number of iterations varies and depends on local data. Incomplete factorizations also fall into the category of complex objectives, except in the level-0 case, where the nonzero pattern of $L + U$ is the same as the pattern of A and thus can be balanced in the traditional way.

Another load-balancing problem that fits into this category is the problem of balancing computation and communication. Models like graph and hypergraph partitioning attempt to balance only computation while minimizing total communication volume. An alternative is to balance both computation and communication simultaneously. Another variation is to balance the weighted sum of computation and communication for each processor, where the weight scaling is machine dependent. This last model may be the most realistic since, in practice, the slowest processor (after doing both computation and communication) determines the overall speed. The main difficulty in balancing computation and communication is that the communication requirements are not known until a data distribution has been computed. The iterative approach described above can be applied naturally to this problem [79].

6.4.2 Flexibly assignable work

In the data-parallel programming model, the data distribution implicitly also distributes the computation among the processors. However, the data distribution does not always uniquely assign all the computations to processors. In many situations, some work can be performed by any of a set of processors. For example, some portions on the data may be replicated on multiple processors, any of which can perform the work. Alternatively, tasks may involve multiple data items that reside on different processors. These are both examples of what is called *flexibly assignable work* [79, 78]. A simple example is molecular dynamics simulations, where a force computation is required between particles that are close to each other. Typically, geometric space is partitioned into regions and assigned to processors. Processors compute forces between particles in the local region, but when two nearby particles reside on different processors, either processor could perform the computation. This computation is flexibly assignable work. Another example is finite element simulations, where some of the computation is node based while other parts are element based. A decomposition assigns either nodes or elements to processors; there is then some flexibility in assigning the other entity.

A *task assignment* problem for flexibly assignable work was formally defined in [78], in which the goal was to minimize the number of tasks assigned to the maximally loaded processor. The authors proposed two different solution methods. The first approach is based on network flow. Formulating the task assignment problem as a network model in which tasks "flow" from task nodes to processor nodes, they minimized the maximum total flow into any processor node. The solution strategy uses parametric search with probes, where each probe operation attempts to find a complete flow (i.e., a flow assigning every task to some processor) for which the maximum total flow into any processor is less than the search parameter. Each probe involves solving or updating a network flow problem (e.g., using augmenting paths). Since network flow algorithms are difficult to parallelize, this method is suitable when the task assignment may be solved in serial as a preprocessing step.

The second approach is applicable when the task assignment has to be done in parallel. A continuous relaxation of the discrete problem can be formulated as an optimization problem of the form min $\|Ax\|_\infty$ subject to $Bx = d$, where Ax represents flow into processor nodes, Bx represents flow out of task nodes, and d is the vector of task sizes. ($Bx = d$ then enforces the requirement that every task is assigned to some processor.) This formulation can be recast as a standard linear program (LP), which is also difficult to solve in parallel. Instead, it is shown [78] that minimizing the 2-norm is equivalent to minimizing the ∞-norm for the problem in question; thus one has to solve only a constrained least-square problem of the form min $\|Ax\|_2$ subject to $Bx = d$. Such problems can be solved efficiently in parallel using iterative methods like Gauss–Seidel. We remark that the 2-norm minimization approach is similar to some diffusive load-balancing schemes [22].

6.4.3 Migration minimization

The cost of moving data from an old decomposition to a new one is often higher than the cost of computing the new decomposition. Not only must data be communicated from the old to the new decomposition, but data structures must be rebuilt on both the sending and receiving processors to account for data removed or added, respectively. Many applications are interested in reducing this data migration cost, through either clever application development or partitioning algorithms.

Within an application, clever techniques can be used to reduce data migration costs. In adaptive FEMs, for example, the amount of migrated data can be reduced by balancing coarse meshes rather than fully refined meshes. One technique, called predictive load balancing [34, 68], performs load balancing after error indicators that guide refinement are computed but before actual refinement occurs. Using the error indicators as weights approximating workloads after refinement, the coarse elements are partitioned and migrated; then the mesh is refined. Because data from the smaller mesh are moved, data migration costs are lower than if the refined mesh were partitioned. In addition, the refinement phase can be better balanced, and memory overflows can be avoided in cases in which there is sufficient global memory for refinement but insufficient local memory before balancing.

Appropriate selection of load-balancing methods can also reduce migration costs. Incremental partitioners (e.g., RCB, SFC, diffusive graph partitioning) are preferred when data migration costs must be controlled. The unified partitioning strategy in ParMETIS computes both a multilevel graph decomposition ("scratch-remap") and a diffusive decomposition [86]; it then selects the better decomposition in terms of load balance and migration costs.

Still greater reduction of migration costs can be achieved by explicitly controlling them within load-balancing algorithms. For example, the similarity matrix in PLUM [69] represents a maximal matching between an old decomposition and a new one. Old and new partitions are represented by the nodes of a bipartite graph, with edges between old and new partitions representing the amount of data they share. A maximal matching, then, numbers the new partitions to provide the greatest overlap between old and new decompositions and, thus, the least data movement. Similar strategies have been adopted by ParMETIS [51] and Zoltan [25, 27].

Load-balancing objectives can also be adjusted to reduce data migration. Heuristics for selecting objects to move to new processors can select those with the lowest migration costs. They can also select a few heavily weighted objects to satisfy balance criteria rather than many lightly weighted objects. Hu, Blake, and Emerson computed diffusive graph-based decompositions to achieve load balance subject to a minimization of data movement [45]. Berzins extended their idea by allowing greater load imbalance when data movement costs are high [7, 8]; he minimized a metric combining load imbalance and data migration to reduce actual time to solution (rather than load imbalance) on homogeneous and heterogeneous networks.

6.5 Beyond traditional architectures

Traditional parallel computers consist of up to thousands of processors, sharing a single architecture and used in a dedicated way, connected by a fast network. Most often these computers are custom built and cost millions of dollars, making it difficult for any organizations except large research centers to own and maintain them. As a result, simpler, more cost-effective parallel environments have been pursued. In particular, clusters have become viable small-scale alternatives to traditional parallel computers. Because they are smaller and are built from commodity parts, they are relatively easy to acquire and run. Their computational capabilities can also be increased easily through the addition of new nodes, although such additions create heterogeneous systems when the new nodes are faster than the old ones. On the other extreme, grid computing ties together widely distributed, widely varying resources for use by applications. Accounting for the heterogeneity of both the processors and the networks connecting them is important in partitioning for grid applications. Moreover, both clusters and grids are shared environments in which resource availability can fluctuate during a computation.

We describe two load-balancing strategies for such environments. The first, resource-aware partitioning, uses dynamic information about the computing environment as input to standard partitioning algorithms. The second, loop scheduling, creates a very fine-grained decomposition of a computation, distributing work on an as-needed basis to processors.

6.5.1 Resource-aware partitioning

In resource-aware partitioning, information about a computing environment is combined with traditional partitioning algorithms (or variations on traditional algorithms) to dynamically adjust processor workloads in the presence of nonhomogeneous or changing computing resources. One approach collects information about the computing environment and processes it for use in partitioning algorithms designed for homogeneous systems. Static information about the computing environment (e.g., CPU MHz ratings, network bandwidth, memory capacity per node) can be provided in a file. Dynamic information must be obtained through monitoring of CPU, network, and memory usage. NWS [107], for example, monitors network and CPU resources and uses mathematical models to forecast resource availability over a given time. The Remos system [59] provides similar network monitoring without sending messages to determine network capacity. Sinha and Parashar [92] use NWS to gather data about the state and capabilities of available resources. They then compute the load capacity of each node as a weighted sum of processing, memory, and communications capabilities and use standard partitioners to generate partitions with sizes proportional to their load capacity. Similarly, the dynamic resource utilization model (DRUM) [24, 33] uses threads to nonintrusively monitor the computing environment; available computational and communication powers are computed and used as percentages of work to be assigned to processors by any standard partitioner. Minyard and Kallinderis [64] monitored process wait times, measuring the time CPUs are idle while waiting for other processors to finish; they used the wait times as weights in an octree partitioning scheme.

A second approach to resource-aware partitioning involves direct incorporation of information about the computing environment into partitioning algorithms. For example, Walshaw and Cross [101] incorporated processor and network information directly into their multilevel graph partitioners. They accept network information through a network cost matrix (NCM), a complete graph with edges representing processor interconnections and edge weights representing the path length between processors. The NCM is incorporated into the cost function used in their multilevel graph partitioners. Teresco and others [95, 96] used information from DRUM to compute decompositions hierarchically. DRUM models a computing environment as a tree, where the root represents the entire system, children represent high-level subdivisions of the system (e.g., routers, switches), and leaves represent computation nodes (e.g., single processors or shared-memory processors). In hierarchical partitioning, work is divided among children at a given level of the DRUM tree, with percentages of work determined by the powers of the subtrees' resources. The work assigned to each subtree is then recursively partitioned among the nodes in the subtrees. Different partitioning methods can be used in each level and subtree to produce effective partitions with respect to the network; for example, graph or hypergraph partitioners could minimize communication between nodes connected by slow networks, while fast geometric partitioners operate within each node.

6.5.2 Load-balancing via dynamic loop scheduling

Load imbalances in scientific applications are induced not only by an application's algorithms or an architecture's hardware but also by system effects, such as data access latency and operating system interference. The potential for these imbalances to become predominant increases in nontraditional environments such as networks of workstations (NOW), clusters of NOW, and clusters of shared-memory processors. The previously discussed load-balancing approaches rely on application and system characteristics that change predictably during computations. For example, adaptive finite element computations can be effectively load balanced by existing repartitioning algorithms that account for changes in the mesh or architecture that occurred in previous iterations. However, these approaches lead to suboptimal results when the number of data points, the workload per data point, and the underlying computational capabilities cannot be predicted well from an a priori evaluation of the computation and architecture.

To address this problem, dynamic work-scheduling schemes can be used to maintain balanced loads by assigning work to idle processors at runtime. By delaying assignments until processors are idle, these schemes accommodate systemic as well as algorithmic variances. A version of this scheme is available in the shared-memory programming model OpenMP [20]. An interesting class of dynamic load-balancing algorithms, well suited to the characteristics of scientific applications, are derived from theoretical advances in scheduling parallel loop iterations with variable running times. For example, Banicescu and her collaborators [1, 2, 4, 3], recently developed and evaluated dynamic loop-scheduling algorithms based on probabilistic analysis called factoring and fractiling. These schemes accommodate imbalances caused by predictable phenomena (e.g., irregular data) as well as unpredictable phenomena (e.g., data access latency and operating system interference). At the same time, they maintain data locality by exploiting the self-similarity property of fractals. Loop iterates are executed in "chunks" of decreasing size, such that earlier, larger chunks have relatively little overhead, and their unevenness in execution time can be smoothed over by later, smaller chunks. The selection of chunk sizes requires that chunks have a high probability of completion before the optimal time. These schemes allow the scheduled batches of chunks (where each batch contains P chunks run on P processors) to be fixed portions of those remaining. For highly heterogeneous computing environments, adaptively weighted versions of these approaches account for the variability in processors' performance.

6.6 Conclusion

Partitioning and load balancing continue to be active areas of research, with efforts addressing new applications, new strategies, new partitioning goals, and new parallel architectures. Applications such as clustering and contact detection for crash simulations require enhancements and clever application of existing technologies. Linear programming, circuit simulations, preconditioners, and adaptive methods require richer models. Partitioners that account for processor and network capabilities and availability are needed for effective decompositions on emerging architectures, such as clusters and grid computers. As described in this chapter, many of these issues are being addressed today, with even greater results expected in the future.

Looking forward, partitioning research will continue to be driven by new applications and architectures. These applications and architectures will be characterized by even less structure than those commonly used today. For example, partitioning extremely large, irregular datasets (e.g., web graphs, social networks, intelligence databases, protein-protein interactions) is only beginning to be addressed. Agent-based computing can have complex, changing relationships between data and only small amounts of computation associated with each agent, making fast, dynamic partitioning with strict control of communication costs important. Differences between computing, memory access, and communication speeds may require partitioners that are sensitive not only to processors and networks but also to memory hierarchies. In all, partitioning and load balancing are exciting and important areas on the frontiers of scientific computing.

Bibliography

[1] I. BANICESCU AND R. CARINO, *Advances in dynamic load balancing techniques for scientific applications*, in Proc. 12th SIAM Conference on Parallel Processing for Scientific Computing, SIAM, Philadelphia, 2004.

[2] I. BANICESCU, S. GHAFOOR, V. VELUSAMY, S. H. RUSS, AND M. BILDERBACK, *Experiences from integrating algorithmic and systemic load balancing strategies*, Concurrency and Computation: Practice and Experience, 13 (2001), pp. 121–139.

[3] I. BANICESCU, V. VELUSAMY, AND J. DEVAPRASAD, *On the scalability of dynamic scheduling scientific applications with adaptive weighted factoring*, Cluster Computing, 6 (2003), pp. 215–226.

[4] I. BANICESCU AND V. VELUSAMY, *Load balancing highly irregular computations with the adaptive factoring*, in Proc. 16th International Parallel and Distributed Processing Symposium, IEEE Computer Society, Los Alamitos, CA, 2002, p. 195.

[5] A. BEN-DOR AND Z. YAKHINI, *Clustering gene expression patterns*, in Third Annual International Conference on Computational Molecular Biology, ACM, New York, 1999, pp. 33–42.

[6] M. J. BERGER AND S. H. BOKHARI, *A partitioning strategy for nonuniform problems on multiprocessors*, IEEE Transactions on Computers, C-36 (1987), pp. 570–580.

[7] M. BERZINS, *A new metric for dynamic load balancing*, Applied Mathematical Modelling, 25 (2000), pp. 141–151.

[8] ———, *A new algorithm for adaptive load balancing*, presented at the 11th SIAM Conference on Parallel Processing for Scientific Computing, SIAM, Philadelphia, 2004.

[9] R. H. BISSELING, *Parallel Scientific Computing: A structured approach using BSP and MPI*, Oxford University Press, Oxford, UK, 2004.

[10] R. BISSELING AND W. MEESEN, *Communication balancing in Mondriaan sparse matrix partitioning*, presented at the 11th SIAM Conference on Parallel Processing for Scientific Computing, SIAM, Philadelphia, 2004.

[11] E. G. BOMAN, *Multicriteria load balancing for scientific computations*, presented at the 11th SIAM Conference on Parallel Processing for Scientific Computing, SIAM, Philadelphia, 2004.

[12] E. BOMAN, K. DEVINE, R. HEAPHY, B. HENDRICKSON, M. HEROUX, AND R. PREIS, *LDRD report: Parallel repartitioning for optimal solver performance*. Tech. Report SAND2004–0365. Sandia National Laboratories, Albuquerque, NM, Feb. 2004.

[13] T. N. BUI AND C. JONES, *A heuristic for reducing fill in sparse matrix factorization*, in Proc. 6th SIAM Conference on Parallel Processing for Scientific Computing, SIAM, 1993, pp. 445–452.

[14] A. E. CALDWELL, A. B. KAHNG, AND I. L. MARKOV, *Improved algorithms for hypergraph bipartitioning*, in Proc. Asia and South Pacific Design Automation Conference, IEEE Press/ACM Press, Piscataway, NJ, 2000, pp. 661–666.

[15] A. CALDWELL, A. KAHNG, AND I. MARKOV, *Design and implementation of move-based heuristics for VLSI hypergraph partitioning*, ACM Journal of Experimental Algorithms, 5 (2000), article no. 5. http://www.acm.org/jea/ARTICLES/Vol5Nbr5.pdf.

[16] Ü. ÇATALYÜREK AND C. AYKANAT, *Decomposing irregularly sparse matrices for parallel matrix-vector multiplications*, Lecture Notes in Computer Science, 1117 (1996), pp. 75 – 86.

[17] ———, *Hypergraph-partitioning-based decomposition for parallel sparse-matrix vector multiplication*, IEEE Transactions on Parallel and Systems, 10 (1999), pp. 673–693.

[18] ———, *A fine-grain hypergraph model for 2d decomposition of sparse matrices*, in Proc. 8th International Workshop on Solving Irregularly Structured Problems in Parallel (Irregular 2001), San Francisco, CA, April 2001.

[19] Ü. ÇATALYÜREK, *Hypergraph models for load balancing irregular applications*, in Proc. Presented at the 11th SIAM Conference on Parallel Processing for Scientific Computing, SIAM, Philadelphia, 2004.

[20] R. CHANDRA, R. MENON, L. DAGUM, D. KOHR, D. MAYDAN, AND J. MCDONALD, *Parallel Programming in OpenMP*, Morgan Kaufmann, Elsevier, 2000.

[21] C. CHANG, T. KURC, A. SUSSMAN, Ü. ÇATALYÜREK, AND J. SALTZ, *A hypergraph-based workload partitioning strategy for parallel data aggregation*, in Proc. 10th SIAM Conference on Parallel Processing for Scientific Computing, SIAM, Philadelphia, 2001, CD-ROM.

[22] G. CYBENKO, *Dynamic load balancing for distributed memory multiprocessors*, Journal of Parallel Distributive Computing, 7 (1989), pp. 279–301.

[23] K. D. DEVINE, E. G. BOMAN, R. T. HEAPHY, R. H. BISSELING, AND U. V. CATALYUREK, *Parallel hypergraph partitioning for scientific computing*, in Proc. of 20th International Parallel and Distributed Processing Symposium, IEEE, Los Alamitos, CA, 2006, pp. 1–10.

[24] K. D. DEVINE, E. G. BOMAN, R. T. HEAPHY, B. A. HENDRICKSON, J. D. TERESCO, J. FAIK, J. E. FLAHERTY, AND L. G. GERVASIO, *New challenges in dynamic load balancing*, Applied Numerical Mathematics, 53 (2005), pp. 133–152.

[25] K. DEVINE, E. BOMAN, R. HEAPHY, B. HENDRICKSON, AND C. VAUGHAN, *Zoltan data management services for parallel dynamic applications*, Computing in Science and Engineering, 4 (2002), pp. 90–97.

[26] K. DEVINE AND J. FLAHERTY, *Parallel adaptive* hp-*refinement techniques for conservation laws*, Applied Numerical Mathematics, 20 (1996), pp. 367–386.

[27] K. DEVINE, B. HENDRICKSON, E. BOMAN, M. ST. JOHN, AND C. VAUGHAN, *Zoltan: A Dynamic Load Balancing Library for Parallel Applications; User's Guide*. Tech. Report SAND99-1377. Sandia National Laboratories, Albuquerque, NM, 1999. http://www.cs.sandia.gov/Zoltan/ug_html/ug.html.

[28] S. DE AMORIM, J. BARTHELEMY, AND C. RIBEIRO, *Clustering and clique partitioning: Simulated annealing and tabu search approaches*, Journal of Classification, 9 (1992), pp. 17–42.

[29] I. S. DHILLON, *Co-clustering documents and words using bipartite spectral graph partitioning*. Tech. Report TR-2001-05. Department of Computer Science, University of Texas, Austin, 2001.

[30] C. H. Q. DING, X. HE, H. ZHA, M. GU, AND H. D. SIMON, *A min-max cut algorithm for graph partitioning and data clustering*, in Proc. IEEE International Conference on Data Mining 2001, pp. 107–114.

[31] R. DUDA, P. HART, AND D. STORK, *Pattern Classification*, John Wiley & Sons, New York, 2001.

[32] H. C. EDWARDS, *A Parallel Infrastructure for Scalable Adaptive Finite Element Methods and its Application to Least Squares C^∞ Collocation*. Ph.D. thesis. The University of Texas, Austin, May 1997.

[33] J. FAIK, *Dynamic load balancing on heterogeneous clusters*, presented at the 11th SIAM Conference on Parallel Processing for Scientific Computing, SIAM, Philadelphia, 2004.

[34] J. E. FLAHERTY, R. M. LOY, M. S. S. BOLESLAW, K. SZYMANSKI, J. D. TERESCO, AND L. H. ZIANTZ, *Predictive load balancing for parallel adaptive finite element computation*, in Proc. Parallel and Distributed Processing Techniques and Applications (PDPTA '97), H. R. Arabnia, ed., vol. I, 1997, pp. 460–469.

[35] J. FLAHERTY, R. LOY, M. SHEPHARD, B. SZYMANSKI, J. TERESCO, AND L. ZIANTZ, *Adaptive local refinement with octree load-balancing for the parallel solution of three-dimensional conservation laws*, Journal of Parallel and Distributed Computing, 47 (1998), pp. 139–152.

[36] J. GARBERS, H. J. PROMEL, AND A. STEGER, *Finding clusters in VLSI circuits*, in Proc. IEEE International Conference on Computer Aided Design, 1990, pp. 520–523.

[37] C. HAGEN AND A. KAHNG, *New spectral methods for ratio cut partitioning and clustering*, IEEE Transactions on Computer-Aided Design of Integrated Circuits and Systems, 11 (1992), pp. 1074–1085.

[38] L. HAGEN AND A. KAHNG, *A new approach to effective circuit clustering*, in Proc. IEEE International Conference on Computer Aided Design, 1992, pp. 422–427.

[39] J. HAN, M. KAMBER, AND A. K. H. TUNG, *Spatial clustering methods in data mining: A survey*, in Geographic Data Mining and Knowledge Discovery, H. Miller and J. Han, eds., Taylor and Francis, Philadelphia, 2001.

[40] R. HEAPHY, *Load balancing contact deformation problems using the Hilbert space filling curve*, in Proc. 12th SIAM Conference on Parallel Processing for Scientific Computing, Feb. 2004.

[41] B. HENDRICKSON AND T. G. KOLDA, *Graph partitioning models for parallel computing*, Parallel Computing, 26 (2000), pp. 1519–1534.

[42] B. HENDRICKSON AND R. LELAND, *The Chaco User's Guide, Version* 2.0. Tech. Report SAND94-2692. Sandia National Laboratories, Albuquerque, NM, Oct. 1994.

[43] ———, *A multilevel algorithm for partitioning graphs*, in Proc. Supercomputing '95, ACM, New York, Dec. 1995.

[44] B. HENDRICKSON, *Graph partitioning and parallel solvers: Has the emperor no clothes?*, Lecture Notes in Computer Science, 1457 (1998), pp. 218–225.

[45] Y. F. HU, R. J. BLAKE, AND D. R. EMERSON, *An optimal migration algorithm for dynamic load balancing*, Concurrency: Practice and Experience, 10 (1998), pp. 467–483.

[46] Y. HU AND R. BLAKE, *An optimal dynamic load balancing algorithm*. Tech. Report DL-P-95-011. Daresbury Laboratory, Warrington, UK, Dec. 1995.

[47] A. K. JAIN, M. N. MURTY, AND P. J. FLYNN, *Data clustering: A review*, ACM Computing Surveys, 31 (1999), pp. 264–323.

[48] M. T. JONES AND P. E. PLASSMANN, *Computational results for parallel unstructured mesh computations*, Computing Systems in Engineering, 5 (1994), pp. 297–309.

[49] S. KARISCH AND F. RENDL, *Semidefinite programming and graph equipartition*, in Topics in Semidefinite and Interior-Point Methods, Fields Inst. Commun., vol. 18, AMS, Providence, RI, 1998, pp. 77–95.

[50] G. Karypis, R. Aggarwal, V. Kumar, and S. Shekhar, *Multilevel hypergraph partitioning: Application in VLSI domain*, in Proc. 34th Conference on Design Automation, ACM, New York, 1997, pp. 526–529.

[51] G. Karypis and V. Kumar, *Parmetis: Parallel graph partitioning and sparse matrix ordering library*. Tech. Report 97-060. Department of Computer Science, University of Minnesota, 1997. http://www.cs.umn.edu/\~metis.

[52] ———, *Multilevel Algorithms for Multiconstraint Graph Paritioning*. Tech. Report 98-019. Dept. Computer Science, University of Minnesota, 1998.

[53] G. Karypis and V. Kumar, *A fast and high quality multilevel scheme for partitioning irregular graphs*, SIAM Journal on Scientific Computing, 20 (1998), pp. 359–392.

[54] G. Karypis, *Multi-constraint mesh partitioning for contact/impact computations*, in Proc. Supercomputing '03, Phoenix, AZ, ACM, New York, 2003.

[55] G. Karypis, *Graph partitioning based data clustering: Problems, models, and algorithms*, presented at the 11th SIAM Conference on Parallel Processing for Scientific Computing, Feb. 2004.

[56] B. W. Kernighan and S. Lin, *An efficient heuristic procedure for partitioning graphs*, Bell System Technical Journal, 49 (1970), pp. 291–307.

[57] J. Lawder and P. King, *Using space-filling curves for multi-dimensional indexing*, in Advances in Databases, Lecture Notes in Computer Science 1832, Springer, New York, 2000, pp. 20–35.

[58] E. Leiss and H. Reddy, *Distributed load balancing: Design and performance analysis*, W.M. Keck Research Computation Laboratory, 5 (1989), pp. 205–270.

[59] B. Lowekamp, N. Miller, D. Sutherland, T. Gross, P. Steenkiste, and J. Subhlok, *A resource query interface for network-aware applications*, in Proc. 7th IEEE Symposium on High-Performance Distributed Computing, IEEE, Los Alamitos, CA, 1998.

[60] B. Maerten, D. Roose, A. Basermann, J. Fingberg, and G. Lonsdale, *DRAMA: A library for parallel dynamic load balancing of finite element applications*, in Proc. Ninth SIAM Conference on Parallel Processing for Scientific Computing, San Antonio, TX, 1999, CD-ROM.

[61] F. Manne and T. Sørevik, *Partitioning an array onto a mesh of processors*, in Proc. Para'96, Workshop on Applied Parallel Computing in Industrial Problems and Optimization, Lecture Notes in Computer Science 1184, Springer, New York, 1996, pp. 467–477.

[62] D. W. Matula, *k-components, clusters and slicings in graphs*, SIAM Journal on Applied Mathematics, 22 (1972), pp. 459–480.

[63] T. MINYARD AND Y. KALLINDERIS, *Octree partitioning of hybrid grids for parallel adaptive viscous flow simulations*, International Journal of Numerical Methods in Fluids, 26 (1998), pp. 57–78.

[64] ———, *Parallel load balancing for dynamic execution environments*, Computer Methods in Applied Mechanics and Engineering, 189 (2000), pp. 1295–1309.

[65] W. F. MITCHELL, *Refinement tree based partitioning for adaptive grids*, in Proc. Seventh SIAM Conference on Parallel Processing for Scientific Computing, SIAM, 1995, pp. 587–592.

[66] ———, *The refinement-tree partition for parallel solution of partial differential equations*, NIST Journal of Research, 103 (1998), pp. 405–414.

[67] D. MOORE, *Fast hilbert curve generation, sorting and range queries*. http://www.caam.rice.edu/~dougm/twiddle/Hilbert.

[68] L. OLIKER, R. BISWAS, AND R. C. STRAWN, *Parallel implementaion of an adaptive scheme for 3D unstructured grids on the SP2*, in Proc. Third International Workshop on Parallel Algorithms for Irregularly Structured Problems, Santa Barbara, CA, 1996.

[69] L. OLIKER AND R. BISWAS, *PLUM: Parallel load balancing for adaptive unstructured meshes*, Journal of Parallel and Distributed Computing, 51 (1998), pp. 150–177.

[70] S. P. OLIVEIRA AND S.-C. SEOK, *Semidefinite approaches to load balancing*, presented at the 11th SIAM Conference on Parallel Processing for Scientific Computing, Feb. 2004.

[71] S. OLIVEIRA, D. STEWART, AND S. TOMA, *A subspace semidefinite programming for spectral graph partitioning*, Lecture Notes in Computer Science 2329, Springer, New York, 2002, pp. 1058–1067.

[72] ———, *Semidefinite programming for graph partitioning with preferences in data distribution*, Lecture Notes in Computer Science, 2565, Springer, New York, 2003, pp. 703–716.

[73] M. OZDAL AND C. AYKANAT, *Hypergraph models and algorithms for data-pattern based clustering*, Data Mining and Knowledge Discovery, 9 (2004), pp. 29–57.

[74] A. PATRA AND J. T. ODEN, *Problem decomposition for adaptive hp finite element methods*, Journal of Computing Systems in Engineering, 6 (1995).

[75] F. PELLIGRINI, *SCOTCH 3.4 User's Guide*. Research Rep. RR-1264-01. LaBRI, Laboratoire Bordelais de Recherche en Informatique, Talence, France, Nov. 2001.

[76] A. PINAR AND C. AYKANAT, *Sparse matrix decomposition with optimal load balancing*, in Proc. International Conference High Performance Computing, Bangalore, India, Dec. 1997, pp. 224–229.

[77] A. PINAR AND B. HENDRICKSON, *Graph partitioning for complex objectives*, in Proc. 15th International Parallel and Distributed Processing Symposium, IPDPS, San Francisco, April 2001.

[78] ———, *Exploiting flexibly assignable work to improve load balance*, in Proc. ACM 14th Symposium Parallel Algorithms and Architectures, Winnipeg, Canada, Aug. 2002, pp. 155–163.

[79] A. PINAR, *Alternative models for load balancing*, presented at the 11th SIAM Conference on Parallel Processing for Scientific Computing, Feb. 2004.

[80] S. PLIMPTON, S. ATTAWAY, B. HENDRICKSON, J. SWEGLE, C. VAUGHAN, AND D. GARDNER, *Transient dynamics simulations: Parallel algorithms for contact detection and smoothed particle hydrodynamics*, Journal of Parallel and Distributed Computing, 50 (1998), pp. 104–122.

[81] A. POTHEN, H. D. SIMON, AND K.-P. LIOU, *Partitioning sparse matrices with eigenvectors of graphs*, SIAM Journal on Matrix Analysis and Applications, 11 (1990), pp. 430–452.

[82] R. PREIS AND R. DIEKMANN, *The PARTY Partitioning Library, User Guide Version 1.1*. Tech. Report tr-rsfb-96-024. Department of Computer Science, University of Paderborn, Paderborn, Germany, Sept. 1996.

[83] L. F. ROMERO AND E. L. ZAPATA, *Data distributions for sparse matrix multiplication*, Parallel Comput., 21 (1995), pp. 585–605.

[84] K. SCHLOEGEL, G. KARYPIS, AND V. KUMAR, *Multilevel diffusion algorithms for repartitioning of adaptive meshes*, Journal of Parallel and Distributed Computing, 47 (1997), pp. 109–124.

[85] ———, *A New Algorithm for Multi-Objective Graph Partitioning*. Tech. Report 99-003. University of Minnesota, Department of Computer Science and Army HPC Center, Minneapolis, 1999.

[86] ———, *A unified algorithm for load-balancing adaptive scientific simulations*, in Proc. Supercomputing, Dallas, 2000.

[87] ———, *Parallel static and dynamic multiconstraint graph partitioning*, Concurrency and Computation—Practice and Experience, 14 (2002), pp. 219–240.

[88] F. SHAHROKHI AND D. MATULA, *The maximum concurrent flow problem*, Journal of the ACM, 37 (1990), pp. 318–334.

[89] R. SHAMIR AND R. SHARAN, *Click: A clustering algorithm for gene expression analysis*, Proc. Eighth International Conference Intelligent Systems for Molecular Biology, AAAI Press, Menlo Park, CA, 2000.

[90] J. SHI AND J. MALIK, *Normalized cuts and image segmentation*, IEEE Transactions on Pattern Analysis and Machine Intelligence, 22 (2000), pp. 888–905.

[91] H. D. SIMON, *Partitioning of unstructured problems for parallel processing*, Computing Systems in Engineering, 2 (1991), pp. 135–148.

[92] S. SINHA AND M. PARASHAR, *Adaptive system partitioning of AMR applications on heterogeneous clusters*, Cluster Computing, 5 (2002), pp. 343–352.

[93] S. TAMURA, *Clustering based on multiple paths*, Pattern Recognition, 15 (1982), pp. 477–483.

[94] V. E. TAYLOR AND B. NOUR-OMID, *A study of the factorization fill-in for a parallel implementation of the finite element method*, Int'l. J. Numer. Methods Engrg., 37 (1994), pp. 3809–3823.

[95] J. D. TERESCO, M. W. BEALL, J. E. FLAHERTY, AND M. S. SHEPHARD, *A hierarchical partition model for adaptive finite element computation*, Comput. Methods Appl. Mech. Engrg., 184 (2000), pp. 269–285.

[96] J. D. TERESCO, *Hierarchical Partitioning and Dynamic Load Balancing for Scientific Computation*. Tech. Report CS-04-04. Department of Computer Science, Williams College, Williamstown, MA, 2004.

[97] A. TRIFUNOVIC AND W. J. KNOTTENBELT, *Parkway 2.0: A parallel multilevel hypergraph partitioning tool*, in Proc. 19th International Symposium on Computer and Information Sciences (ISCIS 2004), Lecture Notes in Computer Science 3280, Springer, New York, 2004, pp. 789–800.

[98] S. VAN DONGEN, *A Cluster Algorithm for Graphs*. Tech. Report INS-R0010. National Research Institute for Mathematics and Computer Science in the Netherlands, Amsterdam, 2000.

[99] B. VASTENHOUW AND R. H. BISSELING, *A two-dimensional data distribution method for parallel sparse matrix-vector multiplication*, SIAM Review, 47 (2005), pp. 67–95.

[100] C. WALSHAW, M. CROSS, AND K. MCMANUS, *Multiphase mesh partitioning*, Applied Mathematical Modelling, 25 (2000), pp. 123–140.

[101] C. WALSHAW AND M. CROSS, *Multilevel mesh partitioning for heterogeneous communication networks*, Future Generation Computer Systems, 17 (2001), pp. 601–623.

[102] C. WALSHAW, *The Parallel JOSTLE Library User's Guide, Version* 3.0, University of Greenwich, London, UK, 2002.

[103] H. WANG, B. ALIDAEE, AND G. KOCHENBERGER, *Evaluating a clique partitioning problem model for clustering high-dimensional data mining*, in Proc. 10th Americas Conference on Information Systems, New York, NY, 2004, pp. 1946–1960.

[104] M. S. WARREN AND J. K. SALMON, *A parallel hashed oct-tree n-body algorithm*, in Proc. Supercomputing '93, Portland, OR, Nov. 1993.

[105] S. WHEAT, *A Fine-Grained Data Migration Approach to Application Load Balancing on MP MIMD Machines*. Ph.D. thesis. Department of Computer Science, University of New Mexico, Albuquerque, 1992.

[106] H. WOLKOWICZ AND Q. ZHAO, *Semidefinite programming relaxations for the graph partitioning problem*, Discrete Applied Mathematics, 96–97 (1999), pp. 461–79.

[107] R. WOLSKI, N. T. SPRING, AND J. HAYES, *The Network Weather Service: A distributed resource performance forecasting service for metacomputing*, Future Generation Computer Systems, 15 (1999), pp. 757–768.

[108] C. W. YEH, C. K. CHENG, AND T. T. LIN, *Circuit clustering using a stochastic flow injection method*, IEEE Transactions on Computer Aided Design of Integrated Circuits and Systems, 14 (1995), pp. 154–162.

[109] H. ZHA, X. HE, C. DING, H. SIMON, AND M. GU, *Bipartite graph partitioning and data clustering*, in Proc. CIKM (Conference on Information and Knowledge Management), ACM, New York, 2001.

Chapter 7
Combinatorial Parallel and Scientific Computing

Ali Pınar and Bruce Hendrickson

Combinatorial algorithms have long played a pivotal enabling role in many applications of parallel computing. Graph algorithms in particular arise in load balancing, scheduling, mapping, and many other aspects of the parallelization of irregular applications. These are still active research areas, mostly due to evolving computational techniques and rapidly changing computational platforms. But the relationship between parallel computing and discrete algorithms is much richer than the mere use of graph algorithms to support the parallelization of traditional scientific computations. Important, emerging areas of science are fundamentally discrete, and they are increasingly reliant on the power of parallel computing. Examples are computational biology, scientific data mining, and network analysis. These applications are changing the relationship between discrete algorithms and parallel computing. In addition to their traditional role as enablers of high performance, combinatorial algorithms are now customers of parallel computing. New parallelization techniques for combinatorial algorithms need to be developed to support these nontraditional scientific approaches.

This chapter describes some of the many areas of intersection between discrete algorithms and parallel scientific computing. The chapter is not a comprehensive survey but rather an introduction to a diverse set of techniques and applications with a particular emphasis on work presented at the Eleventh SIAM Conference on Parallel Processing for Scientific Computing. Some topics highly relevant to this chapter (e.g., load balancing) are addressed elsewhere in this book, and so we do not discuss them here.

7.1 Sparse matrix computations

Solving systems of sparse linear and nonlinear equations lies at the heart of many scientific computing applications, including accelerator modeling, astrophysics, nanoscience, and combustion. Sparse solvers invariably require exploiting the sparsity structure to achieve any of several goals: preserving sparsity during complete or incomplete factorizations, optimizing memory performance, improving the effectiveness of preconditioners, and efficient Hessian and Jacobian construction, among others. The exploitation of sparse structure involves graph algorithms and is probably the best-known example of the role of discrete math in scientific computing.

7.1.1 Sparse direct solvers

Direct methods for solving sparse linear equations are widely used, especially for solving ill-conditioned systems such as those arising in fusion studies or interior point methods for optimization. They are also used when high-accuracy solutions are needed, as with the inversion operator for the shift-and-invert algorithms for eigencomputations, solving coarse grid problems as part of a multigrid solver, and solving subdomains in domain decomposition methods. The sizes of the problems arising in these applications necessitate parallelization, not only for performance but also for memory limitations. Most direct solvers require one processor to hold the whole matrix for preprocessing steps such as reordering to preserve sparsity during factorization, column-row permutations to avoid or decrease pivoting during numerical factorization, and symbolic factorization, and this requirement of having one processor store the whole matrix is an important bottleneck to scalability. Recent studies have addressed parallelization of these less time-consuming parts of sparse direct solvers.

Having large entries on the diagonal at the time of elimination is important for numerical accuracy during LU factorization. The dynamic approach for this problem is to move a large entry to the diagonal at each step during factorization by row and column permutations. However, dynamic pivoting hinders performance significantly. An alternative is the static approach, in which large entries are permuted to the diagonal a priori. Although somewhat less robust numerically, this static pivoting approach achieves much higher performance. The problem of permuting large entries to the diagonal to reduce or totally avoid pivoting during factorization can be fruitfully recast as the identification of a heavy, maximum-cardinality matching in the weighted bipartite graph of the matrix. An example is given in Figure 7.1. In the bipartite graph of a matrix, each row and each column of the matrix is represented by a vertex. An edge connects a row vertex to a column vertex if the corresponding matrix entry at this row and column is nonzero, and the weight of the edge is set equal to the absolute value of the matrix entry. A complete matching between rows and columns identifies a reordering of columns or rows of the matrix, in which all the diagonal values are nonzero. Heavier weighted edges in the matching translate to larger values on the diagonal after permutation. Notice that a maximum weighted matching maximizes the sum of absolute values of diagonal entries. By assigning the logarithms of absolute values of entries to edges, one can maximize the product of diagonal entries with maximum matching.

While bipartite matching is a well-studied problem in graph theory, designing parallel algorithms that perform well in practice remains as a challenge. Most sequential algorithms for bipartite matching rely on augmenting paths, which is hard to parallelize. Bertsekas's auction algorithm is symbolically similar to Jacobi and Gauss–Seidel algorithms for solving linear systems and thus more amenable to parallelization. As the name implies, Bertsekas's algorithm resembles an auction, where the prices of the columns are gradually increased

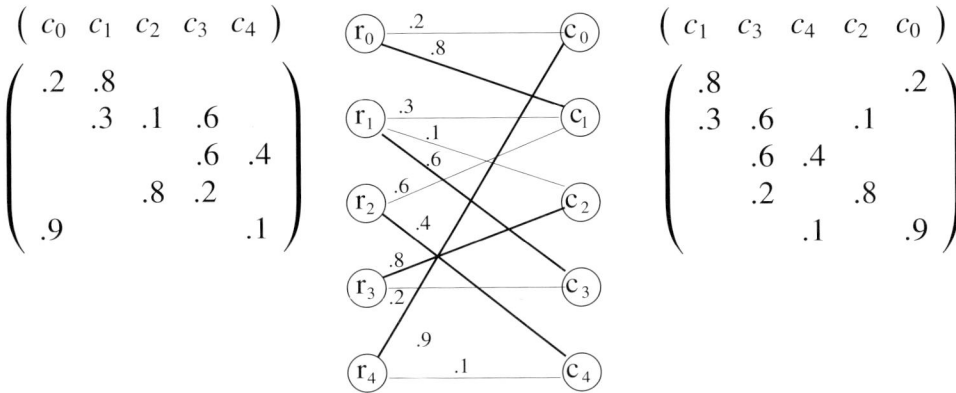

Figure 7.1. *Permuting large entries to the diagonal. Dark edges in the graph correspond to edges in the matching in the bipartite graph of the matrix on the left. The matrix on the right is the permuted matrix with respected to the matching where columns are reordered as mate of the first row, mate of the second row, etc.*

by buyers (rows) that are not matched. Each row bids on the cheapest column, and the process ends when all rows are matched to a column. Riedy and Demmel [25] studied the parallel implementation of Bertsekas's auction algorithm. They observed, as in all parallel search algorithms, speed-up anomalies with superlinear speed-ups and slowdowns. Overall, they showed that the auction algorithm serves very well as a distributed memory solver for weighted bipartite matching.

Another important and challenging problem in sparse direct solvers is the development of parallel algorithms for sparsity preserving orderings for Cholesky or LU factorization. The two most widely used serial strategies for sparsity preserving orderings are instantiations of two of the most common algorithmic paradigms in computer science. Minimum degree and its many variants are greedy algorithms, while nested dissection is an example of a divide-and-conquer approach. Nested dissection is commonly used for parallel orderings since its divide-and-conquer nature has natural parallelism, and subsequent triangular solution operations on the factored matrix grant better efficiency on parallel systems. Nevertheless, parallelizing minimum degree variants remains an intriguing question, although previous attempts have not been very encouraging [9].

Another component of direct solvers that requires a distributed algorithm is the symbolic factorization phase [10] for sparse Cholesky or LU factorization. Symbolic factorization is performed to determine the sparsity structure of the factored matrix. With the sparsity structure known in advance, the numerical operations can be performed much more quickly. Symbolic factorization takes much less time than numerical factorization and is often performed sequentially in one processor. A distributed memory algorithm, however, is critical due to memory limitations. Grigori et al. studied this problem and reported promising initial results [10].

A more in-depth discussion on sparse direct methods can be found in Chapter 9 of this book.

7.1.2 Decompositions with colorings

Independent sets and coloring algorithms are also commonly used in sparse matrix computations. A set of vertices is independent if no edge connects any pair of vertices in the set. A coloring is a union of disjoint independent sets that cover all the vertices. The utility of an independent set arises from the observation that none of the vertices in the set depend upon each other, and so operations can be performed on all of them simultaneously. This insight has been exploited in the parallelization of adaptive mesh codes, in parallel preconditioning, and in other settings. Algebraic multigrid algorithms use independent sets for coarse grid construction. Partitioning problems that arise in the efficient computation of sparse Jacobian and Hessian matrices can be modeled using variants of the graph coloring problem. The particular coloring problem depends on whether the matrix to be computed is symmetric or nonsymmetric, whether a one-dimensional partition or a two-dimensional partition is to be used, whether a direct or a substitution-based evaluation scheme is to be employed, and whether all nonzero matrix entries or only a subset need to be computed. Gebremedhin [8] developed a unified graph theoretic framework to study the resulting problems and developed shared memory parallel coloring algorithms to address several of them.

7.1.3 Preconditioning

Iterative methods for solving linear systems also lead to graph problems, particularly for preconditioning. Incomplete factorization preconditioners make use of many of the same graph ideas employed by sparse direct solvers [13]. Efficient data structures for representing and exploiting the sparsity structure and reordering methods are all relevant here. Domain decomposition preconditioners rely on good partitions of a global domain into subproblems, and this is commonly addressed by (weighted) graph or hypergraph partitioning [3]. Algebraic multigrid methods make use of graph matchings and independent sets in their construction of coarse grids or smoothers [15]. Support theory techniques for preconditioning often make use of spanning trees and graph embeddings [2].

7.2 Utilizing computational infrastructure

Utilization of the underlying computational infrastructure commonly requires combinatorial techniques. Even for applications in which problems are modeled with techniques of continuous mathematics, effective utilization of the computational infrastructure requires decomposition of the problem into subproblems and mapping them onto processors, scheduling the tasks to satisfy precedence constraints, designing data structures for maximum uniprocessors performance, and communication algorithms to exchange information among processors. Solutions to all these problems require combinatorial techniques.

7.2.1 Load balancing

An area in which discrete algorithms have made a major impact in parallel scientific computing is partitioning for load balance. The challenge of decomposing an unstructured computation among the processors of a parallel machine can be naturally expressed as a graph (or hypergraph) partitioning problem. New algorithms and effective software for partitioning have been key enablers for parallel unstructured grid computations. Some problems, e.g., particle simulations, are described most naturally in terms of geometry instead of the language of graphs. A variety of geometric partitioning algorithms have been devised for such problems. In addition, SFCs and octree methods have been developed to parallelize multipole methods. Research in partitioning algorithms and models continues to be an active area, mostly due to evolving computational platforms and algorithms. For instance, with an increasing gap between computation and communication speeds, distribution of the communication work has become an important problem. The next-generation petaflops architectures are expected to have orders of magnitude more processors. An increased number of processors, along with the increasing gap between processor and network speeds, will expose some of the limitations of the existing approaches. Novel decomposition techniques and interprocessor communication algorithms will be required to cope with these problems. Recent advances in load balancing are discussed in depth in Chapter 6.

7.2.2 Memory performance

The increasing gap between CPU and memory performances argues for the design of new algorithms, data structures, and data reorganization methods to improve locality at memory, cache, and register levels. Combinatorial techniques come to the fore in designing algorithms that exhibit high performance on the deep memory hierarchies on current architectures and on the deeper hierarchies expected on the next-generation supercomputers. Cache-oblivious algorithms [7], developed in the last few years, hold the promise of delivering high performance for irregular problems while being insensitive to sizes of the multiple caches. Another approach for better cache utilization is cache-aware algorithms [16], in which the code is tuned to make the working set fit into the cache (e.g., blocking during dense matrix operations), or repeated operations are performed for the data already in the cache (e.g., extra iterations for stationary point methods), since the subsequent iterations come at a much lower cost when the data are already in the cache.

Performance of sparse matrix computations is often constrained by the memory performance due to the irregular memory access patterns and extra memory indirections needed to exploit sparsity. For sparse matrix-vector multiplications, it is possible to reorder the matrix to improve memory performance. Bandwidth or envelope reduction algorithms have been used to gather nonzeros of the matrix around the diagonal for a more regular access pattern, and thus fewer cache misses. A new, more promising method is the blocking techniques that have been used for register reuse and reducing memory load operations [26, 22, 14]. These techniques represent the sparse matrix as a union of dense submatrices. This requires either replacing some structural zeros with numerical zeros so that all dense submatrices are of uniform size [14] or splitting the matrix into several submatrices so that each submatrix covers blocks of different sizes [26, 22]. Experiments show that notable speed-ups can be achieved through these blocking techniques, reaching close to the peak processor performances.

7.2.3 Node allocation

A recent trend for parallel architectures is computational clusters built of off-the-shelf components. Typically in such systems, communication is slower, but it is possible to build very large clusters, due to easy incrementability. With slow communication, along with large numbers of processors, choosing which set of processors to perform a parallel job becomes a critical task for overall performance in terms of both the response time of individual tasks and system throughput. The problem of choosing a subset of processors to perform a parallel job is studied as the node allocation problem, and the objective is to minimize network contention by assigning jobs to maximize processor locality. Leung et al. [18] empirically showed a correlation between the average number of hops that a message has to go through after node allocation and the runtime of tasks. They also proposed node allocation heuristics that increase throughput by 30% on average. Their algorithms linearly order the processors of the computational cluster by using SFCs. Nodes are then allocated for a task, to minimize the span of processors in this linear order. This algorithm requires only one pass over the linearized processor array. To break ties, best-fit or first-fit strategies were studied, and first-fit performed slightly better in the experiments. One direction for further work is to lift the linearized processor array assumption and generalize the node allocation techniques to higher dimensions at which the connectivity of the parallel machine is more explicitly modeled.

7.3 Parallelizing irregular computations

Irregular computations are among the most challenging to parallelize. Irregularity can arise from complex geometries, multiscale spatial or temporal dependencies, or a host of other causes. As mentioned above, graphs and hypergraphs are often used to describe complex data dependencies, and graph partitioning methods play a key role in parallelizing many such computations. However, there are many irregular applications that cannot be parallelized merely by partitioning, because the data dependencies are more complex than the graphs can model. Two examples are discussed below: multipole calculations and radiation transport.

7.3.1 Multipole calculations

Perhaps a better definition of an irregular problem is one whose solution cannot be decomposed into a set of simple, standard, kernel operations. But with this definition, the space of irregular problems depends upon the set of accepted kernels. As parallel computing matures, the set of well-understood kernels steadily increases, and problems that had once seemed irregular can now be solved in a more straightforward manner. An excellent example of this trend can be found in the work of Hariharan and Aluru [11] on multipole methods for many-body problems.

Multipole methods are used to simulate gravitational or electromagnetic phenomena in which forces extend over long ranges. Thus, each object in a simulation can affect all others. This is naively an $O(n^2)$ calculation, but sophisticated algorithms can reduce the complexity to $O(n \log n)$ or even $O(n)$. These multipole algorithms represent collections of objects at multiple scales, combining the impact of a group of objects into a compact representation. This representation is sufficient to compute the effect of all these objects upon faraway objects.

Early attempts to parallelize multipole methods were complex, albeit effective. Space was partitioned geometrically and adaptively, load balancing was fairly ad hoc, communication was complex, and there were no performance guarantees. By anyone's reckoning, this was a challenging, irregular computation. In more recent work, Hariharan and Aluru [11] proposed a set of core data structures and communication primitives that enable much simpler parallelization. In this work, the complexity of early implementations is replaced by a series of calls to standard parallel kernels, like prefix and MPI collective communication operations. By building an application from well-understood steps, Hariharan and Aluru were able to analyze the parallel performance and provide runtime guarantees. With this perspective, multipole algorithms no longer need be seen as irregular parallel computations.

7.3.2 Radiation transport on unstructured grids

Another example of an irregular computation is the simulation of radiation transport on unstructured grids. Radiation effects can be modeled by the discrete-ordinates form of the Boltzmann transport equation. In this method, the object to be studied is modeled as a union of polyhedral finite elements, and the radiation equations are approximated by an angular discretization. The most widely used method for solving these equations is known as source iteration and relies on "sweeps" on each discretized angle. A sweep operation visits all elements in the order of the specified direction. Each face of the element is either "upwind" or "downwind," depending on the direction of the sweep. Computations at each node requires that we first know all the incoming flux, which corresponds to the upwind faces, and the output is the outgoing flux, which corresponds to flux through downwind faces.

As illustrated in Figure 7.2, this process can be formally defined using a directed graph. Each edge is directed from the upwind vertex to the downwind one. The computations associated with an element can be performed if all the predecessors of the associated vertex have been completed. Thus, for each angle, the set of computations is sequenced as a topological sort of the directed graph. A problem arises when the topological sort cannot be completed, i.e., the graph has a cycle. If cycles exist, the numerical calculations need to be modified, typically by using old information along one of the edges in each cycle, thereby removing the dependency. Decomposing the directed graph into strongly connected components will yield groups of vertices with circular dependencies. Thus scalable algorithms for identifying strongly connected components in parallel are essential. Most algorithms for finding strongly connected components rely on depth-first search of the graph, which is inherently sequential. Pinar, Fleischer, and Hendrickson [21] described an $O(n \lg n)$ divide-and-conquer algorithm that relies on reachability searches. McLendon et al. [19] worked on an efficient parallel implementation of this algorithm and applied it to radiation transport problems.

The efficient parallelization of a sweep operation is crucial to radiation transport computations. A trivial solution is to assign a set of sweep directions to each processor; this, however, requires duplicating the mesh at each processor, which is infeasible for large problems. A scalable solution requires distributing the grid among processors and doing multiple sweeps concurrently. This raises the questions of how to distribute the mesh among processors and how to schedule operations on grid elements for performance.

Sweep scheduling is a special case of the precedence-constrained scheduling problem, which is known to be NP-complete. For radiation transport, several heuristic methods have

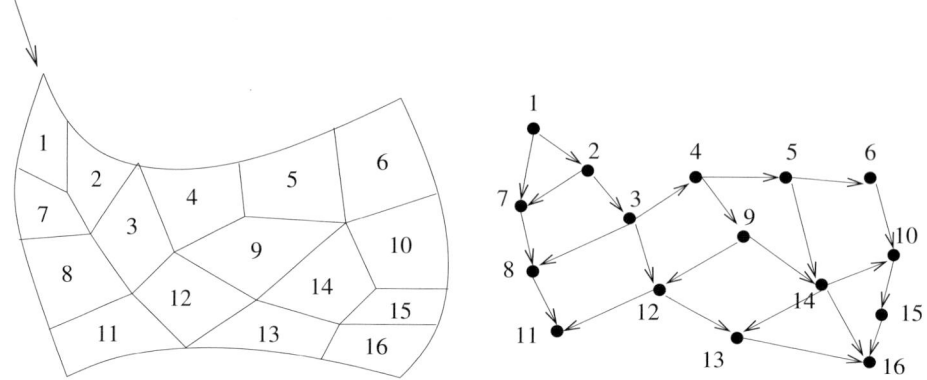

Figure 7.2. *Directed graph for the sweep operation.*

been developed and shown to be effective in practice [20, 24], but they lack theoretical guarantees. Recently, Kumar et al. [17] described the first provably good algorithm for sweep scheduling. Their linear time algorithm gives a schedule of length at most $O(\log^2 n)$ times that of the optimal schedule. Their *random delay* algorithm assigns a random delay to each sweep direction. Each mesh element is then assigned to a processor uniformly at random. Each processor participates in the sweeps without violating the precedence constraints, and by applying a random delay to each sweep. Kumar et al. showed that this algorithm will give a schedule of length at most $O(\log^2 n)$ times the optimal schedule. They also proposed an improved heuristic with the same asymptotic bound on the worst schedule length but that performs better in practice. Experimental results on simulated runs on real meshes show that important improvements are achieved by using the proposed algorithms.

7.4 Computational biology

In recent years, biology has experienced a dramatic transformation into a computational and even an information-theoretic discipline. Problems of massive size abound in newly acquired sequence information of genomes and proteomes. Multiple alignment of the sequences of hundreds of bacterial genomes is a computational problem that can be attempted only with a new suite of efficient alignment algorithms on parallel computers. Large-scale gene identification, annotation, and clustering expressed sequence tags (EST) are other large-scale computational problems in genomics. These applications are constructed from a variety of highly sophisticated string algorithms. More than 5 million human ESTs are available in databases, and this collection continues to grow. These massive datasets necessitate research into parallel and distributed data structures for organizing the data effectively.

Other aspects of biology are also being transformed by computer science. Phylogenetics, the reconstruction of historical relationships between species or individuals, is now intensely computational, involving string and graph algorithms. The analysis of microarray experiments, in which many different cell types can simultaneously be subjected to a range of environments, involves cluster analysis and techniques from learning theory. Understanding the characteristics of protein interaction networks and protein-complex networks formed by all the proteins of an organism is another large computational problem. These networks have the *small-world* property: the average distance between two vertices in the network is small relative to the number of vertices. Semantic networks and models of the worldwide web are some other examples of such small world networks. Understanding the nature of these networks, many with billions of vertices and trillions of edges, is critical to extracting information from them or protecting them from attack. A more detailed discussion on computational problems in biology is provided in Chapter 19 of this book.

One fundamental problem in bioinformatics is sequence alignment, which involves identifying similarities among given sequences. Such alignments are used to figure out what is similar and what is different in the aligned sequences, which might help identify the genomic bases for some biological processes. One application of sequence alignment is finding DNA *signatures*. A signature is a group of subsequences in the DNA that is preserved in all strains in a set of pathogens but is unique when compared to all other organisms. Finding signatures requires multiple sequence alignments at the whole genome level. While dynamic programming is commonly used to optimally align small segments, the complexity of these algorithms is the product of the lengths of the sequences being aligned. The complexity and the gap between their mathematical optimality and biological effectiveness make dynamic programming algorithms undesirable for whole genome level alignments. Hysom and Baldwin [12] worked on an alternative. They used suffix trees to find long subsequences that are common in all sequences. In a suffix tree, each suffix is represented by a path from the root to a leaf, and its construction takes only linear time and space. Once the suffix tree is constructed, long common subsequences can be easily found by looking at internal nodes of the tree. From among these long subsequences *anchors* are chosen for the basis of alignment, so that in the final alignment anchors are matched to each other, and the problem is decomposed to align subsequences between the anchors. Hysom and Baldwin use this decomposition to parallelize the alignment process.

7.5 Information analysis

Advances in technology have enabled production of massive volumes of data through observations and simulations in many scientific applications, such as biology, high-energy physics, climate modeling, and astrophysics. In computational high energy physics, simulations are continuously run, and notable events are stored in detail. The number of events that need to be stored and analyzed is on the order of several million per year. This number will go up dramatically in coming years as new accelerators are completed. In astrophysics, much of the observational data is now stored electronically, creating a *virtual telescope* whose data can be accessed and analyzed by researchers worldwide. Genomic and proteomic technologies are now capable of generating terabytes of data in a single day's experimentation. A similar data explosion is affecting fields besides the conventional scientific computing applications and even the broader societies we live in, and this trend seems likely to continue.

The storage, retrieval, and analysis of these huge datasets is becoming an increasingly important problem, which cries out for sophisticated algorithms and high-performance computing. Efficient retrieval of data requires a good indexing mechanism; however, even the indexing structure itself often occupies a huge space due to the enormous size of the data, which makes the design of compact indexing structure a new research field [23]. Moreover, the queries on these datasets are significantly different than those for traditional databases and so require new algorithms for query processing. For instance, Google's page-ranking algorithm successfully identifies important web pages among those relevant to specified keywords [4]. This algorithm is based on eigenvectors of the link graph of the web. Linear algebra methods are used elsewhere in information processing in latent semantic analysis techniques for information retrieval. In a similar cross-disciplinary vein, understanding the output of large-scale scientific simulations increasingly demands tools from learning theory and sophisticated visualization algorithms.

Graphs provide a nice language to represent the relationships arising in various fields such as the World Wide Web, gene regulatory networks, or human interaction networks. Many such networks have *power law* degree distributions. That is, the number of nodes with d neighbors is proportional to $1/d^\beta$ for some constant $\beta > 0$. This constant has been observed to be between 2 and 3 for a wide assortment of networks. One consequence is that these networks have small diameters, $O(\log \log n)$, where n is the number of nodes. A deeper understanding of the properties of complex networks, and algorithms that exploit these properties, will have a significant impact upon our ability to extract useful information from many different kinds of data.

The analysis of very large networks requires parallel computing. To parallelize the analysis, the network must first be divided among the processors. Chow et al. studied this partitioning problem [5]. Partitioning a network into loosely coupled components of similar sizes is important for parallel query processing, since loosely coupled components enable localizing most of the computation to a processor with limited communication between processors. Although existing partitioning techniques are sufficient for many scientific computing problems, the data dependencies in complex networks are much less structured, and so new parallelization techniques are needed.

7.6 Solving combinatorial problems

The increasing use of combinatorial techniques in parallel scientific computing will require the development of sophisticated software tools and libraries. These libraries will need to be built around recurring abstractions and algorithmic kernels. One important abstraction for discrete problems is that of integer programming. A wide assortment of combinatorial optimization problems can be posed as integer programs. Another foundational abstraction is that of graph algorithms. For both of these general approaches, good parallel libraries and tools will need to be developed.

7.6.1 Integer programming

Many of the combinatorial optimization problems that arise in scientific computing are NP-hard, and thus it is unreasonable to expect an optimal solution to be found quickly. While heuristics are a viable alternative for applications where fast solvers are needed and suboptimal solutions are sufficient, for many other applications a provably optimal or near-optimal solution is needed. Examples of such needs arise in vehicle routing, resource

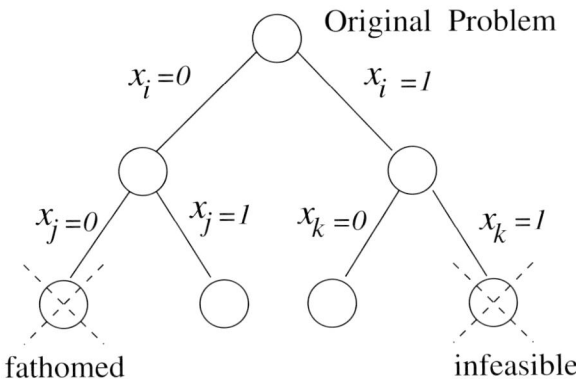

Figure 7.3. *Branch-and-bound algorithm.*

deployment, sensor placement, protein structure prediction and comparison, robot design, and vulnerability analysis. Large instances of such problems can be solved only with high-performance parallel computers.

Mixed-integer linear programming (MILP) involves optimization of a linear function subject to linear and integrality constraints and is typically solved in practice by intelligent search based on branch-and-bound (B&B) and branch-and-cut (constraint generation). B&B recursively subdivides the space of feasible solutions by assigning candidate values to integer variables, i.e., $x_i = 0, 1, 2, \ldots$. Each branch represents the subdomain of all solutions where a variable has the assigned value, e.g., $x_i = 0$. These steps correspond to the branching component of a B&B algorithm. The other important component is bounding, which helps avoid exploring an exponential number of subdomains. For each subdomain a lower bound on the minimum (optimal) value of any feasible solution is computed, and if this lower bound is higher than the value of the best candidate solution, this subdomain is discarded. Otherwise, B&B recursively partitions this subdomain and continues the search in these smaller subdomains. Optimal solutions to subregions are candidates for the overall optimal. The search proceeds until all nodes have been solved or pruned, or until some specified threshold is met between the best solution found and the lower bounds on all unsolved subproblems. See Figure 7.3.

Efficiency of a B&B algorithm relies on availability of a feasible solution that gives a tight upper bound on the optimal solution value and a mechanism with which to find tight lower bounds on problem subdomains, to fathom subdomains early, without repeated decompositions. Since B&B can produce an exponential number of subproblems in the worst case, general and problem-specific lower and upper bound techniques are critical to keep the number of subproblems manageable in practice. Heuristics are commonly used for upper bounds. What makes MILPs attractive for modeling combinatorial models is that a lower bound on an MILP can be computed by dropping the integrality constraints and solving the easier LP relaxation. LP problems can be efficiently solved with today's technology. However, tighter lower bounds necessitate closing the gap between the LP polytope and the MILP polytope, that is, narrowing the LP feasible space to cover only a little more than the integer feasible space. This can be achieved by dynamic constraint

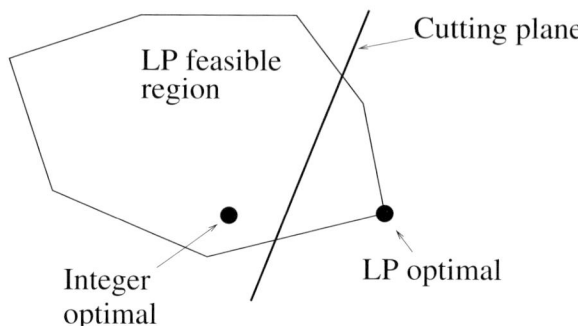

Figure 7.4. *Cutting planes close the gap between IP (Integer Program) and LP feasible regions.*

(cutting plane) generation, as shown in Figure 7.4, either for the whole problem or for the subdomains.

Branch-and-bound algorithms can effectively utilize large numbers of processors in a parallel processing environment. However, the ramp-up phase remains a challenge. Eckstein, Hart, and Phillips [6] designed and developed a parallel integer and combinatorial optimizer (PICO) for massively parallel computing platforms. They observed that the presplitting technique that starts with branching to decompose the problem into one subdomain per processor often leads to poor performance, because it expands many problems that would be fathomed in a serial solution. Alternatively, they studied parallelizing the ramp-up phase, where many processors work in parallel on a single subdomain. This requires parallelization of preprocessing, LP solvers, cutting plane generation, and gradient computations to help with choosing which subdomain to decompose. A more detailed discussion on massively parallel integer programming solvers can be found in Chapter 17 of this book.

7.6.2 Libraries for graph algorithms

The importance of graph algorithms is growing due to the broad applicability of graph abstractions. This is particularly true in bioinformatics and scientific data mining. Scientific problems often generate enormous graphs that can be analyzed only by parallel computation. However, parallelization of graph algorithms is generally very hard and is an extremely challenging research field. Bader and colleagues have studied the parallelization of a number of fundamental graph operations, such as spanning trees and ear decompositions on SMPs for small numbers of processors. In Bader's spanning tree implementation [1], each processor starts growing trees from different vertices by repeatedly adding a vertex adjacent to a vertex in the current tree. Race conditions are handled implicitly by the SMP, and load balancing is achieved by work stealing between processors. Bader and Cong [1] also studied construction of a minimum spanning tree (MST), where the objective is to construct a spanning tree with minimum edge-weight sum. They used Boruvka's MST algorithm, which labels each edge with the smallest weight to join the MST and at each iteration adds the edge with minimum cost to the tree. Bader and Cong experimented with different data structures for Boruvka's algorithm and with a new algorithm where each processor runs Prim's algorithm until it is maximal, and then they switched to Boruvka's algorithm. Their approach was the first to obtain speed-up on parallel MST algorithms.

This and related work needs to be bundled into easy-to-use toolkits to facilitate the greater use of graph algorithms in parallel applications.

7.7 Conclusions

In this chapter, we introduced a few of the areas in which combinatorial algorithms play a crucial role in scientific and parallel computing. Although some of these examples reflect decades of work, the role of discrete algorithms in scientific computing has often been overlooked. One reason for this is that the applications of combinatorial algorithms are scattered across the wide landscape of scientific computing, and so a broader sense of community has been hard to establish. This challenge is being addressed by the emergence of *combinatorial scientific computing* as a recognized subdiscipline.

It is worth noting that some of the most rapidly growing areas within scientific computing (e.g., computational biology, information analysis) are particularly rich in combinatorial problems. Thus, we expect combinatorial ideas to play an ever-growing role in high-performance computing in the years to come.

Acknowledgments

We are grateful to Srinivas Aluru, David Bader, Chuck Baldwin, Michael Bender, Edmond Chow, Jim Demmel, Tina Eliassi-Rad, Assefaw Gebremedhin, Keith Henderson, David Hysom, Anil Kumar, Fredrik Manne, Alex Pothen, Madhav Marathe, and Jason Riedy for their contributions to the Eleventh SIAM Conference on Parallel Processing for Scientific Computing.

Bibliography

[1] D. A. BADER AND G. CONG, *A fast, parallel spanning tree algorithm for symmetric multiprocessors (SMPs)*, in Proc. International Parallel and Distributed Processing Symposium (IPDPS 2004), Santa Fe, NM, April 2004.

[2] M. BERN, J. R. GILBERT, B. HENDRICKSON, N. NGUYEN, AND S. TOLEDO, *Support-graph preconditioners*, SIAM Journal on Matrix Analysis and Applications, 27 (2006), pp. 930–951.

[3] M. K. BHARDWAJ AND D. M. DAY, *Modifications to graph partitioning tools for use with FETI methods*, in Proc. 14th International Conference on Domain Decomposition Methods, Cocoyoc, Mexico, 2003, http://www.ddm.org/DD14/bhardwaj.pdf.

[4] S. BRIN, L. PAGE, R. MOTWANI, AND T. WINOGRAD, *The PageRank Citation Ranking: Bringing Order to the Web*. Tech. Report 1999–0120. Computer Science Department, Stanford University, Stanford, CA, 1999.

[5] E. CHOW, T. ELIASSI-RAD, K. HENDERSON, B. HENDRICKSON, A. PINAR, AND A. POTHEN, *Graph partitioning for complex networks*, Presented at the 11th SIAM Conference on Parallel Processing and Scientific Computing, San Francisco, Feb. 2004.

[6] J. ECKSTEIN, W. HART, AND C. PHILLIPS, Pico: An object-oriented framework for parallel branch-and-bound, in *Inherently Parallel Algorithms in Feasibility and Optimization and Their Applications*, Elsevier Scientific Series on Studies in Computational Mathematics 8, 2001, pp. 219–265.

[7] M. FRIGO, C. LEISERSON, H. PROKOP, AND S. RAMACHANDRAN, *Cache-oblivious algorithms*, in Proc. 40th IEEE Symposium on Foundations of Computer Science (FOCS 99) New York, NY, 1999, pp. 285–297.

[8] A. H. GEBREMEDHIN, *Practical Parallel Algorithms for Graph Coloring Problems in Numerical Optimization*. Ph.D. thesis. Department of Informatics, University of Bergen, Bergen, Norway, 2003.

[9] J. GILBERT, Personal communication, Feb. 2004.

[10] L. GRIGORI, X. S. LI, AND Y. WANG, *Performance evaluation of the recent developments in parallel superlu*, presented at the 11th SIAM Conference on Parallel Processing and Scientific Computing, San Francisco, Feb. 2004.

[11] B. HARIHARAN AND S. ALURU, *Efficient parallel algorithms and software for compressed octrees with application to hierarchical methods*, Parallel Computing, to appear.

[12] D. HYSOM AND C. BALDWIN, *Parallel algorithms and experimental results for multiple genome alignment of viruses and bacteria*, presented at the 11th SIAM Conference on Parallel Processing and Scientific Computing, San Francisco, Feb. 2004.

[13] D. HYSOM AND A. POTHEN, *A scalable parallel algorithm for incomplete factorization preconditioning*, SIAM Journal on Scientific Computing, 22 (2001), pp. 2194–2215.

[14] E.-J. IM, K. YELICK, AND R. VUDUC, *Optimization framework for sparse matrix kernels*, International Journal of High Performance Computing Applications, 18 (2004), pp. 135–158.

[15] H. KIM, J. XU, AND L. ZIKATANOV, *A multigrid method base on graph matching for convection diffusion equations*, Numerical Linear Algebra Applications, 10 (2002), pp. 181–195.

[16] M. KOWARSCHIK, U. RUDE, C. WEISS, AND W. KARL, *Cache-aware multigrid methods for solving poisson's equation in two dimensions*, Computing, 64 (2000), pp. 381–399.

[17] V. A. KUMAR, M. MARATHE, S. PARTHASARATHY, A. SRINIVASAN, AND S. ZUST, *Provable Parallel Algorithms for Radiation Transport on Unstructured Meshes*. Tech. Report LA-UR-04-2811. Los Alamos National Laboratory, Los Alamos, NM, 2004.

[18] V. LEUNG, E. ARKIN, M. A. BENDER, D. BUNDE, J. JOHNSTON, A. LAL, J. MITCHELL, C. PHILLIPS, AND S. SEIDEN, *Processor allocation on cplant: Achieving general processor locality using one-dimensional allocation strategies*, in Proc. Fourth IEEE International Conference on Cluster Computing (CLUSTER), Chicago, IL, 2002, pp. 296–304.

[19] W. MCLENDON III, B. HENDRICKSON, S. PLIMPTON, AND L. RAUCHWERGER, *Finding strongly connected components in distributed graphs*, Journal on Parallel Distributed Computing, submitted for publication.

[20] S. D. PAUTZ, *An algorithm for parallel S_n sweeps on unstructured meshes*, Journal of Nuclear Science and Engineering, 140 (2002), pp. 111–136.

[21] A. PINAR, L. K. FLEISCHER, AND B. HENDRICKSON, *A Divide-and-Conquer Algorithm to Find Strongly Connected Components*. Tech. Report LBNL-51867. Lawrence Berkeley National Laboratory, Berkeley, CA, 2004.

[22] A. PINAR AND M. HEATH, *Improving performance of sparse matrix vector multiplication*, in Proc. IEEE/ACM Conference on Supercomputing, Portland, OR, 1999.

[23] A. PINAR, T. TAO, AND H. FERHATOSMANOGLU, *Compressing bitmap indices by data reorganization*, in Proc. 21st International Conference on Data Engineering (ICDE 2005), Tokyo, Japan, 2005.

[24] S. PLIMPTON, B. HENDRICKSON, S. BURNS, W. MCLENDON III, AND L. RAUCHWERGER, *Parallel algorithms for S_n transport on unstructured grids*, Journal of Nuclear Science and Engineering, 150 (2005), pp. 1–17.

[25] J. RIEDY AND J. DEMMEL, *Parallel weighted bipartite matching*, Proc. SIAM Conference on Parallel Processing and Scientific Computing, San Francisco, Feb. 2004.

[26] S. TOLEDO, *Improving the memory-system performance of sparse matrix vector multiplication*, IBM Journal of Research and Development, 41 (1997).

# Chapter 8
Parallel Adaptive Mesh Refinement

Lori Freitag Diachin, Richard Hornung, Paul Plassmann, and Andy Wissink

As large-scale, parallel computers have become more widely available and numerical models and algorithms have advanced, the range of physical phenomena that can be simulated has expanded dramatically. Many important science and engineering problems exhibit solutions with localized behavior where highly detailed salient features or large gradients appear in certain regions which are separated by much larger regions where the solution is smooth. Examples include chemically reacting flows with radiative heat transfer, high Reynolds-number flows interacting with solid objects, and combustion problems where the flame front is essentially a two-dimensional sheet occupying a small part of a three-dimensional domain.

Modeling such problems numerically requires approximating the governing partial differential equations on a discrete domain, or grid. Grid spacing is an important factor in determining the accuracy and cost of a computation. A fine grid may be needed to resolve key local features, while a much coarser grid may suffice elsewhere. Employing a fine grid everywhere may be inefficient at best and, at worst, may make an adequately resolved simulation impractical. Moreover, the location and resolution of fine grid required for an accurate solution is a dynamic property of a problem's transient features and may not be known a priori. Adaptive mesh refinement (AMR) is a technique that can be used with both structured and unstructured meshes to adjust local grid spacing dynamically to capture solution features with an appropriate degree of resolution. Thus, computational resources can be focused where and when they are needed most to efficiently achieve an accurate solution without incurring the cost of a globally fine grid. Figure 8.1 shows two example computations using AMR. On the left is a structured mesh calculation of an impulsively sheared contact surface [3], and on the right is the fuselage and volume discretization of an RAH-66 Comanche helicopter [37]. Note the ability of both meshing methods to resolve simulation details by varying the local grid spacing.

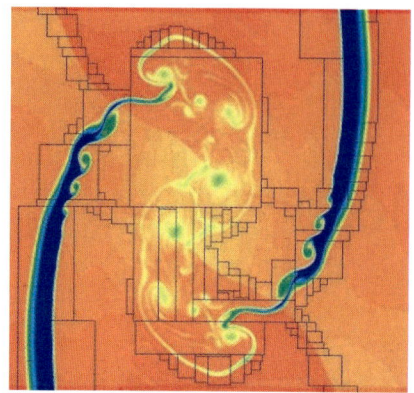 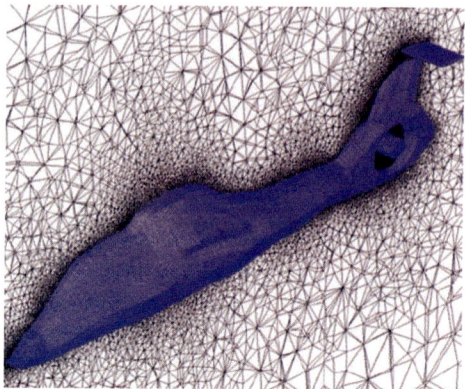

Figure 8.1. *Examples of AMR using structured and unstructured grids. The left figure shows fine detail in an impulsively sheared contact surface computed using patch-based structured AMR* [3]. *The right figure shows the accurate suface and volume representation of the fuselage and engine cowl of an RAH-66 Comanche helicopter with an unstructured AMR grid* [37].

Figure 8.2 illustrates a typical increase in efficiency that AMR provides. Here, the maximum element error is shown as a function of the number of grid points used in a finite element simulation of a three-dimensional pressure vessel with a crack. In the AMR case, grid refinement follows the propagation of a two-dimensional localized feature through the material volume as it transitions from elastic to plastic [8]. The plot compares calculations using a static, uniform grid and an adaptively refined mesh. Note that AMR requires significantly fewer elements to achieve a certain accuracy and that the slopes of lines through each set of points indicates that the uniform mesh solution is converging less rapidly as elements are added. AMR methods have also enabled simulation of problems that may be intractable with other computational approaches. For example, work by Bell et al. [10] has shown that highly detailed features in laboratory-scale methane flames can be revealed using AMR that have not been seen in other simulations. Also, Bryan, Abel, and Norman [17] used AMR in cosmology simulations that span 12 orders of magnitude of spatial resolution.

The basic parallel AMR algorithm is given in Figure 8.3 (adapted from [47]). Most implementations start with a uniform grid that must be partitioned across the processors of a parallel computer. The PDE is solved and the grid locally refined (and/or derefined) as needed based on a posteriori estimates of the error or smoothness of the solution. The refined mesh must then be repartitioned to achieve a balanced load and the solution computed on the new grid configuration. Often, the process of regridding continues iteratively until a specified error tolerance is achieved or some specified finest grid spacing is reached. In time-dependent problems, regridding is performed periodically during the discrete time-stepping sequence. The dynamic nature of the grid results in several difficulties for efficient parallel computation, including dynamic load balancing, data (re-)distribution, and dynamic, complex data communication patterns. Unlike static grid computations, these overheads cannot be amortized over the duration of the calculation. The algorithms developed to meet these challenges are discussed in the remainder of this chapter for both structured adaptive mesh refinement (SAMR) and unstructured adaptive mesh refinement (UAMR) methods.

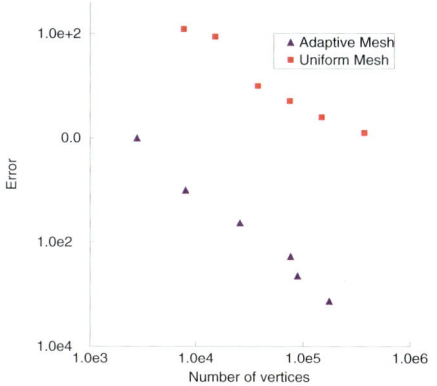 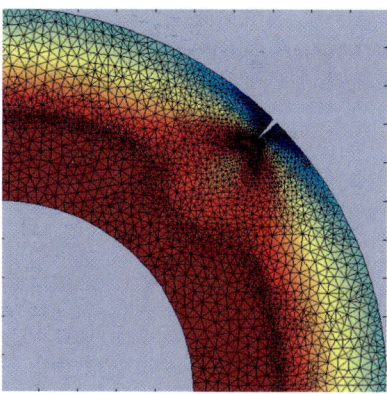

Figure 8.2. *On the left is a comparison of maximum element error as a function of the number of grid vertices in an unstructured, tetrahedral mesh calculation [8]. The AMR computation requires significantly fewer points to achieve a desired accuracy. On the right is an image of the two-dimensional version of this problem showing refinement around the transition region and areas of high elastic stress.*

Partition the initial mesh M_0 on the processors of a parallel computer
Solve the PDE on M_0 and estimate the error on each element
while the maximum element error is larger than a given tolerance **do**
    Based on error estimates, determine a element or subgrid set, S, to
        refine or derefine/merge. Act on these elements or subgrids
        and other elements/subgrids necessary to form the new mesh M
    Repartition the mesh M to achieve a balanced load
    Solve the PDE on M and estimate the error on each element
endwhile

Figure 8.3. *An outline of a parallel adaptive solution method for PDEs.*

The remainder of the chapter is organized as follows. We give an overview of the SAMR and UAMR methods in section 8.1 and section 8.2. We describe the basic features of each approach, along with issues associated with application development and parallel implementation. We also discuss some of the more widely available software packages for each. In section 8.3 we compare and contrast the two methods to highlight the differences between them. In section 8.4, we describe some current investigations by the research community and point out issues for future work including new algorithm development, software interoperability, and scalability to thousands of processors.

8.1 SAMR

SAMR methods are rooted in the work of Berger, Oliger, and Colella [12, 13]. The term *structured* refers to the use of logically rectangular grid concepts in the implementation of the adaptive grid. SAMR utilizes a hierarchy of levels of spatial, and often temporal, grid spacing with each level composed of a union of logically rectangular grid regions. SAMR codes generally adopt one of two implementation strategies that differ with respect to management of the grid hierarchy. We refer to them as the *patch-based* and *tree-based* approaches. While numerical methods for uniform structured grids are generally used in SAMR applications, SAMR algorithms are much more complex because they must properly treat internal mesh boundaries between coarse and fine levels to produce a consistent and accurate solution.

Originally, SAMR was developed for shock hydrodynamics problems [12, 13]. Since then, SAMR methods have been developed for many other problems, including compressible and incompressible fluid dynamics [40, 2, 60], porous media flow [53, 63], solid mechanics [62, 29], radiation diffusion and transport [36], laser-plasma interaction [24], combustion [23, 9], cosmology [17], and astrophysics [28].

Overview of the approach

In both patch-based and tree-based SAMR approaches, the adaptive computational grid is organized as a hierarchy of grid levels, each representing a different grid spacing. The coarsest level covers the entire domain, and the levels are nested so that each finer level covers a portion of the interior of the next coarser level. The formation of each finer level begins by identifying coarser cells that require refinement based on estimating the solution error or local smoothness. Then, these cells are clustered into logically rectangular grid regions, often called *patches*, to form the finer level. Generally, boundaries of fine patches coincide with boundaries of grid cells on the next coarser level to simplify interlevel data communication and the construction of numerical approximations on the grid hierarchy.

In the patch-based scheme [13, 62], an integer index space for the computational domain emerges from the cells on the coarsest global grid level. Each finer level in the hierarchy is a refinement of some subregion of this global index space. Then, patch relationships can be described solely in terms of the level index spaces and grid refinement relations between them. Grid patches may be described compactly using only upper and lower cell indices. Thus, management of the patch hierarchy involves simple bookkeeping and requires very little overhead. The low storage requirements generally make it possible for each processor to own a complete description of the hierarchy and processor assignments. Thus, parallel data communication patterns can be computed efficiently in parallel without extra interprocessor communication.

In the tree-based scheme [25, 50], the grid is also organized into a hierarchy of refinement levels. However, in this case, the grid is usually decomposed into relatively small *blocks* of grid cells. Each grid block is refined into a set of blocks of fine cells, and the grid configuration is managed using a tree-based data structure that maintains explicit child-parent relationships between coarse and fine blocks. While conceptually simple and easy to implement, the tree structure involves greater storage overhead and potentially larger costs to adapt the grid than the patch-based approach. In parallel, it is generally not possible to store the entire tree structure on each processor, so determining how best to split parent and child blocks across processors is important and requires additional interprocessor communication.

Typically, patch-based SAMR employs contiguous, logically rectangular grid regions of various sizes and aspect ratios depending on the problem. Each of these patches usually contains thousands of grid cells. In contrast, tree-based SAMR usually employs relatively small, uniformly sized blocks, each of which may contain up to a few hundred cells. While small blocks make it more difficult to exploit data locality on a large scale, they allow for more flexible grid configurations (e.g., fewer refined cells around local features) and easier computational load balancing. However, the use of smaller blocks and patches increases data communication overhead and storage overhead associated with ghost cells. In the end, both patch and tree approaches present challenges for achieving optimal parallel load balancing and scaling of SAMR applications.

Parallel SAMR

Parallel SAMR codes share aspects with nonadaptive, parallel, structured grid codes. Both employ numerical operations on contiguous, logically rectangular regions of data and communication operations that pass information between the regions to fill ghost cells. However, data communication patterns in SAMR codes are dynamic and more complex because the grid configuration is irregular and changes during the computation. Load balancing numerical and communication operations is also critical for good parallel performance. While nonadaptive codes typically incur the cost of grid generation, load balancing, and constructing data communication dependencies once, these operations are performed frequently by adaptive codes. Thus, efficiency of these operations is paramount so that adaptive gridding overheads are acceptable on large numbers of processors.

Parallel SAMR applications are sufficiently complex and costly to develop that a number of libraries have been built to provide the underlying infrastructure for SAMR applications. While an exhaustive, detailed comparison of such software is beyond the scope of this chapter, a few of the more well-known libraries are Chombo [22] and BoxLib [11] from Lawrence Berkeley National Laboratory, GrACE [49] from Rutgers University, PARAMESH [45] from NASA Goddard, and SAMRAI [35] from Lawrence Livermore National Laboratory.

These libraries support a wide variety of parallel SAMR applications, and all provide programming abstractions for managing parallel data decomposition and distribution on adaptive grid hierarchies. However, they differ in design and features, especially with respect to parallel implementation. GrACE and PARAMESH use the tree-based approach, while BoxLib, Chombo, and SAMRAI are patch based. GrACE developers have extensively researched partitioning strategies for SAMR using SFCs [51]. BoxLib is a pioneering SAMR software library, and many basic concepts found in other SAMR libraries, including Chombo and SAMRAI, are due to BoxLib. Also, BoxLib has been the foundation of an impressive history of SAMR algorithm and CFD application development [11].

SAMRAI and Chombo differ primarily in their design of data management and parallel communication capabilities. Chombo provides data containers templated on the grid data type. Parallel data transfers are performed individually by each data container object for the template parameter [22]. SAMRAI uses an object-oriented composition design pattern for its data management and parallel data communication infrastructure. The parallel data abstractions in SAMRAI are extensions of *communication schedule* ideas found in the

KeLP library [5]. SAMRAI supports an arbitrary number of grid data objects within a single communication operation so that schedule construction costs can be amortized over all data transferred at a communication phase of a calculation. Thus, all data moves in one send-receive message pair per processor pair independent of the number and types of data objects involved. Also, parallel data communication functionality supports new data types, such as irregular user-defined particle data structures, without modifying or recompiling the library [35].

A particularly critical issue in achieving good parallel performance of SAMR calculations is dynamic load balancing. Several researchers have proposed schemes that have shown to be effective. Steensland, Chandra, and Parashar [59] developed partitioning strategies to optimize load balance and/or minimize data migration costs using SFCs in the GrACE library. SFCs are also used in PARAMESH. Lan, Taylor, and Bryan [42] implemented a scheme based on sensitivity analysis of loads for the Enzo [17] code. Rendleman and Beckner [19] proposed a knapsack algorithm to efficiently distribute different-sized patches, which is used in the BoxLib and Chombo libraries. SAMRAI provides greedy algorithms for spatially uniform and spatially nonuniform workloads and an SFC algorithm to help reduce interprocessor communication.

In addition to load balancing, data redistribution and regeneration of data dependencies as the adaptive grid changes are very important for parallel scaling. Scaling studies of SAMR calculations with SAMRAI revealed that these overhead costs can be negligible on a few hundred processors but become unacceptably large on 1,000 or more processors [68]. This observation lead to the investigation of combinatorial techniques for reducing the operational complexity of adaptive gridding operations and improved scaling of large-scale parallel applications. Figure 8.4 shows the scaling properties for a linear advection problem run using SAMRAI. While this problem is particularly simple numerically—a typical physical problem would require much more computationally intensive routines—it exposes the costs associated with adaptive gridding operations. Although numerical operations are minimal

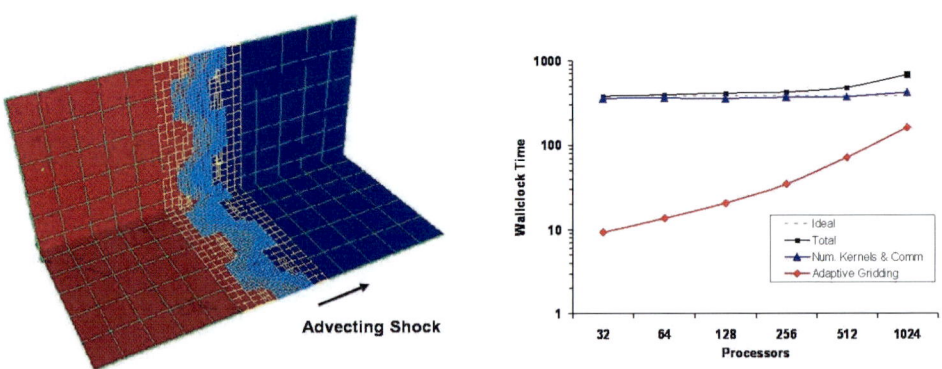

Figure 8.4. *Scaling properties of a three-level scaled SAMR simulation of a moving advecting sinusoidal front [68]. Remeshing occurs every two time-steps. Although the problem scales reasonably, adaptive gridding costs are clearly less scalable than numerical operations. Work to improve scaling of adaptive gridding operations is ongoing.*

and regridding occurs every two time-steps on each grid level, nearly optimal scaling is achieved using more than 1,000 processors. The University of Chicago ASCI Center FLASH code [28], which uses the PARAMESH library, has also demonstrated scaling to several thousand processors [18].

8.2 UAMR

As with SAMR methods, the goal of AMR strategies for unstructured meshes is to place more grid points where the solution error is large. Unlike SAMR methods, the meshes used are called *unstructured* because the local connectivity of elements can vary. Another difference with SAMR methods is that typically the mesh must be *conforming*—the face of an element cannot be adjacent to a subdivided element face. Given the restriction to conforming meshes, the majority of unstructured AMR algorithms have concentrated on simplicial elements (tetrahedra in three dimensions), and we focus on these methods in this section. Unstructured mesh algorithms [14] and adaptive strategies [38] have been extensively studied. In the following section we present an overview of UAMR methods from the perspective of developing scalable parallel implementations of these algorithms. In particular, we focus on aspects of these algorithms that exhibit commonality with SAMR methods.

Overview of the approach

Given the constraint that unstructured meshes must remain conforming, mesh refinement algorithms broadly consist of two steps. First, elements are marked by an error estimation method for refinement (or derefinement) and then these marked elements are subdivided (or merged). Second, the resulting nonconforming mesh is subsequently modified to be remain conforming. The most popular approaches for refinement for simplicial meshes include regular refinement [7] and element bisection [56, 55]. The difference between these two approaches is how they treat an element marked for refinement. With regular refinement, all element edges are simultaneously bisected, producing four triangles from one in two dimensions. With bisection, only one edge is bisected at a time, producing two triangles in two dimensions or two tetrahedra in three dimensions.

The problem with both schemes is that following the refinement, neighboring elements become nonconforming as they contain a subdivided edge. To modify the mesh so that all elements are valid, the refinement must propagate through the mesh by additional refinement until all elements are valid. Although this propagation appears problematic, in practice it is typically limited and serves an additional property of maintaining mesh quality. In Figure 8.5 we give pseudocode for the bisection algorithm proposed by Rivara [56]. The propagation of the refinement of the mesh resulting from nonconforming elements is illustrated for a two-dimensional mesh in Figure 8.6. This process can be extended to three-dimensional, tetrahedral meshes.

Like SAMR methods, the error estimation procedures for UAMR methods are done via a posteriori error estimates [4]. The advantage of this type of error estimation scheme is that for elliptic problems these estimates bound the true error asymptotically, and their computation involves only local element information [6]. However, unlike SAMR methods,

```
i = 0
Q_i = a set of elements marked for refinement
R_i = ∅
while (Q_i ∪ R_i) ≠ ∅ do
        bisect each element in Q_i across its longest edge
        bisect each element in R_i across a nonconforming edge
        all incompatible elements embedded in Q_i are placed in R_{i+1}
        all other incompatible elements are placed in Q_{i+1}
        i = i + 1
endwhile
```

Figure 8.5. *The bisection algorithm.*

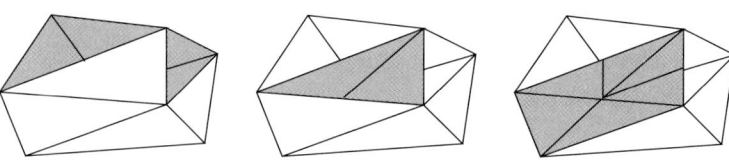

Figure 8.6. *The process of the bisection algorithm is shown from left to right. In the initial mesh the shaded elements are refined; subsequently the shaded elements are refined because they are nonconforming* [14].

many of the technical aspects of unstructured AMR algorithms are based on mesh generation methods. For example, point insertion schemes, where new mesh vertices are placed at edge bisectors or element circumcenters are a fundamental tool for both unstructured mesh generation and adaptive refinement.

A central concern for both mesh generation and mesh refinement methods is their ability to preserve mesh quality—typically this means maintaining well-shaped elements. This problem is especially acute when it comes to the accurate representation of nontrivial (e.g., curved) boundaries [38]. Incorporating a combination of mesh improvement tools such as iterative vertex insertion, flip exchanges, and vertex smoothing into a single mesh refinement loop can be effective [27, 16, 14]. Implementation of these algorithms can be a complex task in three dimensions. For example, the process of flip exchanges for tetrahedra to improve mesh quality has a number of significant technical issues that have been extensively studied [43]. Point insertion schemes for adaptive refinement have also been studied [44].

Parallel UAMR

The basic approach for parallel UAMR methods is given in Figure 8.3. There are two broad areas to consider for these methods: the parallelization of the adaptive mesh refinement algorithm in a manner that ensures a high-quality, conforming mesh, and the issue of repartitioning this mesh as it changes to ensure good load balancing without incurring too much communication overhead.

In early work on parallel UAMR methods, Williams [66, 67] gave an approach for parallel mesh refinement and implemented it in the parallel software package DIME. To ensure a consistent distributed mesh data structure, a parallel *voxel* database was maintained, using vertex coordinate information to help resolve point identity and element neighborhood information. However, a running time analysis of the algorithm was not given, and there are significant issues in maintaining a consistent distributed data structure for the mesh.

An alternative approach [39] uses the refinement of independent sets of elements to ensure that the distributed mesh data structure remains consistent during parallel refinement. A set of mesh elements is said to be independent if they do not share an edge. The independent sets can be efficiently chosen in parallel by a randomization strategy. Random numbers are assigned to every element marked for refinement; an element is in the independent set if its random number is larger than any neighboring marked elements. An analysis and computational experiments for this approach exhibit good parallel scaling to $O(500)$ processors [39].

The implementation of parallel software for UAMR algorithms is a complex task, and several systems have been developed to support these algorithms. For example, the parallel algorithm oriented mesh database (PAOMD) developed at RPI is a mesh management database that provides a variety of services to mesh applications. Their parallel implementation is based on the dupication of mesh entities that are classified on partition boundaries. Partitions are made aware of remote entities through a communication step that happens each time the mesh is modified. Dynamic load balancing is achieved using both global and local mesh migration techniques and the partitioning strategies available in Zoltan [15]. Advanced features of PAOMD include a flexible mesh representation, conforming/nonconforming mesh adaptation, serial and parallel mesh I/O, and dynamic mesh usage monitoring. In addition, this is one of the few groups to consider parallel implementation of time adaptivity on unstructured meshes [25]. The software is written is in C++ and supports a wide variety of element types [54].

Another current system is NWGrid, a library of user-callable tools that provides mesh generation, mesh optimization, and dynamic mesh maintenance in three dimensions. With NWGrid, geometric regions within arbitrarily complicated geometries can be defined as combinations of bounding surfaces, where the surfaces are described analytically or as collections of points in space. A variety of techniques for distributing points within these geometric regions is provided. NWGrid provides grid partitioning functions, reconnection, mesh quality improvement, and remapping [64].

SUMAA3d is a library of scalable algorithms for parallel, adaptive simplicial mesh refinement for two- and three-dimensional unstructured meshes. The AMR scheme is based on edge bisection to refine and de-refine elements in conjunction with Rivara's technique for removing nonconforming points from the mesh. A geometric mesh partitioning heuristic is used to generate a partition tree that strives to minimize both latency and transmission communication costs on distributed-memory computers. The code also includes parallel mesh quality improvement capabilities and has been used in a number of finite element simulations [38, 39].

A common aspect of all of these parallel UAMR implementations is that their efficient parallel performance depends critically on good mesh partitioning. Initially, the mesh must be partitioned to equalize the load on each processor and to minimize the number of elements that share edges but are assigned to different processors (often referred to as ghost elements). As the computation proceeds, the element refinement will not be balanced—some processors are more likely to have refinement. Thus, the mesh must be dynamically rebalanced to maintain the same load distribution as the initial partitioning, while minimizing the interprocessor communication required to move elements between processors.

A number of effective partitioning heuristics have been developed; overall these heuristics can be characterized as being geometric based (using the geometric positions of mesh points) or graph based (using the connectivity structure of the mesh). Mesh migration methods have also been proposed; however, it is generally more efficient in practice to completely repartition the mesh when the element assignments to processors becomes unbalanced. Several software systems have been developed that implement these algorithms, including two widely used packages: Zoltan [15] and ParMetis [58]. There has also been significant research in advanced partitioning algorithms to accommodate heterogeneous computational environments, e.g., [61], and predictive load balancing schemes, e.g., [26].

8.3 A comparison of SAMR and UAMR

Historically, SAMR and UAMR methods have been championed based on their relative strengths when used in particular application areas; a comparison of some of the relevant properties is summarized in Table 8.1. As discussed in section 8.1, SAMR meshes are composed of a hierarchy of regular grids. There are several advantages to this approach compared to the UAMR approach, including efficient storage of the mesh connectivity, fast and efficient computational kernels based on finite difference and finite volume methods, and the ability to easily reuse legacy code developed for Cartesian grids. One of the historical disadvantages of the SAMR approach is that complex geometries are difficult to accurately model, although this is being addressed with current research highlighted in section 8.4. In constrast, complex geometries are typically easier to model using UAMR methods because

Table 8.1. *A comparison of SAMR and UAMR methods.*

Property	SAMR	UAMR
Mesh Configuration	Hierarchy of grids	Single level of elements
Mesh Connectivity	Regular: Implicit *ijk* connectivity	Irregular: explicit connectivity information must be stored
Discretization Method	Typically finite difference/ finite volume	Typically finite element/ finite volume
Kernel Efficiency	Typically highly efficient use of contiguous arrays	Typically less efficient because of indirect addressing
Refinement Issues	Internal boundary discretization	Maintaining mesh quality
Overrefinement Potential	Clustering to form patches	Propagation to maintain conforming meshes
Decomposition Granularity	Blocks of many elements	Individual elements
Partitioning Heuristics	Space filling curves and bin packing	Graph- or geometry-based schemes
Repartitioning Strategy	Create a new level and move the data	Repartition entire mesh or migration strategies

of the increased flexibility in mesh generation. In addition, because all elements are at the same level, legacy physics modules that incorporate finite-element and finite-volume discretization schemes can often be used with no modification when placed into a UAMR framework. However, because the mesh is unstructured, it often requires more resources for storage of the connectivity and geometry information and the computational kernels are typically not as efficient because indirect addressing is often used.

In both SAMR and UAMR methods the grid can be overrefined and more elements subdivided than necessary according to the error estimation process. In the case of SAMR meshes, this is due to the need to create rectangular patches; for UAMR meshes this is due to the need to propagate the refinement to create conforming meshes. Each technique also has discretization issues that must be considered in the refinement process. For example, for UAMR meshes, certain techniques for dividing elements can lead to elements with arbitrarily small angles which can adversely affect discretization accuracy. For SAMR meshes, special discretization techniques must be used at the internal coarse-fine interfaces to maintain stability and accuracy.

Parallelization of the two methods offers different challenges. Parallel SAMR methods work with grid blocks which can contain hundreds or thousands of elements. Typically space-filling or bin-packing algorithms are used to partition the data, and when a new level is created, the blocks are distributed to the processors of the parallel computer. Because the level of granularity is large, there can be challenges associated with achieving good load balance on a parallel computer when the number of blocks does not greatly exceed the number of processors. This is much less a problem for UAMR methods because partitioning is done on the level of individual elements. However, when a UAMR mesh is refined, it is not a matter of distributing the newly created data; typically the entire mesh is repartitioned or mesh migration strategies are used to maintain data locality and good load balance.

8.4 Recent advances and future research directions

To address new simulation problems, researchers are developing new algorithms that combine AMR with other solution methods. In section 8.4.1, we discuss some of these approaches and the issues they present for parallel computing. To make the development of new methods easier in the future, researchers are developing tools to allow software to interoperate in new ways. In section 8.4.2, we describe an effort to define a common abstract data model and interfaces for meshing and discretization tools. In section 8.4.3, we discuss issues associated with scaling of AMR applications on new parallel architectures.

8.4.1 New AMR algorithms and parallel computing issues

AMR technology is being combined with other numerical techniques to expand the range of applicability of adaptive grid methods. Examples include combining AMR with ALE (Arbitrary Langrangian–Eulerian) hydrodynamics methods [3] and coupling continuum and atomistic models via AMR to increase the range of applicability of those models. Other efforts combine structured AMR with embedded boundary methods or overlapping grids to treat problems with complex geometries. We highlight a few recent developments and discuss new research issues they raise.

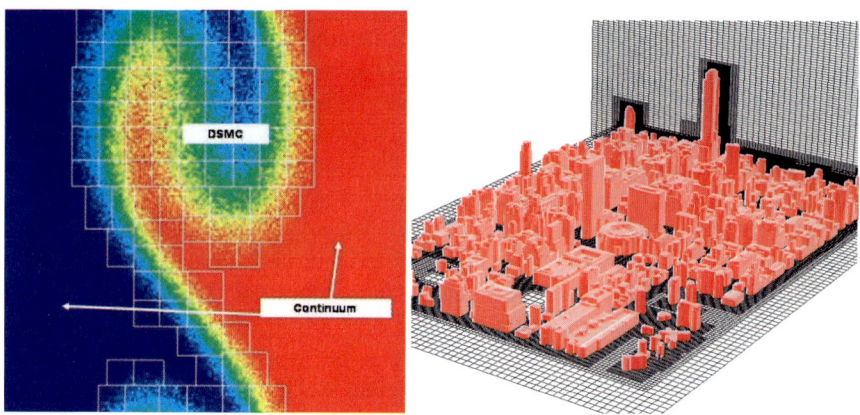

Figure 8.7. *Examples of new AMR applications. The left image shows a continuum-atomistic hybrid coupling using AMR [65]. The right image shows an embedded boundary SAMR mesh around buildings in Manhattan used for flows in urban environments [41].*

Traditionally, AMR has been used to increase grid resolution for numerical methods based on continuum equations. However, many continuum models lack key physical processes that occur at fine scales and which are most accurately modeled using atomistic methods. However, atomistic schemes are often too expensive to apply globally in a computation. AMR techniques can be used to focus the application of atomistic methods in regions where they are needed [30, 65, 57]. The image on the left in Figure 8.7 illustrates an approach in which a continuum fluid model is coupled to a direct simulation Monte Carlo (DSMC) model using AMR to resolve molecular diffusion along a multifluid interface.

Another avenue of development that is being applied to problems in aerospace, geophysics, biology, and others combines AMR with embedded boundaries [52, 1, 48, 46]. These methods provide a viable alternative to unstructured and mapped grid methods for applications involving complex geometries. The image on the right in Figure 8.7 shows an adaptive embedded boundary grid around a complex cityscape used for atmospheric calculations. Another technique for treating complex geometries with structured grids is to combine AMR with overlapping curvilinear grids [34]. This approach yields an accurate boundary representation similar to unstructured grids yet allows structured grid numerical methods to accurately resolve features near the boundaries. Recently, this approach has been used to solve reactive flows in engineering geometries [33].

Apart from numerical challenges, these and other new applications of AMR technology add new considerations for parallel computing. For example, continuum-particle hybrid methods combine irregular particle data structures and standard array-based data, and embedded boundary methods employ additional data in grid regions near the boundary. These approaches introduce additional complexity for dynamic load balancing, due to spatially *nonuniform* workloads, and parallel data communication. Traditionally, many load balancing schemes have assumed that the amount of work required to update the solution in each grid cell is uniform over the entire grid. However, the number of particles associated with a grid cell in an atomistic method typically varies based on local physics. Also, embedded boundary methods require extra numerical operations near boundaries to update the solution. New strategies for balancing nonuniform workloads are being developed to treat these issues. The unstructured grid research community has developed a number of useful schemes for partitioning nonuniform workloads, including those from continuum-particle methods [21], and these techniques may prove useful for structured grid partitioning strategies.

8.4.2 Software interoperability

As applications and algorithms become increasingly complex, there is a growing need to combine tools developed by different groups into a single application code. Most of the tools for parallel adaptive mesh refinement highlighted in section 8.1 fall into the *software framework* category as they provide an overarching infrastructure for AMR computations. Application scientists must adopt the entire framework to take advantage of the meshing services provided. A drawback of this approach is that it can be difficult to incorporate new or complementary tools developed outside the framework or to experiment with different approaches to determine which is best suited for a given application. In general, interchanging meshing technologies, or combining different technologies together, is often a labor-intensive and error-prone process that results in a lengthy diversion from the central scientific investigation.

The recognition of this fundamental problem has led several groups to develop the technologies needed to create interoperable and interchangeable *software components* for scientific computing. Components interact with each other only through well-defined interfaces and are a logical means of facilitating the development of complex applications using software developed by independent groups. Three of the most notable examples of scientific component development are the Cactus Code group [32], the Common Component Architecture Forum [20], and the Terascale Simulation Tools and Technologies (TSTT) DOE SciDAC center [31]. The former two develop general environments for software components for scientific computing; the latter effort is focused on the development of meshing and discretization components, and we highlight that effort here.

The TSTT data model covers a broad spectrum of mesh types and functionalities, ranging from a nonoverlapping, connected set of entities to a collection of meshes that may or may not overlap to cover the computational domain. A key aspect of the TSTT approach is that it does not enforce any particular data structure or implementation within the components, only that certain questions about the mesh data can be answered through calls to the component interface. The challenges inherent in this type of effort include balancing performance of the interface with the flexibility needed to support a wide variety of mesh types. Using these mesh component interfaces, TSTT researchers have developed new hybrid AMR technologies such as SAMR/front-tracking algorithms used in diesel jet spray breakup simulations and astrophysics calculations and insertable, parallel UAMR libraries used in accelerator design.

8.4.3 Scalability

AMR codes have shown that they scale effectively to $O(1,000)$ processors, as previously discussed. In particular, AMR is generally considered to be effective on cluster-based parallel systems in common use today. However, considerable challenges exist for AMR application development to utilize new large-scale parallel architectures such as the IBM BlueGene/L at Lawrence Livermore National Laboratory and the Cray Red Storm at Sandia National Laboratory. These platforms have at least an order of magnitude more processors (30,000 to 120,000), with less memory per processor, than systems in routine use today. Algorithms used to dynamically load balance adaptive applications will have to be extended to efficiently operate on these larger processor systems. At the same time, current data decompositions used to maintain adaptive grid structures will no longer be acceptable within the small amount of memory available.

As AMR researchers begin to address scaling on ever-larger parallel computer systems, it is likely that technologies and algorithms from different AMR methodologies will merge. For example, researchers have developed data structures based on graphs and trees, typically used in tree-based and unstructured AMR, to better manage spatial locality in patch-based AMR [68]. These schemes have significantly improved the efficiency and scaling of communication operations on AMR grids. Other graph-based partitioning algorithms, which have traditionally been used in unstructured AMR, are being explored for tree-based SAMR [59]. These examples show that algorithms developed for one AMR approach can be used to improve the performance of another. The ultimate challenge for both SAMR and UAMR methods will be to achieve the high degree of scalability necessary to take full advantage of a new generation of massively parallel computers.

8.5 Conclusions

AMR methods have proved to be a powerful technique for scientific simulations whose solutions exhibit dynamic, localized features. Two broadly defined approaches, SAMR and UAMR, have developed their own set of algorithms and computational techniques. However, with the increasing availability of high-performance parallel computers, there is significant interest in the development of interoperable parallel algorithms and software to support these AMR methods.

In this chapter we have reviewed the state of the art for both parallel SAMR and UAMR algorithms and existing software implementations. One of the most interesting current areas of research in these algorithms has been the crossover of partitioning techniques commonly used for UAMR methods to the SAMR community. With the use of large numbers (thousands) of processors, the development of methods that are scalable for such machines is essential. A final important area of work has been to develop interoperable software as exemplified by the SciDAC TTST project. As scientists consider more complex multiscale, multiphysics simulations, the ability to coordinate software efforts with this sort of interoperability will become increasingly more important.

Acknowledgments

This work was performed under the auspices of the U.S. Department of Energy by University of California Lawrence Livermore National Laboratory Contract W-7405-Eng-48 and is released under UCRL-JRNL-210250. This work was partially supported by NSF Grants DGE-9987589, CTS-0121573, EIA-0202007, and ACI-0305743.

Bibliography

[1] M. AFTOSMIS, J. MELTON, AND M. BERGER, *Adaptation and surface modeling for cartesian mesh methods*, in Proceedings of the 12th AIAA Computational Fluid Dynamics Conference, San Diego, CA, 1995. AIAA Paper 95-1725.

[2] A. ALMGREN, J. BELL, P. COLELLA, L. HOWELL, AND M. WELCOME, *A conservative adaptive projection method for the variable density incompressible Navier-Stokes equations*, Journal of Computational Physics, 142 (1998), pp. 1–46.

[3] R. W. ANDERSON, N. S. ELLIOTT, AND R. B. PEMBER, *An arbitrary Lagrangian-Eulerian method with adaptive mesh refinement for the solution of the Euler equations*, Journal of Computational Physics, 199 (2004), pp. 598–617.

[4] I. BABUŠKA AND W. C. RHEINBOLDT, *Error estimates for adaptive finite element computations*, SIAM Journal of Numerical Analysis, 15 (1978), pp. 736–754.

[5] S. B. BADEN, *The KeLP programming system*. See http://www-cse.ucsd.edu/groups/hpcl/scg/kelp.html.

[6] R. E. BANK, A. H. SHERMAN, AND A. WEISER, *Refinement algorithms and data structures for regular local mesh refinement*, in Scientific Computing, R. Stepleman et al., ed., IMACS/North-Holland Publishing Company, Amsterdam, 1983, pp. 3–17.

[7] R. E. BANK, *PLTMG: A Software Package for Solving Elliptic Partial Differential Equations. Users' Guide 8.0*, SIAM, Philadelphia, 1998.

[8] W. J. BARRY, M. T. JONES, AND P. E. PLASSMANN, *Parallel adaptive mesh refinement techniques for plasticity problems*, Advances in Engineering Software, 29 (1998), pp. 217–229.

[9] J. B. BELL, M. S. DAY, C. A. RENDLEMAN, S. E. WOOSLEY, AND M. A. ZINGALE, *Adaptive low mach number simulations of nuclear flame microphysics*, Journal of Computational Physics, 195 (2004), pp. 677–694.

[10] J. B. BELL, M. S. DAY, I. G. SHEPHERD, M. JOHNSON, R. K. CHENG, V. E. BECKNER, M. J. LIJEWSKI, AND J. F. GRCAR, *Numerical simulation of a laboratory-scale turbulent v-flame*, Tech. Report LBNL-54198, Lawrence Berkeley National Laboratory, Berkeley, CA, 2003.

[11] J. BELL AND C. RENDLEMAN, *CCSE Application Suite*. http://seesar.lbl.gov/CCSE/Software/index.html.

[12] M. J. BERGER AND J. OLIGER, *Adaptive mesh refinement for hyperbolic partial differental equations*, Journal of Computational Physics, (1984), pp. 484–512.

[13] M. BERGER AND P. COLELLA, *Local adaptive mesh refinement for shock hydrodynamics*, Journal of Computational Physics, 82 (1989), pp. 64–84.

[14] M. W. BERN AND P. E. PLASSMANN, *Mesh generation*, in Handbook of Computational Geometry, J. Sack and J. Urrutia, eds., Elsevier Scientific, 2000, pp. 291–332.

[15] E. BOMAN, K. DEVINE, R. HEAPHY, B. HENDRICKSON, W. MITCHELL, M. ST. JOHN, AND C. VAUGHAN, *Zoltan home page.* http://www.cs.sandia.gov/Zoltan (1999).

[16] F. J. BOSSEN AND P. S. HECKBERT, *A pliant method for anisotropic mesh generation*, in 5th Intl. Meshing Roundtable, Pittsburgh, PA, Oct. 1996, pp. 63–74. http://www.cs.cmu.edu/~ph.

[17] G. L. BRYAN, T. ABEL, AND M. L. NORMAN, *Achieving extreme resolution in numerical cosmology using adaptive mesh refinement: Resolving primordial star formation*, in Proceedings of the 2001 ACM/IEEE conference on Supercomputing (CD-ROM), Denver, CO, 2001.

[18] A. C. CALDER, B. C. CURTIS, L. J. DURSI, B. FRYXELL, G. HENRY, P. MACNEICE, K. OLSON, P. RICKER, R. ROSNER, F. X. TIMMES, H. M. TUFO, J. W. TURAN, AND M. ZINGALE, *High performance reactive fluid flow simulations using adaptive mesh refinement on thousands of processors*, in Proc. Supercomputing '00, IEEE, Los Alamitos, CA, 2000.

[19] C. A. RENDLEMAN, V. E. BECKNER, AND M. LIJEWSKI, *Parallelization of an adaptive mesh refinement method for low mach number*, in Proceedings of the International Conference on Computational Science, Springer-Verlag, London, UK, 2001, pp. 1117–1126.

[20] *Common Component Architecture (CCA) Forum homepage*, 2004. http://www.cca-forum.org/.

[21] J.-R. C. CHENG AND P. E. PLASSMANN, *A parallel algorithm for the dynamic partitioning of particle-mesh computational systems*, in Computational Science — ICCS 2002, The Springer Verlag Lecture Notes in Computer Science (LNCS 2331) Series, Springer, 2002, pp. 1020–1029.

[22] P. COLELLA, D. GRAVES, T. LIGOCKI, D. MARTIN, D. SERAFINI, AND B. V. STRAALEN, *Chombo software package for amr applications design document*, report, Applied Numerical Algorithms Group, NERSC Division, Lawrence Berkeley National Laboratory, Berkeley, CA, September 2003. http://seesar.lbl.gov/ANAG/chombo/index.html.

[23] M. S. DAY AND J. B. BELL, *Numerical simulation of laminar reacting flows with complex chemistry*, Combustion Theory and Modelling, 4 (2000), pp. 535–556.

[24] M. R. DORR, F. X. GARAIZAR, AND J. A. F. HITTINGER, *Simulation of laser plasma filamentation using adaptive mesh refinement*, Journal of Computational Physics, 177 (2002), pp. 233–263.

[25] J. E. FLAHERTY, R. M. LOY, M. S. SHEPHARD, B. K. SZYMANSKI, J. D. TERESCO, AND L. H. ZIANTZ, *Adaptive local refinement with octree load-balancing for the parallel solution of three-dimensional conservation laws*, Journal of Parallel and Distributed Computing, 47 (1997), pp. 139–152.

[26] J. E. FLAHERTY, R. M. LOY, M. S. SHEPHARD, B. K. SZYMANSKI, J. D. TERESCO, AND L. H. ZIANTZ, *Predictive load balancing for parallel adaptive finite element computation*, in Proceeding of PDPTA '97, vol. I, H. R. Arabnia, ed., Las Vegas, NV, 1997, pp. 460–469.

[27] L. FREITAG AND C. OLLIVIER-GOOCH, *Tetrahedral mesh improvement using face swapping and smoothing*, International Journal for Numerical Methods in Engineering, 40 (1997), pp. 3979–4002.

[28] B. FRYXELL, K. OLSON, P. RICKER, F. X. TIMMES, M. ZINGALE, D. Q. LAMB, P. MACNEICE, R. ROSNER, J. W. TRURAN, AND H. TUFO, *FLASH: An adaptive mesh hydrodynamics code for modeling astrophysical thermonuclear flashes*, Astrophysical Journal Supplement, 131 (2000), pp. 273–334.

[29] F. X. GARAIZAR AND J. TRANGENSTEIN, *Adaptive mesh refinement and front-tracking for shear bands in an antiplane shear flow*, SIAM Journal on Scientific Computing, 20 (1999), pp. 750–779.

[30] A. L. GARCIA, J. B. BELL, W. Y. CRUTCHFIELD, AND B. J. ALDER, *Adaptive mesh and algorithm refinement*, Journal of Computational Physics, 154 (1999), pp. 134–155.

[31] J. GLIMM, D. BROWN, AND L. FREITAG, *Terascale Simulation Tools and Technology (TSTT) Center*, 2001. http://www.tstt-scidac.org.

[32] T. GOODALE, G. ALLEN, G. LANFERMANN, J. MASSO, T. RADKE, E. SEIDEL, AND J. SHALF, *The cactus framework and toolkit: Design and applications*, in Vector and Parallel Processing—VECPAR 2002, 5th International Conference, Lecture Notes in Computer Science, Springer, New York, 2002.

[33] W. D. HENSHAW AND D. W. SCHWENDEMAN, *An adaptive numerical scheme for high-speed reactive flow on overlapping grids*, Journal of Computational Physics, 191 (2003), pp. 420–447.

[34] W. D. HENSHAW, *Overture: An object-oriented framework for overlapping grid applications*, in Proceedings of the 32nd American Institute for Aeronautics Fluid Dynamics, St. Louis, MO, June 24–27, 2002. See also http://www.llnl.gov/CASC/Overture.

[35] R. D. HORNUNG AND S. R. KOHN, *Managing application complexity in the samrai object-oriented framework*, Concurrency and Computation: Practice and Experience, 14 (2002), pp. 347–368. See also http://www.llnl.gov/CASC/SAMRAI.

[36] L. H. HOWELL AND J. GREENOUGH, *Radiation diffusion for multi-fluid eulerian hydrodynamics with adaptive mesh refinement*, Journal of Computational Physics, 184 (2003), pp. 53–78.

[37] S. JINDAL, L. LONG, AND P. PLASSMANN, *Large eddy simulations for complex geometries using unstructured grids*, in Proceedings of the 34th AIAA Fluid Dynamics Conference, Portland, OR, 2004. AIAA Paper 2004-2228.

[38] M. T. JONES AND P. E. PLASSMANN, *Adaptive refinement of unstructured finite-element meshes*, Finite Elements in Analysis and Design, 25 (1997), pp. 41–60.

[39] ———, *Parallel algorithms for adaptive mesh refinement*, SIAM Journal on Scientific Computing, 18 (1997), pp. 686–708.

[40] R. KLEIN, J. BELL, R. PEMBER, AND T. KELLEHER, *Three dimensional hydrodynamic calculations with adaptive mesh refinement of the evolution of Rayleigh Taylor and Richtmyer Meshkov instabilities in converging geometry: Multi-mode perturbations*, in Proceedings of the 4th International Workshop on Physics of Compressible Turbulent Mixing, Cambridge, England, March 1993.

[41] B. KOSOVIC, A. WISSINK, AND R. HORNUNG, *Integrated urban dispersion modeling capability*, in Proc. of 84th Annual American Meteorological Society Meeting (AMS04), Seattle, WA, Jan. 11–15, 2004.

[42] Z. LAN, V. TAYLOR, AND G. BRYAN, *Dynamic load balancing for adaptive mesh refinement applications: Improvements and sensitivity analysis*, Computer Physics Communications, 126 (2000), pp. 330–354.

[43] A. LIU AND B. JOE, *Quality local refinement of tetrahedral meshes based on bisection*, SIAM Journal on Scientific Computing, 16 (1995), pp. 1269–1291.

[44] R. LÖHNER, *An adaptive finite element scheme for transient problems in CFD*, Computer Methods in Applied Mechanics and Engineering, 61 (1987), pp. 323–338.

[45] P. MACNEICE, K. M. OLSON, C. MOBARRY, R. DEFAINCHTEIN, AND C. PACKER, *Paramesh: A parallel adaptive mesh refinement community toolkit*, Computer Physics Communications, 126 (2000), pp. 330–354. See http://www.physics.drexel.edu/~olson/paramesh-doc/Users_manual/amr.html.

[46] P. MCCORQUODALE, P. COLELLA, AND H. JOHANSEN, *A cartesian grid embedded boundary method for the heat equation on irregular domains*, Journal of Computational Physics, 173 (2001), pp. 620–635.

[47] W. F. MITCHELL, *A comparison of adaptive refinement techniques for elliptic problems*, ACM Transactions on Mathematical Software, 15 (1989), pp. 326–347.

[48] D. MODIANO AND P. COLELLA, *A higher-order embedded boundary method for time-dependent simulation of hyperbolic conservation laws*, in Proceedings of the ASME 2000 Fluids Engineering Division Summer Meeting, Boston, MA, June 2000. ASME Paper FEDSM00-11220.

[49] M. PARASHAR AND J. C. BROWNE, *System engineering for high performance computing software: The hdda/dagh infrastructure for implementation of parallel structured adaptive mesh refinement*, in IMA Volume on Structured Adaptive Mesh Refinement Grid Methods, 2000, pp. 1–18.

[50] ———, *On partitioning dynamic adaptive grid hierarchies*, in Proceedings of the 29th Annual Hawaii International Conference on System Sciences, Maui, HI, January, 1996, IEEE Computer Society Press, pp. 604–613.

[51] M. PARASHAR, *GrACE–Grid Adaptive Computational Engine*. See http://www.caip.rutgers.edu/TASSL/.

[52] R. PEMBER, J. BELL, P. COLELLA, W. CRUTCHFIELD, AND M. WELCOME, *An adaptive cartesian grid method for unsteady compressible flow in irregular regions*, Journal of Computational Physics, 120 (1995), pp. 278–304.

[53] R. PROPP, P. COLELLA, W. CRUTCHFIELD, AND M. DAY, *A numerical model for trickle-bed reactors*, Journal of Computational Physics, 165 (2000), pp. 311–333.

[54] J.-F. REMACLE AND M. SHEPHARD, *An algorithm oriented mesh database*, International Journal for Numerical Methods in Engineering, 58 (2003), pp. 349–374.

[55] M.-C. RIVARA AND C. LEVIN, *A 3-D refinement algorithm suitable for adaptive and multigrid techniques*, Communications in Applied Numerical Methods, 8 (1992), pp. 281–290.

[56] M.-C. RIVARA, *Algorithms for refining triangular grids suitable for adaptive and multigrid techniques*, International Journal for Numerical Methods in Engineering, 20 (1984), pp. 745–756.

[57] R. E. RUDD AND J. Q. BROUGHTON, *Concurrent coupling of length scales in solid state systems*, Physica Status Solidi B, 217 (2000), p. 251.

[58] K. SCHLOEGEL, G. KARYPIS, AND V. KUMAR, *ParMETIS*, 1999. See http://www-users.cs.umn.edu/\~karypis/metis/parmetis/index.html.

[59] J. STEENSLAND, S. CHANDRA, AND M. PARASHAR, *An application centric characterization of domain-based sfc partitioners for parallel samr*, IEEE Transactions on Parallel and Distributed Systems, (2002), pp. 1275–1289.

[60] M. SUSSMAN, A. ALMGREN, J. BELL, P. COLELLA, L. HOWELL, AND M. WELCOME, *An adaptive level set approach for incompressible two-phase flows*, Journal of Computational Physics, 148 (1999), pp. 81–124.

[61] J. D. TERESCO, M. W. BEALL, J. E. FLAHERTY, AND M. S. SHEPHARD, *A hierarchical partition model for adaptive finite element computation*, Computer Methods in Applied Mechanics and Engineering, 184 (1998), pp. 269–285.

[62] J. A. TRANGENSTEIN, *Adaptive mesh refinement for wave propagation in nonlinear solids*, SIAM Journal on Scientific and Statistical Computing, 16 (1995), pp. 819–839.

[63] J. TRANGENSTEIN AND Z. BI, *Multi-scale iterative techniques and adaptive mesh refinement for flow in porous media*, Advances in Water Resources, 25 (2002), pp. 1175–1213.

[64] H. E. TREASE, L. L. TREASE, AND J. D. FOWLER, *The P3D Code Development Project*. See http://www.emsl.pnl.gov/nwgrid/.

[65] H. S. WIJESINGHE, R. D. HORNUNG, A. L. GARCIA, AND N. G. HADJICONSTANTINOU, *3-dimensional hybrid continuum-atomistic simulations for multiscale hydrodynamics*, Journal of Fluids Engineering, 126 (2004), pp. 768–777.

[66] R. WILLIAMS, *DIME: Distributed Irregular Mesh Environment*, California Institute of Technology, Pasadena, CA, 1990.

[67] ———, *A dynamic solution-adaptive unstructured parallel solver*, Report CCSF-21-92, Caltech Concurrent Supercomputing Facilities, California Institute of Technology, Pasadena, CA, 1992.

[68] A. M. WISSINK, D. HYSOM, AND R. D. HORNUNG, *Enhancing scalability of parallel structured AMR calculations*, in Proceedings of the 17th ACM International Conference on Supercomputing (ICS03), San Francisco, June 2003, pp. 336–347.

Chapter 9
Parallel Sparse Solvers, Preconditioners, and Their Applications

Esmond G. Ng

Systems of linear equations arise at the heart of many scientific and engineering applications. Their solutions often dominate the execution times. The coefficient matrices of these linear systems are often sparse; that is, most of the matrix entries are zeros. For realistic modeling and simulations, the linear systems are very large; some have millions of unknowns. As technology advances, there is a greater demand for extremely high-fidelity simulations. Consequently the systems are becoming even larger than before. To solve them, it is essential to exploit sparsity. Moreover, parallel computing is an essential tool with which to reduce the solution times and, in some cases, may offer the only possibility of solving the systems. There are two main classes of methods for solving sparse linear systems: direct methods and iterative methods. As we will see later, hybrid methods that combine direct and iterative schemes are gaining popularity.

This chapter will sample some of the most recent work on the parallel solution of large sparse linear systems. Section 9.1 deals with issues in parallel sparse direct methods and section 9.2 discusses advances in iterative methods and preconditioning techniques. Hybrid methods that combine techniques in sparse direct methods and iterative schemes are considered in section 9.3. Section 9.4 surveys recent activities on expert systems on sparse matrix computation. Finally, we conclude in section 9.5 with some applications of sparse matrix computations.

9.1 Sparse direct methods

Direct methods, based on triangular factorizations, have provided the most robust and reliable means for solving sparse systems of linear equations $Ax = b$. The solutions are obtained after a finite number of operations. Fill is generally introduced into the factors during the factorization. That is, some entries that correspond to zeros in A become nonzero.

Managing fill during factorization is probably as important as designing efficient algorithms for performing the factorization. The solution process generally consists of three phases: analysis, factorization, and triangular solution. A good introduction to sparse matrix factorization can be found in [22, 30]. During the analysis phase, the matrix is analyzed to determine a (tentative) pivot sequence and perhaps set up the appropriate data structures required for the numerical factorization. This may involve permuting (or ordering) the rows and/or columns of the matrix, as well as constructing tools (such as elimination trees [45, 63] and assembly trees [25]) for efficient numerical factorization. Depending on the characteristics of the matrix, the analysis can be entirely symbolic (e.g., for symmetric positive definite matrices) or can rely on both symbolic and numeric information (e.g., for general unsymmetric matrices). During the numerical factorization, the information from the analysis is used in computing the factors L and U, where L is lower triangular and U is upper triangular. Modifications to the pivot sequence may be needed to maintain numerical stability. The final phase uses the triangular factors to compute the solution to the linear systems. Iterative refinement may be used to improve accuracy.

Permuting the rows and columns during the analysis phase is combinatorial in nature. It often involves graph algorithms, which is the subject of Chapter 7. The numerical factorization is often the most time-consuming step. Consequently, it was the first task that was tackled when parallel computing became available. There is a lot of structure in the triangular factorization. In particular, it is often the case that some consecutive rows and columns of the triangular factors have similar sparsity structures.[1] (This can happen because of fill and in finite-element applications, for example, where there is more than one variable at each node.) Such a group of rows or columns is often referred to as a supernode [6, 46]. The use of supernodes allows dense matrix kernels to be exploited. State-of-the-art sparse direct solvers use Level 3 BLAS [18] and LAPACK [4] routines as much as possible. Once a triangular factorization has been computed, the third phase is relatively straightforward. In a parallel setting, triangular solutions are communication bound; the amount of communication is high compared to the number of floating-point operations required, particularly when solving for a single (or small number of) right-hand sides. As the performance of parallel numerical factorization algorithms improves, parallel sparse triangular solutions can become the bottleneck, particularly when a sequence of right-hand sides has to be solved.

9.1.1 Parallel sparse matrix factorizations

While there has been significant progress in the improvement of the performance of parallel sparse matrix factorizations over the years, sparse direct methods have been less popular for large-scale applications than iterative methods. One reason is the large storage requirement of the numerical factorization phase. Another is the amount of communication required by parallel factorizations. The communication overhead depends, to a large extent, on how the work is partitioned and assigned to the processors.

Li, Grigori, and Wang [35, 48] have recently carried out a careful study of the numerical factorization phase of SuperLU_DIST [47], a state-of-the-art direct solver for sparse

---
[1]Sparsity structure of a matrix refers to the locations of the nonzero elements in the matrix.

unsymmetric systems. The L and U factors are represented in SuperLU_DIST as 2D block matrices and are distributed in a 2D block-cyclic fashion on a 2D process grid. By examining the sparsity structure of L and U, and the communication pattern of the algorithm, Li and others have derived a theoretical bound on the parallel efficiency of the algorithm. They have demonstrated that this bound can be used to predict the performance for any sparse matrix, when the sparseness is measured with respect to the underlying machine parameters, such as floating-point speed, network latency, and bandwidth. The theoretical efficiency bound may be used to determine the most critical hardware parameters that need to be improved to enhance performance for the class of problems under consideration.

Li, Grigori, and Wang analyzed the efficiency of SuperLU_DIST using increasing numbers of processors with increasing problem sizes. They concluded that for matrices satisfying a certain relation between their size and their memory requirements (namely, workload F proportional to $nnz(L+U)^{3/2}$),[2] the factorization algorithm is scalable with respect to memory use. This relation is satisfied by matrices arising from 3D model problems. For these problems, the efficiency is essentially constant when the number of processors increases while the memory requirement per processor is constant. However, for 2D model problems, the algorithm does not scale with respect to memory use. Li, Grigori, and Wang validated their results on an IBM Power3 parallel machine at the National Energy Research Scientific Computing Center (NERSC). It appears that load imbalance and an insufficient work relative to the communication overhead are the main sources of inefficiency on a large number of processors.

In a separate study, Guermouche and L'Excellent [36] considered memory requirements in a parallel implementation of a multifrontal algorithm [25]. They distinguished between storage for the factors (referred to as static) and that for the frontal matrices and the contribution blocks (referred to as dynamic). The static storage grows as the factorization proceeds, while the size of the dynamic storage varies depending on the structure of the assembly tree. In the factorization of a frontal matrix, processors are selected based on their current memory usage. In addition, Guermouche and L'Excellent have taken memory usage into consideration when parallel tasks are scheduled. They have demonstrated that overall memory requirements can be improved using a combination of task distribution and management strategies, without greatly degrading the factorization times.

Another factor that affects the performance of sparse matrix factorization is data mapping. It is well known that parallelism can be identified using a tree structure (e.g., an elimination tree for Cholesky factorization [45, 63] and an assembly tree for multifrontal methods [25]). The *proportional heuristic* [55, 57], which is a generalization of the subtree-to-subcube mapping [29], has typically been used to map the data and computation to processors. However, for sparse systems from finite-element methods on complex domains, the resulting assignments can exhibit significant load imbalances. Malkowski and Raghavan [50] developed a multipass mapping scheme to reduce such load imbalances. The multipass mapping scheme combines the proportional heuristic with refinement steps to adjust the loads on the processors. For a test suite of large sparse matrices, they demonstrated that the new mapping scheme is indeed effective in producing assignments that substantially improve the load balance among processors.

---

[2] $nnz(M)$ denotes the number of nonzeros in the matrix M.

9.1.2 Ordering to increase parallelism

It is well known that for sparse direct methods, the sparsity structure of the triangular factors depends drastically on the ordering of rows and columns [22, 30]. Much work has been done in developing fill-reducing orderings. Examples of fill-reducing ordering algorithms include the Markowitz scheme [51], the minimum degree algorithm [31, 58], and the nested dissection algorithm [32, 43].

It is generally believed that the sparser the triangular factors, the more independent the columns and rows, and hence the higher the degree of available parallelism. However, one can look at the ordering problem differently.

Duff and Scott [21] considered using graph partitioning techniques to permute a unsymmetric matrix A into a *singly bordered block diagonal* form,

$$A \to \begin{bmatrix} A_1 & & & & B_1 \\ & A_2 & & & B_2 \\ & & \ddots & & \vdots \\ & & & A_q & B_q \end{bmatrix},$$

where the diagonal blocks A_i, $1 \le i \le q$, need not be square. A sparse direct solver can be applied to the diagonal blocks A_i independently and in parallel. Since A_i is in general rectangular, its factorization leads to a lower trapezoidal factor and an upper triangular factor,

$$A_i = \begin{bmatrix} L_i \\ \tilde{L}_i \end{bmatrix} U_i,$$

where L_i is square and lower triangular. By putting $\tilde{L}_i U_i$, $1 \le i \le q$, together, one obtains the following partitioning of A:

$$A \to \begin{bmatrix} L_1 U_1 & & & & & C_1 \\ & L_2 U_2 & & & & C_2 \\ & & \ddots & & & \vdots \\ & & & L_q U_q & & C_q \\ \tilde{L}_1 U_1 & & & & & D_1 \\ & \tilde{L}_2 U_2 & & & & D_2 \\ & & \ddots & & & \vdots \\ & & & \tilde{L}_q U_q & & D_q \end{bmatrix}.$$

Here, each B_i, $1 \le i \le q$, has been partitioned according to the row dimensions of L_i and $\tilde{L}_i$. That is,

$$B_i = \begin{bmatrix} C_i \\ D_i \end{bmatrix}.$$

This is termed a *stabilized doubly bordered block diagonal* form. The border is larger than that for a doubly bordered form obtained directly using a graph partitioning algorithm, but the key advantage is that pivots are chosen stably from the diagonal blocks. For efficiency, it is desirable for B_i to have as few columns as possible and to be of a similar size. This is a combinatorial problem. Duff and Scott [21] developed a number of coarse-grained parallel direct solvers based on preordering A to bordered form. These are available in the HSL mathematical software library [24].

9.1.3 Out-of-core methods

One of the primary reasons why sparse direct methods may not be popular among extremely large-scale applications is the amount of storage required for the fill in the triangular factors. A number of codes are available that aim to alleviate the storage bottleneck by incorporating out-of-core techniques [26, 44]. These involve writing part of the matrix factors that have been computed but no longer needed during the factorization to secondary storage (e.g., disks). Only a small portion of the matrix factors is kept in the main memory. As a result, the main memory requirement can be much reduced. Almost all out-of-core implementations have been based on frontal and multifrontal methods [25, 40]. Oblio, an object-oriented library for solving sparse linear systems of equations by direct methods designed and developed by Dobrian and Pothen [17], is designed to handle memory accesses at two levels: in-core and out-of-core. At the in-core level the supernodal nature of the computation provides support for Level 3 dense linear algebra kernels. Most of the time these kernels translate directly into BLAS/LAPACK [4, 18] calls but there are few cases that need to be customized using recursion or blocking. At the out-of-core level, Oblio can store the matrix factors on disk.

9.2 Iterative methods and preconditioning techniques

An iterative method for solving a linear system is based on the generation of a sequence of approximations to the solution. Whether the sequence will converge to the solution depends a great deal on the matrix, the starting guess, and the choice of iterative method. There are many iterative schemes available. Conjugate gradient (CG), minimal residual (MINRES), generalized minimal residual (GMRES), biconjugate gradient (BCG), conjugate gradient squared (CGS), biconjugate gradient stabilized (BiCGSTAB), quasi-minimal residual (QMR), and Chebyshev iteration are some of the most popular schemes [61, 67].

Iterative methods are very popular in large-scale applications because their storage requirements are not as severe as those in sparse direct methods. In most cases, just the original matrix and a few vectors need be stored; there is no fill to worry about. Moreover, the kernels are mostly inner products and sparse matrix-vector multiplications, which are easier to implement and parallelize than sparse direct methods. However, there are few operations to perform so that the efficiency of parallel iterative methods tends to be poor.

The spectral properties of the iteration matrix play a very important role in the rate of convergence. One can change the spectral properties by *preconditioning* the linear system. More specifically, instead of solving $Ax = b$, one can solve

$$PAQQ^{-1}x = Pb,$$

where P and Q are referred to as the left and right preconditioners, respectively. Constructing good preconditioners has been the subject of much research during the last decade.

There are many possibilities. Well-known ones include Jacobi, SSOR, incomplete factorization, approximate inverses, and multilevel preconditioning [61, 67]. The incorporation of the preconditioning step complicates the implementation somewhat but can potentially significantly improve the convergence rate and may be the only way that convergence can be achieved.

9.2.1 Improving the performance of iterative solvers

Matrix-vector multiplication is an important part of many iterative solvers. Its implementation can drastically affect the performance of an entire iterative solver. For sparse problems, this kernel has very little data reuse and a high ratio of memory operations to floating-point operations. Recently, Kaushik and Gropp [41] analyzed the performance based on memory bandwidth, instruction issue rate, and the fraction of floating-point workload. Performance bounds based on these parameters provide a good estimate of achievable performance. To get better performance, they recommend multiplying the sparse matrix by more than one vector whenever possible. They compared the actual performance of this kernel with the derived performance bounds on scalar processors and a vector processor (a Cray X1). They observed that the performance is memory bandwidth limited on most scalar and vector processors. Although memory bandwidth is huge on vector processors (as compared to most scalar machines), sparse matrix-vector multiplication is still memory bandwidth limited: they reported that only 23% of the machine peak is possible under ideal situations for the Cray X1. Similar work can be found in [39, 66, 68].

The work of Baker, Dennis, and Jessup [7] supports the finding of Kaushik and Gropp. Their work attempted to optimize the performance of iterative methods and is based on a variant of the GMRES algorithm, in which the standard Krylov subspace is augmented with approximations to the errors from previous restart cycles. They focused on a block implementation of this variant of GMRES that uses a multivector data structure. The use of this data structure allows groups of vectors to be interlaced together in memory. They examined the memory characteristics of the block variant of GMRES and found that the use of a multivector data structure reduces data movement versus a noninterlaced or conventional approach. The advantage of the multivector data structure is not limited to the matrix-vector multiplication but reduces data movement for all components of the iterative solver. They demonstrated using numerical experiments that reductions in data movement do lead to reductions in execution time

9.2.2 Preconditioning techniques

As noted, preconditioning is crucial for the convergence of iterative methods. Much of the research into iterative methods in recent years has focused on the development of efficient and robust preconditioning techniques. Saad and Hénon [59] proposed computing parallel incomplete LU factorizations in a hierarchical way. An incomplete factorization is basically an approximate factorization of the matrix, in which some of the fill entries in the exact factorization are discarded according to some prescribed criteria [52]. The parallel hierarchical interface decomposition algorithm (PHIDAL), proposed by Hénon and Saad, exploits Schur complements based on independent sets of interfaces. The idea is reminiscent of the so-called wirebasket techniques of domain decomposition [64]. It can also be considered as a variation and an extension of the parallel algebraic recursive multilevel solver (pARMS) of [49]. As the name implies, interfaces (or separators) are constructed in a hierarchical manner. Once the hierarchical interface decomposition is defined, the Gaussian elimination process proceeds by levels: nodes in the first level are eliminated first, followed by those in the second, and so on. Drop tolerance strategies are defined so as to limit fill. More specifically, any nonzero entries that are smaller than a prescribed drop tolerance will be discarded. Hénon and Saad reported that for systems arising from the solution of Poisson equations, the iteration and factorization times scale well by using up to 256 processors and are excellent for a more general unstructured problem.

9.2.3 Ordering for incomplete factorization

One of the most popular approaches to obtaining a preconditioner is to use an incomplete factorization of the original coefficient matrix. As in direct methods, the ordering of the rows and columns can affect the number of fill entries that come up in an incomplete factorization. Since some of these fill entries are discarded, different row and column orderings will generally result in incomplete factors that can behave quite differently as preconditioners.

The most common way to order the rows and columns in an incomplete factorization is to preorder the coefficient matrix using ordering algorithms that have been designed to reduce fill in sparse direct methods (such as the Cuthill–McKee algorithm [13], the minimum degree algorithm [31, 58], and the nested dissection algorithm [32, 43]). Then incomplete factorization is applied to the preordered matrix.

In [53], Munksgaard ordered the rows and columns of a symmetric matrix while he was computing the incomplete factorization. The ordering was based on the minimum degree heuristic. In [15, 16], D'Azevedo, Forsyth, and Tang investigated the use of greedy heuristics (such as minimum degree and minimum deficiency [65]) to order the rows and columns while computing the incomplete factorization. However, numerical information (such as the norm of the discarded fill) was incorporated into the metrics used to select the pivot row and pivot column at each step. While the quality of the resulting incomplete factors (as preconditioners) was quite good, the orderings were quite expensive to compute.

Recently, Lee, Raghavan, and Ng [42] considered an approach similar to Munksgaard's for computing incomplete Cholesky factorization. That is, the minimum degree algorithm and the numerical computation interleave throughout the factorization process. The minimum degree metric is applied to the sparsity pattern of the matrix resulted from incomplete Cholesky factorization. They refer to this as the *interleaved minimum degree* strategy. However, more sophisticated techniques are used to modify the diagonal when the matrix loses positive definiteness. Preliminary results have shown that the conjugate gradient iterations, the incomplete factors produced by the new schemes, often exhibit improved convergence.

9.3 Hybrids of direct and iterative techniques

A relatively new but promising area of research in the solution of sparse linear systems is to combine techniques developed for sparse direct methods and iterative methods. Most of the investigations so far have been focused on the exploitation of techniques developed for sparse direct methods in computing incomplete factorizations. In particular, Ng and Raghavan [54, 56] have considered the use of dense matrix kernels in incomplete Cholesky factorization. More specific, additional constraints are imposed so that dense submatrices are created in the incomplete Cholesky factors. Also, as mentioned in section 9.2.3, ordering techniques for sparse direct methods are often used in the context of computing incomplete factorization, which is then employed as preconditioners.

9.3.1 Applying direct and iterative strategies to partitioned matrices

The singly bordered block diagonal form introduced in section 9.1.2 provides a different approach to the problem. Duff et al. [23] proposed combining direct and iterative methods to solve these large sparse unsymmetric equations. As in section 9.1.2, a direct method is used to partially factorize local rectangular systems. Since the Schur complement matrix is generally quite dense, it can be advantageous to apply an iterative method to solve the subsystem instead of using direct methods.

Another possibility currently being examined is extracting a block diagonal matrix from the bordered form

$$\begin{bmatrix} L_1 U_1 & & & & & & & \\ & L_2 U_2 & & & & & & \\ & & \ddots & & & & & \\ & & & L_q U_q & & & & \\ & & & & D_1 & & & \\ & & & & & D_2 & & \\ & & & & & & \vdots & \\ & & & & & & & D_q \end{bmatrix}$$

and using it as a preconditioner for an iterative scheme on the whole linear system. The advantage is that the matrix $D^T = \begin{bmatrix} D_1^T & D_2^T & \ldots & D_q^T \end{bmatrix}$ should be sparser than the Schur complement matrix. However, D can be singular, so some modifications may be needed to obtain a stable factorization of D.

9.3.2 Mixing direct and iterative methods

Nonoverlapping domain decomposition is a classical approach to solving large-scale PDE problems on parallel distributed computers. This technique often leads to a reduced linear system defined on the interface between the subdomains. Giraud, Mulligan, and Rioual [34] recently considered iterative as well as direct solution techniques that exploit features of the MUMPS package [3]. Their block preconditioner consists of assembling the local Schur complement matrices associated with each subdomain and can be viewed as an additive Schwarz preconditioner. Efficient implementation relies on the capability of MUMPS to compute for each subdomain the local Schur complement matrix as well as the factorization of the local Dirichlet problem. The local Schur complement matrices are factorized by a final parallel application of MUMPS. This step uses the ability of MUMPS to process matrices given in a distributed format. Giraud, Mulligan, and Rioual also considered the solution of the original linear system defined on the complete domain (i.e., not only its restriction to the interface between the subdomains), again using a parallel application of MUMPS and its ability to handle distributed input matrices.

These approaches have been integrated into a mixed finite-element code for the simulation of semiconductor devices in two dimensions where the nonlinear equations are solved using a Newton–Raphson scheme. Experiments have been performed on up to 32 processors for the simulation of a mosfet device. Results show that the iterative approach outperforms a classical direct substructuring technique [33]. Preliminary results for 3D heterogeneous diffusion problems with 9×10^6 degrees of freedom also indicate good scalability of the iterative solver on up to 350 processors.

Another approach that is becoming popular is to add the capability of computing an incomplete factorization using a sparse direct solver. The incomplete factorization can be used as a preconditioner for solving a sparse linear system using an iterative method. The resulting package can be considered a hybrid approach for handling very large problems. An example can be found in PaStiX, a library for solving sparse linear systems on clusters of SMP nodes using supernodal algorithms [37, 38].

9.3.3 Row-projection methods

The block Cimmino method [5, 12, 27], which is a block row-projection method for the solution of large sparse general systems of equations, is another hybrid method. The rows of the system matrix A are first partitioned into blocks. The block Cimmino method projects the current iterate simultaneously onto the manifolds corresponding to the blocks of rows and then takes a convex combination of the resulting vectors.

Drummond [20, 19] investigated the choice of row partitionings. In particular, he considered two different preprocessing strategies that are applied to the matrix AA^T. The goal is to find permutations that transform AA^T into a matrix with a block tridiagonal structure. Doing this provides a natural partitioning of the linear system for row projection methods because these methods use the normal equations to compute their projections. Therefore, the resulting natural block partitioning should improve the rate of convergence of block row projection methods and as block Cimmino and block Kaczmarz. The first preprocessing strategy produces a two-block partition, which naturally induces parallelism and improves the convergence of the block Cimmino method. The second strategy works on matrices with narrower bands, resulting in more blocks that can be processed in parallel. While the latter strategy exploits parallel computing better and could deliver two-block partitions, it is also more dependent on the parameters used to narrow the band of the matrix, the sizes of the resulting blocks, and the interconnection mechanisms between the processing elements.

9.4 Expert approaches to solving sparse linear systems

From the above discussion, it is clear that many algorithms are available for solving sparse systems of linear equations. They come in different flavors: direct methods, iterative methods, and hybrids of the two. These methods represent different trade-offs with respect to metrics such as robustness, scalability, and execution time. Their performance can vary dramatically depending on the characteristics of a given linear system. Attempts are being made to develop expert approaches to ease the selection of methods and to improve the robustness of the solution process.

One such example is the Grid-TLSE project [2, 11]. The goal of the project is to provide one-stop shopping for users of sparse direct methods. To accomplish this goal, the project will maintain a collection of sparse direct solvers and test matrices, as well as a database of performance statistics. A user will be able to interrogate the database for information concerning the sparse direct solvers or matrices that are available in the collection. The user will also be able to perform comparative analysis of selected solvers using user-supplied matrices or specific matrices from the matrix collection available in the GRID-TLSE project.

Another example is the work of Bhowmick, Raghavan, and Teranishi [10]. The purpose of this project is to improve the performance of large-scale simulations. The authors have developed *adaptive* linear solvers, which use heuristics to select a solution method to cope with the changing characteristics of linear systems generated at different stages of an application. They have also developed *composite* linear solvers, which apply a sequence of methods to the same linear system to improve reliability. Preliminary experiments have demonstrated that both approaches can significantly decrease execution times in some nonlinear PDE-based simulations from computational fluid dynamics.

9.5 Applications

As we indicated, there is an abundance of applications that rely on sparse linear solvers. In many cases, the matrix can become very large because of the need to perform high-fidelity modeling and simulations. In this section, we consider two applications: circuit simulations and structural dynamics.

Circuit simulations give rise to very large sparse linear systems, which can be highly ill conditioned and therefore a challenge to solve. Recently, both direct and iterative methods of solution have been considered. Davis and Stanley [14] considered unsymmetrically permuting the matrices to upper triangular form, then applying a symmetric minimum degree algorithm is to the diagonal blocks, which are then factorized using a sparse LU factorization with numerical pivoting. Sosonkina and Saad have employed pARMS [49, 60], a suite of parallel iterative accelerators and multilevel preconditioners for the solution of general sparse linear systems, to solve circuit simulation problems. Partitioning techniques and local ordering strategies play an important role in the solution process. These techniques also are relevant in the work of Basermann et al. [8]. Incomplete LU factorizations [8] and approximate inverses [62] have also been used as preconditioners for iterative methods of solution.

Salinas [9], a massively parallel structural dynamics code developed at Sandia National Laboratories, is a big user of parallel sparse linear solvers. During the early development of Salinas, FETI-DP (dual-primal finite element tearing and interconnecting) [28] was the primary linear solver used. Within each domain, sparse direct solvers are employed. Iterative linear solvers are used to handle the interface variables. Recently, Salinas developers have implemented an abstract interface to linear solvers, which has opened the door to two additional iterative linear solver packages: Prometheus (an algebraic multigrid package) [1] and CLAPS (a multigrid solver developed by Clark Dohrmann at Sandia National Laboratories).

Acknowledgments

The author appreciates the input provided by Leroy Anthony Drummond, Luc Giraud, Laura Grigori, Dinesh Kaushik, Xiaoye Li, and Padma Raghavan. Without their input, it would have been impossible to put this overview together. The author also expresses special thanks to Iain Duff and Jennifer Scott, who read an early draft and provided much feedback to improve the presentation.

Bibliography

[1] M. F. ADAMS, *Multigrid Equation Solvers for Large Scale Nonlinear Finite Element Simulations*, Ph.D. dissertation, University of California, Berkeley, 1998.

[2] P. AMESTOY, I. DUFF, L. GIRAUD, J.-Y. L'EXCELLENT, AND C. PUGLISI, *Grid-tlse: A web site for experimenting with sparse direct solvers on a computational grid*, presented at the 11th SIAM Conference on Parallel Processing for Scientific Computing, San Francisco, CA, 2004.

[3] P. R. AMESTOY, I. S. DUFF, J.-Y. L'EXCELLENT, AND J. KOSTER, *A fully asynchronous multifrontal solver using distributed dynamic scheduling*, SIAM Journal on Matrix Analysis and Applications, 23 (2001), pp. 15–41.

[4] E. ANDERSON, Z. BAI, C. BISCHOF, S. BLACKFORD, J. DEMMEL, J. DONGARRA, J. DU CROZ, A. GREENBAUM, S. HAMMARLING, A. MCKENNEY, AND D. SORENSEN, *LAPACK Users' Guide, Third Edition*, SIAM, Philadelphia, 1999.

[5] M. ARIOLI, I. DUFF, J. NOAILLES, AND D. RUIZ, *Block cimmino and block ssor algorithms for solving linear systems in a parallel environment*, Tech. Report TR/89/11, CERFACS, Toulouse, France, 1989.

[6] C. ASHCRAFT, R. GRIMES, J. LEWIS, B. PEYTON, AND H. SIMON, *Progress in sparse matrix methods for large linear systems on vector supercomputers*, International Journal of Supercomputer Applications, 1 (1987), pp. 10–30.

[7] A. BAKER, J. DENNIS, AND E. JESSUP, *An efficient block variant of GMRES*. Technical Report CU-CS-957-03, Computer Science Department, University of Colorado, Boulder, CO, 2003.

[8] A. BASERMANN, I. JAEKEL, M. NORDHAUSEN, AND K. HACHIYA, *Parallel iterative solvers for sparse linear systems in circuit simulation*, Future Generation Comper. Systems, 21 (2005), pp. 1275–1284.

[9] M. BHARDWAJ, K. PIERSON, G. REESE, T. WALSH, D. DAY, K. ALVIN, J. PEERY, C. FARHAT, AND M. LESOINNE, *Salinas: A scalable software for high-performance*

structural and solid mechanics simulations, in Proc. Supercomputing, ACM, New York, 2002.

[10] S. BHOWMICK, P. RAGHAVAN, AND K. TERANISHI, *A combinatorial scheme for developing efficient composite solvers*, in Lecture Notes in Computer Science, P. Sloot, C. Tan, J. Dongarra, and A. Hoekstra, eds., vol. 2330 of Computational Science (Proc. ICCS 2002), Springer-Verlag, Berlin, New York, 2002.

[11] E. CARON, F. DESPREZ, M. DAYDÉ A. HURAULT, AND M. PANTEL, *On deploying scientific software within the grid-tlse project*, Lectures in Computing Letters, 1 (2005).

[12] G. CIMMINO, *Calcolo approssimato per le soluzioni dei sistemi di equaziono lineari*, La Ricerca Scientifica, II, 9 (1938), pp. 326–333.

[13] E. CUTHILL, *Several strategies for reducing bandwidth of matrices*, in Sparse Matrices and their Applications, D. J. Rose and R. A. Willoughby, eds., New York, 1972, Plenum Press.

[14] T. DAVIS AND K. STANLEY, *Sparse lu factorization of circuit simulation matrices*, presented at Eleventh SIAM Conference on Parallel Processing for Scientific Computing, San Francisco, CA, 2004.

[15] E. F. D'AZEVEDO, P. A. FORSYTH, AND W.-P. TANG, *Ordering methods for preconditioned conjugate gradients methods applied to unstructured grid problems*, SIAM J. Matrix Anal. Appl., 13 (1992), pp. 944–961.

[16] ———, *Towards a cost effective high order ilu preconditioner*, BIT, 32 (1992).

[17] F. DOBRIAN AND A. POTHEN, *OBLIO: Design and performance*, in State of the Art in Scientific Computing, Lecture Notes in Computer Science, 3732, J. Dongarra, K. Madsen, and J. Wasniewski, eds., Springer-Verlag, Berlin, New York, 2005, pp. 758–767.

[18] J. J. DONGARRA, J. D. CROZ, S. HAMMARLING, AND I. DUFF, *A set of level 3 Basic Linear Algebra Subprograms*, ACM Transactions on Mathematical Software, 16 (1990), pp. 1–17.

[19] L. DRUMMOND, I. DUFF, AND D. RUIZ, *Partitioning strategies for the block cimmino algorithm*, presented at the 11th SIAM Conference on Parallel Processing for Scientific Computing, San Francisco, CA, 2004.

[20] L. DRUMMOND, *Block iterative methods for the solution of large sparse linear systems in heterogenous distributed computing environments*, Ph.D. thesis, CERFACS, Toulouse, France, 1995.

[21] I. S. DUFF AND J. A. SCOTT, *Stabilized bordered block diagonal forms for parallel sparse solvers*, Parallel Computing, 31 (2005), pp. 275–289.

[22] I. DUFF, A. ERISMAN, AND J. K. REID, *Direct Methods for Sparse Matrices*, Oxford University Press, Oxford, UK, 1987.

[23] I. DUFF, G. GOLUB, J. SCOTT, AND F. KWOK, *Combining direct and iterative methods to solve partitioned linear systems*, presented at Eleventh SIAM Conference on Parallel Processing for Scientific Computing, San Francisco, CA, 2004.

[24] I. DUFF, R. GRIMES, AND J. LEWIS, *Sparse matrix test problems*, ACM Transactions on Mathematical Software, 15 (1989), pp. 1–14.

[25] I. DUFF AND J. REID, *The multifrontal solution of indefinite sparse symmetric linear equations*, ACM Transactions on Mathematical Software, 9 (1983), pp. 302–325.

[26] I. S. DUFF, *Design features of a frontal code for solving sparse unsymmetric linear systems out-of-core*, SIAM Journal on Scientific Computing, 5 (1984), pp. 270–280.

[27] T. ELFVING, *Block-iterative methods for consistent and inconsistent linear equations*, Numerical Mathematics, 35 (1980), pp. 1–12.

[28] C. FARHAT, M. LESOINNE, P. LETALLEC, K. PIERSON, AND D. RIXEN, *Feti-dp: a dual-primal unified feti method - part i: A faster alternative to the two-level feti method*, International Journal of Numerical Methods in Engineering, 50 (2001), pp. 1523–1544.

[29] A. GEORGE, J. W.-H. LIU, AND E. NG, *Communication results for parallel sparse Cholesky factorization on a hypercube*, Parallel Computing, 10 (1989), pp. 287–298.

[30] A. GEORGE AND J. W.-H. LIU, *Computer Solution of Large Sparse Positive Definite Systems*, Prentice-Hall Inc., Englewood Cliffs, NJ, 1981.

[31] ———, *The evolution of the minimum degree ordering algorithm*, SIAM Review, 31 (1989), pp. 1–19.

[32] A. GEORGE, *Nested dissection of a regular finite element mesh*, SIAM Journal on Numerical Analysis, 10 (1973), pp. 345–363.

[33] L. GIRAUD, A. MARROCCO, AND J. RIOUAL, *Iterative versus direct parallel substructuring methods in semiconductor device modelling*, Numerical Linear Algebra and Applications, 12 (2005), pp. 33–53.

[34] L. GIRAUD, S. MULLIGAN, AND J. RIOUAL, *Algebraic preconditioners for the solution of schur complement systems*, presented at the 11th SIAM Conference on Parallel Processing for Scientific Computing, San Francisco, CA, 2004.

[35] L. GRIGORI AND X. S. LI, *Performance analysis of parallel right-looking sparse lu factorization on two dimensional grids of processors*, in PARA'04 Workshop on State-of-the-art in Scientific Computing, June 20-23, 2004, Copenhagen, Denmark, 2004.

[36] A. GUERMOUCHE AND J.-Y. L'EXCELLENT, *Constructing memory-minimizing schedules for multifrontal methods*, ACM Transactions on Mathematical Software, 32 (2006), pp. 17–32.

[37] P. HÉNON, F. PELLEGRINI, P. RAMET, J. ROMAN, AND Y. SAAD, *High performance complete and incomplete factorizations for very large sparse systems by using Scotch and PaStiX softwares*, presented at the 11th SIAM Conference on Parallel Processing for Scientific Computing, San Francisco, CA, 2004.

[38] P. HÉNON, P. RAMET, AND J. ROMAN, *PaStiX: A High-Performance Parallel Direct Solver for Sparse Symmetric Definite Systems*, Parallel Computing, 28 (2002), pp. 301–321.

[39] E.-J. IM AND K. YELICK, *Optimizing sparse matrix computations for register reuse in SPARSITY*, Lecture Notes in Computer Science, 2073 (2001), pp. 127–136.

[40] B. IRONS, *A frontal solution program for finite element analysis*, Int. J. Num. Meth. Engng., 2 (1970), pp. 5–32.

[41] D. KAUSHIK AND W. GROPP, *Optimizing sparse matrix-vector operations on scalar and vector processors*, presented at the 11th SIAM Conference on Parallel Processing for Scientific Computing, San Francisco, CA, San Francisco, CA, 2004.

[42] I. LEE, P. RAGHAVAN, AND E. G. NG, *Effective preconditioning through ordering interleaved with incomplete factorization*, SIAM Journal on Matrix Analysis and Applications, (2006), pp. 1069–1088.

[43] R. J. LIPTON, D. J. ROSE, AND R. E. TARJAN, *Generalized nested dissection*, SIAM J. Num. Anal., 16 (1979), pp. 346–358.

[44] J. W. H. LIU, *An adaptive general sparse out-of-core Cholesky factorization scheme*, SIAM J. Sci. Stat. Comput., 8 (1987), pp. 585–599.

[45] ———, *The role of elimination trees in sparse factorization*, SIAM J. Matrix Anal., 11 (1990), pp. 134–172.

[46] J. W. H. LIU, E. G. NG, AND B. W. PEYTON, *On finding supernodes for sparse matrix computations*, SIAM Journal on Matrix Analysis and Applications, 14 (1993), pp. 242–252.

[47] X. S. LI AND J. W. DEMMEL, *SuperLU_DIST: A scalable distributed-memory sparse direct solver for unsymmetric linear systems*, ACM Transactions on Mathematical Software, 29 (2003), pp. 110–140.

[48] X. S. LI AND Y. WANG, *Performance evaluation and enhancement of SuperLU_DIST 2.0*, Tech. Report LBNL-53624, Lawrence Berkeley National Laboratory, Berkeley, CA, 2003.

[49] Z. LI, Y. SAAD, AND M. SOSONKINA, *parms: A parallel version of the algebraic recursive multilevel solver*, Numerical Linear Algebra with Applications, 10 (2003), pp. 485–509.

[50] K. MALKOWSKI AND P. RAGHAVAN, *Multi-pass mapping schemes for parallel sparse matrix computations*, in Proceedings of ICCS 2005: 5th International Conference on Computational Science, Lecture Notes in Computer Science, Number 3514, V. Sunderam, G. van Albada, P. Sloot, and J. Dongarra, eds., Springer-Verlag, Berlin, New York, 2005, pp. 245–255.

[51] H. MARKOWITZ, *The elimination form of the inverse and its application to linear programming*, Management Science, 3 (1957), pp. 255–269.

[52] J. MEIJERINK AND H. VANDER VORST, *An iterative solution method for linear systems of which the coefficient matrix is a symmetric M-matrix*, Mathematics of Computation, 31 (1977), pp. 148–162.

[53] N. MUNKSGAARD, *Solving sparse symmetric sets of linear equations by preconditioned conjugate gradients*, ACM Transactions on Mathematical Software, 6 (1980), pp. 206–219.

[54] E. G. NG AND P. RAGHAVAN, *Towards a scalable hybrid sparse solver*, Concurrency: Practice and Experience, 12 (2000), pp. 53–68.

[55] A. POTHEN AND C. SUN, *A mapping algorithm for parallel sparse Cholesky factorization*, SIAM Journal on Scientific Computing, 14 (1993), pp. 1253–1257.

[56] P. RAGHAVAN, K. TERANISHI, AND E. G. NG, *A latency tolerant hybrid sparse solver using incomplete cholesky factorization*, Numerical Linear Algebra and Applications, 10 (2003), pp. 541–560.

[57] P. RAGHAVAN, *Parallel Sparse Matrix Factorization: QR and Cholesky Decompositions*, Ph.D. thesis, The Pennsylvania State University, State College, PA, 1991.

[58] D. ROSE, *A graph-theoretic study of the numerical solution of sparse positive definite systems of linear equations*, in Graph Theory and Computing, R. C. Read, ed., Academic Press, New York, 1972, pp. 183–217.

[59] Y. SAAD AND P. HENON, *PHIDAL: A parallel multilevel linear solver based on a hierarchical interface decomposition*, presented at the 11th SIAM Conference on Parallel Processing for Scientific Computing, San Francisco, CA, 2004.

[60] Y. SAAD AND M. SOSONKINA, *parms: a package for solving general sparse linear systems of equations*, in Parallel Processing and Applied Mathematics, R. Wyrzykowski, J. Dongarra, M. Paprzycki, and J. Wasniewski, eds., vol. 2328 of Lecture Notes in Computer Science, Berlin, 2002, Springer-Verlag, Berlin, New York, pp. 446–457.

[61] Y. SAAD, *Iterative Methods for Sparse Linear Systems, Second Edition*, SIAM, Philadelphia, 2003.

[62] O. SCHENK, *Recent advances in sparse linear solver technology for semiconductor device simulation matrices*, presented at the 11th SIAM Conference on Parallel Processing for Scientific Computing, San Francisco, CA, 2004.

[63] R. SCHREIBER, *A new implementation of sparse Gaussian elimination*, ACM Transactions on Mathematical Software, 8 (1982), pp. 256–276.

[64] B. SMITH, P. BJORSTAD, AND W. GROPP, *Domain Decomposition: Parallel Multilevel Methods for Elliptic Partial Differential Equations*, Cambridge University Press, Cambridge, UK, 1996.

[65] W. TINNEY AND J. WALKER, *Direct solution of sparse network equations by optimally ordered triangular factorization*, Proc. IEEE, 55 (1967), pp. 1801–1809.

[66] S. TOLEDO, *Improving the memory-system performance of sparse-matrix vector multiplication*, IBM Journal of Research and Development, 41 (1997), pp. 711–725.

[67] H. A. VAN DER VORST, *Iterative Krylov Methods for Large Linear Systems*, Cambridge University Press, Cambridge, UK, 2003.

[68] R. VUDUC, J. DEMMEL, K. YELICK, S. KAMIL, R. NISHTALA, AND B. LEE, *Performance optimizations and bounds for sparse matrix-vector multiply*, in Proceedings of Supercomputing, Baltimore, MD, November 2002.

Chapter 10
A Survey of Parallelization Techniques for Multigrid Solvers

Edmond Chow, Robert D. Falgout, Jonathan J. Hu, Raymond S. Tuminaro, and Ulrike Meier Yang

This chapter surveys the techniques that are necessary for constructing computationally efficient parallel multigrid solvers. Both geometric and algebraic methods are considered. We first cover the sources of parallelism, including traditional spatial partitioning and more novel additive multilevel methods. We then cover the parallelism issues that must be addressed: parallel smoothing and coarsening, operator complexity, and parallelization of the coarsest grid solve.

The multigrid algorithm is a fast and efficient method for solving a wide class of integral and partial differential equations. The algorithm requires a series of problems be "solved" on a hierarchy of grids with different mesh sizes. For many problems, it is possible to prove that its execution time is asymptotically optimal. The niche of multigrid algorithms is large-scale problems, where this asymptotic performance is critical. The need for high-resolution PDE simulations has motivated the parallelization of multigrid algorithms. It is our goal in this chapter to provide a brief but structured account of this field of research. Earlier comprehensive treatments of parallel multigrid methods can be found in [26, 61, 71, 52] and in Chapter 6 of [75].

10.1 Sources of parallelism

10.1.1 Partitioning

Most simulations based on PDEs are parallelized by dividing the domain of interest into subdomains (one for each processor). Each processor is then responsible for updating the unknowns associated within its subdomain only. For logically rectangular meshes, partitioning into boxes or cubes is straightforward. For unstructured meshes, there are several tools with which to automate the subdivision of domains [55, 50, 33]. The general goal is to assign each processor an equal amount of work and to minimize the amount of communication between processors by essentially minimizing the surface area of the subdomains.

Parallelization of standard multigrid algorithms follows in a similar fashion. In particular, V- or W-cycle computations within a mesh are performed in parallel but each mesh in the hierarchy is addressed one at a time, as in standard multigrid (i.e., the fine mesh is processed and then the next coarser mesh is processed). For partitioning, the finest grid mesh is usually subdivided ignoring the coarse meshes.[1] While coarse mesh partitioning can also be done in this fashion, it is desirable that the coarse and fine mesh partitions match in some way so that interprocessor communication during grid transfers is minimized. This is usually done by deriving coarse mesh partitions from the fine mesh partition. For example, when the coarse mesh points are a subset of fine mesh points, it is natural to simply use the fine mesh partitioning on the coarse mesh. If the coarse mesh is derived by agglomerating elements and the fine mesh is partitioned by elements, the same idea holds. In cases without a simple correspondence between coarse and fine meshes, it is often easy and natural to enforce a similar condition that coarse grid points reside on the same processors that contain most of the fine grid points that they interpolate [60]. For simulations that are to run on many processors (i.e., much greater than 100) or on networks with relatively high communication latencies, repartitioning the coarsest meshes may be advantageous. There are two such approaches worth noting. The first serializes computations by mapping the entire problem to a single processor at some coarse level in the multigrid cycle [66]. The second replicates computations by combining each processor's coarse mesh data with data from neighboring processors [49, 84]. Both approaches reduce communication costs. Repartitioning meshes is also important in cases where the original fine mesh is not well-balanced, leading to significant imbalances on coarse meshes. Another challenge is when the discretization stencil grows on coarse meshes, as is common with algebraic multigrid. Here, a subdomain on a coarse mesh may need to communicate with a large number of processors to perform its updates, leading to significant overhead.

10.1.2 Specialized parallel multigrid methods

Parallelization of standard multigrid methods yields highly efficient schemes so long as there is sufficient work per processor on the finest mesh. When this is not the case, however, the parallel efficiency of a multigrid algorithm can degrade noticeably due to inefficiencies associated with coarse grid computations. In particular, the number of communication messages on coarse meshes is often nearly the same as that on fine meshes (although messages lengths are much shorter). On most parallel architectures, communication latencies are high compared to current processor speeds, and so coarse grid calculations can be dominated by communication. Further, machines with many processors can eventually reach situations where the number of processors exceeds the number of coarse mesh points, implying that some processors are idle during these computations. To address these concerns, specialized parallel multigrid-like methods have been considered. Most of these highly par-

---

[1]When uniform refinement is used to generate fine grid meshes, it is more natural to partition the coarse mesh first. When adaptive refinement is used, it is useful to consider all meshes during partitioning.

allel multigrid methods fit into four broad categories: concurrent iterations, multiple coarse corrections, full domain partitioning, and block factorizations. The concurrent iteration approach reduces the time per multigrid iteration by performing relaxation sweeps on all grids simultaneously. The multiple coarse grid methods accelerate convergence by projecting the fine grid system onto several different coarse grid spaces. Full domain partitioning reduces the number of communication messages per iteration by only requiring processors to exchange information on the finest and coarsest mesh. Block factorizations use a special selection of coarse and fine points to reveal parallelism.

Concurrent iterations

The principal element of concurrent iteration methods is the distribution of the original problem over a grid hierarchy so that simultaneous processing of the grids can occur. In this way an iteration can be performed more quickly. Methods which fall into this family include any kind of additive multilevel method, such as additive two-level domain decomposition schemes [71] as well as additive hierarchical basis–type methods [90, 86]. In addition to these well-known preconditioning schemes, special multigrid algorithms have been proposed in [42, 43, 73, 79, 40]. All these methods divide the computation over meshes so that the individual problems do not greatly interfere with each other. The general idea is to focus fine grid relaxations on high-frequency errors and coarse grid relaxations on low-frequency errors. This can be done, for example, by first splitting the residual into oscillatory and smooth parts. Then, the oscillatory part is used with the fine grid relaxation while the smooth part is projected onto coarser meshes. Another way to reduce interference between fine and coarse grid computations is to enforce some condition (e.g., an orthogonality condition) when individual solutions are recombined. Unfortunately, while these methods are interesting, convergence rates can suffer, and the efficient mapping of the grid pyramid onto separate processors is a nontrivial task. A more complete discussion of additive multigrid methods can be found in [12]. Theoretical aspects of additive multigrid are established in [17].

Multiple coarse grids

Multiple correction methods employ additional coarse grid corrections to further improve convergence rates. The key to success here is that these additional corrections must do beneficial work without interfering with each other. To illustrate the idea, consider the simple case of one grid point assigned to each processor for a three-dimensional simulation. The number of mesh points is reduced by eight within a standard hierarchy and so most processors are inactive even on the first coarse mesh. However, if each time the current mesh spawns eight coarse grid correction equations, then all the processors are kept active throughout the V-cycle. While this situation of one grid point per processor is academic, communication can so dominate time on coarse meshes within realistic computations that additional subproblems can be formulated at little extra cost.

The most well-known algorithms in this family are due to Frederickson and McBryan [41] and Hackbusch [47, 48]. Each of these algorithms was originally formulated for structured mesh computations in two dimensions. In the Fredrickson and McBryan method the same fairly standard interpolation and projection operators are used for all four subproblems.

The stencils, however, for the different problems are shifted, i.e., coarse points for the first subproblem are exactly aligned with fine mesh points that correspond to the intersection of even numbered mesh lines in both the x and y directions. Coarse points for the second subproblem coincide with the intersection of even-numbered mesh lines in the x direction and odd-numbered mesh lines in the y direction. The third and fourth subproblems are defined in a similar fashion. The similarities in the four subproblems makes for a relatively easy algorithm to implement and analyze. The major benefit of the three additional subproblems is that the combined coarse grid corrections essentially contain no aliasing error.[2] This is due to a beneficial cancellation of aliasing error on the separate grids so that it does not reappear on the fine grid [25]. Further extensions and analysis of this algorithm is pursued in [85]. This work is closely related to methods based on the use of symmetries [35].

For a two-dimensional problem, Hackbusch's parallel multigrid method also uses four projections for two-dimensional problems. The stencils for the four different restriction operators are given by

$$R^{(1)} = \tfrac{1}{8} \begin{pmatrix} 1 & 2 & 1 \\ 2 & 4 & 2 \\ 1 & 2 & 1 \end{pmatrix}, \quad R^{(2)} = \tfrac{1}{8} \begin{pmatrix} -1 & 2 & -1 \\ -2 & 4 & -2 \\ -1 & 2 & -1 \end{pmatrix},$$
$$R^{(3)} = \tfrac{1}{8} \begin{pmatrix} -1 & -2 & -1 \\ 2 & 4 & 2 \\ -1 & -2 & -1 \end{pmatrix}, \quad R^{(4)} = \tfrac{1}{8} \begin{pmatrix} 1 & -2 & 1 \\ -2 & 4 & -2 \\ 1 & -2 & 1 \end{pmatrix},$$
(10.1)

and interpolation is taken as the transpose of restriction. The idea is to project the fine grid problem into spaces associated with both high and low frequencies in the x and y directions, i.e., $R^{(1)}$ projects into low frequency spaces in both the x and y directions, and $R^{(2)}$ projects into a space corresponding to low frequency in the y direction but high frequency in the x direction. These projections into both high- and low-frequency spaces can be useful when it is difficult to smooth in certain directions (e.g., anisotropic problems), or they can be used to reduce the number of smoothing iterations on the fine grid (as the high-frequency subproblems can be used to reduce oscillatory error). It was shown in [31] how to modify this method to be more robust for discontinuous coefficient problems and in [32] how to apply this method with line relaxation on ocean modeling problems. Further extensions and improvements are discussed in [7].

Another interesting and related idea due to Mulder [64] also uses multiple coarse grid corrections to address anisotropic problems. In Mulder's method, different coarse grid corrections are built by applying semicoarsening[3] in different directions. That is, one coarse mesh is built only coarsening in the x direction while another coarsens in the y direction. This is similar to Hackbusch's method in that the idea is to improve robustness by having multiple spaces which are intended to address problems where smoothing is difficult in some direction. Improvements to this idea were presented in [65].

---

[2]Aliasing error arises when high-frequency components are projected onto coarser grids. These frequencies get mapped to low frequency and are often amplified on the coarse grid before returning to the fine mesh.

[3]Semicoarsening refers to coarsening the mesh only in some subset of coordinate directions. The idea is to not coarsen in directions where smoothing is ineffective.

Full domain partitioning

Full domain partitioning takes a different approach that is intended to reduce the number of messages that are sent during each multigrid cycle. The idea was motivated by adaptive grid refinement and is described in the context of hierarchical basis methods [62, 63]. Here, we will give the general flavor of the method in a more traditional multigrid setting.

To illustrate full domain partitioning, consider a one-dimensional PDE discretized on a uniform mesh. Instead of subdividing the mesh and assigning each piece to a different processor as shown in Figure 10.1(a), an auxiliary mesh (with a corresponding discrete PDE operator) for each processor spans the entire domain. A sample is shown for one particular processor in Figure 10.1(b). While each processor's mesh spans the entire domain, only a subregion of the processor's mesh actually corresponds to the fine grid mesh. Additionally,

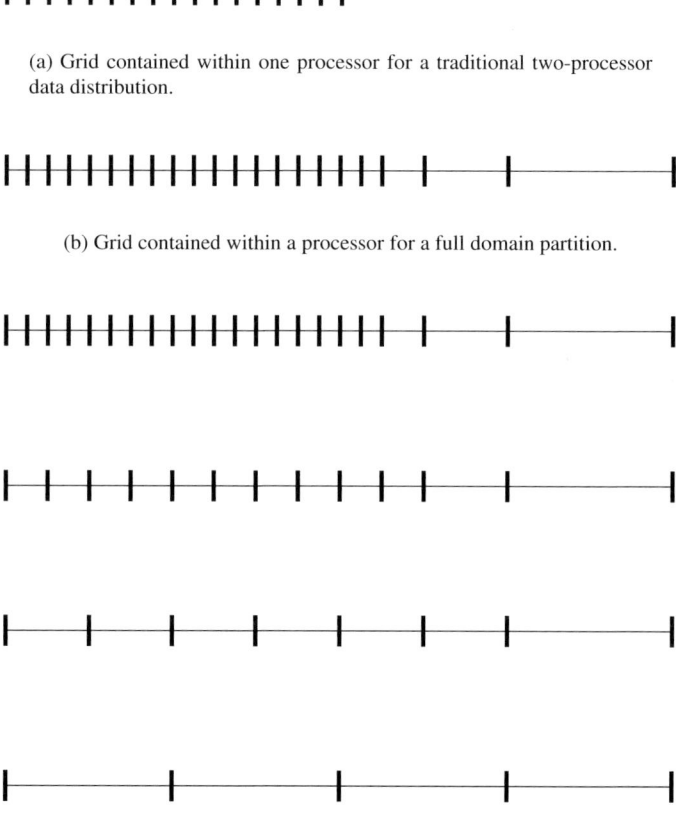

(a) Grid contained within one processor for a traditional two-processor data distribution.

(b) Grid contained within a processor for a full domain partition.

(c) Full multigrid hierarchy for a single processor using full domain partition.

Figure 10.1. *Full domain partitioning example.*

the resolution within a processor's mesh decreases the further we are from the subregion. The basic idea is that each processor performs multigrid on its adaptive grid using a mesh hierarchy suitable for adaptive meshes, such as the one shown in Figure 10.1(c). The multigrid cycle of each processor is almost completely independent of other processors except for communication on the finest level and the coarsest level. This greatly improves the ratio of computation to communication within each multigrid cycle. In [62], convergences rates comparable to standard multigrid are obtained at much higher efficiencies using this full domain partition approach. In [8, 9], these ideas are expanded upon to easily adapt and load balance an existing serial code PLTMG [11] to a parallel environment in an efficient way. Most recently, [10, 59] developed new parallel algebraic multigrid solvers motivated by these ideas.

Parallel multilevel block LU factorizations

Parallel multilevel algorithms have also been developed in the context of approximate block LU factorizations. To illustrate the method with two levels, the variables in a matrix A is partitioned into fine (f) and coarse (c) sets, and the approximate block LU factorization is

$$\begin{pmatrix} A_{ff} & A_{fc} \\ A_{cf} & A_{cc} \end{pmatrix} \approx \begin{pmatrix} A_{ff} & 0 \\ A_{cf} & S \end{pmatrix} \begin{pmatrix} I & -P \\ 0 & I \end{pmatrix},$$

where S is the Schur complement and P is an approximation to $-A_{ff}^{-1} A_{fc}$. The similarity to multigrid methods is evident when $[P, I]^T$ is viewed as a prolongation operator, an approximation to A_{ff} is viewed as a smoother for the fine variables, and S is a suitable coarse grid matrix.

Parallel multilevel versions of this algorithm were first developed by choosing an independent set of fine grid variables, i.e., A_{ff} is diagonal, although actual parallel implementations were not tested [69, 15, 16]. Practical parallel versions were then developed by using a domain decomposition ordering of A, where A_{ff} is block diagonal, possibly with multiple blocks per processor; see [57] and the references therein. Each block represents a small aggregate, and the boundary between the aggregates falls into the coarse grid. If A_{ff} has general form, parallelism can be recovered by using a sparse approximate inverse to approximate the inverse of A_{ff}. See, for example, [27]. This is equivalent to using a sparse approximate inverse smoother, to be discussed later.

10.2 Parallel computation issues

The remainder of this chapter primarily considers parallelization of standard multigrid algorithms (as opposed to those considered in the previous subsection). The main steps in developing multigrid methods are: coarsening the fine grid (or fine matrix graph), choosing grid transfer operators to move between meshes, determining the coarse mesh discretization matrices,[4] and finally developing appropriate smoothers. Developing effective multigrid methods often boils down to striking a good balance between setup times, convergence rates,

---

[4]The coarse grid discretization matrix in an algebraic multigrid method is usually generated by a Galerkin process—the coarsening and grid transfer operators determine the coarse discretization operators.

and cost per iteration. These features in turn depend on operator complexity, coarsening rates, and smoother effectiveness.

10.2.1 Complexity

Complexity issues in geometric solvers

On sequential computers, complexity is not typically a concern for geometric multigrid methods. In parallel, however, implementation issues can lead to large complexities, even for algorithms that exhibit adequate parallelism.

As an illustrative example, consider the three-dimensional SMG semicoarsening multigrid method described in [70]. This SMG method uses a combination of semicoarsening and plane relaxation to achieve a high degree of robustness. It is recursive, employing one V-cycle of a two-dimensional SMG method to effect the plane solves. The computational complexity of the method is larger than standard geometric methods, but it is still optimal.

The storage costs for relaxation can be kept to $O(N^2)$ in the sequential code, which is small relative to the $O(N^3)$ original problem size, where N is the problem size along one dimension. Alternatively, a faster solution time can be achieved by saving the coarse grid information for each of the plane solves, but at the cost of $O(N^3)$ storage for relaxation. In parallel, there is little choice. The solution of one plane at a time in relaxation would incur a communication overhead that is too great and that depends on N. To achieve reasonable scalability, all planes must be solved simultaneously, which means an additional $O(N^3)$ storage requirement for relaxation that more than doubles the memory (see [24, 37]).

Another parallel implementation issue in SMG that exacerbates the storage cost problem is the use of *ghost zones*, which is simply the extra "layer" of data needed from another processor to complete a processor's computation. For parallel geometric methods, the use of ghost zones is natural and widely used. It simplifies both implementation and maintainability and leads to more efficient computational kernels. However, because of the recursive nature of SMG and the need to store all coarse-grid information in the plane solves, the ghost zone memory overhead is quite large and depends logarithmically on N (see [37]).

Complexity issues in algebraic solvers

For algebraic multigrid solvers, two types of complexities need to be considered: the *operator complexity* and the *stencil size*. The operator complexity is defined as the quotient of the sum of the numbers of nonzeros of the matrices on all levels, $A^i, i = 1, \ldots, M$, (M levels) divided by the number of nonzeros of the original matrix $A^1 = A$. This measure indicates how much memory is needed. If memory usage is a concern, it is important to keep this number small. It also affects the number of operations per cycle in the solve phase. Small operator complexities lead to small cycle times. The stencil size of a matrix A is the average number of coefficients per row of A. While stencil sizes of the original matrix are often small, it is possible to get very large stencil sizes on coarser levels. Large stencil sizes can lead to large setup times, even if the operator complexity is small, since various components, particularly coarsening and to some degree interpolation, require that neighbors of neighbors are visited, and so one might observe superlinear or even quadratic growth in the number of operations when evaluating the coarse grid or the interpolation matrix. Large stencil sizes can also increase parallel communication cost, since they might require the exchange of larger sets of data.

Both convergence factors and complexities need to be considered when defining the coarsening and interpolation procedures, as they often affect each other; increasing complexities can improve convergence, and small complexities lead to a degradation in convergence. The user needs therefore to decide on priority. Note that often a degradation in convergence due to low complexity can be overcome or diminished by using the multigrid solver as a preconditioner for a Krylov method.

10.2.2 Coarsening

The parallelization of the coarsening procedure for geometric multigrid methods and block-structured problems in the algebraic case is fairly straightforward. On the other hand, the standard coarsening algorithms for unstructured problems in algebraic multigrid are highly recursive and not suitable for parallel computing. We first describe some issues for coarsening block-structured problems and then move on to unstructured problems.

Coarsening for block-structured problems

Geometric multigrid methods have traditionally been discussed in the context of rectangular structured grids, i.e., Cartesian grids on a square in two dimensions or a cube in three dimensions (see, e.g., [30, 6, 7]). In this setting, computing coarse grids in parallel is a trivial matter, and only the solution phase of the algorithm is of interest. However, in the more general setting where grids are composed of arbitrary unions of rectangular *boxes* such as those that arise in structured adaptive mesh refinement applications, parallel algorithms for coarsening are important [37]. Here, a box is defined by a pair of indexes in the three-dimensional index-space (there is an obvious analogue for two dimensions), $\mathcal{I} = \{(i, j, k) : i, j, k \text{ integers}\}$. That is, a box represents the "lower" and "upper" corner points of a subgrid via the indices $(i_l, j_l, k_l) \in \mathcal{I}$ and $(i_u, j_u, k_u) \in \mathcal{I}$.

In the general setting of a parallel library of sparse linear solvers, the problem data has already been distributed and is given to the solver library in its distributed form. On each processor, the full description of each grid's distribution is not needed, only the description of the subgrids that it owns and their nearest neighboring subgrids. However, to compute this on all grid levels requires that at least one of the processors—one containing a nonempty subgrid of the coarsest grid—has information about the coarsening of every other subgrid. In other words, computing the full set of coarse grids in the V-cycle requires global information.

Assume that we have already determined some appropriate neighbor information (at a cost of $\log(P)$ communications), and consider the following two basic algorithms for coarsening, denoted by A1 and A2. In A1, each processor coarsens the subgrids that it owns and receives neighbor information from other processors. This requires $O(1)$ computations and $O(\log(N))$ communications. In A2, the coarsening procedure is replicated on all processors, which requires $O(P)$ computations and no communications. This latter approach works well for moderate numbers of processors but becomes prohibitive for large P. In particular, the latter approach also requires $O(P)$ storage, which may not be practical for machines with upwards of 100,000 processors, such as BlueGene/L.

The performance of these two basic algorithms is discussed in more detail in [37], and results are also presented that support the analysis. Algorithm A1 is much harder to implement than A2 because of the complexity of determining new nearest-neighbor information on coarser grid levels while storing only $O(1)$ grid boxes.

Sequential coarsening strategies for unstructured problems

Before describing any parallel coarsening schemes, we will describe various sequential coarsening schemes, since most parallel schemes build on these. There are basically two different ways of choosing a coarse grid: classical coarsening [18, 68, 72] and coarsening by agglomeration [82].

Classical coarsening strives to separate all points i into either coarse points (C-points), which are taken to the next level, and fine points (F-points), which are interpolated by the C-points. Since most if not all matrix coefficients are equally important for the determination of the coarse grids, one should consider only those matrix entries which are sufficiently large. Therefore only *strong connections* are considered. A point i depends strongly on j, or conversely, j strongly influences i if

$$-a_{ij} \geq \theta \max_{k \neq i}(-a_{ik}), \tag{10.2}$$

where θ is a small constant. In the classical coarsening process (which we denote Ruge–Stüben or RS coarsening) an attempt is made to fulfill the following two conditions. To restrict the size of the coarse grid, condition (C1) should be fulfilled: the C-points should be a maximal independent subset of all points, i.e., no two C-points are connected to each other, and if another C-point is added then independence is lost. To ensure the quality of interpolation, a second condition (C2) needs to be fulfilled: for each point j that strongly influences an F-point i, j is either a C-point or strongly depends on a C-point k that also strongly influences i.

RS coarsening consists of two passes. In the first pass, which consists of a maximal independent set algorithm, each point i is assigned a measure λ_i, which equals the number of points that are strongly influenced by i. Then a point with a maximal λ_i (there usually will be several) is selected as the first coarse point. Now all points that strongly depend on i become F-points. For all points that strongly influence these new F-points, λ_j is incremented by the number of new F-points that j strongly influences in order to increase j's chances of becoming a C-point. This process is repeated until all points are either C- or F-points. Since this first pass does not guarantee that condition (C2) is satisfied, it is followed by a second pass, which examines all strong F-F connections for common coarse neighbors. If (C2) is not satisfied, new C-points are added.

Experience has shown that often the second pass generates too many C-points, causing large complexities and inefficiency [72]. Therefore condition (C1) has been modified to condition (C1'): each F-point i needs to strongly depend on at least one C-point j. Now just the first pass of the RS coarsening fulfills this requirement. This method leads to better complexities but worse convergence. Although this approach often decreases complexities significantly, complexities can still be quite high and require more memory than desired.

Allowing C-points to be even further apart leads to *aggressive coarsening*. This is achieved by the following new definition of strength: a variable i is *strongly n-connected along a path of length l* to a variable j if there exists a sequence of variables $i_0, i_1, \ldots, i_l$ with $i = i_0$, $j = i_l$ and i_k strongly connected (as previously defined) to i_{k+1} for $k = 0, 1, \ldots, l-1$. A variable i is *strongly n-connected with respect to (p,l)* to a variable j if at least p paths of lengths $\leq l$ exist such that i is strongly n-connected to j along each of these paths. For further details see [72].

Coarsening by aggregation accumulates aggregates, which are the coarse "points" for the next level. For the aggregation scheme, a matrix coefficient a_{ij} is dropped if the following condition is fulfilled:

$$|a_{ij}| \leq \theta \sqrt{|a_{ii} a_{jj}|}. \tag{10.3}$$

An aggregate is defined by a root point i and its neighborhood, i.e., all points j, for which a_{ij} fulfills (10.3). The basic aggregation procedure consists of the following two phases. In the first pass, a root point is picked that is not adjacent to any existing aggregate. This procedure is repeated until all unaggregated points are adjacent to an aggregate. In the second pass, all remaining unaggregated points are either integrated into already existing aggregates or used to form new aggregates. Since root points are connected by paths of length at least 3, this approach leads to a fast coarsening and small complexities. While aggregation is fundamentally different from classical coarsening, many of the same concerns arise. In particular, considerable care must be exercised in choosing root points to limit the number of unaggregated points after the first pass. Further care must be exercised within the second pass when deciding to create new aggregates and when determining what points should be placed within which existing aggregate. If too many aggregates are created in this phase, complexities grow. If aggregates are enlarged too much or have highly irregular shapes, convergence rates suffer.

Parallel coarsening strategies for unstructured problems

The most obvious approach to parallelizing any of the coarsening schemes described in the previous section is to partition all variables into subdomains, assign each processor a subdomain, coarsen the variables on each subdomain using any of the methods described above, and find a way to deal with the variables that are located on the processor boundaries.

The easiest option, a decoupled coarsening scheme, i.e., just ignoring the processor boundaries, is the most efficient one, since it requires no communication, but it most likely will not produce a good coarse grid. For the RS coarsening, it generally violates condition (C1) by generating strong F-F connections without common coarse neighbors and leads to poor convergence [51]. While in practice this approach might lead to fairly good results for coarsening by aggregation [78], it can produce many aggregates near processor boundaries that are either smaller or larger than an ideal aggregate and so lead to larger complexities or have a negative effect on convergence. Another disadvantage of this approach is that it cannot have fewer coarse points or aggregates than processors, which can lead to a large coarsest grid.

There are various ways to deal with the variables on the boundaries. One possible way of treating this problem—after one has performed both passes on each processor independently—is to perform a third pass only on the processor boundary points which will add further C-points and thus ensure that condition (C1) is fulfilled. This approach is called RS3 [51]. One of the disadvantages of this approach is that it can generate C-point clusters on the boundaries, thus increasing stencil sizes at the boundaries where in fact one would like to avoid C-points to keep communication costs low.

Another parallel approach is subdomain blocking [56]. Here, coarsening starts with the processor boundaries, and one then proceeds to coarsen the inside of the domains. Full subdomain blocking is performed by making all boundary points coarse and then coarsening into the interior of the subdomain by using any coarsening scheme, such as one pass of RS coarsening or any of the aggressive coarsening schemes. Like RS3 coarsening, this scheme generates too many C-points on the boundary. A method which avoids this problem is minimum subdomain blocking. This approach uses standard coarsening on the boundaries and then coarsens the interior of the subdomains.

In the coupled aggregation method, aggregates are first built on the boundary. This step is not completely parallel. When there are no more unaggregated points adjacent to an aggregate on the processor boundaries, one can proceed to choose aggregates in the processor interiors, which can be done in parallel. In the third phase, unaggregated points on the boundaries and in the interior are swept into local aggregates. Finally, if there are any remaining points, new local aggregates are formed. This process yields significantly better aggregates and does not limit the coarseness of grids to the number of processors; see [78]. Another aggregation scheme suggested in [78] is based on a parallel maximally independent set (MIS) algorithm, since the goal is to find an initial set of aggregates with as many points as possible with the restriction that no root point can be adjacent to an existing aggregate. Maximizing the number of aggregates is equivalent to finding the largest number of root points such that the distance between any two root points is at least three. This can be accomplished by applying an MIS algorithm, e.g., the asynchronous distributed memory algorithm ADMMA [4], to the square of the matrix in the first phase of the coupled aggregation scheme.

A parallel approach that is independent of the number of processors is suggested in [29, 51] for classical coarsening. It is based on parallel independent set algorithms as described by Luby [58] and Jones and Plassmann [53]. This algorithm, called CLJP coarsening, begins by generating global measures as in RS coarsening and then adding a random number between 0 and 1 to each measure, thus making them distinct. It is now possible to find unique local maxima. The algorithm proceeds as follows. If i is a local maximum, make i a C-point, eliminate the connections to all points j that influence i and decrement j's measure. (Thus rather than immediately turning C-point neighbors into F-points, we increase their likelihood of becoming F-points. This combines the two passes of RS coarsening into one pass.) Further, for any point j that depends on i, remove its connection to i and examine all points k that depend on j to see whether they also depend on i. If i is a common neighbor for both k and j, decrement the measure of j and remove the edge connecting k and j from the graph. If a measure gets smaller than 1, the point associated with it becomes an F-point. This procedure does not require the existence of a coarse point in each processor as the coarsening schemes above and thus coarsening does not slow down on the coarser levels. While this approach works fairly well on truly unstructured grids, it often leads to C-point clusters and fairly high complexities on structured grids. These appear to be caused by fulfilling condition (C1). To reduce operator complexities, while keeping the property of being independent of the number of processors, a new algorithm, the PMIS coarsening [34], has been developed that is more comparable to using one pass of the RS coarsening. While it does not fulfill condition (C1), it fulfills condition (C1'). PMIS coarsening begins just as the CLJP algorithm with distinct global measures and sets local maxima to be C-points. Then points that are influenced by C-points are made into F-points and are eliminated from the graph. This procedure will continue until all points are either C- or F-points.

An approach which has shown to work quite well for structured problems is the following combination of the RS and the CLJP coarsening, which is based on an idea by Falgout (see Henson and Young) [51]. This coarsening starts out as the decoupled RS coarsening. It then uses the C-points that have been generated in this first step and are located in the interior of each processor as the first independent set (i.e., they will all remain C-points) and feeds them into the CLJP-algorithm. The resulting coarsening, which satisfies condition (C1), fills the boundaries with further C-points, and possibly adds a few in the interior of the subdomains. A more aggressive scheme, which satisfies condition (C1'), and uses the same idea, is the HMIS coarsening [34]. It performs only the first pass of the RS coarsening to generate the first independent set, which then is used by the PMIS algorithm.

Another approach is to color the processors so that subdomains of the same color are not connected to each other. Then all these subdomains can be coarsened independently. This approach can be very inefficient since it might lead to many idle processors. An efficient implementation that builds on this approach can be found in [54]. Here the number of colors is restricted to n_c, i.e., processors with color numbers higher than n_c are assigned the color n_c. Good results were achieved using only two colors on the finest level but allowing more colors on coarser levels.

10.2.3 Smoothers

Except for damped Jacobi smoothing, traditional smoothers such as Gauss–Seidel are inherently sequential. In this section, we describe some alternatives that have been developed that have better parallel properties.

Multicolor Gauss–Seidel

One of the most popular smoother choices for multigrid is Gauss–Seidel relaxation, which is a special case of successive over relaxation (SOR) [89]. Although Gauss–Seidel is apparently sequential in nature, one method for exposing parallelism is to use multicoloring. In this approach, the unknown indices are partitioned into disjoint sets $U_1, \ldots, U_k$. Each set is thought of as having a distinct color. Let $A = (a_{ij})$. Each set U_l has the property that if $i, j \in U_l$, then $a_{ij} = a_{ji} = 0$, i.e., the equation for unknown i does not involve unknown j, and vice versa. Unknowns in the same set can be updated independently of each another. Hence, the unknowns of single color can be updated in parallel. In addition to imparting parallelism, reordering the unknowns changes the effectiveness of Gauss–Seidel as a smoother or as a solver. We note that an appropriate ordering depends on the underlying problem.

Much of the literature approaches multicoloring from the viewpoint of using Gauss–Seidel as either a preconditioner to a Krylov method or as the main solver. The underlying ideas, however, are applicable in the context of smoothing. Multicoloring to achieve parallelism for compact stencils on structured grids has been studied extensively. Perhaps the best known instance of multicolor Gauss–Seidel is the use of two colors for the five-point Laplace stencil, i.e., red-black Gauss–Seidel [36]. For a rigorous analysis of red-black Gauss–Seidel as a smoother, see, for instance, [88, 83]. For the nine-point Laplacian, four colors are sufficient to expose parallelism. See [1, 2], for example. Adams and Jordan [1] analyze multicolor SOR and show that for certain colorings the iteration matrix has the same convergence rate as the iteration matrix associated with the natural lexicographic ordering.

Multicoloring can also be extended to block or line smoothing. Multiple unknowns in a line or block of the computational grid are treated as one unknown and updated simultaneously. Each block is assigned a color in such a way that all the blocks of one color have no dependencies on one another. Because multiple unknowns are updated simultaneously, parallel block smoothing tends to have less interprocessor communication than an exact point Gauss–Seidel method. The convergence rate of multigrid using multicolor block Gauss–Seidel, however, depends on the underlying problem. For a problem without strongly varying coefficients, the convergence rate will tend to be worse than point Gauss–Seidel. For strongly anisotropic problems, however, line smoothing may be necessary for acceptable multigrid convergence.

Block, Frommer, and Mayer [14], among others, discussed multicolor block Gauss–Seidel as a solver and provided numerical evidence that the communication overhead is lower for multicolor block Gauss–Seidel. O'Leary [67] showed that for stencils that rely only on eight or fewer nearest neighbors, block colorings exist such that the convergence rate is at least as good as lexicographic ordering. Two-color line Gauss–Seidel as a smoother is analyzed in [83].

For unstructured grids, multicoloring can be problematic, as potentially many more colors may be necessary. Adams [5] implemented a parallel true Gauss–Seidel (i.e., no stale off-processor values) and showed it to be effective on large three-dimensional unstructured elasticity problems.

Hybrid Gauss–Seidel with relaxation weights

The easiest way to implement any smoother in parallel is to just use it independently on each processor, exchanging boundary information after each iteration. We will call such a smoother a *hybrid smoother*. If we use the terminology

$$u_{n+1} = u_n + Q^{-1}(f - Au_n) \tag{10.4}$$

for our relaxation scheme, Q would be a block diagonal matrix with p diagonal blocks $Q_k, k = 1, \ldots, p$, for a computer with p processors. For example, if one applies this approach to Gauss–Seidel, Q_k are lower triangular matrices. (We call this particular smoother hybrid Gauss–Seidel; it has also been referred to as processor block Gauss–Seidel [3].) While this approach is easy to implement, it has the disadvantage of being more similar to a block Jacobi method, albeit worse, since the block systems are not solved exactly. Block Jacobi methods can converge poorly or even diverge unless used with a suitable damping parameter. Additionally, this approach is not scalable, since the number of blocks increases with the number of processors, and with it the number of iterations increases. Despite this, good results can be achieved by setting $Q = (1/\omega) \tilde{Q}$ and choosing a suitable relaxation parameter ω. Finding good parameters is not easy and is made even harder by the fact that in a multilevel scheme one deals with a new system on each level, requiring new parameters. It is therefore important to find an automatic procedure with which to evaluate these parameters. Such a procedure was developed for symmetric positive problems and smoothers in [87] using convergence theory for regular splittings. A good smoothing parameter for a positive symmetric matrix A is $\omega = 1/\lambda_{max}(\tilde{Q}^{-1}A)$, where $\lambda_{max}(M)$ denotes the maximal eigenvalue of M. A good estimate for this value can be obtained by using a few relaxation steps of Lanczos or conjugate gradient preconditioned with $\tilde{Q}$. In [21] this procedure was applied to hybrid symmetric Gauss–Seidel smoothers within smoothed aggregation. Using the resulting preconditioner to solve several structural mechanics problems led to scalable convergence.

This automatic procedure can also be applied to determine smoothing parameters for any symmetric positive definite hybrid smoother, such as hybrid symmetric Gauss–Seidel, Jacobi, Schwarz smoothers, or symmetric positive definite variants of sparse approximate inverse or incomplete Cholesky smoothers.

Polynomial smoothing

While polynomials have long been used as preconditioners, they have not been as widely used as smoothers in multigrid. The computational kernel of a polynomial is the matrix-vector multiply, which means its effectiveness as a smoother does not degrade as the number of processors increases.

One of the major problems associated with traditional polynomial iterative methods and preconditioners is that it is necessary to have the extremal eigenvalues of the system available. While an estimate of the largest eigenvalue is easily available via either Gershgorin's theorem or a few Lanczos steps, estimating the smallest eigenvalue is more problematic. However, when polynomial methods are used as smoothers, this smallest eigenvalue is not really necessary, as only high-energy error needs to be damped. Thus, it is often sufficient to take the smallest eigenvalue as a fraction of the largest eigenvalue. Experience has shown that this fraction can be chosen to be the coarsening rate (the ratio of the number of coarse grid unknowns to fine grid unknowns), meaning more aggressive coarsening requires the smoother to address a larger range of high frequencies [3].

Brezina analyzed the use of a polynomial smoother, called MLS smoothing, in the context of smoothed aggregation [20]. This smoother is essentially a combination of two transformed Chebychev polynomials, which are constructed so as to complement one another on the high-energy error components [19]. Further analysis can be found in [80, 81].

Adams et al. proposed the use of Chebychev polynomials as smoothers in [3]. They showed that such smoothers can often be competitive with Gauss–Seidel on serial architectures. These results are different from earlier experiences with Gauss–Seidel and polynomial methods. These differences arise from unstructured mesh considerations, cache effects, and carefully taking advantage of zero initial guesses.[5] In their parallel experiments, better

---

[5]The initial guess on the coarse grids is typically zero within a V-cycle. Further, when multigrid is used as a preconditioner, the initial guess is identically zero on the finest mesh.

timings were achieved with polynomial smoothers than with basic hybrid Gauss–Seidel smoothers.

Sparse approximate inverse smoothing

A sparse approximate inverse is a sparse approximation to the inverse of a matrix. A sparse approximate inverse can be used as a smoother and can be applied easily in parallel as a sparse matrix-vector product, rather than a triangular solve, for instance. Sparse approximate inverses have only local couplings, making them suitable as smoothers. Other advantages are that more accurate sparse approximate inverse smoothers can be used for more difficult problems, and their performance is not dependent on the ordering of the variables. A drawback of these methods is the relatively high cost of constructing sparse approximate inverses in the general case, compared to the almost negligible cost of setting up Gauss–Seidel. Most studies have focused on very sparse versions that are cheaper to construct.

One common form of the sparse approximate inverse can also be computed easily in parallel. To compute a sparse approximate inverse M for the matrix A, this form minimizes the Frobenius norm of the residual matrix $(I - MA)$. This can be accomplished in parallel because the objective function can be decoupled as the sum of the squares of the 2-norms of the individual rows

$$\|I - MA\|_F^2 = \sum_{i=1}^{n} \|e_i^T - m_i^T A\|_2^2,$$

in which e_i^T and m_i^T are the ith rows of the identity matrix and of the matrix M, respectively. Thus, minimizing the above expression is equivalent to minimizing the individual functions

$$\|e_i^T - m_i^T A\|_2, \quad i = 1, 2, \ldots, n.$$

If no restriction is placed on M, the exact inverse will be found. To find an economical sparse approximation, each row in M is constrained to be sparse. A right approximate inverse may be computed by minimizing $\|I - AM\|_F^2$. The left approximate inverse described above, however, is amenable to the common distribution of parallel matrices by rows.

Sparse approximate inverse smoothers were first proposed by Benson [13] in 1990. Tang and Wan [74] discussed the choice of sparsity pattern and least-squares problems to solve to reduce the cost of the smoother. They also analyzed the smoothing factor for constant coefficient PDEs on a two-dimensional regular grid. Some additional theoretical results are given in [22], including for a diagonal approximate inverse smoother, which may be preferable over damped Jacobi. Experimental results in the algebraic multigrid context are given in [23]. Although none of these studies used parallel implementations, parallel implementations of sparse approximate inverses are available [28].

10.2.4 Coarse grid parallelism

The solver on the coarsest grid can limit the ultimate speedup that can be attained in a parallel computation, for two related reasons. First, the operator at this level is generally small, and the time required for communication may be higher than the time required to perform the solve on a single processor. Second, the coarsest grid operator may couple all pieces of the global problem (i.e., it is dense, or nearly dense), and thus global communication of the right-hand side or other data may be necessary. For these reasons, parallel multigrid solvers often minimize the time spent on coarse grids, i.e., W-cycles and full multigrid (FMG) are avoided.

The coarse grid solver may be a direct solver, an iterative solver, or a multiplication with the full inverse. These are covered briefly in this subsection. Generally, the parallel performance of the setup or factorization stage of the solver is unimportant, since this phase will be amortized over several solves.

A direct solver is perhaps most often used for the coarsest grid problem. However, the solves with the triangular factors are well known to be very sequential. If the problem is small enough, instead of solving in parallel, the coarsest grid problem may be factored and solved on a single processor, with the right-hand side gathered, and the solution scattered to the other processors. The other processors may do useful work during this computation. If the other processors have no work and would remain idle, a better option is to solve the coarsest grid problem on all processors. This redundant form of the calculation does not require communication to distribute the result. For an analysis, see [46].

If the coarsest grid problem is too large to fit on a single processor, then there is no choice but to do a parallel computation. However, the communication complexity can be reduced by solving with only a subset of the processors. Solving redundantly with a subset of the processors is again an option. Related are the techniques of [66, 49, 84], where a smaller set of the processors may be used at coarser levels. We note that for difficult problems the final coarse grid may be chosen to be very large, as the error to be reduced becomes more poorly represented on the coarser grids.

Iterative methods for the coarsest grid solve are less sequential, requiring matrix-vector products for each solve. However, since the matrices are quite dense, it is important that very few iterations are required, or the accumulation of communication costs can become very high. To this end, preconditioning may be used, especially since the cost of constructing the preconditioner will be amortized. Similarly, it is advantageous to exploit previous solves with the same matrix, e.g., Krylov subspace vectors from previous solves may be used as an initial approximation space, e.g., [38].

If the coarse grid problems are small enough, another solution strategy is to first compute the inverse of the coarse grid matrix [45, 44]. Each processor stores a portion of the inverse and computes the portion of the solution it requires. The communication in the solution phase requires the right-hand side to be collected at each processor. However, since the inverses are dense, storage will limit the applicability of this method. To alleviate this problem, Fischer [39] proposed computing a sparse factorization of the inverse of the coarse grid matrix, $A_c^{-1} = XX^T$. The factor X is computed via an A-orthogonalization process and remains sparse if the order of orthogonalization is chosen according to a nested-dissection ordering. Parallel results with this method were reported in [76, 77].

10.3 Concluding remarks

We considered a few of the main research topics associated with the parallelization of multigrid algorithms. These include traditional sources of parallelism such as spatial partitioning as well as nontraditional means of increasing parallelism via multiple coarse grids, concurrent smoothing iterations, and full domain partitioning. We discussed parallel coarsening and operator complexity issues that arise in both classical algebraic multigrid and agglomeration approaches. Finally, we discussed parallel smoothers and the coarsest grid solution strategy.

Acknowledgments

This work was performed under the auspices of the U.S. Department of Energy by the University of California Lawrence Livermore National Laboratory under Contract W-7405-Eng-48. Sandia is a multiprogram laboratory operated by Sandia Corporation, a Lockheed Martin Company, for the U.S. Department of Energy's National Nuclear Security Administration under Contract DE-AC04-94AL85000.

Bibliography

[1] L. M. ADAMS AND H. F. JORDAN, *Is SOR color-blind?*, SIAM Journal on Scientific and Statistical Computing, 7 (1986), pp. 490–506.

[2] L. M. ADAMS, R. J. LEVEQUE, AND D. M. YOUNG, *Analysis of the SOR iteration for the 9-point Laplacian*, SIAM Journal of Numerical Analysis, 25 (1988), pp. 1156–1180.

[3] M. F. ADAMS, M. BREZINA, J. HU, AND R. TUMINARO, *Parallel multigrid smoothing: Polynomial versus Gauss-Seidel*, Journal of Computational Physics, 188 (2003), pp. 593–610.

[4] M. F. ADAMS, *A parallel maximal independent set algorithm*, in Proceedings of the 5th Copper Mountain Conference on Iterative Methods, Copper Mountain, CO, 1998.

[5] ———, *A distributed memory unstructured Gauss-Seidel algorithm for multigrid smoothers*, in ACM/IEEE Proceedings of SC2001: High Performance Networking and Computing, 2001.

[6] S. F. ASHBY AND R. D. FALGOUT, *A parallel multigrid preconditioned conjugate gradient algorithm for groundwater flow simulations*, Nuclear Science and Engineering, 124 (1996), pp. 145–159.

[7] V. A. BANDY, J. E. DENDY, JR., AND W. H. SPANGENBERG, *Some multigrid algorithms for elliptic problems on data parallel machines*, SIAM Journal on Scientific and Statistical Computing, 19 (1998), pp. 74–86.

[8] R. E. BANK AND M. HOLST, *A new paradigm for parallel adaptive meshing algorithms*, SIAM Journal on Scientific and Statistical Computing, 22 (2000), pp. 1411–1443.

[9] R. BANK AND M. HOLST, *A new paradigm for parallel adaptive meshing algorithms*, SIAM Review, 45 (2003), pp. 291–323.

[10] R. BANK, S. LU, C. TONG, AND P. VASSILEVSKI, *Scalable parallel algebraic multigrid solvers*, Tech. report, University of California at San Diego, 2004.

[11] R. E. BANK, *PLTMG:A Software Package for Solving Elliptic Partial Differential Equations: Users' Guide, 8.0*, SIAM, Philadelphia, 1998.

[12] P. BASTIAN, W. HACKBUSCH, AND G. WITTUM, *Additive and multiplicative multi-grid – a comparison*, Computing, 60 (1998), pp. 345–364.

[13] M. W. BENSON, *Frequency domain behavior of a set of parallel multigrid smoothing operators*, International Journal of Computer Mathematics, 36 (1990), pp. 77–88.

[14] U. BLOCK, A. FROMMER, AND G. MAYER, *Block colouring schemes for the SOR method on local memory parallel computers*, Parallel Computing, 14 (1990), pp. 61–75.

[15] E. F. F. BOTTA, A. VAN DER PLOEG, AND F. W. WUBS, *Nested grids ILU-decomposition (NGILU)*, Journal of Computational and Applied Mathematics, 66 (1996), pp. 515–526.

[16] E. F. F. BOTTA AND F. W. WUBS, *Matrix renumbering ILU: An effective algebraic multilevel ILU preconditioner for sparse matrices*, SIAM Journal on Matrix Analysis and Applications, 20 (1999), pp. 1007–1026.

[17] J. BRAMBLE, J. PASCIAK, AND J. XU, *Parallel multilevel preconditioners*, Mathematics of Computation, 55 (1990), pp. 1–22.

[18] A. BRANDT, S. F. MCCORMICK, AND J. W. RUGE, *Algebraic multigrid (AMG) for sparse matrix equations*, in Sparsity and Its Applications, D. J. Evans, ed., Cambridge University Press, Cambridge, UK, 1984.

[19] M. BREZINA, C. HEBERTON, J. MANDEL, AND P. VANĚK, *An iterative method with convergence rate chosen a priori*, Tech. Report UCD/CCM Report 140, University of Colorado at Denver, 1999.

[20] M. BREZINA, *Robust iterative solvers on unstructured meshes*, Ph.D. thesis, University of Colorado at Denver, Denver, CO, 1997.

[21] M. BREZINA, C. TONG, AND R. BECKER, *Parallel algebraic multigrids for structural mechanics*, SIAM Journal on Scientific Computing, 27 (2006), pp. 1534–1554.

[22] O. BRÖKER, M. J. GROTE, C. MAYER, AND A. REUSKEN, *Robust parallel smoothing for multigrid via sparse approximate inverses*, SIAM Journal on Scientific Computing, 23 (2001), pp. 1396–1417.

[23] O. BRÖKER AND M. J. GROTE, *Sparse approximate inverse smoothers for geometric and algebraic multigrid*, Applied Numerical Mathematics, 41 (2002), pp. 61–80.

[24] P. N. BROWN, R. D. FALGOUT, AND J. E. JONES, *Semicoarsening multigrid on distributed memory machines*, SIAM Journal on Scientific Computing, 21 (2000), pp. 1823–1834.

[25] T. CHAN AND R. TUMINARO, *Analysis of a parallel multigrid algorithm*, in Proceedings of the Fourth Copper Mountain Conference on Multigrid Methods, S. McCormick, ed., New York, 1987, Marcel Dekker.

[26] ———, *A survey of parallel multigrid algorithms*, in Proceedings of the ASME Syposium on Parallel Computations and Their Impact on Mechanics, A. Noor, ed., AMD-Vol. 86, The American Society of Mechanical Engineers, Sussex County, NJ, 1987, pp. 155–170.

[27] E. CHOW AND P. S. VASSILEVSKI, *Multilevel block factorizations in generalized hierarachical bases*, Numerical Linear Algebra with Applications, 10 (2003), pp. 105–127.

[28] E. CHOW, *Parallel implementation and practical use of sparse approximate inverses with a priori sparsity patterns*, International Journal of High Performance Computing Applications, 15 (2001), pp. 56–74.

[29] A. J. CLEARY, R. D. FALGOUT, V. E. HENSON, AND J. E. JONES, *Coarse-grid selection for parallel algebraic multigrid*, in Proc. of the Fifth International Symposium on: Solving Irregularly Structured Problems in Parallel, vol. 1457 of Lecture Notes in Computer Science, New York, 1998, Springer-Verlag, Berlin, New York, pp. 104–115.

[30] J. E. DENDY, JR., M. P. IDA, AND J. M. RUTLEDGE, *A semicoarsening multigrid algorithm for SIMD machines*, SIAM Journal on Scientific Computing, 13 (1992), pp. 1460–1469.

[31] J. E. DENDY, JR. AND C. TAZARTES, *Grandchild of the frequency decomposition method*, SIAM Journal on Scientific Computing, 16 (1994), pp. 307–319.

[32] J. E. DENDY, JR., *Revenge of the semicoarsening frequency decomposition method*, SIAM Journal on Scientific Computing, 18 (1997), pp. 430–440.

[33] K. DEVINE, B. HENDRICKSON, E. BOMAN, M. S. JOHN, AND C. VAUGHAN, *Zoltan: A dynamic load-balancing library for parallel applications; user's guide*, Tech. Report SAND99-1377, Sandia National Laboratories, Albuquerque, NM, 1999.

[34] H. DE STERCK, U. M. YANG, AND J. J. HEYS, *Reducing complexity in parallel algebraic multigrid preconditioners*, SIAM Journal on Matrix Analysis and Applications, 27 (2006), pp. 1919–1039.

[35] C. C. DOUGLAS AND W. L. MIRANKER, *Constructive interference in parallel algorithms*, SIAM Journal on Numerical Analysis, 25 (1988), pp. 376–398.

[36] D. J. EVANS, *Parallel S.O.R. iterative methods*, Parallel Computing, 1 (1984), pp. 3–18.

[37] R. D. FALGOUT AND J. E. JONES, *Multigrid on massively parallel architectures*, in Multigrid Methods VI, E. Dick, K. Riemslagh, and J. Vierendeels, eds., vol. 14 of Lecture Notes in Computational Science and Engineering, Springer-Verlag, Berlin, New York, 2000, pp. 101–107.

[38] C. FARHAT AND P. S. CHEN, *Tailoring domain decomposition methods for efficient parallel coarse grid solution and for systems with many right hand sides*, Contemporary Mathematics, 180 (1994), pp. 401–406.

[39] P. F. FISCHER, *Parallel multi-level solvers for spectral element methods*, in Proceedings of International Conference on Spectral and High Order Methods '95, R. Scott, ed., 1996, pp. 595–604.

[40] L. FOURNIER AND S. LANTERI, *Multiplicative and additive parallel multigrid algorithms for the acceleration of compressible flow computations on unstructured meshes*, Applied Numerical Mathematics, 36 (2001), pp. 401–426.

[41] P. FREDERICKSON AND O. MCBRYAN, *Parallel superconvergent multigrid*, in Proceedings of the Third Copper Mountain Conference on Multigrid Methods, S. McCormick, ed., New York, 1987, Marcel Dekker, pp. 195–210.

[42] D. GANNON AND J. V. ROSENDALE, *On the structure of parallelism in a highly concurrent PDE solver*, Journal of Parallel and Distributed Computing, 3 (1986), pp. 106–135.

[43] A. GREENBAUM, *A multigrid method for multiprocessors*, in Proceedings of the Second Copper Mountain Conference on Multigrid Methods, Elsevier Science Inc., S. McCormick, ed., vol. 19 of Applied Mathematics and Computation, 1986, pp. 75–88.

[44] W. D. GROPP AND D. E. KEYES, *Domain decomposition methods in computational fluid dynamics*, International Journal for Numerical Methods in Fluids, 14 (1992), pp. 147–165.

[45] ———, *Domain decomposition with local mesh refinement*, SIAM Journal on Scientific and Statistical Computing, 13 (1992), pp. 967–993.

[46] W. D. GROPP, *Parallel computing and domain decomposition*, in Fifth Conference on Domain Decomposition Methods for Partial Differential Equations, T. F. Chan, D. E. Keyes, G. A. Meurant, J. S. Scroggs, and R. G. Voigt, eds., SIAM, Philadelphia, 1992, pp. 349–362.

[47] W. HACKBUSCH, *A new approach to robust multi-grid methods*, in Proc. First International Conference on Industrial and Applied Mathematics (Paris, 1987), SIAM, Philadelphia, 1988.

[48] ———, *The frequency decomposition multigrid method, part I: Application to anisotropic equaitons*, Numerische Mathematik, 56 (1989), pp. 229–245.

[49] R. HEMPEL AND A. SCHÜLLER, *Experiments with parallel multigrid algorithms using the SUPRENUM communications subroutine library*, Tech. Report 141, GMD, Germany, 1988.

[50] B. HENDRICKSON AND R. LELAND, *A user's guide to Chaco, Version 1.0.*, Tech. Report SAND93-2339, Sandia National Laboratories, Albuquerque, NM, 1993.

[51] V. E. HENSON AND U. M. YANG, *BoomerAMG: a parallel algebraic multigrid solver and preconditioner*, Applied Numerical Mathematics, 41 (2002), pp. 155–177.

[52] J. E. JONES AND S. F. MCCORMICK, *Parallel multigrid methods*, in Parallel Numerical Algorithms, Keyes, Sameh, and Venkatakrishnan, eds., Kluwer Academic, Dordrecht, 1997, pp. 203–224.

[53] M. T. JONES AND P. E. PLASSMANN, *A parallel graph coloring heuristic*, SIAM Journal on Scientific Comput., 14 (1993), pp. 654–669.

[54] W. JOUBERT AND J. CULLUM, *Scalable algebraic multigrid on 3500 processors*, Electronic Transactions on Numerical Analysis, vol. 23, pp. 105–128, 2006.

[55] G. KARYPIS AND V. KUMAR, *Multilevel k-way partitioning scheme for irregular graphs*, Tech. Report 95-064, Army HPC Research Center, Aberdeen Proving Ground, MD, 1995.

[56] A. KRECHEL AND K. STÜBEN, *Parallel algebraic multigrid based on subdomain blocking*, Parallel Computing, 27 (2001), pp. 1009–1031.

[57] Z. LI, Y. SAAD, AND M. SOSONKINA, *pARMS: a parallel version of the algebraic recursive multilevel solver*, Numerical Linear Algebra with Applications, 10 (2003), pp. 485–509.

[58] M. LUBY, *A simple parallel algorithm for the maximal independent set problem*, SIAM Journal on Computing, 15 (1986), pp. 1036–1053.

[59] S. LU, *Scalable Parallel Multilevel Algorithms for Solving Partial Differential Equations*, Ph.D. thesis, University of California at San Diego, 2004.

[60] D. J. MAVRIPLIS, *Parallel performance investigations of an unstructured mesh Navier-Stokes solver*, International Journal of High Performance Computing Applications, 16 (2002), pp. 395–407.

[61] O. A. MCBRYAN, P. O. FREDERICKSON, J. LINDEN, A. SCHÜLLER, K. STÜBEN, C.-A. THOLE, AND U. TROTTENBERG, *Multigrid methods on parallel computers—a survey of recent developments*, Impact of Computing in Science and Engineering, 3 (1991), pp. 1–75.

[62] W. MITCHELL, *A parallel multigrid method using the full domain partition*, Electronic Transcations on Numerical Analysis, 6 (1998), pp. 224–233.

[63] ———, *Parallel adaptive multilevel methods with full domain partitions*, Applied Numerical Analysis and Computational Mathematics, 1 (2004), pp. 36–48.

[64] W. MULDER, *A new multigrid approach to convection problems*, Journal of Computational Physics, 83 (1989), pp. 303–329.

[65] N. H. NAIK AND J. VAN ROSENDALE, *The improved robustness of multigrid elliptic solvers based on multiple semicoarsened grids*, SIAM Journal on Numerical Analysis, 30 (1993), pp. 215–229.

[66] V. K. NAIK AND S. TA'ASAN, *Performance studies of the multigrid algorithms implemented on hypercube multiprocessor systems*, in Proceedings of the Second Conference on Hypercube Multiprocessors, M. T. Heath, ed., SIAM, Philadelphia, 1987, pp. 720–729.

[67] D. P. O'Leary, *Ordering schemes for parallel processing of certain mesh problems*, SIAM Journal on Scientific and Statistical Computing, 5 (1984), pp. 620–632.

[68] J. W. Ruge and K. Stüben, *Algebraic multigrid (AMG)*, in Multigrid Methods, S. F. McCormick, ed., vol. 3 of Frontiers in Applied Mathematics, SIAM, Philadelphia, 1987, pp. 73–130.

[69] Y. Saad, *ILUM: A multi-elimination ILU preconditioner for general sparse matrices*, SIAM Journal on Scientific Computing, 17 (1996), pp. 830–847.

[70] S. Schaffer, *A semicoarsening multigrid method for elliptic partial differential equations with highly discontinuous and anisotropic coefficients*, SIAM Journal on Scientific Computing, 20 (1998), pp. 228–242.

[71] B. Smith, P. Bjorstad, and W. Gropp, *Domain Decomposition: Parallel Multilevel Methods for Elliptic Partial Differential Equations*, Cambridge University Press, Cambridge, UK, 1996.

[72] K. Stüben, *Algebraic multigrid (AMG): an introduction with applications*, in Multigrid, A. S. U. Trottenberg, C. Oosterlee, ed., Academic Press, New York, 2000.

[73] J. Swisshelm, G. Johnson, and S. Kumar, *Parallel computation of Euler and Navier-Stokes flows*, in Proceedings of the Second Copper Mountain Conference on Multigrid Methods, S. McCormick, ed., vol. 19 of Applied Mathematics and Computation, Elsevier, 1986, pp. 321–331.

[74] W.-P. Tang and W. L. Wan, *Sparse approximate inverse smoother for multigrid*, SIAM Journal on Matrix Analysis and Applications, 21 (2000), pp. 1236–1252.

[75] U. Trottenberg, C. Oosterlee, and A. Schüller, *Multigrid*, Academic Press, New York, 2000.

[76] H. M. Tufo and P. F. Fischer, *Terascale spectral element algorithms and implementations*, in Proceedings of Supercomputing, 1999, ACM, New York.

[77] ———, *Fast parallel direct solvers for coarse grid problems*, Journal of Parallel and Distributed Computing, 61 (2001), pp. 151–177.

[78] R. Tuminaro and C. Tong, *Parallel smoothed aggregation multigrid: Aggregation strategies on massively parallel machines*, in Supercomputing 2000 Proceedings, J. Donnelley, ed., IEEE, Los Alamitos, CA, 2000.

[79] R. S. Tuminaro, *A highly parallel multigrid-like method for the solution of the Euler equations*, SIAM Journal on Scientific Computing, 13 (1992), pp. 88–100.

[80] P. Vaněk, M. Brezina, and J. Mandel, *Convergence of algebraic multigrid based on smoothed aggregation*, Numerische Mathematik, 88 (2001), pp. 559–579.

[81] P. Vaněk, M. Brezina, and R. Tezaur, *Two-grid method for linear elasticity on unstructured meshes*, SIAM Journal on Scientific Computing, 21 (1999), pp. 900–923.

[82] P. VANĚK, J. MANDEL, AND M. BREZINA, *Algebraic multigrid based on smoothed aggregation for second and fourth order problems*, Computing, 56 (1996), pp. 179–196.

[83] P. WESSELING, *An Introduction to Multigrid Methods*, John Wiley & Sons, Chichester, 1992. Reprinted by R.T. Edwards, Inc., 2004.

[84] D. E. WOMBLE AND B. C. YOUNG, *A model and implementation of multigrid for massively parallel computers*, International Journal of High Speed Computing, 2 (1990), pp. 239–256.

[85] S. XIAO AND D. YOUNG, *Multiple coarse grid multigrid methods for solving elliptic problems*, in Proceedings of the Seventh Copper Mountain Conference on Multigrid Methods, N. Melson, T. Manteuffel, and S. M. C. Douglas, eds., vol. 3339 of NASA Conference Publication, 1996, pp. 771–791.

[86] J. XU, *Theory of Multilevel Methods*, Ph.D. thesis, Cornell University, Ithaca, NY, 1987.

[87] U. M. YANG, *On the use of relaxation parameters in hybrid smoothers*, Numerical Linear Algebra with Applications, 11 (2004), pp. 155–172.

[88] I. YAVNEH, *On red-black SOR smoothing in multigrid*, SIAM Journal on Scientific Computing, 17 (1996), pp. 180–192.

[89] D. M. YOUNG, *Iterative Methods for Solving Partial Difference Equations of Elliptic Type*, Ph.D. thesis, Harvard University, Cambridge, MA, May 1950.

[90] H. YSERENTANT, *On the multi-level splitting of finite element spaces*, Numerische Mathematik, 49 (1986), pp. 379–412.

Chapter 11
Fault Tolerance in Large-Scale Scientific Computing

Patricia D. Hough and Victoria E. Howle

Large-scale simulation is becoming an increasingly valuable tool in exploring and understanding complex scientific phenomena. Furthermore, the availability of parallel machines with tens or hundreds of thousands of processors makes it possible to conduct computational studies at a level of detail that was never before tractable. Key to the successful use of these machines is the ability of enabling technologies to keep pace with the challenges presented by the massive scale, including scalability, latency, and regular failures. It is on this last category that we focus.

Birman [6] defines fault tolerance as the ability of a distributed system to run correctly through a failure. The system consists not only of the hardware platform, but also of the application software and any middleware upon which it depends. Fault tolerance has long been an active research area in the computer science community. The problem domain for this work has typically consisted of business-, mission-, or life-critical applications, which are characterized by their loosely coupled nature and their need to withstand arbitrary failures. The techniques developed for fault tolerance are usually based on replication of some sort and require little or no knowledge of the application. Therefore, they can be implemented in middleware and used by an application with minimal effort.

The size and complexity of large-scale parallel computers and scientific applications continue to grow at a rapid rate. With that growth comes a corresponding increase in the frequency of failures and thus, a greater concern for fault tolerance. While scientific applications are important, they are notably less critical than those that fall in the traditional problem domain. Coupled with that characterization is the ever-present desire for high performance. The overarching goal, then, is to tolerate the most common failures while introducing only minimal overhead during failure-free execution. The traditional replication-based approaches, while transparent and easy to use, introduce an unacceptable amount of overhead in this setting. Furthermore, the execution model for scientific applications can vary widely, ranging from loosely coupled processes to highly interdependent processes. This variety makes a "silver bullet" solution difficult at best. The result of these combined factors is the emergence of an approach to fault tolerance that depends on application properties and that leverages traditional techniques where possible.

In section 11.1, we discuss recent advances in making algorithms fault tolerant. The algorithms covered include both those that lend themselves to inherent fault tolerance and those in which replication is unavoidable. In section 11.2, we discuss efforts to incorporate support for fault tolerance into various MPI implementations. Since MPI is a key enabling technology for parallel computing, this capability is essential for developing fault-tolerant applications. Finally, we conclude with some thoughts on remaining open questions in the field in section 11.3.

11.1 Fault tolerance in algorithms and applications

As mentioned, the overhead introduced by traditional replication-based fault tolerance techniques is often unacceptable in scientific computing, where high performance is essential. Furthermore, the mean time between failure will continue to decrease as the number of components in large parallel machines grows. Given simple extrapolations of mean time to failure versus number of processors it quickly becomes apparent that traditional disk-based checkpointing will soon become obsolete, as the mean time to failure will fall below the time required to write necessary data to disk or to restart. Faced with these challenges, researchers have begun to explore means of incorporating algorithm-dependent approaches to fault tolerance.

In the following sections, we review recent research in fault-tolerant algorithms and applications. We categorize the methods in the same manner as in Geist and Engelmann [18]. In particular, we group the work into two broad categories: (1) naturally fault-tolerant algorithms, meaning algorithms that can proceed through failure and still achieve the correct result, and (2) algorithms that require some amount of replication, but in which fault tolerance can be achieve more efficiently than with standard schemes of checkpointing large amounts of state information to disk.

11.1.1 Naturally fault-tolerant algorithms

In this section, we describe three recent methods that offer a certain amount of natural fault tolerance. An algorithm is described by Geist and Engelmann [18] as being "naturally fault tolerant" if it is able to compute the correct answer despite the failure of some tasks during the calculation. Naturally fault-tolerant algorithms do not require any checkpointing, so fault tolerance comes at virtually no cost. In some cases, failure detection and notification may still be required to inform the algorithm to adapt to the failure, but the ultimate goal is to eliminate the need for these capabilities as well.

Naturally fault-tolerant algorithms for computing on 100,000 processors

We first examine a class of algorithms known as super-scalable algorithms studied by Geist and Engelmann [18]. They define a super-scalable algorithm as one that is scale-invariant with regard to the number of other tasks a single task must communicate with and that is naturally fault tolerant. Algorithms with both of these properties show the most promise for computing on peta-scale machines.

The first class of problems examined is those that can be formulated to require only information from a local region. Such problems include finite difference and finite element applications. Their approach combines two ideas: chaotic relaxation [5, 12] and meshless methods [30]. Chaotic relaxation was investigated in the 1970s but it never became popular because the conditions under which it converges are more restrictive than for other methods. However, Geist and Engelmann suggest that chaotic relaxation may be competitive in the context of 100,000-processor calculations because it is possible to avoid synchronizing across all nodes between iterations. With chaotic relaxation, nodes update their values and send out their results asynchronously. Chaotic relaxation is combined with a meshless approach to allow a calculation to continue after a fault without a replacement node. On a mesh, standard difference equations, for example, break down when information from one of the stencil nodes is missing. In a meshless setting, the problem can be formulated to avoid the need for a replacement node to fill in the missing hole in the grid.

Geist and Engelmann have also explored super-scalable algorithms for problems requiring global information. Examples of such problems are physics problems involving gravity and radiative transport and convergence tests in most iterative methods. For this case, they restrict their notion of super-scalability to tasks that communicate with only a constant number of neighbors. In their approach, they consider graphs for the global communication that satisfy certain assumptions. In particular, the graph must be connected, and there must be enough degrees to ensure that the removal of several random nodes would be very unlikely to isolate portions of the graph. Studies performed by Geist and Engelmann demonstrate that a random directed graph is the most resilient over a wide range of failure conditions for the example problems they studied.

To analyze the behavior of fault-tolerant algorithms on extremely large-scale computers, Geist and Engelmann have also developed a simulator for peta-scale systems. The simulator is available for download and has been tested for systems of up to 1 million nodes. It can run in parallel on a cluster under Linux or Windows, has an adjustable topology that can be configured at startup, simulates failures on single node and groups of nodes, and supports Java, C, and Fortran applications [17].

Asynchronous parallel pattern search for nonlinear optimization

Another example of natural fault tolerance occurs in asynchronous algorithms. An example of this sort of naturally fault-tolerant algorithm is the asynchronous parallel pattern search (APPS) algorithm for nonlinear optimization developed by Hough, Kolda, and Torczon [25].

Consider solving the unconstrained nonlinear optimization problem, minimize $f(x)$, where $x \in \Re$ and $f : \Re^n \to \Re$. In particular, consider those problems characterized by computationally expensive computer simulations of complex physical processes and by a small number of variables (say, 50 or fewer). Derivative-based methods are often inappropriate for these problems because no procedure exists for the evaluation of the gradient, and the function evaluations are not precise enough to produce an accurate finite-difference gradient. Pattern search is a class of nonlinear optimization methods that is popular for solving these problems because no derivative information is required. At a given iteration, the algorithm samples the function over a predefined pattern of points and simply compares function values to determine the next iterate. The function evaluations are independent and can therefore be performed simultaneously on different processors. This inherent parallelism is the foundation for an asynchronous version of pattern search that has the advantages of reducing processor idle time and facilitating fault tolerance.

The work of Hough, Kolda, and Torczon exploits the algorithmic characteristics of pattern search to design variants that dynamically initiate actions solely in response to messages, rather than routinely cycling through a fixed set of steps. The result is an algorithm in which each processor proceeds based on whatever information is available at the time and is not adversely affected by missing information. This approach allows a high degree of fault tolerance with almost no overhead. In the event of a failure, APPS need only determine if the required mathematical properties of the search pattern are intact. If not, the lost search direction is easily regenerated. Otherwise, the algorithm can continue without modification. No checkpointing or "spare" search directions are required, resulting in no overhead during failure-free execution. A negligible cost is incurred upon failure to check the integrity of the search pattern, but no restart or rollback is needed. Computational results show that failures have little effect on the time it takes APPS to reach a solution.

Fault-tolerant parallelization of time in multidata simulations

Another example of natural fault tolerance can occur in algorithms that address the situation in which communication latencies are high compared to the computational cost. This can happen, for example, when computing a small system for a very long period, when massive parallelism causes the volume per processor to become very small, or in a grid-like environment, where the communication cost is high. Srinivasan and Chandra [43] proposed a new solution strategy for this situation that leads to a natural fault tolerance at the algorithmic level, avoiding the need for checkpointing and restarting.

Srinivasan and Chandra considered the class of applications in which one tracks the evolution of the state of a system with time and in which the change in state is modeled through a differential equation. The usual means of parallelization in this case is domain decomposition, i.e., spatial parallelization, where the physical system is distributed across the processors, and each processor is responsible for computing the next state for a portion of the system. This kind of parallelization requires communication with other processors, and communication costs typically increase proportionally to the surface area of the portion of the system on each processor. The solution strategy of Srinivasan and Chandra is based on scalable functional decomposition. Functional decomposition is a technique whereby data are replicated on each processor, but each processor performs a different, independent action on the data. The result is a more coarse-grained parallel computation with reduced communication overhead. The goal is to increase the number of independent operations that can be performed as the size of the system increases by using scalable functional decomposition coupled with techniques like appropriate time-stepping.

Consider the inherently sequential class of applications where the current state of the system is a function of the previous states, that is, $\text{State}(t_i) = F(\text{State}(t_{i-1}))$. One technique explored by Srinivasan and Chandra for this case is time parallelization. Suppose each processor i starts its simulation at some time t_{i-1} and evolves the state through to time t_i. After one step, each processor would have performed a simulation for a different time interval that would incur no communication overhead. The difficulty is that in general, obtaining the correct starting state at time t_{i-1} requires results from processor $i-1$, making the computation sequential. Baffico et al. [3] got around this problem using a technique based on an approximate-verify-correct sequence. However, their technique leads to certain computational bottlenecks. Srinivasan and Chandra addressed these bottlenecks by a technique of guided simulations. Their method is based on a predict-verify approach, in which the results of old simulations are used to speed up the current simulation. It is often the case in engineering problems that there is a relationship between various problem parameters. The idea is to find such a relationship automatically and use it to predict the state at different times.

This method leads to a natural fault tolerance since the computation on each processor is independent of the others. Therefore, in the event of a processor failure, another processor can take over and fill in the missing time interval. Other computations still running need not be discarded. These methods also show promise for providing a significant improvement in speedup and efficiency for long-time simulations.

11.1.2 Efficient checkpointing

Not all algorithms lend themselves to natural fault tolerance. In these algorithms, the information on each processor is important to the successful completion of the computation. For this sort of application, typically some form of replication is needed to ensure fault tolerance. In this section we discuss methods for efficient, application-dependent checkpointing for those algorithms for which it is unlikely that we can completely avoid checkpoints. The approaches described here seek either to remove some of the bottlenecks associated with checkpointing or to minimize the amount of information that is checkpointed.

Diskless checkpointing applied to FFT

In addition to the problems with checkpointing we have already stated, traditional centralized checkpointing is limited by bandwidth, making it likely that the failure rate will outpace the recovery and checkpointing rate. One solution is decentralized peer-to-peer checkpointing as developed by Engelmann and Geist [16]. In this scheme, each processor holds backup information for its neighbors. A local checkpoint and restart algorithm based on this diskless technique can then be combined with very infrequent checkpointing to some central stable storage.

There are two primary considerations in this approach. The first is the choice of neighbors for the local peer-to-peer diskless checkpointing technique. Physically nearby neighbors allow for low latency, fast backup, and fast recovery. However, physically distant neighbors provide the ability to recover from multiprocessor node failures. Random neighbors give medium latency and bandwidth with an acceptable backup and recovery time. The optimal choice is to select pseudorandom neighbors: random neighbors, but with some attention paid to the system communication infrastructure.

The second consideration is coordination between the local diskless and (infrequent) global checkpoints. This coordination requires both global synchronization and local synchronization. For global synchronization a snapshot (barrier) is taken at a stable global application state. This method backs up all local states and synchronizes the complete application. This is the preferred method for communication-intensive applications. Local synchronization uses asynchronous backup of local state and in-flight messages, making extensive use of message logging. This is the preferred synchronization method for applications that are less communication intensive.

These techniques were demonstrated by Engelmann and Geist through application to the FFT, in particular a distributed FFT (DFFT) and transposed FFT (TFFT). These FFT methods are not scale invariant and use a mixture of local and global communication. A checkpointed DFFT method needs both individual local checkpoints with no synchronization and infrequent coordinated checkpoints with global synchronization. A checkpointed TFFT method requires individual checkpoints with no synchronization and coordinated checkpoints with local synchronization. The coordinated checkpoints are needed only after a transpose, making this method more efficient than the DFFT.

The work of Engelmann and Geist has demonstrated that diskless peer-to-peer checkpointing on super-scale architectures is possible. Their methods have been tested on the cellular architecture simulator [17]. Since this environment does not provide for performance evaluation, tests will need to be run on actual super-scale computers for timing, latency, and bandwidth data. In addition, these methods would require a super-scalable, fault-tolerant MPI or PVM for a real-world implementation.

Diskless checkpointing for linear algebra kernels

Because checkpointing is still necessary for fault tolerance in many applications, another way to improve the efficiency of fault-tolerant methods is to build diskless checkpointing techniques into standard software libraries. A diskless checkpointing method by Plank, Kim, and Dongarra [36] maintains a system checkpoint in memory and uses an extra M processors to encode checkpoints that can restore the data of up to M failed processors. This method avoids the bottlenecks associated with checkpointing to disk. In the case of a fault, all processors can be rolled back if necessary.

Diskless checkpointing is not a transparent checkpointing method; checkpointing must be built into the algorithm. The idea is that if we have N processors executing a computation, each processor maintains its own checkpoint locally, and in addition we have M extra processors ($M \ll N$) maintaining coding information so that if one or more processors fail they can be replaced. If $M = 1$, the extra processor can be used as a parity processor and we can recover from the loss of one processor. If $X = A \otimes B$, then $X \otimes B = A$ and $A \otimes X = B$, where the symbol $\otimes$ represents XOR. Therefore, if the parity processor holds the XOR of the other processors, it can be used to recover data from a lost processor. For example, if we have four processors, $P0$, $P1$, $P2$, and $P3$, and one parity processor $P4$, we can load the parity processor with $P4 = P0 \otimes P1 \otimes P2 \otimes P3$. If we then lose one processor, say, $P1$, the parity processor can take on the role of the missing processor since $P1 = P0 \otimes P2 \otimes P3 \otimes P4$. Similarly, this method can protect against more than one fault if we have M extra processors (to protect against M failures) and use Reed–Solomon coding techniques (e.g., [35, 38]).

Prototype libraries are being developed using this method for various direct linear solver methods, including MM, LU, LL^T, and QR factorizations as well as for sparse iterative solvers (using PVM) [36].

Ongoing research includes determining the checkpointing interval based on the mean time between failures for a particular machine, developing a local checkpointing algorithm where processors hold backups of their neighbors, and developing a restart method with appropriate unwinding computations to get back to the most recent checkpoint. Such an approach may be possible for LU, QR, and LL^T decompositions.

Fault-tolerant linear algebra with partial checkpoints

Another approach to improving the efficiency of checkpointing is simply to checkpoint fewer data. This approach can be applied in the context of both disk-based and diskless checkpointing. Howle [26] considered schemes for reducing the amount of checkpointed information in Krylov solvers for linear systems. Krylov methods frequently account for a large percentage of the computational work in scientific computing applications and are highly synchronous, so the goal is to reduce overhead introduced into failure-free computation by decreasing the frequency and size of required checkpoints within the Krylov methods.

In large-scale linear systems, each vector is typically distributed over many processors. In the naive approach to checkpointing solver data, at every kth iteration all global vectors needed to restart the solver from this iteration are checkpointed. This task is accomplished by instructing each processor to checkpoint its relevant local vectors. This work investigates approaches for checkpointing less information at each kth iteration. We refer to this concept as partial checkpointing. This approach introduces significantly less overhead into failure-free execution than the naive approach. However, additional iterations may be required to reach the solution in the event of a failure because less information is available at restart. Thus, care must be taken when determining what information should be included in a partial checkpoint.

There are several possible ways to define partial checkpoints. One method is to have each processor checkpoint a subvector of every relevant local vector it owns. Another is to have only a subset of the processors checkpoint their complete local vectors. These two approaches are somewhat unsatisfying, as they result in inconsistent checkpoints, and it may be impossible to find consistent global vectors upon restart from a failure. For iterative methods that gradually build up a set of vectors needed for an exact restart (for example, as is the case with GMRES [39]), a more attractive approach is viable. In particular, each processor can checkpoint a globally determined subset of their complete local vectors. This third method results in consistent checkpoints while still reducing the amount of overhead introduced when compared to the naive approach.

The set of Krylov solvers used in this work include the CG method [2], GMRES [39], and flexible variants of these methods, FCG [33] and FGMRES [40]. The motivation for including the latter two methods is that they were developed to allow inconsistency in the preconditioners. More specifically, they allow preconditioners to change at each iteration. Because of this tolerance to inconsistent preconditioners, it was hypothesized that these flexible methods may also be tolerant to other inconsistencies. Not surprisingly, CG is the least amenable to using partial checkpoints and often fails to recover when restarted after a failure. FCG, GMRES, and FGMRES all exhibit behavior similar to each other when recovering using partial checkpoints. That behavior is characterized by a notable rise in the residual upon restart from a failure. In some cases, it was observed that using no checkpointing at all and restarting from the beginning resulted in a faster completion time. This behavior leads to many open questions with regard to characterizing the mathematical impact of restarting Krylov solvers with incomplete information.

A related technique explored by Langou et al. [27] is to avoid checkpointing altogether by computing a new approximate solution using data from the nonfailed processes. The main advantage of this approach is that there is no increase in computational costs during failure-free computation. However, like the partial checkpoints discussed by Howle, convergence is affected by the recovery step.

11.2 Fault tolerance in MPI

Essential to the development of fault-tolerant scientific computing applications is support for fault tolerance in the underlying messaging system. Such support can be found, for example, in the PVM message-passing library [21]. In recent years, however, MPI has become the standard for message passing [31], and most software developers use one of several MPI implementations to build parallel scientific computing codes. The MPI standard specifies that the default behavior in the event of an error is to invalidate the communicator involved. Furthermore, the default error handler is MPI_ERRORS_ARE_FATAL, which causes programs to abort when an error is detected. While this default behavior is clearly unacceptable when trying to make an application fault tolerant, the MPI standard does not preclude the use of more sophisticated error handling. The alternate error handler, MPI_ERRORS_RETURN, is intended to return an error code to the calling application when an error is detected, allowing the application to decide what action is to be taken. In addition, MPI implementors or users can define additional error handlers. Nonetheless, the communicator in which the error occurs is still invalidated, limiting the usefulness of these error handlers in implementing fault tolerance within a parallel application code. More specifically, the application must be written in a manager-worker fashion with a separate intercommunicator for each manager-worker pair, and MPI-2 dynamic process management is needed for failure recovery.

During the last few years, MPI developers have begun to explore means by which they can facilitate the implementation of fault tolerance in parallel applications. Those efforts can be grouped roughly into two categories. We first discuss those that strive to provide fault tolerance to the application in a transparent manner. The second set of approaches seeks to provide a flexible interface to the user to allow the application to define behavior in the event of a failure.

11.2.1 Transparent fault tolerance with MPI

The primary goal for transparent fault tolerance is to make an application fault tolerant without introducing any changes to the code. These approaches typically entail incorporating traditional checkpointing and message-logging techniques directly into the MPI library. We discuss two such efforts here: Egida and the LAM/MPI checkpoint/restart framework. Other related efforts not discussed include Starfish [1], MPICH-V [7], MIST [10], the NCCU MPI implementation [11], Manetho [15], Fail-safe PVM [28], and CoCheck [44]. In addition, we do not discuss compiler-based approaches, such as those being developed by Broneetsky et al. [8] and Norman, Choi, and Lin [32], that seek to use compiler analysis to determine the most efficient placement of checkpoints. We start this section with a discussion of the approach taken by the LA-MPI developers to implement network fault tolerance.

LA-MPI

LA-MPI, developed by Graham et al. [22] at Los Alamos, has two primary goals: high performance and network fault tolerance. While many MPI implementations depend on TCP/IP to provide a reliable message transport layer, the performance is often inadequate when large amounts of data are transferred during an application run. The LA-MPI developers have chosen to take advantage of high-speed network devices and low-latency protocols and to implement their own network fault tolerance to ensure reliable message delivery. Thus, they have incorporated low-overhead techniques for guaranteeing the integrity of delivered messages and for providing the ability to fail over from one network device to another.

To ensure reliable message delivery, LA-MPI makes use of a retransmission scheme coupled with checksums. The sender fragments messages, identifies each with a sequence number and a time stamp, and schedules retransmissions. Upon receipt, the receiver responds with a positive acknowledgment (ACK) once it has successfully verified the fragment checksum and moved it into application memory. A negative acknowledgment (NACK) is sent if the data is corrupt. In the event of a NACK, the sender retransmits the message fragment. A retransmission can also occur when the ACK for a given message fragment has not been received prior to its next scheduled retransmission. The checksum used is a main-memory-to-main-memory 32-bit additive checksum or 32-bit cyclic redundancy code. It is generated by the sender at the time the data are copied out of its main memory and checked by the receiver as the data are copied into its main memory. This approach guards against any network or I/O bus corruption. The checksum can be disabled at runtime if higher performance is desired over data integrity.

The other fault-tolerance technique used by LA-MPI allows fail over from one network device to another if the first is generating an unacceptable number of errors. This responsibility falls on the path scheduler, which binds a given message to a particular route between the message source and destination. In the event of failure or an excessive number of errors, the path scheduler can rebind outstanding messages to other functioning routes, and it will not bind future messages to the failed route. Planned work would allow the failed route to be returned to the set of valid routes if the failure is temporary.

Egida

Egida is an MPICH-based [23] toolkit developed by Rao, Alvisi, and Vin [37] for lightweight, transparent fault tolerance. It includes a range of traditional checkpointing and message-logging protocols with corresponding rollback recovery algorithms. A common interface facilitates experimentation with and comparison of protocols and also allows the application developer to assemble a customized fault-tolerance solution from the available tools. The modules available through Egida provide a set of core functionalities and basic services that support those functionalities, but the modular design of the library allows easy incorporation of new capabilities.

Egida provides three types of checkpointing, the first of which is independent (or uncoordinated) checkpointing. In this approach, each process makes independent decisions about what local information to checkpoint and when. The autonomy lends itself to simplicity and scalability when checkpointing, but the absence of a guaranteed globally consistent state can lead to large storage overhead and excessive rollback in failure recovery. The second approach is coordinated checkpointing. As the name implies, the processes coordinate with each other to ensure that their local checkpoints form a globally consistent state. This guarantee addresses the disadvantages of uncoordinated checkpointing, but the inherent synchronization present in this approach can result in substantial overhead. The final type of checkpointing is communication induced, which combines aspects of the two previous approaches. Each process is allowed to take independent checkpoints but may be forced to take additional checkpoints based on information piggybacked on application messages. Thus, a globally consistent state can be guaranteed without the cost of synchronization.

Regardless of checkpointing approach, the overhead introduced into failure-free execution is often unacceptable. To mitigate that cost, Egida provides an array of message-logging protocols that can be used in conjunction with checkpointing. In short, the combination entails taking fewer checkpoints and logging only nondeterministic events that occur between them. Three approaches to message logging are available in Egida. The first of these is pessimistic logging. This approach ensures that all states on which other processes may depend are recoverable, making rollback straightforward, but it comes with the cost of blocking communication. Optimistic logging does not require blocking communication, but as a result, this protocol cannot guarantee that critical information will be logged before a failure occurs. The outcome can be unrecoverable states that complicate recovery. The final approach, causal logging, strikes a middle ground between these two protocols. It relaxes the blocking requirement of the pessimistic approach but only when no other correct processes depend on the state of interest. Recovery can still be complex, but the overhead incurred by blocking communication is reduced.

Underlying the protocols described here is a common set of services that provide needed resources and a common set of events that drive the execution of the protocols. Services include failure detection and interfaces to stable storage. Events relevant to Egida protocols are categorized as nondeterministic events, failure-detection events, internal-dependency-generating events, external-dependency-generating events, and checkpointing events. These services and events are implemented in a modular fashion, making them accessible by all protocols. Furthermore, the modularity facilitates the incorporation of new protocols, new services, and new events.

The checkpointing, message logging, and rollback recovery protocols described in this section have been integrated with the MPICH implementation of MPI [23]. More specifically, Egida sits between the API and P4, one of the low-level communication layers that manages the actual data transfer between processes. When the application invokes a communication operation via the API, Egida first processes the message according to the chosen protocol. It then calls P4 to complete the operation. The P4 code itself was modified to respawn failed processes and to reestablish the appropriate connections. No changes to the application code are required to make use of Egida capabilities. The user need only link to this modified version of MPICH and specify the desired set of protocols.

LAM/MPI

The LAM implementation of MPI, originally developed by Burns, Daoud, and Vaigl [9], has long provided failure detection and MPI-2 dynamic process management. Both features support incorporating fault tolerance into applications that are written in a manager-worker style. The most current version of LAM/MPI is implemented in a component-based manner [42], greatly enhancing the extensibility of the software. This new architecture is being leveraged to incorporate a transparent checkpoint/restart capability [41] using the Berkeley Lab kernel-level process checkpoint/restart system for Linux (BLCR) [14]. While the focus of the LAM work is on the incorporation of this particular tool, the modular nature of the framework allows for plugging in any of a number of checkpointing tools, such as libtckpt [13], Condor [29], libckpt [34], and CRAK [45].

The infrastructure designed for checkpoint/restart in LAM/MPI is based on coordinated checkpointing. Checkpoint requests are registered by either the user or the runtime system with `mpirun`, which then propagates the requests to the MPI processes. The individual processes interact to reach the globally consistent state required for a coordinated checkpoint. Each process is individually checkpointed by whatever checkpoint mechanism is being used and then continues with normal execution. Restarting processes from a saved image after a failure is also managed through `mpirun`. Once restarted, each process conveys its new process information to `mpirun`, which then broadcasts it to all other processes. Upon receiving that information, each MPI process rebuilds its communication channels with the others and resumes execution from the saved state.

The LAM/MPI software consists of two software layers. The upper layer is the API, and the lower layer is the system services interface (SSI). The SSI is a component framework through which various services can be made available to the MPI layer or to the LAM runtime environment. These services are provided by plug-in modules that can be chosen automatically or by the user at runtime. Checkpoint/restart is one of the services available through the SSI. BLCR is the only module available, but as mentioned, other checkpoint/restart tools can be incorporated as additional modules. The checkpoint/restart component has interfaces to the MPI layer for enabling checkpoints and to `mpirun` for checkpoint management purposes. Those used by the MPI layer are `initialize`, `suspend`, and `finalize`. During the initialization phase, the MPI layer attaches to the underlying checkpointer and registers any callback functions that will be invoked during a checkpoint. The `suspend` function is used to suspend execution when interrupted by a checkpoint request. Finalization includes cleanup and detaching from the underlying checkpointer. The two interfaces used by `mpirun` are `disable checkpoint` and `enable checkpoint`. The former is used when `mpirun` is entering a phase in which it cannot be interrupted by a checkpoint request. The latter is used when that phase is complete.

For an application to make use of the checkpoint/restart services, all other modules selected through the SSI must provide checkpoint/restart functionality in the form of callback functions that can be invoked by the checkpoint/restart module. An example can be found in the LAM request progression interface, which provides device-dependent point-to-point communication modules. The three functions required are `checkpoint`, `continue`, and `restart`. The `checkpoint` function is invoked when a checkpoint is requested and is responsible for bringing the module to a state where it can be checkpointed. In the case of messaging, this usually entails management of in-flight messages. The `continue` function performs any operations required for a process to resume execution after a checkpoint, and `restart` performs any tasks involved with restarting an application from a saved state. As with Egida, no changes to the application are required. The user only needs to specify the appropriate SSI modules.

11.2.2 Application-dependent fault tolerance with MPI

In contrast to the MPI implementations already discussed, FT-MPI and MPI/FT take a nontransparent approach to supporting fault tolerance. While these implementations provide modifications or extensions to the API to facilitate the incorporation of fault tolerance into an application, the user is responsible for implementing any tasks needed to ensure that relevant data are recoverable and that the application takes appropriate actions after a failure has occurred. This approach allows a great deal of flexibility in tailoring the fault-tolerance solution to the specific needs of the application. Thus, the overhead incurred can be significantly less than when using a transparent tool.

FT-MPI

FT-MPI is a relatively recent implementation of MPI being developed by Fagg et al. [19]. Unlike the implementations described in the previous section, it does not provide transparent checkpoint/restart capabilities for fault tolerance. Rather it seeks to provide a flexible set of options from which the application developer can choose to implement fault tolerance in his or her parallel code. These options govern the behavior of FT-MPI in the event of a failure. It is the responsibility of the application developer to define and implement the strategies used to make the application itself fault tolerant.

The options provided by FT-MPI are grouped into four communicator modes, two message modes, and two collective communication modes. The communicator modes define the behavior of `MPI_COMM_WORLD`, the default communicator, in the event of a process failure. The `ABORT` mode induces behavior similar to that of most MPI implementations. In particular, the application will be ended if a process fails. The `BLANK` mode specifies that the communicator should remain intact, with all remaining processes retaining their ranks. The failed process will not be replaced, and there will be a missing process/rank within the communicator. The `SHRINK` mode also keeps the communicator intact without replacing the failed process; however, the processes are reordered to construct a contiguous communicator. Thus, the ranks of some of the processes will change. The final communicator mode is `REBUILD`, which respawns the failed processes and adds them to `MPI_COMM_WORLD`. The resulting configuration appears to the application to be no different than it was before the failure occurred.

The communication modes define how any outstanding messages and communication requests are handled in the event of a failure. The message modes are `RESET` and `CONTINUE`. The `RESET` mode ignores and cancels any active communication or requests, and it is the responsibility of the user to re-post the operations after recovery from the failure. The `CONTINUE` mode allows all successful operations to complete after recovery. The two collective communication modes are `ATOMIC` and `NON-ATOMIC`. In the `ATOMIC` case, either all processes succeed or none of them succeed. The behavior is undefined in the NON-ATOMIC case, though the user can repeat the operation after recovery and/or check to see if the operation completed successfully.

The previous paragraphs describe the means of defining the behavior of FT-MPI in the event of a process failure, but the actions taken do not constitute fault tolerance of the application. It is still the responsibility of the user to ensure that relevant data is recoverable and that the application takes appropriate actions after a failure has occurred. FT-MPI provides two means of failure notification so that the application knows when to initiate recovery. In the first case, FT-MPI returns the MPI_ERR_OTHER error code. The application can check for this after completing an MPI call and invoke a recovery function if appropriate. In the second scenario, the application can implement its own error handler and register it with FT-MPI via MPI_Comm_create_errhandler. The recovery handler is "installed" only once, and the error checking is done automatically. There is clearly much more onus on the user than with the transparent approaches of Egida and LAM/MPI, but the application dependence can result in much more efficient implementations of fault tolerance.

MPI/FT

MPI/FT, developed by Batchu et al. [4], takes a model-based approach to providing support for fault tolerance. The underlying philosophy is that by categorizing applications according to execution models, the fault-tolerance strategy can be tailored to the application, thereby minimizing the overhead incurred. In addition to defining a set of execution models and the requirements for fault tolerance in the middleware, MPI/FT includes several extensions to the API to assist with application-level fault tolerance.

The three criteria identified in [4] for defining execution models are virtual communication topology, program style, and middleware redundancy. The primary cut is made along program style lines, and the two general categories are manager/worker and single program multiple data (SPMD). In the first case, a virtual star communication topology is assumed. In particular, the manager communicates with each worker, but the workers do not communicate with each other. In the typical scenario, the manager assigns work to a worker, and the worker returns the result when the task is complete. If the worker should fail, the MPI/FT middleware returns an error to the manager, who can restart the failed worker if desired and reassign the task. Other workers are unaffected; the only vulnerable process is the manager. There are three approaches to handling redundancy of the master in the middleware. In the first case, the middleware layer provides no redundancy; however, the user can easily implement application-level checkpointing of the master process. The other two possible approaches to redundancy in the middleware layer are passive and active and are not yet implemented in MPI/FT.

In the SPMD case, an all-to-all communication topology is assumed. In addition, it is assumed that the application is synchronous and that communication occurs at regular intervals. As a result, failure notification is propagated in a synchronous manner to all the processes. A single coordinator is responsible for managing recovery of the failed process, and its needs for redundancy are similar to those for the manager in the previous paragraph. The possible levels of coordinator redundancy provided by the middleware are the same as those already mentioned. The current implementation provides no redundancy, and a manual restart is required if the coordinator fails. The two unimplemented approaches are passive and active replication of the coordinator.

MPI/FT provides four API extensions that are intended to assist the user in implementing fault tolerance. The first two are available to both program styles described above. The `MPIFT_GET_DEAD_RANKS()` extension allows the application to poll for failure notification. `MPIFT_RECOVER_RANK()` can be used to initiate the recovery of failed processes. Two additional API extensions are provided for SPMD programs. Those are `MPIFT_CHKPT_DO()` and `MPIFT_CHKPT_RECOVER()`. These are collective operations that facilitate application-level checkpointing by saving and loading data to and from stable storage. Gropp and Lusk [24] also propose the use of API extensions to provide support for fault tolerance. However, their approach is centered around the concept of a process array, which would play the role of a communicator but would be allowed to grow or shrink. Corresponding point-to-point communication operations would be needed, but no collective operations would be implemented for a process array.

11.3 Conclusions

The work presented in this chapter makes it clear that fault tolerance in scientific computing is an active and interesting area of research. The range of activities includes developing naturally fault-tolerant algorithms, developing techniques to reduce overhead incurred by traditional approaches, and incorporating the ability to support fault tolerance in MPI implementations. Furthermore, new activities aimed at pooling resources to better address the problem are starting. One example is the merging of the LA-MPI, FT-MPI, LAM/MPI, and PACX-MPI development teams into the Open MPI effort [20].

In addition to ongoing research, a host of topics remain to be addressed to provide a complete fault-tolerance solution. Among those are failure prediction, process and data migration, load redistribution, verification and validation, managing detection and recovery across multiple software libraries, run-time environments, and system services. As scientific computing platforms continue to evolve, so will the challenges in fault tolerance. Thus, we can expect many years of interesting problems and innovative work in this research area.

Acknowledgments

The authors wish to thank Jack Dongarra, Christian Engelmann, Edgar Gabriel, Al Geist, Rich Graham, Bill Gropp, Tammy Kolda, Andrew Lumsdaine, Jeff Napper, Tony Skjellum, and Ashok Srinivasan for their participation in minisymposia on fault tolerance at the Eleventh SIAM Conference on Parallel Processing for Scientific Computing, and for many informative discussions. The authors would also like to thank Mike Heroux, Padma Raghavan, and Horst Simon for putting this book together and inviting us to participate.

Bibliography

[1] A. AGBARIA AND R. FRIEDMAN, *Starfish: Fault-tolerant dynamic MPI programs on clusters of workstations*, in Proc. Eighth IEEE International Symposium on High Performance Distributed Computing, August 1999, pp. 167–176.

[2] O. AXELSSON, *Iterative Solution Methods*, Cambridge University Press, Cambridge, UK, 1994.

[3] L. BAFFICO, S. BERNARD, Y. MADAY, G. TURINICI, AND G. ZERAH, *Parallel-in-time molecular-dynamics simulations*, Physical Review E (Statistical, Nonlinear, and Soft Matter Physics), 66 (2002), pp. 57701–57704.

[4] R. BATCHU, Y. S. DANDASS, A. SKJELLUM, AND M. BEDDHU, *MPI/FT: A model-based approach to low-overhead fault tolerant message-passing middleware*, Cluster Computing, 7 (2004), pp. 303–315.

[5] G. M. BAUDET, *Asynchronous iterative methods for multiprocessors*, Journal of the ACM, 25 (1978), pp. 226–244.

[6] K. P. BIRMAN, *Building Secure and Reliable Network Applications*, Manning Publications Company, Greenwich, CT, 1996.

[7] G. BOSILCA, A. BOUTEILLER, F. CAPPELLO, S. DJILALI, G. FEDAK, C. GERMAIN, T. HERAULT, P. LEMARINIER, O. LODYGENSKY, F. MAGNIETTE, V. NERI, AND A. SELIKHOV, *MPICH-V: Toward a scalable fault tolerant MPI for volatile nodes*, in Proceedings of SuperComputing, November 2002, IEEE, Los Alamitos, CA.

[8] G. BRONEVETSKY, D. MARQUES, K. PINGALI, AND P. STODGHILL, *Collective operations in an application-level fault-tolerant MPI system*, in International Conference on Supercomputing, June 2003, IEEE, Los Alamitos, CA.

[9] G. BURNS, R. DAOUD, AND J. VAIGL, *LAM An open cluster environment for MPI*, in Proceedings of Supercomputing Symposium, June 1994, IEEE, Los Alamitos, CA, pp. 379–386.

[10] J. CASAS, D. CLARK, P. GALBIATI, R. KONURU, S. OTTO, R. PROUTY, AND J. WALPOLE, *MIST: PVM with transparent migration and checkpointing*, in Proceedings of the Third Annual PVM Users' Group Meeting, Pittsburgh, PA, May 1995.

[11] Y. Z. CHANG, K. S. DING, AND J. J. TSAY, *Interface for clusters of work-stations on local area networks*, International Computer Symposium, Taipai, Taiwan, Dec. 1996.

[12] D. CHAZAN AND M. MIRANKER, *Chaotic relaxation*, Linear Algebra and Its Applications, 2 (1969), pp. 199–222.

[13] W. R. DIETER AND J. E. LUMPP, JR., *A user-level checkpointing library for POSIX threads programs*, in Proceedings of the Twenty-Ninth Annual International Symposium on Fault-Tolerant Computing, Madison, WI, 1999, pp. 224–227.

[14] J. DUELL, P. HARGROVE, AND E. ROMAN, *The design and implementation of Berkeley Lab's Linux checkpoint/restart*. http://crd.lbl.gov/~jcduell, 2003.

[15] E. N. ELNOZAHY AND W. ZWAENEPOEL, *Manetho: Transparent rollback-recovery with low overhead*, IEEE Transactions on Computers, 41 (1992), pp. 526–531.

[16] C. ENGELMANN AND G. A. GEIST, *A diskless checkpointing algorithm for super-scale architectures applied to the fast Fourier transform*, in Proceedings of Challenges of Large-Scale Applications in Distributed Environments (CLADE) Workshop, June 2003, Seattle, WA.

[17] ———, *Java Cellular Architecture Simulator*. http://www.csm.ornl.gov/~engelman, 2004.

[18] ———, *Super-scalable algorithms for computing on 100,000 processors*. Lecture Notes in Computer Science (LNCS), volume 3514, Proceedings of ICCS, 2005, Atlanta, GA, pp. 313–320.

[19] G. E. FAGG, E. GABRIEL, Z. CHEN, T. ANGSKUN, G. BOSILCA, A. BUKOVSKI, AND J. J. DONGARRA, *Fault tolerant communication library and applications for high performance*, in Proc. Los Alamos Computer Science Institute Symposium, Los Alamos, NM, October 2003.

[20] E. GABRIEL, G. E. FAGG, G. BOSILCA, T. ANGSKUN, J. J. DONGARRA, J. M. SQUYRES, V. SAHAY, P. KAMBADUR, B. BARRETT, A. LUMSDAINE, R. H. CASTAIN, D. J. DANIEL, R. L. GRAHAM, AND T. S. WOODALL, *Open MPI: Goals, concept, and design of a next generation MPI implementation*, in Proceedings, Eleventh European PVM/MPI Users' Group Meeting, September 2004, Budapest, Hungary.

[21] A. GEIST, A. BEGUELIN, J. DONGARRA, W. JIANG, R. MANCHEK, AND V. SUNDERAM, *PVM: Parallel Virtual Machine, A Users' Guide and Tutorial for Networked Parallel Computing*, MIT Press, Cambridge, MA, 1994.

[22] R. L. GRAHAM, S.-E. CHOI, D. J. DANIEL, N. N. DESAI, R. G. MINNICH, C. E. RASMUSSEN, L. D. RISINGER, AND M. W. SUKALSKI, *A network-failure-tolerant message-passing system for terascale clusters*, International Journal of Parallel Programming, 31 (2003), pp. 285–303.

[23] W. GROPP, E. LUSK, N. DOSS, AND A. SKJELLUM, *A high-performance, portable implementation of the MPI message passing interface standard*, Parallel Computing, 22 (1996), pp. 789–828.

[24] W. GROPP AND E. LUSK, *Fault tolerance in message passing interface programs*, International Journal of High Performance Computing Applications, 18 (2004), pp. 363–372.

[25] P. D. HOUGH, T. G. KOLDA, AND V. J. TORCZON, *Asynchronous parallel pattern search for nonlinear optimization*, SIAM Journal on Scientific Computing, 23 (2001), pp. 134–156.

[26] V. E. HOWLE, *Fault tolerant linear algebra with Krylov methods*. In preparation.

[27] J. LANGOU, G. BOSILCA, Z. CHEN, AND J. DONGARRA, *Recovery patterns for iterative methods in a parallel unstable environment*. Submitted to SIAM Journal on Scientific Computing, 2005.

[28] J. LEON, A. L. FISHER, AND P. STEENKISTE, *Fail-safe PVM: A portable package for distributed programming with transparent recovery*, Tech. Report CMU-CS-93-124, School of Computer Science, Carnegie Mellon University, Pittsburgh, PA, February 1993.

[29] M. LITZKOW, T. TANNENBAUM, J. BASNEY, AND M. LIVNY, *Checkpoint and migration of Unix processes in the Condor distributed processing system*, Tech. Report CS-TR-1997-1346, University of Wisconsin, Madison, April 1997.

[30] G. R. LIU, *Mesh Free Methods: Moving Beyond the Finite Element Method*, CRC Press, Boca Raton, FL, 2002.

[31] MESSAGE PASSING INTERFACE FORUM, *MPI-2: Extensions to the message passing interface*. http://www.mpi-forum.org, 2003.

[32] A. N. NORMAN, S.-E. CHOI, AND C. LIN, *Compiler-generated staggered checkpointing*, in Proc. 7th ACM Workshop on Languages, Compilers, and Runtime Support for Scalable Systems, October 2004.

[33] Y. NOTAY, *Flexible conjugate gradients*, SIAM Journal on Scientific Computing, 22 (2000), pp. 1444–1460.

[34] J. S. PLANK, M. BECK, G. KINGSLEY, AND K. LI, *Libckpt: Transparent checkpointing under Unix*, in Proceedings of the 1995 Winter USENIX Technical Conference, January 1995, New Orleans, LA, pp. 213–223.

[35] J. S. PLANK, *A tutorial on Reed-Solomon coding for fault-tolerance in RAID-like systems*, Software – Practice and Experience, 27 (1997), pp. 995–1012.

[36] J. PLANK, Y. KIM, AND J. DONGARRA, *Fault tolerant matrix operations for networks of workstations using diskless checkpointing*, Journal of Parallel and Distributed Computing, 43 (1997), pp. 125–138.

[37] S. RAO, L. ALVISI, AND H. M. VIN, *Egida: An extensible toolkit for low-overhead fault-tolerance*, in Proceedings of the 29th Fault-Tolerant Computing Symposium (FTCS-29), Madison, Wisconsin, June 1999, pp. 48–55.

[38] I. S. REED AND G. SOLOMON, *Polynomial codes over certain finite fields*, Journal of the Society for Industrial and Applied Mathematics, 8 (1960), pp. 300–304.

[39] Y. SAAD AND M. H. SCHULTZ, *GMRES: A generalized minimal residual algorithm for solving nonsymmetric linear systems*, SIAM Journal on Scientific and Statistical Computing, 7 (1986), pp. 856–869.

[40] Y. SAAD, *A flexible inner-outer preconditioned GMRES algorithm*, SIAM Journal on Scientific and Statistical Computing, 14 (1993), pp. 461–469.

[41] S. SANKARAN, J. M. SQUYRES, B. BARRETT, A. LUMSDAINE, J. DUELL, P. HARGROVE, AND E. ROMAN, *The LAM/MPI checkpoint/restart framework: System-initiated checkpointing*, International Journal of High Performance Computing Applications, 19 (2005), pp. 479–493.

[42] J. M. SQUYRES AND A. LUMSDAINE, *A component architecture for LAM/MPI*, in Proceedings, Tenth European PVM/MPI Users' Group Meeting, September/October 2003, Venice, Italy, pp. 379–387.

[43] A. SRINIVASAN AND N. CHANDRA, *Latency tolerance through parallelization of time in scientific applications*, in Proceedings of the Eighteenth International Parallel and Distributed Processing Symposium, April 2004, Santa Fe, NM.

[44] G. STELLNER, *CoCheck: Checkpointing and process migration for MPI*, in Proceedings of the Tenth International Parallel Processing Symposium, 1996, Honolulu, Hawaii.

[45] H. ZHONG AND J. NIEH, *CRAK: Linux checkpoint/restart as a kernel module*, Tech. Report CUCS-014-01, Department of Computer Science, Columbia University, New York, NY, November 2001.

Part III

Tools and Frameworks for Parallel Applications

Chapter 12
Parallel Tools and Environments: A Survey

William D. Gropp and Andrew Lumsdaine

Writing parallel programs is difficult. Besides the inherent difficulties associated with writing any kind of software, parallel programs have additional complexities due to data management, process management, and process synchronization. Further, even the basic activities involved in writing and using parallel programs are often more difficult than those same activities on a conventional, uniprocessor computer. Some of this difficulty is due to the traditional dearth of tools for parallel programming and parallel computing. Early users of parallel systems had to write their own tools from scratch, sometimes even including basic system software. Some features, such as robust, fast file systems, were simply unavailable.

Today the situation is quite different. While parallel computing environments are still not as easy to use or as robust as workstation environments, great strides have been made in improving parallel computing for end users. These improved environments have been driven by the rapid expansion in the number of parallel computers and the number of people using them (enabled in large part by the exploitation of commodity components, e.g., by the Beowulf project [7]). Similarly, improved parallel programming has been enabled by the development of a standard programming model and applications programmer interface for developing parallel scientific applications. The MPI standard [3, 5, 6] allows the development of both parallel programs and parallel libraries. By supporting software libraries, MPI allows programmers to build applications in terms of the natural operations for their application, such as solving a system of nonlinear equations, rather than low-level, specialized parallel programming commands. As a result, an active community of builders and users of parallel tools has arisen.

This chapter surveys the categories of tools useful for parallel computing and briefly describes some particular tools in each category. Section 12.1 describes software and tools that can be used to set up and manage a parallel computing cluster. Section 12.2 focuses on tools for computational science, including numerical libraries, software environments, and complete applications.

Many tools and environments are already available; no single chapter (or even book!) could list them all. We cover some of the most widely used open-source and research tools, with particular emphasis on tools that were featured at the Eleventh SIAM Conference on Parallel Processing for Scientific Computing. (The presence or absence of any tool in our survey should not be considered as an endorsement or otherwise. To be fair, we have not specifically named commercial products.) New tools are being developed, and existing tools continue to evolve; we encourage users to ask others what tools they use and to search the Internet for new developments.

12.1 Software and tools for building and running clusters

In the early days of cluster computing, building a cluster meant ordering boxes of computers, unpacking them, loading software onto each one, and then writing custom code to manage the collection of machines as a parallel computer. Today one can order a cluster, complete with all the software needed to operate it, from a vendor who will install it, test it, and service it. Understanding the different system tools available for clusters is still necessary, however, and those who choose to build their own cluster (still often the best choice for small clusters) will need to acquire the tools that operate the cluster and allow users to build and run programs. This section can only touch on these tools; a cluster reference such as [4, 8] will provide a more thorough discussion.

Setting up and running a cluster involves three aspects:

- Node configuration: How will each individual node be configured (e.g,. what operating system and what software will go on each node)?

- Cluster configuration: How will the individual nodes be connected and configured together to make up a parallel computing resource?

- Cluster management: How will the individual nodes and the cluster configuration be managed over time (e.g., how will new software be installed and how will jobs be submitted)?

12.1.1 Node configuration

Clusters comprise a collection of individual computers. An important aspect of cluster setup is therefore the configuration of each of those nodes in the cluster.

Operating system

The most fundamental choice in setting up individual cluster nodes is the operating system. Linux is a common choice in many cases. Linux distributions are available from a number of providers, and the cost of acquisition is typically quite low (often free). Linux has been ported to the various microprocessors that are used in computational clusters, including new 64-bit architectures. Because of the popularity and ubiquity of Linux, a large selection of software packages is available for it (in source and packaged binary form), including most of the tools for parallel computing that are mentioned in this chapter. There are a huge number of Linux distributions (both well known and obscure). Some of the more widely used distributions for cluster computing are RedHat, Debian, SuSE, Fedora, Mandrake, Gentoo, and Yellowdog. In choosing a distribution, one should consider issues such as ease of installation, availability of support, availability of packaged software, and compatibility with specialized hardware, such as high-speed interconnects.

Compilers and debuggers

To develop programs, compilers are needed. The freely available GNU compilers support all of the popular languages in scientific computing (including FORTRAN 95 with the recent release of g95). Higher performance and additional features, such as support for the OpenMP standard [1], are available from a range of commercial compiler vendors. Program development tools, including commercial parallel debuggers, are also available.

Sequential libraries

High levels of parallel performance depend on high levels of sequential performance. Many hardware vendors provide highly tuned versions of sequential libraries such as the BLAS. Many of the BLAS routines are also available as part of the ATLAS project, which uses automatic tuning techniques to provide performance equal to vendor-tuned BLAS in many cases.

12.1.2 Cluster configuration

Beyond the configuration of each individual node, an important aspect of cluster setup is the infrastructure that allows the collection of nodes to work together effectively as a cluster.

Network architecture

The nodes in a computational cluster will almost certainly be equipped out of the box with 100 Mbit/s or even (as is becoming more and more common) 1 Gbit/s Ethernet. This network will be used for cluster administration and most cluster services (such as basic network file system (NFS) file sharing, directory services, and remote login). One important decision is whether to make this a public network or a private network (having public or private IP addresses, respectively). With private addressing, the cluster accesses the public Internet via a gateway machine or router, and this setup can provide certain security and administrative benefits.

For some classes of computational problems, Ethernet may offer sufficient performance. In many cases, however, one will want to add a second high-performance network such as Myrinet, Infiniband, or Quadrics to explicitly support communication for parallel computing. Also desirable will be the availability of an MPI library that is ported (and tuned) for the selected interconnect. Hardware vendors providing high-performance interconnects may also provide a corresponding MPI implementation. Several of the open-source implementations support these interconnects as well.

Basic services

The nodes in a cluster will need basic services such as shared file systems, directory services, gateway services, and cluster administration. For reasons of symmetry (and load balancing), it is best not to use for this purpose nodes that will also be used to run compute jobs. Rather, some number of "head node" servers should be apportioned to handle such services. The exact ratio of service nodes to compute nodes will depend on individual needs, but typically one could expect to support 8 to 32 compute nodes with a single service node.

File system

Any computer needs a file system on which to store data. Unix-base (including Linux-based) clusters will usually provide the NFS. This is the system commonly used on Unix desktop workstations and Unix servers and is often a good choice as the file system for source files. NFS may be a poor choice for use by parallel applications, however, because it was not designed to support multiple processes accessing (particularly writing to) the same file. For I/O to and from parallel applications, a parallel file system should be used. There are a number to choose from, including freely available (such as PVFS2) and commercially supported, such as Lustre (www.clusterfs.com), GPFS (www-1.ibm.com/servers/eserver/clusters/software/gpfs.html), and Panasas (www.panasas.com), and GFS (www.redhat.com/software/rha/gfs).

Middleware

Parallel programs require support for a parallel programming model. While some parallel languages are available with compilers for clusters, most users in computational science use the MPI standard. This standard describes a library of routines that allow processes running on different nodes to communicate and coordinate. There are a number of implementations of the MPI standard; any application that uses MPI may be compiled with the mpi header files provided by the implementation and linked with the MPI library provided by the implementation. Thus, one can use any MPI implementation with any MPI program. Popular MPI implementations are MPICH2 (www.mcs.anl.gov/mpi/mpich2/) and LAM/MPI (www.lam-mpi.org); another implementation, OpenMPI (www.open-mpi.org), should be available when this book is released. Commercial implementations of MPI are also available.

12.1.3 Cluster management

Once a cluster is up and running, various ongoing administrative tasks and policies must be attended to.

Scheduling

A cluster will typically be a shared resource with multiple users. The computational resources for a parallel job should be considered together and allocated as a single resource. Inadvertently sharing even a single node between parallel jobs can cause severe load-balancing problems for those jobs. Manually managing the use of multiple compute nodes (which in a cluster are also essentially workstations) is extraordinarily difficult when even moderate numbers of users and nodes are involved. The most effective way to allocate groups of nodes for exclusive use is via a batch scheduler. Popular batch schedulers include OpenPBS (www.openpbs.org), Torque (http://www.clusterresources.com/pages/products/torque-resource-manager.php), and SLURM (www.llnl.gov/linux/slurm).

Integrated node and cluster configuration management

In a cluster, each node (typically a single PC) needs to have an operating system loaded onto it; the node must also be configured to use the interconnection network that allows the nodes to communicate with each other.

Setting up the individual nodes one by one in a cluster of any size can be a tedious and error-prone task (as would be upgrading a cluster in such a fashion). Fortunately, tools exist to automate this process as well as to automate the process of transforming a collection of nodes into an integrated cluster. Three popular tools are ROCKS (rocks.npaci.edu/Rocks), OSCAR (oscar.openclustergroup.org), and Cplant www.cs.sandia.gov/cplant.

These packages represent different approaches to the management of cluster system software. ROCKS is a *description-based* method. This approach uses tools built into the operating system to describe and assemble the software needed for each node. The advantage of this approach is that it works well with nearly any hardware; but because it is built atop installation tools in an operating system, it limits the choice of operating system. In the case of ROCKS, only certain Linux distributions are allowed.

OSCAR is a *disk-image-based* method. This approach uses a custom installation program to build a disk image that can then be copied to all of the nodes in the cluster. This approach allows greater flexibility in the choice of operating system (some, such as the Chiba City system, allow both Windows and Linux to be used) but may limit the choice of hardware (such as disks or new network interfaces).

Cplant is provided as source code and contains a complete environment targeted at scalability, including runtime utilities and debugging support.

Regardless of which toolkit is chosen, when a cluster management system finishes its initial setup process, the computational cluster will be ready to use. And, since these toolkits are aimed at supporting high-performance science computing, the cluster as initially configured will include the other system software components discussed above.

One of the reasons for the success of clusters is the ability to take advantage of commodity components. This is most obvious in hardware, but it is also true in software. There are multiple commodity operating systems, compilers, file systems, MPI implementations, and parallel programming environments. However, not all these tools work together seamlessly—particularly the tools that manage the cluster. The Scalable Systems Software project (www.scidac.org/ScalableSystems), part of the DoE SciDAC program, seeks to develop standards for interfaces between system software components to enable the development of new functionalities.

12.2 Tools for computational science

Many tools are available for conducting all phases of computational science on clusters. Many of the chapters in this book discuss particular tools in depth; in this chapter, we briefly summarize some of the available tools. Tools chosen for this section were described at the 2004 SIAM parallel processing conference in one or more talks. Not all tools are included, and many other tools are available for clusters. This section is intended to give a sampling that illustrates the breadth of tools available for parallel computing. The section is organized by category, starting with software libraries for solving linear and nonlinear equations.

12.2.1 Solvers for linear and nonlinear equations

The development of solvers for linear and nonlinear systems of equations for parallel computers is as old as parallel computers themselves. As a result, many mature and efficient libraries are available for these problems. Chapters 9 and 13 discuss the state of the art in these areas.

Following are some of the tools featured at the 2004 SIAM meeting on parallel processing.

- pARMS (http://www-users.cs.umn.edu/~saad/software/pARMS) provides preconditioned Krylov solvers for linear systems, using recursive multilevel ILU preconditioning.

- Prometheus (www.cs.berkeley.edu/~madams/prometheus) is a scalable unstructured finite element solver employing multigrid.

- SuperLU (crd.lbl.gov/~xiaoye/SuperLU) is a sparse direct linear solver, with versions for nonparallel machines, shared memory, and distributed memory.

- PETSc (www.mcs.anl.gov/petsc) is a package for solving linear and nonlinear systems of equations, emphasizing support for equations from PDE discretizations.

- hypre (www.llnl.gov/CASC/linear_solvers) provides parallel preconditioners featuring multigrid.

- Petra is part of Trilinos (software.sandia.gov/trilinos) and provides the basic linear algebra support, such as parallel sparse matrix operations.

- PLAPACK (www.cs.utexas.edu/users/plapack) is a parallel dense linear algebra package.

- ScaLAPACK (www.netlib.org/scalapack/scalapack_home.html) is another parallel dense linear algebra package.

In evaluating libraries, beyond the usual issues of correctness and accuracy, one should consider completeness and interoperability. While these terms are not precise, they describe important qualitative properties of a library. A library is *complete* if it provides all the routines needed to create and use the data structures that it needs. For example, a sparse matrix library is not complete if there are no routines to help assemble the sparse matrix data structures. Libraries that are not complete in this sense require more effort to use.

Interoperability is the property that allows an application to use multiple libraries. Some libraries and tools may assume that no other tools are used in the application, an assumption that can limit the applications for which the library is suitable.

12.2.2 Parallel programming and languages

Parallel programming is considered by many to be too difficult. Without question, it is more difficult than programming a single processor; moreover, writing bad parallel programs seems to be easier than writing bad regular programs. Many efforts have been undertaken to simplify parallel programming. One is to develop a new, general-purpose parallel language—often, an extension of an existing language. For example, the partitioned global address space (PGAS) languages provide a unified view of the entire parallel computer, rather than using MPI to connect otherwise separate programs on each node. Important examples of these languages are Unified Parallel C (UPC; upc.gwu.edu) and CoArray FORTRAN (CAF).[1] PGAS languages have the concept of local and remote memory and hence promise efficient implementations on clusters. Users have reported some positive experience with these languages, but they are not yet widely available and do not always offer the highest performance.

Another approach has been to build tools optimized for a particular domain or class of algorithms. For example, both the language Cilk (supertech.lcs.mit.edu/cilk) and the library MasterWorker (www.cs.wisc.edu/condor/mw) provide good support for task-parallelism. Charm++ (charm.cs.uiuc.edu/research/charm) also provides a programming model that supports parallelism through the creation and management of large numbers of virtual tasks.

In the future, we expect to see more such tools. Domain-specific languages are simply programming languages tuned to a particular domain and usually a particular data structure within that domain (data-structure-specific language is often a more accurate description). These languages can take advantage of knowledge about the domain to raise the level of abstraction and hide many of the details of parallel programming from the user. One example is parallel-R (www.aspect-sdm.org/Parallel-R), a parallel version of the statistical language R.

The DARPA high-productivity computer systems project is an important project to watch (www.highproductivity.org). This project seeks to develop a combination of hardware and software (including new computer languages) to significantly increase programmer productivity. Even if these specific efforts never become commercial systems, the ideas developed will undoubtedly stimulate further work in computer architecture and programming languages.

12.2.3 Performance evaluation

Two major factors motivate the use of parallel computing: the need for more computing performance and the need for more memory in which to perform the calculations. Thus,

---
[1] Earlier known as F--.

tools with which to identify and repair performance bugs are a critical part of any parallel computing environment.

For most applications, most of the gap between the performance of an application and the peak performance is due not to the parallelism but to the capabilities of the individual nodes. Thus, tuning the single-node performance is the first and often most important step.

An important step toward making possible high-quality performance evaluation has been the development of a set of routines that provide portable access to the performance counters maintained by most modern CPUs. The PAPI library (http://icl.cs.utk.edu/papi) is available for many operating systems and processors and provides such a portable interface.

Tools that work closely with the compiler or the source code can provide more context for understanding the reasons for the measured performance and suggest ways to improve performance. Tools such as those in the HPCToolkit (www.hipersoft.rice.edu/hpctoolkit) provide detailed information about the behavior of an application.

Once the single-processor or single-node performance of an application has been evaluated and tuned, one should look at the parallel performance. Most tools for understanding the parallel performance of applications fall into two categories: tools that create a log file of every parallel computing event, such as sending or receiving a message, along with tools for analyzing and displaying the contents of this long file, and tools that create a summary of the parallel computing events, for example, by counting the amount of data sent between two processes.

Tuning and Analysis Utilities (TAU; www.cs.uoregon.edu/research/paracomp/tau/tautools) is another package that provides tools for instrumenting and analyzing applications.

Examples of logfile-based tools are Paraver (Chapter 2), SvPablo (www.renci.unc.edu/Project/SVPablo/SvPabloOverview.htm), Jumpshot (www.mcs.anl.gov/perfvis/software/viewers), and Vampir (now part of the Intel Cluster Tools, www.intel.com/software/products/cluster).

Summary tools include FPMPI (www.mcs.anl.gov/fpmpi/WWW) and mpiP (www.llnl.gov/CASC/mpip).

The MPI standard provides support for the development of customized logging tools through what is called the "profiling interface." This feature of MPI provides a way to intercept any MPI call, perform any user-specified action, and then invoke the original MPI operation. In fact, many of the parallel performance tools use this interface. Users that need special kinds of information should consider using the profiling interface (a required part of all MPI implementations).

12.2.4 Problem-solving environments

Parallel programming is not necessary in some applications areas because of the availability of problem-solving environments (PSEs). These provide substantial or complete support for computations, turning a parallel computer into just another source of computer cycles.

Among the PSEs featured at the SIAM 2004 parallel processing meeting were the following:

- BioPSE (www.sci.utah.edu/ncrr/software) is a PSE for biomedical problems and includes, in addition to solver and visualization tools, support for computational steering.
- SCIRun (software.sci.utah.edu/scirun.html) is an environment for building problem solving environments. (BioPSE is built on top of SCIRun.)
- Cactus (www.cactuscode.org) is a PSE supporting the collaborative development of parallel applications in science and engineering, and it is well known for work in CFD and astrophysics.
- NWChem (www.emsl.pnl.gov/docs/nwchem/nwchem.html) is a package for computational chemistry.

Commercial applications include fluid dynamics, structural mechanics, and visualization. More applications can be expected because of the rapidly increasing number of clusters provides a market for them.

12.2.5 Other tools

Many other categories of tools exist in addition to those described above. This book, for example, includes chapters on mesh generation (Chapter 8), component architectures for interoperable software components (Chapter 14), and fault tolerance (Chapter 11). Other sources of information about parallel tools and environments include books such as [2] and [4] as well as online sources such as the Beowulf list (www.beowulf.org). And, of course, using Internet search engines will help one discover new tools as they continue to be developed and deployed.

12.3 Conclusion

For many scientists and engineers, parallel computing has been made practical by the combination of commodity hardware and commodity software, aided by the development of standards—particularly those for parallel computing, such as the MPI standard—and a healthy competition between groups developing software and hardware to these standards.

We close this chapter by summarizing some general recommendations for users and developers of computational science tools for parallel computers.

For users, first and foremost: Don't write code if you don't need to!

1. If you are setting up your own cluster, use one of the setup tools.
2. Use a PSE if possible.
3. Use one or more parallel libraries to raise the level of abstraction, essentially turning MPI into a higher-level, domain-specific language for your application area.
4. Use an appropriate programming model and performance tools.

For tool developers, perhaps the most important recommendation is to ensure that your tool can interoperate with other tools. Tools should also be complete in terms of providing not just the core algorithm but also the routines or tools that get a user from their problem description to your tool.

Bibliography

[1] L. DAGUM AND R. MENON, *Openmp: An industry-standard api for shared-memory programming*, Computing in Science and Engineering, 5 (1998), pp. 46–55.

[2] J. DONGARRA, I. FOSTER, G. FOX, W. GROPP, K. KENNEDY, L. TORCZON, AND A. WHITE, eds., *Sourcebook of Parallel Computing*, Morgan Kaufmann, San Francisco, CA, 2003.

[3] W. GROPP, S. HUSS-LEDERMAN, A. LUMSDAINE, E. LUSK, B. NITZBERG, W. SAPHIR, AND M. SNIR, *MPI—The Complete Reference: Volume 2, The MPI-2 Extensions*, MIT Press, Cambridge, MA, 1998.

[4] W. GROPP, E. LUSK, AND T. STERLING, eds., *Beowulf Cluster Computing with Linux*, 2nd ed., MIT Press, Cambridge, MA, 2003.

[5] MESSAGE PASSING INTERFACE FORUM, *MPI: A Message-Passing Interface standard*, International Journal of Supercomputer Applications, 8 (1994), pp. 165–414.

[6] M. SNIR, S. W. OTTO, S. HUSS-LEDERMAN, D. W. WALKER, AND J. DONGARRA, *MPI—The Complete Reference: Volume 1, The MPI Core,* 2nd edition, MIT Press, Cambridge, MA, 1998.

[7] T. STERLING, D. SAVARESE, D. J. BECKER, J. E. DORBAND, U. A. RANAWAKE, AND C. V. PACKER, *BEOWULF : A parallel workstation for scientific computation*, in International Conference on Parallel Processing, Vol.1: Architecture, Boca Raton, FL, Aug. 1995, CRC Press, pp. 11–14.

[8] T. STERLING, ED., *Beowulf Cluster Computing with Windows*, MIT Press, Cambridge, MA, 2002.

Chapter 13
Parallel Linear Algebra Software

Victor Eijkhout, Julien Langou, and Jack Dongarra

In this chapter we discuss numerical software for linear algebra problems on parallel computers. We focus on some of the most common numerical operations: linear system solving and eigenvalue computations.

Numerical operations such as linear system solving and eigenvalue calculations can be applied to two different kinds of matrix storage: dense and sparse. Dense systems are in general used when essentially every matrix element is nonzero; sparse systems are used whenever a sufficiently large number of matrix elements is zero that a specialized storage scheme is warranted. For an introduction to sparse storage, see [3]. Because the two classes are so different, usually different numerical softwares apply to them.

We discuss ScaLAPACK and PLAPACK as the choices for dense linear system solving (see section 13.1). For solving sparse linear systems, there exist two classes of algorithms: direct methods and iterative methods. We will discuss SuperLU as an example of a direct solver (see section 13.2.1) and PETSc as an example of iterative solvers (see section 13.2.2). For eigenvalue computation, the distinction between sparse and dense matrices does not play so large a role as it does in systems solving; for eigenvalues the main distinction is whether one wants all possible eigenvalues and attendant eigenvectors or just a subset, typically the few largest or smallest. ScaLAPACK and PLAPACK are packages that start with a dense matrix to calculate all or potentially part of the spectrum (see section 13.1), while ARPACK (see section 13.2.3) is preferable when only part of the spectrum is wanted; since it uses reverse communication, PARPACK can handle matrices in sparse format.

In addition to numerical software operations, we discuss the issue of load balancing. We focus on two software packages, ParMetis and Chaco, which can be used in the above-mentioned sparse packages.

We conclude this chapter with a list of software for linear algebra that is freely available on the Internet [16].

13.1 Dense linear algebra software

In the most general way to solve a dense linear system in a parallel distributed environment, the matrix is stored as a distributed array, and the system is solved by Gaussian elimination. This is the basic algorithm in ScaLAPACK and PLAPACK, the two packages we discuss for solving a linear system with a distributed dense coefficient matrix. (Sparse systems are discussed in section 13.2.) On a single processor, the algorithm for dense linear system solving is fairly obvious, although a good deal of optimization is needed for high performance (see section 13.3). In a distributed context, achieving high performance—especially performance that scales up with increasing processor numbers—requires radical rethinking the basic data structures. Both ScaLAPACK and PLAPACK use the same very specific data distribution—2D block-cyclic distribution. This distribution is in fact appropriate for most operations on dense distributed systems and thus represents the key to ScaLAPACK and PLAPACK.

In this section, we explain the 2D block-cyclic distribution and focus on how to specify it in ScaLAPACK to solve a linear system or an eigen problem. We then briefly compare ScaLAPACK and PLAPACK calling style.

13.1.1 ScaLAPACK

ScaLAPACK is a parallel version of LAPACK, both in function and in software design. Like the earlier package, ScaLAPACK targets linear system solution and eigenvalue calculation for dense and banded matrices. In a way, ScaLAPACK is the culmination of a line of linear algebra packages that started with LINPACK and EISPACK. The coding of those packages was fairly straightforward, using at most BLAS level 1 operations as an abstraction level. LAPACK [1, 15] attains high efficiency on a single processor (or a small number of shared-memory processors) through the introduction of blocked algorithms and the use of BLAS level 3 operations. ScaLAPACK uses these blocked algorithms in a parallel context to attain scalably high performance on parallel computers.

The seemingly contradictory demands of portability and efficiency are realized in ScaLAPACK through confining the relevant parts of the code to two subroutine libraries: the BLAS for the computational kernels and the BLACS (basic linear algebra communication subprograms) for communication kernels. While the BLACS come with ScaLAPACK, the user is to supply the BLAS library; see section 13.3.

ScaLAPACK is intended to be called from a FORTRAN environment, as are the examples in this section. The distribution has no C prototypes, but interfacing to a C program is simple, observing the usual name conversion conventions.

13.1.2 ScaLAPACK parallel initialization

ScaLAPACK relies for its communications on the BLACS which offer an abstraction layer over MPI. Their main feature is the ability to communicate submatrices, rather than arrays, and of both rectangular and trapezoidal shape. The latter is of obvious value in factorization algorithms. We will not go into detail about BLACS here; instead, we focus on the aspects that come into play in the program initialization phase.

Suppose a parallel machine is divided into an approximately square grid of `nprows` by `npcols` processors. The following two calls set up a BLACS processor grid—its identifier is `ictxt`—and return the current processor number (by row and column) in it:

```
call sl_init(ictxt,nprows,npcols),
call blacs_gridinfo(ictxt,nprows,npcols,myprow,mypcol).
```

Correspondingly, at the end of the code, the grid is released by

```
call blacs_gridexit(ictxt).
```

A context is to ScaLAPACK what a communicator is in MPI.

ScaLAPACK data format

Creating a matrix in ScaLAPACK unfortunately is not simple. The difficulty lies in the fact that for scalable high performance on factorization algorithms, the 2D block-cyclic storage mode is to be used. The blocking is what enables the use of BLAS level 3 routines; the cyclic storage is needed for scalable parallelism.

Specifically, the block-cyclic storage implies that a global (i, j) coordinate in the matrix gets mapped to a triplet of (p, l, x) for both the i and the j directions, where p is the processor number, l the block, and x the offset inside the block.

The mapping of the data on the processors is dependent on four parameters: `nprows` and `npcols` for the processor grid (see section 13.1.2) and `bs_i` and `bs_j` for the size of the blocks inside the matrix. In Figure 13.1, we give an example of how the data are distributed among the processors.

The block sizes (`bs_i` and `bs_j`) have to be decided by the user; 64 is usually a safe bet. For generality, assuming that block sizes `bs_i` and `bs_j` have been chosen, we explain a general way to map the data onto the processors. First we determine how much storage is needed for the local part of the matrix:

```
mlocal = numroc(mglobal,bs_i,myprow,0,nprows)
nlocal = numroc(nglobal,bs_j,mypcol,0,npcols),
```

where `numroc` is a library function. (The m and n sizes of the matrix need not be equal, since ScaLAPACK also has routines for QR factorization and such.)

Filling in a matrix requires the conversion from (i, j) coordinates to (p, l, x) coordinates. It is best to use conversion functions

```
p_of_i(i,bs,p) = mod(int((i-1)/bs),p),
l_of_i(i,bs,p) = int((i-1)/(p*bs)),
x_of_i(i,bs,p) = mod(i-1,bs)+1
```

that take i or j as input, as well as the block size and the number of processors in that direction. The global matrix element (i, j) is then mapped to

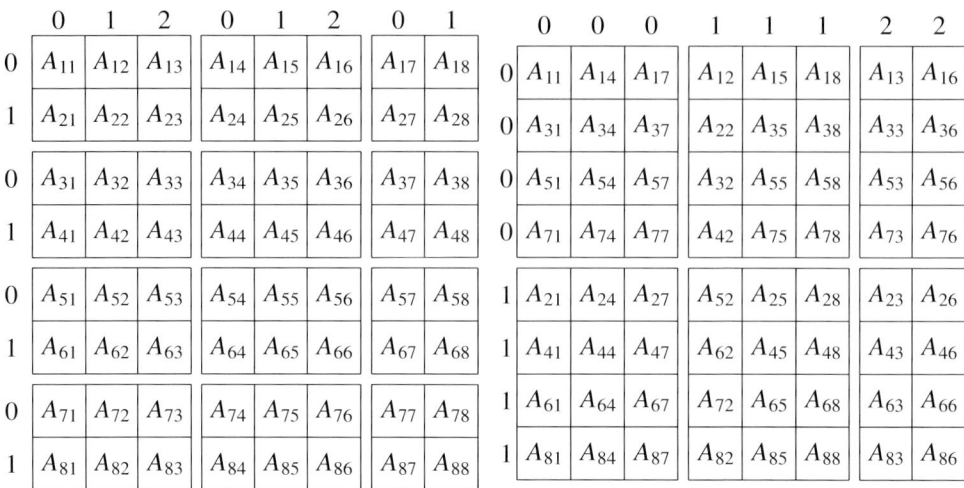

Figure 13.1. *2D block-cyclic distribution of a matrix of order n with parameters* (nprows= $n/8$, npcols= $n/8$, bs_i= 2, bs_j= 3). *On the left, the original data layout, the matrix is partitioned with blocks of size $n/8$; on the right, the data is mapped on a 2×3 processor grid.*

```
pi = p_of_i(i,bs_i,nprows)
li = l_of_i(i,bs_i,nprows)
xi = x_of_i(i,bs_i,nprows)

pj = p_of_i(j,bs_j,npcols)
lj = l_of_i(j,bs_j,npcols)
xj = x_of_i(j,bs_j,npcols)

mat(li*bs_i+xi,lj*bs_j+xj) = mat_global(i,j)
```

if the current processor is (p_i, p_j).

13.1.3 Calling ScaLAPACK routines

ScaLAPACK routines adhere to the LAPACK naming scheme: PXYYZZZ, where P indicates parallel; X is the "precision" (meaning single or double, real or complex); YY is the shape and properties (with GE for general rectangular, TR for triangular, PO for symmetric positive definite ...); and ZZZ denotes the function.

For most functions there is a "simple driver" (for instance, SV for system solving), which makes the routine name in our example PDGESV for double precision, as well as an "expert driver," which has X attached to the name, PDGESVX in this example. The expert driver usually has more input options and usually returns more diagnostic information.

In the call to a ScaLAPACK routine, information about the matrix has to be passed by way of a descriptor:

```
      integer desca(9)
      call descinit(desca,
 >         mglobal,nglobal, bs_i,bs_j, 0,0,ictxt,lda,ierr)
      call pdgesv(nglobal,1, mat_local,1,1, desca,ipiv,
 >         rhs_local,1,1, descb,  ierr)
```

where `lda` is the allocated first dimension of a (`lda>mlocal`).

ScaLAPACK linear solver routines support dense and banded matrices. The drivers for solving a linear system are `PxyySV`, where yy is `GE,GB,PO,PB,PT` for general, general banded, SPD, SPD banded, and SPD tridiagonal, respectively. See the *ScaLAPACK Users' Guide* [4] for more details. The input matrix A of the system is on output overwritten with the LU factorization, and the right-hand side B is overwritten with the solution. Temporary storage is needed only for the (integer) pivot locations for nonsymmetric matrices.

For the symmetric (Hermitian) eigenvalue problem there are the simple and expert driver routines PxSYEV (PxHEEV). The nonsymmetric real problem is tackled in two steps: reduction to upper Hessenberg form by `PDGEHRD`, followed by reduction of the Hessenberg matrix to Schur form by `PDLAHQR`. The non-Hermitian complex problem is not supported. ScaLAPACK has routines for the generalized eigenvalue problem only in the symmetric (Hermitian) definite case: `PxSYGST` (with x=S,D) and `PxHEGST` (with x=C,Z).

13.1.4 PLAPACK

PLAPACK [18] is a package with functionality very similar to ScaLAPACK but with a different calling style. It also relies on optimized BLAS routines and is therefore able to achieve a high performance. Whereas ScaLAPACK uses a calling style that is very FORTRAN in nature, to stay close to its LAPACK roots, PLAPACK uses a more object-oriented style. Its interface is similar in philosophy to that of PETSc (see section 13.2.2).

As an illustration of this object-oriented handling of matrices and vectors, here are matrix-vector multiply and triangular system solve calls:

```
PLA_Gemv( PLA_NO_TRANS, one, A, x, zero, b );
PLA_Trsv( PLA_LOWER_TRIANGULAR, PLA_NO_TRANSPOSE,
                PLA_UNIT_DIAG, A, b );
```

The distribution of the matrix over the processors is induced by a distribution template declared by the user and passed to the matrix creation call:

```
PLA_Matrix_create(  datatype, size, size,
                    templ, PLA_ALIGN_FIRST,
                    PLA_ALIGN_FIRST, &A );
```

PLAPACK wins over ScaLAPACK in user-friendliness in filling in the matrix: like in PETSc, matrix elements can be specified anywhere, and instead of writing them directly into the data structure, they are passed by a `PLA_API_axpy_matrix_to_global` call. On the other hand, PLAPACK seems to lack ScaLAPACK's sophistication of simple and expert drivers, less attention seems to be paid to issues of numerical stability, and the coverage of PLAPACK is not as large as the one of ScaLAPACK.

13.2 Sparse linear algebra software

Software for sparse matrices exploits the sparsity to reduce the storage requirements and the number of floating-point operations performed. Much more than with dense systems, there exists a large variety of software with substantial differences in the algorithms used. Two aspects leads to a particularly complex software environment. First, whereas the best method for dense problem is generally easy to decide, the best method for solving a given sparse problem is highly dependent of the matrix itself, its graph, and its numerical properties. This means that for any given task we can choose from among several packages. Second, software packages are often stronger in some particular aspect of the problem, and an optimal solution is often a combination of packages. This results in a categorization of software along the lines of the various subtasks. Section 13.4 classifies software both ways.

For linear system solving, the most foolproof algorithm is still Gaussian elimination. This is the principle behind SuperLU (section 13.2.1). In certain applications, especially physics-based ones, the matrix has favorable properties that allow the use of so-called iterative solution methods, which can be much more efficient than Gaussian elimination. The PETSc package is built around such iterative methods and also provides the appropriate preconditioners (see section 13.2.2). In section 13.2.3, we address the eigen computation problem and focus on PARPACK. In section 13.2.4, we try to give the reader a notion of the depth of the software environment for sparse problems by mentioning the load balancing issue.

How data are handled by sparse software differs from one package to another, and this can be an important consideration in the choice of the software. There are three main ways to handle sparse matrices: (a) the software does not natively store the matrix but accesses the operator via the matrix-vector operation; this can be realized via reverse communication (e.g., PARPACK) or by having the user provide the matrix-vector product routine; (b) the user provides a pointer to their own data structure to the software (e.g., SuperLU); (c) the user fills the data structure of the software (e.g., PETSc). Pros and cons of these three different methods are discussed at the end of each part.

13.2.1 SuperLU

SuperLU [8, 19] is one of the foremost direct solvers for sparse linear systems. It is available in single-processor, multithreaded, and parallel versions.

Sparse direct solvers aim at finding a reordering of the matrix such that the fill-in during the factorization is as small as possible (see as well Chapter 9). One of the particular features of SuperLU is to find cliques in the matrix graph to obtain a high computational efficiency. Eliminating these cliques reduces the cost of the graph algorithms used; since cliques lead to dense submatrices, it also enables the use of higher-level BLAS routines.

The sequential and threaded versions of SuperLU use partial pivoting for numerical stability. Partial pivoting is avoided in the parallel version, however, because it would lead to large numbers of small messages. Instead, static pivoting is used, with repair of zero pivots during runtime. To compensate for these numerically suboptimal strategies, the solution process uses iterative refinement in a hope to increase the accuracy of the solution.

Like ScaLAPACK, SuperLU has both simple drivers and expert drivers; the latter give the user opportunity for further computational steering, returning more detailed information, and they are more sophisticated in terms of numerical precision.

SuperLU is written in C. The standard installation comes with its own collection of BLAS routines; one can edit the makefile to ensure that an optimized version of the BLAS library is used.

13.2.2 PETSc

PETSc is a library geared toward the solution of PDEs. It features tools for manipulating sparse matrix data structures, a sizable repertoire of iterative linear system solvers and preconditioners, and nonlinear solvers and time-stepping methods. Although it is written in C, there are FORTRAN and F90 interfaces as well as an experimental Python interface.

PETSc distinguishes itself from other libraries in a few aspects. First, it is usable as a toolbox: there are many low-level routines that can be used to implement new methods. In particular, there are tools for parallel computation (the so-called `VecScatter` objects) that offer an abstraction layer over straight MPI communication.

Second, PETSc's approach to parallelism is very flexible. Many routines operate on local matrices as easily as on distributed ones. Impressively, during the construction of a matrix any processor can specify the value of any matrix element. This, for instance, facilitates writing parallel FEM codes, since, along processor boundaries, elements belonging to different processors will contribute to the value of the same matrix element.

A difference between PETSc and other packages (e.g., SuperLU; see section 13.2.1) that is often counted as a disadvantage is that its data structures are internal and not explicitly documented. It is hard for users to provide their own matrices; the user needs to build up a PETSc matrix by passing matrix elements through function calls.

```
MatCreate(comm,...,&A);
for (i=... )
  for (j=... )
    MatSetValue(A,...,i,j,value,...);
```

This implies that the user faces the choice between maintaining duplicate matrices (one in the native user format and one in PETSc format) with the resulting storage overhead or using PETSc throughout the code. As an alternative, the user can supply his or her own matrix-vector product routine, although this requires the user to also write the preconditioner. For yet another solution, the user can add a new matrix data type to PETSc.

Once PETSc data objects have been built, they are used in an object-oriented manner, where the contents and the exact nature of the object are no longer visible:

```
MatMult(A,X,Y);
```

Likewise, parameters to the various objects are kept internal:

```
PCSetType(pc,PCJACOBI);
```

Of particular relevance in the current context is that after the initial creation of an object, its parallel status is largely irrelevant.

13.2.3 PARPACK

Often, in eigenvalue computations, not all eigenvalues or eigenvectors are needed. In such cases one is typically interested in the largest or smallest eigenvalues of the spectrum or in eigenvalues clustered around a certain value.

While ScaLAPACK (section 13.1.1) has routines that can compute a full spectrum, ARPACK focuses on this practically important case of the computation of a small number of eigenvalues and corresponding eigenvectors. It is based on the Arnoldi method.[1]

The Arnoldi method is unsuitable for finding eigenvalues in the interior of the spectrum, so such eigenvalues are found by shift-invert: given some σ close to the eigenvalues being sought, one solves the eigenvalue equation $(A - \sigma)^{-1} x = \mu x$, since eigenvalues of A close to σ will become the largest eigenvalues of $(A - \sigma)^{-1}$.

Reverse communication program structure

The Arnoldi method has the attractive property of accessing the matrix only through the matrix-vector product operation. However, finding eigenvalues, other than the largest, requires solving linear systems with the given matrix or one derived from it.

Since the Arnoldi method can be formulated in terms of the matrix-vector product operation, this means that ARPACK strictly speaking never needs access to individual matrix elements. To take advantage of this fact, ARPACK uses a technique called reverse communication, which dispenses with the need for the user to pass the matrix to the library routines. Thus, ARPACK can work with any user data structure, or even with matrices that are only operatively defined (e.g., FMM).

With reverse communication, whenever a matrix operation is needed, control is passed back to the user program, with a return parameter indicating what operation is being requested. The user then satisfies this request, with input and output in arrays that are passed to the library, and calls the library routine again, indicating that the operation has been performed.

Thus, the structure of a routine using ARPACK will be along these lines:

```
        ido = 0
10      continue
        call dsaupd( ido, .... )
        if (ido.eq.-1 .or. ido.eq.1) then
C           perform matrix vector product
            goto 10
        end if
```

For the case of shift-invert or the generalized eigenvalue problem there will be more clauses to the conditional, but the structure stays the same.

ARPACK can be used in a number of different modes, covering the regular and generalized eigenvalue problem, symmetry of the matrix A (and possibly M), and various

---

[1] In fact, the pure Arnoldi method would have prohibitive memory demands; what is used here is the implicitly restarted Arnoldi method [11].

parts of the spectrum to be computed. Rather than explaining these modes, we refer the reader to the excellent example drivers provided in the ARPACK distribution.

Practical aspects of using ARPACK

ARPACK is written in FORTRAN. No C prototypes are given, but the package is easily interfaced to a C application, observing the usual linker-naming conventions for FORTRAN and C routines. The parallel version of ARPACK, PARPACK, can be based on either MPI or BLACS, the communication layer of ScaLAPACK; see section 13.1.1. ARPACK uses LAPACK and unfortunately relies on an older version than the current one. While this version is included in the distribution, it means that it cannot easily be replaced by a vendor-optimized version.

The flip side of the data independence obtained by reverse communication is that it is incumbent on the user to provide a matrix vector product, which especially in the parallel case is not trivial. Also, in the shift-invert case it is up to the user to provide a linear system solver.

13.2.4 Load balancing

Many applications can be distributed in more than one way over a parallel architecture. Even if one distribution is the natural result of one component of the computation, for instance, setup of a grid and generation of the matrix, a subsequent component, for instance, an eigenvalue calculation, may be so labor intensive that the cost of a full data redistribution may be outweighed by resulting gains in parallel efficiency.

In this section we discuss two packages for graph partitioning: ParMetis and Chaco. These packages aim at finding a partitioning of a graph that assigns roughly equal-size subgraphs to processors, thereby balancing the workload, while minimizing the size of the separators and the consequent communication cost. The reader will also be interested in Chapter 6.

13.2.5 ParMetis

ParMetis [10, 17] is a parallel package for mesh or graph partitioning for parallel load balancing. It is based on a three-step coarsening-partitioning-uncoarsening algorithm that the authors claim is faster than multiway spectral bisection. It can be used in several modes, for instance, repartitioning graphs from adaptively refined meshes or partitioning graphs from multiphysics simulations.

The input format of ParMetis, in its serial form, is a variant on compressed matrix storage: the adjacency of each element is stored consecutively (excluding the diagonal, but for each pair u, v storing both (u, v) and (v, u)), with a pointer array indicating where each element's data start and end. Both vertex and edge weights can be specified optionally. The parallel version of the graph input format takes blocks of consecutive nodes and allocates these to subsequent processors. An array that is identical on each processor then indicates which range of variables each processor owns. The distributed format uses global numbering of the nodes.

The output of ParMetis is a mapping of node numbers to processors. No actual redistribution is performed.

13.2.6 Chaco

The Chaco package [14] comprises several algorithms for graph partitioning, including inertial, spectral, Kernighan–Lin, and multilevel algorithms. It can be used in two modes, stand-alone and library. In stand-alone mode, input and output are done through files. In library mode, Chaco can also be linked to C or FORTRAN codes, and all data are passed through arrays. Unlike ParMetis, Chaco runs only sequentially.

Zoltan [5] is a package for dynamic load balancing that builds on top of Chaco. Thanks to an object-oriented design, it is data structure neutral, so it can be interfaced using existing user data structures.

13.3 Support libraries

The packages in this chapter rely on two very common support libraries: MPI and BLAS. On most parallel distributed platform, there is at least one MPI library installed.

BLAS [7] are fairly simple linear algebra kernels that one could easily code oneself in a few lines. One could also download the source and compile it [13]. However, this is unlikely to give good performance, no matter the level of sophistication of one's compiler. The recommended way is to use vendor libraries, which are available on a number of platforms, for instance, in the `ESSL` library on IBM machines and the `mkl` on Intel. On platforms without such vendor libraries (or sometimes even if they are present), we recommend that one install the ATLAS [12] package, which gives a library tuned to one's specific machine. In a nutshell, ATLAS has a search algorithm that generates many implementations of each kernel, saving the one with the highest performance. This will far outperform anything one can write by hand.

13.4 Freely available software for linear algebra on the Internet

Tables 13.1 through 13.5 present a list of freely available software for the solution of linear algebra problems. The interest is in software for high-performance computers that is available in open source form on the web for solving problems in numerical linear algebra, specifically dense, sparse direct, and iterative systems and sparse iterative eigenvalue problems.

Additional pointers to software can be found at `www.nhse.org/rib/repositories/nhse/catalog/#Numerical_Programs_and_Routines`. A survey of iterative linear system solver packages can be found at `www.netlib.org/utk/papers/iterative-survey`.

Table 13.1. *Support routines for numerical linear algebra.*

Package	Support	Type		Language				Mode		Dense	Sparse
		Real	Complex	f77	c	c++	Seq	Dist			
http://www.netlib.org/atlas/ATLAS	yes	X	X	X	X		X			X	
http://www.netlib.org/blas/BLAS	yes	X	X	X	X		X			X	
http://www.cs.utexas.edu/users/flame/FLAME	yes	X	X	X	X		X			X	
http://www.netlib.org/linalg/LINALG	?										
http://www.lsc.nd.edu/research/mtl/MTL	yes	X				X	X			X	
http://www.robertnz.net/nm_intro.htmNETMAT	yes	X				X	X			X	
http://math.nist.gov/spblas/NIST S-BLAS	yes	X	X	X			X	M			X
http://claudius.ce.uniroma2.it/psblas/PSBLAS	yes	X	X	X			X				X
http://math.nist.gov/sparselib++/SparseLib++	yes	X	X			X	X				X
http://www.boost.org/libs/numeric/ublas/doc/index.htmuBLAS	yes	X	X			X	X			X	

Table 13.2. *Available software for dense matrix.*

Package	Support	Type		Language			Mode	
		Real	Complex	f77	c	c++	Seq	Dist
http://www.netlib.org/lapack/LAPACK	yes	X	X	X	X		X	
http://www.netlib.org/lapack95/LAPACK95	yes	X	X	95			X	
http://www.netlib.org/napack/NAPACK	yes	X		X				
http://www.cs.utexas.edu/users/plapack/PLAPACK	yes	X	X	X		X		M
http://www-unix.mcs.anl.gov/prism/PRISM	yes	X		X			X	M
http://www.netlib.org/scalapack/ScaLAPACK	yes	X	X	X		X		M/P

Table 13.3. *Sparse direct solvers.*

Package	Support	Type		Language			Mode				
		Real	Complex	f77	c	c++	Seq	Dist	SPD		Gen
http://www.cse.psu.edu/~raghavan/Dscpack/DSCPACK	yes	X			X		X	M	X		
http://hsl.rl.ac.uk/archive/hslarchive.html HSL	yes	X	X	X			X		X		X
http://www.cs.utk.edu/~padma/mfact.html MFACT	yes	X		X			X		X		X
http://www.enseeiht.fr/apo/MUMPS/MUMPS	yes	X	X	X			X	M	X		X
http://www.cs.umn.edu/~mjoshi/pspases/index.html PSPASES	yes	X		X				M	X		
http://www.netlib.org/sparse/index.html SPARSE	?	X	X		X		X		X		X
http://www.netlib.org/linalg/spooles/SPOOLES	?	X	X			X	X	M			X
http://www.nersc.gov/~xiaoye/SuperLU/SuperLU	yes	X	X		X		X	M			X
http://www.tau.ac.il/~stoledo/taucs/TAUCS	yes	X	X		X		X		X		X
http://www.cise.ufl.edu/research/sparse/umfpack UMFPACK	yes	X	X		X		X				X
http://www.netlib.org/y12m/index.html Y12M	?	X		X			X				X

Table 13.4. *Sparse eigenvalue solvers.*

Package	Support	Type		Language			Mode				
		Real	Complex	f77	c	c++	Seq	Dist	Sym		Gen
http://www.nersc.gov/~osni/#Software(B/H)LZPACK	yes	X	X	X			X	M/P	X		X
http://www.llnl.gov/CASC/hypre/HYPRE	yes	X			X		X	M	X		
http://www.netlib.org/linalg/qmrpack.tgz QMRPACK	?	X	X	X			X		X		X
http://www.netlib.org/laso/index.html LASO	?	X		X			X				
http://www.caam.rice.edu/~kristyn/parpack_home.html P_ARPACK	yes	X	X	X			X	M/P	X		X
http://www.nersc.gov/research/SIMON/planso.html PLANSO	yes	X		X			X	M	X		
http://www.grycap.upv.es/slepc/SLEPc	yes	X	X			X	X	M	X		X
http://www-unix.mcs.anl.gov/scidac/beskinetics/spam.html SPAM	yes	X	X	90			X		X		X
http://www.nersc.gov/research/SIMON/trlan.html TRLAN	yes	X		X			X	M	X		X

Table 13.5. *Sparse iterative solvers.*

Package	Support	Type		Language			Mode		Precond.		Iterative Solvers	
		Real	Comp.	f77	c	c++	Seq	Dist	SPD	Gen	SPD	Gen
http://www.cs.sandia.gov/CRF/aztec1.html AZTEC	no	X			X		X	M	X	X	X	X
http://www.cs.uky.edu/~jzhang/bilum.html BILUM	yes	X		X			X	M	X	X		X
http://www.mcs.anl.gov/sumaa3d/BlockSolve/index.html BlockSolve95	?	X		X		X		M	X	X		X
http://www-users.cs.umn.edu/~chow/bpkit.html BPKIT	yes	X		X	X	X		M	X	X		
http://www.cerfacs.fr/algor/Softs/CERFACS	yes	X	X	X	X			M		X	X	X
http://www.llnl.gov/CASC/hypre/HYPRE	yes	X		X	X		X	M	X	X	X	X
http://math.nist.gov/iml++/IML++	?	X				X	X				X	X
http://www.lsc.nd.edu/research/itl/ITL	yes	X				X	X				X	X
http://www.netlib.org/itpack/ITPACK	?	X		X				X				X	X
http://www.tu-dresden.de/mwism/skalicky/laspack/laspack.html LASPack	yes	X			X		X				X	X
http://www.stanford.edu/group/SOL/software.html LSQR	yes	X		X		X		X				X	X
http://www-users.cs.umn.edu/~saad/software/pARMS/pARMS	yes	X		X		X		X	M			X	X
http://www.cs.utk.edu/~eijkhout/parpre.html PARPRE	yes	X				X			M	X	X		
http://www.mcs.anl.gov/petsc PETSc	yes	X	X			X		X	M	X	X	X	X
http://www-users.cs.umn.edu/~saad/software/p_sparslib/P-SparsLIB	yes	X		X				X	M				X
http://claudius.ce.uniroma2.it/psblas/PSBLAS	yes	X		X				X	M	X	X	X	X
http://www.netlib.org/linalg/qmrpack.tgz QMRPACK	?	X		X				X				X	X
http://www.netlib.org/slap/SLAP	?	X		X							X		
http://www.sam.math.ethz.ch/~grote/spai/SPAI	yes	X				X		X	M			X	X
http://ftp.cs.indiana.edu/pub/bramley/splib.tar.gz SPLIB	?	X			X		X					X	X
http://www.netlib.org/linalg/spooles/SPOOLES	?	X			X			X				X	X
http://www.stanford.edu/group/SOL/software.html SYMMLQ	yes	X		X				X	M	X	X	X	X
http://www.tau.ac.il/~stoledo/taucs/TAUCS	yes	X			X			X		X		X	X
http://www.netlib.org/templates/index.html Templates	yes	X		X	X			X				X	X
http://software.sandia.gov/trilinos/Trilinos	yes	X				X		X	M	X	X	X	X

Reading List

Linear systems

The literature on linear system solving, like the research in this topic, is mostly split along the lines of direct versus iterative solvers. An introduction that covers both (as well as eigenvalue methods) is the book by Dongarra et al. [6]. A very practical book about linear system solving by iterative methods is the book by Barrett et al. [3], which in addition to the mathematical details contains sections on sparse data storage and other practical matters. More in-depth and less software oriented is the book by Saad [9].

Eigensystems

Along the lines of the Barrett et al. book for linear systems is a similar book for eigenvalues problems [2].

Bibliography

[1] E. ANDERSON, Z. BAI, C. H. BISCHOF, J. DEMMEL, J. J. DONGARRA, J. DU CROZ, A. GREENBAUM, S. HAMMARLING, A. MCKENNEY, S. OSTROUCHOV, AND D. SORENSEN, *LAPACK Users' Guide*, SIAM, Philadelphia, 3rd ed., 1999.

[2] Z. BAI, J. DEMMEL, J. J. DONGARRA, A. RUHE, AND H. A. VAN DER VORST, *Templates for the Solution of Algebraic Eigenvalue Problems, A Practical Guide*, SIAM, Philadelphia, 2000.

[3] R. BARRETT, M. W. BERRY, T. F. CHAN, J. DEMMEL, J. DONATO, J. J. DONGARRA, V. EIJKHOUT, R. POZO, C. ROMINE, AND H. A. VAN DER VORST, *Templates for the Solution of Linear Systems: Building Blocks for Iterative Methods*, SIAM, Philadelphia, 1993. `http://www.netlib.org/templates/`.

[4] L. S. BLACKFORD, J. CHOI, A. CLEARY, E. D'AZEVEDO, J. DEMMEL, I. S. DHILLON, J. J. DONGARRA, S. HAMMARLING, G. HENRY, A. PETITET, K. STANLEY, D. WALKER, AND R. C. WHALEY, *ScaLAPACK Users' Guide*, SIAM, Philadelphia, 1997.

[5] E. BOMAN, D. BOZDAG, U. CATALYUREK, K. DEVINE, L. A. FISK, R. HEAPHY, B. HENDRICKSON, W. MITCHELL, M. ST. JOHN, AND C. VAUGHAN, *Zoltan home page*. `http://www.cs.sandia.gov/Zoltan`, 1999.

[6] J. J. DONGARRA, I. S. DUFF, D. C. SORENSEN, AND H. A. VAN DER VORST, *Numerical Linear Algebra for High-Performance Computers*, SIAM, Philadelphia, 1998.

[7] C. L. LAWSON, R. J. HANSON, D. KINCAID, AND F. KROGH, *Basic linear algebra subprograms for FORTRAN usage*, ACM Transactions on Mathematical Software, 5 (1979), pp. 308–323.

[8] X. S. LI, *Sparse Gaussian Eliminiation on High Performance Computers*, Ph.D. thesis, University of California at Berkeley, 1996.

[9] Y. SAAD, *Iterative Methods for Sparse Linear Systems*, 2nd ed., Society for Industrial and Applied Mathematics, Philadelphia, PA, USA, 2003. First edition published by PWS Publishing Company, Boston, 1996; this edition is available for download from http://www.cs.umn.edu/~saad.

[10] K. SCHLOEGEL, G. KARYPIS, AND V. KUMAR, *Parallel multilevel algorithms for multi-constraint graph partitioning*, in Proceedings of EuroPar-2000, 2000, Munich, Germany.

[11] D. C. SORENSEN, *Implicit application of polynomial filters in a k-step Arnoldi method*, SIAM Journal of Matrix Analysis and Applications, 13 (1992), pp. 357–385.

[12] R. C. WHALEY, A. PETITET, AND J. J. DONGARRA, *Automated empirical optimizations of software and the ATLAS project*, Parallel Computing, 27 (2001), pp. 3–35.

[13] *BLAS home page.* http://www.netlib.org/blas.

[14] *Chaco home page.* http://www.cs.sandia.gov/~bahendr/chaco.html.

[15] *LAPACK home page.* http://www.netlib.org/lapack.

[16] *Freely available software for linear algebra on the web (May 2004).* http://www.netlib.org/utk/people/JackDongarra/la-sw.html.

[17] *ParMETIS home page.* http://www-users.cs.umn.edu/~karypis/metis/parmetis/index.html.

[18] *PLAPACK home page.* http://www.cs.utexas.edu/users/plapack/.

[19] *SuperLU home page.* http://www.nersc.gov/~xiaoye/SuperLU/.

Chapter 14
High-Performance Component Software Systems

Randall Bramley, Rob Armstrong, Lois McInnes, and Matt Sottile

The increasing complexity of software systems for computational science and engineering has led to the adoption of a now-common methodology from business and industrial computing: software components. A component in this context is an independently deployable unit of software, which can be composed together with other components to form a complete program for solving some class of problems [63]. Components must have well-defined interfaces to allow this composition, but the implementation within the component is not specified. This situation implies programming language independence and, as long as the interfaces do not change, the ability to substitute updated or superior implementations. Other desirable features include scalability of the number of interacting components, scalable parallelism both within and between components, and *minimality*. In this context, minimality means that the requirements for a unit of software to function as a component are as lightweight and as few as possible.

Components are typically regarded as peers, so that no component necessarily must be the driver or main component. All component systems provide some level of encapsulation, the idea from object-oriented programming that limits all interactions with the component to defined interfaces. Those interfaces are called *ports*, and often a formal interface definition language (IDL) is used to define ports. Because all interactions are through the ports, defining them completely specifies the component's requirements. Conventional libraries may cause programs linking with them to fail when upgraded to a new version, but components implementing the same interface are interchangeable (although they may differ in performance or resource usage, such as memory).

The setting in which components are connected is called a *framework*, which is responsible for instantiating, running, connecting, and stopping components—in general, the full life cycle. The framework can be a separate process or the process in which components are compiled as libraries. Frameworks can be distributed or local, but one common idea in many of the existing frameworks is to make the framework itself a component, although with some special bootstrapping capability. Some frameworks provide a GUI to choose and "wire" together components with a mouse, as well as some scripting language interface. The user interface can also be built as a component, making customization of interfaces easy.

In business computing, component methodology is now common. Microsoft's COM and DCOM [61] were likely the first widely used component specification, followed by Java Beans [22]. The distributed computing standard CORBA [29] has been extended to include the CORBA component model (CCM) [30], and some scientific component systems have used CORBA as a runtime system [34, 56, 46].

High-performance scientific and engineering computing has some requirements not relevant or important for business computing. Foremost is support for FORTRAN 77 and FORTRAN 90. This capability is not just for legacy software; in some application areas the overwhelming majority of current and newly developed code is in FORTRAN. (In the following, FORTRAN without a qualifier refers to FORTRAN 90.) Another unique requirement is support for high performance and in particular components that are parallel processes. In this chapter the term "parallel" means a single job, run as multiple processes with some message-passing library like MPI [50] or PVM [27]. The term "distributed" refers to computations running on different machines, possibly in a wide area network, which are not being managed by a single instance of a runtime system like MPI. Current scientific component frameworks are either parallel or distributed, but as yet no single framework provides both capabilities. In part this situation is because of the differing needs: collocated parallel components need low latency connections for performance, while most distributed systems require higher-latency network protocols to communicate between different machines and even different architectures. Distributed frameworks also need the ability to perform remote instantiation of processes and to satisfy authentication and authorization requirements. Some recent work has sought to create interframework connection protocols, allowing the differing capabilities to be combined.

Software component systems entail a rich variety of research issues, and this chapter delineates several that require a mathematical formalism. In the same way that programming languages, computability theory, and compilers have benefited from this formalism, it is likely that components will also. Following a brief overview in section 14.1 of current scientific component systems, section 14.2 introduces challenges in parallel model coupling, parallel data redistribution, computational quality of service, and formal representation of component model composition patterns. Section 14.3 concludes with comments about opportunities for future work.

14.1 Current scientific component systems

Several component systems have been developed for scientific and engineering computation, data management, and instrument access. These systems vary in their support of various desirable features: language independence, platform independence, parallel components, distributed components, interface definition standards, interface definition methodology, and conformance to widely accepted standards.

One attribute that all component systems share is their ability to provide standard infrastructure upon which further automation can be performed. Components not only can be composed into applications but also can be parameterized, recomposed, substituted, and proxied in an automated way to improve performance. Such capabilities are most powerful when done dynamically by a component system, while an application is running. One significant advantage of the component-oriented approach is to provide a constituent infrastructure that enables generic middleware devoted to improving performance. Monolithic applications cannot benefit from such middleware because they have no standard infrastructure with which to work. Section 14.2 outlines three different ways in which component infrastructure enables automation, thereby improving performance and code reuse. Section 14.2 also presents a formal development of these concepts, abstracting the similarities and differences in component model patterns of composition.

Common component architecture frameworks

One of the most prominent component systems for high-performance computing is the common component architecture (CCA) [3, 14, 7]. The CCA forum is an open forum that meets quarterly; membership currently includes three universities and five U.S. Department of Energy laboratories (Argonne, Lawrence Livermore, Los Alamos, Oak Ridge, and Sandia) as well as a variety of additional institutions. CCA is not a framework but instead states *how* interfaces are defined and the minimal specifications for ports that will allow components to interoperate. That specification currently consists of one port: setServices [15]. Naturally this approach has enabled several frameworks to be built to the CCA specification. Most CCA frameworks use SIDL [18], the scientific interface definition language created at Lawrence Livermore National Laboratory (LLNL). SIDL is an extension of the CORBA IDL with additional features of common need in scientific computing, such as multidimensional arrays. LLNL has also developed the Babel compiler [38, 6], which from SIDL generates server and client code in any of FORTRAN, FORTRAN77, Python, Java, C, or C++. This ability to interface between different commonly used languages is an important and valuable feature for scientific computing. Babel also provides a runtime system, the code responsible for actually passing arguments and return values across the component interfaces. Additional details regarding the CCA are available in other publications [7, 48, 51, 1].

Ccaffeine. Ccaffeine [2], developed at Sandia National Laboratories, was the first CCA framework to support parallel computing. This framework supports SIDL and Babel, and it allows connecting isocardinal components (ones with the same number of processes). Ccaffeine can also be used without Babel, in its "classic" mode. Ccaffeine can be run using a GUI to choose and connect components, or it can be run in production mode with a scripting language in a resource file. Ccaffeine is being used to support parallel reacting flow simulations [45, 59, 44, 42, 43] and quantum chemistry computations [36] but does not yet support wide-area distributed components.

Decaf. Decaf [39] is an LLNL framework originally developed to help in understanding the CCA specification and to verify during development that SIDL and Babel were self-consistent and able to support the CCA. Decaf, a direct-connect framework for parallel components, uses Babel as its runtime system. Although Decaf does not support distributed components, recent work is bridging between Decaf and the distributed frameworks SCIRun2 and XCAT.

XCAT. XCAT, developed at Indiana University, is actually two frameworks, one for Java and another for C++ components. Both are distributed frameworks that do not support parallel components, and both use the emerging grid standard of web services [26] for distributed component interactions. The C++ version is currently in transition from using SOAP [21] for the underlying intercomponent communications to using the Proteus [16] multiprotocol library. Instead of Babel, XCAT has its own code generator that uses SIDL descriptions of the components. Neither implementation of XCAT currently supports parallel components, but XCAT is likely instead to provide a bridge to distributed grid resources for parallel CCA frameworks through bindings to Proteus.

SCIRun2. SCIRun2 [65] is based on the SCIRun [55] problem-solving environment developed at the University of Utah. SCIRun is a distributed framework that supports parallel components and solves a restricted subset of parallel component interactions when the number of parallel processes in each component differs. In this case, data redistribution occurs automatically for the user. A recent follow-on framework, SCIRun2, is capable of orchestrating CCA-conforming components and bridging among different component models, as discussed in more detail in Chapter 15.

DCA. DCA [9] is an Indiana University research framework for exploring the semantics of parallel remote method invocation (PRMI) and working on parallel data redistribution, both of which are described further in section 14.2.2. DCA provides an MPI-like interface for parallel transfers and handles one-dimensional parallel array data redistribution. Because DCA involves experimenting with the semantics of PRMI, it is not a production framework and is limited to C/C++ components. DCA has a partial implementation of a SIDL parser.

The CCA specification relies almost solely on the *provides/uses* design pattern for composition. (See Figure 14.1; further details and examples are in [15, 7, 48].) An interface, called a *port*, is provided by one component for use by another. Mechanisms are specified to assign types and names, publish *provides* ports, and indicate dependencies on *uses* ports.

The *provides/uses* composition pattern can recover as a degenerate case the familiar data flow pattern, where only data are passed through the ports. However, in the general case, the CCA is much more powerful, supporting the transfer of any functional interface. All the preceding frameworks implement at least a level of functionality for CCA compliance, and in many cases much more. The remaining HPC frameworks implement component models other than the CCA.

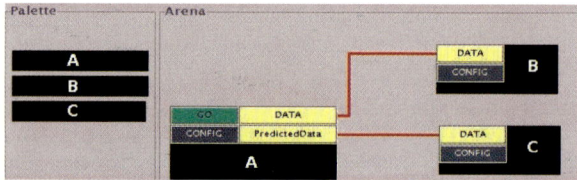

Figure 14.1. *Ccaffeine's graphical builder: the components'* uses *ports appear on their right, while* provides *ports appear on their left.*

PaCO++

PaCO++ [19], a recently introduced framework developed at INRIA, uses CORBA [29] for its runtime system. A PaCO++ component is a collection of identical CORBA objects, connected via an "out-of-band" runtime system like MPI. PaCO++ uses a standard CORBA-compliant code generator to create the interface objects from CORBA IDL, augmented by an XML description of the data distribution for shared parallel objects. In this way extensions for parallelism are not added to the IDL as in SIDL.

Cactus

Cactus [28] is a framework from Louisiana State University designed for solving PDEs, with components (called thorns) divided into application and infrastructure categories. Any application requires a main or driver thorn to manage memory and handle all message passing in a parallel application. Interfaces are implicitly defined in C++ rather than a formal IDL. Cactus is primarily used for PDEs with explicit time-stepping, and applications are supported in numerical relativity, climate modeling, and astrophysics.

Earth Systems Modeling Framework

As its name indicates, the Earth Systems Modeling Framework (ESMF) [37], developed by a multiagency collaboration, is designed for climate and weather modeling. Because of this specialization, the framework can supply several utility infrastructure components (such as time-stepping, parallel input/output (I/O), and visualization) to aid user applications. Components can be hierarchically arranged as in Application Visualization System (AVS) and are generally derived from a gridded component or a coupler component, under the control of an application driver. ESMF components have minimal requirements to be used in the framework—basically object-oriented functions for initialize, run, and finalize. Data interfaces can use the substructure-provided grids but are required only to have import state and export state methods. ESMF components typically are parallel and use an external runtime system for intracomponent communications. Intercomponent connections are handled by a mechanism that wraps MPI but provides architecture awareness, allowing shared memory communications to be used when practical.

Commercial systems

Several scientific component systems were inspired by AVS [5, 54, 11] from Advanced Visual Systems and IBM's Open Visualization Data Explorer (DX) [20], released as an open-source project with restrictions in 2002. Both of these commercial systems provide a visual programming environment: a drag-and-drop GUI palette and a large number of components that can be wired together with a mouse. A composed application can be saved and encapsulated as another component. Both emphasize scientific visualization, are platform independent, and use a data flow model: data start at one component and flow through a pipeline or tree. In AVS components can be written, but at least until 1998 the interface language was a proprietary Scheme-like language. In DX a module description file is used to define components, and then a tool with functionality similar to that of CCA's Babel generates the necessary template code (in C) and makefile. These systems can provide high performance and do allow concurrency by means of a data flow paradigm, but primarily for visualization pipelines, and they do not support parallel component connections or native FORTRAN components.

Understanding commonalities among component systems

Although the number of HPC scientific component frameworks is large and growing, the variety should not conceal the importance of the component methodology: by concentrating on formal definitions of interfaces and not on internal implementations, components introduce a new level of interoperability and portability. Moving a component from one framework to another, or bridging between frameworks, becomes a task in computer systems work, not in physics, chemistry, or other application sciences. It is helpful to identify the different levels of interoperability that frameworks and component models can have in order to exploit similarities and minimize differences.

The preceding frameworks all have component models associated with them explicitly (for example, any CCA framework) or implicitly (for example, ESMF and Cactus). Because frameworks like SCIRun and Ccaffeine are based on a *uses/provides* pattern for composition, they can be considered "close together," as opposed to Cactus, whose principle means of composition is execution order. It is not surprising that the follow-on framework SCIRun2 now orchestrates CCA components that also rely heavily on the *provides/uses* pattern. Rather than resorting to intuition to make judgments of compositional compatibility, a formal representation is introduced in section 14.2.4. While such formal mathematics may not be needed in the practice of framework interoperability, it can inform the vocabulary and reasoning of the discourse. Interoperability can be achieved at many different levels, leveraging compatible binaries, source code, network protocols, etc., and frameworks can benefit from all of these. The idea of compositional interoperability, however, is unique to component concepts and, with the current proliferation of frameworks and component models, will be an increasingly important challenge.

14.2 Mathematical challenges

The software and computer systems challenges of high-performance software components are readily apparent. HPC components need to span multiple runtime systems, be portable to a variety of HPC platforms, make several languages interoperate, manage application data, connect multiple frameworks, and provide user-level interfaces that are flexible and expressive enough for scientists in many application areas.

Less obvious but no less important are the mathematical challenges that this chapter delineates. Mathematical formalism in computer science has enabled advances in programming languages, database systems, compilers, and computability theory. HPC component systems potentially can benefit from the same approach.

14.2.1 Model coupling

A major trend in scientific computing is the need to couple single discipline codes to form larger, multidisciplinary simulations. A prominent example is in climate modeling [17, 37], where modules for the atmosphere, oceans, land ice, sea ice, rivers, and other geophysical phenomena are run simultaneously and mathematically connected via boundary conditions or source terms in PDEs, as described in [40, 48]. Space weather [64] and fusion processes in tokamaks [57] have recently become targets for model coupling. In the past this coupling would have involved merging the codes, typically by refactoring them and creating a new, single code combining all of the physical effects. The advantage of this approach is that a more efficient sharing of data structures and mathematical consistency in discretizations is possible. A disadvantage is that the code developers must acquire some expertise in all the subdisciplines involved. Also, as the original subdiscipline codes evolve and become more refined, these must be reintegrated into the combined version. HPC software component systems are a viable alternative: each subdiscipline code can be maintained and improved by specialists in the individual areas, and the combined simulation can be automatically updated.

Fusion simulation project

The proposed fusion simulation project (FSP) [57, 25] for magnetically confined fusion energy provides an idea of the range of phenomena that need to be integrated. Extended magnetohydrodynamics, radio frequency (RF) current drive, transport of material and energy, microturbulence, and possibly structures and materials properties codes need to be combined to successfully model and ultimately control a burning plasma. This problem is simultaneously multiphysics, multidiscretization, and multiscale. Present-day simulations are based on a variety of techniques, including finite elements, spectral elements, Monte Carlo, particle in cell (PIC), and Burger–Colella adaptive mesh refinement. RF codes have time scales as small as 10^{-10} seconds for electron transit, while transport time scales need to be on the order of 10^4 seconds to model a full burn on the proposed ITER tokamak [33]. Spatial scales range from the size of an electron orbit around a magnetic field line to the tens of meters circumference of ITER's torus. Coupling FSP modules generally increases the time and space scales involved, which are already challenging. Multiscale mathematics not only is vital within each subdiscipline code, but also must be developed to span the useful combinations of physics. Figure 14.2 shows some of the current codes in fusion energy simulation as well as potential couplings among categories.

Coupling different discretizations

Software components provide a computer systems solution, but far more is needed to create the FSP. Integrating multiple physics models will require numerical analysis of conservation properties across the boundaries between the different discretizations. Some projects have successfully merged *two* different discretizations, either by directly passing boundary values from one to the other, or by imposing a third discretization that is used to couple the regimes, such as the ghost fluid method [23] used by the Caltech Center for Simulation of Dynamic

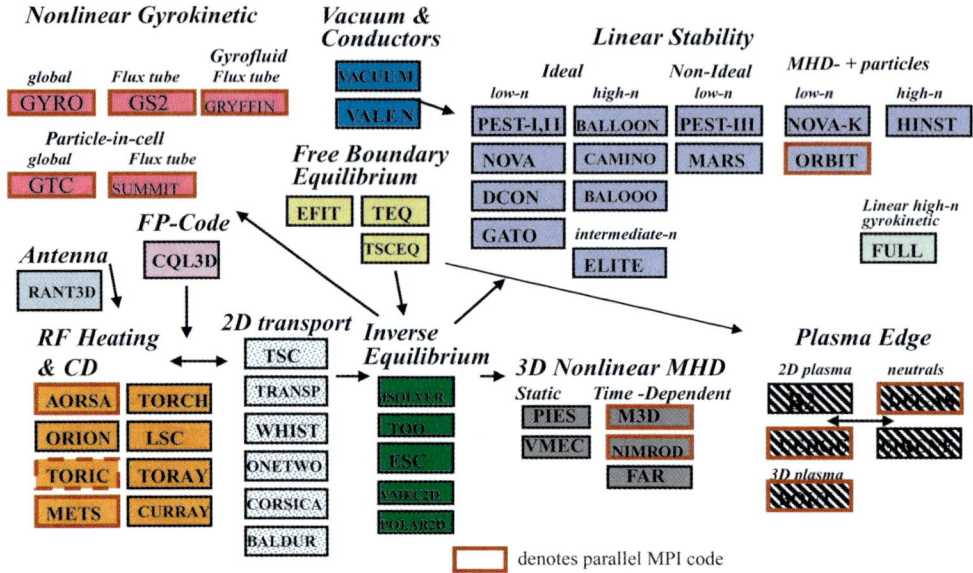

Figure 14.2. *Different codes in fusion energy and potential couplings among categories. (Courtesy of Stephen Jardin, Princeton Plasma Physics Laboratory.)*

Response of Materials [13]. So far, none has done so for the full range of discretization methods used in the fusion subdiscipline codes. A mathematical analysis of the numerical issues will possibly guide the way to a complete mathematical framework for the problem; both are needed. New interpolation methods will be needed between meshes that, in some cases, model the same spatial regions at different time scales. Intermediate translation and filtering components must be defined and created, and automatically correcting for the different units and measurements, a necessity for potentially unforeseen compositions of the computational components, will require the creation of ontologies complete enough to span the necessary physics.

Model coupling is also a motivating example that leads to other issues requiring mathematical methodologies: parallel data redistribution, formal design patterns in component systems, and computational quality of service.

14.2.2 Parallel data redistribution: The MxN problem

The MxN problem is that of connecting two parallel components, one running on M processes and the other on N processes, where M and N may be incommensurate. This situation occurs particularly when different phases of a simulation require different resources and amounts of computation. For example, in the ESMF introduced in section 14.1, an atmospheric model component may require more processors for a weather simulation than an ocean component does, and it would be inefficient globally to allocate the same numbers of processes to both.

MxN Syntax

The MxN problem has two related parts: syntax and data (re)distribution. Parallel components invoking methods on each other is called parallel remote method invocation (PRMI). Java programmers are familiar with RMI, but in the context of scientific components, the term is applied to components written in any language. Also, the term "remote" does not imply distributed components—the encapsulation enforced by component frameworks means that remote and distributed method invocations should be identical from the components' point of view, with the framework providing the actual implementation of what an invocation requires. No well-defined, widely accepted semantics exist yet for the possible wide range of types of parallel invocations. Methods could be invoked between serial or parallel callers and callees, and methods could perform coordinated parallel operations or independently update local state in parallel. Such invocations could require data arguments or return results in either serial or parallel (decomposed or replicated) data arrangements. These problems can occur even when $M = N$, but in that case applications typically pair processes on each side arbitrarily.

In a groundbreaking dissertation, Keahey [35] identified many of the syntax problems that PRMI entails. One issue is process participation: how many and which processes on each component make and handle the method invocation? Because components need to be developed independently and a priori do not know what other components will be connected to them, building in the knowledge of how many processes belong to a cooperating component is not practical. Furthermore, since components may have differing parallel runtime systems (RTS), or different instances of the same RTS, the component cannot rely upon getting that information from the RTS. Thus, communicating the numbers on each side of an MxN connection must be implemented by the framework. That still leaves the problem of deciding which subset of processes actually makes the method call, and which subset of processes on the receiving component will carry out the invoked operations. In the example of coupled ocean and atmospheric components, typically only the processes that own part of the interface between the sea and air need to communicate, and requiring all processes to participate would prevent parallel scalability. Furthermore, the participants may change with time, as in a moving boundary problem.

Each existing framework that handles parallel components resolves the MxN problem in different ways. The most common is to assume each side has the same numbers of processes, $M = N$. Beyond that trivial case there are at least three other approaches [8].

Oak Ridge National Laboratory has developed a CCA MxN component [8], which is collocated with the communicating processes. This component essentially has $M + N$ processes (although fewer if the processes are used for both components) and relies on Parallel Virtual Machine (PVM) functionality to transfer arguments and return values. This approach requires that both components are run on the same set of machines and share a PVM instance. Then each component invokes methods on the MxN component, using whatever subset of processes is required. By sharing a PVM instance, sophisticated efficiency techniques can be applied: a component can signal data readiness and continue processing, while the other component can signal a data request and similarly overlap communications with computation.

SCIRun2 [65] adds PRMI primitives as an extension to SIDL by requiring the methods of a parallel component to be specified as *independent* (one-to-one) or *collective* (all-to-all).

Collective calls are for cases where the parallel component's processes interoperate to solve a problem collaboratively. Collective calls are capable of supporting differing numbers of processes on each side of the call by creating ghost invocations and/or return values so that virtually $M = N$. The user of a collective method must guarantee that all participating caller processes make the invocation; the framework guarantees that all callee processes receive the call and that all callers receive a return value. For consistency, argument and return value data are assumed to be identical across the processes of a component, and the component developer must ensure this. *Independent* invocations in SCIRun2 are for normal serial function call semantics. For each of these invocation types, a SIDL compiler generates the glue code that provides the appropriate behavior.

DCA [9] uses MPI communicator groups to determine process participation. SIDL is extended to specify when arguments are actually parts of a single data structure spread across the parallel processes, by using the special keyword *parallel*. The code generator that parses a SIDL file automatically adds an extra argument to all port methods, of type MPI_Comm, which is used to communicate to the framework which processes participate in the parallel remote method invocation. The framework can then obtain from both of the components the numbers of processes on each side, even when they are using different MPI implementations or instances. This approach also seems to solve the problem of having subsets of processes participating in the method invocation, but a related problem, synchronization, prevents this in some cases.

Synchronization in MxN

The problem of synchronization arises for any component framework in which the components do not share a parallel RTS. DCA uses a *barrier* to guarantee the correct order of invocation when different but intersecting sets of processes make consecutive port calls. Otherwise a deadlock can occur, as illustrated in Figure 14.3. If a PRMI call is delivered as soon as one process reaches the calling point, the remote component will block at some time t_1 waiting for data from processes 2 and 3 and will not accept the second collective call at t_2 and t_3. The remote component will be blocked indefinitely because processes 2 and 3 will never reach t_4 and t_5 to complete the first call. The solution DCA uses is to delay PRMI delivery until all processes are ready by inserting a barrier before the delivery. In other invocation schemes where *all* processes must participate, the barrier is not required because all calls are delivered in order to the remote component.

Synchronization is handled implicitly in SCIRun2 by the restriction of PRMI semantics to either collective or independent calls. In the CCA MxN component, synchronization is handled out-of-band by relying on the PVM mechanisms for parallel data transfer pioneered by CUMULVS [53]. Within ESMF (and in general, most explicit time-stepping PDE solver frameworks), synchronization is provided by a globally shared time clock for the simulation, with each component running for a self-selected number of time-steps between intercomponent communications.

The number of different solutions and approaches shows the importance of the MxN problem. What is lacking now is a formal mathematical framework with which to express issues such as process participation and cross-component synchronization, so that deadlock and permanently blocked processes can be avoided.

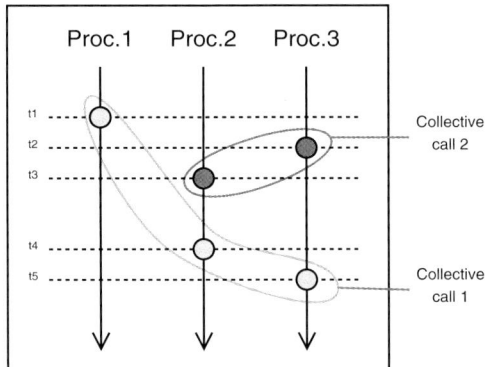

Figure 14.3. *The synchronization problem in PRMI.*

14.2.3 Computational quality of service

Component-based environments provide opportunities to improve performance, numerical accuracy, robustness, and other characteristics of scientific simulations. Not only can applications be assembled from components selected to provide the best performance, but sometimes they can also be changed dynamically during execution to optimize desirable characteristics. Quality-of-service (QoS) research issues for scientific component software differ in important ways from more common QoS approaches, which often emphasize system-related performance effects such as CPU or network loads to implement application priority or bandwidth reservation in networking. Although performance is a shared general concern, high efficiency and parallel scalability are more significant requirements for scientific components. The factors that affect performance are closely tied to a component's parallel implementation, its management of memory, the algorithms executed, the algorithmic parameters employed (for example, the level of fill for incomplete factorization), and other operational characteristics. Scientific component software is also concerned with *functional* qualities, such as the level of accuracy achieved for a particular algorithm.

This concept of the automatic selection and configuration of components to suit a particular computational purpose is called *computational quality of service* (CQoS) [52]. CQoS is a natural extension of the capabilities of the component environment. CQoS embodies the familiar concept of quality of service in networking and the ability to specify and manage characteristics of the application in a way that adapts to the changing (computational) environment.

Metadata and metrics

Component concepts help to manage complexity by providing standard building blocks; these concepts also enable a degree of high-level automation, whereby CQoS metadata may be used to compose or dynamically adapt an application. CQoS meta information includes both the requirements and the capabilities of a given component. This information may be based on historical data, algorithmic convergence theory, and performance models, and it is extensible to other types of metadata for use statically or dynamically. In addition to traditional QoS metrics, CQoS metadata includes metrics such as computational cost (execution time, number of floating point operations, or number of iterations), accuracy, failure rate, convergence rate, and algorithmic quality [32]. A detailed design of an infrastructure for managing CQoS-based component application execution was proposed in [32]. By associating CQoS metadata with a component's *uses* and *provides* ports, as introduced in section 14.1, one can effectively express that component's CQoS requirements and capabilities. Related work has examined the role of higher-level semantic information in component assembly [10, 24, 31, 47, 58].

Performance measurement and monitoring

To evaluate component CQoS, a performance system capable of measuring and reporting metrics of interest is needed. The University of Oregon's TAU system [62] provides a performance monitoring capability for CCA components that collects data for assessing performance metrics for a component, to understand the performance space relative to the metrics and to observe the metrics during execution. After performance data have been accumulated, performance models for single components or entire applications can be constructed. An accurate performance model of the entire application can enable the automated optimization of the component assembly process.

Automated application assembly

CCA scientific simulations are assemblies of components created at run-time. If multiple implementations of a component exist (i.e., they can be transparently replaced by each other), it becomes possible to construct an "optimal" CCA code by choosing the "best" implementation of each component, with added consideration for the overhead of any potentially necessary data transformations. This construction requires the specification of quality attributes with which to discriminate among component implementations. Performance data can be measured and recorded transparently via the proxy-based system described in [60]. Component interface invocations are recorded, resulting in a call graph for the application. The net result of a fully instrumented run is the creation of files containing performance data for every invocation of an instrumented component as well as a call graph with weighted nodes representing components. Performance models are created through regression analysis of this data. At any point before or during the simulation, the performance models of each of the component implementations can be evaluated for the problem's characteristics to obtain the execution times of any component assembly prior to choosing the desired set. Once an optimal set of components has been identified, a performance modeling and optimization component modifies the existing component assembly.

Adaptive multimethod solvers

While application assembly is typically done once before a scientific simulation starts, often the same set of component implementations does not satisfy CQoS requirements throughout the application's entire execution. Argonne National Laboratory and Penn State University are investigating dynamic, CQoS-enhanced *adaptive* multimethod linear solvers in the context of solving nonlinear PDEs via Newton–Krylov methods. Depending on the problem, the linear systems solved in the course of the nonlinear solution can have different numerical properties; thus, a single linear solution method may not be appropriate for the entire simulation. As explained in detail in [49], the adaptive scheme uses a different linear solver during each phase of solution, leading to increased robustness and potentially better overall performance.

As computational science progresses toward ever more realistic multiphysics and multiscale applications, the complexity will become such that no single research group can effectively select or tune all the components in a given application. CQoS employs global information about a simulation's composition and its environment, so that sound choices for implementations and parameters can be made. Building a comprehensive CQoS infrastructure is an enormous task but, given the need to automate the cooperation of algorithmically disparate components, a necessary one. While the research reported in this section is a first step toward this aim, many open mathematical questions remain to be addressed.

14.2.4 Formal representation of component model composition patterns

As shown in section 14.1, a large variety of frameworks and component systems are devoted to high-performance computing, and finding an interoperability among them, even if at just the composition level, has merit. It is advantageous to identify equivalence classes of frameworks for which middleware, operating solely at the level of composition, can be shared among frameworks.

Meta component specifications may be developed, to which no one framework will be solely devoted, but which many will expose as just one facet of their functionality. For example, any framework that exhibits a composition scheme similar to the *provides/uses* design pattern of the CCA can masquerade as a CCA framework without giving up any other value-added that the framework has to offer. The framework must only exhibit the same pattern of component composition as one facet of its structure, while other facets can be treated as extra or orthogonal. The kinds of automation discussed in sections 14.2.1 to 14.2.3 for model coupling, parallel data redistribution, and computational quality of service require only that the pattern of composition and access to properties be the same, without any expectation that frameworks or their components will interoperate. There is no expectation, for example, of being able to connect a CCA component with one from Cactus.

Some formal development is needed to identify sufficiency of a similarity between differing component architectures to accomplish masquerading one as another. A formal derivation aids reasoning about similarities and differences in composition patterns, thereby helping to identify opportunities for automation spanning multiple frameworks. The remainder of this section provides an overview of recent work; further details are in [4].

Formal development: Comparisons of one component model with another

The focus here is to reason about relationships among, but not within, component architectures. A component architecture has sets of state "objects" corresponding to components and connections, as well as morphisms associated with these sets that serve to instantiate, connect, and destroy components within that component architecture.

Because these objects and morphisms need not be exposed beyond their existence, the component model can be simplified to this abstraction. In this terminology, the *component architecture* defines both a set of objects representing component-based structures and a set of morphisms that operate on these structures, requiring that a component architecture is closed under these operations.

A category theoretic definition of component models

To give this concept clearer grounding in an example, we consider a component architecture $\mathcal{M}$ as a set C of component classes l_i, instances c_i, connections between instances k_{ij}, and instance properties p_i, or equivalently, *state*. The component architecture also defines a set of morphisms called F.

$$\mathcal{M} := \left(\begin{array}{l} C = \{\{l_i\}, \{c_i\}, \{k_{ij}\}, \{p_i\}\} \\ F = \{s_1, s_2, \cdots, s_i\} \end{array} \right). \tag{14.1}$$

The morphisms of F are defined within the space of objects for $\mathcal{M}$,

$$C \xrightarrow{s_1} C \xrightarrow{s_2} C \cdots \xrightarrow{s_n} C. \tag{14.2}$$

Using these entities and a suitable identity map for the component architecture, we can establish $\mathcal{M}$ as a mathematical category [41] related to the category $\mathcal{S}^{\circlearrowleft}$ of endomorphs of sets. While others [12] have defined categories for component architectures that are more general and that elucidate richer detail of the internal structure of component composition, this construction suffices for comparisons between component architecture composition schemes.

Without restricting discussion to one or more specific component architectures, we can introduce an abstract component architecture to motivate and illustrate a discussion of intercomponent architecture relationships. In all cases, a component architecture contains components and operators to *compose* them into programs or subprograms.

At the heart of all component models is the composition operation. The fundamental element of this operation carries two components into a composite structure such that dependencies between them are satisfied. This operator is almost always defined to operate not only between individual components but also between structures resulting from previous applications of the operator. In the general case, individual components are simply the smallest, trivial structures within the component architecture.

Mathematically a component structure is an element of the power set $\mathcal{P}(C)$. Each individual component is the trivial structure, represented as a singleton set of $\mathcal{P}(C)$. The base composition to form a structure from two components c_i and c_j is the mapping $\varphi(\{c_i\}, \{c_j\}) \longrightarrow \{c_i, c_j\}$. Thus, the composition operator is a mapping defined as

$$\varphi := \mathcal{P}(C) \times \mathcal{P}(C) \longrightarrow \mathcal{P}(C), \tag{14.3}$$

which leads to the obvious mapping that allows structures of composed components to be themselves composed to form larger structures. Equation (14.3) is required to define the domain and codomain of functors used to relate component architectures.

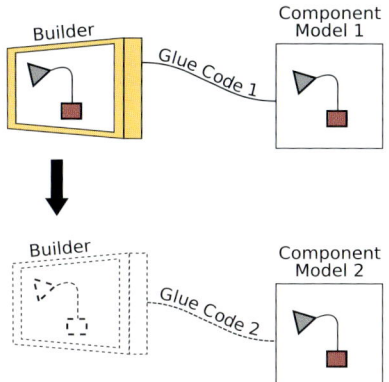

Figure 14.4. *Comparison of two component architectures with a single builder that works interchangeably via model-specific glue code.*

Comparing two component models using a builder

Using the notion of a component architecture as a category is a way to compare two such categories formally, by defining a functor between them. Component architectures often have a builder module that composes applications for users. In Figure 14.1 the builder notionally contains a set of components represented as boxes or widgets and a set of lines or arrows that connect them together to form a control or data-flow graph, or simply to show dependency fulfillment. An idealization of such a builder must be representable as a component model itself and can be a component architecture category. The builder model in practice would naturally be constructed to map onto the component system for which it was designed to build applications. However, the design patterns for composition may, at least partially, be supportable in a different component model (Figure 14.4). The builder category here is referred to as $\mathcal{B}$.

If $C^{\circlearrowleft s_i}$ and $C'^{\circlearrowleft s'_i}$ are two component architectures that are members of $\mathcal{S}^{\circlearrowleft g}$ and defined according to (14.1), then the structure preserving map g between the two categories admits the diagram of (14.4):

$$\begin{array}{ccc} C & \xrightarrow{g} & C' \\ {\scriptstyle s_i}\downarrow & & \downarrow{\scriptstyle s'_i} \\ C & \xrightarrow{g} & C' \end{array}, \qquad (14.4)$$

where $s_i, s'_i \in F$. In practice the kind of glue code used to accomplish the structure preserving map g is irrelevant; the only requirement is that the underlying component architecture supports the metaphor that the builder component architecture exposes. Formally, if a particular component architecture category $\mathcal{C}$ is driven by a builder with a category $\mathcal{B}$,

$$\mathcal{B} \xrightarrow{g} \mathcal{C}, \qquad (14.5)$$

then this expresses the relationship of a builder to a component architecture as a functor between two component architecture categories based on the structure preserving map g. For

$\mathcal{B}$ to be an effective driver for the category $\mathcal{C}$, any state in $B_i \in \mathcal{B}$ must have a representation $C_i \in \mathcal{C}$. Otherwise, transformations of $B \in \mathcal{B}$ would be ambiguous in $C \in \mathcal{C}$, negating the reason for a builder in the first place. Therefore, one requirement of a builder is that every allowable transformation of its representation has a distinguished representation in the target component architecture. This means that the map g must not destroy the information existing in $\mathcal{B}$. Formally g must have a retraction r,

$$\mathcal{B} \xrightleftharpoons[r]{g} \mathcal{C} \,. \tag{14.6}$$

The claim here is that every builder that is a faithful front-end for a given component architecture must share this retraction property. By its nature a state evidenced in a builder must be reflected in the component architecture. However, the converse is generally not true. The component architecture ($\mathcal{C}$) may have operations and state that are orthogonal to the builder ($\mathcal{B}$). Again this means that the builder is always "less than" the component architecture on retraction:

$$\mathcal{B} \overset{\leq}{\underset{r}{=}} \mathcal{C}. \tag{14.7}$$

To compare another component architecture to $\mathcal{C}$ means finding a map from the *same* builder category to the new component architecture:

$$\mathcal{B} \xrightleftharpoons[r']{g'} \mathcal{C}' \,. \tag{14.8}$$

If such a map and its retraction exist, then $\mathcal{C}$ and $\mathcal{C}'$ belong to an equivalence class defined by $\mathcal{B}$.

This approach provides an unambiguous way of identifying similarities among component patterns for composition, and it carries over to any component design patterns that employ automation, such as those discussed in sections 14.2.1 to 14.2.3 for model coupling, parallel data redistribution, and computational quality of service. This situation suggests that if middleware can be written that is generic to a wide-enough class of applications, reuse is possible across multiple component models having similar composition patterns. Different frameworks produced for different HPC application domains will be able to use the same middleware to enhance performance.

14.3 Conclusion

The software component methodology consists of building an application out of interchangeable pieces with well-defined interfaces. Component approaches allow implementation details to be hidden inside the components, as long as the interface specification is met. In scientific computing, this hiding enables the automation of major tasks that end users typically do not want to handle themselves: the complex syntax and bookkeeping associated with connecting components consisting of different numbers of parallel processes, optimizing the settings of different parameters associated with components outside the user's area of expertise, creating new multidisciplinary simulations by composing existing disciplinary codes, and creating performance models and capturing performance characteristics from full applications.

Achieving this utility requires solving unique problems not found in commercial computing. Scientific components require high-performance connections and cannot tolerate slow interface connections. The data that must be transferred between components are orders of magnitude larger in size, and applications require connecting highly heterogeneous computation, data, visualization, and sensor systems. Scientific software component systems present new challenges in mathematical formalism and can benefit from the models and solutions that this formalism can provide. The usefulness of high-performance component systems has led to the need for a higher level of abstraction in reasoning about component frameworks, which category theory may provide.

Acknowledgments

CCA has been under development since 1998 by the CCA forum and represents the contributions of many people, all of whom we gratefully acknowledge. We also thank our collaborators outside the CCA forum, especially the early adopters of the CCA, for the important contributions they have made both to our understanding of component software in the high-performance scientific computing context and to making the CCA a practical and usable environment.

This work was supported in part by NSF Grants ANI-0330568, EIA-0202048, and CDA-0116050 and by the DoE Office of Science through the Center for Component Technology for Terascale Simulation Software SciDAC project.

Bibliography

[1] B. A. ALLAN, R. C. ARMSTRONG, A. P. WOLFE, J. RAY, D. E. BERNHOLDT, AND J. A. KOHL, *The CCA core specification in a distributed memory SPMD framework*, Concurrency and Computation: Practice and Experience, (2002), pp. 1–23.

[2] B. ALLEN, R. ARMSTRONG, S. LEFANTZI, J. RAY, E. WALSH, AND P. WOLFE, *Ccaffeine*. http://www.cca-forum.org/ccafe/ (2005).

[3] R. ARMSTRONG, D. GANNON, A. GEIST, K. KEAHEY, S. KOHN, L. C. MCINNES, S. PARKER, AND B. SMOLINSKI, *Toward a common component architecture for high-performance scientific computing*, in Proceedings of High Performance Distributed Computing, 1999, Los Angeles, CA, pp. 115–124.

[4] R. ARMSTRONG AND M. SOTTILE, *Formal representation of component model composition patterns*, Tech. Report SAND2005-7463, Sandia National Laboratories, Albuquerque, NM, February 2005.

[5] *AVS/Express*. http://www.avs.com/software/soft_t/avsxps.html, 2005.

[6] *Babel*, http://www.llnl.gov/CASC/components/ (2005).

[7] D. E. BERNHOLDT, B. A. ALLAN, R. ARMSTRONG, F. BERTRAND, K. CHIU, T. L. DAHLGREN, K. DAMEVSKI, W. R. ELWASIF, T. G. W. EPPERLY, M. GOVINDARAJU, D. S. KATZ, J. A. KOHL, M. KRISHNAN, G. KUMFERT, J. W. LARSON, S. LEFANTZI, M. J. LEWIS, A. D. MALONY, L. C. MCINNES, J. NIEPLOCHA, B. NORRIS, S. G. PARKER, J. RAY, S. SHENDE, T. L. WINDUS, AND S. ZHOU, *A component architecture for high-performance scientific computing*, 2005. International Journal of High Performance Computing Applications, Vol. 20, No. 2, 2006, pp. 163–202.

[8] F. BERTRAND, R. BRAMLEY, K. DAMEVSKI, J. KOHL, J. LARSON, AND A. SUSSMAN, *MxN interactions in parallel component architectures*, in Proceedings of the International Parallel and Distributed Processing Symposium, Denver, CO, April 4-8, 2005, 2005.

[9] F. BERTRAND AND R. BRAMLEY, *DCA: A distributed CCA framework based on MPI*, in Proceedings of the 9th International Workshop on High-Level Parallel Programming Models and Supportive Environments (HIPS'04), Santa Fe, NM, April 2004, IEEE Press.

[10] A. BEUGNARD, J.-M. JÉZÉQUEL, N. PLOUZEAU, AND D. WATKINS, *Making components contract aware*, IEEE Computer, (1999), pp. 38–45.

[11] R. BRAMLEY, D. GANNON, T. STUCKEY, J. VILLACIS, E. AKMAN, J. BALASUBRAMANIAN, F. BREG, S. DIWAN, AND M. GOVINDARAJU, *The Linear System Analyzer*, Kluwer, Dordrecht, 2000, pp. 123–134.

[12] M. BROY, *Towards a mathematical concept of a component and its use*, Software - Concepts and Tools, 18 (1997).

[13] *Caltech ASCI Center for Simulation of Dynamic Response of Materials.* http://www.cacr.caltech.edu/ASAP/ (2005).

[14] *CCA Forum homepage.* http://www.cca-forum.org/ (2005).

[15] *CCA specification.* http://www.cca-forum.org/specification/ (2005).

[16] K. CHIU, M. GOVINDARAJU, AND D. GANNON, *The proteus multiprotocol library*, in Proceedings of the 2002 Conference on Supercomputing, Baltimore, MD, ACM Press, November 2002.

[17] *Community climate system model.* http://www.cgd.ucar.edu/csm/ (2005).

[18] T. DAHLGREN, T. EPPERLY, AND G. KUMFERT, *Babel User's Guide*, 0.10.8 ed., CASC, Lawrence Livermore National Laboratory, Livermore, CA, July 2005.

[19] A. DENIS, C. PÉREZ, T. PRIOL, AND A. RIBES, *Process coordination and ubiquitous computing*, in Programming the Grid with Distributed Objects, CRC Press, Boca Raton, FL, July 2003, pp. 133–148.

[20] *DX homepage.* http://www.research.ibm/com/dx, 2005.

[21] D. Box et al., *Simple Object Access Protocol 1.1*, Tech. report, W3C, 2000. http://www.w3.org/TR/2000/NOTE-SOAP-20000508/.

[22] R. Englander, *Developing Java Beans*, O'Reilly Medic., Sebastopol, CA, June 1997.

[23] R. P. Fedkiw, *Coupling an Eulerian fluid calculation to a Lagrangian solid calculation with the ghost fluid method on structured adaptively refined meshes*, Journal of Computational Physics, 175 (2002), pp. 200–224.

[24] N. Furmento, A. Mayer, S. McGough, S. Newhouse, T. Field, and J. Darlington, *Optimisation of component-based applications within a grid environment*, in Proceedings of Supercomputing, IEEE, Los Alamitos, CA, 2001.

[25] *Fusion simulation project*. http://www.ofes.fusion.doe.gov/More_HTML/FESAC/FESAC11-02/Dahlburg.pdf.

[26] D. Gannon, R. Bramley, G. Fox, S. Smallen, A. Rossi, R. Ananthakrishnan, F. Bertrand, K. Chiu, M. Farrellee, M. Govindaraju, S. Krishnan, L. Ramakrishnan, Y. Simmhan, A. Slominski, Y. Ma, C. Olariu, and N. Rey-Cenvaz, *Programming the grid: Distributed software components, P2P and grid web services for scientific applications*, Journal of Cluster Computing, 5 (2002), pp. 325–336.

[27] G. A. Geist, A. Beguelin, J. Dongarra, W. Jiang, R. Manchek, and V. Sunderam, *PVM: Parallel Virtual Machine, A User's Guide and Tutorial for Networked Parallel Computing*, MIT Press, Cambridge, MA, 1994.

[28] T. Goodale, G. Allen, G. Lanfermann, J. Masso, T. Radke, E. Seidel, and J. Shalf, *The Cactus framework and toolkit: Design and applications*, in VECPAR'2002, 5th International Conference, Lecture Notes in Computer Science, Springer-Verlag, Berlin, New York, 2002.

[29] O. M. Group, *The Common Object Request Broker: Architecture and Specification*, OMG Document, 1998. http://www.omg.org/corba.

[30] ———, *CORBA Components*, OMG TC Document orbos/99-02-05, March 1999. ftp://ftp.omg.org/pub/docs/orbos/99-02-05.pdf.

[31] X. Gu and K. Nahrstedt, *A scalable QoS-aware service aggregation model for peer-to-peer computing grids*, in Proceedings of High Performance Distributed Computing, 2002, Edinburgh, Scotland, UK.

[32] P. Hovland, K. Keahey, L. C. McInnes, B. Norris, L. F. Diachin, and P. Raghavan, *A quality of service approach for high-performance numerical components*, in Proceedings of Workshop on QoS in Component-Based Software Engineering, Software Technologies Conference, Toulouse, France, 20 June 2003.

[33] *ITER*. http://www.iter.org (2005).

[34] K. Keahey, P. Beckman, and J. Ahrens, *Ligature: Component architecture for high performance applications*, International Journal of High Performance Computing Applications, 14 (2000), pp. 347–356.

[35] K. KEAHEY, *Architecture for Application-Level Parallel Distributed Computing*, Ph.D. thesis, Indiana University, Bloomington, 1996.

[36] J. P. KENNY, S. J. BENSON, Y. ALEXEEV, J. SARICH, C. L. JANSSEN, L. C. MCINNES, M. KRISHNAN, J. NIEPLOCHA, E. JURRUS, C. FAHLSTROM, AND T. L. WINDUS, *Component-based integration of chemistry and optimization software*, Journal of Computational Chemistry, 25 (2004), pp. 1717–1725.

[37] T. KILLEEN, J. MARSHALL, AND A. DA SILVA (PIs), *Earth system modeling framework*. http://www.esmf.ucar.edu/ (2005).

[38] S. KOHN, G. KUMFERT, J. PAINTER, AND C. RIBBENS, *Divorcing language dependencies from a scientific software library*, in Proc. 10th SIAM Conference on Parallel Processing, Portsmouth, VA, March 2001, CD-ROM.

[39] G. KUMFERT, *Understanding the CCA Standard Through Decaf*, Tech. report UCRL-MA-148390-DR, CASC, Lawrence Livermore National Laboratory, Livermore, CA, May 2003.

[40] J. W. LARSON, B. NORRIS, E. T. ONG, D. E. BERNHOLDT, J. B. DRAKE, W. R. ELWASIF, M. W. HAM, C. E. RASMUSSEN, G. KUMFERT, D. S. KATZ, S. ZHOU, C. DELUCA, AND N. S. COLLINS, *Components, the Common Component Architecture, and the climate/weather/ocean community*, in Proceedings of the 84th American Meteorological Society Annual Meeting, Seattle, Washington, 11–15 January 2004, American Meteorological Society.

[41] F. W. LAWVERE AND S. H. SCHANUEL, *Conceptual Mathematics*, Cambridge University Press, Cambridge, UK, 1997.

[42] S. LEFANTZI, C. KENNEDY, J. RAY, AND H. NAJM, *A study of the effect of higher order spatial discretizations in SAMR (Structured Adaptive Mesh Refinement) simulations*, in Proceedings of the Fall Meeting of the Western States Section of the The Combustion Institute, Los Angeles, California, October 2003.

[43] S. LEFANTZI, J. RAY, C. KENNEDY, AND H. NAJM, *A component-based toolkit for reacting flow with high order spatial discretizations on structured adaptively refined meshes*, Progress in Computational Fluid Dynamics: An International Journal, 5 (2005), pp. 298–315.

[44] S. LEFANTZI, J. RAY, AND H. N. NAJM, *Using the Common Component Architecture to design high performance scientific simulation codes*, in Proceedings of the 17th International Parallel and Distributed Processing Symposium (IPDPS 2003), 22-26 April 2003, Nice, France, IEEE Computer Society, 2003.

[45] S. LEFANTZI AND J. RAY, *A component-based scientific toolkit for reacting flows*, in Proceedings of the Second MIT Conference on Computational Fluid and Solid Mechanics, June 17-20, 2003, Cambridge, MA, vol. 2, Elsevier, 2003, pp. 1401–1405.

[46] J. LINDEMANN, O. DAHLBLOM, AND G. SANDBERG, *Using CORBA middleware in finite element software*, in Proceedings of the 2nd International Conference on Computational Science, P. M. A. Sloot, C. J. K. Tan, J. J. Dongarra, , and A. G. Hoekstra, eds., Lecture Notes in Computer Science, Springer, Berlin, New York, 2002. *Future Generation Computer Systems*, Vol. 22, Issue 1, 2006, pp. 158–193.

[47] J. P. LOYALL, R. E. SCHANTZ, J. A. ZINKY, AND D. E. BAKKEN, *Specifying and measuring quality of service in distributed object systems*, in Proceedings of the First International Symposium on Object-Oriented Real-Time Distributed Computing (ISORC '98), 1998, Kyoto, Japan.

[48] L. C. MCINNES, B. A. ALLAN, R. ARMSTRONG, S. J. BENSON, D. E. BERNHOLDT, T. L. DAHLGREN, L. F. DIACHIN, M. KRISHNAN, J. A. KOHL, J. W. LARSON, S. LEFANTZI, J. NIEPLOCHA, B. NORRIS, S. G. PARKER, J. RAY, AND S. ZHOU, *Parallel PDE-based simulations using the Common Component Architecture*, Tech. Report ANL/MCS-P1179-0704, Argonne National Laboratory, 2004. To appear in the book *Numerical Solution of Partial Differential Equations on Parallel Computers*, A. M. Bruaset, P. Bjorstad, and A. Tveito, editors, Springer, in press.

[49] L. MCINNES, B. NORRIS, S. BHOWMICK, AND P. RAGHAVAN, *Adaptive sparse linear solvers for implicit CFD using Newton-Krylov algorithms*, in Proceedings of the Second MIT Conference on Computational Fluid and Solid Mechanics, 2003, Cambridge, MA.

[50] MPI FORUM, *MPI: a message-passing interface standard*, International Journal of Supercomputer Applications and High Performance Computing, 8 (1994), pp. 159–416.

[51] B. NORRIS, S. BALAY, S. BENSON, L. FREITAG, P. HOVLAND, L. MCINNES, AND B. SMITH, *Parallel components for PDEs and optimization: Some issues and experiences*, Parallel Computing, 28 (2002), pp. 1811–1831.

[52] B. NORRIS, J. RAY, R. ARMSTRONG, L. C. MCINNES, D. E. BERNHOLDT, W. R. ELWASIF, A. D. MALONY, AND S. SHENDE, *Computational quality of service for scientific components*, in Proc. of International Symposium on Component-Based Software Engineering (CBSE7), Edinburgh, Scotland, 2004.

[53] P. M. PAPADOPOULOS, J. A. KOHL, AND B. D. SEMERARO, *CUMULVS: Extending a generic steering and visualization middleware for application fault-tolerance of parallel applications*, in Proceedings of the 31st Hawaii International Conference on System Sciences (HICSS-31), vol. 8, Kona, HI, January 1998, pp. 127–136.

[54] P. M. PAPADOPOULOS AND J. A. KOHL, *A library for visualization and steering of distributed simulations using PVM and AVS*, in High Performance Computing Symposium, Montreal, Canada, July 1995.

[55] S. G. PARKER, D. M. WEINSTEIN, AND C. R. JOHNSON, *The SCIRun computational steering software system*, in Modern Software Tools in Scientific Computing, E. Arge, A. M. Bruaset, and H. P. Langtangen, eds., Birkhäuser Press, Basel, 1997, pp. 1–40.

[56] C. Pérez, T. Priol, and A. Ribes, *A parallel CORBA component model for numerical code coupling*, International Journal of High Performance Computing, 17 (2003).

[57] D. Post, D. Batchelor, R. Bramley, J. R. Cary, R. Cohen, P. Colella, and S. Jardin, *Report of the fusion simulation project steering committee*, Tech. Report LA-UR-04-5930, Los Alamos National Laboratory, Los Alamos, NM, November 2004. Journal of Fusion Energy, Vol. 23, No. 1, 2005, pp. 1–26.

[58] R. Raje, B. Bryant, A. Olson, M. Auguston, , and C. Burt, *A quality-of-service-based framework for creating distributed heterogeneous software components*, Concurrency Comput: Pract. Exper., 14 (2002), pp. 1009–1034.

[59] J. Ray, C. Kennedy, S. Lefantzi, and H. Najm, *High-order spatial discretizations and extended stability methods for reacting flows on structured adaptively refined meshes*, in Proceedings of the Third Joint Meeting of the U.S. Sections of The Combustion Institute, March 16-19, 2003, Chicago, Illinois., 2003.

[60] J. Ray, N. Trebon, S. Shende, R. C. Armstrong, and A. Malony, *Performance measurement and modeling of component applications in a high performance computing environment: A case study*, in Proc. of the 18th International Parallel and Distributed Computing Symposium, Santa Fe, NM, 2004.

[61] R. Sessions, *COM and DCOM: Microsoft's Vision for Distributed Objects*, John Wiley & Sons, New York, 1997. See also http://www.microsoft.com/com.

[62] S. Shende, A. D. Malony, C. Rasmussen, and M. Sottile, *A Performance Interface for Component-Based Applications*, in Proceedings of International Workshop on Performance Modeling, Evaluation and Optimization, International Parallel and Distributed Processing Symposium, 2003, Nice, France.

[63] C. Szyperski, *Component Software: Beyond Object-Oriented Programming*, ACM Press, New York, 1998.

[64] G. Toth, O. Volberg, A. J. Ridley, T. I. Gombosi, D. DeZeeuw, K. C. Hansen, D. R. Chesney, Q. F. Stout, K. G. Powell, K. Kane, and R. Oehmke, *A physics-based software framework for sun-earth connection modeling*, in Multiscale Coupling of Sun-Earth Processes, A. T. Y. Lui, Y. Kamide, and G. Consolini, eds., Amsterdam, 2004, Elsevier, pp. 383–397.

[65] K. Zhang, K. Damevski, V. Venkatachalapathy, and S. Parker, *SCIRun2: A CCA framework for high performance computing*, in Proceedings of the 9th International Workshop on High-Level Parallel Programming Models and Supportive Environments (HIPS 2004), Santa Fe, NM, April 2004, IEEE Press, pp. 72–79.

Chapter 15

Integrating Component-Based Scientific Computing Software

Steven G. Parker, Keming Zhang, Kostadin Damevski, and Chris R. Johnson

In recent years, component technology has been a successful methodology for large-scale commercial software development. Component technology combines a set of frequently used functions in a component and makes the implementation transparent to users. Software application developers typically connect a group of components from a component repository, connecting them to create a single application.

SCIRun[1] is a scientific PSE that allows the interactive construction and steering of large-scale scientific computations [20, 19, 21, 11, 23, 25, 10]. A scientific application is constructed by connecting computational, modeling, and visualization elements [8]. This application may contain several computational elements as well as several visualization elements, all of which work together in orchestrating a solution to a scientific problem. Geometric inputs and computational parameters may be changed interactively, and the results of these changes provide immediate feedback to the investigator.

Problem solving environments, such as SCIRun, often employ component technology to bring a variety of computational tools to an engineer or scientist for solving a computational problem. In this scenario, the tools should be readily available and simple to combine to create an application. However, these PSEs typically use a single-component model (such as Java Beans, Microsoft COM, CORBA, or CCA) or employ one of their own design. As a result, components designed for one PSE cannot be easily reused in another PSE or in a stand-alone program. Software developers must *buy in* to a particular component model and produce components for one particular system. Users must typically select a single system or face the challenges of manually managing the data transfer between multiple (usually) incompatible systems.

---

[1]Pronounced "ski-run." SCIRun derives its name from the Scientific Computing and Imaging (SCI) Institute at the University of Utah.

272 Chapter 15. Integrating Component-Based Scientific Computing Software

SCIRun2 [27], currently under development, addresses these shortcomings through a *meta-component model*, allowing support for disparate component-based systems to be incorporated into a single environment and managed through a common user-centric visual interface.

In this chapter, section 15.1 discusses the SCIRun and BioPSE PSEs. Other scientific computing component models are discussed in section 15.2. The remainder of the chapter discusses the design of SCIRun2, including a discussion of meta-components, support for distributed computing, and parallel components. We present conclusions and future work in section 15.6.

15.1 SCIRun and BioPSE

SCIRun is a scientific PSE that allows the interactive construction and steering of large-scale scientific computations [20, 19, 21, 11, 23]. A scientific application is constructed by connecting computational elements (modules) to form a program (network), as shown in Figure 15.1. The program may contain several computational elements as well as several visualization elements, all of which work together in orchestrating a solution to a scientific

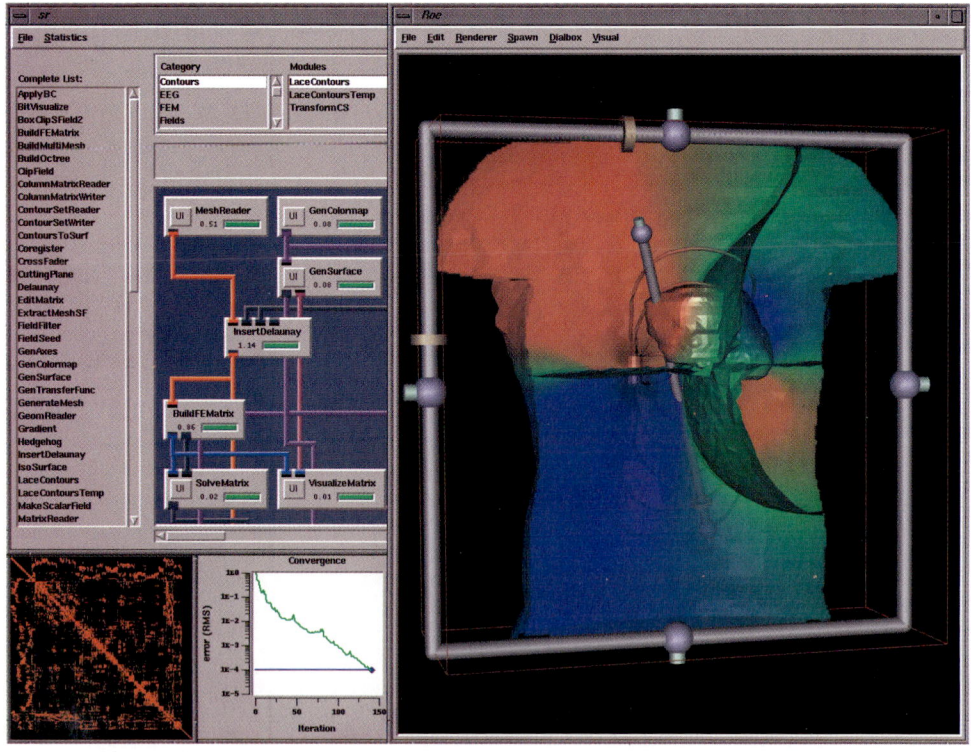

Figure 15.1. *The SCIRun PSE, illustrating a 3D finite element simulation of an implantable cardiac defibrillator.*

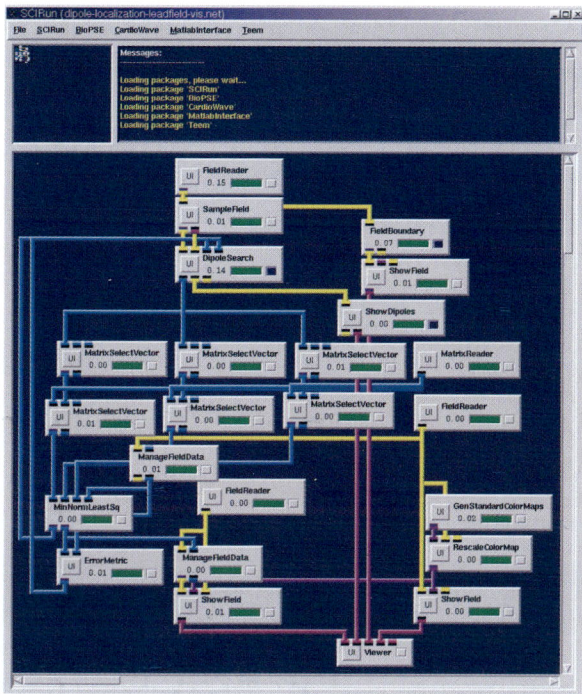

Figure 15.2. *BioPSE neural source localization network. The optimal dipole source is recovered using a multistart optimization algorithm.*

problem. Geometric inputs and computational parameters may be changed interactively, and the results of these changes provide immediate feedback to the investigator. SCIRun is designed to facilitate large-scale scientific computation and visualization on a wide range of architectures from the desktop to large supercomputers.

BioPSE [10] is a PSE based on SCIRun that is targeted to biomedical computing research problems. BioPSE provides the modeling, simulation, and visualization modules; data structures; data converters; and application networks for bioelectric field applications. With these components, researchers can investigate biomedical research issues, such as bioelectric fields produced from epileptic seizures in the brain to atrial arrhythmias in the heart.

An example electroencephalography (EEG) neural source localization application is shown in Figures 15.2 and 15.3. Figure 15.2 contains the dataflow network that implements the inverse EEG application. At the top of the network, the input data files are loaded; these include the finite element mesh that defines the geometry and electrical conductivity properties of the model and a precomputed lead-field matrix that encodes the relationship between electric sources in the domain and the resulting potentials that would be measured at the electrodes. Further down in the network, we have a set of modules that optimize the dipole location in order to minimize the misfit between the measured potentials from the electrodes and the simulated potentials due to the dipole. Finally, we have visualization and

274 Chapter 15. Integrating Component-Based Scientific Computing Software

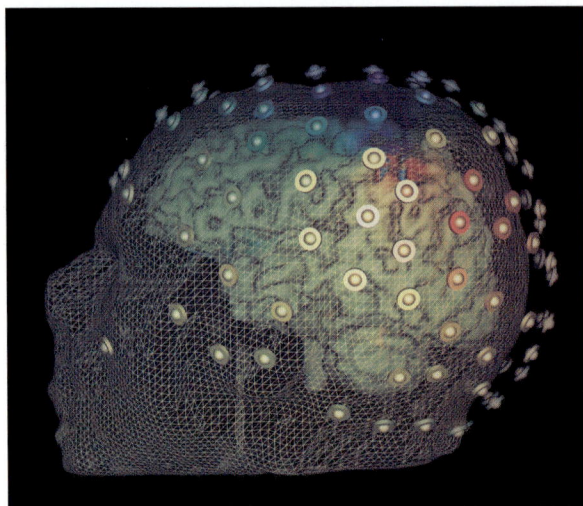

Figure 15.3. *Visualization of the iterative source localization. The voltages of the true solution (disks) and the computed solution (spheres) are qualitatively compared at the electrode positions as the optimization (shown as arrows) converges on a neural source location. The solution misfit can be qualitatively interpreted by pseudocolored voltages at each electrode.*

rendering modules, which provide interactive feedback to the user. The visualization that accompanies this network is shown in Figure 15.3. The potentials that were measured at the electrodes on the scalp are rendered as pseudocolored disks; the potentials originating from the simulated dipole source are shown as pseudocolored spheres embedded within the disks. The rainbow colors of the disks and spheres correspond to voltages, with red mapping to positive potentials, blue mapping to negative potentials, and green mapping to ground. The difference in the color of the sphere and the color of the disk at any particular electrode indicates the misfit between the measured and simulated potentials at that site. The dipoles that are iteratively approaching the true dipole location are shown as gray and blue arrows, and the outside of the head model has been rendered with wire-frame cylinders.

PowerApps

Historically, one of the major hurdles to SCIRun becoming a tool for the scientist as well as the engineer has been SCIRun's dataflow interface. While visual programming is natural for computer scientists and engineers, who are accustomed to writing software and building algorithmic pipelines, it can be overly cumbersome for many application scientists. Even when a dataflow network implements a specific application (such as the forward bioelectric field simulation network provided with BioPSE and detailed in the BioPSE tutorial), the user interface (UI) components of the network are presented to the user in separate UI windows, without any semantic context for their settings. For example, SCIRun provides file browser user interfaces for reading in data. However, on the dataflow network all the file browsers have the same generic presentation. Historically, there has not been a way to present the filename entries in their semantic context, for example, to indicate that one entry should identify the electrodes input file and another should identify the finite element mesh file.

A recent release of BioPSE/SCIRun (in October 2003) addressed this shortcoming by introducing PowerApps. A PowerApp is a customized interface built atop a data flow application network. The data flow network controls the execution and synchronization of the modules that comprise the application, but the generic user interface windows are replaced with entries that are placed in the context of a single application-specific interface window.

BioPSE contains a PowerApp called BioFEM. BioFEM has been built atop the forward finite element network and provides a useful example for demonstrating the differences between the dataflow and PowerApp views of the same functionality. In Figure 15.4, the dataflow version of the application is shown: the user has separate interface windows for controlling different aspects of the simulation and visualization. In contrast, the PowerApp version is shown in Figure 15.5: here, the application has been wrapped up into a single

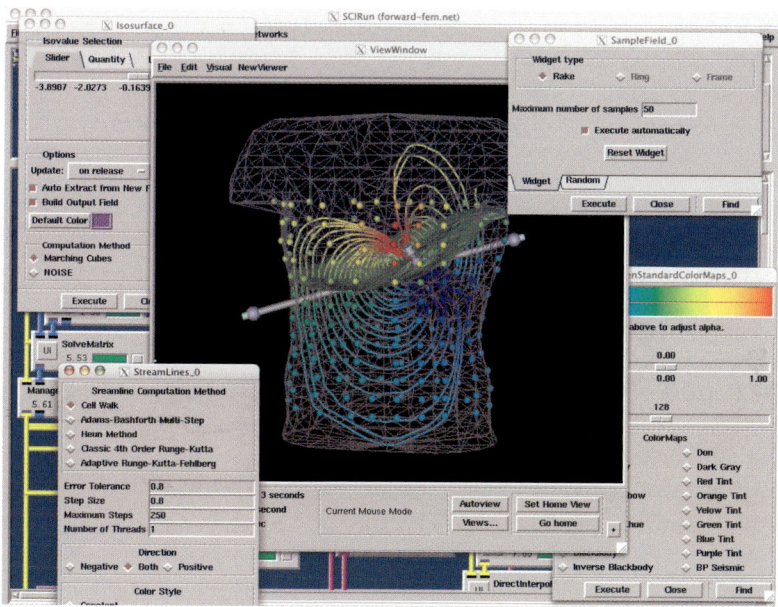

Figure 15.4. *BioPSE dataflow interface to a forward bioelectric field application. The underlying dataflow network implements the application with modular interconnected components called modules. Data are passed between the modules as input and output parameters to the algorithms. While this is a useful interface for prototyping, it can be nonintuitive for end users; it is confusing to have a separate user interface window to control the settings for each module. Moreover, the entries in the user interface windows fail to provide semantic context for their settings. For example, the text-entry field on the SampleField user interface that is labeled "Maximum number of samples" is controlling the number of electric field streamlines that are produced for the visualization.*

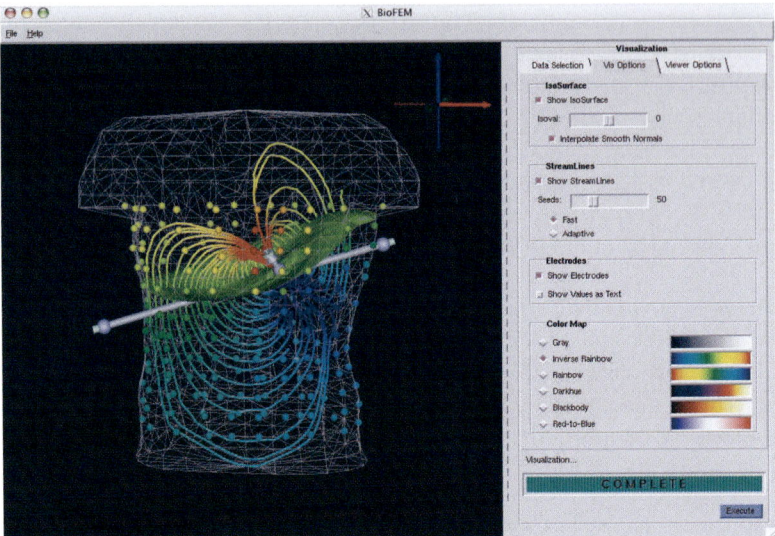

Figure 15.5. *The BioFEM custom interface. Although the application is the functionality equivalent to the data flow version shown in Figure 15.4, this PowerApp version provides an easier-to-use custom interface. Everything is contained within a single window. The user is lead through the steps of loading and visualizing the data with the tabs on the right; generic control settings have been replaced with contextually appropriate labels, and application-specific tooltips (not shown) appear when the user places the cursor over any user interface element.*

interface window, with logically arranged and semantically labeled user interface elements composed within panels and notetabs.

In addition to bioelectric field problems, the BioPSE system can also be used to investigate other biomedical applications. For example, we have wrapped the tensor and raster data processing functionality of the Teem toolkit into the Teem package of BioPSE, and we have used that increased functionality to develop the BioTensor PowerApp, as seen in Figure 15.6. BioTensor presents a customized interface to a 140-module data flow network. With BioTensor the user can visualize diffusion weighted imaging (DWI) datasets to investigate the anisotropic structure of biological tissues. The application supports the import of DICOM and Analyze datasets and implements the latest diffusion tensor visualization techniques, including superquadric glyphs [13] and tensorlines [26] (both shown).

15.2 Components for scientific computing

A number of component models have been developed for a wide range of software applications. Java Beans[9], a component model from Sun, is a platform-neutral architecture for the Java application environment. However, it requires a Java Virtual Machine as the intermediate platform and the components must be written in Java. Microsoft has developed the Component Object Model (COM)[17], a software architecture that allows applications to

Figure 15.6. *The BioTensor PowerApp. Just as with BioFEM, we have wrapped up a complicated data flow network into a custom application. In the left panel, the user is guided through the stages of loading the data, coregistering MRI diffusion weighted images, and constructing diffusion tensors. On the right panel, the user has controls for setting the visualization options. In the rendering window in the middle, the user can render and interact with the dataset.*

be built from binary software components on the Windows platform. The Object Management Group (OMG) developed the common object request broker architecture (CORBA) [18], which is an open, vendor-independent architecture and infrastructure that computer applications can use to work together in a distributed environment.

Many problem solving environments, such as SCIRun, employ these component models or one of their own. As an example, SCIRun provides a dataflow-based component model. The CCA forum, a group of researchers from several DoE national laboratories and academic institutions, has defined a standard component architecture [1] for high performance parallel computing. The CCA forum has defined a minimal set of standard interfaces that a high-performance component framework should provide to implement high-performance components. This standard promotes interoperability between components developed by different teams across different institutions. However, CCA has not yet fully addressed the architecture of parallel components combined with distributed computation.

CCA is discussed in more detail in Chapter 14, but we present an overview here. The CCA model consists of a framework and an expandable set of components. The framework is a workbench for building, connecting, and running the components. A component is the basic unit of an application. A CCA component consists of one or more ports, and a port is a group of method-call-based interfaces. There are two types of ports: **uses** port and **provides** ports. A provides port (or callee) implements its interfaces and waits for other ports to call them. A uses port (or caller) issues method calls that can be fulfilled by a type-compatible provides port on a different component.

A CCA port is represented by an interface, while interfaces are specified through a SIDL. A compiler is usually used to compile a SIDL interface description file into specific language bindings. Generally, component language binding can be provided for many different languages, such as C/C++, Java, Fortran, or Python. The Babel [14] compiler group is working on creating this support for different languages within CCA.

SCIRun2 is a new software framework that combines CCA compatibility with connections to other commercial and academic component models. SCIRun2 is based on the SCIRun [12] infrastructure and the CCA specification. It utilizes parallel-to-parallel remote method invocation to connect components in a distributed memory environment and is multithreaded to facilitate shared memory programming. It also has an optional visual-programming interface.

Although SCIRun2 is designed to be fully compatible with CCA. It aims to combine CCA compatibility with the strength of other component models. A few of the design goals of SCIRun2 are as follows:

1. SCIRun2 is fully CCA compatible; thus any CCA components can be used in SCIRun2 and CCA components developed from SCIRun2 can also be used in other CCA frameworks.

2. SCIRun2 accommodates several useful component models. In addition to CCA components and SCIRun dataflow modules, CORBA components, Microsoft COM components, ITK, and Vtk[24] modules will be supported in SCIRun2.

3. SCIRun2 builds bridges between different component models, so that we can combine a disparate array of computational tools to create powerful applications with cooperative components from different sources.

4. SCIRun2 supports distributed computing. Components created on different computers can work together through a network and build high performance applications.

5. SCIRun2 supports parallel components in a variety of ways for maximum flexibility. This is not constrained to only CCA components, because SCIRun2 employees a M process to N process method invocation and data redistribution (MxN) library [3] that potentially can be used by many component models.

Overall, SCIRun2 provides a broad approach that will allow scientists to combine a variety of tools for solving a particular computational problem. The overarching design goal of SCIRun2 is to provide the ability for a computational scientist to use the right tool for the right job, a goal motivated by the needs of our biomedical and other scientific users.

15.3 Metacomponent model

Systems such as Java Beans, COM, CORBA, CCA, and others successfully employ a component-based architecture to allow users to rapidly assembly computational tools in a single environment. However, these systems typically do not interact with one another in a straightforward manner, and it is difficult to take components developed for one system and redeploy them in another. Software developers must *buy in* to a particular model and

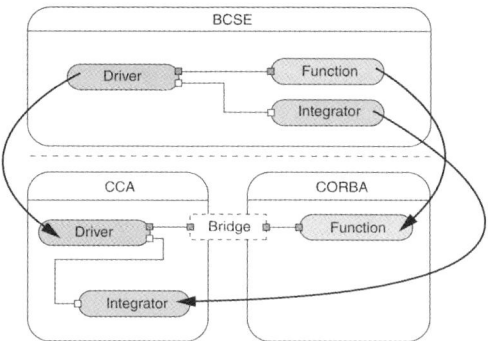

Figure 15.7. *Components of different models cooperate in SCIRun2.*

produce components for one particular system. Users must typically select a single system or face the challenges of manually managing the data transfer between multiple (usually) incompatible systems. SCIRun2 addresses these shortcomings through the meta-component model, allowing support for disparate component-based systems to be incorporated into a single environment and managed through a common user-centric visual interface. Furthermore, many systems that are not traditionally thought of as component models but that have well-designed, regular structures can be mapped to a component model and manipulated dynamically. SCIRun2 combines support for CCA components, "old-style" SCIRun data flow components, and we are planning support for CORBA, COM, and VTK. As a result, SCIRun2 can utilize SCIRun components, CCA components, and other software components in the same simulation.

The meta component model operates by providing a plug-in architecture for component models. Abstract components are manipulated and managed by the SCIRun2 framework, while concrete component models perform the actual work. This facility allows components implemented with disparate component models to be orchestrated together.

Figure 15.7 demonstrates a simple example of how SCIRun2 handles different component models. Two CCA components, Driver and Integrator, and one CORBA component, Function, are created in the SCIRun2 framework. In this simple example, the driver is connected to both the function and the integrator. Inside SCIRun2, two frameworks are hidden: the CCA framework and the CORBA object request broker (ORB). The CCA framework creates the CCA components, driver and integrator. The CORBA framework creates the CORBA component, function. The two CCA components can be connected in a straightforward manner through the CCA component model. However, the components driver and function cannot be connected directly, because neither CCA nor CORBA allows a connection from a component of a different model. Instead, a bridge component is created. Bridges belong to a special internal component model that is used to build a connection between components of different component models. In this example, a bridge has two ports: one CCA port and one CORBA port. In this way it can be connected to both CCA component and CORBA component. The CORBA invocation is converted to request to the CCA port inside the bridge component.

Bridge components can be manually or automatically generated. In situations in which interfaces are easily mapped between one interface and another, automatically generated bridges can facilitate interoperability in a straightforward way. More complex component interactions may require manually generated bridge components. Bridge components may implement heavy-weight transformations between component models and therefore have the potential to introduce performance bottlenecks. For the few scenarios that require maximum performance, reimplementation of both components in a common, performance-oriented component model may be required. However, for rapid prototyping, or for components that are not performance critical, this is completely acceptable.

To automatically generate a bridge component that translates a given pair of components, a generalized translation must be completed between the component models. A software engineer designs how two particular component models will interact. This task can require creating methods of data and control translation between the two models and can be quite difficult in some scenarios. The software engineer expresses the translation into a compiler plugin, which is used as a specification of the translation process. A plugin abstractly represents the entire translation between the two component models. It is specified by an eRuby (embedded Ruby) template document. eRuby templates are text files that can be augmented by Ruby [15] scripts. The Ruby scripts are useful for situations where the translation requires more sophistication than regular text (such as control structures or additional parsing). This provides us with better flexibility and more power inside the plugin, with the end goal of being able to support the translation of a wider range of component models.

The only other source of information is the interface of the ports we want to bridge (usually expressed in an IDL file). The bridge compiler accepts commands that specify a mapping between incompatible interfaces, where the interfaces between the components differ in various names or types but not functionality. Using a combination of the plugin and the interface augmented with mapping commands, the compiler is able to generate the specific bridge component. This component is automatically connected and ready to broker the translation between the two components of different models.

Figure 15.8 shows a more complex example that is motivated by the needs of a biological application. This example works very much like the last: the framework manages components from several different component models through the meta-model interface. Components from the same model interact with each other natively and interact with components in other models through bridges. Allowing components to communicate with each other through their native mechanisms ensures that no performance bottlenecks are introduced and that the original semantics are preserved.

15.4 Distributed computing

SCIRun2 provides support for distributed objects based on remote method invocation (RMI). This support is utilized in the core of the SCIRun framework in addition to distributed components. This section describes the design of the distributed object subsystem.

A distributed object is a set of interfaces defined by SIDL that can be referenced over network. The distributed object is similar to the C++ object, it utilizes similar inheritance rules, and all objects share the same code. However, only methods (interfaces) can be

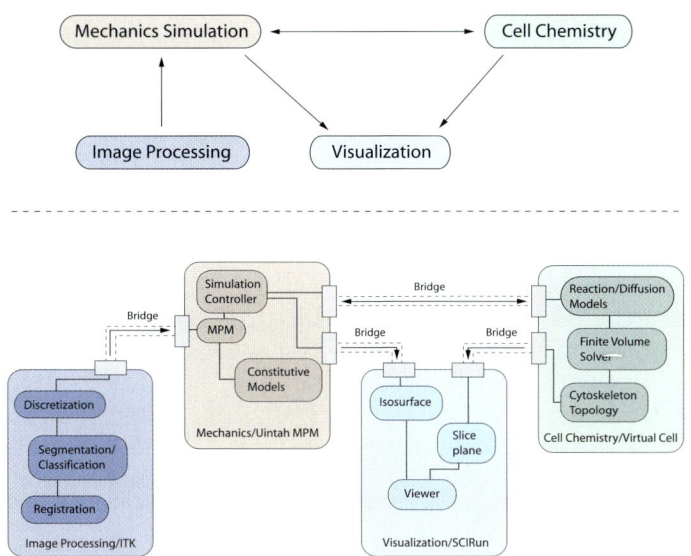

Figure 15.8. *A more intricate example of how components of different models cooperate in SCIRun2. The application and components shown are from a realistic (albeit incomplete) scenario.*

referenced, and the interfaces must be defined in SIDL. Using the SIDL language, we implemented a straightforward distributed object system. We extend the SIDL language and build upon this system for implementing parallel to parallel component connections, as discussed in the next section.

A distributed object is implemented by a concrete C++ class and referenced by a proxy class. The proxy class is a machine-generated class that associates the user-made method calls to a call by the concrete object. The proxy classes are described in a SIDL file, and a compiler compiles the SIDL file and creates the proxy classes. The proxy classes define the abstract classes with a set of pure virtual functions. The concrete classes extends those abstract proxy classes and implement each virtual functions.

There are two types of object proxies: server proxy and client proxy. The server proxy (or skeleton) is the object proxy created in the same memory address space as the concrete object. When the concrete object is created, the server proxy starts and works as a server, waiting for any local or remote methods invocations. The client proxy (or stub) is the proxy created on a different memory address space. When a method is called through the client proxy, the client proxy will package the calling arguments into a single message, send the message to the server proxy, and then wait for the server proxy to invoke the methods and return the result and argument changes.

We created Data Transmitter, a separate layer, that is used by the generated proxy code for handling messaging. We also employ the concept of a data transmission point (DTP), which is similar to the start point and end points used in Nexus [7]. A DTP is a data structure that contains a object pointer pointing to the context of a concrete class. Each memory address space has only one Data Transmitter, and each Data Transmitter uses three communication ports (sockets): one listening port, one receiving port, and one sending port. All the DTPs in the same address space share the same Data Transmitter. A Data Transmitter is identified by its universal resource identifier (URI): IP address + listening port. A DTP is identified by its memory address together with the Data Transmitter URI, because DTP addresses are unique in the same memory address space. Optionally, we could use other type of object identifiers.

The proxy objects package method calls into messages by marshaling objects and then waiting for a reply. Nonpointer arguments, such as integers, fixed sized arrays and strings (character arrays), are marshaled by the proxy into a message in the order in which they are presented in the method. After the server proxy receives the message, it unmarshals the arguments in the same order. A array size is marshaled in the beginning of an array argument, so the proxy knows how to allocate memory for the array. SIDL supports a special opaque data type that can be used to marshal pointers if the two objects are in the same address space. Distributed object references are marshaled by packaging the DTP URI (Data Transmitter URI and object ID). The DTP URI is actually marshaled as a string, and when it is unmarshaled, a new proxy of the appropriate type is created based on the DTP URI.

C++ exceptions are handled as special distributed objects. In a remote method invocation, the server proxy tries to catch an exception (also a distributed object) before it returns. If it catches one, the exception pointer is marshaled to the returned message. Upon receiving the message, the client proxy unmarshals the message and obtains the exception. The exception is then rethrown by the proxy.

15.5 Parallel components

This section introduces the CCA parallel component design and discusses issues of the implementation. Our design goal is to make the parallelism transparent to the component users. In most cases, the component users can use a parallel component as the way they use sequential component without knowing that a component is actually parallel component.

Parallel CCA Component (PCom) is a set of similar components that run in a set of processes respectively. When the number of process is one, the PCom is equivalent to a sequential component. We call each component in a PCom a *member component*. Member components typically communicate internally with MPI [16] or an equivalent message-passing library.

PComs communicate with each other through CCA-style RMI ports. We developed a prototype parallel component infrastructure [5, 2] that facilitates connection of parallel components in a distributed environment. This model supports two types of methods calls: *independent* and *collective*, and as such our port model supports both independent and collective ports.

An independent port is created by a single component member, and it contains only independent interfaces. A collective port is created and owned by all component members in a PCom, and one or more of its methods are collective. Collective methods require that all member components participate in the collective calls in the same order.

As an example of how parallel components interact, let pA be a uses port of component A and pB be a provides port of component B. Both pA and pB have the same port type, which defines the interface. If pB is a collective port and has the interface

```
collective int foo(inout int arg);
```

then getPort("pA") returns a collective pointer that points to the collective port pB. If pB is an independent port, getPort("pA") returns a pointer that points to an independent port.

Component A can have one or more members, so each member might obtain a (collective/independent) pointer to a provides port. The component developer can decide what subset (one, many, or all components) participate in a method call foo(arg). When any member component register a uses port, all other members can share the same uses port. But for a collective provides port, each member must call addProvidesPort to register each member port.

The MxN library takes care of the collective method invocation and data distribution. We repeat only the essentials here; see [3] for details. If an M-member PCom A obtains a pointer ptr pointing to an N-member PCom's B collective port pB, then ptr→foo(args) is a collective method invocation. The MxN library index PCom members with rank 0, 1, ..., M-1 for A and 0, 1, ..., N-1 for B. If $M = N$, then the ith member component of A call foo(args) on the ith component of B. But if M < N, then we "extend" the A's to 0, 1, 2, ..., M, 0, 1, 2, ... M, ... N-1 and they call foo(args) on each member component of B like the M = N case, but only the first M calls request returns. The left panel of Figure 15.9 shows an example of this case with M = 3 and N = 5. If M > N, we extend component B's set to 0, 1, ..., N, 0, 1, ..., N, ..., M-1 and only the first N member components of B are actually called; the rest are not called but simply return the result. We rely on collective semantics

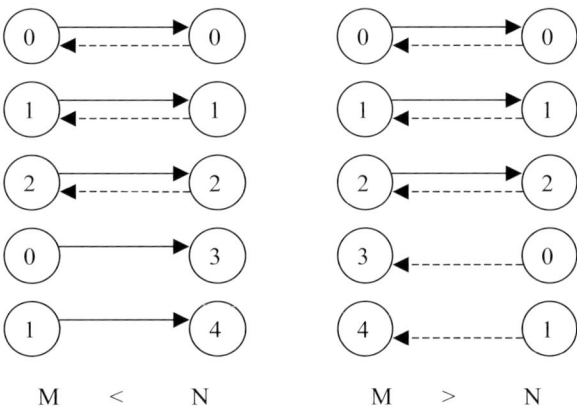

Figure 15.9. MxN *method invocation, with the caller on the left and the callee on the right. In the left scenario, the number of callers is fewer than the number of callees, so some callers make multiple method calls. In the right, the number of callees is fewer, so some callees send multiple return values.*

from the components to ensure consistency without requiring global synchronization. The right panel of Figure 15.9 shows an example of this case with M = 5 and N = 3.

The MxN library also does most of the work for the data redistribution. A multidimensional array can be defined as a distributed array that associates a distribution scheduler with the real data. Both callers and callees define the distribution schedule before the remote method invocation, using a first-stride-last representation for each dimension of the array. The SIDL compiler creates the scheduler and scheduling is done in the background.

With independent ports and collective ports, we cover the two extremes. Ports that require communication among a subset of the member components present a greater challenge. Instead, we utilize a subsetting capability in the MxN system to produce ports that are associated with a subset of the member components and then utilize them as collective ports.

SCIRun2 provides the mechanism to start a parallel component on either shared memory multiprocessors computers or clusters. SCIRun2 consists of a main framework and a set of parallel component loaders (PCLs). A PCL can be started with ssh on a cluster, where it gathers and reports its local component repository and registers to the main framework. The PCL on an N-node cluster is essentially a set of loaders, each running on a node. When the user requests to create a parallel component, the PCL instantiates a parallel component on its processes (or nodes) and passes a distributed pointer to the SCIRun2 framework. PCLs are responsible for creating and destroying components running on their nodes, but they do not maintain the port connections. The SCIRun2 framework maintains all component status and port connections.

Supporting threads and MPI together can be difficult. MPI provides a convenient communication among the processes in a cluster. However, if any process has more than one thread and the MPI calls are made in those threads, the MPI communication may break because MPIs distinguish only processes, not threads. The MPI interface allows an implementation to support threads but does not require it. Most MPI implementations are not threadsafe. We provide support for both threadsafe and nonthreadsafe MPI implementations so that users can choose any available MPI.

A straightforward way to support nonthreadsafe MPIs is to globally order the MPI calls such that no two MPI calls are executed at the same time. We implemented a distributed lock, which has two interfaces:

```
PRMI::lock()
PRMI::unlock()
```

The distributed lock is just like a mutex, but it is collective with respect to all MPI processes in a cluster. The critical section between PRMI::lock() and PRMI::unlock() can be obtained by only one set of threads in different MPI processes. The users must call PRMI::lock() before any MPI calls and call PRMI::unlock() after to release the lock. More than one MPI calls can be made in the critical section. In this way only one set of threads (each from a MPI process) can make MPI calls at one time. Additionally, the overhead of acquiring and releasing this lock is very high because it requires a global synchronization. However, in some cases this approach is necessary for supporting the multi-threaded software framework in an environment where a thread-safe MPI is no available.

It is fairly easier to support threadsafe MPI. Our approach is to create a distinct MPI communicator for the threads that communicate with each other and restrict that those

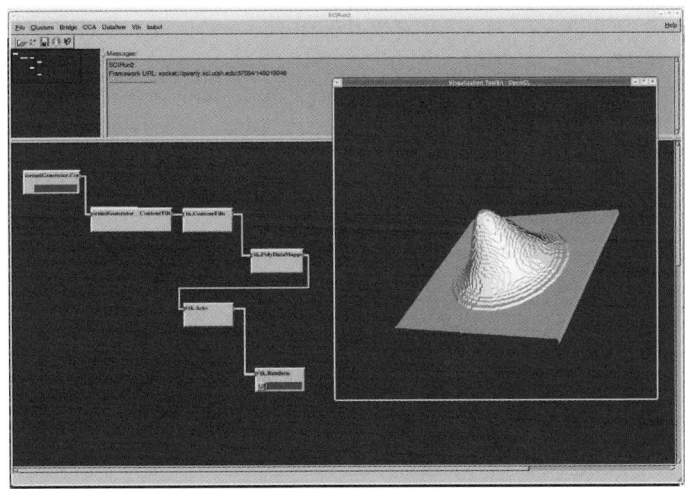

Figure 15.10. *Components of different models cooperate in SCIRun2.*

threads can use only that communicator for MPI communication. The special communicators are created by the PCL and can be obtained through a framework service interface. The threadsafe MPI allows multiple MPI calls executed safely at the same time, and the designated communicators help to identify the group of threads which initiated the MPI calls.

An efficient mechanism allows parallel components to efficient coordinate around error conditions [4].

Figure 15.10 shows a SCIRun2 application that uses bridging to Vtk visualization components. SCIRun2 is currently under development, but we expect a public release in the near future.

15.6 Conclusions and future work

We presented the SCIRun, BioPSE, and SCIRun2 problem solving environments for scientific computing. These systems all employ software components to encapsulate computational functionality into a reusable unit. SCIRun and BioPSE are open source, have biannual public releases, and are used by a number of end users for a variety of different computational applications.

Additionally, we presented an overview of the new SCIRun2 component framework. SCIRun2 integrates multiple component models into a single visual problem solving environment and builds bridges between components of different component models. In this way, a number of tools can be combined into a single environment without requiring global adoption of a common underlying component model. We have also described a parallel component architecture utilizing the common component architecture, combined with distributed objects and parallel MxN array redistribution that can be used in SCIRun2.

A prototype of the SCIRun2 framework has been developed, and we are using this framework for a number of applications in order to demonstrate the SCIRun2 features. Future applications will rely more on the system and will facilitate joining many powerful tools, such as the SCI Institutes' interactive ray-tracing system [22] and the Uintah [6] parallel, multiphysics system. Additional large-scale computational applications are under construction and are beginning to take advantage of the capabilities of SCIRun2. Support for additional component models, such as Vtk, CORBA, and possibly others, will be added in the future.

Acknowledgments

The authors gratefully acknowledge support from NIH NCRR, NSF, and the DoE ASCI and SciDAC programs. The authors would also like to acknowledge contributions from David Weinstein. SCIRun and BioPSE are available as open source at www.sci.utah.edu.

Bibliography

[1] R. ARMSTRONG, D. GANNON, A. GEIST, K. KEAHEY, S. KOHN, L. MCINNES, S. PARKER, AND B. SMOLINSKI, *Toward a Common Component Architecture for High-Performance Scientific Computing*, in Proceedings of the 8th IEEE International Symposium on High Performance Distributed Computing, 1999.

[2] F. BERTRAND, R. BRAMLEY, K. DAMEVSKI, D. BERNHOLDT, J. KOHL, J. LARSON, AND A. SUSSMAN, *Data redistribution and remote method invocation in parallel component architectures*, in Proceedings of The 19th International Parallel and Distributed Processing Symposium, Denver, CO, 2005.

[3] K. DAMEVSKI AND S. PARKER, *Parallel remote method invocation and m-by-n data redistribution*, in Proceedings of the 4th Los Alamos Computer Science Institute Symposium, Los Alamos, NM, 2003.

[4] K. DAMEVSKI AND S. PARKER, *Imprecise exceptions in distributed parallel components*, in Proceedings of the 10th International Euro-Par Conference, vol. 3149 of Lecture Notes in Computer Science, August/September 2004, Springer-Verlag, Berlin, New York, pp. 108–116.

[5] K. DAMEVSKI, *Parallel component interaction with an interface definition language compiler*, Master's thesis, University of Utah, Salt Lake City, UT, 2003.

[6] J. D. DE ST. GERMAIN, J. MCCORQUODALE, S. G. PARKER, AND C. R. JOHNSON, *Uintah: A Massively Parallel Problem Solving Environment*, in Proceedings of the Ninth IEEE International Symposium on High Performance and Distributed Computing, August 2000.

[7] I. FOSTER, C. KESSELMAN, AND S. TUECKE, *The Nexus approach to integrating multithreading and communication*, Journal of Parallel and Distributed Computing, 37 (1996), pp. 70–82.

[8] C. HANSEN AND C. JOHNSON, EDS., *The Visualization Handbook*, Elsevier, Amsterdam, 2005.

[9] JAVABEANS, http://java.sun.com/products/javabeans, 2003.

[10] C. JOHNSON, R. MACLEOD, S. PARKER, AND D. WEINSTEIN, *Biomedical computing and visualization software environments*, Communications of the ACM, 47 (2004), pp. 64–71.

[11] C. JOHNSON AND S. PARKER, *Applications in computational medicine using SCIRun: A computational steering programming environment*, in Supercomputer '95, H. Meuer, ed., Springer-Verlag, Berlin, New York, 1995, pp. 2–19.

[12] C. JOHNSON AND S. PARKER, *The SCIRun Parallel Scientific Compouting Problem Solving Enviroment*, in Talk presented at the 9th SIAM Conference on Parallel Processing for Scientific Computing, 1999.

[13] G. KINDLMANN, *Superquadric tensor glyphs*, in The Joint Eurographics – IEEE TCVG Symposium on Visualization, May 2004, pp. 147–154.

[14] S. KOHN, G. KUMFERT, J. PAINTER, AND C. RIBBENS, *Divorcing language dependencies from a scientific software library*, in Proceedings of the 10th SIAM Conference on Parallel Processing, Portsmouth, VA, March 2001, CD-ROM.

[15] T. R. LANGUAGE, http://www.ruby-lang.org/en, 2004.

[16] MESSAGE PASSING INTERFACE FORUM, *MPI: A Message-Passing Interface Standard*, June 1995.

[17] C. O. MODEL, http://www.microsoft.com/com/tech/com.asp, 2003.

[18] OMG, *The Common Object Request Broker: Architecture and Specification. Revision 2.0*, June 1995. http://www.mpi-forum.org/docs/mpi-11-html/mpi-report.html.

[19] S. G. PARKER, *The SCIRun Problem Solving Environment and Computational Steering Software System*, Ph.D. thesis, University of Utah, Salt Lake City, UT, 1999.

[20] S. PARKER, D. BEAZLEY, AND C. JOHNSON, *Computational steering software systems and strategies*, IEEE Computational Science and Engineering, 4 (1997), pp. 50–59.

[21] S. PARKER AND C. JOHNSON, *SCIRun: A scientific programming environment for computational steering*, in Supercomputing '95, IEEE Press, Los Alamitos, CA, 1995.

[22] S. PARKER, M. PARKER, Y. LIVNAT, P. SLOAN, AND P. SHIRLEY, *Interactive ray tracing for volume visualization*, IEEE Transactions on Visualization and Computer Graphics, 5 (1999).

[23] S. PARKER, D. WEINSTEIN, AND C. JOHNSON, *The SCIRun computational steering software system*, in Modern Software Tools in Scientific Computing, E. Arge, A. Bruaset, and H. Langtangen, eds., Birkhauser Press, Basel, 1997, pp. 1–44.

[24] W. SCHROEDER, K. MARTIN, AND B. LORENSEN, *The Visualization Toolkit, An Object-Oriented Approach to 3-D Graphics*, 2nd ed., Prentice Hall, Upper Saddle River, NJ, 2003.

[25] D. WEINSTEIN, S. PARKER, J. SIMPSON, K. ZIMMERMAN, AND G. JONES., *Visualization in the scirun problem-solving environment*, in The Visualization Handbook, C. Hansen and C. Johnson, eds., Elsevier, Amsterdam, 2005, pp. 615–632.

[26] D. WEINSTEIN, O. POTNIAGUINE, AND L. ZHUKOV, *A comparison of dipolar and focused inversion for EEG source imaging*, in Proc. 3rd International Symposium on Noninvasive Functional Source Imaging (NFSI), Innsbruck, Austria, September 2001, pp. 121–123.

[27] K. ZHANG, K. DAMEVSKI, V. VENKATACHALAPATHY, AND S. PARKER, *SCIRun2: A CCA framework for high performance computing*, in Proceedings of The 9th International Workshop on High-Level Parallel Programming Models and Supportive Environments, April 2004, Santa Fe, NM.

Part IV

Applications of Parallel Computing

Chapter 16
Parallel Algorithms for PDE-Constrained Optimization

Volkan Akçelik, George Biros, Omar Ghattas, Judith Hill, David Keyes, and Bart van Bloemen Waanders

PDE-constrained optimization refers to the optimization of systems governed by PDEs. The *simulation problem* is to solve the PDEs for the *state variables* (e.g., displacement, velocity, temperature, electric field, magnetic field, species concentration), given appropriate data (e.g., geometry, coefficients, boundary conditions, initial conditions, source functions). The *optimization problem* seeks to determine some of these data—the *decision variables*—given performance goals in the form of an objective function and possibly inequality or equality constraints on the behavior of the system. Since the behavior of the system is modeled by the PDEs, they appear as (usually equality) constraints in the optimization problem. We will refer to these PDE constraints as the *state equations*.

Let **u** represent the state variables, **d** the decision variables, $\mathcal{J}$ the objective function, **c** the residual of the state equations, and **h** the residual of the inequality constraints. We can then state the general form of a PDE-constrained optimization problem as

$$\min_{\mathbf{u},\mathbf{d}} \mathcal{J}(\mathbf{u}, \mathbf{d})$$
$$\text{subject to } \mathbf{c}(\mathbf{u}, \mathbf{d}) = \mathbf{0}, \quad (16.1)$$
$$\mathbf{h}(\mathbf{u}, \mathbf{d}) \geq \mathbf{0}.$$

The PDE-constrained optimization problem (16.1) can represent an optimal design, optimal control, or inverse problem, depending on the nature of the objective function and decision variables. The decision variables correspondingly represent design, control, or inversion variables.

Many engineering and science problems—in such diverse areas as aerodynamics, atmospheric sciences, chemical process industry, environment, geosciences, homeland security, infrastructure, manufacturing, medicine, and physics—can be expressed in the form of a PDE-constrained optimization problem. The common difficulty is that PDE solution is just a subproblem associated with optimization. Moreover, while the simulation problem (given **d**, find **u** from **c(u, d)** = **0**) is usually well posed, the optimization problem (16.1) can be ill posed. Finally, when the state equations are evolutionary in nature, the optimality conditions for (16.1) are a boundary value problem in space-time. For these reasons, the optimization problem is often significantly more difficult to solve than the simulation problem.

The size, complexity, and infinite-dimensional nature of PDE-constrained optimization problems present significant challenges for general-purpose optimization algorithms. These features often require regularization, iterative solvers, preconditioning, globalization, inexactness, and parallel implementation that are tailored to the structure of the underlying operators. Continued advances in PDE solvers, and the rapid ascendance of parallel computing, have in recent years motivated the development of special-purpose optimization algorithms that exploit the structure of the PDE constraints and scale to large numbers of processors. These algorithms are the focus of this chapter.

To illustrate the main issues, let us consider a distributed optimal flow control problem for the steady-state Burgers equation:

$$\min_{u,d} \mathcal{J}(u,d) \stackrel{\text{def}}{=} \tfrac{1}{2} \int_\Omega \nabla u \cdot \nabla u \, dx + \frac{\rho}{2} \int_\Omega d \cdot d \, dx$$
$$\text{subject to} \quad -\nu \Delta u + (\nabla u)u = d \quad \text{in } \Omega, \qquad (16.2)$$
$$u = g \quad \text{on } \partial \Omega.$$

Here, $u(x)$ is the velocity field, $d(x)$ is a domain source, $g(s)$ is a boundary source, ν is the viscosity, Ω represents the domain and $\partial \Omega$ its boundary, and ρ is a parameter reflecting the cost of the controls. In the simulation problem we are given the data ν, d, Ω, g and we seek the state u. In the optimization problem the situation is reversed: we wish to determine a portion of the data, for example, g (boundary control), d (distributed control), Ω (shape or topology optimization), or ν (parameter estimation), so that the decision variable and resulting state u minimize some functional of these variables. In the particular example (16.2), the decision variable is just the distributed source d, and ν, Ω, g are taken as knowns. The objective $\mathcal{J}$ represents a balance between the rate of energy dissipation and the L^2 cost of the controls.

A classical way to approach this problem is to introduce a Lagrange multiplier field, $\lambda(x)$, known as the *adjoint state* or *costate* variable, and form a Lagrangian functional $\mathcal{L}$ that incorporates the PDE constraints via an "inner product" with λ,

$$\mathcal{L}(u, \lambda, d) \stackrel{\text{def}}{=} \mathcal{J}(u,d) + \int_\Omega [\nu \nabla u \cdot \nabla \lambda + \lambda \cdot (\nabla u)u - d \cdot \lambda] \, dx. \qquad (16.3)$$

One then requires stationarity of $\mathcal{L}$ with respect to the state (u), decision (d), and adjoint (λ) variables. Taking variations and invoking the appropriate Green identities, we arrive at the following system of equations representing first-order necessary conditions for optimality:

$$-\nu\Delta u + (\nabla u)u = d \quad \text{in } \Omega, \qquad \text{state equation,} \qquad (16.4)$$
$$u = g \quad \text{on } \partial\Omega,$$
$$-\nu\Delta\lambda + (\nabla u)^T\lambda - (\nabla\lambda)u - \lambda \operatorname{div} u = \Delta u \quad \text{in } \Omega, \qquad \text{adjoint equation,} \qquad (16.5)$$
$$\lambda = 0 \quad \text{on } \partial\Omega,$$
$$\rho d + \lambda = 0 \quad \text{in } \Omega, \qquad \text{decision equation.} \qquad (16.6)$$

The state equation (16.4) is just the original Burgers boundary value problem that appears as a constraint in the optimization problem (16.2). The adjoint equation (16.5), which results from stationarity with respect to the state, is a boundary value problem that is linear in the adjoint variable λ and involves the adjoint of the linearized state operator. With appropriate discretization, this adjoint operator is just the transpose of the Jacobian of the discretized state equation. Finally the decision equation (16.6) is in this case algebraic (it would have been differential had the cost of the controls been H^1 instead of L^2). The first-order optimality conditions (16.4)–(16.6) are a system of coupled, nonlinear PDEs and are often known as the Karush–Kuhn–Tucker (KKT) conditions. For theory and analysis of PDE-constrained optimization problems such as (16.2), see, for example, [12, 32, 39, 66, 69]. For recent algorithmic trends and large-scale applications, see [20].

In this chapter we review efficient parallel algorithms for solution of PDE optimality systems such (16.4)–(16.6). Since the coupled optimality system can be formidable to solve simultaneously, a popular alternative is to eliminate state and adjoint variables and, correspondingly, state and adjoint equations, thereby reducing the system to a manageable one in just the decision variable. Methods of this type are known as *reduced space* methods. For example, a *nonlinear elimination* variant of a reduced space method would proceed as follows for the KKT system (16.4)–(16.6). Given d at some iteration, solve the state equation (16.4) for the state variable u. Knowing the state then permits solution of the adjoint equation (16.5) for the adjoint variable λ. Finally, with the state and adjoint known, the decision variable d is updated via an appropriate linearization of the decision equation. This loop is then repeated until convergence. As an alternative to such nonlinear elimination, one often prefers to follow the Newton strategy of *first* linearizing the optimality system and *then* eliminating the state and adjoint updates via block elimination on the linearized state and adjoint equations. The resulting Schur complement operator is known as the *reduced Hessian*, and the equation to which it corresponds can be solved to yield the decision variable update. Since the main components of reduced space method are (linearized) state and adjoint PDE solves, as well as dense decision space solves, parallelism for this reduced Newton solution of the optimization problem is typically as straightforward to achieve as it is for the simulation problem. Algorithms of this class will be reviewed in section 16.1.1.

Reduced space methods are attractive for several reasons. Solving the subsets of equations in sequence exploits the state-adjoint-decision structure of the optimality system, capitalizing on well-established methods and software for solving the state equation. Adjoint PDE solvers are becoming more popular, due to their role in goal-oriented error estimation and efficient sensitivity computation, so they can be exploited as well. Even in their absence, the strong similarities between the state and adjoint operators suggest that an existing PDE solver for the state equation can be modified with reasonable effort to handle the adjoint equation. Finally, exploiting the structure of the reduced Hessian is straightforward (at least for problems of moderate size), since it is a Schur complement of the linearized KKT conditions with respect to the decision variables and is therefore dense.

Another advantage of reduction is that the linearized KKT system is often very ill conditioned (beyond, say, the usual h^{-2} ill conditioning of second-order differential operators); the state and adjoint blocks on the other hand inherit the conditioning properties of the simulation problem. Moreover, the reduced Hessian often has favorable spectral structure (e.g., for many inverse problems its spectrum is similar to that of second kind integral operators), and Krylov solvers can converge in a mesh-independent number of iterations. However, as is the case for most exact Schur-type approaches, the major disadvantage of reduced methods is the need to solve the (linearized) state and adjoint equations exactly at each reduced space iteration, which is a direct consequence of the reduction onto the decision variable space.

In contrast to reduced space methods, *full space* methods solve for the state, decision, and adjoint variables simultaneously. For large-scale problems, this is typically effected via Newton–Krylov iteration. That is, the linear system arising at each Newton iteration on the KKT system is solved using a Krylov iterative method. The difficulty of this approach is the complex structure, indefiniteness, and ill conditioning of the KKT system, which in turn requires effective preconditioning. Since the KKT optimality conditions are usually PDEs, it is natural to seek domain decomposition or multigrid preconditioners for this task. However, stationarity of the Lagrangian is a saddle-point problem, and existing domain decomposition and multilevel preconditioners for the resulting indefinite systems are not as robust as those for definite systems. Furthermore, constructing the correct smoothing, prolongation, restriction, and interface operators can be quite challenging. Despite these difficulties, there have been several successful algorithms based on overlapping and non-overlapping domain decomposition and multigrid preconditioners; these are reviewed in section 16.1.3. Since these methods regard the entire optimality system as a system of coupled PDEs, parallelism follows naturally, as it does for PDE problems, i.e., in a domain-based way.

An alternative full-space approach to domain decomposition or multigrid is to retain the structure-exploiting, condition-improving advantages of a reduced space method but use it as a preconditioner rather than a solver. That is, we solve in the full space using a Newton–Krylov method, but we precondition with a reduced space method. Since the reduced space method is just a preconditioner, it can be applied approximately, requiring just inexact state and adjoint solves at each iteration. These inexact solves can simply be applications of appropriate domain decomposition or multigrid preconditioners for the state and adjoint operators. Depending on its spectral structure, one may also require preconditioners for the reduced Hessian operator. Substantial speedups can be achieved over reduced space methods due to the avoidance of exact solution of the state and adjoint equations at each decision iteration, as the three sets of variables are simultaneously converged. Since the main work per iteration is in the application of preconditioners for the state, adjoint, and decision equations, as well as carrying out PDE-like full space matrix-vector products, these reduced-space-preconditioned full-space methods can be made to parallelize as well as reduced space methods, i.e., as well as the simulation problem. Such methods will be discussed in section 16.1.2.

Numerical evidence suggests that for steady-state PDE-constrained optimization problems, full-space methods can outperform reduced space methods by a wide margin. Typical multigrid efficiency has been obtained for some classes of problems. For optimization of systems governed by time-dependent PDEs, the answer is not as clear. The nonlinearities within each time step of a time-dependent PDE solve are usually much milder than for the corresponding stationary PDEs, so amortizing the nonlinear PDE solve over the optimization iterations is less advantageous. Moreover, time dependence results in large storage requirements for full-space methods, since the full-space optimality system becomes a boundary value problem in the space-time cylinder. For such problems, reduced space methods are often preferable. Section 16.2 provides illustrative examples of optimization problems governed by both steady-state and time-dependent PDEs. The governing equations include convective-diffusive transport, Navier–Stokes flow, and acoustic wave propagation; the decision variables include those for control (for boundary sources), design-like (for PDE coefficients), and inversion (for initial conditions). Both reduced-space and full-space parallel KKT solvers are demonstrated and compared. Parallel implementation issues are discussed in the context of the acoustic inversion problem.

Notation in this chapter respects the following conventions. Scalars are in lowercase italics type, vectors are in lowercase boldface Roman type, and matrices and tensors are in uppercase boldface Roman type. Infinite dimensional quantities are in italics type, whereas finite-dimensional quantities (usually discretizations) are Roman. We will use d or d or $\mathbf{d}$ for decision variables, u or u or $\mathbf{u}$ for the states, and λ or $\boldsymbol{\lambda}$ for adjoint variables.

16.1 Algorithms

In this section we discuss algorithmic issues related to efficient parallel solution of first-order optimality systems by Newton-like methods. Due to space limitations, we omit discussion of adaptivity and error estimation, regularization of ill-posed problems, inequality constraints on state and decision variables, globalization methods to ensure convergence from distant iterates, and checkpointing strategies for balancing work and memory in time-dependent adjoint computations. These issues must be carefully considered to obtain optimally scalable algorithms. The following are some representative references in the infinite-dimensional setting; no attempt is made to be comprehensive. Globalization in the context of PDE solvers is discussed in [63] and in the context of PDE optimization in [51, 76]. For a discussion of active set and interior point methods for inequality constraints in an optimal control setting see [18, 77], and for primal-dual active set methods see [52]. For adaptive methods and error estimation in inverse problems see [11, 16, 17, 73]; for details on regularization see [36, 45, 80]. See [37, 54] for discussions of checkpointing strategies.

Our discussion of parallel algorithms in this section will be in the context of the *discrete form* of a typical PDE-constrained optimization problem; that is, we first discretize the objective and constraints and then form the Lagrangian function and derive optimality conditions. Note that this is the reverse of the procedure that was employed in the optimal flow control example in the previous section, in which the infinite-dimensional Lagrangian functional was first formed and then infinite-dimensional optimality conditions were written. When these infinite-dimensional conditions are discretized, they may result in different discrete optimality conditions than those obtained by first discretizing and then differentiating to form optimality conditions. That is, differentiation and discretization do not necessarily commute. See [1, 31, 39, 53, 70] for details.

Let us represent the discretized PDE-constrained optimization problem by

$$\min_{\mathbf{u},\mathbf{d}} \mathcal{J}(\mathbf{u}, \mathbf{d})$$

$$\text{subject to } \mathbf{c}(\mathbf{u}, \mathbf{d}) = \mathbf{0}, \quad (16.7)$$

where $\mathbf{u} \in \mathbb{R}^n$, $\mathbf{d} \in \mathbb{R}^m$ are the state and decision variables, $\mathcal{J} \in \mathbb{R}$ is the objective function, and $\mathbf{c} \in \mathbb{R}^n$ are the discretized state equations. Using adjoint variables $\boldsymbol{\lambda} \in \mathbb{R}^n$, we can define the Lagrangian function by $\mathcal{L}(\mathbf{u}, \mathbf{d}, \boldsymbol{\lambda}) \stackrel{\text{def}}{=} \mathcal{J}(\mathbf{u}, \mathbf{d}) + \boldsymbol{\lambda}^T \mathbf{c}(\mathbf{u}, \mathbf{d})$. The first-order optimality conditions require that the gradient of the Lagrangian vanish:

$$\left\{ \begin{array}{c} \partial_u \mathcal{L} \\ \partial_d \mathcal{L} \\ \partial_\lambda \mathcal{L} \end{array} \right\} = \left\{ \begin{array}{c} \mathbf{g}_u + \mathbf{J}_u^T \boldsymbol{\lambda} \\ \mathbf{g}_d + \mathbf{J}_d^T \boldsymbol{\lambda} \\ \mathbf{c} \end{array} \right\} = \mathbf{0}. \quad (16.8)$$

Here, $\mathbf{g}_u \in \mathbb{R}^n$ and $\mathbf{g}_d \in \mathbb{R}^m$ are the gradients of $\mathcal{J}$ with respect to the states and decision variables, respectively; $\mathbf{J}_u \in \mathbb{R}^{n \times n}$ is the Jacobian of the state equations with respect to the state variables; and $\mathbf{J}_d \in \mathbb{R}^{n \times m}$ is the Jacobian of the state equations with respect to the decision variables. A Newton step on the optimality conditions gives the linear system

$$\begin{bmatrix} \mathbf{W}_{uu} & \mathbf{W}_{ud} & \mathbf{J}_u^T \\ \mathbf{W}_{du} & \mathbf{W}_{dd} & \mathbf{J}_d^T \\ \mathbf{J}_u & \mathbf{J}_d & 0 \end{bmatrix} \left\{ \begin{array}{c} \mathbf{p}_u \\ \mathbf{p}_d \\ \boldsymbol{\lambda}_+ \end{array} \right\} = -\left\{ \begin{array}{c} \mathbf{g}_u \\ \mathbf{g}_d \\ \mathbf{c} \end{array} \right\}. \quad (16.9)$$

Here, $\mathbf{W} \in \mathbb{R}^{(n+m) \times (n+m)}$ is the Hessian matrix of the Lagrangian (it involves second derivatives of both $\mathcal{J}$ and $\mathbf{c}$) and is block-partitioned according to state and decision variables; $\mathbf{p}_u \in \mathbb{R}^n$ is the search direction in the $\mathbf{u}$ variables; $\mathbf{p}_d \in \mathbb{R}^m$ is the search direction in the $\mathbf{d}$ variables; and $\boldsymbol{\lambda}_+ \in \mathbb{R}^n$ is the updated adjoint variable. This linear system is known as the KKT system, and its coefficient matrix as the *KKT matrix*. The KKT matrix is of dimension $(2n + m) \times (2n + m)$. For realistic 3D PDE problems, n and possibly m are very large, so LU factorization of the KKT matrix is not an option. Iterative methods applied to the full KKT system suffer from ill conditioning and non-positive-definiteness of the KKT matrix. On the other hand, it is desirable to capitalize on existing parallel algorithms (and perhaps software) for inverting the state Jacobian $\mathbf{J}_u$ (and its transpose). Since this is the kernel step in a Newton-based PDE solver, there is a large body of work to build on. For example, for elliptic or parabolic PDEs, optimal or nearly optimal parallel algorithms are available that require algorithmic work that is linear or weakly superlinear in n and that scale to thousands of processors and billions of variables. The ill conditioning and complex structure of the KKT matrix, and the desire to exploit (parallel) PDE solvers for the state equations, motivate the use of reduced space methods, as discussed below.

16.1.1 Reduced space methods

As mentioned, one way to exploit existing PDE solvers is to eliminate the state and adjoint equations and variables and then solve the reduced Hessian system in the remaining decision space. We refer to this as a *reduced Newton* (RN) method. It can be derived by block elimination on the KKT system (16.9): eliminate $\mathbf{p}_u$ from the last block of equations (the state equations), then eliminate $\boldsymbol{\lambda}_+$ from the first block (the adjoint equations), and finally solve the middle block (the decision equations) for $\mathbf{p}_d$. This block elimination on (16.9) amounts to solving the following equations at each Newton step.

RN:

$$\begin{aligned}
\mathbf{W}_z \mathbf{p}_d &= -\mathbf{g}_d - \mathbf{J}_d^T \mathbf{J}_u^{-T} \mathbf{g}_u + \mathbf{W}_{yz}^T \mathbf{J}_u^{-1} \mathbf{c}, & \text{decision step,} \\
\mathbf{J}_u \mathbf{p}_u &= -\mathbf{J}_d \mathbf{p}_d - \mathbf{c}, & \text{state step,} & \quad (16.10) \\
\mathbf{J}_u^T \boldsymbol{\lambda}_+ &= -(\mathbf{g}_u + \mathbf{W}_{uu} \mathbf{p}_u + \mathbf{W}_{ud} \mathbf{p}_d), & \text{adjoint step.}
\end{aligned}$$

The right-hand side of the decision equation involves the *cross-Hessian* $\mathbf{W}_{yz}$, given by

$$\mathbf{W}_{yz} \stackrel{\text{def}}{=} \mathbf{W}_{ud} - \mathbf{W}_{uu} \mathbf{J}_u^{-1} \mathbf{J}_d.$$

The coefficient matrix of the decision step, which is the Schur complement of $\mathbf{W}_{dd}$, is given by

$$\mathbf{W}_z \stackrel{\text{def}}{=} \mathbf{J}_d^T \mathbf{J}_u^{-T} \mathbf{W}_{uu} \mathbf{J}_u^{-1} \mathbf{J}_d - \mathbf{J}_d^T \mathbf{J}_u^{-T} \mathbf{W}_{ud} - \mathbf{W}_{du} \mathbf{J}_u^{-1} \mathbf{J}_d + \mathbf{W}_{dd}$$

and is known as the *reduced Hessian* matrix. Because it contains the inverses of the state and adjoint operators, the reduced Hessian $\mathbf{W}_z$ is a dense matrix. Thus, applying a dense parallel factorization is straightforward. Moreover, since the reduced Hessian is of the dimension of the decision space, m, the dense factorization can be carried out on a single processor when the number of decision variables is substantially smaller than the number of states (as is the case when the decision variables represent discrete parameters that are independent of the mesh size). The remaining two linear systems that have to be solved at each Newton iteration—the state and adjoint updates—have as coefficient matrix either the state Jacobian $\mathbf{J}_u$ or its transpose $\mathbf{J}_u^T$. Since inverting the state Jacobian is at the heart of a Newton solver for the state equations, the state and adjoint updates in (16.10) are able to exploit available parallel algorithms and software for the simulation problem. It follows that the RN method can be implemented with parallel efficiency comparable to that of the simulation problem.

However, the difficulty with the RN method is the need for m solutions of the (linearized) state equations to construct the $\mathbf{J}_u^{-1} \mathbf{J}_d$ term within $\mathbf{W}_z$. This is particularly troublesome for large-scale 3D problems, where (linearized) PDE systems are usually solved iteratively, and solution costs cannot be amortized over multiple right-hand sides as effectively as with direct solvers. When m is moderate or large (as will be the case when the decision space is mesh dependent), RN with exact formation of the reduced Hessian becomes intractable. So while its parallel efficiency may be high, its algorithmic efficiency can be poor.

An alternative to forming the reduced Hessian is to solve the decision step in (16.10) by a Krylov method. Since the reduced Hessian is symmetric and positive definite near a minimum, the Krylov method of choice is conjugate gradients (CG). The required action of the reduced Hessian $\mathbf{W}_z$ on a decision-space vector within the CG iteration is formed in a matrix-free manner. This can be achieved with the dominant cost of a single pair of linearized PDE solves (one state and one adjoint). Moreover, the CG iteration can be terminated early to prevent oversolving in early iterations and to maintain a direction of descent [33]. Finally, in many cases the spectrum of the reduced Hessian is favorable for CG and convergence can be obtained in a mesh-independent number of iterations. We refer to this method as a *reduced Newton CG* (RNCG) method, and we demonstrate it for a large-scale inverse wave propagation problem in section 16.2.1.

While RNCG avoids explicit formation of the exact Hessian and the required m (linearized) PDE solves, it does still require a pair of linearized PDE solves per CG iteration. Moreover, the required second derivatives of the objective and state equations are often difficult to compute (although this difficulty may be mitigated by continuing advances in automatic differentiation tools [61]). A popular technique that addresses these two difficulties is a *reduced quasi-Newton* (RQN) method that replaces the reduced Hessian $\mathbf{W}_z$ with a quasi-Newton (often BFGS) approximation $\mathbf{B}_z$, and discards all other Hessian terms [19].

RQN:

$$\mathbf{B}_z \mathbf{p}_d = -\mathbf{g}_d - \mathbf{J}_d^T \mathbf{J}_u^{-T} \mathbf{g}_u, \qquad \text{decision step,}$$

$$\mathbf{J}_u \mathbf{p}_u = -\mathbf{J}_d \mathbf{p}_d - \mathbf{c}, \qquad \text{state step,} \qquad (16.11)$$

$$\mathbf{J}_u^T \boldsymbol{\lambda}_+ = -\mathbf{g}_u, \qquad \text{adjoint step.}$$

We see that RQN requires just *two* (linearized) PDE solves per Newton iteration (one a linearized state solve with $\mathbf{J}_u$ and one an adjoint solve with $\mathbf{J}_u^T$), as opposed to the m PDE solves required for RN. (The adjoint step to compute the adjoint variable is superfluous in this algorithm.) And with Hessian terms either approximated or dropped, no second derivatives are needed. When the number of decision variables m is small and the number of states n is large, the BFGS update (which involves updates of the Cholesky factors of the BFGS approximation) can be computed serially, and this can be done redundantly across all processors [67]. For problems in which m is intermediate in size, the BFGS update may become too expensive for a single processor, and updating the inverse of the dense BFGS approximation can be done efficiently in parallel. Finally, for large m (such as in distributed control or estimation of continuous fields), a limited-memory BFGS (in place of a full) update [68] becomes necessary. When implemented as an update for the inverse of the reduced Hessian, the required decision-space inner products and vector sums parallelize very well, and good overall parallel efficiency results [25]. A measure of the success of RQN is its application to numerous problems governed by PDEs from linear and nonlinear elasticity, incompressible and compressible flow, heat conduction and convection, phase changes, and flow through porous media. With RQN as described above, the asymptotic convergence rate drops from the quadratic rate associated with RN to two-step superlinear. In addition, unlike the usual case for RN, the number of iterations taken by RQN will typically increase as the decision space is enlarged (i.e., as the mesh is refined), although this also depends on the spectrum of the reduced Hessian and on the difference between it and the initial BFGS approximation. See, for example, [60] for discussion of quasi-Newton methods for infinite-dimensional problems. Specialized quasi-Newton updates that take advantage of the "compact + differential" structure of reduced Hessians for many inverse problems have been developed [42].

As described earlier, one final option for reduced space methods is a nonlinear elimination variant, which we term *nonlinear reduced Newton* (NLRN). This is similar to RN, except elimination is performed on the nonlinear optimality system (16.8). The state equations and state variables are eliminated at each iteration by nonlinear solution of $\mathbf{c}(\mathbf{u}, \mathbf{d}) = \mathbf{0}$.

Similarly, the adjoint equations and adjoint variables are eliminated at each iteration by solution of the linear system $\mathbf{J}_u^T \boldsymbol{\lambda} = -\mathbf{g}_u$. This gives the following form at each Newton step.

NLRN:
$$\mathbf{W}_z \mathbf{p}_d = -\mathbf{g}_d - \mathbf{J}_d^T \mathbf{J}_u^{-T} \mathbf{g}_u, \qquad \text{decision step,} \tag{16.12}$$

where $\mathbf{c}(\mathbf{u}, \mathbf{d}) = \mathbf{0}$ is implicit in (16.12) and the adjoint solve contributes to the right-hand side. Alternatively, one may think of NLRN as solving the optimization problem (16.7) in the space of just the decision variables, by eliminating the state variables and constraints, to give the unconstrained optimization problem:

$$\min_{\mathbf{d}} \mathcal{J}(\mathbf{u}(\mathbf{d}), \mathbf{d}).$$

Application of Newton's method to solve this problem, in conjunction with the implicit function theorem to generate the necessary derivatives, yields NLRN above [65]. NLRN can also be implemented in quasi-Newton and Newton-CG settings. These methods are particularly attractive for time-dependent PDE-constrained optimization problems, in particular those that require a large number of time-steps or are time-integrated accurately or explicitly. In this case the need to carry along and update the current state and adjoint estimates (which are time-dependent) is onerous; on the other hand, there is little advantage to simultaneous solution of the state equations and the optimization problem (in the absence of inequality constraints on the states), if the state equations are weakly nonlinear (as they will be with accurate time-stepping) or explicitly solved. NLRN permits estimates of just the decision variables to be maintained at each optimization iteration.

As successful as the reduced space methods of this section are in combining fast Newton-like convergence with a reduced number of PDE solves per iteration, they do still (formally) require the exact solution of linearized state and adjoint PDE problems at each iteration. In the next section, we see that a method can be constructed that avoids the exact solves while retaining the structure-exploiting advantages of reduced methods.

16.1.2 Lagrange–Newton–Krylov–Schur: Krylov full-space solution with approximate reduced space preconditioning

In this section we return to solution of the full-space Newton step (16.9). We consider use of a Krylov method, in particular, symmetric QMR, applied directly to this system. QMR is attractive because it does not require a positive definite preconditioner. The indefiniteness and potential ill conditioning of the KKT matrix demand a good preconditioner. It should be capable of exploiting the structure of the state constraints (specifically, that good preconditioners for $\mathbf{J}_u$ are available), should be cheap to apply, should be effective in reducing the number of Krylov iterations, and should parallelize readily. The reduced space methods described in the previous section—in particular, an approximate form of RQN—fulfill these requirements.

We begin by noting that the block elimination of (16.10) is equivalent to the following block factorization of the KKT matrix:

$$\begin{bmatrix} \mathbf{W}_{uu} \mathbf{J}_u^{-1} & \mathbf{0} & \mathbf{I} \\ \mathbf{W}_{du} \mathbf{J}_u^{-1} & \mathbf{I} & \mathbf{J}_d^T \mathbf{J}_u^{-T} \\ \mathbf{I} & \mathbf{0} & \mathbf{0} \end{bmatrix} \begin{bmatrix} \mathbf{J}_u & \mathbf{J}_d & \mathbf{0} \\ \mathbf{0} & \mathbf{W}_z & \mathbf{0} \\ \mathbf{0} & \mathbf{W}_{yz} & \mathbf{J}_u^T \end{bmatrix}. \tag{16.13}$$

Note that these factors can be permuted to block triangular form, so we can think of (16.13) as a block LU factorization of the KKT matrix. To derive the preconditioner, we replace the reduced Hessian $\mathbf{W}_z$ in (16.13) by a (usually but not necessarily) limited-memory BFGS approximation $\mathbf{B}_z$ (as in RQN), drop other second derivative terms (also as in RQN), and replace the exact (linearized) state and adjoint operators $\mathbf{J}_u$ and $\mathbf{J}_u^T$ with approximations $\tilde{\mathbf{J}}_u$ and $\tilde{\mathbf{J}}_u^T$. The resulting preconditioner then takes the form of the following approximate block-factorization of the KKT matrix:

$$\begin{bmatrix} \mathbf{0} & \mathbf{0} & \mathbf{I} \\ \mathbf{0} & \mathbf{I} & \mathbf{J}_d^T \tilde{\mathbf{J}}_u^{-T} \\ \mathbf{I} & \mathbf{0} & \mathbf{0} \end{bmatrix} \begin{bmatrix} \tilde{\mathbf{J}}_u & \mathbf{J}_d & \mathbf{0} \\ \mathbf{0} & \mathbf{B}_z & \mathbf{0} \\ \mathbf{0} & \mathbf{0} & \tilde{\mathbf{J}}_u^T \end{bmatrix}. \quad (16.14)$$

Applying the preconditioner by solving with the block factors (16.14) amounts to performing the RQN step in (16.11), but with approximate state and adjoint solves. A good choice for $\tilde{\mathbf{J}}_u$ is one of the available parallel preconditioners for $\mathbf{J}_u$—for many PDE operators, there exist near spectrally equivalent preconditioners that are both cheap to apply (their cost is typically linear or weakly superlinear in problem size) and effective (resulting in iteration counts that are independent of, or increase very slowly in, problem size). For examples of state-of-the-art parallel PDE preconditioners, see [2] for multigrid and [6] for domain decomposition.

With (16.14) used as a preconditioner, the preconditioned KKT matrix becomes

$$\begin{bmatrix} \mathbf{I}_u & \mathcal{O}(\mathbf{E}_u) & \mathbf{0} \\ \tilde{\mathbf{W}}_{yz}^T \tilde{\mathbf{J}}_u^{-1} & \mathcal{O}(\mathbf{E}_u) + \mathbf{W}_z \mathbf{B}_z^{-1} & \mathcal{O}(\mathbf{E}_u) \\ \mathbf{W}_{uu} \tilde{\mathbf{J}}_u^{-1} & \tilde{\mathbf{W}}_{yz} \mathbf{B}_z^{-1} & \mathbf{I}_u \end{bmatrix},$$

where $\mathbf{E}_u \stackrel{\text{def}}{=} \mathbf{J}_u^{-1} - \tilde{\mathbf{J}}_u^{-1}$, $\mathbf{I}_u \stackrel{\text{def}}{=} \mathbf{J}_u \tilde{\mathbf{J}}_u^{-1}$, $\tilde{\mathbf{W}}_{yz} \stackrel{\text{def}}{=} \mathbf{W}_{ud} - \mathbf{W}_{uu} \tilde{\mathbf{J}}_u^{-1} \mathbf{J}_d$. For the exact state equation solution, $\mathbf{E}_u = \mathbf{0}$ and $\mathbf{I}_u = \mathbf{I}$, and we see that the reduced space preconditioner clusters the spectrum of the KKT matrix, with all eigenvalues either unit or belonging to $\mathbf{W}_z \mathbf{B}_z^{-1}$. Therefore, when $\tilde{\mathbf{J}}_u$ is a good preconditioner for the state Jacobian, and when $\mathbf{B}_z$ is a good approximation of the reduced Hessian, we can expect the preconditioner (16.14) to be effective in reducing the number of Krylov iterations.

We refer to this method as Lagrange–Newton–Krylov–Schur (LNKS), since it amounts to a Newton–Krylov method applied to the Lagrangian stationarity conditions, preconditioned by a Schur complement (i.e., reduced Hessian) approximation. See [21, 22, 23, 24] for further details, and [14, 15, 40, 41, 46, 61] for related methods that use reduced space preconditioning ideas for full-space KKT systems.

Since LNKS applies an approximate version of a reduced space method as a preconditioner (by replacing the PDE solve with a PDE preconditioner application), it inherits the parallel efficiency of RQN in the preconditioning step. The other major cost is the KKT matrix-vector product in the Krylov iteration. For many PDE-constrained optimization problems, the Hessian of the Lagrangian and the Jacobian of the constraints are sparse with structure dictated by the mesh (particularly when the decision variables are mesh-related). Thus, formation of the matrix-vector product at each Krylov iteration is linear in both state and decision variables, and it parallelizes well in the usual fine-grained, domain-decomposed manner characteristic of PDE problems. To achieve overall scalability, we require not just parallel efficiency of the components but also algorithmic scalability in the sense of mesh-independence (or near-independence) of both Newton and Krylov iterations. Mesh-independence of Newton iterations is characteristic of a wide class of smooth nonlinear operator problems, and we have observed it for a variety of PDE-constrained optimization problems (see also [81]). Mesh-independence of LNKS's Krylov iterations depends on the efficacy of the state and adjoint PDE preconditioners and the limited memory BFGS (or other) approximation of the reduced Hessian. While the former are well studied, the performance of the latter depends on the nature of the governing PDEs as well as the objective functional. In section 16.2.2 we demonstrate parallel scalability and superiority of LNKS over limited memory RQN for a large-scale optimal flow control problem.

16.1.3 Domain decomposition and multigrid methods

As an alternative to the Schur-based method described in section 16.1.2 for solution of the full-space Newton step (16.9), one may pursue domain decomposition or multigrid preconditioners for the KKT matrix. These methods are more recent than those of section 16.1.1 and are undergoing rapid development. Here we give just a brief overview and cite relevant references.

In [71] an overlapping Krylov–Schwarz domain decomposition method was used to solve (16.9) related to the boundary control of an incompressible driven-cavity problem. This approach resulted in excellent algorithmic and parallel scalability on up to 64 processors for a velocity-vorticity formulation of the 2D steady-state Navier–Stokes equations. One key insight of the method is that the necessary overlap for a control problem is larger than that for the simulation problem. More recently a multilevel variant has been derived [72].

Domain-decomposition preconditioners for linear-quadratic elliptic optimal control problems are presented in [48] for the overlapping case and [49] for the nonoverlapping case. Mesh-independent convergence for two-level variants is shown. These domain decomposition methods have been extended to advection-diffusion [13] and time-dependent parabolic [47] problems. Parallelism in the domain-decomposition methods described above can be achieved for the optimization problem in the same manner as it is for the simulation problem, i.e., based on spatial decomposition. Several new ideas in parallel time domain decomposition have emerged recently [43, 50, 78] and have been applied in the parabolic and electromagnetic settings. Although parallel efficiency is less than optimal, parallel speed-ups are still observed over non-time-decomposed algorithms, which may be crucial for real-time applications.

Multigrid methods are another class of preconditioners for the full-space Newton system (16.9). An overview can be found in [35]. There are three basic approaches: multigrid applied directly to the optimization problem, multigrid as a preconditioner for the reduced Hessian $\mathbf{W}_z$ in RNCG, and multigrid on the full space Newton system (16.9). In [64] multigrid is applied directly to the optimization problem to generate a sequence of optimization subproblems with increasingly coarser grids. It is demonstrated that multigrid may accelerate solution of the optimization problem even when it may not be an appropriate solver for the PDE problem. Multigrid for the reduced system (in the context of shape optimization of potential and steady-state incompressible Euler flows) has been studied in [7, 8] based on an analysis of the symbol of the reduced Hessian. For a large class of problems, especially with the presence of a regularization term in the objective functional, the reduced Hessian operator is spectrally equivalent to a second-kind Fredholm integral equation. Although this operator has a favorable spectrum leading to mesh-independent convergence, in practice preconditioning is still useful to reduce the number of iterations. It is essential that the smoother be tailored to the "compact + identity" structure of such operators [44, 58, 59, 62]. The use of appropriate smoothers of this type has resulted in successful multigrid methods for inverse problems for elliptic and parabolic PDEs [4, 34, 57].

Multigrid methods have also been developed for application to the full KKT optimality system for nonlinear inverse electromagnetic problems [9] and for distributed control of linear elliptic and parabolic problems [28, 29]. In such approaches, the state, adjoint, and decision equations are typically relaxed together in pointwise manner (or in the case of L^2 regularization, the decision variable can be eliminated and pointwise relaxation is applied to the coupled state-adjoint system). These multigrid methods have been extended to optimal control of nonlinear reaction-diffusion systems as well [26, 27]. Nonlinearities are addressed through either the Newton-multigrid or the full approximation scheme (FAS). Just as with reduced space multigrid methods, careful design of the smoother is critical to the success of full space multigrid.

16.2 Numerical examples

In this section we present numerical results for parallel solution of three large-scale 3D PDE-constrained optimization problems. Section 16.2.1 presents an inverse acoustic scattering problem that can be formulated as a PDE-constrained optimization problem with hyperbolic constraints. The decision variables represent the PDE coefficient, in this case the squared velocity of the medium (and thus the structure is similar to a design problem). Because of the large number of time-steps and the linearity of the forward problem, a full-space method is not warranted, and instead the reduced space methods of section 16.1.1 are employed. In section 16.2.2 we present an optimization problem for boundary control of steady Navier–Stokes flows. This problem is an example of an optimization problem constrained by a nonlinear PDE with dominant elliptic term. The decision variables are velocity sources on the boundary. The LNKS method of section 16.1.2 delivers excellent performance for this problem. Finally, section 16.2.3 presents results from an inverse problem with a parabolic PDE, the convection-diffusion equation. The problem is to estimate the initial condition of an atmospheric contaminant from sparse measurements of its transport. In these three examples, we encounter elliptic, parabolic, and hyperbolic PDE constraints; forward solvers that are explicit, linearly implicit, and nonlinearly implicit; optimization problems that are linear, nonlinear in the state, and nonlinear in the decision variable; decision variables that represent boundary condition, initial condition, and PDE coefficient fields; inverse, control, and design-like problems; reduced-space and full-space solvers; and domain decomposition and multigrid preconditioners. Thus, the examples provide a glimpse into a wide spectrum of problems and methods of current interest.

All the examples presented in this section have been implemented on top of the parallel numerical PDE solver library PETSc [10]. The infinite-dimensional optimality conditions presented in the following sections are discretized in space with finite elements and (where applicable) in time with finite differences. For each example, we study the algorithmic scalability of the parallel method, i.e., the growth in iterations as the problem size and number of processors increase. In addition, for the acoustic scattering example, we provide a detailed discussion of parallel scalability and implementation issues. Due to space limitations, we restrict the discussion of parallel scalability to this first example; however, the other examples will have similar structure and similar behavior is expected. The key idea is that the algorithms of section 16.1 can be implemented for PDE-constrained optimization problems in such a way that the core computations are those that are found in a parallel forward PDE solver, e.g., sparse (with grid structure) operator evaluations, sparse matvecs, vector sums and inner products, and parallel PDE preconditioning. (In fact, this is why we are able to use PETSc for our implementation.) Thus, the optimization solvers largely inherit the parallel efficiency of the forward PDE solver. Overall scalability then depends on the algorithmic efficiency of the particular method, which is studied in the following sections.

16.2.1 Inverse acoustic wave propagation

Here we study the performance of the reduced space methods of section 16.1.1 on an inverse acoustic wave propagation problem [5, 75]. Consider an acoustic medium with domain Ω and boundary Γ. The medium is excited with a known acoustic energy source $f(x, t)$ (for simplicity we assume a single source event), and the pressure $u^*(x, t)$ is observed at N_r receivers, corresponding to points x_j on the boundary. Our objective is to infer from these measurements the squared acoustic velocity distribution $d(x)$, which is a property of the medium. Here d represents the decision variable and $u(x, t)$ the state variable. We seek to minimize, over the period $t = 0$ to T, an L^2 norm difference between the observed state and that predicted by the PDE model of acoustic wave propagation, at the N_r receiver locations. The PDE-constrained optimization problem can be written as

$$\min_{u,d} \mathcal{J}(u, d) \stackrel{\text{def}}{=} \frac{1}{2} \sum_{j=1}^{N_r} \int_0^T \int_\Omega (u^* - u)^2 \delta(x - x_j) \, dx \, dt + \rho \int_\Omega (\nabla d \cdot \nabla d + \varepsilon)^{\frac{1}{2}} dx \, dt$$

$$\text{subject to} \quad \ddot{u} - \nabla \cdot d\nabla u = f \quad \text{in } \Omega \times (0, T),$$
$$d\nabla u \cdot n = 0 \quad \text{on } \Gamma \times (0, T), \quad (16.15)$$
$$u = \dot{u} = 0 \quad \text{in } \Omega \times \{t = 0\}.$$

The first term in the objective function is the misfit between observed and predicted states, the second term is a *total variation* (TV) regularization functional with regularization parameter ρ, and the constraints are the initial boundary value problem for acoustic wave propagation (assuming constant bulk modulus and variable density).

TV regularization preserves jump discontinuities in material interfaces, while smoothing along them. For a discussion of numerical issues and comparison with standard Tikhonov regularization, see [5, 79]. While regularization eliminates the null space of the inversion operator (i.e., the reduced Hessian), there remains the difficulty that the objective function can be highly oscillatory in the space of material model d, meaning that straightforward solution of the optimization problem (16.15) can fail by becoming trapped in a local minimum [74]. To overcome this problem, we use multilevel grid and frequency continuation to generate a sequence of solutions that remain in the basin of attraction of the global minimum;

304　　　　**Chapter 16. Parallel Algorithms for PDE-Constrained Optimization**

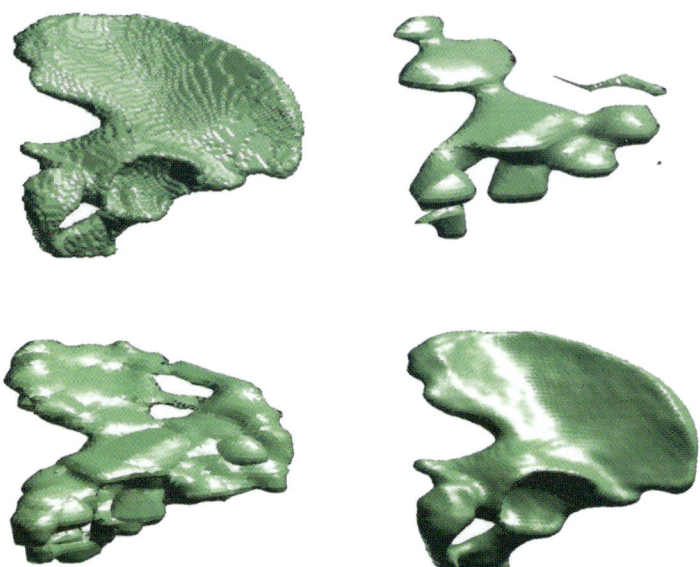

Figure 16.1. *Reconstruction of hemipelvic bony geometry via solution of an inverse wave propagation problem using a parallel multiscale reduced (Gauss) Newton conjugate gradient optimization algorithm with TV regularization.*

that is, we solve the optimization problem (16.15) for increasingly higher frequency components of the material model, on a sequence of increasingly finer grids with increasingly higher frequency sources [30]. For details see [5].

Figure 16.1 illustrates this multiscale approach and the effectiveness of the TV regularizer. The inverse problem is to reconstruct a piecewise-homogeneous velocity model (pictured at top left) that describes the geometry of a hemipelvic bone and surrounding volume from sparse synthetic pressure measurements on four faces of a cube that encloses the acoustic medium. The source consists of the simultaneous introduction of a Ricker wavelet at each measurement point. Two intermediate-grid models are shown (upper right, lower left). The fine-grid reconstructed model (lower right) is able to capture fine-scale features of the ground truth model with uncanny accuracy. The anisotropic behavior of the TV regularizer in revealed by its smoothing of ripple artifacts along the interface of the original model. The fine-scale problem has 2.1 million material parameters and 3.4 billion total space-time variables and was solved in 3 hours on 256 AlphaServer processors at the Pittsburgh Supercomputing Center.

We next discuss how the optimization problem (16.15) is solved for a particular grid level in the multiscale continuation scheme. The first-order optimality conditions for this problem take the following form:

$$
\begin{aligned}
\ddot{u} - \nabla \cdot d\nabla u &= f \quad \text{in } \Omega \times (0, T), \\
d\nabla u \cdot n &= 0 \quad \text{on } \Gamma \times (0, T), \quad \text{state equation,} \quad (16.16) \\
u = \dot{u} &= 0 \quad \text{for } \Omega \times \{t = 0\},
\end{aligned}
$$

$$\ddot{\lambda} - \nabla \cdot d\nabla\lambda + \sum_{i=1}^{N_r} \left(u^* - u\right) \delta(\boldsymbol{x} - \boldsymbol{x}_j) = 0 \quad \text{in } \Omega \times (0, T),$$

$$d\nabla\lambda \cdot n = 0 \quad \text{on } \Gamma \times (0, T), \qquad \text{adjoint equation,} \tag{16.17}$$

$$\lambda = \dot{\lambda} = 0 \quad \text{for } \Omega \times \{t = T\},$$

$$\int_0^T \nabla u \cdot \nabla\lambda \, dt - \beta \nabla \cdot (|\nabla d|_\varepsilon^{-1} \nabla d) = 0 \quad \text{in } \Omega, \qquad \text{decision equation,} \tag{16.18}$$

$$\nabla d \cdot n = 0 \quad \text{on } d\Gamma.$$

The state equation (16.16) is just the acoustic wave propagation initial boundary value problem. Since the wave operator is self-adjoint in time and space, the adjoint equation (16.17) has the same form as the state equation, i.e., it too is acoustic wave equation. However, the adjoint wave equation has *terminal*, as opposed to initial, conditions on λ in (16.17), and it has a different source, which depends on the state variable u. Finally, the decision equation (16.18) is integro-partial-differential and time independent.

When appropriately discretized on the current grid level, the dimension of each of u and λ is equal to the number of grid points N_g multiplied by time-steps N_t, d is of dimension N_g, and thus the system (16.16)–(16.18) is of dimension $2N_g N_t + N_g$. This can be very large for problems of interest—for example, in the largest problem presented in this section, the system contains 3.4×10^9 unknowns. The time dimension cannot be hidden with the usual time-stepping procedures, since (16.16)–(16.18) couples the initial and final value problems through the decision equation. The optimality system is thus a boundary value problem in four-dimensional (4D) space-time. Full space methods require storage of at least the entire time history of states and adjoints; moreover, because the state and adjoint equations are linear, there is no advantage in folding the state and adjoint solver iterations into the decision iteration, as would be done in a full space method. For this reason, the reduced space methods of section 16.1.1 are preferable. Since the state equation is linear in the state u, there is no distinction between the linear and nonlinear variants RN and NLRN.

The numerical results in this section are based on the RNCG method with a limited memory BFGS variant of RQN as a preconditioner. Since this is a least-squares problem, we do not use exact Hessian information; instead we use a Gauss–Newton approximation that neglects second derivative terms that involve λ. Spatial approximation is by Galerkin finite elements, in particular, piecewise trilinear basis functions for the state u, adjoint λ, and decision d fields. For the class of wave propagation problems we are interested in, the Courant-limited time step size is on the order of that dictated by accuracy considerations, and therefore we choose to discretize in time via explicit central differences. Thus, the number of time steps is of the order of cube root of the number of grid points. Since we require time accurate resolution of wave propagation phenomena, the 4D problem dimension scales with the $\frac{4}{3}$ power of the number of grid points.

The overall work is dominated by the cost of the CG iteration, which, because the preconditioner is time independent, is dominated by the Hessian-vector product. With the Gauss–Newton approximation, the CG matvec requires the same work as the reduced gradient computation: a forward wave propagation, an adjoint wave propagation, possible checkpointing recomputations based on available memory, and the reduction of the state and adjoint spatiotemporal fields onto the material model space via terms of the form $\int \nabla u \cdot \nabla \lambda \, dt$. These components are all PDE-solver-like, and can be parallelized effectively in a fine-grained domain-based way, using many of the building blocks of sparse PDE-based parallel computation: sparse grid-based matrix-vector products, vector sums, scalings, and inner products.

We report results of fixed-size scaling on the Cray T3E at PSC. We expect the overhead due to communication, synchronization, and sequential bottlenecks to be very low, since one of the key features of the method is that it recasts the majority of the work in solving the inverse problem in terms of explicitly solved wave propagation problems, both forward and backward in time, and local tensor reduction operations to form the reduced gradient and reduced Hessian-vector product. Because the communication patterns for these components are nearest-neighbor, and because there are no barriers to excellent load balance, the code should scale well. There are also some inner products and global reduction operations, associated with each iteration of CG and with the application of the preconditioner, that require global communication. In a standard Krylov-based forward PDE solver, such inner products can start to dominate as processor counts reach into the thousands. Here, however, it is the PDE solver that is on the inside, and the (inversion-related) Krylov iterations that are on the outside. Communication costs associated with inner products are thus negligible. Table 16.1 demonstrates the good parallel efficiency obtainable for an eightfold increase in number of processors on a Cray T3E, for a fixed problem size of 262,144 grid points (and thus material parameters) and the same number of state and adjoint unknowns per time step.

Table 16.1 shows a mild decrease in parallel efficiency with increasing problem size. Note the very coarse granularity (a few thousand grid points per processor) for the last few rows of the table. For many forward problems, one would prefer finer granularities, for greater computation-to-communication ratios. However, for most optimization problems, we are necessarily compute bound, since a sequence of many forward-like problems has to be solved, and one needs as much parallelism as possible. We are therefore interested in appropriating as many processors as possible while keeping parallel efficiency reasonable.

We should point out that this particular inverse problem presents a very severe test of parallel scalability. For scalar wave propagation PDEs, discretized with low-order finite elements on structured spatial grids (i.e., the grid stencils are very compact) and explicit central differences in time, there is little workload for each processor in each time step. So while we can express the inverse method in terms of (a sequence of) forward-like PDE problems, and while this means we follow the usual "volume computation/surface communication" paradigm, it turns out for this particular inverse problem (involving acoustic wave

Table 16.1. *Fixed-size scalability on a Cray T3E-900 for a 262,144–grid point problem corresponding to a two-layered medium.*

processors	grid pts/processor	time (s)	time/gridpts/proc (s)	efficiency
16	16,384	6756	0.41	1.00
32	8192	3549	0.43	0.95
64	4096	1933	0.47	0.87
128	2048	1011	0.49	0.84

propagation), the computation to communication ratio is about as low as it can get for a PDE problem (and this will be true whether we solve the forward or inverse problem). A nonlinear forward problem, vector unknowns per grid point, higher-order spatial discretization, and unstructured meshes would all increase the computation/communication ratio and produce better parallel efficiencies.

By increasing the number of processors with a fixed grid size, we have studied the effect of communication and load balancing on parallel efficiency in isolation of algorithmic performance. We next turn our attention to algorithmic scalability. We characterize the increase in work as problem size increases (mesh size decreases) by the number of inner (linear) CG and outer (nonlinear) Gauss–Newton iterations. The work per CG iteration involves explicit forward and adjoint wave propagation solutions, and their cost scales with the $\frac{4}{3}$ power of the number of grid points; a CG iteration also requires the computation of the integral in (16.18), which is linear in the number of grid points. Ideally, the number of linear and nonlinear iterations will be independent of the problem size.

Table 16.2 shows the growth in iterations for a limited memory BFGS variant of reduced quasi-Newton (LRQN), unpreconditioned reduced (Gauss) Newton conjugate gradient (RNCG), and LRQN-preconditioned RNCG (PRNCG)) methods as a function of material model resolution. LRQN was not able to converge for the 4,913 and 35,937 parameter problems in any reasonable amount of time, and larger problems were not attempted with the method. The Newton methods showed mesh-independence of nonlinear iterations, until the finest grid, which exhibited a significant increase in iterations. This is most likely due to the TV regularizer, which results in an increasingly ill-conditioned reduced Hessian

Table 16.2. *Algorithmic scaling by LRQN, RNCG, and PRNCG methods as a function of material model resolution. For LRQN, the number of iterations is reported, and for both LRQN solver and preconditioner, 200 L-BFGS vectors are stored. For RNCG and PRNCG, the total number of CG iterations is reported, along with the number of Newton iterations in parentheses. On all material grids up to 65^3, the forward and adjoint wave propagation problems are posed on 65^3 grid $\times$ 400 time steps, and inversion is done on 64 PSC AlphaServer processors; for the 129^3 material grid, the wave equations are on 129^3 grids $\times$ 800 time steps, on 256 processors. In all cases, work per iteration reported is dominated by a reduced gradient (LRQN) or reduced-gradient-like (RNCG, PRNCG) calculation, so the reported iterations can be compared across the different methods. Convergence criterion is 10^{-5} relative norm of the reduced gradient. * indicates lack of convergence;* † *indicates number of iterations extrapolated from converging value after 6 hours of runtime.*

grid size	material parameters	LRQN its	RNCG its	PRNCG its
65^3	8	16	17 (5)	10 (5)
65^3	27	36	57 (6)	20 (6)
65^3	125	144	131 (7)	33 (6)
65^3	729	156	128 (5)	85 (4)
65^3	4913	*	144 (4)	161 (4)
65^3	35, 937	*	177 (4)	159 (6)
65^3	274, 625	—	350 (7)	197 (6)
129^3	2, 146, 689	—	$1470^\dagger$ (22)	409 (16)

as the mesh is refined. On the other hand, the inner conjugate gradient iterations in PRNCG appear to remain relatively constant within each nonlinear iteration. To verify that the inner iteration would keep scaling, we ran one nonlinear iteration on a 257^3 grid (nearly 17 million inversion parameters) on 2,048 AlphaServer processors at PSC. This required 27 CG iterations, which is comparable to the smaller grids, suggesting that the preconditioner is effective.

These results show that the quasi-Newton-preconditioned Newton-CG method seems to be scaling reasonably well for this highly nonlinear and ill-conditioned problem. Overall, the method is able to solve a problem with over 2 million unknown inversion parameters in just 3 hours on 256 AlphaServer processors. However, each CG iteration involves a forward/adjoint pair of wave propagation solutions, so that the cost of inversion is over 800 times the cost of the forward problem. Thus, the excellent reconstruction in Figure 16.1 has come at significant cost. This approach has also been applied to elastic wave equation inverse problems in the context of inverse earthquake modeling with success [3].

16.2.2 Optimal boundary control of Navier–Stokes flow

In this second example, we give sample results for an optimal boundary control problem for 3D steady Navier–Stokes flow. A survey and articles on this topic can be found in [38, 55, 56]. We use the velocity-pressure $(u(x), p(x))$ form of the incompressible Navier–Stokes equations. The boundary control problem seeks to find an appropriate source $d(s)$ on the control boundary $\partial\Omega_d$ so that the H^1 seminorm of the velocity (i.e., the rate of dissipation of viscous energy) is minimized:

$$\min_{u,p,d} \mathcal{J}(u, p, d) \stackrel{\text{def}}{=} \frac{\nu}{2}\int_{\Omega} \nabla u \cdot \nabla u \, dx + \frac{\rho}{2}\int_{\partial\Omega_d} |d|^2 \, ds$$

$$\text{subject to } -\nu\Delta u + (\nabla u)u + \nabla p = \mathbf{0} \text{ in } \Omega,$$

$$\nabla \cdot u = 0 \text{ in } \Omega, \quad (16.19)$$

$$u = u_g \text{ on } \partial\Omega_u,$$

$$u = d \text{ on } \partial\Omega_d,$$

$$-p\mathbf{n} + \nu(\nabla u)\mathbf{n} = \mathbf{0} \text{ on } \partial\Omega_N.$$

Here the decision variable is the control, i.e., the velocity vector d on $\partial\Omega_d$, and the objective reflects an $L^2(\partial\Omega_d)$ cost of the control. There are both Dirichlet (with source u_g) and Neumann boundary conditions, and ν is the inverse Reynolds number. For the simulation problem we need not distinguish between $\partial\Omega_d$ and $\partial\Omega_u$ since both boundary subdomains are part of the Dirichlet boundary. In the optimization problem, however, d is not known. Figure 16.2 illustrates the effect of the optimal boundary control in eliminating the separated flow around a cylinder.

To derive the optimality conditions, we introduce adjoint variables $\lambda(x)$, $\mu(x)$ for the state variables u, p, respectively. See [24] for details. The optimality system then takes the following form:

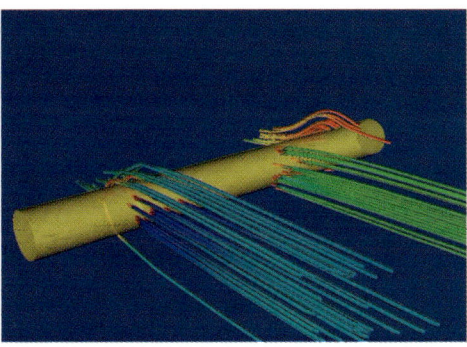 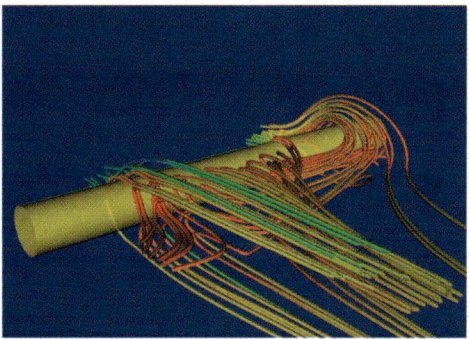

Figure 16.2. *An optimal boundary control problem to minimize the rate of energy dissipation (equivalent here to the drag) by applying suction or injection of a fluid on the downstream portion of a cylinder at Re = 40. The left image depicts an uncontrolled flow; the right image depicts the optimally controlled flow. Injecting fluid entirely eliminates recirculation and secondary flows in the wake of the cylinder, thus minimizing dissipation. The optimization problem has over 600,000 states and nearly 9,000 controls and was solved in 4.1 hours on 256 processors of a Cray T3E at PSC.*

state equations:

$$\begin{aligned}
-\nu \Delta \boldsymbol{u} + (\nabla \boldsymbol{u})\boldsymbol{u} + \nabla p &= \boldsymbol{0} \text{ in } \Omega, \\
\nabla \cdot \boldsymbol{u} &= 0 \text{ in } \Omega, \\
\boldsymbol{u} &= \boldsymbol{u}_g \text{ on } \partial \Omega_u, \\
\boldsymbol{u} &= \boldsymbol{d} \text{ on } \partial \Omega_d, \\
-p\boldsymbol{n} + \nu(\nabla \boldsymbol{u})\boldsymbol{n} &= \boldsymbol{0} \text{ on } \partial \Omega_N;
\end{aligned} \qquad (16.20)$$

adjoint equations:

$$\begin{aligned}
-\nu \Delta \boldsymbol{\lambda} + (\nabla \boldsymbol{u})^T \boldsymbol{\lambda} - (\nabla \boldsymbol{\lambda})\boldsymbol{u} + \nabla \mu &= \nu \Delta \boldsymbol{u} \text{ in } \Omega, \\
\nabla \cdot \boldsymbol{\lambda} &= \boldsymbol{0} \text{ in } \Omega, \\
\boldsymbol{\lambda} &= \boldsymbol{0} \text{ on } \partial \Omega_u, \\
\boldsymbol{\lambda} &= \boldsymbol{0} \text{ on } \partial \Omega_d, \\
-\mu \boldsymbol{n} + \nu \nabla(\boldsymbol{\lambda})\boldsymbol{n} + (\boldsymbol{u} \cdot \boldsymbol{n})\boldsymbol{\lambda} &= -\nu(\nabla \boldsymbol{u})\boldsymbol{n} \text{ on } \partial \Omega_N;
\end{aligned} \qquad (16.21)$$

decision equations:

$$\nu(\nabla \boldsymbol{\lambda} + \nabla \boldsymbol{u})\boldsymbol{n} - \rho \boldsymbol{d} = \boldsymbol{0} \text{ on } \partial \Omega_d. \qquad (16.22)$$

Since the flow equations are steady and highly nonlinear for the separated flow, there is significant benefit to integrating state solutions iterations with optimization iterations, and therefore we study the performance of the LNKS method of section 16.1.2 in comparison with a limited memory BFGS variant of the reduced quasi-Newton method. We refer to the latter as LRQN. In Table 16.3 we quote a set of representative results from many

Table 16.3. *Algorithmic scalability for Navier–Stokes optimal flow control problem on 64 and 128 processors of a Cray T3E for a doubling (roughly) of problem size.*

states controls	method	Newton iter	average KKT iter	time (hours)
389,440	LRQN	189	—	46.3
6,549	LNKS-EX	6	19	27.4
(64 procs)	LNKS-PR	6	2,153	15.7
	LNKS-PR-TR	13	238	3.8
615,981	LRQN	204	—	53.1
8,901	LNKS-EX	7	20	33.8
(128 procs)	LNKS-PR	6	3,583	16.8
	LNKS-PR-TR	12	379	4.1

we have obtained for up to 1.5 million state variables and 50,000 control variables on up to 256 processors. Approximation is by Taylor–Hood Galerkin finite elements, both for state and decision variables. The table provides results for 64 and 128 Cray T3E processors for a doubling (roughly) of problem size. LNKS-EX refers to exact solution of the linearized Navier–Stokes equation within the LRQN preconditioner, whereas LNKS-PR refers to application of a block-Jacobi (with local ILU(0)) approximation of the linearized Navier–Stokes forward and adjoint operators within the preconditioner. LNKS-PR-IN uses an inexact Newton method, which avoids fully converging the KKT linear system for iterates that are far from a solution.

The results in the table reflect the independence of Newton iterations on problem size, the mild dependence of KKT iterations on problem size and the resulting reasonable scalability of the method. It is important to point out here that the Navier–Stokes discrete operator is very ill conditioned, and there is room for improvement of its domain-decomposition preconditioner (single-level block Jacobi–ILU). The scalability of the LNKS methods would improve correspondingly. A dramatic acceleration of the LNKS algorithm is achieved by truncating the Krylov iterations. More detailed results are given in [21, 23, 24]. The important result is that LNKS solves the optimization problem in 4.1 hours, which is five times the cost of solving the equivalent simulation problem and over an order of magnitude faster than a conventional reduced space method (LRQN).

16.2.3 Initial condition inversion of atmospheric contaminant transport

In this section we consider an inverse problem governed by a parabolic PDE. Given observations of the concentration of an airborne contaminant $\{u_j^*\}_{j=1}^{N_s}$ at N_s locations $\{x_j\}_{j=1}^{N_s}$ inside a domain Ω, we wish to estimate the initial concentration $d(x)$ using a convection-diffusion transport PDE model. The inverse problem is formulated as a constrained, least-squares optimization problem:

$$\min_{u,d} \mathcal{J}(u,d) \stackrel{\text{def}}{=} \frac{1}{2} \sum_{j=1}^{N_s} \int_\Omega (u-u^*)^2 \,\delta(\boldsymbol{x}-\boldsymbol{x}_j)\, d\boldsymbol{x}\, dt + \frac{\beta}{2} \int_\Omega d^2\, d\boldsymbol{x}$$

$$\text{subject to} \quad \dot{u} - \nu\Delta u + \boldsymbol{v}\cdot\nabla u = 0 \quad \text{in } \Omega \times (0,T), \tag{16.23}$$
$$\nu\nabla u \cdot \boldsymbol{n} = 0 \quad \text{on } \Gamma \times (0,T),$$
$$u = d \quad \text{in } \Omega \times \{t=0\}.$$

The first term in the objective functional $\mathcal{J}$ represents the least-squares misfit of predicted concentrations $u(\boldsymbol{x}_j)$ with observed concentrations $u^*(\boldsymbol{x}_j)$ at sensor locations, over a time horizon $(0,T)$, and the second term provides L^2 regularization of the initial condition d, resulting in a well-posed problem. The constraint is the convection-diffusion initial-boundary value problem, where u is the contaminant concentration field, d is the initial concentration, $\boldsymbol{v}$ is the wind velocity field (assumed known), and ν is the diffusion coefficient. For simplicity, a steady laminar incompressible Navier–Stokes solver is used to generate wind velocity fields over a terrain of interest.

Optimality conditions for (16.23) can be stated as as follows:

state equation:

$$\dot{u} - \nu\Delta u + \boldsymbol{v}\cdot\nabla u = 0 \quad \text{in } \Omega \times (0,T),$$
$$\nu\nabla u \cdot \boldsymbol{n} = 0 \quad \text{on } \Gamma \times (0,T), \tag{16.24}$$
$$u = d \quad \text{in } \Omega \times \{t=0\};$$

adjoint equation:

$$-\dot{\lambda} - \nu\Delta\lambda - \nabla\cdot(\lambda\boldsymbol{v}) = -\sum_{j=1}^{N_s}(u-u^*)\delta(\boldsymbol{x}-\boldsymbol{x}_j) \quad \text{in } \Omega\times(0,T),$$
$$(\nu\nabla\lambda + \boldsymbol{v}\lambda)\cdot\boldsymbol{n} = 0 \quad \text{on } \Gamma\times(0,T), \tag{16.25}$$
$$\lambda = 0 \quad \text{in } \Omega\times\{t=T\};$$

decision equation:

$$\beta u_0 - \lambda|_{t=0} = 0 \quad \text{in } \Omega. \tag{16.26}$$

The equations of (16.24) are just the original forward convection-diffusion transport problem for the contaminant field. The adjoint convection-diffusion problem (16.25) resembles the forward problem, but with some essential differences. First, it is a terminal value problem; that is, the adjoint λ is specified at the final time $t = T$. Second, convection is directed backward along the streamlines. Third, it is driven by a source term given by the negative of the misfit between predicted and measured concentrations at sensor locations. Finally, the initial concentration equation (16.26) is in the present case of L^2 regularization an algebraic equation. Together, (16.24), (16.25), and (16.26) furnish a coupled system of linear PDEs for (u, λ, d).

The principal difficulty in solving this system is that—while the forward and adjoint transport problems are evolution equations—the KKT optimality system is a *coupled boundary value problem in 4D space-time*. As in the acoustic inversion example, the 4D space-time nature of (16.24)–(16.26) presents prohibitive memory requirements for large-scale problems, and thus we consider reduced space methods. In fact, the optimality system is a linear system, since the state equation is linear in the state, and the decision variable appears linearly. Block elimination produces a reduced Hessian that has condition number independent of the mesh size. (It is spectrally equivalent to a compact perturbation of the identity.) However, a preconditioner capable of reducing the number of iterations is still critical, since each CG iteration requires one state and one adjoint convection-diffusion solve. We are unable to employ the limited memory BFGS preconditioner that was used for the acoustic inverse problem, since for this linear problem there is no opportunity for the preconditioner to reuse built-up curvature information. Instead, we appeal to multigrid methods for second-kind integral equations and compact operators [34, 44, 57, 58, 62] to precondition the reduced Hessian system. Standard multigrid smoothers (e.g., for elliptic PDEs) are inappropriate for inverse operators, and instead a smoother that is tailored to the spectral structure of the reduced Hessian must be used; for details see [4].

The optimality system (16.24)–(16.26) is discretized by streamline upwind/Petrov Galerkin (SUPG) stabilized finite elements in space and Crank–Nicolson in time. We use a logically rectangular topography-conforming isoparametric hexahedral finite element mesh on which piecewise-trilinear basis functions are defined. Since the Crank–Nicolson method is implicit, we invert the time-stepping operator using a restarted GMRES method, accelerated by an additive Schwarz domain decomposition preconditioner, both from the PETSc library. Figure 16.3 illustrates solution of the inverse problem for a contaminant release scenario in the Greater Los Angeles Basin. As can be seen in the figure, the reconstruction of the initial condition is very accurate.

We next study the parallel and algorithmic scalability of the multigrid preconditioner. We take synthetic measurements on a $7 \times 7 \times 7$ sensor array. CG is terminated when the residual of the reduced system has been reduced by six orders of magnitude. Table 16.4 presents fixed-size scalability results. The inverse problem is solved on a $257 \times 257 \times 257 \times 257$ grid, i.e., there are 17×10^6 inversion parameters and 4.3×10^9 total space-time unknowns in the optimality system (16.9). Note that while the CG iterations are insensitive to the number of processors, the forward and adjoint transport simulations at each iteration rely on a single-level Schwarz domain decomposition preconditioner, whose effectiveness deteriorates with increasing number of processors. Thus, the efficiencies reported in the table reflect parallel as well as (forward) algorithmic scalability. The multigrid preconditioner incurs nonnegligible overhead as the number of processors increases for fixed problem size, since the coarse subproblems are solved on ever-larger numbers of processors. For example, on 1,024 processors, the $65 \times 65 \times 65$ coarse grid solve has just 270 grid points per processor, which is far too few for a favorable computation-to-communication ratio.

On the other hand, the unpreconditioned CG iterations exhibit excellent parallel scalability since the forward and adjoint problems are solved on just the fine grids. Nevertheless, the multigrid preconditioner achieves a net speedup in wall-clock time, varying from a factor of 2.5 for 128 processors to 1.5 for 1,024 processors. Most important, the inverse problem is solved in less than 29 minutes on 1,024 processors. This is about 18 times the wall-clock time for solving a single forward transport problem.

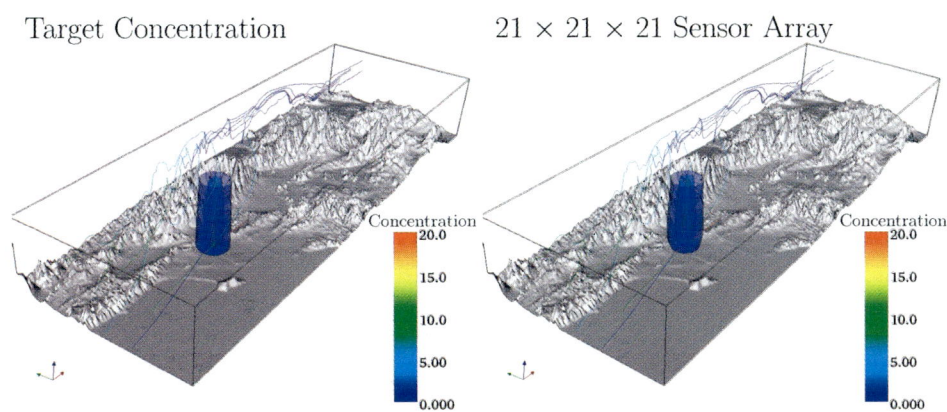

Figure 16.3. *Solution of a airborne contaminant inverse problem in the Greater Los Angeles Basin with onshore winds; Peclet number = 10. The target initial concentration is shown at left and reconstructed initial condition on the right. The measurements for the inverse problem were synthesized by solving the convection-diffusion equation using the target initial condition and recording measurements on a $21 \times 21 \times 21$ uniform array of sensors. The mesh has 917,301 grid points; the problem has the same number of initial condition unknowns and 74 million total space-time unknowns. Inversion takes 2.5 hours on 64 AlphaServer processors at PSC. CG iterations are terminated when the norm of the residual of the reduced space equations is reduced by five orders of magnitude.*

Table 16.4. *Fixed size scalability of unpreconditioned and multigrid preconditioned inversion. Here the problem size is $257 \times 257 \times 257 \times 257$ for all cases. We use a three-level version of the multigrid preconditioner. The variables are distributed across the processors in space, whereas they are stored sequentially in time (as in a multicomponent PDE). Here* hours *is the wall-clock time, and η is the parallel efficiency inferred from the runtime. The unpreconditioned code scales extremely well since there is little overhead associated with its single-grid simulations. The multigrid preconditioner also scales reasonably well, but its performance deteriorates since the problem granularity at the coarser levels is significantly reduced. Nevertheless, wall-clock time is significantly reduced over the unpreconditioned case.*

CPUs	no preconditioner		multigrid	
	hours	η	hours	η
128	5.65	1.00	2.22	1.00
512	1.41	1.00	0.76	0.73
1024	0.74	0.95	0.48	0.58

Table 16.5 presents isogranular scalability results. Here the problem size ranges from 5.56×10^8 to 1.39×10^{11} total space-time unknowns, while the number of processors ranges from 16 to 1,024. Because we refine in time as well as in space, and because the number of processors increases by a factor of 8 with each refinement of the grid, the total

Table 16.5. *Isogranular scalability of unpreconditioned and multigrid preconditioned inversion. The spatial problem size per processor is fixed (stride of 8). Ideal speed-up should result in doubling of wall-clock time. The multigrid preconditioner scales very well due to improving algorithmic efficiency (decreasing CG iterations) with increasing problem size. Unpreconditioned CG is not able to solve the largest problem in reasonable time.*

grid size	problem size		CPUs	no preconditioner		multigrid	
	d	(u, λ, d)		hours	iterations	hours	iterations
129^4	2.15E+6	5.56E+8	16	2.13	23	1.05	8
257^4	1.70E+7	8.75E+9	128	5.65	23	2.22	6
513^4	1.35E+8	1.39E+11	1024	—	—	4.89	5

number of space-time unknowns is not constant from row to row of the table; in fact it doubles. However, the number of grid points per processor does remain constant, and this is the number that dictates the computation to communication ratio. For ideal overall (i.e., algorithmic + parallel) scalability, we would thus expect wall-clock time to double with each refinement of the grid. Unpreconditioned CG becomes too expensive for the larger problems and is unable to solve the largest problem in reasonable time. The multigrid preconditioned solver, on the other hand, exhibits very good overall scalability, with overall efficiency dropping to 95% on 128 processors and 86% on 1,024 processors, compared to the 16-processor base case. From the fixed-size scalability studies in Table 16.4, we know that the parallel efficiency of the multigrid preconditioner drops on large numbers of processors due to the need to solve coarse problems. However, the isogranular scalability results of Table 16.5 indicate substantially better multigrid performance. What accounts for this? First, the constant number of grid points per processor keeps the processors relatively well populated for the coarse problems. Second, the algorithmic efficacy of the multigrid preconditioner improves with decreasing mesh size; the number of iterations drops from eight to five over two successive doublings of mesh resolution. The largest problem exhibits a factor of 4.6 reduction in CG iterations relative to the unpreconditioned case (5 versus 23). This improvement in algorithmic efficiency helps keep the overall efficiency high.

16.3 Conclusions

This chapter gave an overview of parallel algorithms for PDE-constrained optimization problems, focusing on reduced-space and full-space Newton-like methods. Examples illustrate application of the methods to elliptic, parabolic, and hyperbolic problems representing inverse, control, and design problems. A key conclusion is that an appropriate choice of optimization method can result in an algorithm that largely inherits the parallelism properties of the simulation problem. Moreover, under certain conditions, the combination of linear work per Krylov iteration, weak dependence of Krylov iterations on problem size, and independence of Newton iterations on problem size can result in a method that scales well with increasing problem size and number of processors. Thus, overall (parallel + algorithmic) efficiency follows.

There is no recipe for a general-purpose parallel PDE-constrained optimization method, just as there is no recipe for a general-purpose parallel PDE solver. The optimizer must be built around the best available numerical techniques for the state PDEs. The situation is actually more pronounced for optimization than it is for simulation, since new operators—the adjoint, the reduced Hessian, the KKT—appear that are not present in the simulation problem. PDE-constrained optimization requires special attention to preconditioning or approximation of these operators, a consideration that is usually not present in the design of general purpose optimization software.

However, some general themes do recur. For steady PDEs or whenever the state equations are highly nonlinear, a full-space method that simultaneously iterates on the state, adjoint, and decision equations can be significantly more effective than a reduced-space method that entails satisfaction of (a linear approximation of) the state and adjoint equations at each optimization iteration. For example, in the optimal flow control example in section 16.2.2, the LNKS method was able to compute the optimal control at high parallel efficiency and at a cost of just five simulations. LNKS preconditions the full-space KKT matrix by an approximate factorization involving subpreconditioners for state, adjoint, and reduced Hessian operators, thereby capitalizing on available parallel preconditioners for the state equation. Alternatively, methods that seek to extend domain decomposition and multigrid preconditioners for direct application to the KKT matrix are being developed and show considerable promise in also solving the optimization problem in a small multiple of the cost of the simulation. Careful consideration of smoothing, intergrid transfer, and interface conditions is required for these methods. Like their counterparts for the PDE forward problem, parallelism comes naturally for these methods.

At the opposite end of the spectrum, for time-dependent PDEs that are explicit, linear, or weakly nonlinear at each time step, the benefit of full-space solution is less apparent, and reduced-space methods may be required, if only for memory reasons. For small numbers of decision variables, quasi-Newton methods are likely sufficient, while for large (typically mesh-dependent) decision spaces, Newton methods with inexactly terminated CG solution of the quadratic step are preferred. Preconditioning the reduced Hessian becomes essential, even when it is well conditioned, since each CG iteration involves a pair of PDE solves (one state, one adjoint). For many large-scale inverse problems, the reduced Hessian has a compact + identity or compact + differential structure, which can be exploited to design effective preconditioners. Nevertheless, when the optimization problem is highly nonlinear in the decision space but weakly nonlinear or linear in the state space, such as for the inverse wave propagation problem described in section 16.2.1, we can expect that the cost of solving the optimization problem will be many times that of the simulation problem.

A number of important and challenging issues were not mentioned. We assumed that the appropriate Jacobian, adjoint, and Hessian operators were available, which is rarely the case for legacy code. A key difficulty not discussed here is globalization, which must often take on a problem-specific nature (as in the grid/frequency continuation employed for the inverse wave propagation problem). Design of scalable parallel algorithms for mesh-dependent inequality constraints on decision and state variables remains a significant challenge. Parallel adaptivity for the full KKT system complicates matters considerably. Nonsmoothness and singularities in the governing PDEs, such as shocks, localization phenomena, contact, and bifurcation, can alter the convergence properties of the methods described here. Choosing the correct regularization is a crucial matter.

Nevertheless, parallel algorithms for certain classes of PDE-constrained optimization problems are sufficiently mature to warrant application to problems of exceedingly large scale and complexity, characteristic of the largest forward simulations performed today. For example, the inverse atmospheric transport problem described in section 16.2.3 has been solved for 135 million initial condition parameters and 139 billion total space-time unknowns in less than 5 hours on 1,024 AlphaServer processors at 86% overall efficiency. Such computations point to a future in which optimization for design, control, and inversion—and the decision making enabled by it—become routine for the largest of today's terascale PDE simulations.

Acknowledgments

This work was supported in part by the U.S. Department of Energy through the SciDAC Terascale Optimal PDE Simulations Center and Grants DE-FC02-01ER25477 and DE-FG02-04ER25646; the Computer Science Research Institute at Sandia National Laboratories; and the National Science Foundation under ITR Grants ACI-0121667, EAR-0326449, and CCF-0427985 and DDDAS Grant CNS-0540372. Computing resources at the Pittsburgh Supercomputing Center were provided under NSF PACI/TeraGrid Awards ASC-990003P, ASC-010025P, ASC-010036P, MCA01S002P, BCS020001P, and MCA04N026P. We thank the PETSc group at Argonne National Laboratory for their work in making PETSc available to the research community.

Bibliography

[1] F. ABRAHAM, M. BEHR, AND M. HEINKENSCHLOSS, *The effect of stabilization in finite element methods for the optimal boundary control of the Oseen equations*, Finite Elements in Analysis and Design, 41 (2004), pp. 229–251.

[2] M. F. ADAMS, H. BAYRAKTAR, T. KEAVENY, AND P. PAPADOPOULOS, *Ultrascalable implicit finite element analyses in solid mechanics with over a half a billion degrees of freedom*, in Proceedings of ACM/IEEE Supercomputing, Pittsburgh, 2004.

[3] V. AKÇELIK, J. BIELAK, G. BIROS, I. EPANOMERITAKIS, A. FERNANDEZ, O. GHATTAS, E. KIM, D. O'HALLARON, AND T. TU, *High-resolution forward and inverse earthquake modeling on terascale computers*, in Proceedings of ACM/IEEE Supercomputing, Phoenix, November 2003.

[4] V. AKÇELIK, G. BIROS, A. DRĂGĂNESCU, O. GHATTAS, J. HILL, AND B. VAN BLOEMAN WAANDERS, *Dynamic data-driven inversion for terascale simulations: Real-time identification of airborne contaminants*, in Proceedings of ACM/IEEE Supercomputing, Seattle, November 2005.

[5] V. AKÇELIK, G. BIROS, AND O. GHATTAS, *Parallel multiscale Gauss-Newton-Krylov methods for inverse wave propagation*, in Proceedings of ACM/IEEE Supercomputing, Baltimore, Maryland, November 2002.

[6] W. K. ANDERSON, W. D. GROPP, D. KAUSHIK, D. E. KEYES, AND B. F. SMITH, *Achieving high sustained performance in an unstructured mesh CFD application*, in Proceedings of ACM/IEEE Supercomputing, Portland, November 1999.

[7] E. ARIAN AND S. TA'ASAN, *Multigrid one shot methods for optimal control problems: Infinite dimensional control*, Tech. Report ICASE 94-52, ICASE, NASA Langley Research Center, Hampton, VA, July 1994.

[8] ———, *Analysis of the Hessian for aerodynamic optimization*, Tech. Report 96-28, ICASE, NASA Langley Research Center, Hampton, VA, 1996.

[9] U. ASCHER AND E. HABER, *A multigrid method for distributed parameter estimation problems*, Electronic Transaction on Numerical Analysis, 15 (2003), pp. 1–12.

[10] S. BALAY, K. BUSCHELMAN, W. D. GROPP, D. KAUSHIK, M. G. KNEPLEY, L. C. MCINNES, B. F. SMITH, AND H. ZHANG, *PETSc Web page*, 2001. http://www.mcs.anl.gov/petsc.

[11] W. BANGERTH, *Adaptive Finite Element Methods for the Identification of Distributed Parameters in Partial Differential Equations*, Ph.D. thesis, University of Heidelberg, Heidelberg, Germany, 2002.

[12] H. T. BANKS AND K. KUNISCH, *Estimation Techniques for Distributed Parameter Systems*, Birkhauser, Basel, 1989.

[13] R. BARTLETT, M. HEINKENSCHLOSS, D. RIDZAL, AND B. VAN BLOEMEN WAANDERS, *Domain decomposition methods for advection dominated linear-quadratic elliptic optimal control problems*, Tech. Report SAND 2005-2895, Sandia National Laboratories, Albuquerque, NM, April 2005.

[14] A. BATTERMANN AND M. HEINKENSCHLOSS, *Preconditioners for Karush-Kuhn-Tucker matrices arising in the optimal control of distributed systems*, in Optimal control of partial differential equations, W. Desch, F. Kappel, and K. Kunisch, eds., vol. 126 of International Series of Numerical Mathematics, Birkhäuser-Verlag, Berlin, 1998, pp. 15–32.

[15] A. BATTERMANN AND E. W. SACHS, *Block preconditioner for KKT systems in PDE-governed optimal control problems*, in Workshop on Fast Solutions of Discretized Optimization Problems, R. H. W. Hoppe, K.-H. Hoffmann, and V. Schulz, eds., Birkhäuser, Basel, 2001, pp. 1–18.

[16] R. BECKER AND B. VEXLER, *A posteriori error estimation for finite element discretization of parameter identification problems*, Numerische Mathematik, 96 (2004), pp. 435–459.

[17] L. BEILINA, *Adaptive hybrid FEM/FDM methods for inverse scattering problems*, Applied and Computational Mathematics, 2 (2003), pp. 119–134.

[18] M. BERGOUNIOUX, M. HADDOU, M. HINTERMÜLLER, AND K. KUNISCH, *A comparison of a Moreau–Yosida-based active set strategy and interior point methods for constrained optimal control problems*, SIAM Journal on Optimization, 11 (2000), pp. 495–521.

[19] L. T. BIEGLER, J. NOCEDAL, AND C. SCHMID, *A reduced Hessian method for large-scale constrained optimization*, SIAM Journal on Optimization, 5 (1995), pp. 314–347.

[20] L. BIEGLER, O. GHATTAS, M. HEINKENSCHLOSS, AND B. VAN BLOEMEN WAANDERS, eds., *Large-Scale PDE-Constrained Optimization*, vol. 30 of Lecture Notes in Computational Science and Engineering, Springer-Verlag, Berlin, New York, 2003.

[21] G. BIROS AND O. GHATTAS, *Parallel Newton-Krylov algorithms for PDE-constrained optimization*, in Proceedings of ACM/IEEE Supercomputing, Portland, November 1999.

[22] ———, *Parallel preconditioners for KKT systems arising in optimal control of viscous incompressible flows*, in Parallel Computational Fluid Dynamics 1999, D. E. Keyes, A. Ecer, J. Periaux, and N. Satofuka, eds., North-Holland, Amsterdam, 1999.

[23] ———, *Parallel Lagrange–Newton–Krylov–Schur methods for PDE-constrained optimization. Part I: The Krylov–Schur solver*, SIAM Journal on Scientific Computing, 27 (2005), pp. 687–713.

[24] ———, *Parallel Lagrange–Newton–Krylov–Schur methods for PDE-constrained optimization. Part II: The Lagrange–Newton solver and its application to optimal control of steady viscous flows*, SIAM Journal on Scientific Computing, 27 (2005), pp. 714–739.

[25] G. BIROS, *Parallel Algorithms for PDE-Constrained Optimization and Application to Optimal Control of Viscous Flows*, Ph.D. thesis, Carnegie Mellon University, Pittsburgh, PA, August 2000.

[26] A. E. BORZÌ, K. KUNISCH, AND M. VANMAELE, *A multigrid approach to the optimal control of solid fuel ignition problems*, Lecture Notes in Computational Science and Engineering, (2000), pp. 59–65.

[27] A. BORZÌ AND K. KUNISCH, *The numerical solution of the steady state solid fuel ignition model and its optimal control*, SIAM Journal on Scientific Computing, 22 (2000), pp. 263–284.

[28] A. E. BORZÌ, *Multigrid methods for optimality systems*, Habilitation thesis, University of Graz, Austria, 2003.

[29] ———, *Multigrid methods for parabolic distributed optimal control problems*, Journal of Computational and Applied Mathematics, 157 (2003), pp. 365–382.

[30] C. BUNKS, F. M. SALECK, S. ZALESKI, AND G. CHAVENT, *Multiscale seismic waveform inversion*, Geophysics, 50 (1995), pp. 1457–1473.

[31] S. S. COLLIS AND M. HEINKENSCHLOSS, *Analysis of the streamline upwind/Petrov Galerkin method applied to the solution of optimal control problems*, Tech. Report CAAM TR02-01, Rice University, Houston, TX, March 2002.

[32] M. DELFOUR AND J.-P. ZOLÉSIO, *Shapes and Geometries: Analysis, Differential Calculus, and Optimization*, SIAM, Philadelphia, 2001.

[33] R. S. DEMBO, S. C. EISENSTAT, AND T. STEIHAUG, *Inexact Newton methods*, SIAM Journal on Numerical Analysis, 19 (1982), pp. 400–408.

[34] A. DRĂGĂNESCU, *Two investigations in numerical analysis: Monotonicity preserving finite element methods, and multigrid methods for inverse parabolic problems*, Ph.D. thesis, University of Chicago, August 2004.

[35] T. DREYER, B. MAAR, AND V. SCHULZ, *Multigrid optimization in applications*, Journal of Computational and Applied Mathematics, 120 (2000), pp. 67–84.

[36] H. ENGL, M. HANKE, AND A. NEUBAUER, *Regularization of Inverse Problems*, Kluwer, Dordrecht, 1996.

[37] A. GRIEWANK, *Achieving logarithmic growth of temporal and spatial complexity in reverse automatic differentiation*, Optimization Methods and Software, 1 (1992).

[38] M. D. GUNZBURGER, ed., *Flow Control*, vol. 68 of Institute for Mathematics and Its Applications, Springer-Verlag, New York, 1995.

[39] M. D. GUNZBURGER, *Perspectives in Flow Control and Optimization*, SIAM, 2003.

[40] E. HABER AND U. C. ASCHER, *Preconditioned all-at-once methods for large, sparse parameter estimation problems*, Inverse Problems, 17 (2001).

[41] E. HABER, U. ASCHER, AND D. OLDENBURG, *Inversion of 3D electromagnetic data in frequency and time domain using an inexact all-at-once approach*, Geophysics, 69 (2004), pp. 1216–1228.

[42] E. HABER, *Quasi-Newton methods for large scale electromagnetic inverse problems*, Inverse Problems, 21 (2004), pp. 305–317.

[43] ———, *A parallel method for large scale time domain electromagnetic inverse problems*. To appear, IMACS Journal, 2005.

[44] W. HACKBUSCH, *Multigrid methods and applications*, vol. 4 of Springer Series in Computational Mathematics, Springer-Verlag, Berlin, 1985.

[45] P. C. HANSEN, *Rank-Deficient and Discrete Ill-Posed Problems: Numerical Aspects of Linear Inversion*, SIAM, Philadelphia, 1997.

[46] S. B. HAZRA AND V. SCHULZ, *Simultaneous pseudo-timestepping for PDE-model based optimization problems*, BIT, 44 (2004), pp. 457–472.

[47] M. HEINKENSCHLOSS AND M. HERTY, *A spatial domain decomposition method for parabolic optimal control problems*, Tech. Report CAAM TR05-03, Rice University, Houston, TX, May 2005.

[48] M. HEINKENSCHLOSS AND H. NGUYEN, *Domain decomposition preconditioners for linear-quadratic elliptic optimal control problems*, Tech. Report CAAM TR04-20, Rice University, Houston, TX, November 2004.

[49] ———, *Neumann-Neumann domain decomposition preconditioners for linear-quadratic elliptic optimal control problems*, Tech. Report CAAM TR04-01, Rice University, Houston, TX, August 2004.

[50] M. HEINKENSCHLOSS, *Time-domain decomposition iterative methods for the solution of distributed linear quadratic optimal control problems*, Journal of Computational and Applied Mathematics, 173 (2005), pp. 169–198.

[51] M. HINTERMÜLLER AND M. HINZE, *Globalization of SQP-methods in control of the instationary Navier-Stokes equations*, Mathematical Modelling and Numerical Analysis, 36 (2002), pp. 725–746.

[52] M. HINTERMÜLLER, K. ITO, AND K. KUNISCH, *The primal-dual active set strategy as a semismooth Newton method*, SIAM Journal on Optimization, 13 (2003), pp. 865–888.

[53] M. HINZE AND T. SLAWIG, *Adjoint gradients compared to gradients from algorithmic differentiation in instantaneous control of the Navier-Stokes equations*, Optimization Methods and Software, 18 (2003).

[54] M. HINZE, J. STERNBERG, AND A. WALTHER, *An optimal memory-reduced procedure for calculating adjoints of the instationary Navier-Stokes equations*, Optimal Control Applications and Methods, 27 (2006), pp. 19–40.

[55] L. S. HOU AND S. S. RAVINDRAN, *Numerical approximation of optimal flow control problems by a penalty method: Error estimates and numerical results*, SIAM Journal on Scientific Computing, 20 (1999), pp. 1753–1777.

[56] L. S. HOU, *Analysis and Finite Element Approximation of Some Optimal Control Problems Associated with the Navier-Stokes Equations*, Ph.D. thesis, Carnegie Mellon University, Department of Mathematical Sciences, Pittsburgh, August 1989.

[57] B. KALTENBACHER, M. KALTENBACHER, AND S. REITZINGER, *Identification of nonlinear $B - H$ curves based on magnetic field computations and multigrid methods for ill-posed problems*, European Journal of Applied Mathematics, 14 (2003), pp. 15–38.

[58] B. KALTENBACHER, *V-cycle convergence of some multigrid methods for ill-posed problems*, Mathematics of Computation, 72 (2003), pp. 1711–1730.

[59] C. T. KELLEY AND E. W. SACHS, *Multilevel algorithms for constrained compact fixed point problems*, SIAM Journal on Scientific and Statistical Computing, 15 (1994), pp. 645–667.

[60] ——, *Quasi-Newton methods and unconstrained optimal control problems*, SIAM Journal on Control and Optimization, 25 (1987), pp. 1503–1516.

[61] D. E. KEYES, P. D. HOVLAND, L. C. MCINNES, AND W. SAMYONO, *Using automatic differentiation for second-order matrix-free methods in PDE-constrained optimization*, in Automatic Differentiation of Algorithms: From Simulation to Optimization, Springer, Berlin, New York, 2002, pp. 35–50.

[62] J. T. KING, *Multilevel algorithms for ill-posed problems*, Numerische Mathematik, 61 (1992), pp. 311–334.

[63] D. A. KNOLL AND D. E. KEYES, *Jacobian-free Newton-Krylov methods: A survey of approaches and applications*, Journal of Computational Physics, 193 (2004), pp. 357–397.

[64] R. M. LEWIS AND S. G. NASH, *Model problems for the multigrid optimization of systems governed by differential equations*, SIAM Journal on Scientific Computing, 26 (2005), pp. 1811–1837.

[65] R. M. LEWIS, *Practical aspects of variable reduction formulations and reduced basis algorithms in multidisciplinary optimization*, Tech. Report 95-76, Institute for Computer Applications in Science and Engineering (ICASE), NASA Langley Research Center, Hampton, VA, 1995.

[66] J.-L. LIONS, *Some Aspects of the Optimal Control of Distributed Parameter Systems*, SIAM, Philadelphia, 1972.

[67] I. MALČEVIĆ, *Large-scale unstructured mesh shape optimization on parallel computers*, Master's thesis, Carnegie Mellon University, Pittsburgh, PA, 1997.

[68] J. NOCEDAL AND S. J. WRIGHT, *Numerical Optimization*, Springer, Berlin, New York, 1999.

[69] O. PIRONNEAU, *Optimal Shape Design for Elliptic Systems*, Springer-Verlag, Berlin, New York, 1983.

[70] E. POLAK, *Optimization: Algorithms and Consistent Approximations*, Springer, Berlin, New York, 1997.

[71] E. E. PRUDENCIO, R. BYRD, AND X.-C. CAI, *Parallel full space SQP Lagrange–Newton–Krylov–Schwarz algorithms for PDE-constrained optimization problems*, SIAM Journal on Scientific Computing, 27 (2006), pp. 1305–1328.

[72] E. PRUDENCIO AND X.-C. CAI, *Parallel multi-level Lagrange-Newton-Krylov-Schwarz algorithms with pollution removing for PDE-constrained optimization*, 2006. Submitted.

[73] R. RANNACHER AND B. VEXLER, *A priori error estimates for the finite element discretization of elliptic parameter identification problems with pointwise measurements*, SIAM Journal on Control and Optimization, 44 (2005), pp. 1844–1863.

[74] W. W. SYMES AND J. J. CARAZZONE, *Velocity inversion by differential semblance optimization*, Geophysics, 56 (1991), pp. 654–663.

[75] A. TARANTOLA, *Inversion of seismic reflection data in the acoustic approximation*, Geophysics, 49 (1984), pp. 1259–1266.

[76] M. ULBRICH, S. ULBRICH, AND M. HEINKENSCHLOSS, *Global convergence of trust region interior-point algorithms for infinite-dimensional nonconvex minimization subject to pointwise bounds*, SIAM Journal on Control and Optimization, 37 (1999), pp. 731–764.

[77] M. ULBRICH AND S. ULBRICH, *Superlinear convergence of affine-scaling interior-point Newton methods for infinite-dimensional nonlinear problems with pointwise bounds*, SIAM Journal on Control and Optimization, 6 (2000), pp. 1938–1984.

[78] S. ULBRICH, *Generalized SQP-methods with "parareal" time-domain decomposition for time-dependent PDE-constrained optimization*. Submitted, 2004.

[79] C. R. VOGEL AND M. E. OMAN, *Iterative methods for total variation denoising*, SIAM Journal on Scientific Computing, 17 (1996), pp. 227–238.

[80] C. R. VOGEL, *Computational Methods for Inverse Problems*, SIAM, Philadelphia, 2002.

[81] S. VOLKWEIN, *Mesh-independence for an augmented Lagrangian-SQP method in Hilbert spaces*, SIAM Journal on Optimization, 38 (2000), pp. 767–785.

Chapter 17
Massively Parallel Mixed-Integer Programming: Algorithms and Applications

Cynthia A. Phillips, Jonathan Eckstein, and William Hart

Mixed-integer programming (MIP), optimization of a linear function subject to linear and integrality constraints, is a standard technology for computing an efficient allocation of limited resources. In this chapter, we survey MIP applications at Sandia National Laboratories. We describe scalability features of the massively parallel MIP solver in PICO (parallel integer and combinatorial optimizer), designed to effectively use thousands of processors to solve national-scale problems.

A MIP in standard form is

$$(\text{MIP}) \quad \text{minimize} \quad c^T x,$$
$$\text{where} \quad \begin{cases} Ax = b, \\ \ell \leq x \leq u, \\ x_j \in \mathcal{Z} \quad \forall j \in D \subseteq \{1, \ldots, n\}, \end{cases}$$

where x and c are n-vectors, A is an $m \times n$ matrix, b is an m-vector, and $\mathcal{Z}$ is the set of integers. Although in principle all input data are reals, for practical solution on a computer they are rational. Frequently the entries of A, c, and b are integers. We can convert an inequality constraint to an equality by adding a variable to represent slack between the value of ax and its bound b. For example, a constraint of the form $ax \leq b$ becomes $ax + s = b, s \geq 0$. If all variables are integer variables, this is a (pure) integer program (IP). If none are integer, this is a linear program (LP). The objective can be a maximization if that is the more natural optimization direction.

The only nonlinearity in MIP is the integrality constraints. These give MIP its enormous practical modeling power, but they are also responsible for MIP's theoretical difficulty and its practical difficulty, especially for large problems. Integer variables can represent decisions. In particular, binary variables (those for which 0 and 1 are the only possible values) can represent yes/no decisions. For example, a company must either build a factory or not build it; one cannot half build a factory at half the cost to achieve half the benefit.

MIPs easily express resource allocation problems such as scheduling, inventory planning, facility location, or general budget allocation. Therefore, they are a workhorse technology for human decision support and operations research. They also model hypothesized resource allocation decisions made by natural systems. For example, one might assume that it is cheaper for a species to inherit a trait from an ancestor species than to evolve a trait de novo. Therefore a good phylogeny (evolutionary tree) on a set of species might imply a minimum number of trait evolutions.

MIP is NP-complete, meaning it is formally intractable. Any algorithm that solves all instances of MIP to optimality will require an unacceptable amount of compute time in the worst case [20]. However, one may still wish to find a (near) optimal solution to a specific MIP instance using an algorithm that will not succeed on all instances. For example, when the instance involves significant cost, human safety, or national security, it's usually worth extra time to find the optimal solution. Sometimes a solution that's a few percent better than a previous one saves millions of dollars. Also, one can test the practical quality of a heuristic method by comparing the heuristic solution to the optimal for each instance in a benchmark suite that is representative of normal instances. This provides confidence in the quality of the current tool or indicates the value of investment in higher-quality approximation algorithms. In the latter case, studying the structure of optimal solutions can provide insight that leads to better algorithms. Because representing other NP-complete problems as MIPs is usually direct and natural, a first choice strategy for finding an optimal solution to a particular instance of an NP-complete problem is to formulate the instance as a MIP and try a general-purpose MIP solver.

Current general-purpose MIP solvers compute (approximately) optimal solutions by intelligent search based on branch-and-bound and branch-and-cut. In section 17.1, we describe this basic strategy. The IP formulation (precise choice of variables and constraints) critically affects running time. To at least partially understand what makes one formulation better than another when both are correct or equivalent at optimality, one must understand these search algorithms.

ILOG's commerical MIP solver CPLEX [10] is excellent for moderate-size instances. CPLEX runs in serial or on small SMPs. MINTO [34], ABACUS [22], lp_solve, CBC[18], and GLPK (Gnu linear programming kit) are free serial MIP solvers. Most of the Sandia National Laboratories MIP applications surveyed in section 17.2 have instances large enough to require parallel solution. For example, analyzing a national-scale infrastructure or computing a 30-year manufacturing production plan can tax the best current serial solvers in both time and memory requirements.

There are a number of parallel MIP solvers, none of which are commercial. SYMPHONY [38] and COIN/BCP [25, 31] are designed for small-scale, distributed-memory systems such as clusters. BLIS [37], under development, is designed as a more scalable version of SYMPHONY and BCP. It will be part of the optimization software available through COIN-OR (computational infrastructure for operations research) [8] once it is available. Ralphs, Ladányi, and Saltzman discuss of all three [36]. FATCOP [7] is designed for grid systems. The grid offers vast computational resources, but it is not a suitable platform for sensitive computations such as those involving national security or company proprietary information. The parallel branch-and-bound search strategy in PICO (parallel integer and combinatorial optimizer) [12] is particularly well suited for solving MIPs on tightly coupled massively parallel distributed-memory architectures, such as those available at the National

Laboratories. In section 17.3 we survey sources of parallelism in MIP computations and discuss features of the PICO solver designed to scalably exploit that parallelism.

17.1 Basic branch and bound for MIP

All general integer programming solvers are based on branch and bound (B&B) and/or branch and cut. In this section we describe the fundamental algorithms applied to solve general MIPs. See, for example, [2] for a more general description of (parallel) branch and bound.

Basic B&B iteratively subdivides the feasible region (the set of all x that satisfy the linear and integrality constraints) and recursively searches each piece. B&B is often more efficient than straight enumeration because it eliminates regions that provably contain no optimal solution. For a minimization problem, it computes a lower bound on the value of the optimal solution in each subregion. If this bound is worse (higher) than the value of the *incumbent* (the best feasible solution found so far), then there is no optimal feasible solution in the subregion. We now describe bounding and splitting methods for general MIPs. One can modify these and other basic B&B pieces to exploit problem-specific structure.

Every MIP has a natural, usually nontrivial bound. If we relax (remove) the integrality constraints, a MIP becomes an LP. The optimal value of this *LP relaxation* is a lower bound for a minimization problem and an upper bound for a maximization; we assume minimization for this discussion. If the LP solution coincidentally obeys all integrality constraints, then it is an optimal solution to the MIP as well. LPs are theoretically solvable in polynomial time [23] and are usually solved efficiently in practice with commercial tools such as CPLEX [10], XPRESS [45], or free tools such as COIN-LP [8].

The B&B algorithm grows a search tree as follows. The first incumbent value is infinity. The initial problem is the root r. Compute the LP bound $z(r)$ for the root. If the LP is infeasible, then the MIP is infeasible. If the LP solution is integer feasible, this is an optimal solution for the MIP. Optionally, search for an incumbent using either a problem-specific heuristic that exploits problem structure or a general MIP heuristic method. If the incumbent value matches the lower bound $z(r)$, then we can *fathom* (eliminate) the node; there is nothing there that is better than the incumbent. Otherwise, *branch* or *split* the problem. When the LP relaxation is not an integer-feasible solution, there is some $j \in D$ such that the optimal solution to the LP relaxation x^* has value $x_j^* \notin \mathcal{Z}$. For the simplest MIP branching, create two new sub-MIPs as children of the root: one with the restriction $x_j \leq \lfloor x_j^* \rfloor$ and one with the restriction $x_j \geq \lceil x_j^* \rceil$. For binary variables, one child has $x_j = 0$ and the other has $x_j = 1$. The feasible regions of the two children are disjoint and any solution with $\lfloor x_j^* \rfloor < x_j < \lceil x_j^* \rceil$, including x^*, is no longer feasible in either child. Thus the LP relaxation of a child differs from the LP relaxation of the parent. Then recursively solve each subproblem. At any point in the computation, let P be the pool of active (unresolved) subproblems. Then $L = \min_{p \in P} z(p)$ is a global lower bound on the original problem. B&B terminates when there are no active subproblems or when the relative or absolute gap between L and the incumbent value is sufficiently small.

Splitting causes exponential work explosion in cases where the B&B strategy fails. Therefore most MIP systems use branch and cut: they add general and/or problem-specific valid inequalities (cutting planes) to improve the lower bound on a subproblem to delay branching as long as possible (or avoid it altogether if the lower bound rises above the incumbent value). Given x^*, an optimal nonintegral solution to the LP relaxation of a (sub)problem, a cutting plane is a constraint $ax = b$ such that $ax' = b$ for all possible (optimal) integer solutions x' but $ax^* \neq b$. Adding this constraint to the system (cutting) makes the current LP optimal infeasible. In the branch-and-cut algorithm, processing a subproblem involves solving the LP relaxation, finding and adding cuts, resolving the LP, and iterating until cutting becomes too difficult or unproductive. Finally the node splits as before.

Multiple processors can grow a given (static) search tree faster than one. But the key to practical solution of MIPs is keeping the search tree to a tractable size. This requires strong lower bounds, since this is the primary way to prune the tree. For MIP that means formulating the problem so that the LP relaxation gives a good approximation of the value of the integer optimal solution. A poor formulation can eliminate the benefits of parallelization. One measure of the quality of an LP lower bound is the *integrality gap*, the ratio between the value of the optimal MIP solution and its LP relaxation. It is generally good to add constraints to a MIP formulation to strengthen the LP relaxation even if the constraints are redundant for an optimal integer solution. Frequently one can achieve a provably smaller integrality gap (and faster solution in practice) by adding a family of constraints too large to enumerate in practice. One can still compute the LP solution for the entire set by enforcing only a polynomial number of the constraints, but only if the class has an efficient *separation algorithm*. A separation algorithm accepts a proposed solution x and either determines that x satisfies all constraints in the family or returns a violated inequality. Theoretically, one can use this separation algorithm within the ellipsoid algorithm [32] to solve the LP relaxation in polynomial time. However, in practice, it is faster to iteratively add a most violated cut and resolve the LP using dual simplex until the separation algorithm determines that all constraints are satisfied.

17.2 Applications

In this section we describe several MIP applications solved at Sandia National Laboratories (SNL) for real data. We describe some MIPs in detail, giving one possible formulation for each. SNL researchers have also solved MIPs for nuclear weapon evaluation planning (determining minumum extra resources necessary to complete a set of tasks) [1, 24] and computing well-shaped meshes of physical objects for simulation codes [43]. They have studied other MIPs in research settings.

17.2.1 Shortest-path network interdiction

In the shortest-path network interdiction problem, we wish to interfere with an adversary who is traversing a network from a start node to a target node. We represent the network as a graph $G = (V, E)$ with start node $s \in V$ and target node $t \in V$. Each edge $e = (u, v) \in E$ has length ℓ_{uv} (or ℓ_e) representing the distance between nodes u and v. Distance is additive. The length of the path between two nodes is the sum of the lengths of the edges on the path. We assume the adversary can plan his route through the network, and in the worst case, the adversary will choose a shortest path from start point s to target t.

Distance can represent time, cost, effort, etc. Distance can also measure probability such as probability of detection. For example, suppose the probability of detecting the adversary while he traverses edge e is p_e and therefore the probability of his evading detection is $q_e = 1 - p_e$. Then, assuming these probabilities are all independent, the probability of evading detection from s to t along a path P is $\prod_{e \in P} q_e$. We can turn the evasion-probability (multiplication) calculation into a path-length (addition) computation by using length $\ell_e = -\ln(q_e)$ for each edge e. For any source-to-target path through the network, the sum of the ℓ_e (path lengths) is the negative logarithm of the probability of traversing that entire path undetected. An intruder has a probability $1 - e^{-L}$ of evading detection along a path with length L. Thus the shortest path corresponds to the path with maximum evasion probability (and is the most dangerous path for the intruder to take).

In the shortest-path interdiction problem, we pay to increase edge lengths in a network to maximize the resulting shortest path. This maximally delays an omniscient adversary who takes the best path through the network. For each edge (u, v), we can pay c_{uv} to increase the edge length by λ_{uv}. We have limited edge-reinforcement resources, given as a budget B.

An integer-programming formulation for this problem uses a variable d_v for each node v. In any optimal solution, d_v is the length of the shortest path from the start node s to node v after the edge-length increases. We also have binary decision variables x_{uv} for each edge (u, v). If $x_{uv} = 1$, then we pay to increase the length of edge (u, v), and if $x_{uv} = 0$, then we do not alter the length of edge (u, v). This models the case in which one must pay the whole price and add the full delay. For example, the cost to install a speed bump in a road is roughly the same regardless of the height of the bump, so one cannot pay half the cost to gain half the delay. In this version, we assume the edges are symmetric (undirected) and that one can increase the travel time in either direction when adding a delay to an edge. If we cannot add a delay to a particular edge (u, v), then we set $x_{uv} = 0$, logically. Practically, we simply do not have the variable in the formulation.

The integer program is

$$(\text{SPI}) \quad \text{maximize} \quad d_t,$$

$$\text{where} \quad \begin{cases} d_v \leq d_u + \ell_{uv} + \lambda_{uv} x_{uv} & \forall (u, v) \in E, \\ d_u \leq d_v + \ell_{uv} + \lambda_{uv} x_{uv} & \forall (u, v) \in E, \\ \sum_{(u,v) \in E} c_{uv} x_{uv} \leq B, \\ d_s = 0, \\ x_{uv} \in \{0, 1\} & \forall (u, v) \in E. \end{cases}$$

The first constraint enforces a shortest-path computation. If node u is a neighbor for node v (that is, there is an edge (u, v)), then the adversary can travel to node v via node u. Therefore, the length of the shortest path from start node s to node v is at most the length of the shortest from start node s to node u plus the length of the edge (u, v). The length of edge (u, v) is its original length ℓ_{uv} if we choose to leave it unchanged ($x_{uv} = 0$) and it is $\ell_{uv} + \lambda_{uv}$ if we choose to lengthen it ($x_{uv} = 1$). The second constraint is symmetric, representing traversing the edge in the other direction. The third constraint enforces the budget, limiting the number of edges we can lengthen. The fourth constraint says that the shortest path from the start point to itself has length zero. And the last constraint enforces integrality for the decision variables.

In the special case where $\ell_{uv} = 0$ and $\lambda_{uv} = 1$ for all $(u, v) \in E$ and $B = k \leq |E|$, we may instead wish to minimize the budget B and constrain the distance d_t from the start point to the target to be at least k. This is the *k-hurdle problem*. This models the case in which we wish to ensure that every intruder must pass k hurdles, such as cameras or guard posts, on any start-to-target path. The constraint matrix in this case is totally unimodular, which means that all the decision variables will be integral at optimality even if we don't explicitly enforce the integrality constraints. (We need only enforce the upper bound of 1.) Thus we can solve this variation provably optimally using only linear programming.

Though the problem applies naturally to physical transportation networks such as building or road networks, it also applies to logical networks. In the Netv computer security analysis system [42], each node represents the state of an attack on a computer network, such as aquired privileges. Each edge represents an attack step. The start node represents the attacker's initial set of privileges (usually none, but possibly significant for insiders), and the target is the security breach the attacker wishes to achieve. Any start-to-target path is a plausible way to achieve the target breach and the length of the path represents the difficulty of the attack. In this case, when one pays to harden the system, a single cost can increase the length of multiple graph edges. Thus the decision variable x_i is associated with defense measure i. Each measure can contribute to the length of multiple edges and each edge can be increased by multiple defense measures.

17.2.2 Network flow interdiction

In the network flow interdiction (or inhibition) problem we wish to maximally damage the ability of a network to transport material from a start node to a destination node. As with shortest-path interdiction, the network is a graph $G = (V, E)$. Now each edge (u, v) has a capacity c_{uv}. Material moves through the network from start node s to destination node t according to the classic maximum flow problem. That is, (material) flow is conserved at every node other than s and t, and for each edge, the flow per unit time does not exceed the edge capacity. We can remove an edge $e = (u, v)$ from the graph at cost r_{uv}. We wish to expend at most a fixed budget B removing edges of G to minimize the resulting maximum possible s-t flow.[1]

If we partition the nodes of a network into two sets, S and T with $s \in S$ and $t \in T$, the set of edges with one endpoint in S and the other endpoint in T is called a *cut*. The *capacity* of a cut is the sum of the capacities of the edges in the cut. By Ford and Fulkerson's classic theorem [17], the value of a maximum flow per unit time from s to t equals the minimum capacity of any s-t cut. Thus to minimize the resulting postattack maximum flow, we must minimize the resulting minimum cut.

We base the IP for network flow interdiction on the classic minimum-cut integer program [40]. We specify a cut by specifying the vertex partition S and T. The IP has a binary decision variable d_v for each vertex $v \in V$. The IP sets $d_v = 1$ if vertex v is on the t side of the partition and $d_v = 0$ if v is on the s side. There are also two binary variables for each edge. Variable $y_{uv} = 1$ if edge (u, v) is in the cut specified by the d_v variables and

---

[1] Our algorithmic work for the problem allows partial removal of an edge at proportional partial cost. This does not change the complexity of the problem. Furthermore, there is always an optimal solution with at most one edge partially removed [35].

we do not remove it ($y_{uv} = 0$ otherwise), and variable $z_{uv} = 1$ if edge (u, v) is in the cut and we do remove it ($z_{uv} = 0$ otherwise).

The network-inhibition mixed-integer program is

$$\text{(NI)} \quad \text{minimize} \quad \sum_{(u,v) \in E} c_{uv} y_{uv},$$

$$\text{where} \quad \begin{cases} \sum_{(u,v) \in E} r_{uv} z_{uv} \leq B, \\ y_{uv} + z_{uv} \geq d_u - d_v & \forall (u, v) \in E, \\ y_{uv} + z_{uv} \geq d_v - d_u & \forall (u, v) \in E, \\ d_s = 0, \ d_t = 1, \\ d_v, y_{uv}, z_{uv} \in \{0, 1\} & \forall v \in V, (u, v) \in E. \end{cases}$$

This IP chooses a cut to attack and attacks it optimally. The quality of an attack (the objective function) is the residual capacity left in the cut. The first constraint enforces the budget. The second and third sets of constraints compute the edges in the cut based on the vertex partition. If exactly one of u and v is on the s side, then edge (u, v) is in the cut. We must either remove it (paying for it in the first constraint) or leave it to contribute to the residual cut capacity (paying for it in the objective function). Burch et.al. [5] show that the LP relaxation of this problem is highly structured, so one can quickly find an incumbent solution, frequently a provably good one. Wood [44] describes some variations on this model and gives some valid inequalities (cuts) one might use in practice.

Although the network flow interdiction problem has obvious applications to attacking an adversary's transportation network, one can also use it defensively. Optimal and near-optimal attack strategies on a network expose vulnerabilities that a network owner may wish to reinforce. For example, Sandia researchers have used this problem to analyze the denial-of-service effect of attacks on water networks.

17.2.3 Sensor placement in water networks

In this problem, we wish to place a limited number of sensors in a municipal water network to minimize the expected damage from a malicious attack or an accidental contamination. We model the water network as a graph $G = (V, E)$. Nodes represent water sources, such as tanks, or consumption points, which could be as small as a single faucet or as large as a neighborhood, depending upon model granularity. Edges are pipes, valves, or other means of transporting water between nodes. We assume a normal daily pattern of water use and network management, so the network has predictable hydraulics. Given an attack (contaminant injection parameters, time of day, location), an offline simulator tracks the contaminant plume for a specified number of days. For example, it determines when each node is hit by the plume (if at all) and where and when the contaminant exits the system. We wish to choose $S_{\max}$ sensor locations from the set $L \subseteq V \cup E$ of feasible locations to minimize the expected amount of contamination released to the network before detection. The expectation is taken over a probability distribution on attacks where α_a is the probability of attack $a \in A$ and we assume exactly one attack in A occurs. We assume the sensors are perfect and that there is a general alarm as soon as any sensor detects contamination. Hence no consumers are at risk after detection.

To determine parameters for the integer program, we run the simulator for each attack $a \in A$ to determine L_a, the set of feasible sensor locations hit by the plume, and w_{ai}, the amount of contaminant released from the network before location $i \in L_a$ is first hit during attack a. We add a dummy location q and define $\mathcal{L}_a = L_a \cup \{q\}$ and set w_{aq} to the full contaminant dose for all attacks $a \in A$.

The IP has a decision variable s_i for each potential sensor location $i \in L$, where $s_i = 1$ if we place a sensor at location i and $s_i = 0$ otherwise. There are also derived variables b_{ai} for $a \in \mathcal{A}$ and $i \in \mathcal{L}_a$. Variable $b_{ai} = 1$ if location i witnesses attack a and $b_{ai} = 0$ otherwise. That is, $b_{ai} = 1$ if there is a sensor at location i and it is the first sensor hit for attack scenario a. These variables need not have formal integrality constraints. They will always be binary in any optimal solution provided the s_i variables are binary. Omitting these unnecessary constraints can improve the practical performance of IP solvers. Formally, the IP to minimize consumption is

$$(\text{MC}) \quad \text{minimize} \quad \sum_{a \in \mathcal{A}} \sum_{i \in \mathcal{L}_a} \alpha_a w_{ai} b_{ai},$$

$$\text{where} \quad \begin{cases} \sum_{i \in \mathcal{L}_a} b_{ai} = 1 & \forall a \in \mathcal{A}, \\ b_{ai} \leq s_i & \forall a \in \mathcal{A}, i \in \mathcal{L}_a, \\ \sum_{i \in L} s_i \leq S_{\max}, \\ s_i \in \{0, 1\} & \forall i \in L. \end{cases}$$

The first constraints ensure exactly one witness for each attack. The second set enforces that a sensor cannot witness an attack if it is never installed. Objective-function pressure then ensures that the first installed sensor hit in attack a is the witness. The last constraint enforces the limit on the total number of sensors. The objective minimizes the total consumption over all attacks (weighted by risk).

This IP is equivalent to the classic unconstrained facility location problem. In that problem, we wish to build facilities to serve customers. Each customer must be served by an open facility, and we wish to minimize the initial cost of building the facilities plus the cost of serving the customers' regular demands from the open facilities. In our case, the sensors are the facilities and the attacks are the customers. Our only costs are the building costs. The term "unconstrained" means there is no limit on the number of customers a facility can serve.

17.2.4 Processor allocation

On large commodity-based cluster systems such as Sandia's Cplant system [39], jobs should be allocated to localized clusters of processors to minimize communication costs and to avoid bandwidth contention caused by overlapping jobs. Leung et. al. [28] showed that the *average number of communication hops* between the processors allocated to a job strongly correlates with the job's completion time. On Cplant, the number of switches (hops) between a pair of processors is its Manhattan distance in the grid (the sum of the horizontal and vertical differences for two dimensions). Although one would not solve a MIP for real-time scheduling, studying the behavior of optimal placements for this metric did yield insight into the quality of the metric as a basis for processor-allocation algorithms. The following MIP computes an optimal placement of a single job with respect to the average-hop metric.

We have a set P of free processors upon which we have imposed an arbitrary order. We wish to select k processors with minimum average distance, where d_{pq} is the distance between processors p and q. The MIP has a binary variable x_p for each free processor p, where $x_p = 1$ if we choose processor p and $x_p = 0$ otherwise. Variable $y_{pq} = 1$ if we choose both processor p and q where $p < q$. The IP is

(NA) minimize $\sum_{p \in F} \sum_{q > p \in F} d_{pq} y_{pq}$,

where
$$\begin{cases} \sum_{p \in F} x_p = k, & \\ y_{pq} \leq x_p & \forall q \in F, \\ y_{pq} \leq x_q & \forall p \in F, \\ y_{pq} \geq x_p + x_q - 1 & \forall p \in F, q \in F, p < q, \\ \sum_{q > p} y_{pq} + \sum_{h < p} y_{hp} = (k-1) x_p & \forall p \in F, \\ x_p \in \{0, 1\} & \forall p \in F. \end{cases}$$

The first constraint forces the selection of exactly k processors. The next three sets of constraints set $y_{pq} = x_p \wedge x_q$ as long as the x_i are binary. The next set of constraints tightens the formulation by forcing every selected processor to contribute $k-1$ distances to the objective.

17.2.5 Contact map overlap

One approach to understanding a newly discovered protein's function is to compare it to known proteins. SNL researchers have developed combinatorial techniques to compute protein-protein similarity using knowledge of the structure of both proteins.

A protein is a chain of amino acids (called *residues*). The *sequence* of a protein is the order of residues along this *backbone*. This one-dimensional chain folds into a three-dimensional form in its working environment. This is called the protein's *native state*. A protein's function is closely related to its native state. It is difficult to determine the native state in a living creature, but researchers can crystalize proteins and determine crystal structure with magnetic reasonance or x-ray technology. Two residues that are not adjacent on the backbone but are sufficiently close in the native state form a *contact*. For example, two nonadjacent residues could form a contact if the Euclidean distance between any atom in the first residue and any atom in the second is below a given threshold in the folded protein.

The *contact* map of a protein is a graph with a node for each residue and an edge connecting each contact. Given contact maps for two proteins, $G_1 = (V_1, E_1)$ and $G_2 = (V_2, E_2)$, a similarity measure is the maximum number of shared contacts in two aligned subgraphs [21]. To compute this measure, pick k nodes from each contact map (for some $k \leq \min(|V_1|, |V_2|)$) and number the selected nodes from each map from 1 to k in sequence order. The ith node from the first sequence is *aligned* with the ith node of the second sequence. For some $1 \leq i < j \leq k$, there is a shared contact if the ith and jth nodes are neighbors in each subgraph (form a contact). For example, in Figure 17.1, seven nodes and five shared contacts are selected from each map. The dashed lines connect aligned nodes (those with the same rank in the selected subsequences). Since the alignment respects the sequence order, no pair of dashed lines intersects. This is called a *noncrossing alignment*.

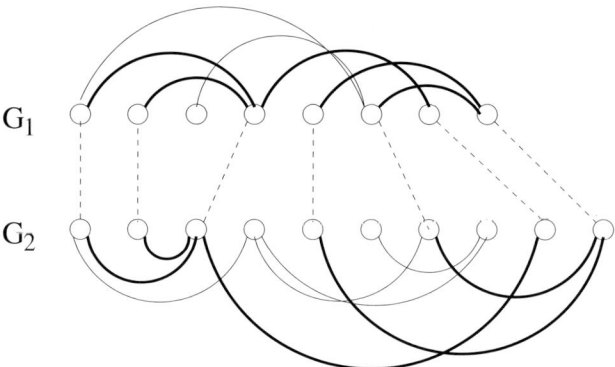

Figure 17.1. *Example contact map alignment with isomorphic subgraphs with seven nodes and five edges corresponding to an alignment of seven amino acid residues with five shared contacts (bold edges)* [27].

The contact map overlap IP uses two types of variables: one to choose an alignment of nodes and the other to indicate shared contacts. In a feasible solution, variable $x_{ij} = 1$ if $i \in V_1$ is aligned with $j \in V_2$ and is 0 otherwise. Variable $y_{(i,k)(j,l)} = 1$ if edges $(i,k) \in E_1$ and $(j,l) \in E_2$ are a shared contact (the edges exist, i is aligned with j, and k is aligned with l). The integer program is

$$\text{(CMO)} \quad \text{maximize} \quad \sum_{(i,k) \in E_1} \sum_{(j,l) \in E_2} y_{(i,k)(j,l)},$$

$$\text{where} \quad \begin{cases} y_{(i,k)(j,l)} \leq x_{ij} & \forall (i,k) \in E_1, (j,l) \in E_2, \\ y_{(i,k)(j,l)} \leq x_{kl} & \forall (i,k) \in E_1, (j,l) \in E_2, \\ \sum_{i \in V_1} x_{ij} \leq 1 & \forall j \in V_2, \\ \sum_{j \in V_2} x_{ij} \leq 1 & \forall i \in V_1, \\ x_{ij} + x_{kl} \leq 1 & \forall 1 \leq i < k \leq |V_1| \text{ and } 1 \leq l < j \leq |V_2|, \\ x_{ij}, y_{(i,k)(j,l)} \in \{0,1\}. \end{cases}$$

The first pair of constraints enforces endpoint alignment for shared contacts. The second pair of constraints allows each node of a contact map to align with at most one node of the other contact map. The fifth set of constraints disallows alignments that cross (violate the sequence orderings). This IP formulation is correct, but in practice, it is important to use a set of valid inequalities (cuts) described in [27].

Lancia et al. used this IP to compute exact CMO measures on small proteins in the Protein Data Bank [27]. On test sets of known protein families, this measure provided insight consistent with known protein functionality.

17.3 A scalable parallel MIP solver

PICO is an MPI-based C++ branch-and-bound engine with a derived MIP solver. In this section, we describe features of PICO's B&B and MIP solvers that are particularly well suited for solving MIPs on tightly coupled massively parallel distributed-memory architectures, such as those available at the National Laboratories for solution of national-scale problems. For these architectures, one has exclusive use of perhaps thousands of processors for the entire computation. Thus one major concern is effectively using all these processors during the initial *ramp-up* phase, when the search tree is small.

Good parallel speed up depends critically upon keeping the total tree size close to the size of that generated by a good serial solver. Given an incumbent, serial solvers usually expand the active subproblem with the lowest bound (the "best" node). This node *must* be processed to either find a better solution or prove that there is no solution better than the incumbent (within tolerance). Precomputing a large set of independent subproblems (e.g., the $(\log M)$th level of a complete binary tree for some branching choices where M is the number of processors) deviates significantly from this careful growth strategy. In pathological cases the parallel computation performs so much more work than its serial counterpart that there is a slowdown anomaly (e.g., [14, 26, 29, 30]). That is, adding processors increases the wall-clock time. Section 17.3.1 describes other ways to use parallelism during ramp-up. After ramp-up, when there are more active independent subproblems, PICO enters a *parallel-subproblem* phase. In section 17.3.2, we sketch strategies for scalably managing this asynchronous parallel search. For example, PICO uses multiple load-balancing strategies to ensure that all worker processes are solving sufficiently high-quality subproblems. This combination of strategies can use massive parallelism effectively. In preliminary experiments on some problems PICO had near-perfect speed up through 512 processors [12]. In section 17.3.3 we sketch high-productivity features of PICO, those that assist in rapid development of fast MIP applications.

17.3.1 Managing ramp-up

PICO uses an explicit ramp-up phase in which all processors work on a single subproblem, parallelizing the individual subproblem evaluation steps. In particular, one could parallelize (1) problem-specific preprocessing, (2) root bounding, (3) initialization of gradient estimation (used for branching prioritization), (4) incumbent generation (problem-specific or PICO's general-purpose parallel incumbent generator), and (5) cutting-plane generation. Some processors could search for incumbents and cutting planes independently from those growing the tree. One could generalize this approach to allow multiple processors to evaluate a single node while evaluating multiple nodes in parallel. Efficient management of this hybrid approach is an open research problem that we will address in later versions of PICO. PICO currently supports ramp up parallelism of types (3) and (4). We now describe how to exploit subproblem-level MIP parallelism.

Preprocessing recognizes problem structure that can partially solve a problem a priori. To parallelize problem-specific preprocessing, processors can cooperate on individual preprocessing steps or they can compute independent separate steps. Real-world MIP instances frequently have special structure that is captured by a small upper bound on a parameter k (e.g., the degree of a graph, maximum contention for a resource). To solve these fixed-parameter-tractable problems, one first *kernelizes* the problem, transforming it in polynomial time into a new instance of the same problem with size bounded by a function of k. These preprocessing steps are frequently local (such as replacing a subgraph with a smaller subgraph) and therefore good candidates for parallelization. See Fellows [16] for an excellent summary of the theory and practice of kernelization.

Computing LP bounds can be the most time-consuming part of evaluating a subproblem, so it is an obvious candidate for parallelization. PICO does not yet do this because of limitations in current parallel LP technology. PICO's serial solver uses a primal simplex algorithm to solve the root. This finds a corner of the feasible region and repeatedly moves to a new corner with a better objective value till it finds an optimal (corner or vertex) solution. PICO uses a dual simplex LP solver to compute the LP bound of a subproblem. Starting this computation at the (vertex) solution of the closely related parent problem can speed subproblem solution by orders of magnitude compared to the root solve.

A parallel interior point solver such as pPCx [9] could provide moderate speed-up at the root. The core computational problem is the solution of a linear system of the form $AD^2A^Tx = b$, where A is the original constraint matrix and D is a diagonal matrix that changes each iteration. Parallel direct Cholesky solvers for such systems are robust but do not provide reasonable speed up beyond a few dozen processors. Unfortunately, interior-point LP solvers do not generally return a vertex solution when there are multiple optimal solutions. Although PICO could solve all problems during ramp-up with a parallel interior-point method, when it switches to serial solution of independent subproblems, it requires starting points for dual simplex. This requires a *crossover* procedure to produce a vertex solution from a standard interior-point solution. There is still no accepted efficient crossover method. Current methods could take as long as a primal simplex solve in the worst case, although in practice one can expect significantly better performance.

Developing parallel LP solvers that give higher speed-ups or are useful beyond the root are open research areas. SNL is leading a research effort to find more scalable interior-point solvers using iterative linear systems solvers [4]. The primary difficulty is the lack of preconditioner classes that work well on combinatorially structured problems.[2] Alternatively, PICO could use (massively) parallel sparse (primal and dual) simplex codes. We are not aware of any such codes, although Eckstein et al. [11] have developed a dense simplex code.

PICO must be able to use free LP solvers because (faster) commercial LP codes do not have licensing schemes for massively parallel (MP) machines, and individual processor licenses would be prohibitively expensive. PICO has a coping strategy to avoid making thousands of processors wait for slow root solves in MP computations. The user can solve the root LP offline (e.g., using a fast commercial solver) and give this LP solution to a subsequent parallel computation.

Good branching choices, especially early in the computation, can significantly affect final search tree size. PICO maintains pseudocosts (branching gradients) to estimate the value of branching on each variable. For the simple branching described above, the pseudocost for a variable is the average change in LP objective per unit change in the variable (with up/down pseudocosts tracked separately). When a variable is a branching candidate for the first time, PICO initializes its pseudocosts by pretending to branch in each direction. All these LP solves (two per fractional variable) are independent, so the processors partition the work and share the results.

For any given bounding and splitting strategy there is a minimum-size search tree, obtained by knowing the optimal value at the start. All other nodes must be evaluated to

---

[2]A notable exception is support preconditioners [3, 41] for the case in which A is symmetric and diagonally dominant, such as the incidence matrix of a graph. None of the graph-based MIPs in section 17.2 have this pure network structure except the k-hurdle problem.

prove optimality. Thus incumbent heuristics that find near-optimal solutions early allow early pruning and can lead to much smaller search trees.

PICO's general cut-pivot-dive heuristic [33] can exploit multiple processors during ramp-up. This discussion applies to MIPs with binary variables only, although it generalizes to arbitrary MIPs. The heuristic guides its search with an integrality-measuring merit function. It can use any merit function that is 0 for integer vectors, positive for fractional vectors, differentiable, and strictly concave. In particular, PICO uses a family of merit functions parametrized by $0 < \alpha < 1$, where the merit function attains its maximum at α. Processors can use a random value of α for each variable, resulting in different search biases. Processors can also fix some fractional variables, giving preference to those with a history of improving integrality.

Sometimes problem-specific incumbent heuristics can use multiple processors. For example, α-point heuristics for scheduling compute multiple schedules based on a single LP relaxation. If a scheduling IP uses a variable for each possible (job, finish time) pair, then the α-point of a job for $0 < \alpha \leq 1$ is the time when the LP relaxation has (fractionally) completed an α fraction of the job. An α-point heuristic greedily schedules jobs in α-point order. The number of values of α that result in different lists is usually polynomial in the number of jobs. Taking the best of these schedules can be provably better than using any fixed value of α [6].

Finally, one can parallelize the generation of cutting planes by cooperating on the generation of one plane or by generating different planes in parallel. For example, Gomory cuts apply to any MIP. There are m independent computatations (for m equal to the number of constraints), each of which could produce a Gomory cut. These computations are reasonably fast so the problem would likely have to be large for this parallelization to help. However, clique cuts for problems with packing structure (all variables and matrix coefficients 0-1, $b = 1$, no $\geq$ inequalities) have a similar number of independent computations and these are much more expensive.

17.3.2 Managing independent subproblems

PICO's ramp-up phase usually terminates when there are enough subproblems to keep most processors busy. After ramp-up, PICO switches to a phase where processors work on separate subproblems. Hub processors coordinate this search. Each hub controls a set of worker processors, few enough that the workers are not significantly slowed by contention for service from the hub. A hub plus its workers form a *cluster*. Initially each hub takes control of an equal share of active subproblems. Since all processors have grown the tree together, this requires no communication. Each worker has a local pool of subproblems to reduce dependence on its hub. Though PICO has considerable flexibility in subproblem selection criteria, once there is an incumbent both hubs and workers generally use a best-first strategy.

PICO has three load-balancing mechanisms. First, if, based on information from the hub, a worker determines it controls too much of the (good) work in its cluster, it sends a block of subproblems back to the hub. Second, when a worker creates a subproblem and decides not to keep it locally, it sends the problem to its hub or probabilistically scatters it to a random hub. The probability of scattering depends upon the load controlled in its cluster relative to average system load. The third mechanism is global load balancing. The hubs use a tree to determine overloaded (donor) and underloaded (receiver) hubs based on both quantity and quality of subproblems. They use parallel prefix operations to rank the donors and receivers. The donors and receivers then pair by rendezvous based on rank. See [2, 13, 15, 12] for more details.

Because hub communication can become a bottleneck, hubs do not handle all the data associated with the subproblems they control. Instead they keep a small *token* containing only the information needed to control the problem. In particular, the token contains the subproblem bound and the ID of the worker that created the subproblem. When a worker creates a subproblem and relinquishes control to a hub, it stores all the subproblem data and sends this small token to the hub. When a hub wants to dispatch a subproblem to processor p_i, it sends a message to the processor p_j that created the subproblem telling processor p_j to send the subproblem data to processor p_i. Thus the communication pattern in a MIP computation has many small messages to and from the hubs and, because of the load balancing, long messages going point to point in a reasonably random pattern.

17.3.3 High-productivity computing

PICO has a number of features that aid in rapid application development.

Because PICO is written in C++, any derived application automatically inherits all the parallel search management just described. A developer need only develop the serial application that customizes the search to exploit problem-specific structure. Then to use the parallel solver, they need only implement methods to pack and unpack problem-specific data. PICO supplies a `PackBuffer` data object that packs or unpacks any type of object using stream operators. Thus the developer need only stream the data into the buffer and remove it in the same order.

Mathematical programming languages like AMPL [19] allow developers to express a MIP using natural (multidimensional) variables rather than the usual linear representation of general MIP solvers. AMPL models are a formalization of the mathematical MIP representation we used in section 17.2. For example, there are classes of constraints. PICO provides scripts that accept an AMPL MIP model and automatically generate derived PICO classes that are aware of the AMPL names. A developer can then write incumbent heuristics and cut separation algorithms using the natural problem variables. AMPL generates the constraint matrix.

PICO has an *early output* feature. Whenever PICO finds a new incumbent it writes the solution to a file (with a delay to prevent too much I/O in a flurry of incumbent finds). Thus if a computation stalls, one can abort the computation and still have the solution to seed a future computation.

Long computations on large numbers of processors can sometimes fail after a considerable amount of computation. For example, a processor can fail, the computation could hit a system-imposed time limit, or, especially in B&B, the job could exceed the processors' memory. PICO has a checkpoint feature which, when enabled, saves the full computation state regularly. The computation can restart after a failure, on a different number of processors if necessary.

Bibliography

[1] A. ASGEIRSSON, J. BERRY, C. PHILLIPS, D. PHILLIPS, C. STEIN, AND J. WEIN, *Scheduling an industrial production facility*, in Proceedings of the 10th Conference on Integer Programming and Combinatorial Optimization, 2004, pp. 116–131.

[2] D. BADER, W. HART, AND C. PHILLIPS, *Parallel algorithm design for branch and bound*, in Tutorials on Emerging Methodologies and Applications in Operations Research, H. J. Greenberg, ed., Kluwer Academic Press, Dordrecht, 2004.

[3] E. G. BOMAN AND B. HENDRICKSON, *Support theory for preconditioning*, SIAM Journal on Matrix Analysis and Applications, 25 (2003), pp. 694–717.

[4] E. G. BOMAN, O. PAREKH, AND C. PHILLIPS, *LDRD final report on massively-parallel linear programming: the parPCx system*, Tech. Report SAND2004-6440, Sandia National Laboratories, Albuquerque, NM, January 2005.

[5] C. BURCH, R. CARR, S. KRUMKE, M. MARATHE, C. PHILLIPS, AND E. SUNDBERG, *A decomposition-based pseudoapproximation algorithm for network flow inhibition*, in Network Interdiction and Stochastic Integer Programming, D. L. Woodruff, ed., Kluwer Academic Press, Dordrecht, 2003, pp. 51–68.

[6] C. CHEKURI, R. MOTWANI, B. NATARAJAN, AND C. STEIN, *Approximation techniques for average completion time scheduling*, SIAM Journal on Computing, 31 (2001), pp. 146–166.

[7] Q. CHEN AND M. C. FERRIS, *FATCOP: A fault tolerant Condor-PVM mixed integer programming solver*, SIAM Journal on Optimization, 11 (2001), pp. 1019–1036.

[8] *Computational Infrastructure for Operations Research*, http://www.coin-or.org/.

[9] T. COLEMAN, J. CZYZYK, C. SUN, M. WAGNER, AND S. WRIGHT, *pPCx: Parallel software for linear programming*, in Proceedings of the Eighth SIAM Conference on Parallel Processing for Scientific Computing, SIAM, Philadelphia, 1997.

[10] *ILOG CPLEX*, http://www.ilog.com/products/cplex/.

[11] J. ECKSTEIN, I. BODUROGLU, L. POLYMENAKOS, AND D. GOLDFARB, *Data-parallel implementations of dense simplex methods on the connection machine CM-2*, ORSA Journal on Computing, 7 (1995), pp. 402–416.

[12] J. ECKSTEIN, W. E. HART, AND C. A. PHILLIPS, *PICO: An object-oriented framework for parallel branch-and-bound*, in Inherently Parallel Algorithms in Feasibility and Optimization and Their Applications, Elsevier Scientific Series on Studies in Computational Mathematics, Elsevier, Amsterdam, 2001, pp. 219–265.

[13] J. ECKSTEIN, *Control strategies for parallel mixed integer branch and bound*, in Proceedings of Supercomputing '94, IEEE Computer Society Press, Los Alamitos, CA, 1994, pp. 41–48.

[14] ——, *Parallel branch-and-bound algorithms for general mixed integer programming on the CM-5*, SIAM Journal on Optimization, 4 (1994), pp. 794–814.

[15] ——, *Distributed versus centralized storage and control for parallel branch and bound: Mixed integer programming on the CM-5*, Computational Optimization and Applications, 7 (1997), pp. 199–202.

[16] M. FELLOWS, *Parameterized complexity*, in Experimental Algorithmics, R. Fleischer, E. Meineche-Schmidt, and B. M. E. Moret, eds., vol. 2547 of Lecture Notes in Computer Science, Springer-Verlag, Berlin, New York, 2002, pp. 51–74.

[17] L. R. FORD AND D. R. FULKERSON, *Flows in Networks*, Princeton University Press, Princeton, NJ, 1962.

[18] J. FORREST AND R. LOUGEE-HEIMER, *The CBC user guide*, 2005. http://www.coin-or.org/Cbc/cbcuserguide.html.

[19] R. FOURER, D. GAY, AND B. KERNIGHAN, *AMPL: A Modeling Language for Mathematical Programming*, Boyd & Fraser Publishing Company, Danvers, MA, 1993.

[20] M. GAREY AND D. JOHNSON, *Computers and Intractability – A Guide to the Theory of NP-Completeness*, W. H. Freeman, San Francisco, CA, 1979.

[21] D. GOLDMAN, C. PAPADIMITRIOU, AND S. ISTRAIL, *Algorithmic aspects of protein structure similarity*, in Proceedings of the 40th Annual Symposium on Foundations of Computer Science, IEEE, Los Alamitos, CA, 1999.

[22] M. JÜNGER AND S. THIENEL, *The ABACUS system for branch-and-cut-and-price algorithms in integer programming and combinatorial optimization*, Software: Practice and Experience, 30 (2001), pp. 1325–1352.

[23] L. KHACHIAN, *A polynomial time algorithm for linear programming*, Soviet Mathematics Doklady, 20 (1979), pp. 191–194.

[24] E. A. KJELDGAARD, D. A. JONES, G. F. LIST, M. A. TURNQUIST, J. W. ANGELO, R. D. HOPSON, J. HUDSON, AND T. HOLEMAN, *Swords into plowshares: Nuclear weapon dismantlement, evaluation, and maintenance at pantex*, Interfaces, 30 (2000), pp. 57–82.

[25] L. LADÁNYI, *BCP (Branch, Cut, and Price)*. Available from http://www-124.ibm.com/developerworks/opensource/coin/.

[26] T.-H. LAI AND S. SAHNI, *Anomalies in parallel branch-and-bound algorithms*, Communications of the ACM, 27 (1984), pp. 594–602.

[27] G. LANCIA, R. CARR, B. WALENZ, AND S. ISTRAIL, *101 optimal PDB structure alignments: A branch-and-cut algorithm for the maximum contact map overlap problem*, in Proceedings of the Fifth Annual International Conference on Computational Biology, New York, NY, 2001, ACM Press, pp. 193–202.

[28] V. LEUNG, E. M. ARKIN, M. A. BENDER, D. BUNDE, J. JOHNSTON, A. LAL, J. S. B. MITCHELL, C. PHILLIPS, AND S. SEIDEN, *Processor allocation on Cplant: achieving general processor locality using one-dimensional allocation strategies*, in Proceedings of the International Conference on Cluster Computing, 2002, Chicago, IL.

[29] G.-J. LI AND B. WAH, *Coping with anomalies in parallel branch-and-bound algorithms*, IEEE Transactions on Computing, C-35 (1986), pp. 568–573.

[30] ———, *Computational efficiency of parallel combinatorial OR-tree searches*, IEEE Transactions on Software Engineering, 18 (1990), pp. 13–31.

[31] F. MARGOT, *BAC: A BCP based branch-and-cut example*, Tech. Report RC22799, IBM, New York, 2003.

[32] L. L. M. GRÖTSCHEL, L. LOVÁSZ, AND A. SCHRIJVER, *Geometric Algorithms and Combinatorial Optimization*, Springer-Verlag, Berlin, Germany, 1988.

[33] M. NEDIAK AND J. ECKSTEIN, *Pivot, cut, and dive: A heuristic for mixed 0-1 integer programming*, Tech. Report RRR 53-2001, RUTCOR, Piscataway, NJ, October 2001.

[34] G. L. NEMHAUSER, M. W. P. SAVELSBERGH, AND G. C. SIGISMONDI, *Minto, a mixed integer optimizer*, Operations Research Letters, 15 (1994), pp. 47–58.

[35] C. PHILLIPS, *The network inhibition problem*, in Proceedings of the 25th Annual ACM Symposium on the Theory of Computing, May 1993, pp. 776–785.

[36] T. K. RALPHS, L. LADÁNYI, AND M. J. SALTZMAN, *Parallel branch, cut, and price for large-scale discrete optimization*, Mathematical Programming, 98 (2003).

[37] ———, *A library for implementing scalable parallel search algorithms*, The Journal of SuperComputing, 28 (2004), pp. 215–234.

[38] T. K. RALPHS, *Symphony 4.0 users manual*, 2004. Available from www.branchandcut.org/SYMPHONY.

[39] R. RIESEN, R. BRIGHTWELL, L. A. FISK, T. HUDSON, J. OTTO, AND A. B. MACCABE, *Cplant*, in Proc. 2nd Extreme Linux workshop at the 1999 USENIX Annual Technical Conference, 1999, Monterey, CA.

[40] A. SCHRIJVER, *Theory of Linear and Integer Programming*, John Wiley & Sons, New York, 1986.

[41] D. SPIELMAN AND S.-H. TENG, *Solving sparse, symmetric, diagonally-dominant linear systems in time $O(m^{1.31})$*, in Proc. of IEEE Foundations of Computer Science, 2003, pp. 416–427.

[42] L. P. SWILER, C. PHILLIPS, AND D. ELLIS, *Computer-attack graph generation tool*, in Proceedings of the DARPA Information Survivability Conference and Exposition, 2001, Anaheim, CA.

[43] W. R. WITKOWSKI, J. J. JUNG, C. R. DOHRMANN, AND V. J. LEUNG, *Finite element meshing approached as a global minimization problem*, Tech. Report SAND2000-0579, Sandia National Laboratories, Albuquerque, NM, March 2000.

[44] K. WOOD, *Deterministic network interdiction*, Mathmatical and Computer Modeling, 17 (1993), pp. 1–18.

[45] *Dash Optimization, XPRESS-MP*, 2004. `http://www.dashoptimization.com/`.

Chapter 18
Parallel Methods and Software for Multicomponent Simulations

Michael T. Heath and Xiangmin Jiao

Computational simulation is an increasingly important technique both for understanding natural phenomena and for designing engineered devices. Many engineering systems and physical phenomena of interest are composed of various components that interact with each other, often in a very complex manner. Spatial decomposition, in which components occupy distinct regions within the overall domain of the system, is one of the most common and important examples. Such a spatial decomposition may arise naturally (e.g., land, ocean, and atmosphere in a climate model) or may be artificially induced as part of a numerical discretization, especially when partitioned for parallel implementation. Interactions between adjacent components typically occur at the interfacial surfaces where their geometric subdomains abut. A further complication is that the problem geometry may change over time, and the interfacial surfaces between components may move.

At the Center for Simulation of Advanced Rockets (CSAR) at the University of Illinois (www.csar.uiuc.edu), we have been developing a software system, Rocstar, for detailed simulation of solid rocket motors. This system involves many disciplines, including three broad physical disciplines—fluid dynamics, solid mechanics, and combustion—that interact with each other at the primary system level, with additional subsystem level interactions, such as particles and turbulence within fluids. To accommodate the diverse and dynamically changing needs of individual physics disciplines, we have adopted a *partitioned* approach, to enable coupling of individual software components that solve problems in their own physical and geometrical domains. With this approach, the physical components of the system are naturally mapped onto various software components (or modules), which can then be developed and parallelized independently. These modules are then integrated into a coherent system through an integration framework, which, among other responsibilities, manages distributed data objects and performs intermodule communications on parallel machines.

The partitioned approach also introduces new challenges in computational mathematics. One such challenge is how to transfer data between components in a numerically accurate and physically conservative manner. In simulating mechanical systems, for example, conservation of energy, mass, and momentum must be maintained in all component interactions. Another challenge is dealing with changing problem geometry as a system evolves over time. For example, processes such as burning, erosion, etching, deposition, or phase changes alter the size and shape of subdomains and cause the boundaries between them to move. Propagating or tracking moving surfaces is a longstanding problem in computational mathematics, and it is further complicated in a partitioned parallel setting. Another implication of geometric change is potential deterioration of mesh quality, as the mesh representing a subdomain may become compressed, distended, or otherwise distorted. Maintaining or improving mesh quality during multicomponent simulations is another major challenge, especially in a parallel setting, where mesh modifications must be coordinated across processors.

In this chapter we overview some of our recent progress in addressing these issues. The remainder of the chapter is organized as follows. Section 18.1 overviews the parallel, multiphysics software system developed at CSAR and describes the key characteristics of the physics modules and their parallel implementations. Section 18.2 presents our integration framework for multicomponent systems and some middleware services built on top of it. Section 18.3 surveys some key computational problems arising from the integration of such systems and our solutions to them. Section 18.4 presents sample simulation results obtained with our coupled code, followed by performance results. Section 18.5 concludes the chapter with a discussion of some remaining challenges.

18.1 System overview

To enable parallel simulations of rocket motors, we have developed a large number of software modules. Figure 18.1 shows an overview of the components of the current generation of Rocstar. These modules are grouped into four categories: physics modules, service modules, integration interface, and control (orchestration) modules, corresponding to the components at the lower left, right, center, and top in Figure 18.1, respectively. In addition,

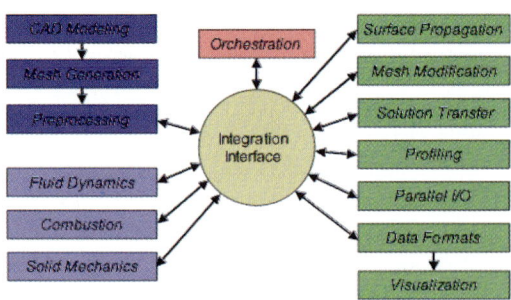

Figure 18.1. *Overview of Rocstar software components.*

our system uses some *offline tools*, such as those in the upper-left corner of the figure, which provide specific pre- or postprocessing utilities for physics modules.

18.1.1 Physics modules

The physics modules solve physical problems in their respective geometric domains and are similar to stand-alone applications. They are the primary components of Rocstar, and their needs drive the development of other modules. We next briefly summarize the key features and parallel implementations of these modules, focusing on their interactions and the characteristics that are most critical to the coupling of Rocstar.

Fluid dynamics solvers. Rocflo [3] and Rocflu [8] are advanced CFD solvers developed at CSAR for modeling core flow and associated multiphysics phenomena. Both modules solve the integral form of the 3D time-dependent compressible Euler or Navier–Stokes equations using finite-volume methods. In addition, they are both designed to interact with other physics submodules, including turbulence, particles, chemical reactions, and radiation [17]. Rocflo, developed by Blazek, Wasistho, and colleagues, uses a multiblock structured mesh. Rocflu, developed primarily by Haselbacher, uses a mixed unstructured mesh. Both solvers provide second- or higher-order accuracy in both space and time [8]. To accommodate dynamically changing fluid domains, these solvers allow for moving meshes using an arbitrary Lagrangian–Eulerian (ALE) formulation. The geometric conservation law (GCL) [24] is satisfied in a discrete sense to within machine precision to avoid the introduction of spurious sources of mass, momentum, and energy due to grid motion.

Solid mechanics solvers. Rocsolid and Rocfrac are two general-purpose finite-element solvers for linear and nonlinear elastic problems with large deformations for modeling the propellant, insulation, case, and nozzle of a rocket. Both modules support moving meshes using an ALE formulation. Rocsolid, developed by Namazifard, Parsons, and colleagues, is an implicit solver using unstructured hexahedral meshes [18]. It provides a scalable geometric multigrid method for symmetric linear systems [19] and a BiCGSTAB method for nonsymmetric systems. Rocfrac, developed by Breitenfeld and Geubelle, is an explicit solver that uses linear (4-node) or quadratic (10-node) tetrahedral elements for complex geometries, with additional support for other types of elements for anisotropic geometries. Rocfrac can also simulate complex dynamic fracture problems using an explicit cohesive volumetric finite element (CVFE) scheme [6].

Combustion modules. The combustion module Rocburn provides the regression rate of solid propellant at the burning propellant surface. Developed by Tang, Massa, and colleagues, Rocburn comprises three interchangeable 1D combustion models plus an adaptor module. The combustion models calculate the burning rate at any given point on the burning surface using either a quasi-steady combustion model [10] or one of two unsteady combustion models [22, 23]. The adaptor module manages data and interacts with other modules at the level of the burning surface. In addition, Rocburn simulates the ignition of the propellant under convective heat flux, when a thermal boundary layer is present in

344 Chapter 18. Parallel Methods and Software for Multicomponent Simulations

the fluids modules. The models in Rocburn are in turn informed by more detailed results from Rocfire, developed by Massa, Jackson, and Short [16], which models combustion of heterogeneous solid propellant at micron-scale resolution. These scales are small enough to capture the interaction between gas phase fields and solid phase morphology. The models implemented in Rocfire are on too fine a scale to be integrated directly into Rocstar, but they are critical for calibrating the homogenized combustion models used in Rocburn.

18.1.2 High-performance implementations

All the physics modules are implemented in FORTRAN 90 and employ derived data types and pointers extensively to achieve data encapsulation and modularity. To achieve high serial performance, computationally intensive parts of the codes are written in FORTRAN 77 style (e.g., avoiding use of pointers) or utilize LAPACK routines [1] whenever possible.

Each physics module is parallelized for distributed memory machines using a domain-decomposition approach. For Rocflo, which uses multiblock structured meshes, parallelization is based on the block topology, where each processor may own one or more blocks. For other modules using unstructured meshes, their parallel implementations are based on element-based partitioning of meshes, typically with one partition per process. For interblock or interpartition data exchange, the finite-volume fluids codes utilize the concept of ghost cells, with the difference that Rocflo uses nonblocking persistent communication calls of MPI [7], whereas Rocflu utilizes the services provided by the finite element framework built on top of MPI [2]. For the finite-element solids modules, the nodes along partition boundaries are shared by multiple processes, and their values are communicated using nonblocking MPI calls. Rocburn is solved on the burning patches of either the fluid or solid surface meshes, and its decomposition is derived from that of the volume mesh of the corresponding parent module.

All the physics modules are designed to take advantage of AMPI, which is a multi-threaded version of MPI that supports virtual processes and dynamic migration [9]. Developed in Kalé's group at Illinois, AMPI is based on Charm++, provides virtually all the standard MPI calls, and can be linked with any MPI code with only minor changes to driver routines. Its virtual processes allow emulating larger machines with smaller ones and overlapping communication with computation, as demonstrated by the example in Figure 18.2. To take full advantage of virtual processes, we have eliminated global variables in nearly all

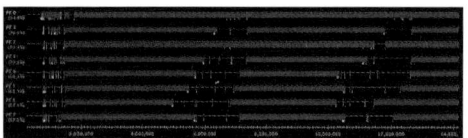
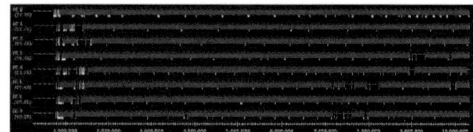

(a) 8 virtual on 8 physical processors.   (b) 64 virtual on 8 physical processors.

Figure 18.2. *AMPI minimizes idle times (gaps in plots) by overlapping communication with computation on different virtual procs. Courtesy of Charm group.*

modules in Rocstar. For each physics module, whose data are well encapsulated to begin with, a context object (of a derived data type) is introduced to contain pointers to all the data used by the module. The context object of each physics module is privatized for each virtual process with the aid of the data registration and function invocation mechanisms of Roccom, which we describe shortly. Utilizing AMPI, our physics code developers and users can, for example, run a 480-process dataset by using 480 virtual AMPI processes on just 32 physical processors of a Linux cluster, and they can take advantage of parallelism within a process, without having to use a complex hybrid MPI plus OpenMP programming paradigm.

18.2 Integration framework and middleware services

To facilitate interactions between physics modules, we have developed an object-oriented, data-centric integration framework called Roccom that allows individual components to be developed as independently as possible and then integrated subsequently with little or no change. Roccom provides maximum flexibility for physics codes and can be adapted to fit the diverse needs of components, instead of requiring the components to be adapted to fit the framework. Roccom differs from many traditional software architectures and frameworks, which are often designed for extension instead of integration and typically assume that the framework is in full control.

18.2.1 Management of distributed objects

The design of Roccom is based on the notion of persistent objects. An object is said to be persistent if it lasts beyond a major coupled simulation step. In a typical physics module, especially in the high-performance regime, data objects are allocated during an initialization stage, reused for multiple iterations of calculations, and deallocated during a finalization stage, so that most objects are naturally persistent in multipcomponent simulations.

Based on the assumption of persistence, Roccom organizes data into distributed objects called *windows* and provides a registration mechanism for them. A window encapsulates a number of *data attributes*, such as the coordinates, connectivities, and field variables associated with a mesh. A window can be partitioned into multiple *panes* for exploiting parallelism or for distinguishing different types of materials or boundary conditions. In a parallel setting, a pane belongs to a single process, while a process may own any number of panes. A module constructs windows at runtime by creating attributes and registering their addresses. Different modules can communicate with each other only through windows, as illustrated in Figure 18.3.

The window-and-pane data abstraction of Roccom drastically simplifies intermodule interaction: data objects of physics modules are registered and reorganized into windows, so that their implementation details are hidden from the framework and need not be altered extensively to fit the framework. Service utilities can now also be developed independently, by interacting only with window objects. Window objects are self-descriptive, and in turn the interface functions can be simplified substantially, frequently reducing the number of functions or the number of arguments per function by an order of magnitude. Roccom also introduces the novel concept of *partial inheritance* of windows to construct a subwindow

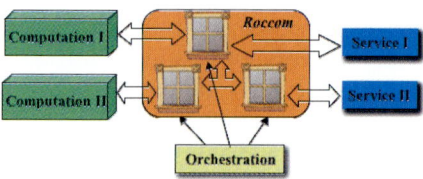

Figure 18.3. *Windows and panes.*

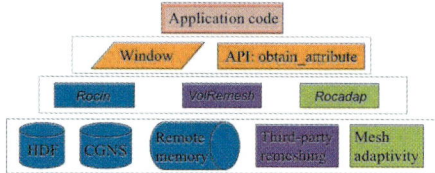

Figure 18.4. *Abstraction of data input.*

by *using* or *cloning* a subset of the mesh or attributes of another window. In addition, the registered attributes in Roccom can be referenced as an aggregate, such as using "mesh" to refer to the collection of nodal coordinates and element connectivity. These advanced features enable performing complex tasks, such as reading or writing data for a whole window, with only one or two function calls. For more information on the novel features of Roccom, see [11].

On top of Roccom, we have developed a number of reusable service modules, including *middleware* services, such as I/O, communication, and performance tools, which we describe in the following subsections, as well mathematical services, which we discuss in the next section.

18.2.2 Data I/O

In scientific simulations, data exchange between a module and the outside world can be very complex. For file I/O alone, a developer already must face many issues, including various file formats, parallel efficiency, platform compatibility, and interoperability with offline tools. In a dynamic simulation, the situation is even more complex, as the code may need to exchange its mesh and data attributes with mesh repair or remeshing services or to receive data from remote processes.

To meet these challenges, we use the window abstraction of Roccom as the medium or "virtual file" for all data exchanges for a module, regardless of whether the other side is a service utility, files of various formats, or remote machines, and let middleware services take care of the mapping between the window and the other side. For example, file I/O services map Roccom windows with scientific file formats (such as HDF and CGNS), so that the details of file formats and optimization techniques become transparent to application modules. Furthermore, as illustrated in Figure 18.4, all application modules obtain data from an input window through a generic function interface, obtain_attribute(), which is supported by a number of services, including file readers and remeshing tools. This novel design allows physics modules to use the same initialization routine to obtain data under different circumstances, including initial startup, restart, restart after remeshing, or reinitialization after mesh repair.

18.2.3 Interpane communication

Traditional message-passing paradigms typically provide general but low-level interprocess communications, such as send, receive, and broadcast. In physical simulations using finite element or finite volume methods, communications are typically across panes or partitions, whether the panes or partitions are on the same or different processes. The Roccom framework provides high-level interpane communication abstractions, including performing reductions (such as sum, max, and min operations) on shared nodes, and updating values for ghost (i.e., locally cached copies of remote values of) nodes or elements. Communication patterns between these nodes and elements are encapsulated in the *pane connectivity* of a window, which can be provided by application modules or constructed automatically in parallel using geometric algorithms. These interpane communication abstractions simplify parallelization of a large number of modules, including surface propagation and mesh smoothing, which we discuss in the next section.

18.2.4 Performance monitoring

There is a large variety of tools for the collection and analysis of performance data for parallel applications. However, the use of external tools for performance tuning is too laborious a process for many applications, especially for a complex integrated system such as Rocstar. Many tools are not available on all the platforms for which we wish to collect data, and using a disparate collection of tools introduces complications as well. To obviate the need for external tools, we have extended the Roccom framework's "service-based" design philosophy with the development of a performance profiling module, Rocprof.

Rocprof provides two modes of profiling: module-level profiling and submodule-level profiling. The module-level profiling is fully automatic, embedded in Roccom's function invocation mechanism, and hence requires no user intervention. For submodule-level profiling, Rocprof offers profiling services through the standard `MPI_Pcontrol` interface, as well as a native interface for non-MPI based codes. By utilizing the `MPI_Pcontrol` interface, applications developers can collect profiling information for arbitrary, user-defined sections of source code without breaking their stand-alone codes. Internally, Rocprof uses PAPI [4] or HPM from IBM to collect hardware performance statistics.

18.3 Parallel computational methods

In Rocstar, a physical domain is decomposed into a volume mesh, which can be either block structured or unstructured, and the numerical discretization is based on either a finite element or finite volume method. The interface between fluid and solid moves due to both chemical burning and mechanical deformation. In such a context, we must address a large number of mathematical issues, three of which we discuss here.

18.3.1 Intermodule data transfer

In multiphysics simulations, the computational domains for each physical component are frequently meshed independently, so that geometric algorithms are required to correlate the surface meshes at the common interface between each pair of interacting domains to exchange boundary conditions. These surface meshes in general differ both geometrically and combinatorially and are also partitioned differently in a parallel setting. To correlate such interface meshes, we have developed a novel algorithm to construct a *common refinement* of two triangular or quadrilateral meshes modeling the same surface, that is, a finer mesh whose polygons subdivide the polygons of the input surface meshes [14]. To resolve geometric mismatch, the algorithm determines a *conforming homeomorphism* between the meshes and utilizes locality and duality to achieve optimal linear time complexity. Because the problem is nonlinear, our algorithm uses iterative solution methods and floating-point arithmetic but nevertheless achieves provable robustness by identifying a set of consistency rules and an intersection principle to resolve any inconsistencies due to numerical errors.

After constructing the common refinement, we must transfer data between the nonmatching meshes in a numerically accurate and physically conservative manner. Traditional methods, including pointwise interpolation and some weighted residual methods, can achieve either accuracy or conservation, but none could achieve both simultaneously. Leveraging the common refinement, we developed more advanced formulations and optimal discretizations that minimize errors in a certain norm while achieving strict conservation, yielding significant advantages over traditional methods, especially for repeated transfers in multiphysics simulations [12]. In a parallel setting, the common refinement also identifies the correlation of elements across partitions of different meshes and hence provides the communication structure needed for intermodule, interprocess data exchange. This communication structure is precise and can be reused for many iterations of a simulation. If both input meshes are well balanced across processors, our parallel data transfer scheme delivers excellent scalability, as demonstrated in Figure 18.5 for a scaled, well-balanced problem on up to 960 processors on ALC (ASC Linux Cluster with 2.4GHz Pentium IV processors and QsNet interconnection; www.llnl.gov/asci/platforms).

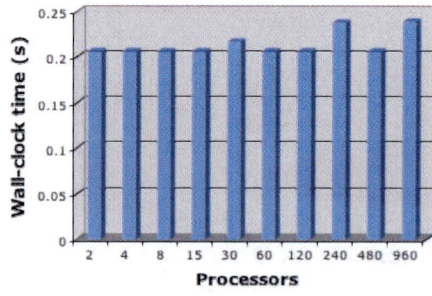

Figure 18.5. *Scalability of data transfer on Linux cluster.*

18.3.2 Mesh optimization

In Rocstar, each physics module operates on some type of mesh. An outstanding issue in integrated rocket simulations is the degradation of mesh quality due to the changing geometry resulting from consumption of propellant by burning, which causes the solid region to shrink and the fluid region to expand and compresses or inflates their respective meshes. This degradation can lead to excessively small time-steps when an element becomes poorly shaped, or even outright failure when an element becomes inverted. Some simple mesh motion algorithms are built into our physics modules. For example, simple Laplacian smoothing is used for unstructured meshes, and a combination of linear transfinite interpolation (TFI) with Laplacian smoothing is used for structured meshes in Rocflo. These simple schemes are insufficient, however, when a mesh undergoes substantial deformation or distortion. To address this issue, we take a three-tiered approach, in increasing order of aggressiveness: mesh smoothing, mesh repair, and global remeshing.

Mesh smoothing copes with gradual changes in the mesh. We provide a combination of in-house tools and integration of external packages. Our in-house effort focuses on parallel, feature-aware surface mesh optimization and provides novel parallel algorithms for mixed meshes with both triangles and quadrilaterals. To smooth volume meshes, we utilize the serial MESQUITE package [5] from Sandia National Laboratories, which also works for mixed meshes, and we have adapted it for use in parallel by leveraging our across-pane communication abstractions. The blue (lower) curve in Figure 18.6 shows the speed-ups of the parallelized MESQUITE for a tetrahedral mesh with approximately 0.8 million elements on up to 128 processors of the Turing Linux cluster at UIUC, with 1GHz Pentium III processors and Myrinet interconnection network.

If the mesh deforms more substantially, then mesh smoothing becomes inadequate and more aggressive mesh repair or even global remeshing may be required, although the latter is too expensive to perform very frequently. For these more drastic measures, we currently focus on only tetrahedral meshes and leverage third-party tools offline, including Yams and TetMesh from Simulog and MeshSim from Simmetrix, but we have work in progress to integrate MeshSim into our framework for online use. Remeshing requires that data be mapped from the old mesh onto the new mesh, for which we have developed parallel algorithms to transfer both node- and cell-centered data accurately, built on top of

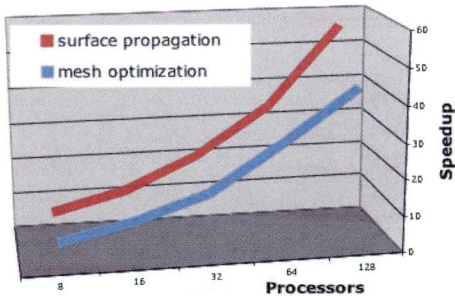

Figure 18.6. *Speed-ups of mesh optimization and surface propagation.*

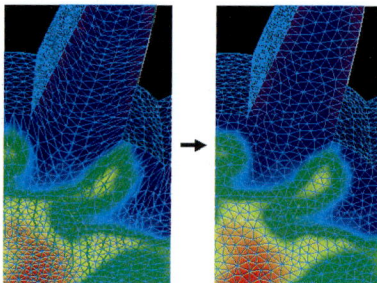

Figure 18.7. *Example of remeshing and data transfer for deformed star grain.*

the parallel collision detection package developed by Lawlor and Kalé [15]. Figure 18.7 shows an example where a deformed star-shaped section of solid propellant is remeshed, with the temperature field of the fluid volume transferred from the old to the new mesh.

18.3.3 Surface propagation

In Rocstar, the interface between fluid and solid domains must be tracked as it regresses due to burning. In recent years, Eulerian methods, especially level set methods, have made significant advancements and have become the dominant methods for moving interfaces [20, 21]. In our context, Lagrangian representation of the interface is crucial to describe the boundary of volume meshes of physical regions, but there was no known stable numerical method for Lagrangian surface propagation.

To meet this challenge, we have developed a novel class of methods, called *face-offsetting methods*, based on a new *entropy-satisfying Lagrangian (ESL) formulation* [13]. Our face-offsetting methods exploit some fundamental ideas used by level set methods, together with well-established numerical techniques to provide accurate and stable entropy-satisfying solutions, without requiring Eulerian volume meshes. A fundamental difference between face-offsetting and traditional Lagrangian methods is that our methods solve the Lagrangian formulation face by face and then reconstruct vertices by constrained minimization and curvature-aware averaging, instead of directly moving vertices along some approximate normal directions. Figure 18.8 shows a sample result of the initial burn of a star grain section of a rocket motor, which exhibits rapid expansion at slots and contraction at fins.

Our method also lends itself to parallelism, with communication patterns similar to those in finite element solvers, which are easily implemented using our interpane communication abstractions. The red (upper) curve in Figure 18.6 shows sample speed-up results for a surface mesh with approximately 60,000 triangles on up to 128 processors of the Turing Linux cluster. Our algorithm includes an integrated node redistribution scheme that suffices to control mesh quality for moderately moving interfaces without perturbing the geometry. Currently, we are coupling it with more sophisticated geometric and topological

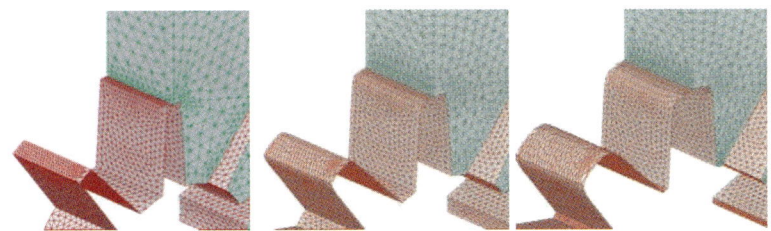

Figure 18.8. *Initial burn of star slice exhibits rapid expansion at slots and contraction at fins. Images correspond to 0%, 6%, and 12% burns, respectively.*

algorithms for mesh adaptivity and topological control to provide a more complete solution for a broader range of applications.

18.4 Results of coupled simulations

18.4.1 Verification and validation

The Rocstar code suite has been tested on a number of 3D problems, some of which are used for qualitative validation, while others have specific analytical results that should be matched. One of our major test problems is the propellant slumping in the Titan IV SRMU Prequalification Motor #1 [25]. Figure 18.9 shows the propellant deformation nearly 1 second after ignition for an incompressible neo-Hookean material model, obtained from 3D simulations with Rocstar. The deformation is due to an aeroelastic effect and is particularly noticeable near joint slots. The resulting flow restriction led to catastrophic failure of the real rocket on the test stand. The space shuttle reusable solid rocket motor (RSRM) is another example. The results shown in Figure 18.10, in which the ignition and dynamic burn rate models are used in simulating the entire RSRM [22], match well qualitatively with experimental data obtained from NASA. These simulations are performed on 500 or more processors and may run for several weeks.

18.4.2 Performance results

In high-performance computing, serial performance is frequently critical to achieving good overall performance. With the aid of Rocprof, code developers have been able to tune their modules selectively. Figure 18.11 shows sample statistics of hardware counters for Rocfrac, obtained by Rocprof on ALC (ASC Linux Cluster). Figure 18.12 shows the absolute performance of Rocstar and the computationally intensive Rocfrac and Rocflo on a number of platforms. Overall, Rocstar achieves a respectable 16% of peak performance on ALC and 10% or higher on other platforms.

To measure the scalability of Rocstar, we use a *scaled* problem, in which the problem size is proportional to the number of processors, so that the amount of work per process remains constant. Ideally, the wall-clock time should remain constant if scalability is

352 Chapter 18. Parallel Methods and Software for Multicomponent Simulations

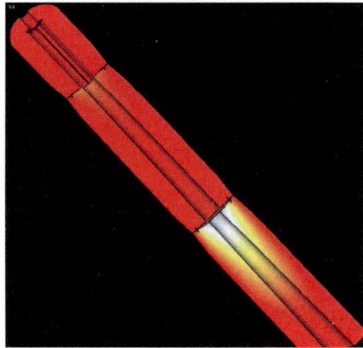

Figure 18.9. *Titan IV propellant deformation after 1 second.*

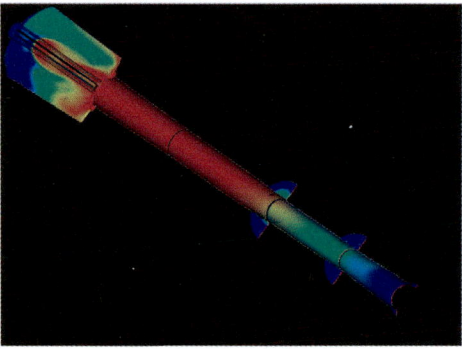

Figure 18.10. *RSRM propellant temperature at 175 ms.*

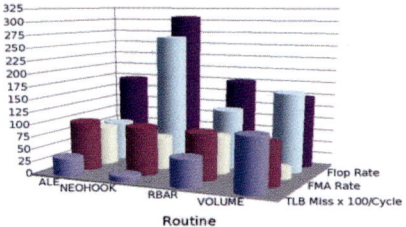

Figure 18.11. *Hardware counters for Rocfrac obtained by Rocprof.*

perfect. Figure 18.13 shows the wall-clock times per iteration using explicit-implicit coupling between Rocflo and Rocsolid, with a five-to-one ratio (i.e., five explicit fluid timesteps for each implicit solid time-step), on up to 480 processors on ASC White (Frost), based upon IBM's POWER3 SP technology. Figure 18.14 shows wall-clock time for the explicit-explicit coupling between Rocflu and Rocfrac, on up to 480 processors on ALC. In both cases scalability is excellent, even for very large numbers of processors. The interface code, which is predominantly data transfer between fluid and solid interfaces, takes less than 2% of the overall time. Times for other modules are negligible and hence are not shown.

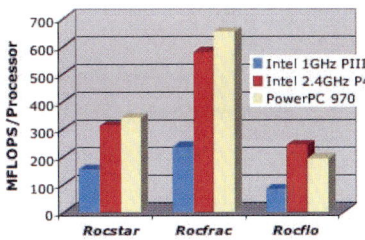

Figure 18.12. *Absolute performance of Rocstar on Linux and Mac.*

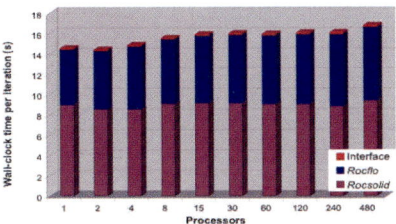

Figure 18.13. *Scalability with Rocflo and Rocsolid on IBM SP.*

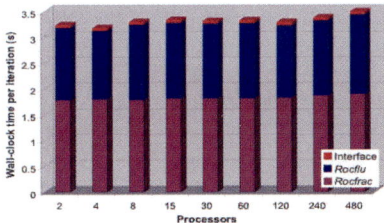

Figure 18.14. *Scalability with Rocflu and Rocfrac on Linux cluster.*

18.5 Conclusion

In this chapter, we have given an overview of some software and algorithmic issues in developing high-performance simulation tools for multicomponent systems, based on our experience in coupled simulation of solid propellant rockets. Working as an interdisciplinary team, we have made substantial progress in advancing the state of the art for such simulations, especially in data transfer between components, propagation of and adaptation to geometric change, and the flexible software integration framework in which these and other novel algorithmic and software technologies are incorporated.

Many challenging research issues remain, however, including distributed algorithms and data structures for parallel mesh repair and adaptivity, generation and partitioning of extremely large meshes under memory constraints, parallel mesh adaptation for crack propagation in three dimensions, and data transfer at sliding and adaptive interfaces. These issues offer new research opportunities and will require close collaboration between computer and engineering scientists to devise effective and practical methodologies to deal with them.

Acknowledgments

The research results presented in this chapter are snapshots of many research contributions made by our colleagues at CSAR, as we have noted in the text. The CSAR research program is supported by the U.S. Department of Energy through the University of California under Subcontract B523819.

Bibliography

[1] E. ANDERSON, Z. BAI, C. BISCHOF, S. BLACKFORD, J. DEMMEL, J. DONGARRA, J. DU CROZ, A. GREENBAUM, S. HAMMERLING, A. MCKENNEY, AND D. SORENSEN, *LAPACK Users' Guide*, SIAM, Philadelphia, 3rd ed., 1999.

[2] M. BHANDARKAR AND L. V. KALÉ, *A parallel framework for explicit FEM*, in Proc. Internat. Conf. High Performance Computing (HiPC 2000), M. Valero et al., eds., Springer, Berlin, 2000, pp. 385–395.

[3] J. BLAZEK, *Flow simulation in solid rocket motors using advanced CFD*, in 39th AIAA/ASME/SAE/ASEE Joint Propulsion Conf. and Exhibit, Huntsville Alabama, 2003. AIAA Paper 2003-5111.

[4] S. BROWNE, J. DONGARRA, N. GARNER, G. HO, AND P. MUCCI, *A portable programming interface for performance evaluation on modern processors*, International Journal of High Performance Computing Applications, 14 (2000), pp. 189–204.

[5] L. FREITAG, T. LEURENT, P. KNUPP, AND D. MELANDER, *MESQUITE design: Issues in the development of a mesh quality improvement toolkit*, in Proceedings of 8th Intl. Conf. Numer. Grid Gener. Comput. Field Sim., 2002, Honolulu, pp. 159–168.

[6] P. H. GEUBELLE AND J. BAYLOR, *Impact-induced delamination of composites: a 2D simulation*, Composites B, 29B (1998), pp. 589–602.

[7] W. GROPP, E. LUSK, AND A. SKJELLUM, *Using MPI: Portable Parallel Programming with the Message-Passing Interface*, 2nd ed., MIT Press, Cambridge, MA, 1999.

[8] A. HASELBACHER, *A WENO reconstruction method for unstructured grids based on explicit stencil construction*, in 43rd AIAA Aerospace Sciences Meeting and Exhibit, Reno, NV, Jan. 2005. AIAA Paper 2005-0879, to appear.

[9] C. HUANG, O. S. LAWLOR, AND L. V. KALÉ, *Adaptive MPI*, in Proc. 16th Internat. Workshop on Languages and Compilers for Parallel Computing (LCPC 03), October 2003, College Station, TX.

[10] C. HUGGETT, C. E. BARTLEY, AND M. M. MILLS, *Solid Propellant Rockets*, Princeton University Press, Princeton, NJ, 1960.

[11] X. JIAO, M. T. CAMPBELL, AND M. T. HEATH, *Roccom: An object-oriented, datacentric software integration framework for multiphysics simulations*, in 17th Annual ACM International Conference on Supercomputing, 2003, pp. 358–368.

[12] X. JIAO AND M. T. HEATH, *Common-refinement based data transfer between non-matching meshes in multiphysics simulations*, International Journal for Numerical Methods in Engineering, 61 (2004), pp. 2402–2427.

[13] ———, *Face-offsetting methods for entropy-satisfying Lagrangian surface propagation*. In preparation, 2006.

[14] ———, *Overlaying surface meshes. I. Algorithms*, International Journal of Computational Geometry and Applications, 14 (2004), pp. 379–402.

[15] O. S. LAWLOR AND L. V. KALÉ, *A voxel-based parallel collision detection algorithm*, in Proc. International Conference Supercomputing, June 2002, New York, NY, pp. 285–293.

[16] L. MASSA, T. L. JACKSON, AND M. SHORT, *Numerical simulation of three-dimensional heterogeneous propellant*, Combustion Theory and Modelling, 7 (2003), pp. 579–602.

[17] F. M. NAJJAR, A. HASELBACHER, J. P. FERRY, B. WASISTHO, S. BALACHANDAR, AND R. D. MOSER, *Large-scale multiphase large-eddy simulation of flows in solid-rocket motors*, in 16th AIAA Computational Fluid Dynamics Conf., Orlando, FL, June 2003. AIAA Paper 2003-3700.

[18] A. NAMAZIFARD, I. D. PARSONS, A. ACHARYA, E. TACIROGLU, AND J. HALES, *Parallel structural analysis of solid rocket motors*, in AIAA/ASME/SAE/ASEE Joint Propulsion Conf., 2000. AIAA Paper 2000-3457.

[19] A. NAMAZIFARD AND I. D. PARSONS, *A distributed memory parallel implementation of the multigrid method for solving three-dimensional implicit solid mechanics problems*, International Journal for Numerical Methods in Engineering, 61 (2004), pp. 1173–1208.

[20] S. OSHER AND R. FEDKIW, *Level Set Methods and Dynamic Implicit Surfaces*, Springer, Berlin, New York, 2003.

[21] J. A. SETHIAN, *Level Set Methods and Fast Marching Methods*, Cambridge University Press, Cambridge, UK, 1999.

[22] K. C. TANG AND M. Q. BREWSTER, *Dynamic combustion of AP composite propellants: Ignition pressure spike*, 2001. AIAA Paper 2001-4502.

[23] ———, *Nonlinear dynamic combustion in solid rockets: L^*-effects*, J. Propulsion and Power, 14 (2001), pp. 909–918.

[24] P. D. THOMAS AND C. K. LOMBARD, *Geometric conservation law and its application to flow computations on moving grids*, AIAA Journal, 17 (1979), pp. 1030–1037.

[25] W. G. WILSON, J. M. ANDERSON, AND M. VANDER MEYDEN, *Titan IV SRMU PQM-1 overview*, 1992. AIAA Paper 92-3819.

Chapter 19
Parallel Computational Biology

Srinivas Aluru, Nancy Amato, David A. Bader, Suchindra Bhandarkar, Laxmikant Kale, and Dan C. Marinescu

The emerging field of computational biology is replete with challenging, large-scale problems that could benefit from effective use of high-performance parallel computing. Many problems in biology are irregular in structure, and significantly challenging to parallelize and often involve integer-based abstract data structures. Biological problems may require high-performance computing due either to problems involving massive datasets or to optimization problems that lie between difficult and intractable. Many problems use seemingly well-behaved polynomial-time algorithms (e.g., all-to-all comparisons) but have massive computing requirements because of the large datasets analyzed, for example, the assembly of an entire genome. Other problems are compute intensive due to their inherent algorithmic complexity, such as protein folding and reconstructing evolutionary histories from molecular data. Some of these problems are known to be NP-hard and often require approximations that are themselves complex.

In this chapter, we briefly summarize the work by the authors and their respective research groups in solving an assortment of large-scale or compute-intensive problems in computational molecular biology. This chapter is based on the SIAM minisymposium presentations given by the authors and should not be taken as representative of the breadth of research in high-performance computational biology. Nevertheless, the research presented here spans a number of subfields of computational biology, including genomics, phylogenetics, and protein structural biology.

19.1 Assembling the maize genome

As the best studied biological model for cereals and an economically important crop, there is strong rationale for sequencing the maize genome. While comparable in size to the human genome [1], it is estimated that 65% to 80% of maize genome is composed of highly similar repetitive sequences, dominated by tens of thousands of copies of large, highly homogeneous retrotransposons [5]. This renders traditional strategies such as whole genome shotgun assembly ineffective. At the risk of oversimplification, whole genome shotgun assembly can be thought of as the problem of identifying an unknown sequence, given a large number of uniformly sampled short fragments of it. Overlaps between fragments derived from the same region of the genome are the primary source of information in generating the assembly. The presence of an overwhelming number of repeats does not allow one to draw the conclusion that overlapping fragments can be meaningfully assembled.

The most important goal of a genome sequencing project is to decipher the portion of the genome containing genes and to map the approximate locations and the relative orientations of the genes along the chromosomes. In case of maize, the gene space constitutes 10% to 15% of the genome and is largely outside the repetitive regions [5]. In light of this, alternative sequencing strategies to bias the sampling toward the gene space are recommended [5]. The National Science Foundation funded two projects to compare three strategies for sequencing the maize genome (DBI 0221536 and DBI 0211851 [16, 25]). The first strategy, methyl filtration (MF), utilizes strains of *E. coli* that degrade methylated DNA to enrich for the gene-rich fraction of the genome [19]. This approach is effective because plant genes tend to be hypomethylated relative to transposons and other nongenic sequences. The second strategy enriches for genes by sequencing only the high $C_o t$ (HC) fraction of the genome in which the frequency of low-copy sequences has been normalized [17, 26]. Repetitive sequences hybridize more often in a heterogeneous mixture of single-stranded genomic DNA fragments; consequently, removing double-stranded sequences after some elapsed time enriches for lower-copy sequences. The third approach involves sequencing bacterial artificial chromosomes (BACs) and BAC ends to obtain a "random" sample of the genome. Later, it was also decided to sequence a number of "gene-rich" BACs. As a result, 450,197 MF, 445,631 HC, and 50,877 shotgun (unfiltered) sequences from the inbred line B73 have been deposited in GenBank.

Traditional assembly programs are designed to assemble shotgun sequence data, which approximates a uniform random sampling of the genome. Most assembly programs function by finding overlaps between fragments. Because of sequencing errors, potential overlaps must be detected using a dynamic programming based alignment algorithm, whose runtime is proportional to the product of the lengths of the fragments being aligned. As aligning all pairs of fragments is computationally expensive, faster methods typically using lookup tables were developed to first identify pairs of sequences that have an exact match of a minimum threshold size. Alignments are then restricted to only such pairs, which we term promising pairs. The number of promising pairs is proportional to the number of fragments for random shotgun data. In contrast, for highly nonuniform sampling such as results from gene enrichment (MF and HC), this number can, in the worst case, be proportional to the square of the number of fragments. The memory required by these programs scales similarly, causing exorbitant memory usage. Furthermore, as the lookup table data structure is useful only in detecting exact matches of a specific size (say, k), long exact matches are revealed as multiple overlapping matches of size k. If not done carefully, this causes additional memory usage as well.

To overcome these limitations, we developed algorithmic techniques for the accurate assembly of maize fragments [7]. Our methodology limits memory usage to linear in the size of input, contains heuristic strategies that significantly reduce the number of pairwise alignments without affecting quality, and uses parallel processing to accelerate the assembly and facilitate assembling of large-scale data. This resulted in the first published draft genome assembly of the complete set of fragments described above (http://www.plantgenomics.iastate.edu/maize) and was carried out in only 3 hours on a 64-processor Myrinet commodity cluster. We briefly describe the methodology adopted in parallel assembly of the maize genome.

Because of the nature of the sequencing strategies employed, the resulting assembly is expected to be a large number of genomic islands separated by vast stretches of the genome dominated by repetitive sequences. If we could cluster the sequences that belong to each genomic island, the multiple clusters can be assembled trivially in parallel using a traditional sequence assembly program such as CAP3 [11]. The memory and runtime issues of a traditional assembler would no longer be an issue because the size of each cluster is significantly smaller than the complete set of input fragments. This approach was adopted to avoid duplicating the functionality of the assembler and accelerate the production of public availability of the assembly.

Given a set of n input fragments, we define the clustering problem as that of computing a partition of the set of fragments with the following property. Two fragments are in the same subset (cluster) of the partition if there exists a sequence of overlaps leading from one fragment to the other. Each cluster is expected to correspond to fragments forming a genomic island. The clusters are computed as follows. Initially, each fragment is considered a cluster by itself. If a pair of fragments from two different clusters can be identified such that they exhibit strong overlap as computed by the alignment algorithm, then the clusters can be combined into a single cluster. The clusters can be maintained using the classic union-find data structure [12]. Note that the maximum number of union operations required to compute the correct answer is $O(n)$, irrespective of whether the fragments constitute a uniform sampling or biased sampling. The difficulty is in identifying those pairs that will quickly lead us to the final set of clusters.

Because of low frequency of sequencing errors, any good alignment must contain long regions of exact matches. Taking advantage of this, we generate promising pairs of fragments that share an exact match of at least a prespecified threshold size. Once a pair is generated, the current set of clusters is consulted to identify the clusters containing the two fragments of the pair (Find operation). If they are already in the same cluster, no alignment is performed. If they belong to different clusters, an alignment is performed and detection of a good alignment will lead to combining the respective clusters. Significant savings in run-time can be achieved by fast identification of pairs that yield a positive outcome when the pairwise alignment algorithm is run. Although all promising pairs are generated by the algorithm, forming clusters early will eliminate the need to align many of the generated pairs. To increase the chance of finding successful alignments early, we generate promising pairs in decreasing order of the length of a shared maximal common substring.

The parallel clustering framework is described in Figure 19.1. We first compute a distributed representation of the generalized suffix tree (GST) of all the input fragments in parallel [14]. Each internal node in a suffix tree corresponds to a common substring shared by all the strings represented in the subtree underneath it. As we are not interested in short exact matches, the top levels of the tree are irrelevant. Pair generation is internal to a subtree. Therefore, each processor can independently generate promising pairs. We designed an

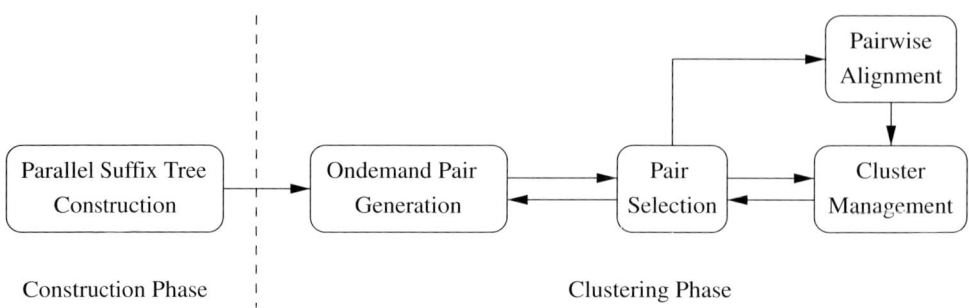

Figure 19.1. *Parallel clustering framework.*

Table 19.1. *Assembly statistics and runtime on a 64-processor Pentium III 1.26 GZH Myrinet Cluster.*

Number of fragments	946,705
Post repeat masking	875,523
Assembly size (Mb)	176.9
Number of islands	114,173
Avg. fragments per contig	5.85
Avg. island length (bp)	1550
Max. island length (bp)	12498

Stage	Approximate runtime (mins)
Contaminated fragment removal	10
Repeat Masking	20
Parallel Clustering	120
CAP3 Assembly	30
Total	180

algorithm that generates pairs on demand in decreasing order of maximal common substring length, without the need to store any previously generated pairs. Thus, the total memory requirement of our algorithm over all processors is that required for maintaining the GST, which is $O(n)$. The clusters are maintained at one designated master processor. The other processors are expected to both generate promising pairs based on the subtrees contained in it, and perform alignments as necessary. The generated pairs are communicated to the master processor which filters the list to generate pairs to be aligned based on current set of clusters. The pairs are then sent for alignment to one of the processors. Additional flexibility is achieved by not requiring the processor generating the pair and that performing the alignment to be identical.

Once the clusters are formed, each cluster is assembled into a genomic island using CAP3. If a more relaxed overlap criteria is used in forming clusters, each cluster can result in a small number of genomic islands. The clusters are distributed to processors in a load balanced fashion and CAP3 is run on each cluster to form the genomic islands. The statistics of the assembly and runtime are presented in Table 19.1. Removal of contaminated fragments and known and statistically defined repetitive fragments can be trivially done in parallel by partitioning the sequences across processors and each processor processing the sequences allocated to it. The clustering took only 2 hours on 64 Pentium III 1.26 GHZ processors. The same was carried out in about half an hour on 512 nodes of the IBM BlueGene/L.

Genome assembly is often viewed as a complex process taking weeks to months of computational effort by specialized assembly groups. The main contribution of the presented work is to use a combination of improved algorithms and parallel processing to drastically reduce the runtime. This allows quick dissemination of the resulting analysis and encourages experimentation of the assembly process (e.g., How sensitive is the assembly to parameter choices?). More recently, the DoE Joint Genome Institute deposited more than a million shotgun maize fragments. The Institute of Genome Research and the Whitehead Institute have deposited more than 800,000 fragments from maize BACs. The NSF Plant Genome Research program, in conjunction with DoE and USDA, is planning funding for large-scale sequencing of the maize genome. As these projects continue to generate large numbers of maize fragments, we hope to continue to provide assemblies at a rapid pace through the use of high-performance parallel computing.

19.2 An information theoretic approach to genome reconstruction

Creating maps of entire chromosomes, which could then be used to reconstruct the chromosome's DNA sequence, has been one of the fundamental problems in genetics right from its inception [35]. These maps are central to the understanding of the structure of genes, their function, their transmission, and their evolution. Chromosomal maps fall into two broad categories—*genetic maps* and *physical maps*. Genetic maps are typically of low resolution (1 to 10 Mb) and represent an ordering of genetic markers along a chromosome where the distance between two genetic markers is related to their recombination frequency. While genetic maps enable a scientist to narrow the search for genes to a particular chromosomal region, it is a physical map that ultimately allows the recovery and molecular manipulation of genes of interest.

A physical map is an ordering of distinguishable (i.e., sequenced) DNA fragments called *clones* or *contigs* by their position along the entire chromosome where the clones may or may not contain genetic markers. The physical mapping problem is therefore one of reconstructing the order of clones and determining their position along the chromosome. A physical map has a much higher resolution than a genetic map of the same chromosome i.e., 10,000 to 100,000 base pairs (Kb). Physical maps have provided fundamental insights into gene development, gene organization, chromosome structure, recombination, and the role of sex in evolution and have also provided a means for the recovery and molecular manipulation of genes of interest.

We model the problem of physical map generation on the information theoretic concept of maximum likelihood reconstruction of signals that have been corrupted by noise when transmitted through a communications channel. The chromosome is modeled as the original signal, the hybridization experiment as the process of transmission through a communications channel, the hybridization errors as the noise introduced by the communications channel, the binary hybridization matrix as the observed corrupted signal at the receiving end of the communications channel, and the desired physical map as the reconstructed signal. In particular, the maximum likelihood (ML) estimation-based approach to physical map construction proposed in [29, 32] is described. In this approach, the probe ordering and interprobe spacings are determined such that the probability of occurrence of the experimentally observed binary hybridization matrix H is maximized under a probabilistic model of hybridization errors consisting of false positives and false negatives. The binary hybridization matrix H is generated using the sampling without replacement protocol under which the probes are selected to be a maximal nonoverlapping subset of the clones that covers the length of the chromosome. If the probes are ordered with respect to their position along a chromosome, then by selecting from H a common overlapping clone for each pair of adjacent probes, a minimal set of clones and probes that covers the entire chromosome (i.e., a minimal tiling) is obtained. The minimal tiling in conjunction with the sequencing of each individual clone or probe in the tiling and a sequence assembly procedure that determines the overlaps between successive sequenced clones or probes in the tiling [31] is then used to reconstruct the DNA sequence of the entire chromosome.

The ML estimation procedure involves a combination of discrete and continuous optimization where determining the probe ordering entails discrete (i.e., combinatorial) optimization, whereas determining the interprobe spacings for a particular probe ordering entails continuous optimization. The problem of determining the optimal probe ordering is intractable and is isomorphic to the classical NP-hard traveling salesman problem (TSP) [30]. Moreover, the ML objective function is nonlinear in the probe ordering, thus rendering the classical linear programming or integer linear programming techniques inapplicable. However, for a given probe ordering, determining the optimal interprobe spacings is a tractable problem that is solvable using gradient descent-based search techniques.

We investigated three stochastic combinatorial optimization algorithms for computation of the optimal probe ordering based on simulated annealing (SA) [27], large-step Markov chains (LSMC) [33], and genetic algorithms (GA) [34]. The computation of the optimal interprobe spacings for a specified probe ordering is shown to be best achieved by the conjugate gradient descent (CGD) algorithm. The high computational complexity of the ML-estimation-based physical mapping algorithm demands the use of parallel computing.

A two-tier parallelization strategy for efficient implementation of the ML-estimation-based physical mapping algorithm is implemented. The upper level represents parallel discrete optimization using the aforementioned stochastic combinatorial optimization algorithms, whereas the lower level comprises of parallel CGD search. The resulting parallel algorithms are implemented on a networked cluster of shared-memory symmetric multiprocessors (SMPs) running the message passing interface (MPI) environment. The cluster of SMPs offers a hybrid of shared-memory (within a single SMP) and distributed-memory (across the SMP cluster) parallel computing. A shared-memory data parallel approach where the components of the gradient vector are distributed among the individual processors within an SMP is deemed more suitable for the parallelization of the CGD search procedure. A distributed-memory control parallel scheme where individual SMPs perform noninteracting or periodically interacting searches is deemed more suitable for the parallelization of SA, the LSMC algorithm, and the GA. The GA is further enhanced by the incorporation of a stochastic hill-climbing search similar to the LSMC algorithm. The GA-LSMC hybrid algorithm is observed to be more resilient to premature convergence to a local optimum when compared to the canonical GA.

Experimental results on simulated clone-probe data show that the payoff in data parallelization of the CGD procedure is better realized for large problem sizes (i.e., large numbers of probes and clones). A similar trend is observed in the case of the parallel versions of SA, the LSMC algorithm, and the GA. In the case of the parallel GA, superlinear speed-up is observed in some instances, which can be attributed to population caching effects. The parallel exhaustive local 2-opt search algorithm, which is a component of the LSMC algorithm, is observed to be the most scalable in terms of speed-up. This is expected since the parallel exhaustive local 2-opt search algorithm entails minimal interprocessor communication and synchronization overhead. Overall, the experimental results are found to be in conformity with expectations based on formal analysis.

Future research will investigate extensions of the ML function that encapsulate errors due to repeat DNA sequences in addition to false positives and false negatives. The current MPI implementation of the ML estimator is targeted toward a homogeneous distributed processing platform such as a network of identical SMPs. Future research will explore and address issues that deal with the parallelization of the ML estimator on a heterogeneous distributed processing platform such as a network of SMPs that differ in processing speeds, a scenario that is more likely to be encountered in the real world. Other combinatorial optimization techniques such as those based on Lagrangian-based global search and tabu search will also be investigated. Extensions of the ML-estimation-based approach to a Bayesian MAP estimation-based approach, where the ordering of clones or probes containing genetic markers, as inferred from a genetic map, are used as a prior distribution will also be investigated.

19.3 High-performance computing for reconstructing evolutionary trees

A phylogeny is a representation of the evolutionary history of a group of genes, gene products, or species of organisms (taxa). Phylogenies have been reconstructed by experts, without use of computing, for more than a century. The availability of genetic sequence data has made it possible to infer phylogenetic trees from the genetic sequences—those sequences of molecules that are acted upon by evolution—and thus record evolution's end effects.

Phylogenetic analysis uses data from living organisms to attempt to reconstruct the evolutionary history of genes, gene products, or taxa. Because phylogenies are crucial to answering so many fundamental open questions in biomolecular evolution, biologists have a strong interest in algorithms that enable resolution of ancient relationships. Much applied research depends on these algorithms, as well. Pharmaceutical companies use phylogenetic analysis in drug discovery, for instance, in discovering biochemical pathways unique to target organisms. Health organizations study the phylogenies of such organisms as HIV to understand their epidemiologies and to aid in predicting the course of disease over time within an individual. Government laboratories work to develop improved strains of basic foodstuffs, such as rice, wheat, and potatoes, using an understanding of the phylogenetic distribution of variation in wild populations. Finally, the reconstruction of large phylogenies has yielded fundamental new insights into the process of evolution. (See [3].) In a well-known computational study, Rice, Donoghue, and Olmstead [20] used DNA data for a gene common to most seed plants (rbcL) to build an evolutionary history for more than 500 taxa of seed plants using a maximum-parsimony-based analysis. Their study used independently seeded, heuristic parsimony searches and ran for approximately 1 year of CPU time on a parallel cluster.

Existing phylogenetic reconstruction techniques suffer from serious problems of running time (or, when fast, of accuracy). The problem is particularly serious for large data sets: although datasets comprising a sequence from a single gene continue to pose challenges (e.g., some analyses are still running after 2 years of computation on medium-size clusters), using whole-genome data (such as gene content and gene order) gives rise to even more formidable computational problems, particularly in datasets with large numbers of genes and highly rearranged genomes. Although new algorithmic developments are clearly desirable, high-performance computing can still reduce the running time of current algorithms significantly and turn tomorrow's algorithms into fast and effective tools. Almost every model of speciation and genomic evolution used in phylogenetic reconstruction has given rise to NP-hard optimization problems. Three major classes of methods are in common use: heuristics (such as neighbor-joining) [21], maximum parsimony [8], and maximum likelihood [9]. Heuristics (a natural consequence of the NP-hardness of the problems) run quickly but may offer no quality guarantees and may not even have a well-defined optimization criterion. Parsimony-based methods take exponential time (as a function of the number of taxa), but at least for DNA and amino acid data they can often be run to completion on datasets of moderate size. Maximum likelihood methods come with a larger set of conditions and assumptions than parsimony methods, but when these conditions are met they appear capable of outperforming the others in terms of the quality of solutions. However, maximum likelihood methods take time that rises factorially with the number of taxa and require massive amounts of computing time for large data sets.

Until recently, most phylogenetic algorithms focused on DNA or protein sequence data, using a model of evolution based mostly on nucleotide substitution. Another type of data has recently become available through the characterization of entire genomes: gene content and gene order data. For a few animals, several plants and microorganisms, and a fair sampling of cell organelles (mitochondria and chloroplast), we have a thorough catalog of genes and their physical locations on chromosomes. Several mechanisms of evolution operate at the genome level, including gene duplication, loss, and reordering. These mechanisms operate on time scales that are much slower than nucleotide mutations and as a result are potentially useful in resolving ancient evolutionary relationships. This new source of data has thus been embraced by biologists interested in the evolution of major divisions of plants, animals, and microorganisms.

Exploiting data about gene content and gene order has proved extremely challenging from a computational perspective. Tasks that can easily be carried out in linear time for DNA data have required entirely new theories (such as the computation of inversion distance [10, 4]) or appear to be NP-hard. Thus gene ordering approaches have been used most extensively on simple genomes—bacteria and organelles such as chloroplasts and mitochondria. Mitochondria are organelles found in all eukaryotic cells (plants, animals, and protozoans). They are instrumental in processing energy in cells. Chloroplasts are found in photosynthetic protozoans and plants and are responsible for turning sunlight into energy-storing compounds. Mitochondria and chloroplasts have their own bacteria-like DNA. The genetic information of bacteria, mitochondria, and chloroplasts consists of a single chromosome and, unlike eukaryotes, all the genetic material is expressed. Furthermore, the order of genes in prokaryote-like DNA (bacteria, mitochondria, chloroplasts) is very important in gene expression and cell function. The evolutionary relationships of bacteria may be studied by examining the order of genes in bacterial DNA. Since mitochondria and chloroplasts have their own DNA that is independent of the genetic material of the eukaryotic organisms of which they are a part, the evolutionary relationships of the eukaryotes can likewise be studied by examining the gene order of their mitochondria or chloroplasts.

We can think of the gene order along a chromosome as an ordering of signed integers, with each integer representing a single gene (the sign denotes the relative orientation of the gene along the DNA). Sankoff and Blanchette [22] developed a method called "breakpoint phylogeny" to infer the structure of phylogenetic trees based on analysis of changes in gene order.

GRAPPA (genome rearrangement analysis through parsimony and other phylogenetic algorithms) extends and makes more realistic the underlying evolutionary theory of breakpoint analysis and provides a highly optimized parallel program that performs well on a variety of supercomputer systems [15, 3]. We have used GRAPPA on the University of New Mexico's 512-processor Linux cluster to analyze the evolutionary relationships of the bellflower family (*Campanulaceae*), a group of bluebell flowers. We demonstrated a linear speed-up with number of processors (that is, essentially perfect parallel scaling) [2] and a speed-up of a million fold as compared to the original implementation of breakpoint analysis. The latest version of GRAPPA includes significantly improved underlying algorithms to model the evolutionary process and shows a speed-up of more than 1 billion as compared to the original algorithm!

GRAPPA is a prime example of the potential of high-performance algorithm development and use of high-performance computer systems in computational biology. Such potential is likely to be especially great for problems involving complex optimizations. Our reimplementation did not require new algorithms or entirely new techniques, yet it achieved gains that turned what had been an impractical approach into a usable one. Of course, even large speed-ups have only limited benefits in theoretical terms when applied to NP-hard optimization problems. The 1-billion-fold speed-up with GRAPPA enabled expansion of datasets from 10 taxa to 18 taxa. Thus a high-performance computing approach is not a substitute for innovative algorithm design but rather is a natural complement. Much faster implementations, when mature enough, can alter the practice of research in biology and medicine. Research activities regarded as impossible due to computational challenges become feasible both in theoretical biological research and applied biomedical research. Thus, approaches to both scale and algorithmic design will enable the high-performance computing and biomedical research communities to solve grand challenge problems in computing and biology.

19.4 Scaling classical molecular dynamics to thousands of processors

Molecular dynamics simulation is a tool used by researchers in biophysics to study the function of biomolecules such as proteins and DNA. A protein, for example, typically folds into a shape specific to that protein, and its function is decided by this shape, the electrostatic landscape created by the atoms around it, and its dynamic properties (e.g., how it would respond to being tugged in some direction). Molecular dynamics simulations help us understand how a particular molecular system (consisting of, say, proteins, cell membranes, water, and other molecules and ions) carries out a particular biological function and helps uncover the specific mechanisms in its operation. As a result, it is increasingly becoming an important tool in science as well as in rational drug design.

Classical molecular dynamics ignore quantum effects but model and compute other atomic forces in detail. In particular, it involves computing, in each time-step, forces on atoms due to (1) coulombic (electrostatic) interactions between atoms, (2) van der Waal's forces, and (3) forces due to bonds. Movements of atoms are then computed using an appropriate numerical integration scheme.

Each time-step is usually of the order of a femtosecond (10^{-15} seconds), while typical simulations may need to model several nanoseconds of behavior. The number of atoms in a simulation may vary from tens of thousands to hundreds of thousands. So, the computational complexity of these simulations arises from having to do millions of time-steps, each of which involves a relatively small amount of computation. For example, a simulation consisting of around 92,000 atoms takes about 8 seconds on the older Alpha processors of the LeMieux machine at Pittsburgh Supercomputing Center (PSC). Since smaller computations are harder to parallelize (and since there cannot be parallelism across time-steps), MD simulations are challenging to efficiently parallelize and scale to exploit a large number of processors. Further complicating effective parallelization is the idea of multiple time-stepping: since electrostatic forces due to faraway atoms vary slowly, it is more efficient to compute long-range component every few time-steps (say, four), while computing forces due to nearby atoms (within a cutoff radius of few 10 Angstroms, for example).

The NAMD2 code was designed to address this challenge. It has an (admittedly unfair) advantage over existing codes such as CHARM, AMBER, and GROMOS to which was designed as a parallel code. It has an (admittedly unfair) advantage because it was designed as a parallel code unlike most other MD codes such as CHARM, AMBER, and GROMOS, which were well-established sequential codes before use of parallel machines became prevalent. NAMD2 exploits parallelism by utilizing the Charm++ parallel programming system.

Charm++ is a C++-based parallel language. Programs are written in normal C++, with the exception that some of the C++ objects may be on remote processors. Methods (function calls) to such objects are asynchronously invoked—this is equivalent to sending a message to the remote object. Objects are grouped into collections, and they are assigned to processors under the control of a dynamic load balancer. More important, this assignment can be changed at runtime as needed. Charm++ is a mature system, ported to most parallel machines, with tools for performance visualization and debugging; it is distributed to researchers via the web (http://charm.cs.uiuc.edu). Since Charm++ allows multiple objects per processor, it leads to a natural latency-tolerant behavior—objects waiting for data from remote processors don't hold up the processor, allowing other ready objects to compute, thus overlapping communication with computation automatically and adaptively.

To take advantage of Charm++ capabilities and to handle the challenge of scalability mentioned above, NAMD uses an aggressive parallelization strategy: the set of atoms is dynamically decomposed into a set of cubic cells of size slightly larger than the cut-off radius. Every k time-steps (typically between 8 and 20 in the case of NAMD) atoms are migrated to a different cell if they have moved out of their original cells. NAMD creates a separate set of objects for calculating electrostatic forces between atoms in neighboring cells, which creates $14 * C$ objects available for load balancing, where C is the number of cells. In addition, it creates a similar number of objects for computing three- and four-atom

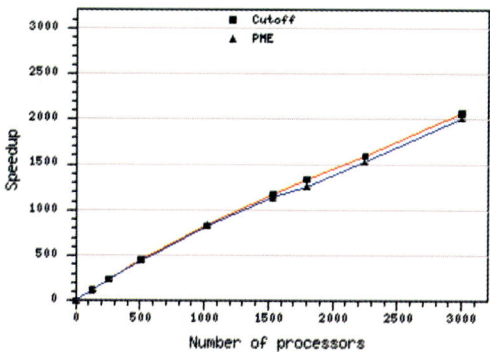

Figure 19.2. *Speed-up on PSC LeMieux.*

bonded forces using a dynamic scheme for assigning specific bonds to specific objects [13]. The long-range electrostatics are handled via an efficient implementation of the particle mesh Ewald (PME) algorithm that uses sequential Fastest Fourier Transform in the West (FFTW) library with a Charm++ based parallel FFT implementation. This allows PME-related computations and communications to overlap with other force computations. Since PME is communication intensive operation, with large latencies, this helps improve the efficiency.

Electrostatics force computation constitutes most of the time of the overall computation. To increase parallelism of this component further, we subdivide the task of computing forces between adjoining cells when they connect at a face (or for self-interactions), which is a case where a large number of atom pairs are found to be within the cutoff distance. With these schemes we can generate a high degree of parallelism. For example, in a simulation of ATPase involving about 320,000 atoms, there were about 700 cells plus bonded-force objects—about 350 objects for PME and about 30,000 objects for within-cutoff electrostatics. These objects were assigned to processors under the control of the load balancer.

NAMD has achieved excellent performance on clusters as well as large parallel machines. Despite its C++ implementation, which is often perceived to be slower than FORTRAN, its sequential performance is comparable to that of other MD programs. Its scaling is much better than most other MD programs: we have demonstrated speed-ups of up to 3,000 processors of the PSC LeMieux machine, leading to a Gordon Bell award (shared) in 2002 [18].

Figure 19.2 shows the performance of NAMD running a large benchmark with about 320K atoms (including water molecules) on the PSC Lemieux. Speed-up of more than 2,000 is achieved on 3,000 processors with a time-step of about 10 ms. Further, speed-up in runs with and without PME is similar.

NAMD is being used extensively by biophysicists around the world. It is distributed via the web at http://www.ks.uiuc.edu. Several high-profile simulations have been carried out using NAMD, including the aquaporin simulation [24]. The most recent application has been "snap fastener on biological cells," which revealed a dynamic picture of the interactions used by cells to link themselves to the extracellular matrix. The simulation showed that it is actually a brave water molecule that is recruited by integrins as a protective shield for the interaction. The simulations provide for the first time a detailed view of how cell tissues are stabilized through surface ions against mechanical stress [6]. Another example is the Japanese lantern protein, which functions as a mechanosensitive channel of small conductance (MscS) to protect the bacterial cell against osmotic stress, when a bacterium finds itself suddenly in an aqueous environment, entering water can burst the cell [23]. Embedding the large protein into a lipid bilayer and water led to a simulation encompassing 220,000 atoms. Surprisingly, the protein balloon was found to control the arrangement of positive and negative ions through a peculiar pattern of charged, polar, and nonpolar amino acids on its internal and external surfaces.

In the near future, we plan to port NAMD to upcoming large parallel machines. In particular, IBM's blueGene/L machine, with about 130,000 processors, will be installed at Lawrence Livermore National Lab during 2005. We have already ported NAMD to a smaller prototype of this machine with 1,000 processors and demonstrated good preliminary performance. Significant redesign and new strategies will be needed to scale to the full machine efficiently. A challenge from another direction is that of interactive molecular dynamics: here, we need to obtain high speed-ups for relatively small molecular systems (e.g., 10,000 atoms) on modest-size parallel machines with several hundred processors.

19.5 Cluster and grid computing for 3D structure determination of viruses with unknown symmetry at high resolution

Viruses are large macromolecules with hundreds of thousands of amino acids and millions of atoms. They cause various human, animal, and plant diseases. Viruses infect healthy cells by attaching and then delivering their nucleic acid to the host cell. Instead of expressing the cellular gene, the biosynthetic system of an infected cell is forced to facilitate the replication, transcription, and translation of the viral gene. Then the virus particle created in the infected cell leaves it to infect another host.

The knowledge of the 3D structure of viruses is invaluable for the design of antiviral drugs. X-ray crystallography and electron microscopy can be used to study the 3D atomic structure of large macromolecules. X-ray crystallography is capable of producing very-high-resolution electron density maps, in the 2.0 to 3.0 Å range, but it is difficult to crystallize large macromolecules. Preparing samples for cryo transmission electron microscopy (cryoTEM) is easier, but the typical resolution is lower. In the last few years, several groups, including ours, have reported results at 6 to 10 Å resolution. Figure 19.3(a) shows the 3D reconstruction of Sindbis virus at 10 Å resolution. Recently, we have successfully reconstructed the structure of reo virus at 7 Å resolution [38].

The steps for virus particle reconstruction using information collected experimentally by cryoTEM are as follows:

Step 1. Extract particle images from cryo-electron micrographs or charge-coupled device (CCD) images.

Step 2. Determine the orientations of individual projections.

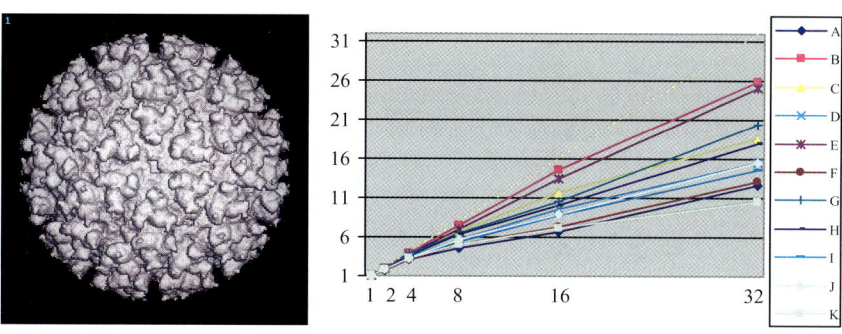

Figure 19.3. (a) 3D reconstruction of Sindbis at 10 Å resolution. (b) The speed-up of one 3D reconstruction algorithm for several virus structures.

Table 19.2. The increase of the amount of data and the corresponding increase in memory requirements for very-high-resolution reconstruction of the reo virus with a diameter of about 850 Å.

Resolution	12 Å	6 Å	3 Å
Pixel Size (Å)	4	2	1
Particle Image Size (pixels/Mbytes)	256 x 256 256 KB	512 x 512 1 MB	1024 x 1024 4 MB
Number of Particles	1000	10,000	1,000,000
Image Data Set Size	256 MB	10 GB	4 TB
The Size of the 3D Map	256^3 64 MB	512^3 0.5 GB	1024^3 4 GB

Step 3. Reconstruct the 3D object from 2D projections. Repeat Steps 2 and 3 until the electron density map no longer improves (convergence).

Step 4. Dock an atomic model into the map using information from protein databases.

The computational challenges for cryoTEM are to (1) increase resolution to 3 to 6 Å; to do so we have to increase number of particle projections collected experimentally by several orders of magnitude; (2) increase the size of pixel frames; (3) support reconstruction of asymmetric objects; and (4) optimize the algorithms to reduce the computation time by one to two orders of magnitude.

The development of parallel algorithms for orientation refinement and 3D reconstruction becomes a critical task due to the massive amount of data necessary to study virus structures at increasingly high resolution. Table 19.2 illustrates the dramatic increase of computer resources, memory, and CPU cycles (see [37] for an analysis of the complexity of algorithms) when the resolution increases from 12 Å to 6 Å and then to 3 Å for a virus with icosahedral symmetry and a diameter of about 850 Å.

We use a model-based approach for the refinement of orientations that is less sensitive to the noise caused by experimental errors and allows us to compute the actual orientation of an experimental view with a precision only limited by the quality of the experimental data (see [36]). We first compute a 2D discrete Fourier transform (DFT) of each experimental view, apply a contrast transfer function (CTF) correction to it, and then compare the corrected 2D DFT with a series of central sections or cuts of the 3D DFT of the electron density map. This series of central sections is chosen such that their orientations span the current best estimate of the object's approximate orientation. Once we define the distance between the 2D DFT of an experimental view and a calculated cut of the 3D DFT of the electron density map, the goal of the search is to identify the calculated cut which most closely matches (i.e., is at minimum distance from) the 2D DFT of an experimental view. The distance is a function of the real and imaginary part of two 2D arrays of complex numbers. The orientation refinement is optimized; given an approximate orientation we search a range for the three angles defining the orientation, first in steps of $1°$, then we decrease the step size to $0.1°$ and search around the more precise value obtained during the previous iteration; and finally we search with a step size of $0.01°$ (see Table 19.3). A similar strategy is used for refining the centers of the experimental views. The algorithm does not make any assumptions about the symmetry of the object, but it can detect symmetry if it is present. An important advantage of our algorithm for orientation refinement is a straightforward implementation of the CTF correction (see [37]). To study the limitations of our algorithm we project the electron density map of a virus structure at known angles and then apply the algorithm to determine the orientation of each projection known to us. Our experiments show that we can refine the angles to a precision of $0.001°$; the execution time increases considerably and such a precision is not necessary for most virus structures.

A family of parallel algorithms for the reconstruction of asymmetric objects in Cartesian coordinates, with different memory and CPU cycle requirements, is described in [37]. We consider the DFT of a pixel frame to be a slab and use bilinear interpolation to obtain

Table 19.3. *The time for different steps of the orientation refinement for reo virus using 4,422 views with 511×511 pixels/view. DFT size is $512 \times 512 \times 512$. Refinement steps of $1°$, $0.1°$, and $0.01°$. The refinement time increases three to five times when the refinement step size decreases from $0.1°$ to $0.01°$ because of a larger number of operations and also due to the memory access time to much larger data structures. The orientation refinement time is the dominant component of the total execution time, hundreds of minutes, as compared with the computation of the 3D DFT, the reading time, and the DFT analysis, which take a few hundred seconds.*

Refinement Step Size (degree)	1	0.1	0.01
Search Range	9^3	9^3	11^3
3D DFT (seconds)	175	206	178
Read Images (seconds)	550	533	573
DFT Analysis (seconds)	138	142	137
Refine Time (minutes)	332	366	1161
Total Time (minutes)	347	381	1176

values at points of the 3D grid. The speed-ups of one of the algorithms in the family is summarized in Figure 19.3(b).

The parallel algorithms for orientation refinement and reconstruction currently runs on parallel machines (SP2) and clusters. The results reported here are obtained using a cluster with 44 nodes, each consisting of two 2.4 GHz Pentium 4 processors and a shared memory of 3 GB per node.

19.6 Using motion planning to study protein folding

Protein folding research is typically focused on two main problems: protein structure prediction and the study of the protein folding process. The goal of large and ongoing research efforts is to determine the native structure of a protein from its amino acid sequence [59, 65]. Determining a protein's so-called native state—an energetically stable, three-dimensional configuration—is important because the protein's function is related its structure. Knowledge of the dynamic folding process by which a protein folds to its native state is also of great practical importance since some devastating diseases, such as Alzheimer's and bovine spongiform encephalopathy (mad cow), are associated with the misfolding of proteins [56].

Several computational approaches have been applied to compute protein folding pathways or to study other issues related to the folding process such as folding rates (see Table 19.4). These include lattice models [48], energy minimization [60, 68], molecular dynamics [58, 52, 50, 51], Monte Carlo methods [49, 55], and genetic algorithms [47, 67]. Molecular dynamics and Monte Carlo methods provide a single, high-quality folding pathway, but each run is computationally intensive. Statistical mechanical models [62, 39, 46], while computationally efficient, are limited to studying global averages of folding kinetics and are unable to produce folding pathways.

Parallel protein folding techniques have been restricted to molecular dynamics simulations. Peter Kollman pioneered work in this area with AMBER [69]. The NAMD parallel molecular dynamics framework is presented in greater detail in a previous section. Folding@Home [57] uses a distributed computing technique to run molecular dynamics simulations. It overcomes the huge computation barrier of molecular dynamics simulations by making use of more than 40,000 machines. Still, only relatively small motions have been simulated with this method.

Table 19.4. *A comparison of protein folding models.*

Comparison of Models for Protein Folding					
Approach	Folding Landscape	# Paths Produced	Path Quality	Compute Time	Native State Required
Molecular Dynamics	No	1	Good	Long	No
Monte Carlo	No	1	Good	Long	No
Statistical Model	Yes	0	N/A	Fast	Yes
PRM-Based	Yes	Many	Approx	Fast	Yes
Lattice Model	Not used on real proteins				

We have developed a new computational technique for studying protein folding [42, 41, 66] that provides an alternative approach to those listed in Table 19.4. It is based on a class of motion-planning techniques, called probabilistic roadmap methods (PRMs) [54], that have proved effective on a wide range of applications, from robotics to computer animation to molecules. Briefly, given the known native structure of a protein, our PRM-based method computes an approximate map of a protein's potential and free energy landscapes that contains thousands of feasible folding pathways and enables the study of global properties of the folding landscape. We study issues related to the folding process such as secondary and tertiary structure formation and their dependence on the initial denatured configuration. We obtained promising results for several small proteins (60 to 100 amino acids) [42] and validated our pathways by comparing secondary structure formation order with known experimental results [61]. In one case study, we demonstrated that our technique is sensitive enough to identify subtle differences in folding behaviors for structurally similar proteins G and L [66].

Apaydin et al. [45, 44] have also used PRM-based techniques to study protein folding; however, their work differs from ours in several aspects. First, they model the protein at a much coarser level, considering each secondary structure to be rigid. Second, while our focus is on studying the folding process, their focus has been to compare the PRM approach with methods such as Monte Carlo simulation. They have shown that the PRM-based technique converges to the same stochastic distribution as Monte Carlo simulation but is much faster.

Our technique, although significantly more computationally efficient than previous methods, still requires large amounts of computational resources. For example, it takes several hours on a desktop PC to compute a map approximating the potential landscape of a small protein when using a coarse approximation for the energy calculations. With a more accurate and detailed energy calculation, the running time increases to 2 weeks. It is imperative that we find a faster technique if we are to study larger proteins with higher accuracy. Fortunately, PRMs are "embarrassingly parallel" [40]. In particular, as we will see, the running time of our technique is dominated by energy calculations, and most are independent of each other.

We have used the standard template adaptive parallel library (STAPL) [64, 43] to parallelize our existing PRM-based protein folding code. We chose STAPL for the following reasons: STAPL allows for an easy transition from sequential code to parallel code by extending the ANSI C++ standard template library [63] and STAPL provides portable efficiency to different systems, both shared-memory and distributed-memory models, without requiring user code modification. We have obtained good speed-ups on a variety of systems, including the IBM BlueGene/L supercomputer, a distributed shared-memory machine, a homogeneous dedicated Linux cluster, and a heterogeneous nondedicated Linux cluster. These results demonstrate the capability of STAPL to enable one to run the same parallel application on several different platforms without modifying user code.

While we believe our new PRM-based technique is very promising, many issues remain to be addressed before we will obtain a computational method that is both efficient and accurate enough to be used as a tool for studying the dynamic protein folding process. These challenges are both computational (e.g., developing better algorithms or sampling strategies, or understanding the relative merits of known methods) and biological (e.g., determining appropriate validation mechanisms for processes that are difficult or impossible to capture experimentally).

Bibliography

[1] K. ARUMUGANATHAN AND E. D. EARLE, *Nuclear DNA content of some important plant species*, Plant Molecular Biology Reporter, 9(3):211–215, 1991.

[2] D. A. BADER AND B. M. E. MORET, *GRAPPA runs in a record time*, HPCwire, 9(47), 2000. Available online at www.hpcwire.com/archives/18961.html.

[3] D. A. BADER, B. M. E. MORET, AND L. VAWTER, *Industrial applications of high-performance computing for phylogeny reconstruction*, In H. J. Siegel, editor, Proc. SPIE Commercial Applications for High-Performance Computing, volume 4528, pages 159–168, Denver, CO, 2001. SPIE.

[4] D. A. BADER, B. M. E. MORET, AND M. YAN, *A linear-time algorithm for computing inversion distance between signed permutations with an experimental study*, Journal of Computational Biology, 8(5):483–491, 2001.

[5] B. L. BENNETZEN, V. L. CHANDLER, AND P. SCHNABLE, *National Science Foundation-sponsored workshop report - Maize genome sequencing project*, Plant Physiology, 127:1572–1578, 2001.

[6] D. CRAIG, M. GAO, K. SCHULTEN, AND V. VOGEL, *Structural insights into how the midas ion stabilizes integrin binding to an rgd peptide under force*, Structure, 12:2049–2058, 2004.

[7] S. J. EMRICH, S. ALURU, Y. FU, ET AL., *A strategy for assembling the maize (Zea mays) genome*, Bioinformatics, 20:140–147, 2004.

[8] J. S. FARRIS, *The logical basis of phylogenetic analysis*. In N. I. Platnick and V. A. Funk, editors, Advances in Cladistics, pages 1–36. Columbia University Press, New York, 1983.

[9] J. FELSENSTEIN, *Evolutionary trees from DNA sequences: a maximum likelihood approach*, Journal of Molecular Evolution, 17:368–376, 1981.

[10] S. HANNENHALLI AND P. A. PEVZNER, *Transforming cabbage into turnip (polynomial algorithm for sorting signed permutations by reversals)*, In Proc. 27th Annual Symposium on Theory of Computing (STOC95), pages 178–189, Las Vegas, NV, 1995.

[11] X. HUANG AND A. MADAN, *CAP3: A DNA sequence assembly program*, Genome Research, 9:868–877, 1999.

[12] R. E. TARJAN, *Efficiency of a good but not linear set union union algorithm*, Journal of the ACM, 22(2) (1975), pp. 215–225.

[13] L. KALÉ, R. SKEEL, M. BHANDARKAR, R. BRUNNER, A. GURSOY, N. KRAWETZ, J. PHILLIPS, A. SHINOZAKI, K. VARADARAJAN, AND K. SCHULTEN, NAMD2: *Greater scalability for parallel molecular dynamics*, Journal of Computational Physics, 151:283–312, 1999.

[14] A. KALYANARAMAN, S. ALURU, V. BRENDEL, AND S. KOTHARI, *Space and time efficient parallel algorithms and software for EST clustering*, IEEE Transactions on Parallel and Distributed Systems, 14(12):1209–1221, 2003.

[15] B. M. E. MORET, S. WYMAN, D. A. BADER, T. WARNOW, AND M. YAN, *A new implementation and detailed study of breakpoint analysis*, In Proc. 6th Pacific Symposium on Biocomputing (PSB 2001), pages 583–594, Hawaii, 2001.

[16] L. E. PALMER ET AL., *Maize genome sequencing by methylation filtration*, Science, 302:2115–2117, 2003.

[17] D. G. PETERSON, ET AL., *Integration of Cot analysis, DNA cloning and high-throughput sequencing facilitates genome characterization and gene discovery*, Genome Research, 12:795–807, 2002.

[18] J. C. PHILLIPS, G. ZHENG, S. KUMAR, AND L. V. KALÉ, *NAMD: Biomolecular simulation on thousands of processors*, In Proceedings of Supercomputing 2002, Baltimore, MD, September 2002.

[19] P. E. RABINOWICZ ET AL., *Differential methylation of genes and retrotransposons facilitates shotgun sequencing of maize genome*, Nature Genetics, 23:305–308, 1999.

[20] K. RICE, M. DONOGHUE, AND R. OLMSTEAD, *Analyzing large datasets: rbcl500 revisited*, Syst. Biol., 46:554–562, 1997.

[21] N. SAITOU AND M. NEI, *The neighbor-joining method: A new method for reconstruction of phylogenetic trees*, 4:406–425, 1987.

[22] D. SANKOFF AND M. BLANCHETTE, *Multiple genome rearrangement and breakpoint phylogeny*, Journal of Computational Biology, 5:555–570, 1998.

[23] M. SOTOMAYOR AND K. SCHULTEN, *Molecular dynamics study of gating in the mechanosensitive channel of small conductance mscs*, Biophysical Journal, 87:3050–3065, 2004.

[24] E. TAJKHORSHID, P. NOLLERTA, M. Ã. JENSEN, L. J. W. MIERCKE, J. O'CONNELL, R. M. STROUD, AND KLAUS SCHULTEN, *Control of the selectivity of the aquaporin water channel family by global orientational tuning*, Science, 296:525–530, 2002.

[25] C. A. WHITELAW, W. B. BARBAZUK, G. PERTEA, ET AL., *Enrichment of gene-coding sequences in maize by genome filtration*, Science, 302:2118–2120, 2003.

[26] Y. YUAN, P. SANMIGUEL, AND J. L. BENNETZEN, *High-Cot sequence analysis of the maize genome*, Plant Journal, 49:249–255, 2003.

[27] E. H. L. AARTS AND K. KORST, *Simulated Annealing and Boltzman Machines: A Stochastic Approach to Combinatorial Optimization and Neural Computing*, Wiley, New York, 1989.

[28] G. ANDREWS, *Foundations of Multithreaded, Parallel, and Distributed Programming*, Addison Wesley Pub. Co., Reading, MA, 2000.

[29] S. M. BHANDARKAR, S. A. MACHAKA, S. S. SHETE, AND R. N. KOTA, *Parallel Computation of a Maximum Likelihood Estimator of a Physical Map*, Genetics, special issue on Computational Biology, Vol. 157, No. 3, pp. 1021–1043, March 2001.

[30] M. S. GAREY AND D. S. JOHNSON, *Computers and Intractability: A Guide to the Theory of NP–Completeness*, W.H. Freeman, New York, NY, 1979.

[31] J. D. KECECIOGLU AND E. W. MYERS, *Combinatorial algorithms for DNA sequence assembly*, Algorithmica, Vol. 13, pp. 7–51, 1995.

[32] J. D. KECECIOGLU, S. S. SHETE, AND J. ARNOLD, *Reconstructing distances in physical maps of chromosomes with nonoverlapping probes*, Proc. ACM Conf. Computational Molecular Biology, Tokyo, Japan, pp. 183–192, April 2000.

[33] O. MARTIN, S. W. OTTO, AND E. W. FELTEN, *Large-Step Markov Chains for the Traveling Salesman Problem*, Complex Systems, Vol. 5, No. 3, pp. 299–326, 1991.

[34] M. MITCHELL, *An Introduction to Genetic Algorithms*, MIT Press, Cambridge, MA, 1996.

[35] A. H. STURTEVANT, *The linear arrangement of six sex-linked factors in Drosophila as shown by their mode of association*, Jour. Exp. Zool., Vol. 14, pp. 43–49, 1913.

[36] Y. JI, D. C. MARINESCU, T. S. BAKER, AND W. ZHANG, *Orientation refinement of virus structures with unknown symmetry*, in Proc. 17th Annual International Symposium on Parallel and Distributed Computing, (Nice, France) IEEE Press, 2003.

[37] D. C. MARINESCU AND Y. JI, *A computational framework for the 3D structure determination of viruses with unknown symmetry*, Journal of Parallel and Distributed Computing, 63 (2003), pp. 738–758.

[38] X. ZHANG, Y. JI, L. ZHANG, M. A. AGOSTO, S. C. HARRISON, D. C. MARINESCU, M. L. NIBERT, AND T. S. BAKER, *New Features of Reovirus Outer-Capsid Protein 1 Revealed at 7.0-Ã . . . Resolution or Better by Electron Cryomicroscopy and Image Reconstruction of the Virion*, (in preparation).

[39] E. ALM AND D. BAKER, *Prediction of protein-folding mechanisms from free-energy landscapes derived from native structures*, Proceedings of the National Academy of Sciences USA, 96(20):11305–11310, 1999.

[40] N. M. AMATO AND L. K. DALE, *Probabilistic roadmap methods are embarrassingly parallel*. In Proc. IEEE International Conference on Robotics and Automation (ICRA), pp. 688–694, 1999.

[41] N. M. AMATO, KEN A. DILL, AND G. SONG, *Using motion planning to map protein folding landscapes and analyze folding kinetics of known native structures*, Journal of Computational Biology, 10(3-4):239–256, 2003.

[42] N. M. AMATO AND G. SONG, *Using motion planning to study protein folding pathways*, Journal of Computational Biology, 9(2):149–168, 2002.

[43] P. AN, A. JULA, S. RUS, S. SAUNDERS, T. SMITH, G. TANASE, N. THOMAS, N. AMATO, AND L. RAUCHWERGER, *STAPL: An adaptive, generic parallel programming library for C++*. In Proc. of the 14th International Workshop on Languages and Compilers for Parallel Computing (LCPC), Cumberland Falls, Kentucky, Aug. 2001.

[44] M. S. APAYDIN, D. L. BRUTLAG, C. GUESTRIN, D. HSU, AND J.-C. LATOMBE, *Stochastic roadmap simulation: An efficient representation and algorithm for analyzing molecular motion*. In Proc. International Conference on Computational Molecular Biology (RECOMB), pp. 12–21, 2002.

[45] M. S. APAYDIN, A. P. SINGH, D. L. BRUTLAG, AND J.-C. LATOMBE, *Capturing molecular energy landscapes with probabilistic conformational roadmaps*. In Proc. IEEE International Conference on Robotics and Automation (ICRA), pp. 932–939, 2001.

[46] D. BAKER, *A surprising simplicity to protein folding*, Nature, 405:39–42, 2000.

[47] J. U. BOWIE AND D. EISENBERG, *An evolutionary approach to folding small α-helical proteins that uses sequence information and an empirical guiding fitness function*, Proceedings of the National Academy of Sciences USA, 91(10):4436–4440, 1994.

[48] J. D. BRYNGELSON, J. N. ONUCHIC, N. D. SOCCI, AND P. G. WOLYNES, *Funnels, pathways, and the energy landscape of protein folding: A synthesis*, Proteins Structure Function Genetics, 21:167–195, 1995.

[49] D. G. COVELL, *Folding protein α-carbon chains into compact forms by Monte Carlo methods*, Proteins: Structure Function Genetics, 14(4):409–420, 1992.

[50] V. DAGGETT AND M. LEVITT, *Realistic simulation of naive-protein dynamics in solution and beyond*, Annual Review of Biophysics and Biomolecular Structure, 22:353–380, 1993.

[51] Y. DUAN AND P. A. KOLLMAN, *Pathways to a protein folding intermediate observed in a 1-microsecond simulation in aqueous solution*, Science, 282:740–744, 1998.

[52] J. M. HAILE, *Molecular Dynamics Simulation: elementary methods*, Wiley, New York, 1992.

[53] L. KALÉ, R. SKEEL, M. BHANDARKAR, R. BRUNNER, A. GURSOY, N. KRAWETZ, J. PHILLIPS, A. SHINOZAKI, K. VARADARAJAN, AND K. SCHULTEN, *Namd2: Greater scalability for parallel molecular dynamics*, Journal of Computational Physics, 151:283–312, 1999.

[54] L. E. KAVRAKI, P. SVESTKA, J. C. LATOMBE, AND M. H. OVERMARS, *Probabilistic roadmaps for path planning in high-dimensional configuration spaces*, IEEE Transactions on Rotobics and Automation, 12(4):566–580, August 1996.

[55] A. KOLINSKI AND J. SKOLNICK, *Monte Carlo simulations of protein folding*, Proteins Structure Function Genetics, 18(3):338–352, 1994.

[56] P. T. LANSBURY, *Evolution of amyloid: What normal protein folding may tell us about fibrillogenesis and disease*, Proc. of the National Academy of Sciences USA, 96(7):3342–3344, 1999.

[57] S. M. LARSON, C. D. SNOW, M. SHIRTS, AND V. S. PANDE, *Foldinghome and genomehome: Using distributed computing to tackle previously intractable problems in computational biology*, Computational Genomics, 2003. To appear.

[58] M. LEVITT, *Protein folding by restrained energy minimization and molecular dynamics*, Journal of Molecular Biology, 170:723–764, 1983.

[59] M. LEVITT, M. GERSTEIN, E. HUANG, S. SUBBIAH, AND J. TSAI, *Protein folding: the endgame*, Annual Review of Biochemistry, 66:549–579, 1997.

[60] M. LEVITT AND A. WARSHEL, *Computer simulation of protein folding*, Nature, 253:694–698, 1975.

[61] R. LI AND C. WOODWARD, *The hydrogen exchange core and protein folding*, Protein Science, 8(8):1571–1591, 1999.

[62] V. MUÑOZ, E. R. HENRY, J. HOFERICHTER, AND W. A. EATON, *A statistical mechanical model for β-hairpin kinetics*, Proceedings of the National Academy of Sciences USA, 95:5872–5879, 1998.

[63] D. MUSSER, G. DERGE, AND A. SAINI, *STL Tutorial and Reference Guide, Second Edition*, Addison-Wesley, New York, 2001.

[64] L. RAUCHWERGER, F. ARZU, AND K. OUCHI, *Standard Templates Adaptive Parallel Library*. In Proc. of the 4th International Workshop on Languages, Compilers and Run-Time Systems for Scalable Computers (LCR), Pittsburgh, PA, May 1998.

[65] G. N. REEKE, JR., *Protein folding: Computational approaches to an exponential-time problem*, Annual Review of Computer Science, 3:59–84, 1988.

[66] G. SONG, S. L. THOMAS, K. A. DILL, J. M. SCHOLTZ, AND N. M. AMATO, *A path planning-based study of protein folding with a case study of hairpin formation in protein G and L*. In Proc. Pacific Symposium of Biocomputing (PSB), pp. 240–251, 2003, Lihue, Hawaii.

[67] S. SUN, *Reduced representation model of protein structure prediction: statistical potential and genetic algorithms*, Protein Science, 2(5):762–785, 1993.

[68] S. Sun, P. D. Thomas, and K. A. Dill, *A simple protein folding algorithm using a binary code and secondary structure constraints*, Protein Engineering, 8(8):769–778, 1995.

[69] P. K. Weiner and P. A. Kollman, *Amber: Assisted model building with energy renement, a general program for modeling molecules and their interactions*, Journal of Computational Chemistry, 2:287–303, 1981.

Chapter 20
Opportunities and Challenges for Parallel Computing in Science and Engineering

Michael A. Heroux, Padma Raghavan, and Horst D. Simon

This chapter surveys some of the most important opportunities and challenges for parallel computing in science and engineering. Although we focus specifically on a time frame of 5 to 10 years, at the same time we attempt to present these topics from a higher level view in the context of perennial issues.

Our discussion proceeds in a hierarchical fashion, starting with computer hardware and system software, followed by algorithms and applications development and finally large-scale modeling and simulation.

20.1 Parallel computer systems

20.1.1 Processors

One of the most critical enabling technology trends in the last two to three decades has been the unrelenting performance improvements of microprocessors. Moore's Law has been stated in many forms since Gordon Moore's original declaration in 1965. One interpretation of Moore's Law predicts that processor performance will double every 18 months. Although any exponential model must eventually fail, Moore's Law has been amazingly accurate and even at times pessimistic. We believe that Moore's Law will remain valid for the next decade and we can continue to expect a steady improvement of microprocessor performance.

Beyond this general statement, we do not expect processor clock speeds to improve exponentially during the next 10 years. Instead, performance improvements will be a combination of clock speed and architectural improvements. One of the most important developments for parallel computing is the recent introduction of *multicore processors*. A multicore processor contains on a single chip two or more processor cores that can work in parallel. This is not a fundamental architecture change, but it is important because our ability to exploit the full potential of a multicore processor will require higher-level parallelism.

With the advent of multicore processors, the definition of a processor becomes less clear. As an illustration, the Cray X1 computer system contains multiple single-stream scalar processors that, through a light-weight synchronization mechanism, can be utilized as a single multistream processor. This kind of dual view of multicore processors may also be appropriate.

In addition to microprocessor improvements, we will continue to see improvements in novel processor architectures. The primary goal of novel architectures is to reduce the effective memory latency, and this will continue to be the driver. Vector architectures continue to be a good approach in principle. However, commercial vector systems continue to have a narrow market exposure outside of the very-high-end customer base and certain industries such as automotive engineering. Of course there is a modest vectorization capability in modern microprocessors via the multimedia instruction set that supports two to four vector floating pointer operations per clock, but there are no signs of increasing the size of these registers in future microprocessors. An alternative approach to vectorization that has reappeared uses the concept of a coprocessor. For example, the ClearSpeed [6] coprocessor attaches to a PC system via the PCI-X interface and supports $O(10)$ GFLOPS double-precision vector floating point capabilities.

Massively threaded architectures such as the Cray MTA provide another approach to hiding memory latency by allowing a large number of active thread states that the processor can attach to at each clock cycle. From one perspective this is a generalization of vectorization that allows any type of rich loop construct to be processed effectively. Once again, the market exposure of this type of system is very limited and will remain so for the next decade.

A final category of processor architecture we discuss is that of multimedia processors, especially graphics processing units (GPUs). GPUs have a remarkable floating point computing capability since the introduction of single-precision functional units several years ago. Although this special-purpose hardware is solely intent on making realistic visual images, a number of research efforts have been able to exploit GPUs as vector processors and obtain promising initial results [8]. However, to our knowledge there has been no practical success to date, and a number of hurdles remain in making GPUs truly effective for certain computations. First and foremost is that the type of operation that can benefit from the specialized instruction set capabilities is restricted to single instruction, multiple data (SIMD)-like operations with lots of data. Second, most GPUs do not support IEEE double-precision floating point in hardware and there is no automatic software support to simulated double precision. Since most technical applications use double precision, this is a serious issues. Third, GPU memory is separate from main CPU memory, so data transfer is a significant overhead. Finally, there are no compilers to support easy development of technical application code for GPUs in languages such as FORTRAN, C, and C++. None of these issues is a singular show stopper, but collectively they represent a serious challenge to widespread use of GPUs for technical computing. The Cell architecture [3, 22], a novel combination of a PowerPC processor and eight SIMD cores intended for multimedia gaming, promises to provide a significant improvement for both single- and double-precision processing. If this architecture is successful and programming environments are developed for it, we could see practical use of it for scientific and engineering computing, especially for applications that require only single-precision floating point arithmetic.

Processors for parallel computers have generally come from two primary sources: commodity and custom vendors. Commodity processors such as microprocessors are not well designed for most scientific and engineering applications, as is illustrated by the typically poor fraction of peak performance we obtain. At the same time, they are attractive because mass production makes them inexpensive and reliable. Custom processors, such as vector processors from Cray, are typically much better suited for scientific and engineering computing but do not enjoy the same cost models. This competition between making the best of commodity processors and designing custom processors will continue. However, as microprocessor clock speed increases taper off, and their architectures become more difficult to program, the attractiveness of GPUs, including the Cell architecture, will likely increase. These processors have the same attractive cost model and promise significant performance.

Finally, in addition to improvements in silicon-based processors, the advent of quantum computers, based on exploiting atomic structure for very rapid calculations, remains a possibility in the coming decade. The raw computing capability promised by these systems will surely change the scientific and engineering computing landscape.

20.1.2 Interconnect networks

After the processor, the second principle architectural component of a parallel computer is its interconnect networks (ICNs). Any parallel computer has at least one ICN to support the transfer of data from processor to processor, and in many cases the ICN has hardware support for synchronization and other important network events. Some parallel computers have more than one network. For example, large-scale systems typically have an ICN with a mesh topology for use via calls to MPI functions and a second tree-type network for rapid deployment of program executables and systemwide functionality.

ICNs emerged in the 1980s in two forms: the custom-designed network for parallel computers such as the Cray X-MP and the network that connected workstations together for the purposes of remote system access and email, for example, Ethernet. With the advent of so-called Beowulf clusters in the 1990s and similar networks of workstations, the distinction between these two types of network started on a path to rapid convergence. Some custom-designed interconnect networks still exploit the inherent advantage that tight integration and custom design can provide. This is especially true of some of the very-high-end computers. This will continue to be true as we are able to build custom ICNs that will couple 1 million or more processors in the next few years. At the same time, the performance improvement in both bandwidth and latency of commodity external ICNs rivals those of custom design and separates the choice of processors from the choice of the ICN.

Future trends include improvements in both custom and commodity ICNs. In the custom ICN area we will see increasingly large processor counts, reaching 1 million and more processors in the near future and 10,000 processor systems becoming commonplace. These systems will push us above the petaflop (10^{15} operations per second) mark in capability within the next 5 years. These systems will also place strenuous demands on application developers to produce applications that can exploit large processor counts. We discuss these issues in sections 20.2 and 20.3. Interestingly, our ability to reach such large processor counts is a function of several engineering advances that have a multiplicative effect: large-count multicore processors, integration of tens of processors into a single 1U form-factor chassis, and advances in the interchassis ICN.

Commodity-like ICNs such as Gigabit Ethernet, Myrinet, and Quadrics will continue to improve latency and bandwidth, but major improvements will come from better integration of communication protocols into the global computer system. In particular, a global shared address space will be available, giving us the ability to directly address any memory location on the parallel machine regardless of physical location. This capability provides an inherent advantage because fewer messages are required in the implementation of a parallel application when processors are able to read and write directly from memory, even if that memory is remote. This hardware capability will be an important enabling technology as we push forward with parallel (partitioned) global address space (PGAS) programming models such as CoArray FORTRAN (CAF) and UPC.

20.1.3 Parallel programming models

Most application programmers view a parallel machine through a conceptual model that abstracts away many of the details of the parallel computer. In fact, practically speaking, in our experience, the vast majority of parallel application development is done on single-processor workstations or laptops since this type of platform is far more convenient to program and is a dedicated personal and portable resource. Although parallel performance cannot be accurately obtained on these platforms, correct parallel execution can usually be simulated even on a single processor.

Because of this reality, we cannot overstate the importance of parallel programming models. Many models are used in technical computing: Posix threads and OpenMP are probably the most commonly used shared memory models. MPI is by far the most common distributed memory model and is singular as a truly portable programming model across all parallel computing architectures. CAF and UPC are emerging standards that support effective global shared address space parallel computing.

For the foreseeable future, MPI will continue to be the dominant parallel programming model for scientific and engineering computing. Its ubiquity, flexibility, and clarity of data and work ownership has been the right blend for many application developers to guarantee a portable, high-performance, and expressive parallel computing environment. At the same time, MPI has definite weaknesses that PGAS languages such as CAF and UPC can address. In particular, a well-written CAF or UPC application code, with a compiler that can effectively aggregate remote memory reference, on a computer platform that has an effective PGAS implementation will be faster than an equivalent MPI version because remote references can be prefetched and brought straight into register without the multiple buffers that MPI would require [10].

Although PGAS programming models are intrinsically superior, we do not expect them to be adopted quickly. The lack of PGAS hardware support, good optimizing compilers, and applications that can see dramatic improvement for a small effort means that adoption will be slow. Also, many of the best parallel application developers are very comfortable with MPI programming and are reluctant to migrate to a new model when they lose portability and do not see uniform performance improvement across all platforms.

Shared memory programming models will continue to persist in some application spaces, but we do not see them gaining much popularity. Use of Posix threads or OpenMP alone is not a scalable model since the underlying computer must have a single system image in addition to a global address space. Furthermore, incremental introduction of these models into an existing serial code has disappointing performance results in many cases. Issues of memory locality, false cache-line sharing, and ambiguous work distribution have made shared memory programming a challenge and disappointing to many parallel application developers. Of course there are notable exceptions, but we believe that most parallel applications should not be solely developed using threads or OpenMP.

Hybrid models that combine threads or OpenMP with MPI have been used with some success on platforms that have multiprocessor nodes, and such will also be true for parallel machines with multicore processors. However, this programming model has not been as effective as many people initially speculated. In particular, most performance analysis has shown that hybrid use of threads or OpenMP along with MPI has not been any more effective than simply using MPI. For example, a 32-processor system composed of 8 4-processor nodes can be utilized via 8 MPI processes, each of which spawn 4 threads, or it can be utilized via 32 MPI processes. Most research has shown that the latter approach is just as effective as the former and allows the application to retain a much simpler and more portable parallel programming model. Again, there are notable exceptions to this general statement, but we do not expect hybrid models to substantially increase in popularity, even with the advent of multicore processors.

20.1.4 Power consumption

One issue that is receiving increasing attention is the cost of ownership of high-end computer systems. Power consumption in particular is a major concern for large data centers. Recent processor implementations have started to provide power detection and management features that allow a processor to be put to sleep or have its clock speed reduced. Such features can provide a vehicle for significantly reducing the total cost of ownership of a parallel computer. Power consumption can be managed by the operating system, especially during idle cycles, but user applications can also directly manage clock speed, especially if analysis shows that reduced clock speed does not adversely affect the overall performance of the application when compared to the cost savings.

Although this issue may not affect many users, some large-scale applications that run for many hours or days will benefit from a performance–power consumption analysis, which may find that significant power consumption costs can be cut without greatly reducing application performance [5, 17, 12, 15]. Furthermore, low-power architectural features could be added to enhance performance, thus improving both performance and power attributes [7, 13, 18].

20.2 Robust and scalable algorithms

The technical computing community has long recognized the importance of algorithm research and development. Although more difficult to measure, algorithmic improvements have played an equally important role as hardware improvements in advancing the impact of technical computing on science and engineering. Even more important, advances in hardware and algorithms have a multiplicative effect on capabilities that has been nothing short of remarkable.

20.2.1 The importance of forward solves

At the heart of many scientific and engineering applications is the ability to solve the state of system in the domain of interest, such that the results are physically meaningful. This is often called the *forward problem* and is the solution of single problem with a prescribed model, and known boundary and initial conditions. Accurate solution of the forward problem is important in the discovery phase of simulation, leading to "eureka" experiences in which insight into the behavior of the problem is needed. However, scientific and engineering computing becomes even more valuable when the forward problem can be solved quickly enough to support repeated forward solves of a family of problems. In particular, accurate transient behavior, stability of the solution, optimization, and quantification of uncertainty require fast and accurate forward solves.

20.2.2 Multilevel algorithms

Use of parallel computers requires effective parallel algorithms. Although many phases of a scientific or engineering application can be effectively programmed such that a problem of twice the size can be run on twice as many processors in the same amount of time, this is not true for implicit solvers. Since implicit solvers are a key kernel for many applications, scalable solvers are vital. Multilevel algorithms (see Chapter 10), which either geometrically or algebraically introduce a nested sequence of coarse problems to drive rapid convergence, are an important area of algorithm development, directly addressing this scalability issue. At the same time, multilevel algorithms are notoriously fragile in the sense that they require a great deal of specific problem information to obtain this convergence. Thus, a multilevel solver for one class of problems is not general purpose and useful for another class of problems.

We foresee continued research in multilevel algorithms, especially preconditioners for Krylov methods. The primary focus of the work will be to develop automated and semiautomated techniques for deriving coarse problems that can be more general purpose. These algorithms will be essential for resolution of large-scale, high-fidelity numerical solutions that are required to get an accurate solution to a detailed model of a particular scientific or engineering problem.

20.2.3 Multiscale algorithms

To reach the next level of model fidelity, increasing emphasis has been seen in multiscale algorithms. This class of algorithms takes into account phenomena at multiple time and length scales. One basic approach to this problem is to loosely couple a code that models one scale with another that models on another scale, passing information as boundary and initial conditions between the two applications, e.g., a molecular dynamics application with a fluid dynamics application. Such coupling is a good first step and was discussed in sections 14.2.1 and 16.2.1 and much of Chapter 18.

Recent efforts are focused on incorporating fine-scale information more carefully into the coarse scale, providing more accurate modeling of how the fine scale affects coarse scale and at the same time providing more rapid and robust solutions. We foresee continued efforts in multiscale algorithms, since model accuracy demands this coupling and is necessary for realistic physical solutions.

20.2.4 Model accuracy, speed, and uncertainty quantification

As our ability to accurately and rapidly resolve the forward problem increases, our use of computer modeling and simulation will mature. Ultimately, one primary outcome of our work will be the ability determine an optimal result to our problem with guaranteed range of accuracy. Scientific and engineering computing for any particular problem class will have reached maturity when this capability is realized.

Computer modeling and simulation have not matured to this level for many, if any, problem classes beyond the simplest models. We foresee that growth in this direction will continue, but maturity across a broad set of problems is still more than a decade away. Progress depends heavily on incremental advances in the accuracy and speed of the forward solve, as well as on advances in optimization algorithms and modeling of uncertainty.

20.2.5 Load balancing

Another critical issue for scalable parallel computations is load balance. This is especially true for obtaining the best parallel execution for a fixed-size problem. As we discussed in Chapter 6, there are a variety of efforts and tools to aid application and library developers in determining a good distribution of load. For uniform meshes, load balancing is typically not an issue. However, for irregular and adaptive meshes, and meshless applications, the tools discussed in Chapter 6 are critical. In fact, it is becoming increasingly necessary to maintain two or more data distributions within a single application. For example, we may need one partitioning for the load phase of a finite-element application and another for the solve phase, or, in a multiscale application, we may have different partitionings for each scale. We foresee that load balancing will continue to be an important topic, especially for large-scale applications.

20.3 Application development and integration

Increasingly, scientific and engineering applications are becoming complex, multideveloper software efforts built on existing capabilities delivered as libraries or components. In terms of reuse, this is a positive trend. However, it brings with it a complexity in terms of human and software interaction and increases the importance of good software engineering practices and processes.

20.3.1 Application building blocks: Libraries and components and application programming interfaces

In the early days of scientific and engineering computing, it was typical for an application to be completely self-contained. All source code was native to the application and there were no external dependencies. As more reusable software modules are available, such as libraries for solvers (Chapters 9 and 13), load balancers (Chapter 6), meshers (Chapters 8 and 13), material properties, etc., application developers are creating dependencies on external software to cut down on development time and exploit external expertise. For some modern applications, the amount of native source code is a small fraction of the amount of source code access in the external modules. We foresee this trend continuing and believe it is essential to rapid application development.

Scientific and engineering computing environments, also called application programming interfaces (APIs), such as Matlab [14], and computing languages such as Python [19] also play a role in rapid application development. Matlab is *the* scientific programming environment for many users. However, although a number of parallel Matlab environments have been developed in the last 10 years, to date none has emerged as a full-featured parallel programming environment. We expect this situation to change within the next few years, allowing at least modest parallel programming to be possible via a Matlab interface. We also expect that an increasing number of external libraries will be available via Matlab, so that Matlab can be used as a full-featured application development environment.

In addition to Matlab, Python has become a popular scientific programming language and environment. Python supports interactive use. Also, there are several tools available, such as the simple wrapper interface generator (SWIG) [1] and SIDL/Babel [21] (discussed in section 14.1), that assist or automate the wrapping of existing libraries, written in other languages, as Python classes. Because of this, Python is an attractive environment for users to develop applications and still gain access to external high-performance libraries. This approach has been successful for PyTrilinos [20].

To make scientific and engineering computing more accessible to the large audience of scientist and engineers, easier-to-use tools and APIs must be developed. We will continue to see sophisticated users rely on advanced programming languages and software environments, but other potential users are unable or unwilling to invest in these efforts. Efforts to develop and promote reusable libraries will continue, and the ability to access these libraries via Matlab-like interfaces and interactive languages such as Python will increase.

20.3.2 Software quality: Engineering and assurance

As computer modeling and simulation applications become more capable tools and are placed on the critical path for decision making in research and industry, software quality becomes a major concern. To date, many scientific software engineering efforts have not adopted rigorous quality processes or standards, at least not in a formal sense. However, as we come to rely more heavily on this software, saying "We do a good job" will not be sufficient assurance.

Slowly, the scientific software community is studying the gains made in the business software community and adopting ideas and practices as appropriate for the particular needs of the scientific community. A number of government customers, recognizing the requirements for rigorous software processes, have placed strong software quality requirements on funded projects. For example, the Accelerated Strategic Computing Initiative (ASCI) [16], now ASC [11], requires that projects it funds develop and adopt a software quality plan [2].

We foresee that this trend will continue, but not rapidly. Since most scientific software is written by experts in science or engineering, not software, and since algorithms research is such a critical component to most scientific software development, the focus on formal software tools, practices, and processes will be a lower priority. However, as software life-cycle models are developed to respect the strong research emphasis and as scientific software becomes increasingly critical in decision making, software quality will be an essential part of scientific software engineering.

20.4 Large-scale modeling and simulation

Any serious scientific or engineering computing effort eventually evolves to tackling large-scale problems. Such problems are complex by their very nature since they typically involve high-fidelity, large-dimension problems and multiple applications working in collaboration, worked on by one or more teams with diverse talents. Chapters 14 and 15 in particular deal with this type of effort. In this section we discuss the trends in efforts to make large-scale modeling and simulation easier, pointing out, in particular, software and algorithms issues.

20.4.1 Software components and frameworks

Chapters 14 and 15 focused on formal software componentization as an approach to easing the coupling of separately developed modeling and simulation applications. By formally defining a component interface that applications can adapt to, efforts like CCA [4] provide a scalable process for making applications interoperable. On the solver level, the Trilinos project [9] provides a similar capability by formally defining a solver package and making abstract interfaces available for access solver services. In this way, solver capabilities within Trilinos can be developed in a scalable way with a loosely coupled organizational approach, and external software can easily adapt to the Trilinos package architecture to become interoperable.

We expect that components and frameworks will become increasingly important as formal techniques to aid the rapid development of new scientific and engineering software and to make legacy software compatible. This is especially true as we increase our focus on specialized solver components and tackle multiscale problems. In addition, as software quality becomes increasingly important, components and frameworks will also be an important vehicle for testing software. Rigorous conceptual testing done at the abstract component level, within the component framework, provides an excellent reusable testing environment for software developed within or brought into the framework. We have already seen the advantage of this with CCA and Trilinos.

20.4.2 Analysis, design, and optimization: Beyond the forward problem

As mentioned in section 20.2, a robust, scalable forward solver enables other critical capabilities. One of the brightest areas of scientific and engineering computing is our ever-improving predictive capability. Although high-fidelity forward solves are still a challenge in many problem domains, predictive capabilities are becoming ever more possible. We foresee that scientific computing will become qualitatively more useful as analysis, design, and optimization become more prevalent. When simulation begins to address the issue of what is an optimal, stable result and can provide a family of solutions that can then be used to support decision in a broader context, it will be a kind of must-have capability. We have reached this point in some areas, such as automotive engineering, and will continue to make progress in the next 10 years.

At the same time, within this larger context, some of the advances we have made in high-fidelity forward solutions may be unattractive in this larger context. This is especially true of techniques that are nonsmooth. Good forward solutions based on ad hoc techniques for determining material properties and other physical parameters may be inappropriate for situations in which smooth behavior is needed. As a result, even in mature problem domains, we will continue to need new algorithms for the forward problem.

20.5 Concluding remarks

In this final chapter we have reviewed many of the major themes of this book, bringing together the present capabilities and some idea of the future trends. Parallel scientific and engineering computing has been a very active field since its beginnings in the late 1980s. However, the present landscape is particularly exciting in almost every respect. The advent of new processors, interconnect networks, and parallel software environments gives us unprecedented system capabilities. Advances in algorithms and coupling of multiple physics and scales provides new opportunities for fidelity of modeling and results. Finally, the impact of computer modeling and simulation as a third branch of scientific discover, along with theory and experimentation, is reason for excitement about the work presented in this book.

Acknowledgments

Sandia is a multiprogram laboratory operated by Sandia Corporation, a Lockheed Martin Company, for the U. S. Department of Energy's National Nuclear Security Administration under Contract DE-AC04-94AL85000.

Bibliography

[1] D. M. BEAZLEY, *Automated scientific software scripting with SWIG*, Future Generation Computer Systems, 19 (2003), pp. 599–609.

[2] E. A. BOUCHERON, R. R. DRAKE, H. C. EDWARDS, M. A. ELLIS, C. A. FORSYTHE, R. HEAPHY, A. L. HODGES, C. PAVLAKOS, J. R. SCHOFIELD, J. E. STURTEVANT, AND C. M. WILLIAMSON, *Sandia national laboratories advanced simulation and computing (asc) software quality plan part 1: Asc software quality engineering practices version 1.0*, Tech. Report SAND2004-6602, Sandia National Laboratories, Albuquerque, NM, 2005.

[3] J. A. KAHLE, M. N. DAY, H. P. HOFSTEE, C. R. JOHNS, T. R. MAEURER, AND D. SHIPPY, *Introduction to the cell multiprocessor*, Tech. Report IBM JRD 49-4/5, IBM, 2005. http://www.research.ibm.com/journal/rd/494/kahle.html.

[4] *CCA Forum.* http://www.cca-forum.org/.

[5] G. Chen, K. Malowski, M. Kandemir, and P. Raghavan, *Reducing power with performance constraints for parallel sparse applications*, in Proceedings of 19th IEEE International Parallel & Distributed Processing Symposium (IPDPS'05)—Workshop 11, 2005, p. 231a. http://doi.ieeecomputersociety.org/10.1109/IPDPS.2005.378.

[6] *Clearspeed homepage*, 2006. http://www.clearspeed.com/.

[7] V. Freeh and D. L. (Co-Chairs), *The second workshop on high-performance, power-aware computing workshop, in conjunction with the IEEE international parallel & distributed processing symposium*, 2006. http://fortknox.csc.ncsu.edu/proj/hppac/.

[8] *General-purpose computation using graphics hardware*, 2006. http://www.gpgpu.org/.

[9] M. A. Heroux, *Trilinos home page*, 2004. http://software.sandia.gov/trilinos.

[10] A. A. Johnson, *Aerodynamics of hummingbirds*, 2005. http://www.cray.com/downloads/science/hummingbirds_flyer.pdf.

[11] Sandia National Laboratories, *Advanced simulation and computing (asc)*, 2005. http://www.sandia.gov/NNSA/ASC/.

[12] K. J. Lee and K. Skadron, *Using performance counters for runtime temperature sensing in high-performance processors*, in Proceedings of 19th IEEE International Parallel & Distributed Processing Symposium (IPDPS'05)—Workshop 11, 2005, p. 232a. http://doi.ieeecomputersociety.org/10.1109/IPDPS.2005.448.

[13] K. Malkowski, I. Lee, P. Raghavan, and M. Irwin, *Conjugate gradient sparse solvers: Performance-power characteristics*, in Proceedings of 20th IEEE International Parallel & Distributed Processing Symposium (IPDPS'06), 2006, pp. 1–8.

[14] The MathWorks, *MATLAB.* http://www.mathworks.com/.

[15] H. Nakashima, H. Nakamura, M. Sato, T. Boku, S. Matsuoka, D. Takahashi, and Y. Hotta, *Megaproto: A low-power and compact cluster for high-performance computing*, in Proceedings of 19th IEEE International Parallel & Distributed Processing Symposium (IPDPS'05)—Workshop 11, 2005, p. 231b. http://doi.ieeecomputersociety.org/10.1109/IPDPS.2005.278.

[16] United States Department of Energy Defense Programs, Lawrence Livermore National Laboratory, Los Alamos National Laboratory, and Sandia National Laboratories, *Accelerated strategic computing initiative program plan*, 1996. http://www.sandia.gov/NNSA/ASC/pubs/progplanFY96.html.

[17] F. PAN, V. W. FREEH, AND D. M. SMITH, *Exploring the energy-time tradeoff in high performance computing*, in Proceedings of 19th IEEE International Parallel & Distributed Processing Symposium (IPDPS'05)—Workshop 11, 2005, p. 234a. `http://doi.ieeecomputersociety.org/10.1109/IPDPS.2005.213`.

[18] P. RAGHAVAN, M. J. IRWIN, L. C. MCINNES, AND B. NORRIS, *Adaptive software for scientific computing: Co-managing quality-performance-power tradeoffs*, in Proceedings of 19th IEEE International Parallel & Distributed Processing Symposium (IPDPS'05)—Workshop 10, 2005, p. 220b. `http://doi.ieeecomputersociety.org/10.1109/IPDPS.2005.83`.

[19] G. V. ROSSUM, *The Python Language Reference Manual*, Network Theory Ltd., 2003.

[20] M. SALA, W. F. SPOTZ, AND M. A. HEROUX, *Pytrilinos: High-performance distributed-memory solvers for python*, ACM Transactions on Mathematical Software, (2006). Accepted.

[21] *Babel home page*, 2005. `http://www.llnl.gov/CASC/components/babel.html`.

[22] S. WILLIAMS, J. SHALF, L. OLIKER, S. KAMIL, P. HUSBANDS, AND K. YELICK, *The potential of the cell processor for scientific computing*, in Proceedings of Third Conference on Computing Frontiers, ACM, New York, 2006, pp. 9–20.

Index

adaptive linear solvers, 172
adaptive mesh refinement, 143
adaptive MPI, 344
adaptive multimethod solvers, 261
additive Schwarz preconditioner, 170
adjoint equation, 293
adjoint state or costate, 292
algorithm-dependent fault tolerance, 204
Altix, 78
Apex-MAP, 89
applications, 4
    circuit simulations, 172
    computational biology, 5
    engineering, 4
    optimization, 4
    structural dynamics, 172
arbitrary Lagrangian–Eulerian, 343
architectural probes, 88
architecture-aware computation, 33
ASCI Red, 61
astrophysics, 81
asynchronous parallel pattern search
    fault tolerant, 205
atmospheric contaminant transport, 310

Babel, 251, 386
bandwidth, 22
basic linear algebra subprograms (BLAS), 234
batch scheduler, 227
Beowulf, 223
binary variable, 323
BioPSE, 231, 273
bipartite graph, 128

bipartite matching, 128
BLAS, 164, 167, 234
block Cimmino method, 171
block row-projection method, 171
BlueGene/L, 59
branch and cut, 325
branch-and-bound, 137, 325
bugs, performance, 230

cache-oblivious algorithms, 131
Cactus, 231, 253
canonical program variant, 38
Car–Parrinello molecular dynamics, 69
CCA, 251, 277, 387
Ccaffeine, 251
Charm++, 39, 344
checkpoint/restart
    algorithm-dependent, 207
    diskless, 207, 208
    in MPI, 210
CLAPS, 173
clones, 361
cluster configuration, 227
clustering, 105
CoArray FORTRAN, 229, 382
combinatorial algorithms, 127
combinatorial scientific computing, 127
commodity, 231
Common Component Architecture (CCA), 251, 387
common refinement, 348
communication abstractions, 347
components, 249, 276
composite linear solvers, 172

computational biology, 127, 357
computational fluid dynamics, 83
computational quality of service, 259
configuration
    description-based, 227
    disk image-based, 227
configuration, cluster, 227
Conforming unstructured mesh, 149
conservation, 348
contact detection, 102
contigs, 361
continuum-particle methods, 154
cosmology, 82
costate, 292
Cplant, 227
crossover, 334

data mapping
    multipass mapping, 165
    proportional heuristic, 165
    subtree-to-subcube mapping, 165
data migration, 114
data transfer, 348
DCA, 252
decision equation, 293
decision variables, 291
dense systems, 233
design pattern, 252
developers
    recommendations, 231
direct simulation Monte Carlo, 154
discrete algorithms, 127
distributed computing, 280
distributed objects, 345
DNA fragments, 361
domain decomposition, 301
domain-specific languages, 229
dual-primal finite element tearing and interconnecting (FETI-DP), 172
dynamic load balancing, 42, 151
dynamic migration, 344
dynamic resource utilization model (DRUM), 42

Earth Systems Modeling Framework (ESMF), 253

element bisection refinement, 149
embedded boundaries, 154
engineering and scientific subroutine library (ESSL), 62
Enzo, 71
Ethernet, 225
evolutionary trees, 363

face offsetting, 350
fathom, 325
fault tolerance, 203
    checkpoint/restart in MPI, 210
    in algorithms, 204
    MPI application interfaces, 214
fault-tolerant algorithms
    asynchronous parallel pattern search, 205
    FFT, 207
    Krylov solvers, 209
    linear algebra kernels, 208
    molecular dynamics, 206
    natural fault tolerance, 204
fault-tolerant MPI
    application interfaces, 214
    checkpoint/restart, 210
    Egida, 211
    FT-MPI, 214
    LA-MPI, 211
    LAM/MPI, 213
    MPI/FT, 215
    Open MPI, 216
FETI-DP, 172
FFT
    fault-tolerant, 207
file system, parallel, 226
flexibly assignable work, 113
framework, 249, 387
full space methods, 294

Gaussian elimination, 234, 238
GenBank, 358
genetic maps, 361
genome reconstruction, 361
geometric conservation law, 343
geometric partitioning, 101
geophysics, 85

GFS, 226
global address space, language, 229, 382
GPFS, 226
graph algorithms, 127, 136, 138
graph coloring, 130
graph embeddings, 130
graph partitioning techniques, 100, 130, 166
GRAPPA, 365
grid spacing, 143
Grid-TLSE, 172
GridARM, 46

HDF5, 72
heterogeneous environments, 42
hierarchical partitioning, 44
high-performance scientific components, 250
high-productivity computing, 229
HPCToolkit, 230
HSL mathematical software library, 167
hybrid direct/iterative techniques, 169
hypergraph, 106, 109
hypergraph partitioning, 130
hypre, 228

incumbent, 325
independent sets, 130
Infiniband, 225
information retrieval, 136
input/output (I/O), 346
integer program (IP), 323
integer programming, 136
integrality gap, 326
integration framework, 341, 345
interoperability, 228
inverse acoustic wave propagation, 303
irregular applications, 127, 132
Itanium2, 78
iterative methods, 167
    BCG, 167
    BiCGSTAB, 167
    CG, 167
    CGS, 167
    Chebyshev iteration, 167
    GMRES, 167, 168
    MINRES, 167
    QMR, 167

Japanese Earth Simulator (JEP), 79
Jostle, 45

Karush–Kuhn–Tucker (KKT), 293
Krylov solvers
    fault tolerant, 209

LAM/MPI, 213
languages, domain-specific, 229
languages, R, 229
languages, statistical, 229
LAPACK, 164, 167
latency, 22
library
    completeness, 228
    hypre, 228
    interoperability, 228
    pARMS, 228
    Petra, 228
    PETSc, 228
    PLAPACK, 228
    Prometheus, 228
    ScaLAPACK, 228
    SuperLU, 228
    Trilinos, 228
linear program, 325
linear programming (LP), 137
    relaxation, 325
linear solvers
    in ScaLAPACK, 237
Linux distribution, 224
load balance, 20
load balancing, 99, 130
locality, 131
logfiles, 230
Lustre, 226

magnetic fusion, 84
maize genome, 357
MASS library, 68
materials science, 80
math acceleration subsystem vector (MASSV), 62
MATLAB, 386

matrix-vector multiplication, 108, 168
memory access probe (MAP), 89
memory performance, 128, 131
mesh optimization, 349
mesh quality, 150
mesh repair, 349
mesh smoothing, 349
Message Passing Interface (MPI), 223, 382
metacomponents, 278
metrics, 20
middleware, 345, 346
migration, 114
mixed integer program, 323
    formulation, 324
model coupling, 255
molecular dynamics
    fault tolerant, 206
MPI, 22, 223, 382
    Egida, 211
    FT-MPI, 214
    interfaces for application fault tolerance, 214
    LA-MPI, 211
    LAM/MPI, 213
    MPI/FT, 215
    open MPI, 216
    profiling interface, 230
    with checkpoint/restart, 210
MPI implementation
    LAM/MPI, 226
    MPICH2, 226
    OpenMPI, 226
    others, 226
MPICH2, 226
multigrid methods, 301
multigrid, coarsening
    algebraic, parallel
        CLJP, 189
        coupled aggregation, 189
        decoupled, 188
        Falgout, 190
        HMIS, 190
        MIS aggregation, 189
        PMIS, 190
        processor coloring, 190

        RS3, 189
        subdomain blocking, 189
    algebraic, sequential
        aggregation, 188
        aggressive, 188
        Ruge–Stüben, 187
    geometric
        block-structured problems, 186
        Cartesian grids, 186
        semicoarsening, 185
        SMG method, 185
multigrid, coarsest grid parallelism, 193
    direct solvers, 194
    iterative methods, 194
    processor subsets, 194
multigrid, complexity
    algebraic
        operator, 185
        stencil size, 185
    geometric, 185
multigrid, parallel methods
    block factorizations, 184
    concurrent iterations, 181
    full domain partitioning, 183
    multiple coarse corrections, 181
multigrid, smoothing
    hybrid, 191
    multicolor Gauss–Seidel, 190
    polynomial smoothing
        Chebychev, 192
        MLS, 192
    processor block Gauss–Seidel, 191
    sparse approximate inverses, 193
multigrid, sources of parallelism
    partitioning, 179
multilevel algorithms, 384
multipole methods, 132
MUMPS, 170
Myrinet, 225

NAS (NASA Advanced Supercomputing) parallel benchmarks, 87
NAS parallel benchmarks, 37, 64
Navier–Stokes flow, 308
network analysis, 127
networks, 381

Ethernet, 225
Infiniband, 225
Myrinet, 225
Quadrics, 225
Newton–Krylov iteration, 294
nonlinear elimination, 293
nonoverlapping domain decomposition, 170
normalized resource metric (NRM), 47
normalized work metric (NWM), 47
NP-complete, 324
NP-hard, 357
numerical factorization, 128
numerical software for linear algebra problems, 233
NWChem, 231

Oblio, 167
OpenMP, 22, 225, 382
OpenMPI, 226
OpenPBS, 227
optimization problem, 291
ordering algorithms
    Cuthill–McKee, 169
    interleaved minimum degree, 169
    Markowitz scheme, 166
    minimum deficiency, 169
    minimum degree, 166, 169, 172
    nested dissection, 166, 169
OSCAR, 227

PaCO++, 253
Panasas, 226
PAPI, 230
parallel algebraic recursive multilevel solver (pARMS), 169
parallel algorithms, 2
    combinatorial, 3
    fault tolerance, 3
    mesh refinement, 3
    partitioning, 3
    scalability, 2
    sparse linear solvers, 3
parallel components, 282
parallel data redistribution, 256
parallel file system, 226

parallel hierarchical interface decomposition algorithm (PHIDAL), 168
parallel mesh partitioning, 151
parallel structured mesh refinement, 147
parallel unstructured mesh refinement, 150
Paraver visualization tool, 9
ParMetis, 45
pARMS, 169, 172, 228
partial inheritance, 345
partitioned approach, 341
partitioned global address space (PGAS), 229
partitioning, 99
    complex objectives, 112
    geometric, 101
    graph, 100
    resource-aware, 116
PaStiX, 171
patch-based refinement, 146
PDE-constrained optimization, 291
PERC, 91
performance
    evaluation, 80, 86
    modeling, 2, 90
    sensitivity, 92
performance analysis, 9
performance analysis tools, 11
performance bugs, 230
Performance Evaluation Research Center (PERC), 90
performance models, 29
performance monitoring, 347
performance tools
    logfiles, 230
    summary, 230
persistent objects, 345
Petra, 228
PETSc, 228, 238, 302
PGAS, 229, 382
PHIDAL, 168
phylogeny, 363
physical maps, 361
PLAPACK, 228
polycrystal, 73
port, 249

Power3, 77
Power4, 78
PowerPC (PPC) 440 processors, 60
preconditioning techniques, 167, 168, 172
    approximate inverses, 168
    incomplete factorization, 168
    Jacobi, 168
    multilevel preconditioning, 168
    ordering issues, 169
    SSOR, 168
processors, 379
    massively threaded, 380
    multicore, 379
    multimedia, 380
    vector, 380
profiling
    module-level, 347
profiling interface, MPI, 230
Prometheus, 173, 228
Prophesy, 35
provides port, 252
PVFS2, 226
Python, 386

quadrics, 225
query processing, 136

radiation transport, 133
recommendations, for tool developers, 231
recommendations, for users, 231
reduced Hessian, 293
reduced space methods, 293, 296
regular mesh refinement, 149
remeshing, 349
remote method invocation (RMI), 280
resource-aware partitioning, 116
ROCKS, 227
ROSE, 39

Salinas, 172
scalability, 23, 351
ScaLAPACK, 228, 234
scheduler, batch, 227
scientific data mining, 127

scientific interface definition language (SIDL), 251, 276, 386
SCIRun, 231
SCIRun2, 252
semidefinite programming, 111
separation algorithm, 326
sequence alignment, 135
SIDL, 251, 276, 386
simulation problem, 291
Single Program Multiple Data (SPMD), 19
singly bordered block diagonal form, 166, 170
slack variable, 323
SLURM, 227
software components, 155
software quality, 386
spanning trees, 130
sparse direct methods, 163
sparse matrices, 238
sparse matrix solvers, 128
sparse matrix-vector multiplication, 131, 167
sparse systems, 233
sparse triangular factorization
    assembly trees, 164, 165
    elimination trees, 164, 165
    fill, 163
    frontal methods, 167
    multifrontal methods, 165, 167
    ordering algorithms, 166
    out-of-core techniques, 167
    supernode, 164
SPMD, 34
sPPM, 67
Sqmat, 89
stabilized doubly bordered block diagonal form, 166
state equation, 293
state equations, 291
state variables, 291
steady-state Burgers equation, 292
strongly connected components, 133
structured adaptive mesh refinement, 145
suffix tree, 135
SuperLU, 228, 238

SuperLU_DIST, 164
support theory, 130
surface propagation, 350
symbolic factorization, 128, 129

Tarragon, 39
the Karush–Kuhn–Tucker (KKT), 293
tools and frameworks, 3
    linear algebra, 4
    software components, 4
    survey, 3
torque, 227
torus interconnect, 61
tree-based refinement, 146
triangular factorizations, 163
Trilinos, 228, 387

UMT2K, 69
Unified parallel C (UPC), 229, 382
unstructured adaptive mesh refinement, 149
users
    recommendations, 231
uses port, 252

validation, 351
verification, 351
virtual processes, 344

X1, 79, 380
XCAT, 252

Zoltan parallel data services toolkit, 43